ColdFusion® MX:
The Complete Reference

About the Author

Jeffry Houser has been working in web development for over seven years. He graduated from Central Connecticut State University with a computer science degree in 1997. He accumulated a wide range of experience as the tech guy at a small advertising firm, and has worked with numerous technologies including Lotus Notes, iCat, and ColdFusion. His experience touched upon all aspects of the IT world including application and web development, server administration, and help desk support. Jeffry has achieved numerous certifications in ColdFusion and Lotus Notes.

Jeffry started the company DotComIt in 2000. Its unique business model is designed to alleviate the load of overworked development teams. DotComIt works with small web development firms that are lacking in technical skill and corporate IT departments.

In his spare time, Jeffry plays guitar as half of Connecticut's premiere original alternative folk rock duo, Far Cry Fly. You can check out Far Cry Fly on the web at www.farcryfly.com. When not gigging or programming, he likes to play computer adventure games, and hopes that the rumors of a new Space Quest game come to fruition.

Check out the web site for Jeff's books at www.instantcoldfusion.com. Jeffry can be reached via e-mail at jeff@instantcoldfusion.com, and he loves hearing feedback from people who read his books.

ColdFusion® MX:
The Complete Reference

Jeffry Houser

McGraw-Hill/Osborne

New York   Chicago   San Francisco
Lisbon   London   Madrid   Mexico City
Milan   New Delhi   San Juan
Seoul   Singapore   Sydney   Toronto

McGraw-Hill/Osborne
2600 Tenth Street
Berkeley, California 94710
U.S.A.

To arrange bulk purchase discounts for sales promotions, premiums, or fund-raisers, please contact **McGraw-Hill/**Osborne at the above address. For information on translations or book distributors outside the U.S.A., please see the International Contact Information page immediately following the index of this book.

ColdFusion® MX: The Complete Reference

1234567890 DOC DOC 0198765432

ISBN 0-07-222556-4

Publisher
Brandon A. Nordin

Vice President & Associate Publisher
Scott Rogers

Acquisitions Editor
Jim Schachterle

Project Editor
Janet Walden

Acquisitions Coordinator
Timothy Madrid

Technical Editors
Michael Dinowitz, Michael Buffington, Craig Fisher

Copy Editor
William McManus

Proofreader
Karen Mead

Indexer
Rebecca Plunkett

Production
Apollo Publishing Services

Illustrators
Michael Mueller, Lyssa Wald

Series Design
Peter F. Hancik

This book was composed with Corel VENTURA™ Publisher.

Angela said if I dedicated the book to her, it would go to number 1.
This book is dedicated to her.

Contents at a Glance

Part IV **Demonstrating Advanced Application Development Concepts**

Part V **Integrating ColdFusion with Other Technologies**

Part VI   Appendixes

Contents

Part II

Administering Your ColdFusion Server

Part IV

Demonstrating Advanced Application Development Concepts

Part V

Integrating ColdFusion with Other Technologies

Part VI

Appendixes

Acknowledgements

I'd like to thank Jim, Tim, Janet, and all the folks at McGraw-Hill/Osborne for once again working with me through the toils of writing a book. An ultra-big-extra-special thanks goes out to Tim, who has been with me for all three of my books, but won't be around for the next book. I also want to thank Michael, Craig, and Michael for helping out with tech edits, and Simon and Chris for lending their skills to a few of the chapters.

I want to send out an extra-special thanks for everyone who bought and read my other books, *Instant ColdFusion* and *ColdFusion: A Beginner's Guide*. Mad props go out to the folks who actually took time to e-mail feedback to me. I hope you found those books useful enough to give this one a try. I want to thank Macromedia for continuing to make ColdFusion a priority, and thank the community of ColdFusion developers, especially HouseofFusion.com for hosting the important mailing list. I also want to tip my hat to the makers of all the software programs that I wrote about in this book. Many were kind enough to give me fully functional versions of their software, just so I could write about them.

I want to thank everyone I ever worked with, including Stephenie, Laura, Krista, Barry, Lou, Karl, Suzanne, Jim, Aaron, Judy, and Kristen. I want to thank my parents, siblings, and their respective significant others for their continued support in everything I do. I want to thank my friends: Tammi, Jude (and Tom), Angela, Jenni (and Luke),

Lori (and Blaine), Bonnie, Tim, Shadow, and anyone who ever bought Far Cry Fly merchandise.

Last, I want to thank everyone who is buying this book. (The people who hold my mortgage will be truly thankful.) I hope you find this to be a valuable resource for all of your ColdFusion needs. Please check out the web site, www.instantcoldfusion.com, and send me an e-mail at jeff@instantcoldfusion.com to let me know what you think.

Introduction

ColdFusion MX promises great things for the future of web development in ColdFusion. Macromedia has rewritten the entire code base to be J2EE compliant and run on J2EE servers. This book will be one of the few on the shelves written from scratch with ColdFusion MX in mind. I was lucky enough to be accepted into the beta cycle by Macromedia and was able to learn about the new MX release through lots of trial and error, while wading through the unfinished documentation. I'm very pleased with the amount of information that we were able to stuff into this reference.

Who Should Read This Book

This book is designed for everyone who writes ColdFusion code. If you are new to ColdFusion, you will have no problem understanding this book. If you are an intermediate developer, you can use this book to expand and polish your current skills. If you are an advanced developer, this book will offer you great information about ColdFusion MX and is a great reference to keep by your computer as you develop.

How to Read This Book

This book is designed to be a cross between a reference and a tutorial on the ColdFusion language. You do not have to sit down and read it cover to cover, although you are welcome to do so if you wish. You can go directly to the topic you wish to learn about and read away. If a chapter covers a concept that is discussed in more depth in a different chapter, a cross-reference to the relevant chapter is provided.

This book was designed to highlight information about ColdFusion MX and how to accomplish tasks in ColdFusion MX. Each individual chapter does not deal with changes between ColdFusion MX and previous versions of ColdFusion. If you have worked with previous versions of ColdFusion and want to know about migrating your applications, Chapter 14 is dedicated to the topic.

ColdFusion MX: The Complete Reference is divided into these parts:

Part I: Getting Started

- Chapter 1, "The Evolution of ColdFusion," introduces ColdFusion and talks about the benefits of the J2EE Server.

- Chapter 2, "Installing the ColdFusion Server," teaches you to install and set up the ColdFusion server.

- Chapter 3, "Getting Around in the ColdFusion Administrator," introduces the ColdFusion Administrator.

Part II: Administering Your ColdFusion Server

- Chapter 4, "Securing Your Server," teaches techniques about securing your ColdFusion server.

- Chapter 5, "Monitoring and Load Testing Your Server," talks about how to monitor your server and load test your applications.

- Chapter 6, "Applying Advanced Administration Techniques," discusses advanced features of the ColdFusion Administrator.

Part III: Coding in ColdFusion

- Chapter 7, "Introducing Programming Languages," provides an introduction to programming.

- Chapter 8, "Learning CFML Basics," introduces CFML basics, including the application framework.

- Chapter 9, "Designing Your Database," introduces database concepts, including good database design and the SQL language.

- Chapter 10, "Picking a Development Methodology," introduces the software development lifecycle and some common ColdFusion methodologies, such as Fusebox.

- Chapter 11, "Writing ColdFusion Code," teaches you how to use Dreamweaver MX to maintain your ColdFusion applications.

- Chapter 12, "Sharing Variables Between Templates," teaches you about form and URL variables.
- Chapter 13, "Controlling Your ColdFusion Code," teaches you about conditional and looping logic.
- Chapter 14, "Migrating Your Applications to ColdFusion MX," talks about tags and functions that have been deprecated or changed.

Part IV: Demonstrating Advanced Application Development Concepts

- Chapter 15, "Scripting Inside ColdFusion," contains a complete guide to CFScript.
- Chapter 16, "Modularizing Your Code," teaches you about includes, CFML custom tags, user-defined functions, and ColdFusion Components.
- Chapter 17, "Securing Your ColdFusion Applications," teaches you about ColdFusion MX's new security model.
- Chapter 18, "Debugging and Optimizing Your Applications," talks about ways to build error handling into your application.
- Chapter 19, "Maintaining File and Directory Structures," discusses the file and directory handling abilities of ColdFusion MX.
- Chapter 20, "Creating Graphs with ColdFusion," talks about the brand-new ColdFusion MX cfchart tag.
- Chapter 21, "Learning Advanced Database Concepts," teaches you about advanced SQL concepts such as stored procedures and SQL grouping.

Part V: Integrating ColdFusion with Other Technologies

- Chapter 22, "Mixing ColdFusion with Internet Standards," teaches you how to work with Internet standards, such as HTTP web surfing and FTP, and how to send and receive e-mail.
- Chapter 23, "Using ColdFusion with Java and J2EE Application Servers," shows how to integrate ColdFusion with Java servers.
- Chapter 24, "Creating Search Engines with Verity," demonstrates how to make use of the Verity search engine included in ColdFusion MX.
- Chapter 25, "Writing ColdFusion for Wireless Applications," introduces WML and how to make wireless applications with it.
- Chapter 26, "Extending ColdFusion with CFX Custom Tags," shows you how to extend ColdFusion with CFX custom tags.

- Chapter 27, "Sharing Data with WDDX or XML," teaches you about XML and WDDX.
- Chapter 28, "Integrating ColdFusion MX and Flash MX," demonstrates how ColdFusion and Flash integrate with each other.
- Chapter 29, "Adding Web-Based Content Editors to Your Site," shows you how to use web-based content editors.
- Chapter 30, "Calling COM and CORBA Objects from ColdFusion," teaches you how to create PDFs using COM with ColdFusion.
- Chapter 31, "Using Web Services in ColdFusion," teaches you how to create and consume Web services with ColdFusion.
- Chapter 32, "Discovering BlueDragon," introduces BlueDragon, a third-party CFML interpreter.

Part VI: Appendixes

- Appendix A, "ColdFusion Tag and Function List," is a complete reference of all ColdFusion tags and functions.
- Appendix B, "Discovering Special ColdFusion Variables," shows you some special ColdFusion variables.
- Appendix C, "Finding Additional Online and Print Resources," shows you where to go for more information.
- Appendix D, "Using the Online Files," tells you how to use the online files.

Special Features

Throughout this book, you will find some special features:

- **Notes**   Notes give you some useful information related to the current topic.
- **Tips**   Tips give you some advice about how to best implement the current topic.
- **Cautions**   Cautions warn you about snags to avoid.

Using the Online Files

All the files that are used in this book are available online at **www.instantcoldfusion.com** and **www.osborne.com**. The files come in a single zip archive. You need a program, such as WinZip (www.winzip.com), to unzip the archive. The files are separated into folders, by chapter. Files for Chapter 1 are located in the Chapter1 directory, files for Chapter 2 are located in the Chapter2 directory, and so on. The zip archive includes ColdFusion templates, database files, and any other applicable files.

The
Complete
Reference

ColdFusion MX

Part I

Getting Started

The
Complete
Reference

ColdFusion
MX

Chapter 1

The Evolution
of ColdFusion

This chapter introduces you to the Web and ColdFusion. We'll discuss how the Web was invented and how corporations came to use it to promote their business through activities such as supporting current customers, creating new customers, and selling products. Next, we will examine ColdFusion's humble beginnings and trace its history to the powerhouse that it has become today.

The Advent of ColdFusion

This section will give you an explanation of what the World Wide Web is and how the Web developed. We will then go on to discuss why more functionality was needed on the Web and how ColdFusion fills that need.

The Emergence of the Dynamic Web

In the 1960s, a government-funded research project laid the foundation for what is known today as the Internet. As time passed, more and more people became connected to the Internet, leading to the creation of the World Wide Web in the 1990s. If you already know a lot of this background material, you can jump right to "ColdFusion MX: The New Frontier," later in this chapter.

Growing the Web?

Tim Berners-Lee had an idea. He wanted to create a common place for sharing information. Taking this idea and combining it with the mathematical concept of a *web* (meaning any one item can link to any other item), Berners-Lee created the World Wide Web in the early 1990s. He defined the Hypertext Transfer Protocol (HTTP), Hypertext Markup Language (HTML), and Uniform Resource Locator (URL) protocols, which make up the foundation of today's Web.

In the beginning, the Web was primarily used to share information between academic types. In the mid-1990s, businesses started to take notice of the Web. New companies were created based entirely on the Web and traditional businesses moved operations onto the Web.

Creating Advanced Functionality on the Web

As the Web grew, its functionality needs increased. In the beginning, the main purpose of the Web was to pass information from the web server to the web browser. Such a model was fine for sharing information, but it did not fill the needs of most web-based businesses.

To conduct business on the Web, these companies needed a way to take and process orders. They needed to be able to distinguish one user from another, something not done inherently by web browsers or servers. They needed to be able to create specific sorts and searches of data. At first, this functionality was accomplished by writing Common Gateway Interface (CGI) programs that would run on the server. HTML forms would execute these programs when submitted.

> **Note**   *ColdFusion was originally implemented as a CGI program.*

On high-volume sites, it became inefficient to run a program every time a form was submitted. If 12 people submitted the form at once, then 12 instances of the program would be running at once. To solve this problem, programs were moved from CGI implementation to web server API (application programming interface) implementation. This means that instead of running the program each time someone submitted the form, the program was run once and kept in memory. The web server would take the form information and pass it to the program, and then pass the results back to the web browser. This allowed for a single instance of the program to run and process all requests. Macromedia's ColdFusion is implemented in this way.

ColdFusion's Role in Today's Web

ColdFusion is implemented using a web server's API, so we'll start by examining the two parts of ColdFusion. Then, we'll trace ColdFusion's history, and finish off by comparing ColdFusion to some other related technologies.

Understanding ColdFusion

There are two separate portions of ColdFusion: the ColdFusion Application Server and ColdFusion Markup Language (CFML). We will look at each of these pieces and how they relate to each other.

CFML is the language of ColdFusion and is composed of a set of tags that defines the functionality you want to accomplish. ColdFusion can be programmed to do things like manipulate database data (Chapter 9), create search engines (Chapter 24), and even check your e-mail (Chapter 22). CFML tags have a similar format to HTML, thus making ColdFusion an easy language for nonprogrammers to learn.

The ColdFusion Application Server runs on the web server machine, integrating with the server software through that software's API. When a web browser requests a ColdFusion page, the web server recognizes that you are asking for a ColdFusion page, usually by seeing that the page has a .cfm extension, and passes the page onto the ColdFusion Application Server. Next, the ColdFusion Application Server processes the CFML tags in that page and sends the results back to the web server. The web server then passes these results directly to the web browser that requested them.

The History of ColdFusion

Let's take a look at the history of ColdFusion to understand how it has evolved from a simple CGI program to the powerhouse it has become today. Two brothers, J. J. and Jeremy Allaire, created ColdFusion. As the story goes, Jeremy was looking for an easy way to update the web site for a print publication that he worked for. So, he went to his programmer brother, J. J., and asked for help. J. J. created what became the first version of ColdFusion in 1995. Understanding the potential applications of the software, the two brothers formed Allaire Corporation, with ColdFusion as their flagship product.

The original version of ColdFusion was built to work as a CGI program, although future versions were developed to access web servers through the API. ColdFusion works on a variety of web servers including the Apache Web Server and Microsoft Internet Information Server (IIS). It will integrate with a variety of operating systems such as Windows, Linux, Unix, and Solaris.

Allaire added some additional products to its line, including HomeSite, a code editor; JRun, a J2EE-compliant Java server; and Spectra, a content management system. In 2001, Macromedia, most famous for its Flash file format, merged with Allaire and released ColdFusion 5, a release much anticipated by the developer community. ColdFusion 5 was focused on speeding up the inner workings of ColdFusion as well as adding some much-requested functionality such as user-defined functions (Chapter 16) and the ability to query a query (Chapter 21). A whole new version of ColdFusion was released in 2002: ColdFusion MX.

ColdFusion MX: The New Frontier

ColdFusion MX is an important release to the ColdFusion community. This section will explain why it is so important. We'll talk about Macromedia's commitment to standards and how the Java platform has become increasingly important to the future of ColdFusion.

Overview of ColdFusion MX

In June of 2002, Macromedia released ColdFusion MX, starting a new era in the ColdFusion product line. ColdFusion MX is the next version of the ColdFusion technology. It was in development for over two years, even before ColdFusion 5 was released. This section will talk about the changes that ColdFusion MX brings to the table.

Understanding New Language Features

There are many important new features that make the upgrade to ColdFusion MX pay for itself ten times over. These are some of them:

- **Expanded XML support** ColdFusion MX has added native XML support for parsing XML data. XML can now be treated as a native data type in ColdFusion. We'll explore this more in Chapter 27.

- **ColdFusion Components** ColdFusion Components (CFC) will allow you to bring code modularity to a whole new level. This feature is discussed in depth in Chapter 16.

- **Native Flash connectivity and server-side ActionScript** With ColdFusion 5 came the Flash Component Kit add-in, to allow Flash movies and ColdFusion to interact with each other. ColdFusion MX now allows greater interactivity between the two programs. Flash developers can also create ActionScript files that can access ColdFusion resources directly. We'll discuss this in Chapter 28.

- **Enhanced integration option** ColdFusion MX easily passes information to and from Java Server Pages and servlets pages. You will be able to import JSP tag libraries directly into your ColdFusion applications. This is discussed in Chapter 23.

- **Improved error handling and debugging** ColdFusion MX makes it even easier to catch and handle the run-time errors in your program. We will talk about these enhancements in Chapter 18.

- **Verity improvements** ColdFusion MX brings forth many new features for dealing with searches using the Verity engine. These are discussed in Chapter 24.

- **Security enhancements** For companies that are hosting ColdFusion sites in a shared environment, it is now much easier to set up your security sandbox and you have more control over the resources that each developer can use. This is discussed in Chapter 4.

- **Its own web server** That's right folks, now ColdFusion comes loaded with its own web server. This web server isn't suitable for production hosting, but it's just the thing you need for your development purposes. We'll talk about this in Chapter 2.

These features only scratch the surface of the new enhancements that are available in ColdFusion MX. Read on for more information.

Understanding ColdFusion Administrator Choices

As previously stated, there are two parts to ColdFusion: the CFML language and the ColdFusion Application Server. One reason that ColdFusion is the premier choice for many web sites is that it is able to work on many operating systems, with many different web servers. A platform for ColdFusion consists of two components: the operating system and the web server.

Any given platform starts at the operating system level. ColdFusion will work on both Windows and Unix operating systems. Of course, your operating system choice is not that easy, because each type of OS contains various flavors, geared toward different markets. In the Windows world, ColdFusion will work on Windows NT, Windows 2000, Windows XP, and Windows 95/98/ME. In the Unix world, ColdFusion will work with Red Hat Linux, SuSE Linux, Cobalt Linux, Solaris, and HP-UX.

On top of the operating system is placed a web server. ColdFusion will integrate with Microsoft IIS, Netscape iPlanet, and the Apache web server. Additionally, ColdFusion MX includes a web server of its own. This web server is not designed for the hosting of applications that have been put in production, but will suit the needs of any developer.

ColdFusion MX adds a new component to the way that ColdFusion will operate. You will be able to use ColdFusion as a plug-in to any stand-alone J2EE-compliant Java server, such as Macromedia JRun and IBM's Websphere. This allows for even more deployment options for your ColdFusion applications, because you can run ColdFusion on top of any Java server.

Placing ColdFusion in Macromedia's MX Product Line

Macromedia is bringing us a new wave of programs to help push the limits of today's Web. Three products reside at the center of Macromedia's strategy: ColdFusion, Flash, and Dreamweaver. Together they present the full range of integrated services needed to build dynamic web sites.

Flash MX is the ultimate front-end tool for web site development. It offers everything that dynamic HTML (DHTML) promised and more. Since Flash is included with both Internet Explorer and Netscape Navigator, it has an extremely high penetration rate for a browser plug-in. Just about anyone can interact with a Flash movie. Flash is a powerful tool for developing web interfaces.

Dreamweaver MX is Macromedia's new editor for creating web pages and templates in any number of languages. It includes some specialized features, making it a great choice for developing web sites in ColdFusion. We discuss Dreamweaver MX in Chapter 11.

ColdFusion MX, as you probably already know, acts as a middleman between the web browser and a database server. It brings great functionality to a web site in terms of the dynamic display of data, processing of user input, and session management capabilities. Its tight integration with Flash MX, as discussed in Chapter 28, allows you to deliver dynamic content to Flash movies.

The Benefits of the Java Platform

ColdFusion MX was rebuilt from scratch to work on the Java platform. This section will go over some of the benefits of this change.

Moving into Java

When ColdFusion was created by J. J. and Jeremy Allaire in 1995, it was built as a CGI program, coded in C++. As ColdFusion grew, its code base in C++ had limitations. Macromedia's leadership decided it was time for a change. ColdFusion MX was rewritten entirely from scratch using standards-compliant Java.

ColdFusion 5 consisted of four major subsystems, as shown in Figure 1-1. At the top of the chain is the CFML compiler, which turns CFML code into p-code. The CFML language runtime unit comes next, executing the p-code. The CFML language runtime unit interacts at the next level with built-in application services, such as the search and graphing engines. The next level consists of the infrastructure services. This level deals with the operating system and database operations. Underneath the infrastructure services lies the operating system.

ColdFusion MX operates conceptually in much the same way, as shown in Figure 1-2. One primary component has changed. The proprietary infrastructure component is now replaced with a standards-compliant Java 2 Enterprise Edition (J2EE) server. The CFML compiler now compiles down to Java byte code instead of p-code. J2EE servers provide a standardized approach to creating enterprise applications. By adhering to

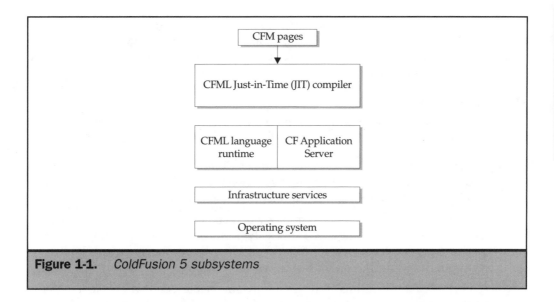

Figure 1-1.   *ColdFusion 5 subsystems*

this body of standards, Macromedia can concentrate on writing ColdFusion, without having to deal with issues such as resource management or security models that are built into the J2EE engines. Macromedia developers can just call upon the Java methods inherent in the J2EE engine.

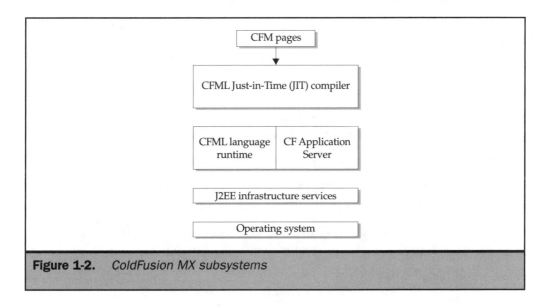

Figure 1-2.   *ColdFusion MX subsystems*

If you have developed applications in ColdFusion in past versions, you should have no fear. ColdFusion still works the way you are used to it working, as a tag-based language that easily integrates with HTML. The difference is that there are plenty more options available to you if you need to advance your programming.

Benefits of Java

Why did Macromedia choose Java as the base for the next version of ColdFusion? Here are some reasons:

- **Faster development**   If you thought that ColdFusion was a rapid development tool before, then you haven't seen anything yet. The use of Java components and ability to create ColdFusion Components will make things even easier.

- **Portability**   It was the Java technology that coined the phrase "write once and run anywhere." Java languages are easily portable between operating systems and web servers. That means we can expect less discrepancy between ColdFusion for Linux and ColdFusion for Windows, for example.

- **Distributed applications**   The use of Java in the back end will make it easier to distribute Java applications from within ColdFusion. There are many choices for J2EE servers.

- **Native support for double-byte languages**   Java has built-in support for languages, such as Chinese and Japanese, that need to be encoded in double-byte formats.

- **Seamless interoperability with other languages**   The Java servers open up ColdFusion to a whole array of web services and standards, such as XML, SOAP, and even Microsoft's .NET services.

Overall, ColdFusion MX is a great platform for all your development needs.

Summary

In this chapter, you learned about the following:

- ColdFusion's place in the Web
- New features in ColdFusion MX
- The benefits of ColdFusion's new Java architecture

The next chapter will teach you how to get up and running with your ColdFusion Application Server.

ColdFusion
MX

Chapter 2

Installing the ColdFusion Server

This chapter teaches you how to set up and configure your ColdFusion machine. It shows you how to gauge the system requirements and steps you through the installation process of your server.

Evaluating Your Requirements

This section gives you an overview of the four different ColdFusion MX versions available. It shows you the differences between each version and tells you how to choose the hardware that meets your needs.

Choosing Which Version of ColdFusion MX You Need

The four different versions of ColdFusion MX are

- ColdFusion MX Professional Edition
- ColdFusion MX Enterprise Edition
- ColdFusion MX Developer Edition
- ColdFusion MX for J2EE Servers

The ColdFusion MX Developer Edition is a version of ColdFusion MX Enterprise that can only be accessed by a single IP address at a time. It is provided as a service to the developers who create ColdFusion applications. It cannot be licensed for production use.

ColdFusion MX for J2EE Servers is designed to act as a library plug-in for any stand-alone J2EE server. At the time of this writing, ColdFusion MX for J2EE Servers is not yet available, but versions have been announced for Macromedia JRun, IBM WebSphere Application Server, and Sun ONE Application Server. Only ColdFusion MX Professional and ColdFusion MX Enterprise are valid choices for your live production server. Table 2-1 shows a side-by-side comparison of features.

If you need to run on Solaris or HP-UX, then ColdFusion MX Enterprise is for you. If you need Security Sandbox, load balancing, built-in connectivity to advanced databases, or other advanced server management facilities, then ColdFusion MX Enterprise is for you. If you need to integrate with JSP pages, then get ColdFusion MX Enterprise. For anything else, save yourself some money and get ColdFusion MX Professional.

Evaluating Your System Requirements

The next choice you have to make is that of your operating system. Do you want to run on Windows, or do you want to run on Unix? ColdFusion MX will run on all versions of Windows. For production hosting, it is recommended that you use a server operating system, such as Windows 2000 Server, XP Professional, or NT Server. ColdFusion MX

Feature	ColdFusion MX Professional	ColdFusion MX Enterprise
Operating systems	Windows and Linux	Windows, Linux, Solaris, HP-UX
Database connectivity	**Windows:** ODBC, desktop databases, SQL Server, MySQL **Linux:** SQL Server, MySQL	**Windows:** ODBC, Access, SQL Server, Oracle, Informix, Sybase, DB2 **Linux:** SQL Server, MySQL, Oracle, Informix, Sybase, DB2
Verity search	125,000 documents	250,000 documents
Advanced deployment and management	No	Yes
Load balancing and failover	No	Yes
Enhanced Java integration	No	Yes, through a Java Server Page include or a Java Tag Library import
Security Sandbox	No	Yes

Table 2-1.   *Comparison of ColdFusion MX Professional with ColdFusion MX Enterprise*

Professional will run on Red Hat Linux and SuSE Linux. ColdFusion MX Enterprise also adds support for Solaris and HP-UX.

Once you choose you operating system, you can choose your web server. ColdFusion MX comes with an internal web server. It is great for development, but is not designed for hosting. If you are on a Windows unit, Microsoft IIS is the ideal choice. Apache is a common choice on Unix machines. The iPlanet or Netscape servers are also good choices for either Windows or Unix units. With the OS and web server choices behind you, you'll want to decide upon the hardware for your machine. Table 2-2 shows a list of the requirements that you should keep in mind as you pick your hardware.

Tip   *WebSite Pro is not officially supported, but its creator is working on creating a wrapper that will make it work. You can find out more information at www.deerfield.com.*

Resource	Windows	Unix
Processor	Pentium	Pentium for Linux SPARC for Solaris PA-RISC 1.1 or 2.0 for HP-UX
Minimum RAM	256MB	256MB
Recommended RAM	512MB	512MB
Disk space to install	400MB	350MB
Disk space to run	250MB	250MB
Web servers	ColdFusion MX Internal Server Microsoft IIS 4.0+ Netscape Enterprise Server 3.6+ iPlanet Enterprise Server 4.x, 6.x Apache Web Server 1.3.12 and higher	ColdFusion MX Internal Server Netscape Enterprise Server 3.6 and higher iPlanet Enterprise Server 4.x, 6.x Apache Web Server 1.3.12 and higher
Java Virtual Machine	Sun JDK/JRE 1.3.1 + IBM JVM 1.2.2 +	Sun JDK/JRE 1.3.1 + IBM JVM 1.2.2 +

Table 2-2.   *System Requirements for ColdFusion MX*

As a general rule, you want to have at least 512MB of RAM on your development machine. Since RAM is currently so cheap, I recommend bumping up RAM to 1,024MB or more. You need 400MB of disk space free to install on a Windows machine, or 350MB on a Unix machine. ColdFusion MX ships with its own Java Virtual Machine. For best results, I recommend using the version that ships with it.

Tip   *Development machines often have slightly lower memory requirements than server machines.*

Installing ColdFusion MX

This section steps you through the installation process for ColdFusion MX. It teaches you some things that you can do to help prepare for the installation and then steps you through the process of installing the software.

Preparing to Install

Here are some important things you should be aware of before you start to install ColdFusion MX:

- If you plan to interact with Flash and ColdFusion MX, you must install the Flash Remoting components in your Flash MX authoring environment.

- In ideal production environments, each ColdFusion application is hosted on a dedicated server. The database server, mail server, and other servers should not be running on the same machine.

- If you are installing on a Windows unit, do not configure ColdFusion MX as a primary or backup domain controller. Macromedia follows the Microsoft network model, and the primary and backup domain controllers are designed to manage a network or domain, not to run an application server.

- If you are installing on Unix, the installer creates a file called Macromedia_ColdFusion_MX_install.log file in the ColdFusion root directory.

Installing the Software

This section steps you through the installation process, and offers some post-installation advice. It also shows you the directory structure that the ColdFusion installation creates.

Stepping Through the Install Process

This section steps you through the installation process of ColdFusion MX. You can download the latest version from the Macromedia site. You may want to review the release notes before installing the software. They are located at www.macromedia.com/support/coldfusion/releasenotes.html. You can also read the ColdFusion MX installation documentation at http://livedocs.macromedia.com.

 Close all applications before installing ColdFusion MX.

Here are the steps to install ColdFusion MX on a Windows server:

1. Launch the Installer file. After some initial setup, you will see the Install Wizard Welcome page.

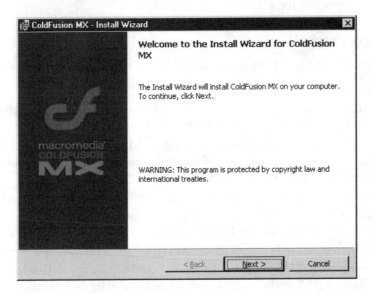

2. Click Next to move to the License Agreement wizard page. Read the agreement, and select the radio button that says you accept the terms of the agreement.

3. Click Next to move to the Customer Information wizard page. In the User Name, Organization, Serial Number, and Upgrade Serial Number boxes, enter your name, company, and serial number or upgrade serial number. You can leave the serial number blank if you are installing the evaluation or developer versions of the software.

4. Click Next to move to the Web Server wizard page, and then choose your web server.

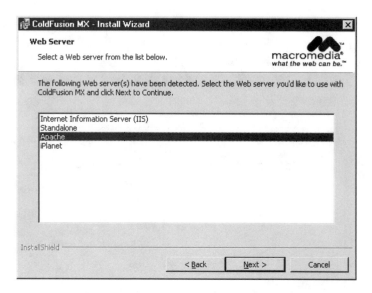

ColdFusion automatically detects the installed web servers. You most likely do not need more than one web server on your machine. ColdFusion automatically configures itself for the web server that you choose.

5. Click Next to move to the Webroot Folder wizard page.

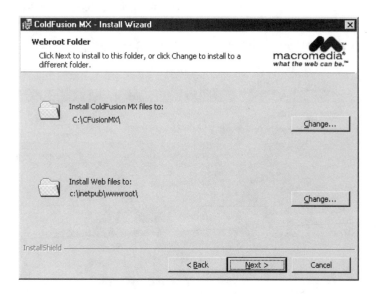

This screen allows you to select your ColdFusion installation directory and the root directory of your web server. ColdFusion automatically detects the correct root directory of your web server.

6. Click Next to move to the Custom Setup wizard page. You want to install the ColdFusion MX Application.

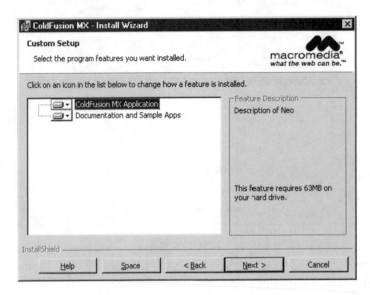

If you are installing on a production box, I recommend that you do not install the documentation and sample applications. If installed, a sneaky hacker can use them to break into your system.

7. Click Next to move to the Select Passwords wizard page, and choose your passwords.

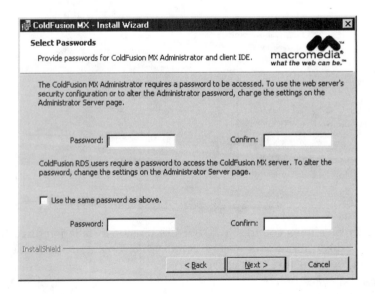

Enter the password that you want to use when you log in to the ColdFusion Administrator. You can also set the password that you want to use when logging in to the machine via Remote Development Services (RDS). If you want to use the same password for both the Administrator and RDS, you can select the checkbox. If necessary, you can disable the password from the ColdFusion Administrator later.

8. Click Next and review your settings. Click install. The software will install. Then click Finish to launch the ColdFusion Administrator and test your installation. You can start and stop your ColdFusion server from the Services control panel. There are three ColdFusion-related services: ColdFusion MX Application Server, ColdFusion MX ODBC Agent, and ColdFusion MX ODBC Server.

If you are running on Windows 9*x* or Windows Me, there are two executables that you can use to start services. Links are automatically placed in the Macromedia ColdFusion MX folder of the Start menu: ColdFusion Application Server will start the server, and ColdFusion RDS will shut down the server. Icons appear on the taskbar when these programs are launched. They can be shut down by right-clicking the icon and selecting Stop.

To install ColdFusion MX on a Unix machine, use these steps:

1. Log in to the operating system as root. Choose your proper installation file: cfusionmx_solaris_us.bin for Solaris installations, cfusionmx_linux_us.bin for Linux installations, and cfusionmx_hp_us.bin for HP-UX installations.

2. Modify the installation file with this command:

```
chmod 755 filename
```

Then start the installation process by executing the file with this command:

```
./<filename>
```

3. Step through the installation process. This process is similar to the installation for Windows units. For security purposes, it is recommended that you do not use the root user as the run-time user for ColdFusion MX.

4. Once the installation is complete, you can start the ColdFusion Application Server using this command:

```
/CFusionMX/bin/coldfusion start
```

The server can be stopped using this command:

```
/CFusionMX/bin/coldfusion stop
```

In normal circumstances, ColdFusion MX is set up to start when the computer is booted and to stop when the computer is turned off. You can restart ColdFusion Application Server using the restart parameter instead of start or stop.

Running ColdFusion MX for the First Time

If you had a previous installation of ColdFusion 5, the first time that you enter the ColdFusion Administrator, you will be given the option to copy over existing settings from CF5 into ColdFusion MX. If you decide not to migrate settings now, but wish to do so later, you can modify the value of the following Windows Registry key from 0 to 1:

```
HKEY_LOCAL_MACHINE\SOFTWARE\Macromedia\Install Data\
ColdFusionMX\migrate
```

You can perform the same task on a Unix machine by creating a blank upgrade file in the bin directory of the ColdFusion installation.

 When you migrate your ColdFusion 5 settings, you may lose settings that you already set up in ColdFusion MX.

Understanding the ColdFusion Files

Table 2-3 shows a list of subdirectories that will be installed on your machine. These directories contain the files that make ColdFusion MX run, configuration files, sample applications, and documentation.

Changing or Uninstalling Your ColdFusion MX Setup

On a Windows unit, you can change your ColdFusion setup by selecting ColdFusion MX from the Control Panel. This opens the Program Maintenance page of the Install Wizard. This page has three options from which you can choose:

- **Modify** Choose this if you want to change your ColdFusion MX installation, perhaps by removing or adding sample applications.

- **Repair** Choose this if something is wrong with your ColdFusion MX installation. It will fix your problems.

- **Uninstall** Choose this if you want to remove ColdFusion MX from the current machine. If you uninstall, the ColdFusion installation directory may not be deleted automatically. You want to make sure that you back up any custom files, such as custom tags, CFX tags, or web files, before deleting this directory.

On a Unix machine, you can uninstall ColdFusion MX by going into the uninstall directory of the ColdFusion root directory and running the following command:

```
./uninstall.sh
```

GETTING STARTED

Directory	Description
bin	Contains the binary files that make ColdFusion MX run.
cache	Contains temporary files created by ColdFusion MX when it is running.
cfx	Contains sample CFX custom tags. You can read about how to create these in Chapter 26.
charting	Contains files for the ColdFusion MX charting engine.
customtags	Contains all CFML custom tags.
db	Contains the databases for the sample applications.
jintegra	Contains files to integrate Java and COM, manage ActiveX access, and perform other actions that need the jintegra programs.
jre	In Unix, contains the Java Runtime Engine. In Windows, it is under the runtime directory.
lib	Contains JAR, XML, and other files that are the foundation of ColdFusion MX functionality.
logs	Contains many of the ColdFusion MX logs.
mail	Contains spooled mail and undelivered mail.
META-INF	Contains XML metadata for the ColdFusion Administrator.
registry	In Unix, contains flat files that mimic a Windows Registry. This will become obsolete in future versions of ColdFusion.
runtime	Contains programs that support ColdFusion runtime. In Windows, the Java Runtime Engine is located here.
uninstall	On Unix, contains files to tell how to uninstall ColdFusion MX.
verity	Contains Verity collections.
wwwroot	The default web root directory for the stand-alone server.

Table 2-3.   *Directories of ColdFusion MX*

Performing Configuration Tasks

This section shows some of the different settings that you may need to configure for different web servers. It starts by looking at the built-in web server and then goes on to explain some other configuration tasks that you may want to deal with.

Working with the Internal Web Server

A new feature in ColdFusion MX is that it comes with a built-in web server. This web server is great for development and is set up automatically by the ColdFusion MX installation. This helps you to avoid the headache of installing and setting up an external web server, such as Apache or Windows Personal Web Server.

The internal web server is set up to listen to port 8500. You can surf it by pointing your browser to localhost:8500. The web server's root directory is located in the wwwroot directory of the ColdFusion MX installation directory.

You can configure settings of the internal web server by modifying the jrun.xml file, which contains configuration information for the core services of the internal web server. It is located in the directory CFusionMX\runtime\servers\default\SERVER-INF. Near the end of the file, you will see this group of lines:

```
<service class="jrun.servlet.jrpp.JRunProxyService"
         name="ProxyService">
 <attribute name="port">8500</attribute>
 <attribute name="deactivated">false</attribute>
</service>
```

You can change the port number to anything that you wish. After you do so, you have to restart the ColdFusion Application Server for the changes to take effect.

If you want to create virtual directories for your web server, you can add lines, similar to these, to the jrun.xml file:

```
<virtual-mapping>
 <resource-path>/htdocs/*</resource-path>
 <system-path>C:\htdocs</system-path>
</virtual-mapping>
```

The resource-path tag is the name of the virtual directory. The system-path tag defines the file location that the virtual path will point to when called from a browser.

Changing Your Web Server

This section shows you how you can configure web servers manually from the command line. After the configuration, it shows you how to verify the installation for various web servers.

Configuring Your Web Server

If you want to configure a different web server after ColdFusion MX has been installed, there is a way to do it. By running the Java program with various parameters, you can configure any particular web server. On Unix machines, the java file is located in the CFusionMX/jre/bin directory. On Windows machines, it is located in the CFusionMX\runtime\jre\bin directory.

To set up Microsoft IIS, use this command at the command prompt (it must reside all on one line):

```
C:\CFusionMX\runtime\jre\bin\java -cp cf_root\runtime\lib
-jar C:\CFusionMX\runtime\lib\wsconfig.jar -wd IIS -site "0"
-map .cfm,.cfc,.cfml,.jsp -v
```

Since Microsoft IIS won't work on Unix machines, there is no Unix version of the command for IIS. Versions of this command do exist for other web servers, though.

To configure Netscape Enterprise Server or iPlanet Server, use this command (it must reside all on one line):

```
C:\CFusionMX\runtime\jre\bin\java -cp cf_root\runtime\lib
-jar C:\CFusionMX\runtime\lib\wsconfig.jar -ws <Iplanet or NES>
-dir <Netscape/iPlanet config directory> -v
```

The method is similar if you want to configure Netscape or iPlanet on a Unix machine (again, should be all on one line):

```
opt/CFusionMX/jre/bin/java
-jar opt/CFusionMX/runtime/lib/wsconfig.jar -ws <Iplanet or NES>
-dir <Netscape/iPlanet config directory> -v
```

The cp parameter is left out when running on a Unix-based box, but otherwise the concepts are the same.

Apache on Windows can be set up like this (all on one line):

```
c:\cfusionmx\runtime\jre\bin\java -cp c:\cfusionmx\runtime\lib
-jar c:\cfusionmx\runtime\lib\wsconfig.jar -ws Apache
-dir c:\Program Files\Apache Group\Apache\conf -v
```

Configuring Apache on Unix is similar, except that the cp parameter is left out and the directories are different (code should be all on one line):

```
opt/CFusionMX/jre/bin/java
-jar opt/CFusionMX/runtime/lib/wsconfig.jar -ws Apache
-dir c:\Program Files\Apache Group\Apache\conf -v
```

Verifying the New Installation

You can verify your updated configuration in a number of ways. The easiest way to make sure that something is working is to browse to a ColdFusion page residing on the web server. You can also manually check the settings. This section shows you what to look for.

1. Launch the Internet Services Manager.
2. Open the Properties dialog box for the web site and click the Home tab.
3. Click the Configuration button to open the Application Configuration dialog box.
4. Click the App Mappings tab and make sure that there are mappings pointing to the .cfm, .cfc, .cfml, and .jsp files.

To verify your configuration in IIS, first make sure that the jrun.dll file was created in the runtime\libs\wsconfig directory. Then verify that the mappings were created for your web sites. Follow these steps:

1. Launch the Internet Services Manager.
2. Right click on your web site's name and select properties.
3. Click the Home tab.
4. Click the Configuration button to open the Application Configuration dialog box. Click on the App Mappings tab.
5. Verify that mappings exist for.cfm, .cfc, .cfml, and .jsp files:

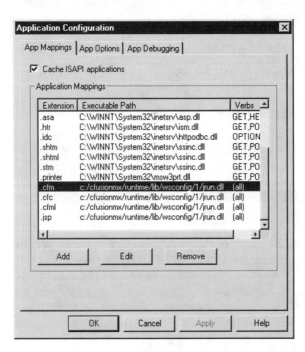

Then make sure that a virtual directory called JRunScripts exists on each of your web sites. This directory should point to the CFusionMX/runtime/lib/wsconfig/1 directory.

In iPlanet or Netscape, the pertinent DLL is run_nsapi35.dll. Make sure that it is created. Open the obj.conf file in your web server directory and make sure that the following line is in the file:

```
NameTrans fn="jrunfilter"
```

Also make sure that JRun was added to the prefix of this line:

```
#JRun NameTrans fn="pfx2dir"
        from="/servlet" dir="e:/netscape/servers/docs/servlet"
```

Near the end of the file, an object should have been added that looks like this:

```
<Object name="jrun">
 PathCheck fn="jrunfilter"
 Service fn="jrunservice"
</Object>
```

If all these actions have occurred, then your Netscape and iPlanet configurations are all set and ready to go.

The Apache configuration can also be verified by some setting changes and the existence of certain files. Look for a file named mod_jrun.so, in the CFusionMX\runtime\lib\wsconfig\1\ directory. Then check the apache configuration file, usually httpd.conf. This information should have been added to it:

```
# JRun Settings
LoadModule jrun_module
                "c:/CFusionMX/runtime/lib/wsconfig/1/mod_jrun.so"
<IfModule mod_jrun.c>
    JRunConfig Verbose false
    JRunConfig Apialloc false
    JRunConfig Ssl false
    JRunConfig Serverstore
            "c:/CFusionMX/runtime/lib/wsconfig/1/jrunserver.store"
    JRunConfig Bootstrap 127.0.0.1:51000
    #JRunConfig Errorurl <URL for errors>
</IfModule>
```

The Serverstore parameter will contain different values for Unix or Windows machines or if you used a custom installation directory.

Performing Miscellaneous Configuration Tasks

There are some other actions that you may want to perform on your ColdFusion MX installation. The first thing that you may want to do is to enable or disable Remote Development Services. Follow these steps:

1. Find the web.xml file in the wwwroot\WEB-INF directory of your ColdFusion MX installation.

2. Find the servlet-mapping tag that contains a servlet-name tag with the value of RDSServlet. It will look like this:

```
<servlet-mapping>
 <servlet-name>RDSServlet</servlet-name>
 <url-pattern>/CFIDE/main/ide.cfm</url-pattern>
</servlet-mapping>
```

3. Comment out the mapping with HTML comments to disable RDS. Remove the comments to enable RDS.

4. Restart your ColdFusion Application Server for the settings to take effect.

If you are running on a Windows Server machine, the next thing you will want to do is to change the user that the ColdFusion services runs under. Here is how you can do it:

1. From the Administrative Tools section of the Control Panel, launch Computer Management.

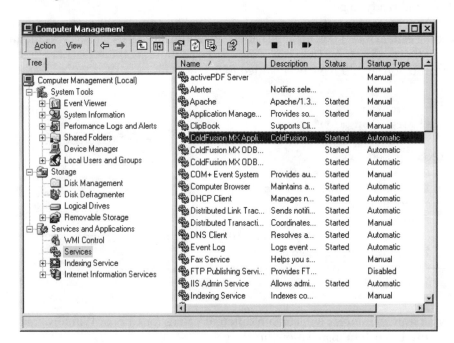

GETTING STARTED

2. Expand the Services And Applications menu and select Services.

3. Right-click the ColdFusion MX Application Server service, select Properties, and choose the Log On tab.

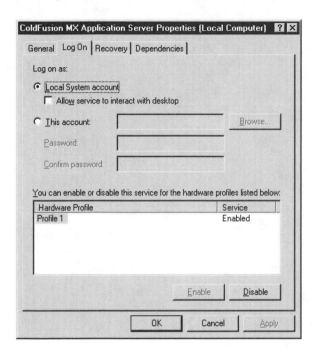

4. Select This Account and enter the account information. Click OK to save your changes.

5. Restart the service.

Summary

In this chapter, you learned about the following:

■ The differences between ColdFusion MX Enterprise and ColdFusion MX Professional

■ The installation process for ColdFusion MX

■ How to set up ColdFusion MX for Apache and configure the ColdFusion MX internal web server

The next chapter will show you how to get around in the ColdFusion Administrator.

ColdFusion
MX

Chapter 3

Getting Around
in the ColdFusion
Administrator

Afler you have finished installing your ColdFusion server, you are ready to start hosting sites on your web box. This chapter teaches you how to get around in the web-based ColdFusion Administrator and demonstrates its abilities.

Learning the Basics

This section gives you a broad overview of the ColdFusion Administrator, and then introduces the security features of the Administrator, telling you how to log in and deal with your password.

Introducing the Administrator

This section describes some of the functions of the ColdFusion Administrator, and where to go to access those functions. Table 3-1 shows the functionality that can be achieved from the ColdFusion Administrator and where you can learn more about each function in this book.

If You Want To	Go Here in ColdFusion Administrator	Go Here in This Book
Create a site-wide error handler	General Settings	Chapter 18
Create a default missing template handler	General Settings	Chapter 18
Modify the request timeout	General Settings	This chapter, in "Understanding the General Settings"
Set the simultaneous request limit	General Settings	This chapter, in "Understanding the General Settings"
Set cftoken to be a UUID	General Settings	This chapter, in "Understanding the General Settings"
Modify whitespace management	General Settings	This chapter, in "Understanding the General Settings"
Control caching of templates and queries	Caching	This chapter, in "Handling Memory Management"

Table 3-1.   *Capabilities of the ColdFusion Administrator*

If You Want To	Go Here in ColdFusion Administrator	Go Here in This Book
Set up client variable management	Client Variables	This chapter, in "Working with Client Variables"
Set up session variable defaults	Memory Variables	This chapter, in "Handling Memory Management"
Set application variable defaults	Memory Variables	This chapter, in "Handling Memory Management"
Control directory mappings	Mappings	Chapter 6
Configure mail server settings	Mail Server	Chapter 6
Set chart cache settings	Charting	This chapter, in "Handling Memory Management"
Set Java settings	Java and JVM Settings	Chapter 6
Maintain archives	Manage Archives	Chapter 6
Create datasources	Data Sources	This chapter, in "Dealing with Databases"
Maintain Verity collections	Verity Collections	Chapter 24
Configure Verity K2 Server	Verity K2 Server	Chapter 24
Maintain Web services	Web Services	Chapters 6 and 31
Modify debug output	Debugging Settings	Chapters 6 and 18
Limit debugging output to specific IP address	Debugging IP Addresses	Chapters 6 and 18
Change the log directory	Logging Settings	Chapter 6
Modify logging settings	Logging Settings	Chapter 6
View log files	Log Files	Chapter 6
Maintain scheduled tasks	Scheduled Tasks	This chapter, "Automated Tasks"
Maintain system probes	System Probes	This chapter, "Automated Tasks"
Test ColdFusion code for ColdFusion MX compatibility	Code Analyzer	Chapter 12

Table 3-1. *Capabilities of the ColdFusion Administrator* (continued)

If You Want To	Go Here in ColdFusion Administrator	Go Here in This Book
Register Java applets for use with cfform	Java Applets	Chapter 6
Maintain CFX tags	CFX Tags	Chapters 6 and 26
Add a new custom tag path	Custom Tag Paths	Chapter 6
Maintain CORBA connector	CORBA Connectors	Chapter 6
Set up security sandbox	Settings	Chapter 4
Change admin password	CF Admin Password	This chapter, "Changing Your Passwords"
Change RDS password	RDS Password	This chapter, "Changing Your Passwords"
Configure sandbox security	Sandbox Security	Chapter 4

Table 3-1. *Capabilities of the ColdFusion Administrator* (continued)

Securing the Administrator

As you can see from the preceding section, a lot of things can be done from the ColdFusion Administrator. You will want to take pains to make sure that it is as secure as possible. Thankfully, the ColdFusion installer asked for some passwords when you installed it that help you protect your Administrator.

Logging In

To access the web-based Administrator, just point your browser to http://localhost/cfide/administrator/. If you are trying to access the Administrator remotely, you have to enter the IP address or web server instead of using the name localhost. If you are on a server with multiple domains, the Administrator will have to be mapped.

When you get there, you will see a screen much like this:

When you installed your ColdFusion server, as described in Chapter 2, you were asked for a password. Enter this password here and click the Login button. Congratulations! You have now entered the ColdFusion Administrator, as shown in Figure 3-1.

Changing Your Passwords

You can easily change the relevant passwords from within the ColdFusion Administrator if you need to. At the bottom of the navigation bar are two password change links, one for the admin password and one for the RDS password. We used the ColdFusion admin password to log in, so let's change that first.

Click the CF Admin Password link, and the password change screen will open.

Click the button on the right to update ColdFusion Administrator Password... | Submit Changes |

☑ **Use a ColdFusion Administration Password.**

The ColdFusion Administrator should be restricted exclusively to trusted users. By default, an administrative password is required to access these pages. If you configure your web server to restrict access to these pages you may opt to disable this administrative password and rely on your web server's security instead. (Consult your web server documentation for details on securing pages.) To change the ColdFusion administrator password, enter a new password and confirm it below:

New Password [   ]   Confirm Password [   ]

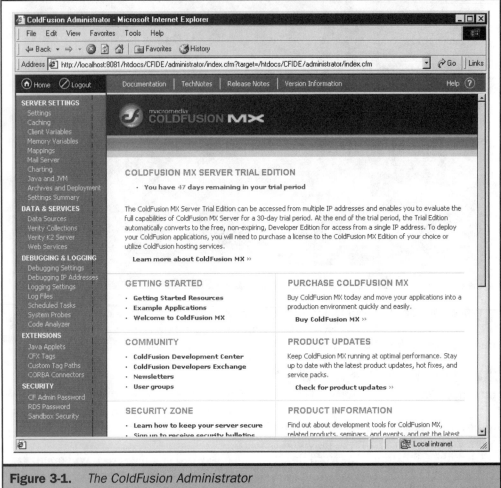

Figure 3-1. *The ColdFusion Administrator*

If you want to forgo the password altogether, clear the Use A ColdFusion Administration Password checkbox. If this is unchecked, you are able to bypass the login screen. Unless you are on a development machine that is protected from outside intruders, it is not a good idea to uncheck this checkbox. To change the password, type your new password in the New Password box and in the Confirm Password box. Click the Submit Changes button to change the password.

The RDS password allows users to access Remote Development Services (RDS) from within ColdFusion Studio or through a Dreamweaver MX site. The password change screen operates in much the same way as the CF Administrator Password change screen. There is a check box to disable the password if you do not want to use it, and two boxes for your new password. Pressing the Submit Changes button will change the password.

Resetting a Forgotten Password

What happens when you forget your password and cannot log in to the Administrator? Thankfully, even if you forget your password, there is still a way to reset it. Follow this procedure:

1. Open up the neo-security.xml file in the lib directory of your ColdFusion installation.

2. Look for this line:

```
<var name='admin.security.enabled'>
 <boolean value='true'/>
</var>
```

3. Change the Boolean value from true to false.

4. Restart your ColdFusion server.

5. You can now change your password normally from within the Administrator. If you cannot, go directly to the page localhost/CFIDE/administrator/security/cfadminpassword.cfm.

If you are using a version of ColdFusion 5 or earlier, you can reset the password by editing the Registry. Go to the key HKEY_LOCAL_MACHINE | Software | Allaire | ColdFusion | CurrentVersion | Server. Find the UseAdminPassword attribute, and set it to 0. Repeat Steps 4 and 5 in the preceding list.

Understanding the General Settings

Now that you are in the ColdFusion Administrator, you can start to poke around at specific settings. This section teaches you about some of the basic things you can do from the Administrator.

Global Settings

To review and change server settings, begin by clicking Settings under Server Settings in the navigation bar. Many different items can be controlled from this page:

- **Limit Simultaneous Requests To** x This setting restricts the number of requests that ColdFusion will try to process at the same time. If ColdFusion has more requests than this number, then additional requests will have to wait until one is finished before starting to execute. If you expect a lot of users to access your application at one time, then giving this value a greater number will increase performance.

- **Timeout Requests After** x **Seconds**   When this box is checked, the ColdFusion server will terminate specific requests that are taking too long to process, based on the time that you specify. This will prevent unusually long requests from wasting server resources.

■ **Use UUID For CFToken**   The cftoken is a special variable used in conjunction with session variables. When this is box is unchecked, ColdFusion chooses a random number for this value. When it is checked, ColdFusion creates a UUID value. UUID values are 35-character string representations of 128-bit integers. You can use the CreateUUID function to create them on your own if necessary (see Appendix A and the ColdFusion documentation for more on the CreateUUID function).

■ **Enable HTTP Status Codes**   Check this box to allow ColdFusion to set status codes when unhandled exceptions occur.

■ **Enable Whitespace Management**   Check this box to remove the extraneous whitespace created by many ColdFusion tags when streaming results back to the browser. To do this on a template basis, you can use the cfsetting or cfsilent tags.

■ **Missing Template Handler**   The filename you enter here will be called whenever a link points to a missing file. This can be overridden by application-specific error handling, such as described in Chapter 18.

■ **Site-Wide Error Handler**   The filename you enter here will be called upon whenever there is an error anywhere in the site. This can be overridden by application-specific error handling, such as described in Chapter 18.

Handling Memory Management

Understanding the inner workings of your server is important. This section discusses some settings that control how ColdFusion can access and use the memory on the server machine.

Caching Issues

A *cache* is something that is stored in memory, as opposed to on disk, for easy and fast retrieval. First, click the Caching link under Server Settings to open the Caching page. There are three different values you can change here:

■ **Template Cache Size**   This value represents the number of templates that you want to be able to cache on your server. The more templates that are in memory, the faster the templates will execute. If you are after high performance values, then setting this to a very high number would serve you well. ColdFusion will collect memory as it needs it, so you do not need to worry about losing all your memory instantly by setting this to a high number.

■ **Trusted Cache**   If this box is checked, then any templates found to already reside in the cache will not be compared to the uncached copy. If you do not update templates, then this will increase the performance of your server.

■ **Limit the Maximum Number of Cached Queries on the Server to** x This number specifies the maximum number of cached queries that can be located on the server. We discuss queries in more detail in Chapter 9. A query is the result of getting data from a database. Storing the results in memory improves performance.

The Caching page doesn't contain everything we need to discuss regarding memory management. Click the Charting link.

The Charting Settings page deals with ColdFusion's cfgraph tag. We will examine the cfchart tag in more detail in Chapter 20. Basically, it is a way to create dynamic graphs in your ColdFusion application, using a variety of formats. This page has four settings:

■ **Cache Type**   There are two options, either memory or disk. Memory caching is much more efficient, but will suck up your memory. Disk caching is the default. Unless you have high use of the cfgraph tag, you will want to keep this to disk caching.

■ **Maximum Number of Images in Cache**   This specifies the number of charts to store in the cache. When you reach the limit, the oldest one will be discarded in favor of the newest. If you are going to have multiple requests for identical charts, this increases performance because the chart doesn't have to be generated each time.

■ **Maximum Number of Charting Threads**   This value accepts a range of 1 to 5. The higher the number, the more memory-intensive the chart creation process is.

■ **Disk Cache Location**   This field can be used to specify the location of your disk cache. If you need to change this, you will want to point it to a temporary directory.

Both the Charting Settings and Caching pages deal with the data that ColdFusion stores in the server's memory. Caching is not the only item ColdFusion needs memory for. Read on!

Working with Application and Session Variables

Click the Memory Variables link to open the Memory Variables page. Application and session variables are two types of variables stored in ColdFusion's memory. They are discussed in detail in Chapter 8. This is the list of operations you can perform on this page:

■ **Use J2EE Session Variables**   If you want to share session data between ColdFusion and JSP pages, then make sure that this option is checked.

■ **Enable Application Variables**   This allows you to turn on, or off, application variables.

- **Enable Session Variables**   This allows you to turn on, or off, session variables.
- **Maximum Timeout**   You can specify the maximum timeout for application and session variables in days, hours, minutes, and seconds. These values cannot be overridden in the code.

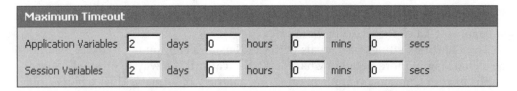

- **Default Timeout**   These values specify the default timeouts for application and session variables, in days, hours, minutes, and seconds (the setup is the same as was shown for the Maximum Timeout values). These values can be overridden in ColdFusion code.

Dealing with Databases

The meat and potatoes of your ColdFusion applications will be a database. We discuss how to access databases from a programmer's standpoint in Chapter 9. But, that chapter assumes that the system administrator has already set up ColdFusion to access the database by creating a database. This section shows you how to set up a datasource for use from within your ColdFusion applications.

Creating a Datasource

Databases are accessed from ColdFusion via an ODBC connection. These are the steps to create an ODBC datasource:

1. From your ColdFusion Administrator, click the Data Sources link under Data & Services to open the Data Sources page.

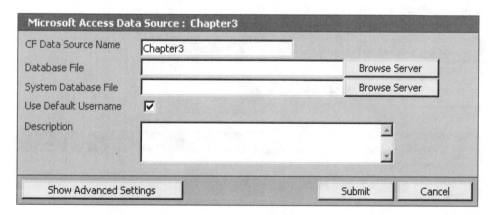

Add New Data Source

Data Source Name	
Driver	DB2 UDB for OS/390 ▼

Add

Connected Data Sources

Actions	Data Source Name	Driver	Status
🔲 ☑ ⊠	cfsnippets	ODBC Socket	
🔲 ☑ ⊠	Chapter17	Microsoft Access	
🔲 ☑ ⊠	CompanyInfo	ODBC Socket	
🔲 ☑ ⊠	exampleapps	ODBC Socket	

Verify All Connections

2. Type the name of the datasource you want to create and select the driver you are going to use for the datasource. I named the datasource Chapter3 and selected Microsoft SQL Server [Macromedia]. Click Add, and you will see this page:

Microsoft Access Data Source : Chapter3

CF Data Source Name	Chapter3
Database File	[ ] Browse Server
System Database File	[ ] Browse Server
Use Default Username	☑
Description	[ ]

Show Advanced Settings   Submit   Cancel

3. Fill out the appropriate data. The data that you are asked to enter will change for each datasource. For a SQL Server datasource, I entered the IP address of the server, the username, and the password. The data you need to enter will vary depending upon the driver.

4. Click the Submit button. You will be redirected back to the Data Sources main page. Your new datasource should be listed and verified. The ok next to the datasource shows you the verification.

You can also verify all connections from the Data Sources page. When you click the Verify All Connections button, each datasource will be queried and will state "ok" if it verified okay, or "failed" if it did not.

 As long as the datasource is on the server machine and the Java ODBC services are activated, ColdFusion will be able to access it.

Working with Client Variables

This section describes how to work with client variables. Client variables do not inherently relate to databases, but that is the most common storage repository for them, which is why the information on client variables is placed here.

Client variables are an important part of session management and ColdFusion's application framework, as described in Chapter 8. They are a way to store information regarding a particular user. Click the Client Variables link under Server Settings to open the Client Variables page.

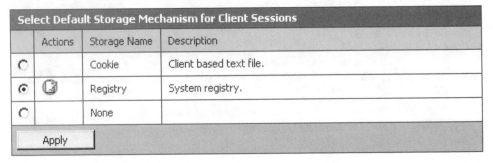

There are three options you can choose for client variable storage. The first is cookies. This means that for each user, the client variables are stored as cookies on the user's machine. This is functional, although it does have some limitations. Browsers will usually restrict the number of cookies that can be placed by any one domain. Additionally, there is a limit to the total amount of space that those cookies can take up. Storing client variables as cookies is easy to set up, with no additional work by the administrator. It also makes for quick data retrieval.

The next option is to store client variables in the Registry of the server machine. This is generally considered a bad move. With high-traffic sites, the Registry can easily become too big, causing problems with the server machine. Additionally, the Registry is not designed for mass storage or retrieval of data. Client variables are often used on every page request. The Registry is considered the worst choice for client variable storage. The benefits of Registry storage are that retrieval of the values is quick and easy.

There is a third choice that is the preferred by many hosts, and that is storing client variables in a database. The main drawback to database storage is speed. Getting data from a database is slower than retrieving data from the Registry or as cookies. Storing in a database does not have any storage limitations, other than hard drive space, and it will not cause harm to the machine, as might happen if the Registry balloons beyond its maximum size. Storing in a database is the preferred method.

The Client Variables page has two radio button options for storing client variables. You can choose Registry or Cookie by selecting the option and clicking the Apply button. To use a datasource, you can follow this procedure:

1. Create the database as an empty database, using whatever database software you choose. SQL Server is a common choice.

2. Set up the datasource as described earlier in this chapter.

3. Choose your datasource name from the list on top of the screen and click Add.

4. In the next screen that appears, enter a description in the box at the top of the page. This may contain any text you want.

5. Keep the Create Client Database Tables box checked, unless you have created them manually. I don't recommend creating them manually.

6. Select the Purge Data For Clients That Remain Unvisited For *x* Days checkbox. Enter the number of days after which you want to purge unvisited variables. Client variables do not need to be stored forever.

7. Choose whether you want to select the Disable Global Client Variable Updates checkbox. There are two global client variables for each user: HitCount and LastVisit. If updates are enabled, these values are modified on each page request.

8. Click the Submit Changes button. This returns you to the Client Variables home page. You'll notice that the datasource is not selected yet. Select it and click Apply.

You have now set up your server to use client variables.

Before ending this section, I want to specify what tables are created for client variable storage. Two tables, CData and CGlobal, are created. These are the columns in CData:

- **CFID**   Contains a unique identifier for the user
- **App**   Contains the name of the application that the variables are associated with
- **Data**   Contains the client variables

The CGlobal table contains these columns:

- **CFID**   Contains a unique identifier for the user
- **Data**   Contains the HitCount, LastVisit, and TimeCreated variables
- **LVisit**   Contains the date of the user's last visit

Client variables are a very powerful tool in the developer's toolbox. Making sure that they are set up with the developer's best interests in mind will pay off.

Automating Tasks

This section describes some of the automation functions in ColdFusion. There are two important automation features built into the server administrator. One is called a probe, and the other is called a scheduled task.

Creating Probes and Scheduling Tasks

A *probe* is a way to routinely check a specific URL and send an e-mail message if the results it returns are unexpected. *Scheduled tasks* are a way to execute a certain CFML template at a specified interval. This section shows you how to set up each.

Creating a Probe

Click the System Probes link under Debugging & Logging in your ColdFusion Administrator to open the System Probes page.

Click the button on the right to update System Probes... | Submit Changes |

System probes can monitor the health of a web application by checking the contents of a URL at a regular interval. If the contents are not what was expected, probes can send a failure notification email or execute a script.

Define New Probe

System Probes

Actions	Probe Name	Status	Interval	URL

No probes have been defined.

Notification Email Recipients	
Notification Sent From	ColdFusionProbe@localhost
Probe.cfm URL	http://127.0.0.1:8081/CFIDE/probe.cfm
Probe.cfm Username	
Probe.cfm Password	

The first thing that you want to do is to define who will receive notification in case of a problem. You fill this out in the Notification Email Recipients field. The Probe.cfm URL field contains the generic code used to execute a probe. You will probably not ever have to change this. The Notification Sent From field specifies the e-mail address in the From field of the notification e-mail. The Probe.cfm Username and Probe.cfm Password fields specify the authentication method you want to use to get to the page in case it resides in a password-protected directory.

This is how you create a new probe:

1. Click the Define New Probe button.

2. In the screen that appears, enter a name for the probe. I used CheckMySite.

3. Set the frequency of the probe. I set my probe to run every four hours.

4. Enter the URL that you want to verify. I entered index.cfm. If you wanted to check for a database query or other item, you could write a page specifically for that purpose.

5. Enter the username and password, if applicable, to reach your test page.

6. Enter the Proxy Server information, if applicable.

7. Define how the probe fails or succeeds. You can check whether the results contain (or do not contain) a specific value. The value could be a string or a regular expression. Regular expressions are beyond the scope of this book.

8. Set the probe's failure action. There are two different actions that the probe can do upon failure. First, you could set it up to send an e-mail to the e-mail address that you specified in the previous page. The second option is to execute a program. You can set this up to run a batch file that will restart your server services, for example.

9. Choose your Publish action. If you check this box, the results will be output to a file. You can enter the filename you wish to output to.

10. Set the Resolve URL attribute. In the return e-mail, this will send you absolute URLs instead of return URLs.

11. Click Submit. You will now see your probe listed on the System Probes page.

System Probes				
Actions	Probe Name	Status	Interval	URL
🖉 🜨 🜨 🜨	CheckMySite	Unknown	Every 4 hour(s) from 10:00:00	http://localhost:8081/htdocs/farcryfly/index.cfm

The Actions column contains four buttons for actions that you can perform on the probe; from left to right they are Edit, Run, Disable (or Enable), and Delete. Only the Disable probe or Enable probe buttons will displayed, depending upon the current status of the probe.

A probe has one of four different statuses, as indicated in the Status column on the System Probes page:

■ **OK**   The probe was successfully executed.

■ **Failed**   The probe failed the last time it was run.

- **Unknown**   The probe has not run since the last server restart.
- **Disabled**   The probe has been disabled.

   Probes run as scheduled tasks in ColdFusion and therefore will not run if the ColdFusion server goes offline.

Scheduling a Task

A probe is actually just a specialized version of a scheduled task. Scheduled tasks are a way to automatically execute a ColdFusion template. The most common use for scheduled tasks that I have come across is for automatic report generation. You can create a CFML page to parse your data, and create reports and store them in a database. Click Scheduled Tasks under Debugging & Logging to open the Scheduled Tasks page.

This is how you create a scheduled task:

1. Click the Schedule New Task Button to open the Add/Edit Scheduled Task page.

Add/Edit Scheduled Task

Task Name	
Duration	Start Date May 13, 2002 End Date (optional)
Frequency	⦿ **One-Time** at 22:07:20
	○ **Recurring** Daily ▾ at
	○ **Daily every** Hours 0 Minutes 0 Seconds 0
	Start Time End Time
URL	http://
User Name	
Password	
Timeout (sec)	
Proxy Server	:
Publish	☐ Save output to a file
File	
Resolve URL	☐ Resolve internal URLs so that links remain intact

Submit   Cancel

2. Enter a Task Name. I entered MyNewTask.

3. The Start Date is automatically filled in to today's date, but you change it to any date of your choosing.

4. You can set up your scheduled task to run once, run once a day (or week or month) at a specific time, or daily on a specific interval.

5. Enter the URL of your scheduled task.

6. Enter the User Name and Password, if applicable, to access the scheduled task.

7. Enter the Timeout value, in seconds.

8. Enter the Proxy Server, if applicable.

9. Select whether you want to publish the results. Publishing the results will save the output to a file. You can specify the name of the file you want to save the output to.

10. Select whether to resolve the URL link. In the file, this will change relative URLs to absolute URLs.

11. Once the task is created, you will see it on the Scheduled Tasks list, and you can modify, run, or delete it as needed.

Tip *You can also create scheduled tasks using the cfschedule tag.*

Summary

In this chapter, you learned about the following:

- Basic information about the ColdFusion Administrator
- How to create a datasource
- How to implement scheduled tasks and probes
- Session, application, and client variables

The next chapter will talk about securing your server.

The
Complete
Reference

ColdFusion
MX

Part II

Administering Your
ColdFusion Server

The Complete Reference

ColdFusion MX

Chapter 4

Securing Your Server

When you put a server out on the Internet, many people have access to it. Often that is what you want. You want people to come to your site and reap the benefits that you have to offer. Due to the public nature of web servers, you want to take care to protect the information on your web server. This chapter teaches you some of the pitfalls that you should avoid in order to protect your ColdFusion applications.

Learning Some Security Best Practices

This section looks at some security best practices with regard to your ColdFusion application. We will look at where you should place your files, how they are accessed, and pitfalls to watch out for.

Some Security Basics

First, we want to examine some basic security definitions. Next, we will discuss some basic security practices that you can apply to your own machine.

Understanding Security Definitions

Before we start talking about how to secure your server, you need to know the language. Much of this language probably is not new to you, but you may not have thought about these issues with security in mind. The following are the basic definitions you should understand:

- **User**   A single entity that has access to your system. Everything regarding security starts with the user. A user is the root of all security concerns, whether good or bad. Without users, you would have no need for security.

- **Resource**   The item that needs to be protected, whether it is a machine, hard drive, datasource, or specific file.

- **Rule**   Another name for a resource.

- **Login**   Usually a username and password combination that a user can use to access resources. Most security problems occur when a user uses a login that was not intended for that user.

- **Group**   A collection of users. It is easier to maintain access to specific resources on a group basis than on an individual basis.

- **Directory**   Another name for a group (also called *user directory*).

- **Permissions**   The type of access that a user has to a particular resource. The four types of permissions to data are usually grouped by read, write, execute, and delete. Read means that the user can view the files. Write means the user can write files. Delete means the user can remove files. Execute means that the user can run the programs.

- **Policy**   A collection of resources (rules) and groups (directories). It means that these users can access these resources.

For various reasons, security has not been an important issue in the past. The main reason, in my experience, is finances. An application doesn't always have to be secure to be functional. Sometimes developers end up setting up servers because it is cheaper than hiring a server administrator. The primary concern of a developer is, of course, functionality, not security. Security concerns are not always obvious.

There are three areas where breaches can take place in your web application. One is on the operating system level of the web server. The second is with regard to the database, or database server. The third is from within ColdFusion itself.

Practicing Web Server Security

There are some basic things that you can do, as a server administrator, to help protect your server from the infamous hacking community. Many of them are simple, as the following list demonstrates:

- **Document your company's policies**   While this doesn't directly relate to anything in hardware or software, it does provide a reference that you can use to determine what constitutes a security breach and what doesn't. Policies will also help support your legal case if you ever end up in court.

- **Limit access to servers**   If anybody can walk in and sit down at your computer's console and use it, that computer is not secure. Make sure that you use a "need to know" type of policy when providing access to your servers. If a user does not need access, there is no reason to provide it. Don't provide users with more access than they need.

- **Change passwords**   Changing passwords on a routine basis is considered to be a good security practice. Making sure that the passwords and login names are not the default will increase security.

- **Turn off unused services**   The more features that are on a web server, the more likely it is that one of them will allow hackers a back door into the machine. If you aren't using services, extensions, shells, or other programs, remove them from the server. For instance, if you don't use Perl scripts, don't install Perl on your machine.

- **Set permissions**   Make sure that permissions are properly set. You probably want your web server directory to be available to anonymous users, but not the root directory of your main drive. Make sure that execute capability is limited to web users. You probably want them to be able to execute only in a single directory, often called the Scripts directory.

Space is limited in this book, so unfortunately I am unable to go into specific operating system details for each of these safeguards. Reading the documentation of your operating system of choice would be a good start. Also check out these books: *Hacking Exposed: Network Security Secrets & Solutions, Third Edition* by Stuart McClure, Joel Scambray, and George Kurtz (McGraw-Hill/Osborne, 2001) and *Hacking Exposed Web Applications* by Joel Scambray and Mike Shema (McGraw-Hill/Osborne, 2002).

For more information, you can check out the World Wide Web Consortium's security FAQ at www.w3.org/Security/Faq or Macromedia's Security Zone at www.macromedia.com/v1/developer/SecurityZone/.

Securing Databases and Files

This section discusses some issues regarding databases and files. Most client/server databases have some form of built-in user-based security. Most file-based databases do not.

File-based databases, such as Microsoft Access, are not built for security or to be accessed by many people at once. Microsoft Access can add a single password to the database. With that password, the user can open it and have access to all information contained in the database.

The easiest way to avoid some of the problems with file-based databases is to not use them for web development. If you have to use such a database, make sure that you store it in a directory that is not accessible via the Web. You wouldn't want someone to be able to guess a URL and be able to download your whole database. Password-protecting the database, if possible, is also a good option.

Client/server databases, on the other hand, have good built-in security. They have users with logins, and groups. Database server programs allow you to limit access based on user login to specific databases. Within the database, you can limit access to specific tables or operations. Most web sites are created so that one web user accesses the database, as opposed to creating a database user for every single web user.

Directories and Files

What happens when you are streaming protected content, such as music files or photographs? In sites like this, you want to protect your images from people who are not properly registered. ColdFusion has a mechanism that allows you to do this: Keep your protected files in directories that are not accessible to the Web. When a properly verified user requests the file, you can use the cfcontent tag to deliver it to them.

Another thing that you can do to add that extra layer of security to your web site is to change the default virtual directories. Everybody who reads this book knows that cfide/administrator/ is the default directory path to get to the ColdFusion Administrator. If you move the directory on the server or change the name of the virtual directory that points to the ColdFusion administrator files, you put one more step between you and the hacker.

Setting Up a Security Sandbox

ColdFusion has two types of security: basic security and advanced security. Basic security just forces a user to log in to get into the ColdFusion Administrator or through Remote Development Services (RDS). We discussed some basic security features in Chapter 3. This section discusses advanced security, or as it is sometimes called, the *security sandbox.*

Understanding the Security Sandbox

This section shows you how to activate advanced security from within the ColdFusion Administrator, and then teaches you how to configure the security sandbox settings. The sandbox relates to directories.

Activating Advanced Security

Before you can configure and use ColdFusion's advanced security, you must activate it. Here is how:

1. Log in to the ColdFusion Administrator and click the Sandbox Security link under Security in the lower-left corner. You will see the Sandbox Security Permissions page, shown in Figure 4-1.

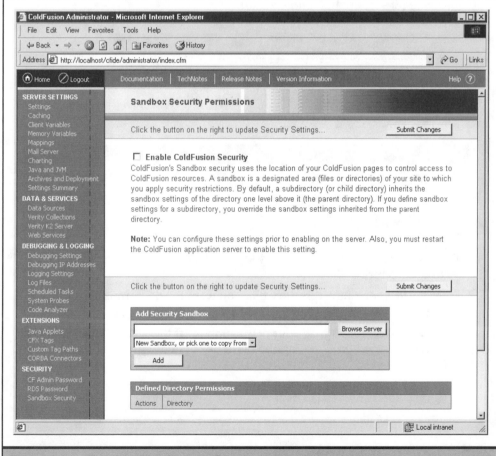

Figure 4-1.   *The Sandbox Security Permissions page*

2. Check the Enable ColdFusion Security checkbox and click the Submit Changes button.

3. Restart your ColdFusion server.

Now you are ready to start configuring your security sandbox.

Creating Your Security Sandbox

After you have enabled advanced security, you can start to configure it. Advanced security allows you to restrict access to ColdFusion functions, ColdFusion tags, datasources, and file permissions. The security allows certain permissions based on the directory that the commands are being executed in.

Here is how you can create a new sandbox:

1. Log in to the ColdFusion Administrator, if you are not already logged in. Click the Sandbox Security link under Security.

Add Security Sandbox

	Browse Server

New Sandbox, or pick one to copy from ▾

Add

Defined Directory Permissions

Actions	Directory
◔	(ColdFusion WEB-INF system directory)
◔	(ColdFusion CFIDE system directory)

The bottom of the Sandbox Security screen allows you to create the sandbox security directories.

2. Enter the location of the directory that you want to add permissions to. I entered htdocs.

3. You have the option to base your new sandbox off the settings of another one. If you don't select one, the sandbox will be created with settings from the default sandbox.

4. Click Add. You will see your sandbox listed in the list of sandboxes.

 Sandboxes do not automatically inherit permissions from their parent directory.

Configuring Your Sandbox

Creating your sandbox is only half the battle. Next, you have to configure the sandbox:

1. Log in to the ColdFusion Administrator and click the Sandbox Security link under Security. Select the sandbox that you want to edit. You should see a screen similar to this:

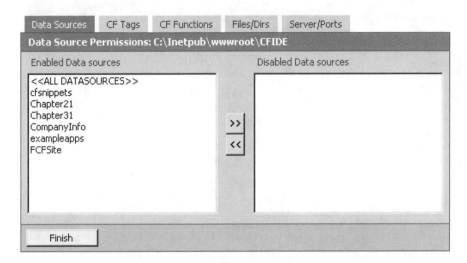

2. The first screen allows you to select the datasources that the given directory will not have access to. You can select the datasource in either window and use the arrow buttons to give and remove access.

3. Click the CF Tags tab.

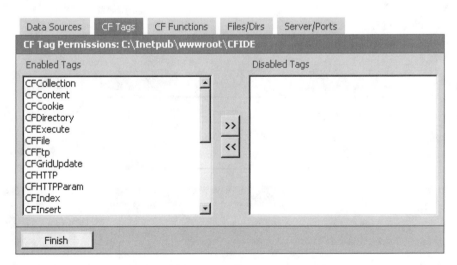

You will see the list of ColdFusion tags that you can limit the use of in your specific directory. The two select boxes operate similarly to the way the Data Sources window operates. Selecting a tag name and clicking the appropriate arrow will move the functions to the other window.

4. Click the CF Functions tab.

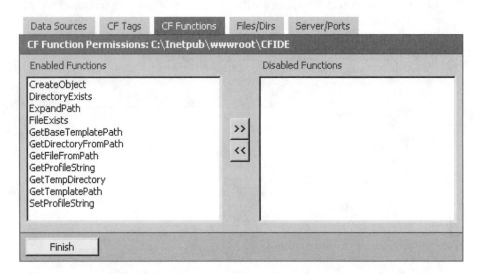

Here you have a list of ColdFusion functions that you are allowed to limit access to.

You may want to limit the use of these tags and functions, because they can be used to create or modify server settings and access the directories and files. These operations open your server to potential security breaches.

5. Click the Files/Dirs tab.

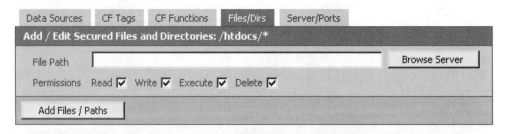

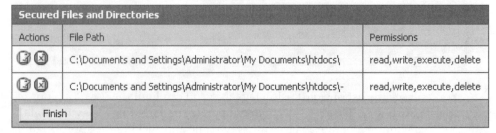

You can use this screen to add access to new directories or modify access to existing directories. To add a new directory, just type the name of the directory, set the permissions, and click the Add Files/Paths button.

To edit a directory, click the directory name. The screen will refresh with the directory name automatically added into the File Path box.

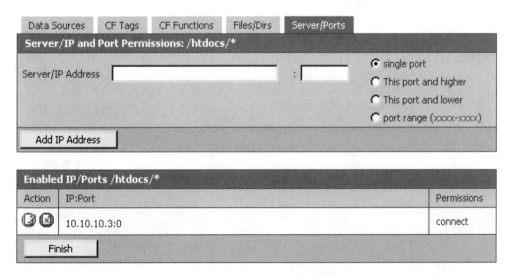

You can change the permissions and click the Edit Files/Paths button to modify the settings.

Tip   *If you add a minus sign (−) after the directory slash at the end of the directory, the permissions will be set for all files and directories underneath the current directory, and the files and directories underneath those directories, and so on until you are out of directories.*

6. Click the Server/Ports tab.

You can limit the access that tags running within your sandbox directory have to other IP addresses and ports. The reason for specifying a port is that you may want to specify a port for the mail server, but not for an HTTP server. Enter the IP address and port and then click the Add IP Address button. To edit the IP address, click the Edit IP Address button.

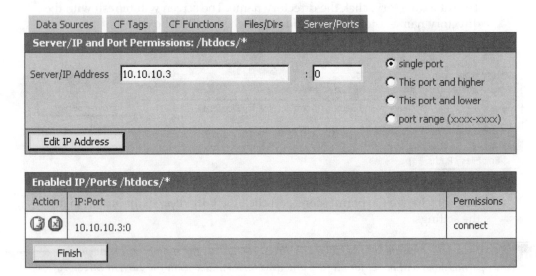

You can change the various settings that you need to.

7. Click the Finish button and you will be brought back to the Sandbox Security main page. Congratulations! You have just completed your first Sandbox Security main page.

Summary

In this chapter, you learned about the following:

- Some basic security considerations
- How to enable ColdFusion's advanced security
- How to configure advanced security settings

The next chapter will teach you how to load test your applications and monitor your server.

The Complete Reference

Chapter 5

Monitoring and Load Testing Your Server

Now that your server is installed and fully functional, you are ready to start hosting applications, whether they are your own or a third party's. The amount of time that your web application is available is called its *uptime*. Ideally, you will strive for 100 percent uptime, so that your application is available 24 hours a day, seven days a week. This chapter discusses ways to monitor the health of your server.

Using Software to Monitor Your Server

The first thing that you are going to want to do to monitor your server is to keep an eye on it. You will want to be notified if the server is down, or if certain applications are causing errors. This section first examines different software programs that check whether a server is up and functioning. Then it shows you how to use your ColdFusion log files to identify weak areas in your application.

Determining Whether Your Server Is Still Running

There are many software programs that will check whether a server is still up and running. Some check the server across the Internet, while others check it via a local network. They all offer some form of notification when a specified server goes down.

The concept of server monitoring is to check the status of one machine from another machine. If the server monitoring software is on the same machine you are monitoring, you will never receive notifications if the server goes down. The monitoring software needs a working machine to send notifications from. There are things that you can do while sitting at a machine to verify its health and check its resource usage, but server monitoring software is for those times when you are not at your machine.

Here are some products you can use for monitoring your server:

- **ColdFusion probes** ColdFusion probes (discussed in Chapter 3) are included as part of the ColdFusion Administrator. They check on a regular basis a URL that you specify, and e-mail you if there are problems with it.

- **AlertSite** AlertSite (www.alertsite.com) is a product that allows you to check your site from multiple geographic locations, receive notifications of problems via e-mail, pager, or mobile phone, and verify existing content on your site. It offers extensive reporting on different response times.

- **Monitor Magic** Monitor Magic is a program from Advanced Toolware (www.advtoolware.com) that monitors, over a network connection, items including logs, disks, files and directories, and system processes of a server. It can automatically restart a server or service, send e-mails, or execute batch scripts when it finds problems.

- **WebSitePulse.com** WebSitePulse.com is a completely web-based solution. Instead of buying a product to monitor your servers, you pay them to monitor your servers. When problems occur, they will notify you via e-mail, cell phone, or pager.

■ **IPCheck**   IPCheck, available at www.paessler.com, is a program used for monitoring network traffic.

■ **Windows Task Monitor**   Windows Task Monitor, available in most Windows server systems, allows you to check the current status of a machine, including programs that are running, CPU usage, and memory usage. This can be useful if you are trying to discover what process is bringing down your machine.

Analyzing ColdFusion Logs for Errors

Server monitoring aside, you can use ColdFusion logs to troubleshoot application problems. Although server monitoring software is great, it has a major flaw insofar as it only lets you know about problems after they have occurred. It would be better to spot potential problems before they occur. One method of doing this is to watch your ColdFusion logs.

You can access the ColdFusion logs from the ColdFusion Administrator. Chapter 6 talks in depth about the different types of logs, including how to access and search through them. To access logs in the ColdFusion Administrator, you can follow these simple steps:

1. Log in to your ColdFusion Administrator.

2. Click Log Files under Debugging & Logging on the navigation bar.

3. You will see a list of all logs available on your machine. Click the specific log to view that log's information.

You can also access the log files directly by looking in the logs subdirectory of your ColdFusion installation directory.

 Tip   *From within a ColdFusion application, you can easily create your own logs, or add entries into an existing log, using ColdFusion's cflog tag. We will discuss this in Chapter 18.*

When you are looking at a log, you want to look for errors that occur frequently. A one-time database error probably doesn't warrant investigation, but if you have 100 Page Not Found errors, then you definitely have a problem that needs to be investigated more thoroughly.

There are many programs that can be used to analyze the log files of your applications, with varying degrees of complexity and cost:

■ **WebTrends Log Analyzer**   WebTrends is the most famous log analyzer. It works in multiserver environments, and offers graphical reporting. You can find out more at www.webtrends.com.

- **123LogAnalyzer**   123LogAnalyzer is a program that is designed for speed in analyzing log files, being able to process 1GB of information per minute. It allows for customizable reports, which include information such as bandwidth usage and the number of hits that a user made on the web site, as well as specific errors and what IP address had errors. You can find out more at http://123LogAnalyzer.com.

- **Webalizer**   The Webalizer software is a free log analysis program located at www.webalizer.com. Other than being available on many operating systems, its main advantage over the other options is that it is free.

- **Atomic Log**   Atomic Log is a real-time log analyzer. The information that resides in the logs updates as the program runs, and keeps track of who is accessing your machine and from where. You can find more about this product at http://atomiclog.com.

These programs are just a few of the many log analyzers out there. You can find more by searching on Google or in your favorite shareware library.

Using cfstat to Watch Your Server

ColdFusion includes a program called cfstat that enables you to monitor your ColdFusion Server in real time, so that you can get real-time metrics, or analysis, of your application's performance.

Cfstat is a command-line program that is located in the bin directory of your ColdFusion installation. ColdFusion MX installs to the default directory of ColdFusion MX, so unless you changed that location, the cfstat program resides in CFusionMX\bin\. The way that cfstat works is to collect the information that ColdFusion writes to the system monitor, before it is written. Table 5-1 shows the type of information that you can collect with cfstat.

To run cfstat, just type **cfstat** from the console, with the specific options that you are after. Here are the switch options:

- **n**   Suppresses or displays the column headers

- **s**   Forces cfstat to display output in a single line

- **#**   Contains an integer that specifies the delay before the next listing of stats will be collected

- **h**   Contains the host of the web server that you are using; its default is localhost

- **p**   Contains the port of the web server that you are monitoring; its default value is 80

Name	Abbreviation	Comment
Page Hits per Second	pg/sec	The number of ColdFusion page hits per second
Database Access per Second	db/sec	The number of database accesses per second
Cache Pops per Second	cp/sec	The number of cached templates that are removed from the cache per second
Number of Queued Requests	req q'ed	The number of requests that are waiting to be processed by ColdFusion
Number of Running Requests	req run'g	The number of requests that are currently running
Number of Timed Requests	req to'ed	The number of requests that have timed out
Average Queue Time	avgq time	The number of milliseconds that a page waits to be processed
Average Request Time	avgreq time	The number of milliseconds that it takes to process a page
Average Database Transaction Time	avgdb time	An average of the time ColdFusion spends communicating with databases
Bytes Incoming per Second	bytes in/sec	The number of bytes ColdFusion accepted in the last second
Bytes Outgoing per Second	bytes out/sec	The number of bytes ColdFusion wrote in the last second

Table 5-1.   *Information Collected by cfstat*

Running the cfstat program with the relevant parameters will give you output like this:

```
MS-DOS Prompt                                                    _ □ ×
C:\CFUSIO~1\BIN>cfstat 3

JAVA_HOME is not set.  If cfstat doesn't run, please
set the JAVA_HOME environment variable.

Pg/Sec  DB/Sec  CP/Sec  Reqs  Reqs   Reqs   AvgQ  AvgReq AvgDB  Bytes   Bytes
Now Hi  Now Hi  Now Hi  Q'ed  Run'g  TO'ed  Time  Time   Time   In/Sec  Out/Sec
0   0   0   0   -1  -1  0     0      0      0     1326   0      0       0
0   0   0   0   -1  -1  0     0      0      0     1326   0      0       0
0   0   0   0   -1  -1  0     0      0      0     1326   0      0       0
0   0   0   0   -1  -1  0     0      0      0     1326   0      0       0
0   0   0   0   -1  -1  0     0      0      0     1326   0      0       0
0   0   0   0   -1  -1  0     0      0      0     1326   0      0       0
0   0   0   0   -1  -1  0     0      0      0     1326   0      0       0
0   0   0   0   -1  -1  0     0      0      0     1326   0      0       0
0   0   0   0   -1  -1  0     0      0      0     718    0      247     0
2   2   0   0   -1  -1  0     0      0      0     71     0      2135    0
0   2   0   0   -1  -1  0     0      0      0     466    0      598     0
0   2   0   0   -1  -1  0     1      0      0     466    0      307     0
0   2   0   0   -1  -1  0     1      0      0     1389   0      300     0
0   2   0   0   -1  -1  0     1      0      0     1171   0      296     0
0   2   0   0   -1  -1  0     0      0      0     1027   0      311     6
```

Testing Your Applications Under Load

This section explains what load testing is and why you should do it. It then discusses different software programs that can be used to perform load testing.

Understanding Load Testing

Consider the following scenario. You've sat down with the client and mapped out the functionality of an application. You spent six weeks writing the application and two weeks testing it before releasing it to go live. The application was launched on the Internet, with a big party, including balloons, bands, and a lot of food. Now, all of a sudden, you are getting errors galore. People can't view pages, the databases are timing out, and the server is crashing on a routine basis. Why is this happening?

Somewhere in the software development cycle, something was done wrong. The application could have been written poorly, missing important elements such as variable locking. The queries may not have been optimized to take advantage of the database features. Perhaps the hardware is not sufficient to support the number of people on the site. Whatever the reason, you should have discovered this beforehand. The way to do this is through load testing.

Load testing is the act of testing your application to see how it will perform when numerous visitors are visiting your site. Programs that perform load testing simulate a specific number of page requests on your site. The site may perform great when you, the developer, are surfing it, but what happens when 10, 25, 100, 10,000, or even more users are surfing your site at once? Load testing software helps you to find out.

 Load testing should never be done on the server that you are testing. The software will use valuable resources, thus skewing your results.

The Microsoft Web Application Stress Tool

The first tool to examine comes from software giant Microsoft. It has a product designed for load testing that is called Web Application Stress (WAS). You can download the software from its web site at http://webtool.rte.microsoft.com.

Defining Scripts

WAS works by having you define a series of actions that you want the web server to test. This list of actions is called a script. There are five different ways that you can define a script:

- **Manually**   You can manually define the script's actions.
- **Recording browser activity**   You can define the script's actions by surfing the site through your browser and having WAS record your actions.
- **Using an IIS log file**   You can have WAS analyze a log file and use it to design a plan of attack, targeting the most used portions of your site.
- **Selecting files**   You can select the files that you want WAS to hit.
- **Importing**   You can create a script by importing actions from another WAS installation.

When you launch WAS, you are shown this dialog box:

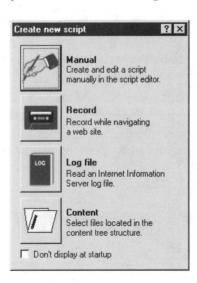

ADMINISTERING YOUR COLDFUSION SERVER

This box allows you to create a script in four of the five ways listed. The fifth, importing, can be accessed from the File menu. To find menu alternates for any of the four selections in the Create New Script dialog box, look under Create in the Scripts menu.

Close the dialog box, and you will return to the main WAS screen.

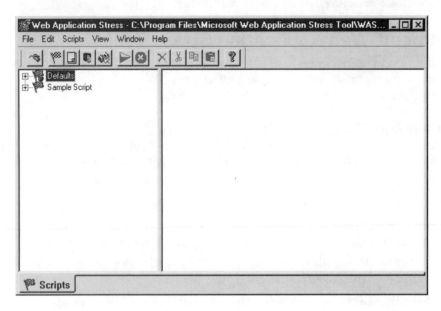

The area on the left shows a list of all scripts. As you expand the scripts, specific information is displayed in the pane on the right.

This is how you create a new script from scratch:

1. Launch the Web Application Stress tool. Select Manual from the Create New Script dialog box. If WAS is already running, select Scripts | Create | Manual.

2. You will see the main screen (see Figure 5-1). Type the domain name of the server you are testing in the Server box. You can use the Notes box to enter your description of this script.

3. Enter the links for specific files you want to check. This is how to manually define a script.

4. If you have directory access to the server, expand the New Script entry, and click the Content Tree selection. In the window that opens, you can select the file location of the site you are load testing. You define the script by selecting the files to test.

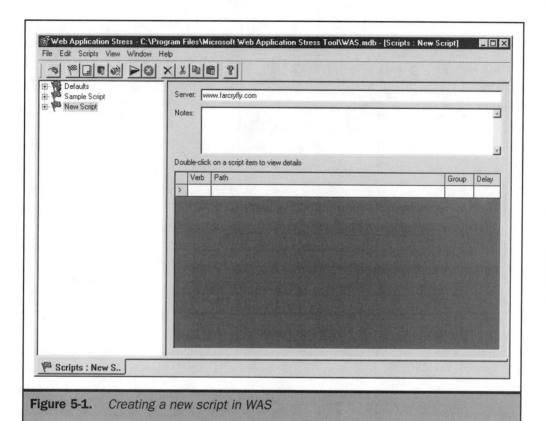

Figure 5-1. *Creating a new script in WAS*

5. Expand the New Script entry and click Settings. In the window that opens (see Figure 5-2), enter the number of threads. This is the number of users that you want to throw at the site at once. Choose a number for the stress multiplier. A *stress multiplier* is used to expand the total number of concurrent requests. WAS multiplies the Stress Level times the Stress Multplier to get the total number of concurrent requests. Choose values for the length of the test run. The longer that you run the test, the more likely you are to get accurate data.

A random delay is used to help simulate the Internet bottlenecks that may exist between your user and your site. You can test your site for a specific bandwidth by checking the Throttle Bandwidth checkbox.

6. Under New Script, you can configure several other settings. Click Users to specify users who are going to access the site. Click Clients to test from multiple

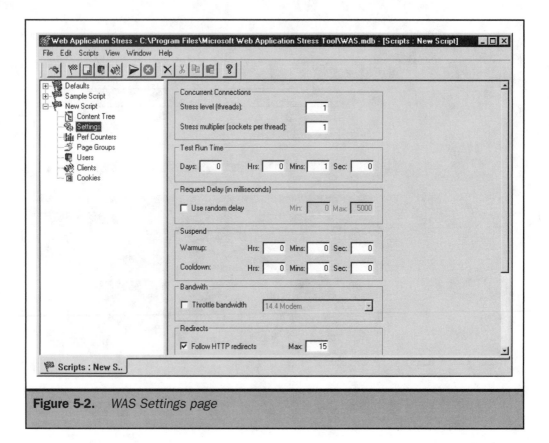

Figure 5-2. *WAS Settings page*

machines at once. Click Cookies to specify cookie values for a specific client. Click Page Groups to group specific pages together. Click Perf Counters to store performance counters with the script. After modifying all the settings, you can now run your script, as is defined in the upcoming section of this chapter.

You can find more information about performance counters on the Web at http://webtool.rte.microsoft.com/tutor/perf.htm.

This is how you can create a script using the log files:

1. Launch the Web Application Stress tool. Select Log File in the Create New Script dialog box. If WAS is already running, select Scripts | Create | Log.

2. In the IIS Log - Step 1 of 2 dialog box, click the button with the ellipses (...) to select the log file. The default log directory for IIS is C:\WINNT\SYSTEM32\ LogFiles\W3SVC1.

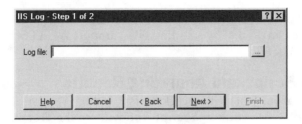

3. Click Next to open the IIS Log - Step 2 of 2 dialog box. I like to stick with the default settings, which is to read the entire log file and to skip duplicates.

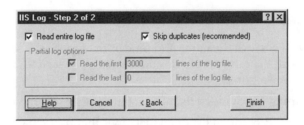

4. Click Finish. WAS will automatically create the new script.

The fourth way to create a script is to record your browsing activity. This is how you do it:

1. Launch the Web Application Stress tool. Select Record from the Create New Script dialog box. If WAS is already running, select Scripts | Create | Record.

2. In the Browser Recorder - Step 1 of 2 dialog box, I like to select the Record Delay Between Requests and Record Browser Cookies options. You can also select Record The Host Header checkbox if you wish.

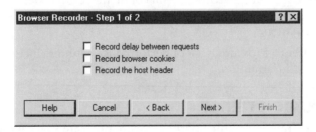

3. Click the Next button. In the Browser Recorder - Step 2 of 2 dialog box, click Finish. Your browser will open. As you browse, WAS will keep track of your actions in a window.

4. Click the Stop Recording button when you have finished your sample application. You will see the newly recorded script in the script list on the Scripts tab.

The fifth way to create a script is to import it from Windows Capacity Analysis Tool (WCAT). You can do that by selecting File | Import WCAT Script. WAS was created to replace WCAT.

Running the Script and Analyzing Results

To run the script that you just created, click the Play button. You can also choose Scripts | Run to run a script. Once you run a script, you will see the Test Status dialog box. It will show you the amount of time left in your script and give you the option to stop the script from running. Once the script is finished running, you can view the reports (see Figure 5-3) by either clicking the Reports tab at the bottom of the window or choosing View | Reports.

The report will give you this information:

- **Overview**   Provides the name and date of the report, the software version that ran the report, the number of hits and requests per second, and statistics about the socket connections.

- **Script Settings**   Provides a list of the settings that you ran the script under.

- **Test Clients**   Provides a list of all machines that participated in the test, as well as specific information related to that particular host.

- **Result Codes**   Contains the categorized number of responses from the web server. You can look here to find the errors.

- **Page Summary**   Includes a summary of the links that were selected, how many hits each page got, the query string, the Time to First Byte average, and the Time to Last Byte average.

- **Page Groups**   Provides a list of the page groups included in the test and related information.

- **Page Data**   Provides information relating to each specific page that was included in the test. It includes the URL, the hit count, the result codes, breakdowns of the time to first byte and time to last byte, downloaded content length, and other page information.

- **Perf Counters**   Provides a list of performance counters included in the test and their related information.

Web Performance Trainer

Web Performance Trainer is a third-party software program that can perform load testing. It is designed for the purpose of making load testing easy. Web Performance Trainer is very easy to use and understand, and is packed with great documentation and tutorials. You can download Web Performance Trainer and view the online documentation at www.webperformanceinc.com.

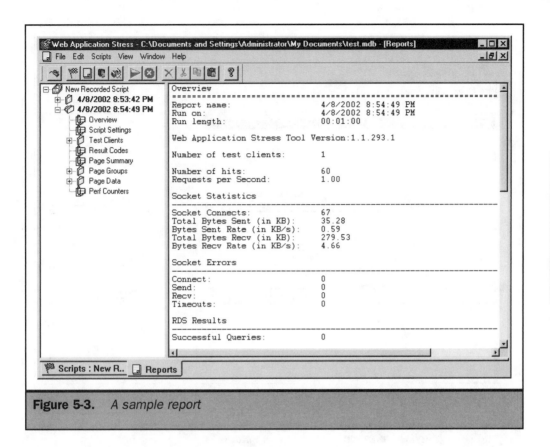

Figure 5-3.   *A sample report*

Creating a Load Profile

A *load profile* is a group of actions that Web Performance Trainer will use to load test your software. Load profiles are made up of separate business cases. A business case is akin to a script in Microsoft's Web Application Stress tool. It is a series of actions that a common user might perform on your web site. A business case can be something as simple as filling out a customer service form to something as complicated as viewing the home page.

This is how you create a business case:

1. Launch Web Performance Trainer, and you will see the screen shown in Figure 5-4.

2. To create a new business case, you can either click the green Play button or select Record | Start Recording.

3. Once you start the business case, your browser launches. Your browser will test the proxy and SSL settings inside Web Performance Trainer.

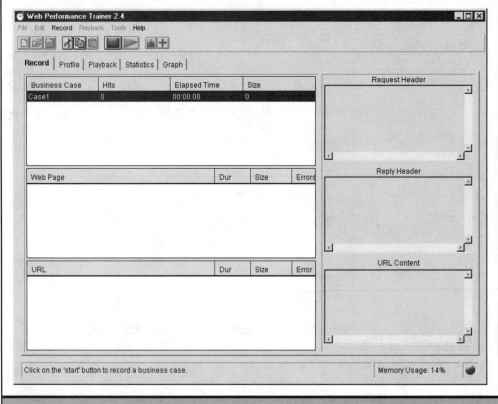

Figure 5-4. *Web Performance Trainer main screen*

4. After the browser check, you can surf the web site that you want to test. The Record tab of the business case will fill up with the pages and associated files, such as images, that you surf.

5. Go back to Web Performance Trainer and click the red Stop button to create the case.

6. Repeat this process until you have created all the business cases that you need.

Once you have your business cases, the next step is to create your load profile:

1. Launch Web Performance Trainer and select the Profile tab, as shown in Figure 5-5.

2. Select Edit | Create | Load Profile to create a load profile. This creates an empty profile. You will have to add your business cases to it.

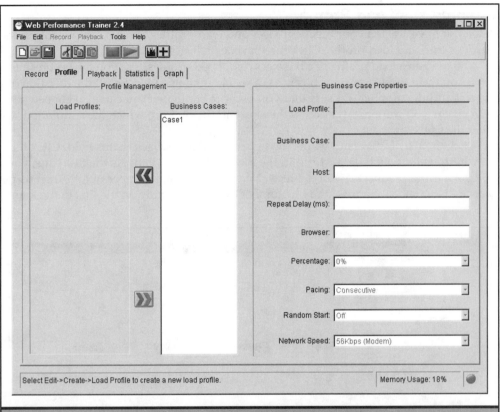

Figure 5-5. *Web Performance Trainer Profile tab*

3. Select the load profile in the Load Profiles list. Select a business case in the Business Cases list. You can use the right and left arrow buttons to add or remove a business case from a profile.

4. For each business case, you can specify the name of the host, the length of the delay between each execution of a business case, the HTTP value that the browser used, the percentage of total users assigned to this case, and the network connection speed.

   You can also specify a random start so that all users don't start slamming the server at once, and the pace at which the server is accessed. A Consecutive pace maintains a steady byte stream accessing the server. If you choose Recorded, then the web pages will play back at the speed that they loaded when they were recorded.

Running the Load Profile

After you have created your business cases and load profiles, the next step is to run the business case and load profile. Click the Playback tab (see Figure 5-6).

You can run a load profile or a business case. Load profiles give you the best results, but if you want to test a specific business case, that is allowed too. Select the duration of the test and the number of users that you want to simulate. You can also choose how many users you want to have access the site, and the order in which the simulation will enter the site.

Click the Play button and watch the test run in the Playback Status field. Click the Play button and watch the test run in the Playback Status field. As the test runs, you will get various feedback about the tests. You'll see the total number of hits, the hits per second, the number of errors, and the number of users currently on the site. In the lower

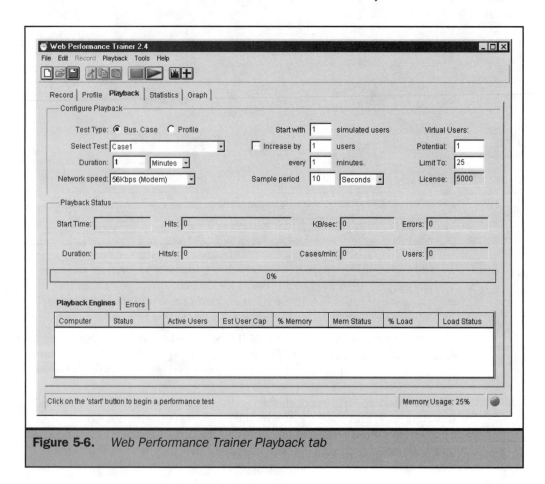

Figure 5-6. *Web Performance Trainer Playback tab*

portion of the window, on the Playback Engines tab, you'll see the current number of active users, the memory allocated for internal buffers, and the memory status. It also shows the percentage load on the playback computer and the load status.

Reporting with Statistics and Graphs

Web Performance Trainer provides two different views to get information about your test. You can look at the Statistics tab or the Graph tab. They both contain the same data, but the Graph tab is a graphical view of the data, whereas the Statistics tab is a textual view.

Click the Statistics tab (see Figure 5-7). The interface is presented in a standard drill-down fashion, starting with the load profile, and then moving to the business cases, the web page, and the URL. You can reduce or expand your results as much as necessary.

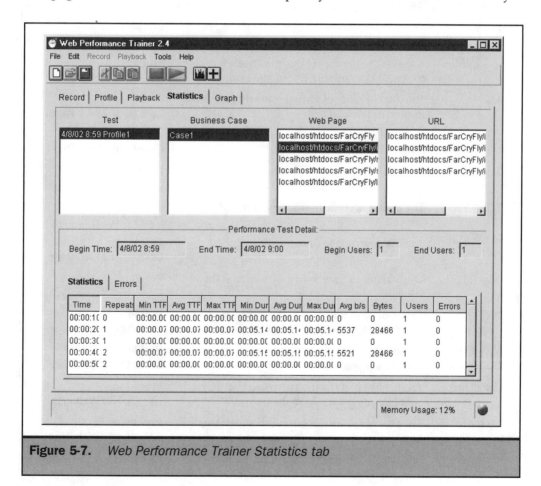

Figure 5-7.   *Web Performance Trainer Statistics tab*

ADMINISTERING YOUR
COLDFUSION SERVER

The available statistics will depend on what you are showing statistics on—the full load test or a specific case/URL. The available data is described in Table 5-2.

Statistic	Description	Where Available
Time	The number of seconds into the test that the statistics occurred.	Profile Case/URL/Web Page
Total Hits	The total number of hits of all business cases. This is available if you select a load test.	Profile
Hits/S	The average number of hits per second during the length of the load test.	Profile
kbytes/S	The average number of bytes transferred per second during the load test.	Profile
Cases/Min	The average number of business cases that were completed per minute during the load test.	Profile
Users	The total number of virtual users that existed at the end of the load test.	Profile Case/URL/Web Page
Errors	The total number of errors that were generated during the load test.	Profile Case/URL/Web Page
Repeats	The number of times the business case, URL, or web page was repeated.	Profile Case/URL/Web Page
Min TTFB	The minimum time to first byte during the test run.	Profile Case/URL/Web Page
Avg TTFB	The average time to first byte during the test run.	Profile Case/URL/Web Page
Max TTFB	The maximum time to first byte during the test run.	Profile Case/URL/Web Page
Min Dur	The minimum time it took the virtual user to get all information back from the server.	Profile Case/URL/Web Page
Avg Dur	The average time it took to get all information back from the user.	Profile Case/URL/Web Page
Max Dur	The longest that it took the virtual user to get all information back from the user.	Profile Case/URL/Web Page
Avg b/s	The average bytes per second that each user received.	Profile Case/URL/Web Page
Bytes	The total data transferred during the test.	Profile Case/URL/Web Page

Table 5-2.   *Web Performance Trainer Statistics*

You can create graphs using the statistics. Click the Graph tab (see Figure 5-8). Graphs are set up so that the X axis is the time, in the format of hours:minutes:seconds. The Y axis can mean many things depending upon the type of statistic that you are graphing. You can graph any of the statistics that appear in Table 5-2.

If you have already run some test cases, then you have some statistics and can start to add elements to your graph. Here is how to do it:

1. While on the Graph tab, select Edit | Add To Chart to open the Add Statistic Dialog dialog box.

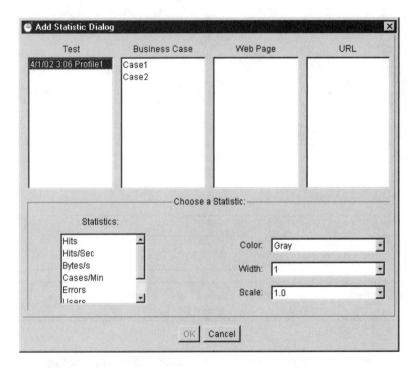

2. The drill-down interface is similar to that of the Statistics tab. You can select the load profile, and the case, down to the web page and URL.

3. Select the value that you want to graph from the Statistics list.

4. Select the Color, Width, and Scale of the graph.

5. Click OK, and you will see your graph.

6. Repeat until you have added all the elements to your graph that you want to graph.

  If you try to delete the last graph, Web Performance Trainer will not let you. There must be at least one graph at all times.

The power of Web Performance Trainer does not end here. Advanced features of the product allow you to deal with Java applets, ActiveX, cookie-based authentication,

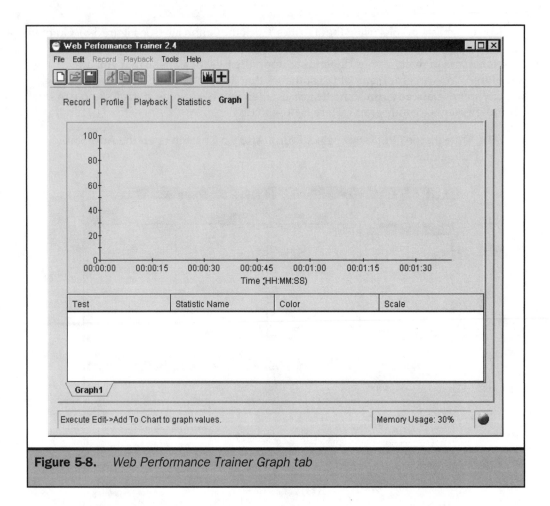

Figure 5-8. *Web Performance Trainer Graph tab*

session management, and modification of form data that was entered into during the recording of a business case.

Summary

In this chapter, you learned about the following:

- Software programs that allow you to monitor your server
- Monitoring your server with cfstat
- The concepts behind load testing
- How to use two different software programs to perform load testing

The next chapter will move on to discuss some more advanced server administration techniques.

The Complete Reference

Chapter 6

Applying Advanced Administration Techniques

This chapter covers some of the advanced Administrator functionality that was not covered in Chapter 3. If you haven't read Chapter 3 yet, I suggest you take a look at it, although it is not a prerequisite for this chapter. This chapter covers directory mappings, custom tags, archives, and debugging options.

Directory Mappings

This section explains what directory mappings are, the various types available in ColdFusion, and how to set them up.

Understanding Mappings

Although directory mappings are an important concept in development, my experience is that many people do not have a full understanding of them. A *directory mapping* is a specific name that refers to a directory. It is like an alias. Let's look at a simple example. Suppose you have a web site:

www.instantcoldfusion.com

This web name is an alias for a specific directory located on a hard drive. The hard drive directory is

C:\InetPub\wwwroot\InstantColdFusion

Putting the domain name in the browser will show you the contents of this directory. One name refers to the other. This is the basic concept behind directory mappings. Let's follow this with a more expansive example.

Let's say that we have three different web sites:

www.mysite.com
www.mysite2.com
www.mysite3.com

This is the directory structure of the server:

C:\InetPub\wwwroot\MySite\
C:\InetPub\wwwroot\MySite\MySite2
C:\InetPub\wwwroot\MySite\MySite3

We want our first site, www.mysite.com, to point to the MySite directory. We want www.mysite2.com to point to the MySite2 directory, and www.mysite3.com to point to the MySite3 directory; both reside one directory beneath the www.mysite.com directory.

Your web server of choice most likely allows you to set this up using virtual servers, so having each domain point to the specific directory is not a problem. Let's suppose you go ahead and create www.mysite.com and make it live. One of the directories for this site is an image directory

C:\InetPub\wwwroot\MySite\Images

You can reference the image directory through the web site like this:

www.mysite.com/Images/

Next, you start developing www.mysite2.com and www.mysite3.com. You find that you are able to use a lot of images from the initial site in the two subsites, but there is a problem: You cannot access the Images directory from either of the subsite domains. You certainly don't want to keep multiple copies of all the images, so what do you do?

The answer is to create a virtual directory, or mapping, on the server. In this case, I would create a mapping called /Images that points to the image directory

C:\InetPub\wwwroot\MySite\Images

That way, you can access the same directory in either of three ways:

www.mysite.com/Images
www.mysite2.com/Images
www.mysite3.com/Images

All three mappings point to the Images directory.

By now you may be wondering how the information about mappings applies to ColdFusion. ColdFusion doesn't deal with images. The previous example described mappings from a web server. ColdFusion is an application server, built to work in conjunction with a web server. ColdFusion mappings work the same way as web server mappings, but won't be checked when you are surfing the Web or creating relative links to images. They are used for custom tags and includes (discussed in Chapter 16).

Creating ColdFusion Mappings

As stated, ColdFusion mappings are used in conjunction with two tags: cfinclude and cfmodule. This is how you can create a mapping:

1. From the ColdFusion Administrator, click the Mappings link under Server Settings. You will see the ColdFusion Mappings page:

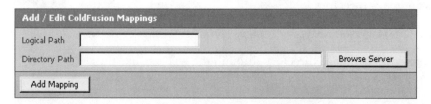

2. Enter the logical path. This is the name that you want to use to access the directory.

3. Enter the directory path. This is the location that you want to access. You can click the Browse Server button to choose a directory instead of typing it in.

4. Click the Add Mapping button to create your mapping. It is now ready for use from within ColdFusion.

In addition to the mappings, the ColdFusion Administrator also allows you to create custom tag directories. When calling a custom tag, ColdFusion will automatically look in these directories for the custom tag if the custom tag is not found in the current directory. This is how you add a custom tag directory to your site:

1. Click the Custom Tag Paths link underneath Extensions. You will see a screen similar to the ColdFusion Mappings page shown previously.

2. You can type the file directory path of the server that you want to use or you can click the Browse Server button to choose it graphically.

3. Click Add Path.

When ColdFusion goes looking for a custom tag, it checks the current directory first, then the CustomTags directory of the ColdFusion directory, then the subdirectories in the CustomTags directory, and, finally, the directories you specified in the ColdFusion Administrator.

Putting Archives to Use for You

This section describes archives. An archive is a group of files that make up a ColdFusion web site. You can use archives to back up ColdFusion applications and/or deploy those backups on a new server. This section shows you how.

Understanding Archives

Archives are an important enhancement to the deployment of ColdFusion applications. In the past, if you wanted to move a ColdFusion site from one server to another, you had to move all the files, custom tags, mappings, and other server settings manually. With archives, that is a thing of the past. This section shows you how to put archives to work for you.

Archives are a way to back up specific ColdFusion settings for later retrieval. Before you learn how to set them up, you need to know which settings can be stored in an archive:

- **File locations**   You can specify the locations of specific files that you want to archive.
- **Sever settings**   You can save any server settings from the General Settings page.
- **ColdFusion mappings**   You can choose from any ColdFusion mappings on the server.
- **Datasources**   You can back up datasource information, so you do not have to re-create it when the site is finished.
- **Verity collections**   You can add Verity collections to your archive. Creating Verity collections is discussed in Chapter 24.
- **Scheduled tasks and probes**   You can add any scheduled tasks or probes to your archive.
- **Java applets**   You can put any Java applets that have been registered with this server into your archive.
- **CFX tags**   You can put CFX tags that are installed on the server into your archive.
- **Archive to-do lists**   You can create to-do lists as part of the archive to remind you of the things to do before you restore the archive and after you restore the archive.

Creating and Restoring Archives

This section shows you how to put archives to work for you. It starts by stepping you through the process of creating an archive. Then, it shows you how to deploy, or restore, an archive.

Creating an Archive

These are the steps that you must take to create an archive:

1. Log in to the ColdFusion Administrator and click the Archives and Deployment link under Server Settings.

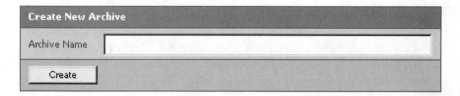

2. Type the archive name in the Create New Archive box and click Create. The Archive Wizard will pop up (see Figure 6-1).

3. Enter a description if you desire.

4. Click the Assoc. Files/Dirs link to add your files to the archive.

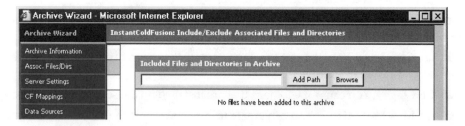

Fill in the Included Files And Directories In Archive box and click the Add Path button. That path and all directories underneath it are now in your archive.

5. You now have the option to exclude directories from the archive. You do so the same way that you add directories to the archive.

6. Click the Server Settings link. This gives you a list of all the server settings that you may want to back up. You can select as many or as few items that you want to back up.

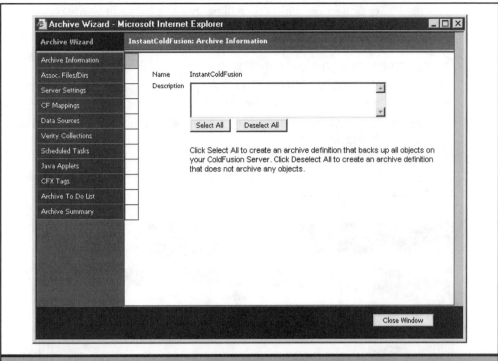

Figure 6-1.   *The Archive Information panel of the Archive Wizard*

7. Click the CF Mappings link. You will be shown a list of all existing ColdFusion mappings. You can check the ones that you want to save in your archive.

8. Click the Data Sources link. You can back up the settings, which allows ColdFusion to restore the datasource information.

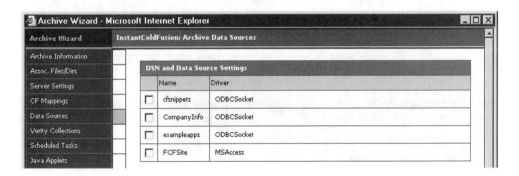

9. Click the Verity Collections link. You will be shown a list of all Verity collections on your current server.

10. Click the Scheduled Tasks link. You will see a list of all scheduled tasks. Select the ones you want to put in this archive.

11. Select Java Applets to see a list of all Java Applets available to this server. You can back up as many or as few of them as you need.

12. Clicking the CFX Tags link will show all registered CFX tags. You will learn how to register CFX tags later in this chapter. You can back up the ones you need. My server does not have any.

13. Click the Archive To Do List link. You are able to create a list of things to do before, and after, you restore the archive.

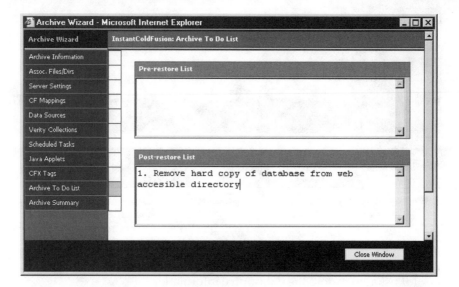

14. Click the Archive Summary link. This will show you a summary of all the archive information.

15. Click the Close Window button at the bottom of the screen to return to the Archives and Deployment screen. You will see your new archive in the Current Archive Definition list.

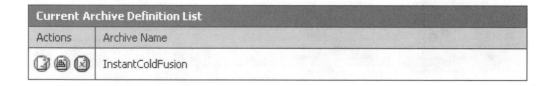

Current Archive Definition List	
Actions	Archive Name
🔲 🖨 ⊠	InstantColdFusion

16. All we have done up to this point is define the list of steps that must be taken to create an archive. Click the Build Archive button, which is the middle yellow button between Delete and Edit. An archive summary opens, as shown in Figure 6-2. Verify your archive information and click Next.

17. Choose a location for your archive. The filename you specify must have a .car extension. I suggest that you do not store them in a web-accessible directory. Click Next.

18. You will see status messages flash by as the archive is created.

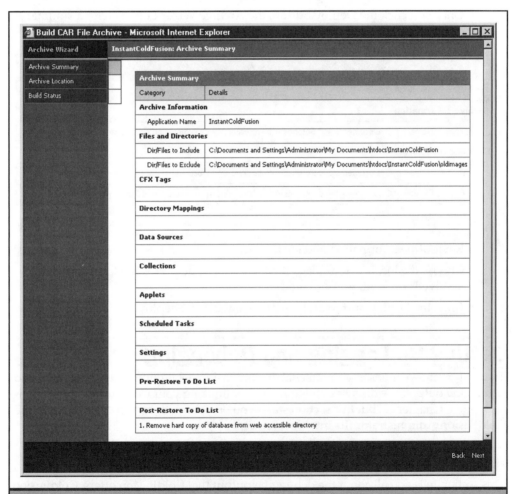

Figure 6-2.   *The Archive Summary panel of the Archive Wizard*

Deploying an Archive

The archive file is potentially useless if you do not have a way to unarchive it. The Administrator provides this functionality. Here is how to do it:

1. Log in to the Administrator and select the Archives and Deployment link under Server Settings.

2. Enter the name and location of your archive in the Deploy An Existing Archive box and click the Deploy button. You can browse the server to find the archive, as opposed to just typing in the location manually.

3. Once you click the Deploy button, the Archive Wizard opens with a summary of things on the archive.

Archive Summary	
Category	Details
Archive Information	
Application Name	C:\Documents and Settings\Administrator\My Documents\htdocs\Instantcf.car
Files and Directories	
Dir/Files to Include	C:\Documents and Settings\Administrator\My Documents\htdocs\InstantColdFusion
Dir/Files to Exclude	C:\Documents and Settings\Administrator\My Documents\htdocs\InstantColdFusion\oldimages
CFX Tags	

Review the information and click Next.

4. Choose the location to replace the archive. The default is the location it was archived from, but you can modify it.

5. Click the Deploy button and the archive will start deploying.

Setting Up Logging and Debugging

Two important weapons in your arsenal of ColdFusion debugging tools are log files and debugging output. We discuss debugging and optimizing your ColdFusion applications in depth in Chapter 17, but this section starts you on your path by showing you how the ColdFusion Administrator fits into the picture.

Debugging Your ColdFusion Information

This section tells you all about the debugging output that ColdFusion offers. ColdFusion presents debugging output on a per-template basis. The information that is shown can be used to highlight problem areas in the templates, or specific templates that are taking too long to process.

Debugging Output

The first thing we want to examine is the type of information that we can get from the ColdFusion debugging output. Log in to your Administrator and click Debugging Settings under Debugging & Logging. There is a lot of information that can be turned on or off from this page:

- **Enable Debugging**   Indicates whether you want debugging output on or off.

- **Debugging Format**   ColdFusion MX offers two ways to view debugging output. The classic view is one that users of previous versions of ColdFusion will recognize. The dockable view is a new way to view debugging. It offers a tree-based debugging panel.

- **Report Execution Times**   Select this checkbox to log templates whose execution times take longer than the specified amount.

- **Database Activity**   Select this checkbox to display all queries and their execution times, as well as the number of results returned by the query.

- **Exception Information**   Select this checkbox to display all information related to errors that occurred on the page.

- **Tracing Information**   Select this checkbox to allow a developer to track the efficiency of the template using the cftrace tag.

- **Variables**   Select this checkbox to show all the checked variable scopes in the output. If using debugging output, I recommend turning on URL, Session, Application, and Cookie variables at the least.

- **Enable Robust Exception Information**   Select this checkbox to allow the user to see the physical path of the template, the URL of the template, the line that the code error occurred on, the SQL statement, the name of the datasource, and the Java Stack trace if an error occurs.

- **Enable Performance Monitoring**   Select this checkbox to allow the Windows NT Performance Monitor to display information on the ColdFusion Application Server.

- **Enable CFStat**   Select this checkbox to enable cfstat to collect information on the ColdFusion Application Server. This is designed for systems that do not support performance monitoring.

ADMINISTERING YOUR COLDFUSION SERVER

This is the kind of information that can be displayed when debugging output. Here is an example of the debugging output:

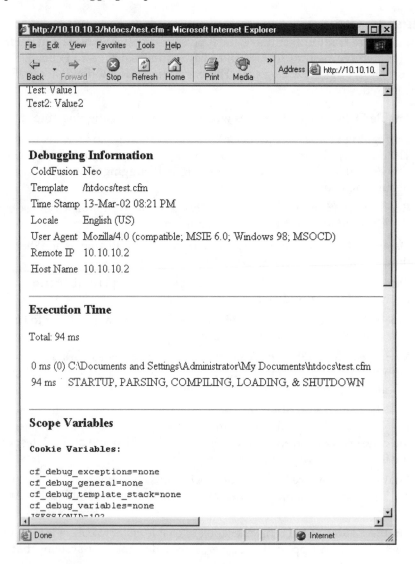

Caution *Turning on debugging output will slow down the server.*

Limiting Debugging Output by IP Address

Sometimes, you want to turn debugging output on, but don't want it available for all users to see. ColdFusion allows you to restrict the debugging output to a specific number of IP addresses or domains. This is how:

1. Log in to the ColdFusion Administrator, and select Debugging IP Addresses under Debugging & Logging to open the following screen:

Select IP Addresses for Debug Output

| IP Address | | Add | Add Current |

View / Remove Selected IP Addresses for Debug Output

127.0.0.1

Remove Selected

You are now looking at a list of all IP addresses that have debugging turned on. If there is nothing listed, then all IP addressees will show debugging output.

2. Type an IP address in the IP Address box and click the Add button. The IP address is now listed in the box on the lower part of the screen.

3. You can also click the Add Current button to add your current IP address automatically.

Using Logs

This section teaches you about the different types of logs. As a server administrator, you want to monitor your logs to identify errors in the server configuration or the applications that you are hosting. This section tells you about the different types of logs, where to go to activate them, and where to go to view them.

Different Types of Logs

The different types of logs that are available in ColdFusion MX are described in Table 6-1.

Logging Settings

There are various settings that can be set in relation to ColdFusion log files. Log in to the Administrator and click the Logging Settings link under Debugging & Logging.

You can control various settings with regard to logs from this page:

- **Log Directory** This allows you to change the log directory.

- **Maximum File Size** This specifies the maximum file size of the log.

- **Maximum Number of Archives** This specifies the largest number of log archives that can be created. After reaching the limit, the oldest file will be deleted to make room for the new one.

- **Log Slow Pages...** If a page takes too long to load, this setting will have ColdFusion add a log entry to let you know.
- **Log All CORBA Calls** When checked, all CORBA calls will be tracked in server.log file.he.
- **Enable Logging for Scheduled Tasks** When checked, scheduled tasks are added to the logs.

Additionally, you can also change mail log settings from the Mail Server page.

Viewing Logs

This section shows you how to view logs and get information out of them. First, log in to your Administrator and click the Log Files link under Debugging & Logging. You will see a list of all the available logs.

Log	Description
rdservice.log	Records all errors that occur within Remote Development Services (RDS). We discussed RDS in Chapter 11.
application.log	Records all errors that are reported to a user by the ColdFusion Application Server.
car.log	Contains errors associated with site archiving and deployment.You can also look for archive-specific logs at car_archive_*archivename.log* and car_deploy_*archivename*.log.
customtag.log	Keeps track of all errors generated by the processing of custom tags.
exceptions.log	Records the stack information for all errors that occur on the server.
mail.log	Records all errors related to mail server–related issues.
mailsent.log	Maintains all mail messages sent by the ColdFusion server.
Probes.log	Contains all errors associated with probes.
scheduler.log	Contains all scheduled tasks.
server.log	Records all errors on the ColdFusion server.

Table 6-1. *Types of Log Files*

This page shows a list of all the logs on your server. You have four options for each log: View, Download, Store, and Delete. You can also check any number of logs and click the View Log Files button to view multiple logs at once.

Click the application.log file to view it.

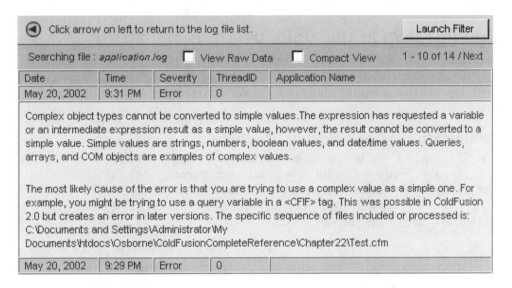

You can order the log entries by clicking the relevant header: Date, Time, Severity, ThreadID, or Application Name. Clicking the Compact View checkbox will extend description entries.

Click the Launch Filter button. A search box opens that allows you to filter log files:

This is a powerful way to search for specific entries in your log files. You can choose among the type of log entries: Fatal, Error, Warning, or Information. You can limit a date range or time span, perform a keyword search, and search on specific ThreadIDs or application names.

Advanced Miscellaneous Settings

This section covers the remaining features of the ColdFusion Administrator that have not been covered yet. We'll talk a little about a bunch of miscellaneous features, starting with Java.

Configuring Java in the ColdFusion Administrator

Since its code base was developed in Java, Java is an integral part of ColdFusion MX. But, Java and ColdFusion always coexisted peacefully, as complements to each other. This section shows you some of the features you can control regarding ColdFusion's flirtation with Java.

Setting Up the Java Virtual Machine

Select the Java and JVM link under Server Settings in the ColdFusion Administrator. From this page, you can control how ColdFusion interacts with the Java Virtual Machine (JVM). This is separate from the J2EE server that ColdFusion runs on top of; this functionality is designed for use with applets that will run in the browser.

Here are the features you can modify:

- **Java Virtual Machine Path**   This contains the location of the JVM. ColdFusion provides a path by default, but you can specify a different one.
- **Initial Memory Size**   This is the initial amount of memory that the JVM ColdFusion server will take when loading.
- **Maximum Memory Size**   This is the maximum amount of memory that the ColdFusion server can use for Java.
- **Class Path**   This is a path where the JVM will look for Java class files. You can list multiple class paths here.
- **JVM Arguments**   These are command-line arguments that will be added to the JVM when it loads.

Registering Java Applets

The other important Java feature in the ColdFusion Administrator is the ability to register an applet for use with the cfform tag. Within a cfform tag, you can call one of these applets by using the cfapplet tag. Here is how to register an applet:

1. Log in to the Administrator and click the Java Applets link under Extensions. You should see a page similar to this:

Register New Applet

Registered Java Applets

Actions	Applet	Code	Method	Code Base
🖉 ⊠	copytext	copytext.class		/cfide/Classes/allaire/controls/codebase

2. Click the Register New Applet button to open the Add/Edit Registered Java Applet page.

Add/Edit Registered Java Applet

Applet Name	
Code	
Code Base	
Archive	
Method	
Height	Width
VSpace	HSpace
Align	LEFT
Not Supported Message	

Applet Parameters

Parameter Name	Value	
		Add

Submit   Cancel

3. Enter the applet name. This will be used to reference the applet from the cfapplet tag.

4. Enter the Code and Code Base attributes. These will be identical to the HTML code and codebase attributes of the applet tag. Code contains the name of the class file, and Code Base specifies the URL of the codebase file.

5. Enter the Archive attribute. This is a comma-separated list of resources that contain classes upon which this applet is dependant.

6. Enter the Method variable. This is usually post or get. It refers to the type of form that the applet is placed on.

7. Enter the Height, Width, Vspace, and Hspace values. These values specify how much real estate on the screen the applet will take when it loads.

8. Select the alignment options for the applet.

9. Enter a message in case the browser does not support the applet.

10. Enter parameters for the applet. Registering a Java applet in this way allows you to specify its full configuration. You can enter as many parameters as you need, but note that parameters specified when the cfapplet tag is called will override these defaults.

11. Click the Submit button to save the applet.

Final Features of the Administrator

This section wraps up our discussion of the ColdFusion Administrator by discussing some remaining features.

Configuring Your Mail Server

You can send mail from ColdFusion using the cfmail tag. We discuss using the cfmail tag in Chapter 22. ColdFusion is not a mail server, though, nor does it include a mail server as part of the package. ColdFusion must refer to an already existing and configured mail server. The cfmail tag can be used to specify the server that you are using to send mail, or you can specify a default mail server in the ColdFusion Administrator.

Log in to the ColdFusion Administrator and select Mail Server under Server Settings. From this screen you can control these features:

- **Mail Server**   This is the domain name, or IP address of your mail server.

- **Server Port**   This contains the port that the mail server is located on. You won't usually have to change this from 25.

- **Connection Timeout**   This specifies how long ColdFusion will wait for a connection to the mail server before timing out.

- **Spool Interval**   This specifies how often the ColdFusion mail spooler will process the mail.

- **Verify Mail Server Connection**   Click this checkbox and click the Submit Changes button on the page. ColdFusion will see if it can find a mail server and provide you with a status message.

- **Error Log Severity**   This specifies the type of errors that you want to store in the mail log.

■ **Log All E-Mail Messages Sent by ColdFusion**   If checked, then all mail will
be logged in the mailsent.log file. Otherwise, it will not be logged.

Creating a Web Service

Web services are the way of the future, and as such the ColdFusion developers at
Macromedia have included Web service features into the release of ColdFusion MX.
A Web service is a way to describe the communications between two applications.

The ColdFusion Administrator allows you to register a program to act as a Web
service. Here is how:

1. Log in to the Administrator and click the Web Services link under Data &
Services. You will see this form:

Add / Edit ColdFusion Web Service	
Web Service Name	
WSDL URL	
Username	
Password	

Add Web Service

Active ColdFusion Web Serivces		
Actions	Web Service Name	WSDL URL
⊡ ⊡ ⊠	http://127.0.0.1:8500/neo/regression/webservices/wscf/echocomplex_2.cfc?wsdl	http://127.0.0.1:8500/neo/regression/webservices/wscf/echocomplex_2.cfc?wsdl
⊡ ⊡ ⊠	http://127.0.0.1:8500/neo/regression/webservices/wscf/basic.cfc?wsdl	http://127.0.0.1:8500/neo/regression/webservices/wscf/basic.cfc?wsdl
⊡ ⊡ ⊠	http://127.0.0.1:8500/neo/regression/webservices/wscf/echosimple.cfc?wsdl	http://127.0.0.1:8500/neo/regression/webservices/wscf/echosimple.cfc?wsdl
⊡ ⊡ ⊠	http://127.0.0.1:8500/neo/regression/webservices/wscf/echosimple.cfc?wsdl	http://127.0.0.1:8500/neo/regression/webservices/wscf/echosimple.cfc?wsdl
⊡ ⊡ ⊠	http://127.0.0.1:8500/neo/regression/webservices/wscf/basic.cfc?wsdl	http://127.0.0.1:8500/neo/regression/webservices/wscf/basic.cfc?wsdl
⊡ ⊡ ⊠	http://127.0.0.1:8500/neo/regression/webservices/wscf/echocomplex_2.cfc?wsdl	http://127.0.0.1:8500/neo/regression/webservices/wscf/echocomplex_2.cfc?wsdl

2. Type the Web service name and the WSDL URL. WSDL stands for Web Services
Description Language. It is an XML format for describing how Web services
operate. The URL that you enter is the location of your WSDL document.

3. Click the Add Web Service button to save your Web service.

All of this makes it easier to access the Web service from within ColdFusion. Without
registering the Web service, you can still access it, but you have to specify all the
information in the cfinvoke tag.

Registering a CFX Tag

CFX tags are ColdFusion custom tags that were written in C++ or Java. They are great
for expanding the functionality of ColdFusion. We discuss how to write custom tags

in Chapter 26. After you have written a CFX custom tag, you must register it with the ColdFusion server before it can be used. Here is how you do it:

1. Log in to the ColdFusion Administrator and click the CFX Tags link. You will see this page:

Registered CFX Tags			
Actions	Tag Name	Type	Description
			No CFXs found.

2. There are two types of CFX custom tags, Java and C++. Click the appropriate button for the type you want to register.

3. If you click the Register Java CFX button, you will see this screen:

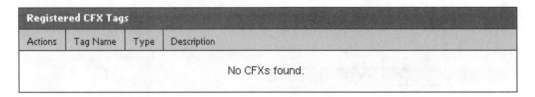

If you click the Register C++ CFX button, you will see this screen:

4. Enter the tag name and a description of the tag. If you are registering a Java tag, enter the name of the class that contains the Java tag. If you are registering a C++ tag, enter the name of the DLL and the procedure. If you want to retain the library in memory, leave the checkbox checked.

5. Click the Submit button to finish registration.

CORBA Connectors

CORBA (Common Object Request Broker Architecture) is just another way to share data between two different applications. ColdFusion loads ORBs (object request brokers) via a connector, but does not include a connector built into ColdFusion. You can set up ColdFusion to use any third-party connector. Here is how:

1. Log in to the ColdFusion Administrator and select the CORBA Connectors link under Extensions. You will see this page:

Register CORBA Connector

Registered CORBA Connectors		
Actions	Name	Classpath
No ORBs have been registered.		

2. Click the Register CORBA Connector button, and you'll see this page:

CORBA Connector		
ORB Name		
ORB Class Name		
Classpath		Browse Server
ORB Property File		Browse Server
	Submit	Cancel

3. Enter the ORB name and the name of its class in the appropriate boxes.

4. Enter, or select, the classpath and ORB property file.

5. Click Submit to finish your registration.

You are now ready to access CORBA objects via ColdFusion.

Summary

In this chapter, you learned about the following:

- ColdFusion directory mappings
- How the ColdFusion Administrator deals with Java applets and custom tags
- How to implement archives from the ColdFusion Administrator
- Logging and debugging settings

The next chapter will teach you how to cluster a ColdFusion server.

The Complete Reference

ColdFusion MX

Part III

Coding in ColdFusion

Chapter 7

Introducing Programming Languages

To understand how to program in ColdFusion, you need to understand the language it was built to work with, HTML. This chapter introduces the elements that make up an HTML page. It then starts to explore programming languages and talks about how CFML was built as a language to work with HTML.

Understanding HTML

This section gives you a brief history of HTML. It teaches you about the HTML tag-based syntax and introduces some common HTML tags that will be used throughout this book.

Exploring HTML's History

Hypertext Markup Language (HTML) is the language of the Web. It is a language that defines the look and feel of a web page. HTML is called a markup language, which is a term that comes from the days before computers, when printers had to format, or mark up, their text before passing it through a printing press. The term *markup* means to define the look, feel, and placement of text, images, or other content in regard to one other.

Tim Berners-Lee included the first definition of HTML when he released his first web program in 1991. HTML is an implementation of Standard Generalized Markup Language (SGML). SGML is a language that is used to define other languages. HTML was later turned over to an independent standards body called the World Wide Web Consortium (W3C). You can find more information about this organization at http://w3.org.

The HTML standard is currently in its fourth rendition. In the past, there have been many extensions to HTML that have been custom-coded directly into browsers, most notably Microsoft Internet Explorer and Netscape Navigator. W3C acts feverishly to incorporate these new features into the written standard. As Microsoft's market share grows larger and the Netscape browser gets used less and less, the push for new tags has lessened, but the standard continues to evolve and grow.

Understanding HTML Syntax

This section examines the syntax of the HTML language and explores the elements that make up an HTML document.

Using HTML Tags

HTML is said to be a tag-based language. It uses tags to tell the web browser how to display text and images to the end user. A standard HTML tag usually consists of an open tag and a close tag. The text you want to format is placed after the open tag and before the end tag.

This is an example of a tag:

```
<tagname>
 Your Text Here
</tagname>
```

The tag opens up with a <. Next comes the tag name. The name of the tag is followed by a >, finishing up your open tag.

The text that you want to format is placed between the begin and end tag. The browser will view the start tag and understand that it has to process the text that follows it. After the text comes the end tag. The end tag starts with </ and is followed by the name of the tag. It is closed with a >. End tags do not have a parameter list.

 *Not all tags have an end tag, such as the line break tag (
).*

You can use attributes to further refine the operation of a tag. The specific names and values of an attribute depend upon the tag. Some tags have a lot of attributes, while others have none at all. The attribute list is always located in the start tag, like this:

```
<tagname attribute1="AttributeValue" attribute2="AttributeValue">
 Your Text Here
</tagname>
```

As this example shows, attributes are put in the start tag after the tag name but before the closing >. The attribute starts with the attribute name. It is usually, but not always, followed by an equal sign and an open quote. After the open quote comes the attribute value. The value is followed by the close quote. A space is used to separate an attribute from the tag name, and to separate multiple attributes.

Putting Together an HTML Document

HTML tags can be grouped together to form an HTML document, or HTML page. HTML pages are split into two parts: the header and the body. The header is defined using the head tag, while the body is placed inside a body tag. Headers are relatively simple, but the body is much more complex, because it contains the content that makes up your document.

This is a sample HTML document:

```
<html>

 <head>
  <title>Sample HTML Document</title>
```

```
</head>

<body>
 Some Sample HTML Document Text
</body>
</html>
```

The document starts with the html tag, which is a wrapper for both the header and body of an HTML document. Next comes the head tag. Inside the head tag is the title of the document. This value will show up in the title bar of the web browser. After the head tag is closed, the body tag begins. The body tag contains all the text for the HTML document.

 Most browsers do not need the body or head tags to correctly translate an HTML document. For the sake of brevity, these tags are left out of most of the code in this book, but it is a best practice to write your code so that it adheres to the HTML standard.

Using Common HTML Tags

This section examines some of the common HTML tags that will be used throughout this book. The first tag is called the line break tag. By default, HTML displays all text on a single line. Carriage returns are removed, and any number of spaces will only display as a single space. The line break tag is br. It does not have an end tag. This is an example:

```
Here is the Broken <br>
Text
```

Line breaks are great for the simple formatting demands of this book, but you will often find that they are not complex enough for your formatting needs.

Tables are a simple means for formatting your data in a spreadsheet-like format. They are a bit more complex than just using the br tag, but are still a simple, yet powerful, formatting tool. HTML tables are anchored with the table tag. Rows are specified using the table row tag, tr. Columns are specified using the table data tag, td. Rows must be specified inside a table tag. Columns must be specified inside a row.

This is an example of a table with two rows and two columns:

```
<table>
 <tr>
  <td>Row 1, Column 1</td>
  <td>Row 1, Column 2</td>
 </tr>

 <tr>
  <td>Row 2, Column 1</td>
```

```
   <td>Row 2, Column 2</td>
  </tr>
</table>
```

The HTML code starts with the table tag. It defines two different rows, with two columns each. This is an example of the table:

Row 1, Column 1	Row 1, Column 2
Row 2, Column 1	Row 2, Column 2

There are many attributes that can be used to change the behavior of tables, but discussion of those attributes is beyond the scope of this book.

Perhaps one of the most important tags in web development is the anchor tag. The anchor tag is used to define links from the existing page to some other page. The anchor tag consists of a single letter, a. The most common attribute of this tag is the href attribute, which is used to specify the location that the link will go to when clicked. This is an example:

```
<a href="MyPage.cfm">My Link</a>
```

This anchor will create a link called My Link on the current page. When the My Link text is clicked, the user will move from the current page to MyPage.cfm.

Introducing Programming Languages

This section introduces you to the concept of a programming language and talks about some of the different types of programming languages. It then discusses some important concepts in computer programming and shows you where to look in this book for more information.

Choosing Between Different Types of Languages

Programming languages, at their core, exist to tell a computer how to solve a problem. The main difference between a programming language and a spoken language is that a programming language is designed for communication between a computer and a person, whereas a spoken language is designed to help two people communicate with each other.

The four important aspects of a programming language are the *programmer*, who tells the computer what to do, the *computer*, which solves the problem, the *process* that the program performs, and the *problem* that needs to be solved. Programming languages can be classified into the following five different types, the first four of which are based on the perspective of one of these aspects, and the fifth of which combines all aspects:

- **Imperative** Based on the perspective of the computer. Commands are written to execute in sequential order. This is the most common type of language, with C and Pascal being two examples. Imperative languages are also called procedural languages.

- **Functional** Based on the process that is used to solve the problem. It is very easy to design a process in a functional language. FP is a pure functional language.

- **Logic-oriented** Based on the perspective of the programmer. Logic-oriented languages try to mimic the way a human brain would solve the problem. SQL is a logic-oriented language that has particular relevance to ColdFusion development.

- **Object-oriented** Based on the perspective of the problem. Object-oriented languages became popular in the late '80s and early '90s. They are based on objects that correspond to real things, such as people, places, or things. Smalltalk is one of the few truly object-oriented languages, but object-oriented concepts have been applied to many imperative languages to create hybrids, such as Java or C++.

- **Distributed parallel** Based on all perspectives. Distributed parallel languages are designed to take features from all the four other types of languages and combine them so the program can travel down different paths simultaneously. Ada is a good example of a distributed parallel language.

The two most common types of languages in use today are imperative and object-oriented languages. ColdFusion's language, CFML, has historically been an imperative language, processing all templates from the top to the bottom. It is still an imperative language, but ColdFusion MX introduces some object-oriented features, making it a hybrid language able to use the best of both worlds.

Understanding Different Aspects of Programming

There are many important aspects of programming languages and software design that will be covered elsewhere in this book, as shown in Table 7-1.

Summary

In this chapter, you were introduced to the following:

Concept	Description
Assignment	Used to create variables and manipulate values. See Chapter 8.
Conditional logic	Allows you to make decisions in your code. See Chapter 13.
Looping logic	Allows you to repeat sections of your code. See Chapter 13.
Code modularization	Used to create blocks of code that you want to reuse multiple times or in multiple places. See Chapter 16.
Database design	The heart of many web applications is the database. See Chapter 9.
Development methodologies	Used to define an approach to solve a problem. See Chapter 10.

Table 7-1.   *Programming Language Concepts*

- HTML and some common HTML tags
- The different types of programming languages
- Important programming concepts

Understanding HTML is a good first step to understanding CFML, which is the language of ColdFusion. The next chapter starts to delve into features of CFML.

CODING IN COLDFUSION

The Complete Reference

ColdFusion MX

Chapter 8

Learning CFML Basics

I f the ColdFusion Application Server is the meat of your ColdFusion dinner, then
ColdFusion Markup Language (CFML) is the potato. CFML is the language that tells
ColdFusion what to do. This chapter introduces CFML, variables, and expressions.

Understanding CFML

This section explains how you can use CFML. If you already know HTML, then you
should have no problems learning CFML. First, you need to understand how to use
ColdFusion tags in a ColdFusion document.

Comparing CFML Tags to HTML Tags

ColdFusion tags are set up the same way as HTML tags. They just happen to perform
different functions. HTML tags are used to define the look and feel of data. ColdFusion
tags are used to modify and manipulate data before that data is displayed.

The web browser parses the HTML document and formats the text that the end user
sees, but it is the ColdFusion Application Server that processes CFML tags. ColdFusion
and HTML documents are the same, with one major exception. ColdFusion documents
end with .cfm as an extension, whereas HTML documents use .htm or .html. When a
web server sees an .htm extension, it sends the document to the web browser, but when
it sees a .cfm extension, it sends the document to the ColdFusion Application Server
(CFAS). The CFAS processes the various ColdFusion tags and sends them back to the
web server, which then sends the output to the web browser.

*ColdFusion tags are in the form of cftagname. The cf prefix is located before the name
of the tag. You can use this to distinguish CFML tags from HTML tags.*

Learning Different Types of Tags

HTML and CFML tags coexist very peacefully next to each other. It is easy to use CFML
to enhance the functionality of your web site. Let's examine some of the things that can
be done with CFML:

- **Database operations**   ColdFusion's most important use is to maintain data
  located in a database. This will be discussed in Chapter 9.

- **Controlling the logic in your code**   ColdFusion can conditionally display text
  or repeat certain sections of code, as described in Chapter 13.

- **Graphing**   ColdFusion has advanced graphing capability, as described in
  Chapter 20.

- **Search engines**   ColdFusion's built-in Verity search engine makes creating
  a search on your site very easy. We discuss this in Chapter 24.

- **Collect user data**   ColdFusion can take data entered through user forms and
  manipulate it in various ways. We discuss this in Chapter 12.

Next, this chapter looks at variables in ColdFusion.

All About Variables

One of the most important programming concepts is that of a variable. This section teaches you what variables are and demonstrates how to use them in ColdFusion.

Understanding Variable Basics

A variable is a name-value pair. That means that the name of the variable is used to refer to its given value. Variables in programming are similar to variables in algebra or physics. We all know (or used to know, when taking a physics course) that the gravity of the earth is 32.2 feet/second^2, yet we use the letter g as a placeholder for gravity instead of using the number 32.2. This allows us to apply the same equations if the value for gravity changes, such as when an equation refers to a planet other than earth; only one value, g, has to be changed as opposed to every equation that uses gravity. Let's look at variables in ColdFusion.

Simple Variable Types

A simple variable type in ColdFusion is one that contains a single value. Table 8-1 lists and describes all the variable types. One example of a simple variable type is a number, of which there are two types: integers and reals. A *real* is a number with a decimal, and an *integer* is a number without a decimal. A *string* is a group of zero or more characters. The difference between a number and a string is that strings are enclosed in quotes. Look at these values:

```
"This is a Variable"
1234
"1234"
12.5
```

CODING IN COLDFUSION

Variable Type	Description
Numeric	Contains an integer or a real number
Date	Can be interpreted in a date format
Boolean	Can have either of two values
String	A collection of one or more characters
List	A specialized version of a string, where a specified delimiter separates elements

Table 8-1.   *Simple Variable Types*

Out of these three values, can you tell which ones are strings? The first and third values are strings, whereas the second is an integer and the fourth is a real. Why is the third value not an integer? Even though it would pass as a number, it is enclosed in quotes and therefore ColdFusion considers it a string.

Two of the simple variable types in Table 8-1 need further discussion. A Boolean variable is one that can contain one of two values. The value pairs are usually 1 or 0, On or Off, Yes or No, or, most commonly, True or False. Computers are built on top of switches and switches only have either of two states: on or off (ignoring mutant light switches that are designed to dim lights). A Boolean can be stored in a single bit, and therefore is memory efficient. ColdFusion treats integers as Boolean values, where 0 is considered false and anything else is considered true. Strings can be Boolean if their values are Yes or No, or True or False.

Lists are a specialized version of a string. A list is a collection of values, separated by a delimiter, usually a comma. In addition to standard variable usage, ColdFusion provides some special functions designed exclusively for string access. We'll examine ColdFusion functions later in this module. This is an example list:

```
"A, B, C, D, E, F, G"
```

This list contains the first seven letters of the alphabet, separated by commas. Since ColdFusion stores lists as strings, the list can be used just as any other string.

If you have experience with some traditional programming languages, you will be happy to learn that ColdFusion is a loosely typed language. This means that you can easily change a variable from one type to another—from an integer to a string, for example. You also do not have to declare the type of the variable before using it. Typed languages do not allow this.

You can easily change a simple variable's type from one type to another, but it is not possible with complex variables.

Complex Variable Types

A complex variable can be defined simply as a collection of simple variables. There are two different types of complex variables: structures and arrays. Let's look at each type individually.

To understand complex variable types, let's examine a shopping cart, which is a common application for complex variables. If you think of the traditional shopping cart that you push through a grocery store, you can probably isolate some properties specific to it. The shopping cart holds many different items, but all the items are still referred to collectively as a shopping cart. It is not until you are done with your grocery shopping that you need to worry about individual items in the shopping cart.

To refer to an item individually, you use something called an *index*. The main difference between arrays and structures is the type of index. Arrays use a numerical index, while structures use a string as the index. An array is good for any collection of similar elements, and is often used to keep track of lists of numbers because of the built-in mathematical functions associated with arrays. Structures are called *associative* arrays, because the index is a string and you are associating that string with the value. Structures are akin to objects and are best used when there is no specific relation between the types of data.

With this information in mind, let's revisit the shopping cart example. Each item in the shopping cart is best represented as a structure. They have differing qualities, such as the price, weight, and name of the item. The shopping cart as a unit is best represented as an array of structures.

"But, hold up, Jeffry. Lists consist of a collection of simple data types. Aren't lists also complex variables?" Thanks for asking; you are correct insofar as lists act like complex data types. A list is a collection of simple variables. However, there is one important difference: Lists are stored internally as strings. All functions performed on lists are variations on string processing. This is not the case with structures or arrays.

Variable Scopes

A variable scope is something that defines the length of time that the variable exists and in what aspects that variable can be used. The variable scopes are described in Table 8-2.

Scope	Prefix	How Created	Availability	Comment
Local	variables	Using cfset or cfparam	During a single template's execution	Custom tags called by the template cannot access this scope
Form field	form	Submitting an HTML form	During a single template's execution	Discussed in Chapter 12
URL parameter	url	In the URL's query string	During a single template's execution	Custom tags called by the template cannot access this scope; discussed in Chapter 12
CGI environment	cgi	By the server	Available in all templates	Offer information about a browser and may change on each request

Table 8-2.   *ColdFusion Scopes*

Scope	Prefix	How Created	Availability	Comment
HTTP cookies	cookies	Using cfcookie tag	During a single template's execution	Stored on a user's machine
Request	request	Using cfset or cfparam	During a single template's execution	Available in custom tags
Server	server	Using cfset or cfparam	In all templates by all applications on a server	
Application	application	Using cfset or cfparam	During a single template's execution	These variables persist between templates
Session	session	Using cfset or cfparam	During a single template's execution	These variables persist between templates
Client	client	Using cfset or cfparam	During a single template's execution	These variables persist between templates; discussed later in this chapter
Caller	caller	When calling a custom tag	Available in custom tags	Discussed in Chapter 16
Attributes	attributes	When calling a custom tag	Available in custom tags	Discussed in Chapter 16
Arguments	arguments	When calling a custom function	Available in a custom function	Discussed in Chapter 16
Local custom tag	thistag	When calling a custom function	Available in a custom function	Discussed in Chapter 16
Local function	this	When calling a custom function or ColdFusion Component	Available in a custom function and ColdFusion Component	Discussed in Chapter 16
Flash	flash	When calling a template from a Macromedia Flash movie	During a single template's execution	Discussed in Chapter 28

Table 8-2. *ColdFusion Scopes* (continued)

Creating Simple Variables

Now that you know all this great information about variable types and scopes, it is time to put it all to use. This section teaches you how to create a variable. It also introduces you to your first CFML tags; isn't it about time?

Using cfset to Create Variables

One of the simplest tags in ColdFusion is the cfset tag. It is used to create variables and assign a value to the variable. This is its format:

```
<cfset variablename = variablevalue>
```

The cfset tag is one that does not contain an end tag.

The cfset tag is the primary tag used for variable creation and assignment. If you use cfset on a variable that already exists, it will change its value. If you use cfset on a variable that does not yet exist, it will be created and assigned the value that you specify.

Let's look at some sample ColdFusion code:

```
<cfset MyVariable = "MyVar">
<cfset MyVariable = "1,2,3,4,5">
<cfset MyVariable2 = 45>
<cfset MyVariable3 = 45.2>
```

The first line creates a variable called MyVariable, and gives it a string value of MyVar. The second line works a little differently. Since the MyVariable variable is already defined, the second line simply replaces the existing string value MyVar with the list 1,2,3,4,5. The third line creates the variable MyVariable2 and gives it an integer value of 45. The fourth line creates MyVariable3 and gives it the real value of 45.2.

The cfset tag is almost an anomaly in the tag world. It does not have a consistent or well-defined attribute. Developers have a lot of flexibility with variable naming conventions, as we'll discuss later in this chapter. Most tags are not as lenient.

Using cfparam to Create Variables

The cfparam tag is kind of like a superhuman cfset tag. In addition to creating new variables, it can perform verification on a variable's data type. If the variable already exists, cfparam will opt not to change its data type.

The following are the attributes for cfparam:

- **name**   The name of the variable you want to create (required attribute).
- **default**   The default value for the variable (optional attribute).
- **type**   The default type for the variable that you want to create. Valid values are any, array, binary, Boolean, date, numeric, query, string, struct, UUID, and variablename (optional attribute).

CODING IN COLDFUSION

The only required attribute of this tag is the name attribute. If you use the cfparam tag with just the name, then the tag will check for a variable's existence. If the variable exists, then ColdFusion continues processing; if it does not exist, then an error is thrown. This is an example of cfparam with only the name attribute:

```
<cfparam name="MyVariable">
```

If you use cfparam with both the name and default attributes, then a nonexistent variable will be created and assigned the default value. This is an example:

```
<cfparam name="MyVariable" default="My Value">
```

Finally, you can use the cfparam tag with the name and type attributes. Here is an example:

```
<cfparam name="MyVariable" default="numeric">
```

In this case, ColdFusion checks whether the variable, MyVariable, exists. If it does, ColdFusion checks whether it has a numeric type. Numeric types are integers or reals. If MyVariable does not have the correct type, then an error is thrown. The cfparam tag will check for these variable types:

- **Any**   Check for any data type (this is the default value).
- **Array**   Checks whether the given variable is an array.
- **Binary**   Checks whether the given string value is in Binary format.
- **Boolean**   Checks whether the current value passes for a Boolean.
- **Date**   Checks for a date value.
- **Numeric**   Checks whether the value is a number, either Integer or Real.
- **Query**   A specialized complex data type. We will discuss queries in Chapter 9.
- **String**   Checks whether the given value is a string.
- **Struct**   Checks whether the given variable is a structure.
- **UUID**   A universally defined unique identifier in the format xxxxxxxx-xxxx-xxxx-xxxxxxxxxxxxxxxx, created using ColdFusion's CreateUUID function.
- **Variablename**   Checks whether a string value is an acceptable variable name. We discuss variable naming conventions next.

Note   *If ColdFusion does throw an error, you have ways to handle the error, as described in Chapter 18.*

Naming Conventions for Variables

ColdFusion is not completely open-ended when it comes to variable names. You must follow specific rules to name your variables. These are some important naming conventions:

- The first character in a variable name must be a letter.
- The variable name, excepting the first character, can be any combination of letters, numbers, and the underscore character.
- Variable names cannot have spaces in them.
- Variable names cannot have periods in them.

 If you use a period in a variable name, ColdFusion MX does not throw an error. It creates a complex variable type called a structure, in which the part to the left of the period is the name of the structure, and the part to the right of the variable is the name of the key.

Here are some sample variable names:

Correct Variable Names	Incorrect Variable Names
A1234	1234
My_Variable	My Variable
X	SX$

Developing ColdFusion Expressions

A ColdFusion expression is a way to process a variable or other piece of data. Expressions unleash the real power of ColdFusion by manipulating multiple data, functions, or even other expressions. Expressions always evaluate to a single piece of data. This section shows you how they work.

Creating a ColdFusion Expression

As with variables, there are simple expressions and complex expressions. Since a complex expression is just a group of simple expressions, we will start by examining simple expressions. Then we will examine the different types of operators that can be used to create complex expressions.

Understanding the Elements of a ColdFusion Expression

First we want to look at the elements of a ColdFusion expression. They are listed and described in Table 8-3.

CODING IN COLDFUSION

Type	Description
Literals numeric	All the simple data types—numeric data types, strings, Boolean, date-time values, and lists—can be used explicitly in a ColdFusion expression.
Structures	A complex data type.
Arrays	A complex data type.
Queries	A specialized version of a complex data type. We discuss queries in Chapter 9.
COM objects	Common Object Model (COM) objects are components that encapsulate specific functionality. These are discussed in Chapter 30.
Variables	When a variable is used in an expression, its value is returned. Variables must contain simple variable types when used in an expression.
Functions	ColdFusion functions return a simple variable type. These are discussed later in this chapter.

Table 8-3.   *Elements of a ColdFusion Expression*

Creating a Simple ColdFusion Expression

ColdFusion expressions can be used within the attributes of a ColdFusion tag, or mixed within HTML. When you are integrating ColdFusion expressions with normal HTML, ColdFusion needs a way to be able to separate the ColdFusion elements from standard HTML elements. There are two elements that ColdFusion will use to do this: the cfoutput tag and the pound sign, #.

ColdFusion's cfoutput tag is used to distinguish ColdFusion output from normal output. When processing a CFM page, the ColdFusion server will stream any text that isn't a ColdFusion tag, or in between two cfoutput tags. When a cfoutput block is processed, ColdFusion looks for the pound sign. The pound sign tells your CFAS that it needs to do some special processing. To display a variable, you need to use two pound signs.

Let's look at a sample template:

```
<cfset MyVariable = "My Sample Text">
<cfoutput>
 My Variable: #MyVariable#
</cfoutput>
```

The first line of the template uses cfset to create a variable. Then it processes the cfoutput tag. This tells ColdFusion to start looking for the pound signs, which delineate an expression. It passes the first group of text, "My Variable:", right back to the web server. Then it discovers the pound sign, and processes the expression, which is just a variable name. The value of the variable is returned. ColdFusion then finds the end cfoutput tag and finishes processing the template. This will be the resulting output:

```
My Variable: My Sample Text
```

Creating Complex Expressions

A complex expression is made up of multiple simple expressions. Depending on the type of data that you are operating upon, there are multiple operators that you can use to create complex expressions, as shown in Table 8-4.

Operator	Expression Type	Use	Order of Operations
+	Numeric	Tells you that the number is positive.	First
-	Numeric	Tells you that the number is negative.	First
^	Numeric	Exponent	Second
*	Numeric	Multiplication	Third
/	Numeric	Division	Third
\	Numeric	Div operator, performs division and returns the integer result without a remainder.	Fourth
MOD	Numeric	Performs division and returns the integer remainder.	Fifth
+	Numeric	Addition	Sixth
-	Numeric	Subtraction	Sixth
&	String	Concatenates two strings.	Seventh
IS EQ EQUAL	Decision	Performs a case-insensitive comparison and returns true if the values are identical.	Eighth

Table 8-4. *ColdFusion Operators*

Operator	Expression Type	Use	Order of Operations
IS NOT NEQ NOT EQUAL	Decision	Performs a case-insensitive comparison and returns false if the values are identical.	Eighth
CONTAINS	Decision	If the value on the left is contained in the value on the right, returns true.	Eighth
DOES NOT CONTAIN	Decision	If the value on the left is contained in the value on the right, returns false.	Eighth
GREATER THAN GT	Decision	If the value on the left is greater than the value on the right, returns true.	Eighth
LESS THAN LT	Decision	If the value on the left is greater than the value on the right, returns false.	Eighth
GREATER THAN OR EQUAL TO GTE GE	Decision	If the value on the left is greater than the value on the right, returns true.	Eighth
LESS THAN OR EQUAL TO LTE LE	Decision	If the value on the left is greater than the value on the right, returns false.	Eighth
NOT	Boolean	If the condition is true, then it becomes false. If the condition is false, then it becomes true.	Ninth
AND	Boolean	If both conditions are true, the result is true; otherwise, the result is false.	Tenth
OR	Boolean	If both conditions are false, the result is false; otherwise, the result is true.	Eleventh

Table 8-4. *ColdFusion Operators* (continued)

Operator	Expression Type	Use	Order of Operations
XOR	Boolean	If both conditions are true or both conditions are false, the result is false. If one condition is true and one condition is false, the result is true.	Twelfth
EQV	Boolean	If both conditions are true, or both values are false, the result is true. If one condition is true and the other is false, then the result is false.	Thirteenth
IMP	Boolean	If the first condition is true and the second is false, then the result is false; otherwise, the result is true.	Fourteenth

Table 8-4. *ColdFusion Operators* (continued)

Let's examine this code segment as an example of how you can create a complex expression:

```
<cfset MyVariable1 = "My Variable">
<cfset MyVariable2 = "My Variable 2">
<cfset MyVariable3 = MyVariable1 & MyVariable2>
```

There are three lines in this template. The first creates a variable, MyVariable1. The value given to the variable is a simple expression, in the form of a string literal. The second line, creating MyVariable2, performs a similar operation. The third line creates a third variable using the string concatenation operator. The complex expression MyVariable1 & MyVariable2 evaluates to "My VariableMy Variable 2" and that is what MyVariable3 is set to.

Using Functions

ColdFusion functions are designed to provide further refinements to data. You can use them to format your data for output, and to manipulate complex variable types. Mathematical functions can be performed using ColdFusion functions, as well as verification of a variable's type and existence. This section shows you how to use functions and illustrates some commonly used functions.

How to Use Functions

A ColdFusion function is really just an element of an expression. The general format of a function is this:

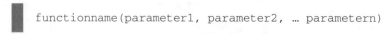

```
functionname(parameter1, parameter2, … parametern)
```

The function name is followed by a parameter list. The specific parameters depend on the function. Parameters in functions are similar to attributes in tags. In ColdFusion tags, you define tag attributes using name-value pairs, where the name is equal to the value. With functions, you simply list the values in the parameter list, without specifying the name of the parameter.

Let's take a look at an example function, NumberFormat, to see how this all works. NumberFormat is a function that is used to format numbers for output. It accepts two parameters, the number and a mask. The mask is the text that defines the output. We are going to use two elements in our mask. The underscore is a placeholder for a digit and will be either an empty digit or a number. The decimal shows where the decimal will show up on the number. This code:

```
<cfoutput>
  #NumberFormat(3.141592654, "__.__")#
  #NumberFormat(125, "__.__")#
  #NumberFormat(19, "__.__")#
  #NumberFormat(19.521456, "__.__")#
</cfoutput>
```

produces these results:

```
3.14
125.0
19.00
19.52
```

This is an example of how functions can be used when creating output within ColdFusion.

Functions can be used anywhere a ColdFusion expression can be used, including inside other ColdFusion functions.

List Functions

This section examines some of the most common list functions. You'll remember that a list is just a specialized version of a string. All string functions can be used on lists and vice versa. List functions are described in Table 8-5.

Function Name	Parameters	Usage
ListAppend	**List:** The list **Value:** The value you are adding **Delimiters:** The optional delimiter for the list	Adds a value to the end of a list.
ListPrepend	**List:** The list **Value:** The value you are adding **Delimiters:** The optional delimiter for the list	Adds a value to the beginning of a list.
ListDeleteAt	**List:** The list **Position:** The position you are modifying **Delimiters:** The optional delimiter for the list	Deletes a specific list element.
ListInsertAt	**List:** The list **Position:** The position you are modifying **Value:** The value you are adding **Delimiters:** The optional delimiter for the list	Inserts a value into a list.
ListSetAt	**List:** The list **Position:** The position you are modifying **Value:** The value you are adding **Delimiters:** The optional delimiter for the list	Sets a specific list item.
ListFirst	**List:** The list **Delimiters:** The optional delimiter for the list	Returns the first element of a list.

Table 8-5. *Common List Functions*

Function Name	Parameters	Usage
ListLast	**List:** The list **Delimiters:** The optional delimiter for the list	Returns the last element of a list.
ListRest	**List:** The list **Delimiters:** The optional delimiter for the list	Returns all list elements except the first one.
ListGetAt	**List:** The list **Position:** The position you are modifying **Delimiters:** The optional delimiter for the list	Returns the element located at the given position.
ListContains ListContainsNoCase ListFind ListFindNoCase	**List:** The list **Substring:** The value you're searching for **Delimiters:** The optional delimiter for the list	Returns the list index of the first list element that contains the specified substring. The ListContains function returns true for partial matches. The ListFind function needs a complete match to return true. ListContainsNoCase and ListFindNoCase perform non-case-sensitive searches, while ListContains and ListFind perform case-sensitive searches.
ListLen	**List:** The list **Delimiters:** The optional delimiter for the list	Returns the number of elements in the list.
ListSort	**List:** The list **SortType:** The type of sort you want to perform: Numeric, Text, or TextNoCase **Delimiters:** The optional delimiter for the list	Returns a sorted list.
ListValueCount ListValueCountNoCase	**List:** The list **Value:** The value you are checking for **Delimiters:** The optional delimiter for the list	Returns the number of instances of a specific value in the given list. ListValueCountNoCase is not case sensitive, while ListValueCount is.

Table 8-5. *Common List Functions* (continued)

Since lists are stored internally as strings, they can be created just like any other simple variables using cfset or cfparam. The elements of a list are numbered internally. The first element of the list is numbered 1, the second element is numbered 2, and so on. When accessing an element in the center or at the end of the list, you specify the element. Since the delimiter of a list can be specified, a little creativity gives you a lot of flexibility. A sentence could be a list with the space a delimiter, or a URL could be a list with the forward slash as a delimiter, for example.

Tip   *List functions are great for processing form checkboxes on the form-processing page. We discuss this in Chapter 12.*

Array Functions

This section displays some of the most common array functions, which are listed and described in Table 8-6.

Function Name	Parameters	Usage
ArrayNew	**Dimension:** The dimension of the array you are creating	Creates a new array, of 1, 2, or 3 dimensions
ArrayAppend	**Array:** The array **Value:** The value you want to add to the array	Adds an item at the end of the array
ArrayPrepend	**Array:** The array **Value:** The value you want to add to the array	Adds an item at the beginning of the array
ArrayInsertAt	**Array:** The array **Position:** The position at which you want to insert an item into the array **Value:** The value you want to add to the array	Adds an item into the array at the specified position
ArrayDeleteAt	**Array:** The array **Position:** The position at which you want to delete an item from the array	Deletes an item on the array at the specified position
ArraySum	**Array:** The array	Returns the sum of all array elements
ArrayAvg	**Array:** The array	Returns the average of all array elements
ArrayMax	**Array:** The array	Returns the largest value in the array

Table 8-6. *Common Array Functions*

Function Name	Parameters	Usage
ArrayMin	**Array:** The array	Returns the smallest value in the array
IsArray	**VariableName:** The name of the value you want to check to see if it's an array	Returns true if the given variable is an array; returns false otherwise
ArrayIsEmpty	**Array:** The array	Returns true if the given array is empty; returns false otherwise
ArraySort	**Array:** The array **SortType:** Defines how you want to sort the array: numeric, text, and textnocase are the options **SortOrder:** Defines how you want the results to be sorted: asc for ascending or desc for descending	Returns true if the array was sorted; returns false otherwise

Table 8-6.   *Common Array Functions* (continued)

The ArrayNew function can be used in combination with cfset to create an array. Arrays can be created in up to three dimensions, although if the element of one array is another array, you can build in more dimensions. Arrays are designed to be memory efficient and will automatically expand and collapse according to the number of elements that they have in them.

Note   *Array and Structure functions modify the variable in memory, while List functions return an updated value without modifying the original variable.*

Examine the following code:

```
<cfset MyArray = ArrayNew(1)>
<cfset Added = ArrayAppend(MyArray, "First")>
<cfset Added = ArrayAppend(MyArray, "Second")>
<cfset Added = ArrayAppend(MyArray, "Third")>
```

The Added variable is the Boolean result, if you ever need to check it for proof that your element was added to your array. The code creates this one-dimensional array, called MyArray, with these elements:

Index	Element
1	First
2	Second
3	Third

You access the values in these arrays by using the array name, MyArray, followed by the index surrounded in open and close brackets, [ ]. This code will display the three items in the array:

```
<cfoutput>
  #MyArray[1]# <br>
  #MyArray[2]# <br>
  #MyArray[3]# <br>
</cfoutput>
```

You can also use this syntax to set array values, instead of using the ArrayAppend, ArrayPrepend, or ArraySetAt functions. This will create a two-dimensional array and set some values:

```
<cfset MyArray = ArrayNew(2)>
<cfset MyArray[1][1] = "First First")>
<cfset MyArray[1][2] = "First Second")>
<cfset MyArray[2][1] = "Second First" )>
```

This will create the following array:

Index	1	2
1	First First	First Second
2	Second First	*Blank*

There is nothing located at array spot 2, 2, and there won't be until we add something there. This is a part of ColdFusion's efficient memory handling. Blank spots in the array do not exist. The following code will delete the entry at 1, 1:

```
<cfset deleted = ArrayDeleteAt(MyArray[1],1)>
```

Notice that we must send a one-dimensional array to the ArrayDeleteAt function, so we do so by only specifying the dimension in the function argument. Our resulting array would be like this:

Index	1	2
1	First Second	*Blank*
2	Second First	*Blank*

No values would be located in the second dimension.

Structure Functions

This section examines some of the common structure functions. Structures are like arrays, except the index is a string instead of a number. Table 8-7 lists and describes common structure functions.

The first thing you need to know is how to create a structure, which is similar to how we create arrays:

```
<cfset MyStruct = StructNew()>
```

The StructNew function does not take any arguments. Unlike arrays, structures do not have multiple dimensions, so there are no parameters to the StructNew function.

We use this code to add some elements into our structure:

```
<cfset Added = StructInsert(MyStruct,"Test","Value1")>
<cfset Added = StructInsert(MyStruct,"Test2","Value2")>
```

The preceding code creates the following structure:

Index	Value
Test	Value1
Test2	Value2

There are three different ways in which we can access the values in the structure. The first is to use the structure functions, StructFind:

```
<cfoutput>
 Test: #StructFind(MyStruct, "Test")#<br>
 Test2: #StructFind(MyStruct, "Test2")#<br>
</cfoutput>
```

Function Name	Parameters	Usage
StructNew	N/A	Creates a new structure.
StructInsert	**Structure:** The structure **Key:** The key you want to insert **Value:** The value you want to insert **AllowOverWrite:** A Boolean value that tells the function whether to overwrite an already existing value	Inserts the given value into the structure at the specified key.
StructUpdate	**Structure:** The structure **Key:** The key you want to change **Value:** The value you want to update	Updates the specified key with the given value.
StructFind	**Structure:** The structure **Key:** The key whose value you want to return	Returns the value located at the given key.
StructClear	**Structure:** The structure	Deletes all elements in the structure.
StructDelete	**Structure:** The structure **Key:** The key whose value you want to return **IndicateNonexisting:** If set to yes, the function will return true if the key doesn't exist	Removes the specified key from the structure.
IsStruct	**VariableName:** The name of the variable you're checking	Checks whether the given variable is a structure.
StructIsEmpty	**Structure:** The structure	Checks whether the structure has any keys.
StructKeyExists	**Structure:** The structure **Key:** Any given key	Checks whether the given key exists in the given structure.
StructCount	**Structure:** The structure	Returns the number of keys in the structure.
StructAppend	**Structure1:** The first structure **Structure2:** The second structure **OverWriteFlag:** A Boolean value if you want repeat keys in Structure2 to overwrite values in Structure 1	Adds all keys and values from Structure2 into Structure1. This function always returns yes.

Table 8-7.   *Common Structure Functions*

The second way is similar to how we access one-dimensional arrays and is called associative array notation. Instead of placing a number between the open and close brackets, we place a string:

```
<cfoutput>
  Test: #MyStruct["Test"]#<br>
  Test2: #MyStruct["Test2"]#<br>
</cfoutput>
```

There is yet a third way to accomplish the same thing. It is called object property notation, and is my personal preference when dealing with structures. It stems from the object-oriented programming world. After the name of the structure variable, we place a period followed by the name of the key:

```
<cfoutput>
  Test: #MyStruct.Test#<br>
  Test2: #MyStruct.Test2#<br>
</cfoutput>
```

All three of these options will produce the same output:

```
Test: Value1
Test2: Value2
```

Setting Up a ColdFusion Application

The last issue that we want to cover in this chapter is ColdFusion's application framework. You use the application framework to set up the breadth of your application, control sessions, track users, and control other application-specific related issues.

Using the cfapplication Tag

To start to use ColdFusion's application framework, you must set up the cfapplication tag. This section teaches you how to use the cfapplication tag, which is the tag that sets up ColdFusion's application framework. It allows you to define how your application will use Application, Session, and Client variables, and also provides a name for your application. These are the attributes:

- **name**   Defines the name of your application. It is required if you want to use Application, Session, or Client variables.

- **clientmanagement**   Defines whether or not Client variables are enabled for use within the current application (optional attribute). If set to yes, Client variables are enabled.

- **clientstorage**   Defines where client variables will be stored. The three options are registry, cookie, or the name of a datasource. If this attribute is left out, it defaults to the settings set up in the ColdFusion Administrator.

- **setclientcookies**   Defines whether or not the CFID and CFTOKEN cookies are created as cookies on the user's machine. If the value is yes, it's the default, and then the CFID and CFTOKEN cookies are created on the user's machine. ColdFusion uses these two cookies to keep track of a user between page requests. If you choose no, then you must explicitly pass the CFID and CFTOKEN values to each request, as URL variables.

- **sessionmanagement**   Defines whether or not the session variables are enabled for the application. If set to yes, they are enabled; if set to no (the default), they are not enabled.

- **sessiontimeout**   Defines how long a session variable will exist idle in memory before it is automatically cleared (optional attribute). You set this value using the CreateTimeSpan function, which accepts four values: days, hours, minutes, and seconds. The value you specify can override the default value, which is set in the ColdFusion Administrator, but it cannot override the maximum value set in the Administrator. We discussed these settings in Chapter 3.

- **applicationtimeout**   Acts in the same way that the sessiontimeout attribute does, but is designed for application variables, not session variables (optional attribute). You set its value with the CreateTimeSpan function. The default and maximum values can be set in the ColdFusion Administrator.

- **setdomaincookies**   Defines whether or not the CFID and CFTOKEN values are available for all subdomains to see. If you are running your application on a clustered server, give this attribute a yes value so that the CFID and CFTOKEN values are available for all subdomains to see. ColdFusion will create a third cookie, CFMAGIC, to tell ColdFusion whether or not to look for domain cookies.

Tip   *Whenever you are using clustered servers that are not session-aware, you will want to use client variables to store your session data. Session variables will be lost if a user moves from one computer in the cluster to another.*

The cfapplication tag is one that only contains a start tag, without needing an end tag. It does not need additional input or processing. This is a common example:

```
<cfapplication name="Chapter8" sessionmanagement="Yes"
               sessiontimeout="#CreateTimeSpan(0,6,0,0)#"
               applicationtimeout="#CreateTimeSpan(1,0,0,0)#"
               clientmanagement="Yes">
```

This tag gives our application the name of Chapter8. We turn on session management with a timeout of six hours for session variables. Application variables will time out in one day, and client variables are enabled.

CODING IN COLDFUSION

Application.cfm and OnRequestEnd.cfm

You may be wondering where to put the cfapplication tag. It doesn't make sense to put it on every single template. If you were to make a change to the cfapplication tag, you would have to make it manually on every single page in your applications. Thankfully, ColdFusion provides two files, Application.cfm and OnRequestEnd.cfm, to handle issues such as these.

You'll remember from Chapter 1 that ColdFusion will process a page like this:

1. The web browser requests a page ending with .cfm.

2. The web server sees that the page ends with a .cfm extension and passes it to the ColdFusion Application Server.

3. The ColdFusion Application Server processes the page and sends the results to the web server.

4. The web server sends the results to the web browser.

There is a hidden step that is not explicitly defined in this chain of events. When the ColdFusion Application Server is sent a page to process, it first looks for the Application.cfm file and executes it. If it doesn't find the Application.cfm file in the current directory, it looks in the directory above it. It continues to drill up the directory structure until it reaches the root directory of the web site or finds the Application.cfm file.

After finding the Application.cfm file, ColdFusion executes the code inside it, and then executes the page that was requested. Before sending the results back to the browser, ColdFusion looks for a file called OnRequestEnd.cfm in the same directory in which it found the Application.cfm file. It executes this file, appends the results to the text, and streams the results of all three files (Application.cfm, the requested page, and OnRequestEnd) to the web server, which passes it on to the browser.

> **Tip** *Application.cfm and OnRequestEnd.cfm are case-sensitive filenames.*

The Application.cfm file is the best place to put the cfapplication tag because it is automatically executed for each template. You can set up your application in a single file, and all subsequent files and subdirectories will be able to use it. If you make a change, it is automatically trickled down through the application. You can also add site headers in the Application.cfm file. The OnRequestEnd.cfm file is good for standard footers, or any processing that you need to perform to finalize your page's processing.

Summary

In this chapter, you learned about the following:

- How to create and manipulate simple and complex variable types
- Variable scopes
- How to use ColdFusion expressions and functions
- How to define a ColdFusion application framework, using the cfapplication tag

The next chapter will delve into the world of databases.

CODING IN COLDFUSION

The Complete Reference

Chapter 9

Designing Your Database

Behind the scenes of just about every ColdFusion site lies a database. Some developers have even said that understanding database design and database concepts is more important to your ColdFusion sites than understanding ColdFusion. I don't want to downplay the importance of understanding ColdFusion, mind you, but since one of ColdFusion's primary purposes is to transfer data between a web or application server and a web browser, understanding a database will complement your ColdFusion skills greatly.

Learning Important Database Concepts

Before you can understand how to access databases from within ColdFusion, you need to understand exactly what a database is. A database is, basically, any collection of data.

Explaining Database Elements

Unlike web technology, databases have been around since the advent of computers. They have been studied, researched, implemented, and then studied some more. The concepts surrounding databases have been set in stone. With that said, let's blow the dust off these old stone tablets and review the basics.

Understanding Database Software

As I said earlier, a database is any collection of data. The collection of books in a library is a database. All the receipts associated with last year's business ski trip tax loss could be a database. If we want to be able to use that data, we need it to be in a digital format. Computers aren't yet smart enough to go to the library and search for every book regarding nuclear physics, and come back home with a list of them.

When we speak of databases with regard to ColdFusion, we are actually referring to a relational database management system (RDBMS). An RDBMS is a collection of components. One component is the interface for maintaining the data. Another component is the storage mechanism that stores the data. There is a component that sits in the middle, which transfers data between the user interface and the data storage. The reason for having these separate components is that the way users access or use the data is not necessarily always the most efficient way to store the data.

There are two main types of RDBMS: file-based databases and client/server databases. File-based systems are usually all-in-one packages, offering the interface and data storage in a single package. Microsoft Access is one of the most common file-based databases. As a general rule, file-based databases are not very good for web development. File-based databases were designed to support only one user at a time, which does not satisfy the requirement for any web site that receives visitors.

Microsoft Access is used on the Web a lot because it is widely available, as part of Microsoft Office. Refer to Chapter 4 for some best practices using Access on your web site.

Client/server databases are designed from the ground up to handle a whole lot of users at the same time. That makes them great for supporting web sites. There are two parts to a client/server database: the client and the server. You probably already know about client/server activity, even if you don't know you know it. Browsing the Web is a client/server experience. Your web browser is a client. You are accessing information that resides on a web server computer. The web server computer accepts different requests at the same time, and processes them by sending HTML pages and graphics files to the user who requested them.

Client/server databases operate in much the same way as web browsers and servers. Any number of database clients can access the server. It is the server that handles each request and sends data back to the respective client. Common client/server databases are Microsoft SQL Server, Oracle, and Sybase SQL Anywhere.

Explaining Tables and Columns

Now let's get down to the nitty-gritty. What does an RDBMS actually do? This section discusses how the data is stored in an RDBMS.

Databases are made up of one or more tables. Tables are made up of columns and rows. A *column* is a single piece of data. A *row*, or record, is the set of values for each column in a table. In a single table, no two rows can be identical. It is good to think of a single table as a spreadsheet. Rows are horizontal and columns are vertical.

This is a sample database table:

Name	Email	ZIP	State
Jeffry Houser	jeff@instantcoldfusion.com	12345	Connecticut
Postmaster	postmaster@instantcoldfusion.com	67890	New York

This table has four columns: Name, Email, ZIP, and State. It has two rows, one starting with Jeffry Houser and the second starting with Postmaster.

Understanding Relationships

The real power behind a database is how your tables relate to each other. Without the ability to relate your tables, a database's usability would decrease drastically. You'd be stuck with disjointed data and no way to use it.

Keys

Before we can understand relationships between our data, we need to understand what a key is. A *key* is a way that you can uniquely identify a row in a table. No two keys can be identical in a single table. A key can be a single column or a combination of multiple columns. In practice, most people create a single field to be used as the key of that table, usually an auto-incrementing integer.

There are two types of keys: primary keys and foreign keys. The primary key is used to identify a row in the current table. A foreign key is used to identify the row in another table. A foreign key in one table is the primary key of another. We can add a primary key to our example table from the previous section as follows:

UserID	Name	Email	ZIP	State
1	Jeffry Houser	jeff@instantcoldfusion.com	12345	Connecticut
2	Postmaster	postmaster@instantcoldfusion.com	67890	New York

We added a column, UserID, to this table. This would be the primary key. Let's say that you were working with an e-commerce site and had a table to hold the various shopping cart data. Some columns in the table are: ShoppingCartID, the primary key; TotalCost, the total cost of the order; and ShippingCost, the shipping and handling charge on the order. We need a way to sync up the shopping cart with the user who did the shopping. This is where a foreign key comes into play. We place the UserID from our original table into the ShoppingCart table, like so:

ShoppingCartID	TotalCost	ShippingCost	UserID
1	$15.37	$5.00	1
2	$19.95	$5.00	1
3	$49.99	$23.00	2

One-to-One Relationships

After we understand what a key is, we can start looking at relationships between data. The first type of relationship is a one-to-one relationship. Consider two pieces of data, X and Y. In a one-to-one relationship, there are two defining factors:

- Only one piece of data X exists for every piece of data Y.
- Only one piece of data Y exists for every piece of data X.

We can refer to the user table in the previous section for some examples.

Start by taking a look at yourself. What are pieces of data associated with you? You have a name, an address, and a social security number. These are one-to-one relationships. Any given person has only one name, and each name is associated with only one person. Any given social security number belongs to only one person and any given person only has one social security number. This is the nature of a one-to-one relationship.

Look at the bank statement for one of your accounts. You will find many one-to-one relationships that reside on it. What are some of the pieces of data associated with your account? There is an account number and a current balance, to give an example. For any given account number, there is only one balance. Any given balance is associated with only one account.

With all this talk of theoretical examples, you are probably wondering how you can turn this information into a database table. In most cases, one-to-one relationships are stored in the same table. To turn your bank account information into a table, you might use a table structure like this:

AccountID	AccountNumber	AccountBalance
1	123-45-6789	$13.99
2	456-12-3456	$15.00
3	85-58-1264	$1,256.00

There is a primary key column, AccountID, along with two data columns. Our Customer table might be formatted like this:

CustomerID	FirstName	LastName	SSN
1	Jeffry	Houser	123-45-6789
2	Mike	Thompson	456-12-3456
3	Nick	Solder	85-58-1264

The Customers table contains a primary key, CustomerID, along with the customer's name and social security number. In some cases, it may make sense to implement one-to-one relationships in a separate table.

 When modeling someone's name, make sure you separate the first and last name in case you ever have to do a mail merge on the data.

If you were developing a system under the assumption that a customer can never have more than one account, you would have a one-to-one relationship between tables. To implement this relationship, we take the primary key of one table and add it to the other as a foreign key. In a one-to-one relationship, it does not matter which key gets moved. Let's move the CustomerID:

AccountID	AccountNumber	AccountBalance	CustomerID
1	123-45-6789	$13.99	1
2	456-12-3456	$15.00	2
3	85-58-1264	$1,256.00	3

"Hey, Jeff! I hate to burst your bubble, but I have more than one bank account." I'm glad you brought that up. Thankfully, the theoretical database gods were aware of such a situation. Read on.

One-to-Many Relationships

The next type of relationship to examine is a one-to-many relationship. Examine two pieces of data, X and Y. A one-to-many relationship has these defining factors:

- Only one piece of data X exists for every piece of data Y.
- For any pieces of Y that exist, there may exist many pieces of data X.

Referring to the bank example, you noticed that an assumption was made that every customer only has one bank account. This may, or may not, be the case. Most customers will, in fact, have more than one account. That is a one-to-many relationship. Every account has one customer, but each customer may have more than one account.

In a one-to-many situation, you must take the primary key from the "one" side of the relationship and add it to the table, as a foreign key, to the "many" side of the relationship. In our case, we have a one-to-many relationship between the Customers table and the Accounts table. Customers is on the one side, so we take the CustomerID and add it to the Accounts side. With a thought to the future, the CustomerID was placed correctly in the Accounts table as a foreign key.

"You know, Jeff, I think you may have messed up again. Did I forget to tell you that I have a joint account with my [mother, father, son, girlfriend, wife, daughter]?" Other than wishing you had told me that before I started developing the system, we can remain thankful that the database gods have that covered too.

Many-to-Many Relationships

The final type of relationship to learn about is a many-to-many relationship. If you have two pieces of data, X and Y, you can discover whether they have a many-to-many relationship by following this guide:

- For every piece of data X, there are many pieces of data Y.
- For every piece of data Y, there are many pieces of data X.

Many-to-many relationships are perhaps the most common relationships to find between your data; however, they can be the most complicated to understand.

Following in the footsteps of our bank account example, we have decided that there is a many-to-many relationship between the Customers and Accounts tables. This will expand the system enough to allow for joint accounts. Another example of a many-to-many relationship might be the number of computers on a network. A network can contain many computers, and a computer can be hooked into multiple networks. Links on a web site would be another example. A web site can contain many links, but a link can be located on many web sites.

To implement a many-to-many relationship, we need to create a new table. This table is called an intersection, or linking, table, and usually contains the primary keys from the two tables that it is associating. In the bank account example, this would be the intersection table:

CustomerID	AccountsID
1	1
2	2
3	3

Neither the Customers table nor the Accounts table will receive a foreign key.

 The primary key for most intersection tables is the sum of all columns. This is the one case where it is common to use multiple tables as the unique identifier for a table.

Normalizing Your Data

Before you start your project and database design, you will most likely have the opportunity to collect your data. Chances are you are not going to get your data in perfect relational-database form. In some cases, you may be lucky to get it in a digital format, such as a Word document or Excel file.

When you are examining the data, you will decide how you want to store the data as tables. One purpose of a relational database is to prevent the replication of data. You do this by splitting data up into its simplest form and using primary and foreign keys to piece the data back together when you need it. The process of designing and optimizing a database table structure is called *normalizing*. When you normalize, you are trying to avoid insertion and deletion anomalies.

To explain these anomalies, suppose you are developing a product catalog for an e-commerce site and you have this data:

ProductID	ProductName	ProductPrice	Brand	ProductCategory
1	Banana Dance	$15.99	Monkey Music	CD
2	Insanely Ripe the Movie	$15.99	Garman	DVD
3	Forever Ending	$23.02	Electric	CD
4	Insanely Ripe the Movie	$3.99	Garman	VHS

Close examination of this table reveals that you cannot add a product category without also adding a product. This is an insertion anomaly. If we were to try to delete ProductID 2, Insanely Ripe the Movie, we would also permanently remove the ProductCategory, DVD. This is a deletion anomaly. Both insertion and deletion anomalies are not desirable.

To change the preceding table into a more suitable table structure, you will want to separate the ProductPrice, Brand, and ProductCategory fields into separate tables. Start with ProductCategory:

ProductCategoryID	ProductCategory
1	CD
2	DVD
3	VHS

Next, create the Brand table:

BrandID	Brand
1	Monkey Music
2	Garman
3	Electric

Create the ProductPrice table:

PriceID	Price
1	$15.99
2	$23.02
3	$3.99

Finally, update the Product table:

ProductID	ProductName	ProductPriceID	BrandID	ProductCategoryID
1	Banana Dance	1	1	1
2	Insanely Ripe the Movie	1	2	2
3	Forever Ending	2	3	2
4	Insanely Ripe the Movie	3	2	3

You can see the final table structure in the following screenshot:

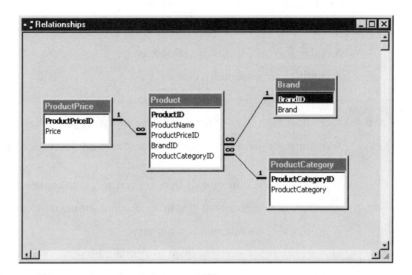

Learning Structure Query Language

Structure Query Language (SQL) is the language of databases. It is a standard language universally supported by most database software. While this language is very easy to learn, it can be tough to master. This section will demonstrate the basics.

Understanding Basic SQL Terminology

There are some basic definitions that are helpful to know when dealing with SQL. These definitions are listed in Table 9-1. Some of them we have already discussed.

There are some terms in this list that we have not yet discussed. A query is a group of SQL statements. It is a way to combine and filter your data before displaying it to the user. After executing a query, a recordset is created. A recordset is the result returned by executing a query.

Advanced database topics such as aggregate functions, triggers, and stored procedures are discussed in Chapter 21.

Using SQL Commands

You may need to perform any of four different actions on any piece of data: select it, insert it, update it, or delete it. SQL provides a command for each one of those actions.

Term	Definition
Database	A collection of tables
Table	A collection of columns in a database
Column	A single piece of data in a table
Row	A single set of all columns in a table
Primary key	A column, or group of columns, that uniquely identifies a row
Foreign key	A column, or group of columns, that uniquely identifies a row from another table
Query	A group of SQL commands that are written to execute together
Record	Another name for row, a single set of all columns in a table
Recordset	A group of rows returned by a query
Join	The act of retrieving data from multiple tables

Table 9-1.   *Database Terminology*

Selecting Data

The most common operation you will want to perform on data is to retrieve it. For this, SQL provides the SELECT command. This is the format for a select statement:

```
SELECT ColumnList
FROM Table
WHERE conditions
```

This select statement starts with the keyword SELECT. Following that is a comma-delimited list of columns that we want to select from the table. Best practices dictate that we should list every column we want to retrieve; however, a wildcard, the asterisk *, is available for those times when we want to select everything.

The next portion of our select statement is the FROM keyword. Following the FROM keyword, we list the name of the table that we are selecting data from. Then, we have an optional clause in our select statement. The WHERE keyword is followed by a list of conditions. These conditions define ways to filter our data. This will be explained with an example.

The product database table structure from the last section can be used to form some queries. This is a simple query that will return all of the products:

```
SELECT *
FROM Products
```

Notice in this query that we used the asterisk to return all columns from the table. We also do not use a WHERE clause to limit the data. All rows from the table will be returned, like this:

ProductID	ProductName	ProductPriceID	BrandID	ProductCategoryID
1	Banana Dance	1	1	1
2	Insanely Ripe the Movie	1	2	2
3	Forever Ending	2	3	2
4	Insanely Ripe the Movie	3	2	3

In the WHERE clause of a SQL statement, you can test for various conditions, as shown in Table 9-2. This example will get all products where the ProductID is less than or equal to 2:

```
SELECT *
FROM Products
WHERE Products.ProductID <= 2
```

Condition Tested	Operator
Equal	=
Greater than	>
Less than	<
Not equal to	<>
Greater than or equal to	>=
Less than or equal to	<=

Table 9-2. *SQL Operators*

The following is the recordset from this query:

ProductID	ProductName	ProductPriceID	BrandID	ProductCategoryID
1	Banana Dance	1	1	1
2	Insanely Ripe the Movie	1	2	2

You can use Boolean operators, such as AND and OR, to further refine your search criteria. If we were to execute this code:

```
SELECT *
FROM Products
WHERE Products.ProductID < 2 and Products.ProductID > 3
```

it will return these records:

ProductID	ProductName	ProductPriceID	BrandID	ProductCategoryID
1	Banana Dance	1	1	1
4	Insanely Ripe the Movie	3	2	3

At this point, you may be thinking that the data is returning a lot of keys, but not a lot of data. You are correct. We will remedy this situation in the next section as we discuss joins.

Understanding Inner and Outer Joins

A *join* is the act of selecting data from multiple tables and returning it in one query. The two types of joins are inner and outer joins. Inner joins between two tables return all rows that the two tables have in common. An outer join returns all rows from one table, and elements from the second table where the join condition is met. First, let's examine inner joins, since they are much more common.

There are two syntaxes you can use when creating an inner join. This is the first:

```
SELECT Products.*, ProductPrice.Price
FROM Products, ProductPrice
WHERE Products.ProductPriceID = ProductPrice.ProductPriceID
```

After the SELECT keyword, we have our list of columns. To distinguish which table we are selecting the column from, we add the name of the table it is coming from before the column name. Then comes the FROM keyword, followed by a comma-separated list of the tables that we are selecting from. In this case, we are selecting all information from the Products table, and the Price column from the ProductPrice table.

After the list of tables, we come to the WHERE clause of our statement. To perform the join, we are selecting rows where the ProductPriceID in the Products table is equal to the ProductPriceID in the ProductPrice table.

This is what happens when the join is performed. First, the union of the two tables is taken. That means that every record in the first table is matched with every record in the second table, giving us this table:

Product ProductID	Product ProductName	Product ProductPriceID	Product BrandID	Product ProductCategoryID	ProductPrice PriceID	ProductPrice Price
1	Banana Dance	1	1	1	1	$15.99
2	Insanely Ripe the Movie	1	2	2	1	$15.99
3	Forever Ending	2	3	2	1	$15.99
4	Insanely Ripe the Movie	3	2	3	1	$15.99
1	Banana Dance	1	1	1	2	$23.02
2	Insanely Ripe the Movie	1	2	2	2	$23.02
3	Forever Ending	2	3	2	2	$23.02
4	Insanely Ripe the Movie	3	2	3	2	$23.02
1	Banana Dance	1	1	1	3	$3.99
2	Insanely Ripe the Movie	1	2	2	3	$3.99
3	Forever Ending	2	3	2	3	$3.99
4	Insanely Ripe the Movie	3	2	3	3	$3.99

Then, the condition is applied to the resulting table, where the PriceID in the Product table is equal to the PriceID in the ProductPrice table:

Product ProductID	Product ProductName	Product ProductPriceID	Product BrandID	Product ProductCategoryID	ProductPrice PriceID	ProductPrice Price
1	Banana Dance	1	1	1	1	$15.99

Product ProductID	Product ProductName	Product ProductPriceID	Product BrandID	Product ProductCategoryID	ProductPrice PriceID	ProductPrice Price
2	Insanely Ripe the Movie	1	2	2	1	$15.99
3	Forever Ending	2	3	2	2	$23.02
4	Insanely Ripe the Movie	3	2	3	3	$3.99

The final result eliminates the columns that were not requested:

Product ProductID	Product ProductName	Product ProductPriceID	Product BrandID	Product ProductCategoryID	ProductPrice Price
1	Banana Dance	1	1	1	$15.99
2	Insanely Ripe the Movie	1	2	2	$15.99
3	Forever Ending	2	3	2	$23.02
4	Insanely Ripe the Movie	3	2	3	$3.99

That is how a join works.

I mentioned that there were two syntaxes for an inner join. This is the second:

```
SELECT Products.*, ProductPrice.Price
FROM Products JOIN ProductPrice
    ON Products.ProductPriceID = ProductPrice.ProductPriceID
```

The results will be the same no matter which syntax you use. This syntax starts with the name of the first table, and then uses the keyword JOIN. After that you have the name of the second table, followed by the keyword ON. After the keyword, the condition in which the tables are being joined is stated.

An outer join is set up in a similar syntax to what we previously looked at. An outer join takes all the rows from one table and the rows that meet the defined criteria from the second. This is the syntax:

```
SELECT Products.*, ProductPrice.Price
FROM Products RIGHT OUTER JOIN ProductPrice
    ON Products.ProductPriceID = ProductPrice.ProductPriceID
```

You'll notice that the syntax is very similar to the previous syntax. We added two keywords before JOIN: RIGHT and OUTER. The OUTER keyword specifies that we are performing an outer join. The RIGHT keyword specifies that the table on the right will be the table that all elements are returned from. We can also specify the keyword LEFT. In our case, every element in the Price table is located in the Product table, so the resulting recordset will be similar whether or not we do an outer join.

Creating Data

To create data in your database table, SQL gives us the insert query. This is the format of an insert statement:

```
INSERT INTO tablename(ColumnList)
VALUES (ValueList)
```

The statement starts with the keywords INSERT and INTO. Following that we state the name of the table that we want to insert data into. Parentheses surround the list of columns that we are adding into the table. Commas separate columns. Next we have the VALUES keyword and the list of values that we are adding into the table. The values will match the columns in the order that they are listed.

 Select statements are the only statements in which joins apply. Insert, update, and delete queries will only relate to a single table.

We can insert a new entry into the Product table:

```
INSERT INTO Product(ProductName, ProductPriceID, BrandID, ProductCategoryID)
VALUES ('Insanely Ripe -- the Soundtrack', 3, 2, 1)
```

This statement will update our Product table like so:

ProductID	ProductName	ProductPriceID	BrandID	ProductCategoryID
1	Banana Dance	1	1	1
2	Insanely Ripe the Movie	1	2	2
3	Forever Ending	2	3	2
4	Insanely Ripe the Movie	3	2	3
5	Insanely Ripe— the Soundtrack	3	2	1

Note   *You might notice in our insert statement that string values are surrounded by single quotes and numerical values are left open. This is standard in all SQL statements.*

Updating Data

Unfortunately, data rarely stays the same, because it needs to be changed and updated over time. You can do this by using the SQL UPDATE command. Here is the format:

```
UPDATE TableName
SET Column1 = Value1,
 Column2 = Value2,
...
 ColumnN = ValueN
WHERE Conditions
```

The query starts with the UPDATE keyword, followed by the table name. Then, it has the SET keyword and a list of name-value pairs. The name-value pairs consist of the column that you want to update, followed by an equal sign and the value that you want to update it to. You separate each pair with a comma. The update statement is finished off with a WHERE clause. Without the WHERE clause, every item would be updated.

When learning about the insert statement, a new product was created in the Product table. This will update the row:

```
UPDATE Product
SET ProductName = 'Insanely Ripe the Soundtrack'
WHERE ProductID = 5
```

The newly updated Product table is shown here, with only entry five modified:

ProductID	ProductName	ProductPriceID	BrandID	ProductCategoryID
1	Banana Dance	1	1	1
2	Insanely Ripe the Movie	1	2	2
3	Forever Ending	2	3	2
4	Insanely Ripe the Movie	3	2	3
5	Insanely Ripe the Soundtrack	3	2	1

Deleting Data

That last action we will ever want to perform on a piece of data is to remove it from existence. We do this with a SQL DELETE command. This is the format:

```
DELETE FROM tablename
WHERE Conditions
```

Our delete query starts with the DELETE and FROM keywords. It is followed by the name of the table that we want to delete elements from. As with select and update statements, the WHERE clause comes next. It is used to limit the data that you are deleting; without it, you would delete all data in the table.

 Instead of deleting data immediately, you may want to keep a Boolean flag in your table. Have all your queries filter out results where this flag is true. When someone wants you to restore data that they deleted, you only have to change the flag back to false.

We can create a delete query to remove the same record that we created and updated in the previous section:

```
DELETE FROM Product
WHERE ProductID = 5
```

Notice in the following updated Product table that the ProductID of 5 is missing:

ProductID	ProductName	ProductPriceID	BrandID	ProductCategoryID
1	Banana Dance	1	1	1
2	Insanely Ripe the Movie	1	2	2
3	Forever Ending	2	3	2
4	Insanely Ripe the Movie	3	2	3

Applying Queries in ColdFusion

Databases provide the meat of all dynamic web sites. With a strong understanding of SQL and query concepts behind you, you are now set to learn how to mix SQL with ColdFusion. There are three different tags that allow us to easily access a database: cfquery, cfinsert, and cfupdate.

CODING IN COLDFUSION

Using the cfquery Tag

The cfquery tag is the most powerful of the three database tags, so we will examine it first. The most important, and commonly used, SQL tag in ColdFusion is the cfquery tag. It allows you to pass any query onto your database. First, we will examine how to use the cfquery tag.

Putting the cfquery Tag to Work for You

The cfquery tag has an open tag and a close tag, with your query statements located between. These are the attributes to cfquery:

- **name**   The name of the variable that the query results will be stored in. A query object is stored internally as an array of structures, with each row being an element of the array and each column being an element of the structure. The name attribute is required if you want to access values returned by your query.

- **datasource**   The name of the datasource that the query is being passed to. This is optional if you are performing a query of a query, as described in Chapter 21.

- **dbname**   Overrides the default database specified in the datasource. This is an optional attribute for Sybase System 11 drivers only.

- **username**   Optional attribute that will override the username information listed in the datasource.

- **password**   Optional attribute that will override the password information listed in the datasource.

- **maxrows**   Optional attribute that specifies the maximum number of rows to return. The default is to return all rows.

- **blockfactor**   Optional attribute that specifies how many rows at a time are returned from the database. The range of numbers is between 1 and 100, with the default being 1.

- **timeout**   Optional attribute that specifies the largest amount of time that ColdFusion will wait for the query to execute before returning an error.

- **cachedafter**   Optional attribute that accepts a date object. If the specified date is after the current date, ColdFusion will use a cached query; otherwise, the query will run new.

- **cachedwithin**   Optional attribute that accepts a time span created with the CreateTimeSpan function. If the original query date is within the time span specified, the cached query is used; otherwise, the query is executed again.

Note   *The time span returns numerical values. For example, one day is equal to the number 1, and 12 hours is equal to .5. You can give less processing to the ColdFusion server by using constant values instead of the function.*

- **provider**   Optional attribute that contains the COM provider for OLE datasources only.
- **providerdsn**   Optional attribute that contains the data source name for the COM provider.
- **debug**   Optional attribute that specifies whether the number of records returned by the query and the SQL code that was passed to the datasource is displayed. If debugging is turned off in the administrator, this has no effect; if debugging is turned on, then setting this to No will suppress the debug output.

After executing a query, some special variables are created:

- **cfquery.ExecutionTime**   Holds the execution time of the query. It is not part of the query object and will change for each query executed.
- **query_name.CurrentRow**   When processing the query results, contains the current row that you are examining.
- **query_name.ColumnList**   Contains a list of all columns in the query.
- **query_name.RecordCount**   Contains the number of records returned by the query.

We can easily take some of the SQL examples and turn them into full-blown ColdFusion queries.

Caution   *ColdFusion does not verify your SQL statements within a cfquery tag. It just passes them on to the database.*

You can download the database for this chapter from InstantColdFusion.com. Create a datasource, point it to our product database, and call it Chapter9. Chapter 3 taught you how to create a datasource from the ColdFusion Administrator. This is our cfquery tag:

```
<cfquery name="Chapter9Query" datasource="Chapter9">
 SELECT Products.*, ProductPrice.Price
 FROM Products, ProductPrice
 WHERE Products.ProductPriceID = ProductPrice.ProductPriceID
</cfquery>
```

This will create a query object called Chapter8Query. Now that you have it, what are you going to do with it? Read on!

Tip   *ColdFusion provides two tags, cfupdate and cfinsert, that make it easy to create or update records from within ColdFusion.*

Displaying Query Results

The most common type of processing that you want to do with query results is to output them. ColdFusion provides two different tags that will accomplish this: cfoutput and cfloop. Here we will examine the cfoutput tag. The cfloop tag is discussed in more detail in Chapter 13.

You have already used the cfoutput tag in its simplest form. Here we are using it to execute specific code for each row in a query. It has these attributes:

- **query** The name of the query object that you want to display
- **startrow** The first row in the query
- **maxrows** The maximum number of rows you want to loop over in the query
- **group** The column that you want to group on (grouping is discussed in more detail in Chapter 21)
- **groupcasesensitive** Tells whether or not the grouping action should be case sensitive

None of the attributes are required, as shown in previous chapters. You can use cfoutput without any attributes to output variables.

Here is some code to loop over a query:

```
<cfoutput query="Chapter9Query">
  #Chapter9Query.ProductName# #Chapter9Query.Price#<br>
</cfoutput>
```

The code between the open and close cfoutput tags will execute once for each row in the recordset. This is our output:

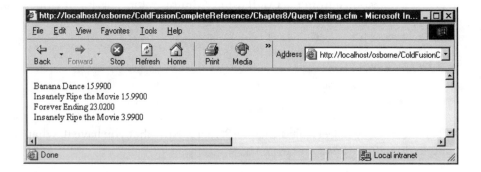

Inserting and Updating Without SQL

ColdFusion provides two tags that allow you to easily insert and update data in a database: cfinsert and cfupdate. Both of these tags are designed to work with forms, as described in Chapter 12. We will go over each one briefly here.

The cfinsert tag is used to create a new record in a given table. The cfupdate tag is used to update an existing record. You can use either on a form's processing page, and ColdFusion will create the SQL query automatically, using values from the form fields.

Both cfupdate and cfinsert have the same attributes. Here is a list:

- **datasource**   The name of the datasource that you want to create the new record in. It is required.

- **username**   Contains the username required to access the database. It is optional, if there is no username or password needed.

- **password**   Contains the password required to access the database. It is optional, if you don't need a username or password combination to access the database.

- **tablename**   Accepts the name of the table that you are inserting a new record into. It is required.

- **tableowner**   Use to specify the owner of a table, if it is needed to create the record.

- **tablequalifer**   Used to specify a table qualifier. The use of a table qualifier will vary from database to database.

- **formfields**   Accepts a comma-delimited list of field names from the form that was submitted. Use this if you have fields on your form that you do not want submitted to the database. I find that I have best results with both cfupdate and cfinsert by using the formfields attribute.

The main difference between the cfinsert and cfupdate tags is that cfinsert creates a new record and cfupdate updates an existing one. When using cfupdate, you must have a valid primary key identified, or else the tag will not know which record to update.

Tip   *For both cfinsert and cfupdate, your form fields must be named identically to the database field names.*

Summary

In this chapter, you learned the following:

- Important database concepts
- How to relate your data with primary and foreign keys
- How to maintain data through the use of SQL

■ How to call SQL statements from within ColdFusion

The next chapter will examine some coding methodologies, and list some best practices.

The
Complete
Reference

Chapter 10

Picking a Development Methodology

This chapter will teach you about development methodologies. Without a methodology or approach to a problem, you will probably not develop code that is easy to read, understand, or maintain, even by its author (you). We'll talk a little about the software development cycle and then go on to introduce some standard elements of any methodology. We will finish off our discussion by referencing Fusebox and cfObjects, some of the most popular ColdFusion development methodologies.

Understanding the Software Development Cycle

People have been developing software for many years, even before the Web and ColdFusion came into play. Certain ways to approach software development have been invented. This section will talk about some common elements of many of the methods, and then give you a brief overview of some of those methods.

Understanding Phases of the Software Development Lifecycle

There are some common elements in many of the software development models. Here is a list of some common phases in the life of a software program:

- **Requirements** The requirements phase is usually the first stage of software development. This is when the client, or software program user, has an idea for a program. They talk to you and try to explain it to you. I like to think of the requirements phase as the phase during which the client says, "This is what I want." In the ideal world, the client would offer you documentation explaining what is wanted. However, most of the time, the requirements phase may just be a conversation between you and the client. I strongly suggest that you create a requirements document during this phase.

- **Specification** The specification phase is where you take your information from the client and decide the best way to implement it. If the requirements phase is one where the client says, "This is what I want," then the specification phase is the one where you say, "This is what I'm going to give you." In the ideal world, the stars will align and you will be giving the client what he or she wants. It doesn't always happen that way. You will probably want to create a specification document in this phase.

 Sometimes the requirements and specification phases are combined. I don't recommend this. How can you give a client something before the client tells you what they want?

- **Design** With an approved specification document in your hands, you can start to design the software. This is where you would make flowcharts to illustrate the flow of the program, mock up an interface, create database diagrams, and flush out the columns in all database tables. This step is where you do all the preparation for the implementation. A requirements document tells you what the client wants, and the specification document tells you what you are going to give the client. A design document tells you how you are going to make the specifications work.

Note *The line between requirements, specifications, and design can sometimes be blurred. Building an application in ColdFusion MX may be introduced in any phase.*

- **Implementation** The implementation phase is where you take the software design and code the program. Often, the design and implementation phases are combined as one phase. In the implementation phase, you are just making the design work.

- **Debugging and testing** This is where you test the application as a whole, from start to finish, looking for obvious and less than obvious bugs. Some debugging will most likely be done during the implementation phase. I often like to have the customer involved in this phase, so they can see the progress and help discover bugs. Be careful of "creeping featuritis" though. That is when the customer tries to get you to add new features or change existing features at this, or later, phases.

- **Integration and rollout** After you finish debugging and testing the system, it is now time to make it available. In the web world, this is usually pretty easy. You can roll it out just telling your users where to go to access the new features, or just adding a link from the existing web application to the new features that you just developed. During this phase, you will also want to train the users, or at least provide documentation, on how to use the new product or features.

- **Maintenance** After the application is finished, you get paid and you'll be happy. The client will have this brand-new application that is going to make their business more efficient, and therefore profitable, in some manner. They are happy. This won't last for long. Not that the client will be unhappy with your work, mind you, it is just that their needs will change and the application will have to be changed to suit the needs. The bulk of a software program's life will be in the maintenance phase.

- **Retirement** I like to refer to this phase as the "All Good Things Must Come to an End" phase. The retirement phase happens because the software, or application, that you developed just no longer meets the need of the users. Retirement is not a bad thing; change is hard to avoid. It is time for this application to be backed up, archived, and stuck in a damp box in a dark basement never to be seen again.

Comparing Different Models of Software Development

Now that we have examined some of the phases of software development, we can examine some ways that these are pieced together to form a fully functional approach method for developing software.

Build and Fix Model

The build and fix model operates like this:

1. The client asks you to build something.

2. You build it.

3. The client looks at it and tells you if it is right or wrong.

4. You modify it.

5. Repeat Steps 3 and 4 until the cows come home.

Under the build and fix model, software programs or web sites are created without any thought, planning, rhyme, or reason. Unfortunately, especially in the web development world, this is often the model that is followed. There are better ways.

Waterfall Model

The waterfall model of software development is my favorite. You can see how the outline works in Figure 10-1.

This is called the waterfall model because you start at the top, and go to the bottom, like water trickling or cascading down a waterfall. There are also built-in checks and balances during each phase of the project.

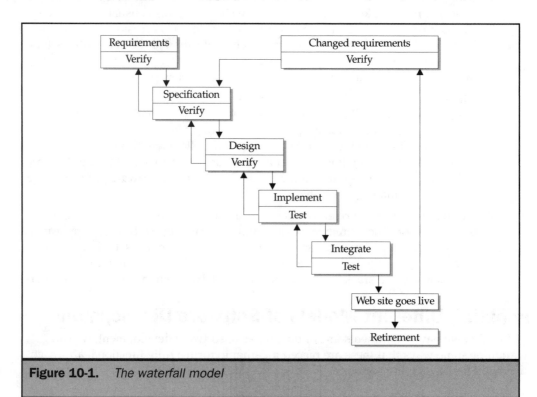

Figure 10-1.   *The waterfall model*

During the requirements, specification, and design phases, you must verify that you are still on track with what took place in the previous phases. During the implementation and integration phases, you must test the functionality against the plans that were created in the previous phases. If there are problems with the tests in any phase, you can go back to the previous phase to adjust. In the worst-case scenario, you have to go all the way back to the requirements phase.

When maintenance occurs, the operations phase ("Web site goes live") can go back to the beginning and run through the cycle again with the changed requirements. This structure gives a good base for developing software.

Rapid Prototype Model

The next model that we want to examine is the rapid prototype model. This model is very similar to the waterfall model, except prototyping is added in. A prototype is a quick mockup of the functionality. You can see an outline of the rapid prototype model in Figure 10-2.

A prototype is usually a quick click-through of the site that demonstrates limited functionality of the final product. The users can play around with the product before it is made live. In the rapid prototype model, verifying and testing each phase is generally quicker and less prone to errors than the waterfall method because you have

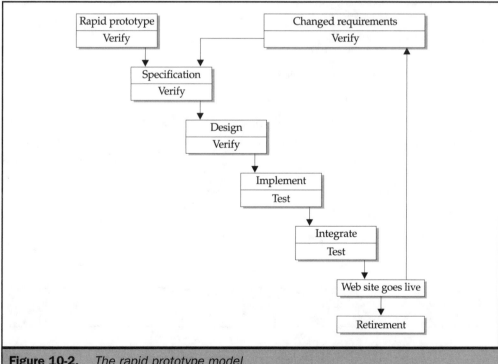

Figure 10-2.   *The rapid prototype model*

a working mockup before you start the other phases. Since it is so easy to develop in CFML, ColdFusion is an ideal rapid prototype tool.

Incremental Model

The incremental model of software development is one in which the application is built step by step, or block by block, as if you were putting a building together. This is very similar to the waterfall model, except in the scope of the work done. Instead of designing, implementing, and integrating the whole product at once, you do it in small increments. You don't start the next increment until the first one is rolled out. You can see the incremental method illustrated in Figure 10-3.

The main difference between this method and the waterfall or rapid prototyping method is that you are not delivering the client a piece of software that satisfies all requirements or specifications. You are just giving them a piece and then later continuing to give them more. The incremental method is great in situations where you want to space out development due to a limited budget.

Extreme programming (XP) is a version of the incremental model that creates only one feature at a time, includes built-in tests, and promotes team development. "XP" has nothing to do with the Windows operating system of the same name.

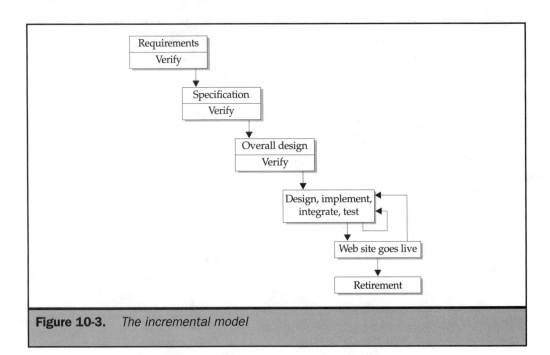

Figure 10-3. *The incremental model*

Choosing the Elements of Your Coding Methodology

The previous section examined ways to approach developing your software. The remainder of this chapter will discuss best practices for writing code. There is no one coding method that will work well in every case, but this section will give you some basics that are important and that you can apply to suit your own needs.

Writing Detailed Documentation

Perhaps one of the most important portions of your code writing will be documentation. This may be the writing of specification, requirement, or design documents, as discussed in the last section, or it may be the documentation of your code, as we discuss here.

Understanding Different Types of Documentation

After all is said and done, documentation can be grouped into two different types: HTML documentation and CFML documentation. HTML documentation is streamed to the web browser, but is ignored when displaying an HTML page. CFML documentation is ignored completely by the ColdFusion Application Server; therefore, it does not get streamed back to the web browser.

To create HTML documentation, you use a tag like this:

```
<!-- Your HTML documentation here -->
```

Like most tags, it starts with a bracket (<). Unlike most other tags, the next character is an exclamation point. After the exclamation point come two dashes. After that, you can place your comments. The browser will ignore everything up until the end comment qualifier, which is two dashes and a bracket, -->.

ColdFusion comments are very similar to HTML comments. The main change in syntax is that there are three dashes instead of two:

```
<!--- Your ColdFusion Documentation Here --->
```

I strongly recommend using ColdFusion comments to document the ColdFusion portion of your code. You would not want any person using a browser to view the code and discover the business logic that is behind the scenes making the site work.

Writing a Documentation Header

I like to include a documentation header at the top of every template I create. I include information relating to the template's purpose and the code dependencies in the documentation header. This is the list of items:

- **Description**   This category contains a description of the template. What does it do? Why does it exist? These are questions I would answer in the description.

■ **Entering/Exiting**   I use these categories to describe the flow of the template. When you enter this template, where are you coming from? When you leave, where are you likely to go in the normal processing of the template? I find that including this information is most useful when dealing with forms, although that is not its only application. We discuss forms in Chapter 12.

■ **Dependencies**   I use this category to list any files that are expected to be preexisting when this template is executed. This could be custom tags, CFX tags, ColdFusion components, or special includes that are used to make this chapter work.

■ **Expecting**   This category describes the variables that you expect to be defined when entering this template. I use this, mainly, to list URL or form variables that are required to make the current template work.

■ **Modification History**   This category is an important part of the documentation, and is especially useful in situations where you have multiple developers. I add the current date, my name, the company I work for, and a description of the modification that I made. I will usually place my contact information in there, too. The first entry in the Modification column is almost always "Created."

Here is an example of a standard documentation header:

```
<!---
Description:

Entering: N/A
Exiting: N/A

Dependencies: N/A
Expecting: N/A

Modification History
Date       Modifier            Modification
********************************************************
03/17/2002 Jeff Houser, DotComIt   Created
           jeff@instantcoldfusion.com

--->
```

You can enter the relevant information as needed in your templates. You can see further examples of this technique in many other places throughout this book.

Tip   *I create my documentation header as a snippet for ColdFusion Studio and Dreamweaver MX. I can drop it into any given template and fill in the appropriate information.*

Inline Documentation

In addition to a documentation header, I like to use comments sprinkled throughout my ColdFusion code, describing the actions that I am taking as I take them. These snippets of documentation are called inline documentation. Let's look at a simple example (which you might recognize from Chapter 9):

```
<!--- Run query to get all products and their prices --->
<cfquery name="Chapter9Query" datasource="Chapter9">
 SELECT Products.*, ProductPrice.Price
 FROM Products, ProductPrice
 WHERE Products.ProductPriceID = ProductPrice.ProductPriceID
</cfquery>

<!--- Output all products and their prices --->
<cfoutput query="Chapter9Query">
 #Chapter9Query.ProductName# #Chapter9Query.Price#<br>
</cfoutput>
```

We wrote all of this code in Chapter 9. This segment puts the code together and documents it as we go. The first block of code, the cfquery tag, gets data from the database. We get all the products and their prices. The next block of code outputs all the products and prices. That is an example of inline documentation.

Creating Code

While documenting your code is great, and I strongly suggest doing it, you will probably spend more time writing your code than documenting it. This section examines some best practices for writing your code.

Code Formatting

When you are writing your code, you will want to format it in some way. The best-formatted code is in a format that makes it easy to read not only for you, but for other readers also.

Whenever I have code with a start and end tag, I like to indent everything between those two tags. We saw an example in the last section:

```
<cfquery name="Chapter9Query" datasource="Chapter9">
 SELECT Products.*, ProductPrice.Price
 FROM Products, ProductPrice
 WHERE Products.ProductPriceID = ProductPrice.ProductPriceID
</cfquery>
```

All code between the start and end cfquery tags is indented by one space.

For *nested tags,* where one tag is inside another tag, I just indent further. If we want to perform a cfquery inside a cfoutput tag, we can set it up like this:

```
<cfoutput>
 <cfquery name="Chapter9Query" datasource="Chapter9">
  SELECT Products.*, ProductPrice.Price
  FROM Products, ProductPrice
  WHERE Products.ProductPriceID = ProductPrice.ProductPriceID
 </cfquery>
</cfoutput>
```

You can see how the code indents as we go further in the nested chain.

Another thing to be aware of is how you format information in your templates. I like to start my templates with a documentation header, as described earlier in this chapter. Beyond that, it is a good idea to keep business logic, or functional code, in the top half of the template. The bottom half is reserved for display code, to format the data from the page you are creating.

To give code a consistent feel, I like to keep my formatting consistent. In this book, you will always find code segments with HTML or CFML tags in lowercase. Attribute names and variable scopes will be in lowercase. Variable names will be in a mix of upper- and lowercase. Although ColdFusion is not case-sensitive, this formatting makes the code easy to read and consistent. ColdFusion functions will be a mix of upper- and lowercase. SQL statements will be in uppercase. Reserved words and operators, such as IS or GREATER THAN, will be put into all uppercase.

Variable Naming Conventions

We discussed valid variable naming conventions in Chapter 8, but we didn't discuss how we might apply those naming conventions. This section will teach you how you might apply those naming conventions.

First off, I always recommend trying to choose variable names that make sense. For instance, take a look at this code:

```
<!--- create a loop variable --->
<cfset x = 10>

<!--- Display Output, from 1 to 10--->
<cfloop index="y" from="1" to="#x#">
 <cfoutput>
  #y#<br>
 </cfoutput>
</cfloop>
```

This code makes use of an index loop, outputting the numbers 1 to 10. Is the code readable? Yes. Is it self-documenting? No. We use variable names such as x and y. It is not easy to guess what x and y accomplish.

Note   *We discuss looping in more detail in Chapter 13.*

We can update the preceding code like this:

```
<!--- create a loop variable --->
<cfset LoopMax = 10>

<!--- Display Output, from 1 to 10--->
<cfloop index="LoopIndex" from="1" to="#LoopMax#">
 <cfoutput>
  #LoopIndex#<br>
 </cfoutput>
</cfloop>
```

Is this code more easily readable? Yes, instead of x we use a variable called LoopMax, which stands for the maximum that the loop will execute. Instead of y, we use a variable called LoopIndex, which is the current iteration, or index, of the loop. Will we know what these variable names mean when we come back to them in a year? It is easy to distinguish that both of these variables have something to do with a loop. The remainder of each variable's name finishes off the story nicely.

Tip   *When using variables, it is always best to scope your variables. We discussed variable usage in Chapter 8.*

There is one more thing I want to point out to you here, and that is Hungarian notation. Hungarian notation does not have anything to do with the restaurant right around the corner from where I grew up that my mom used to buy goulash from. It is a way to tell the type of variable based on the variable's name. Hungarian notation was created by one of the first Windows programmers, Charles Simonyi. The only person that can put Hungarian notation to work for your site is you.

Hungarian notation takes certain qualifiers and either appends or prepends those qualifiers to the variable name. You can see a list of potential qualifiers in Table 10-1. There is nothing about ColdFusion that enforces this type of convention; it is just one way to approach naming things, and programmers that use it may even use a different flavor of their own creation. Some variable types, such as queries, are fairly unique to ColdFusion, so I provided some suggestions in Table 10-1.

Qualifier	Type	Example
Str s	String	sMyString StrMyString
n	Integer or Numeric	nMyNumber
b	Boolean	bMyBoolean
d	Date	dDate
a	Array	aMyArray
sc	Structure	scMyStructure
q	Query	qMyQuery
i	Integer	iMyInteger
x	XML	xMyXML
w	WDDX	wMyWDDX
o	Object	oMyObject

Table 10-1. *Hungarian Notation in ColdFusion*

Note *If you want to know more about Hungarian notation, you can do a search on Google or your favorite search engine. I only listed the types here that will most commonly apply to ColdFusion.*

Directory Naming Conventions

Here is a list of some standard directory structures that I like to use when creating sites:

- **Root** The root directory is where I usually store the home page and the Application.cfm of the site. You can find information about this in Chapter 8.

- **Images** The images directory is where I store images for the site.

- **Administration** The administration directory contains all the templates that perform special admin functions to maintain users, process orders, update data, or do whatever administrative things need to be done. I like to name this directory a nonsensical name that hackers will not easily be able to guess, such as JellyBean or FruitLoop. If you have sensitive data that needs protection, you should always have this directory password-protected in some way.

- **Includes**   This directory contains all modular code, such as includes, custom tags, or ColdFusion components. Code modularization is discussed in more detail in Chapter 16.

- **Section Name**   I like to give each section of the site its own directory. This allows me to easily group specific files for specific sections all together in one nice package. When I have to edit something, it makes it easy to find where it goes.

Types of Files

With an understanding of the directories in a web site, we can now discuss the types of templates that reside in a web site. When creating ColdFusion applications, I try to keep the purpose of templates very specific, each performing only one main function. It avoids the creation of additional processing where you have to figure out which mode the template is in, and which block of code will be processed accordingly.

Here is a list of file types I commonly use in a web site:

- **Index**   The index file is the home page of the site. Some web servers are trained to look for default.cfm instead of index.cfm, but many are set up to look for both.

- **Includes or custom tags**   Both includes and custom tags are modularized bits of code that are called upon from other templates. We mentioned these in the last section and will discuss them in more depth in Chapter 16.

Tip   *I like to specify the name of templates that contain custom tags by adding a ct to the beginning of the filename.*

- **Input**   When dealing with forms (see Chapter 12), there are two types of form pages: the input page and the processing page. The input page is where you enter data, and the processing page is where you process it, usually creating database records. I use input pages when creating new data. I name these files with the convention of typeofdatai.cfm. For creating a form to create a new topic, I would name the form Topici.cfm.

- **Update**   Update forms are similar to input forms, except that they are used for updating a form's data. I name them with the letter *u*. So, to update a topic, I would name the file Topicu.cfm.

- **Verification**   Verification forms are a specialized version of a processing page for the form. They present users with the information that was just submitted and allow them to verify before creating the final processing page. I name verification forms with the letter *v* at the end. To create a topic verify form, I would name the page Topicv.cfm.

- **Processing**   The processing page is usually the last page that is processed in the form. It takes the data that was entered or modified and places it in the database or performs other processing on it. I name processing pages with a *p*. So, the processing page for the topic form would be Topicp.cfm.

- **Delete**   The delete page is one that is used when we are deleting data from the database. I name these files with a *d* at the end. So, to delete a topic, the filename would be Topicd.cfm.

Those are some of the conventions that I use when creating web sites. Next, we look at some of the conventions that are commonly used throughout the ColdFusion community.

Learning Other Development Methodologies

No single development methodology will suit the needs of every application every time, so it is good to remain flexible when choosing a development methodology. There are some common methodologies that have taken hold in the real world. This section examines some of them.

Creating a Site in Fusebox

One of the most popular methodologies in the development community is Fusebox. Seventy percent of all custom software projects fail, and Fusebox was created to address this issue. As with any methodology, Fusebox provides a standard way of approaching development. It is currently in its third rendition, although the most commonly used is the second. This section examines the basics of Fusebox 2.

Understanding Fusebox

It is hard to follow the structure of a web application. One web page can link to any other, by its very nature. Trying to map out the functional flow of a web site can be frustrating and confusing. Fusebox uses two concepts to avoid this: the fuse and the fusebox.

A *fuse* is a ColdFusion template that contains a block of code that performs a single action. Fuses can perform a query, contain navigational or display elements, or perform any type of ColdFusion action. By creating fuses in this way, they are easy to write, debug, and reuse.

How, you might ask, do we put fuses together to form an application? The answer is within the fusebox. A *fusebox* is a single template that contains all the potential actions of the application. Based on the action that is passed into it, called a *fuseaction*, the template decides what action to perform. Every link or form in the site points back to the fusebox, with a different fuseaction. The fusebox reminds me of a main routine from traditional programming. It is the main routine that directs the action and calls all other routines. Figure 10-4 shows a graphical representation of how the Fusebox model works.

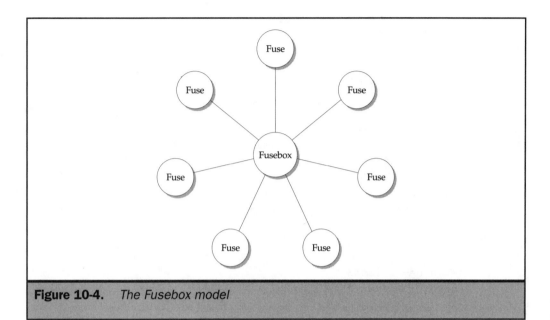

Figure 10-4. *The Fusebox model*

This is a very simple example to illustrate the concept of Fusebox:

```
<!--- www.instantcoldfusion.com

Description: A sample Fusebox Index Page

Entering: N/A
Exiting: N/A

Dependencies: N/A
Expecting: N/A

Modification History
Date       Modifier              Modification
*********************************************************
03/21/2002 Jeff Houser, DotComIt   Created
--->


<!--- Call this custom tag to move form and URL variables into
      the attributes scope --->
```

CODING IN COLDFUSION

```
<cf_formurl2attributes>

<!--- Set a default fuseaction --->
<cfparam name="attributes.fuseaction" default="Home">


<!--- Process the Fuse Action --->
<cfswitch expression = "#attributes.fuseaction#">

 <!--- the Home Fuse --->
 <cfcase value="Home">
  <cfinclude template="dsp_home.cfm">

 </cfcase>

 <cfcase value="Sales">
  <cfinclude template="dsp_sale.cfm">
 </cfcase>

 <!--- the default fuse --->
 <cfdefaultcase>
  Sorry, that was an invalid Action
 </cfdefaultcase>

</cfswitch>
```

The preceding page is a sample Fusebox page. It starts with a standard documentation header. Following that is a custom tag. Custom tags will be discussed in more depth in Chapter 16. This custom tag is called formurl2attributes. It copies all form and URL variables into the attributes scope.

 You can get the formurl2attributes tag from www.fusebox.org.

Following the custom tag, we use the cfparam tag to set a default fuse. Our default fuse value is Home. Following that we enter the body of our template. We are using conditional logic to include the proper template based on the value of the fuse. Conditional logic is discussed in Chapter 13, and includes are discussed in Chapter 16.

Our conditional logic comes in the form of a cfswitch tag. Given a variable, ColdFusion will look at each case until it finds one that is equal to the value of the variable. It will process the commands in that case, a cfinclude, and end the switch statement. In our default case, it includes the dsp_home.cfm page:

```
<!--- www.instantcoldfusion.com

Description: A Home Page

Entering: N/A
Exiting: N/A

Dependencies: N/A
Expecting: N/A

Modification History
Date         Modifier                Modification
*********************************************************
03/21/2002 Jeff Houser, DotComIt    Created
--->

<!DOCTYPE HTML PUBLIC "-//W3C//DTD HTML 4.01 Transitional//EN">

<html>
<head>
 <title>Home</title>
</head>
<body>

This is the Home Page.  Check out our
<A href="index.cfm?fuseaction=sales">Sales page</A>.

</body>
</html>
```

This is a simple HTML page that just displays some text, and a link to another fuse. The link is called an exit point. It is where we leave one fuse to go to another. This sample application only consists of two fuses. Most applications are more advanced than this.

One of the benefits of the Fusebox methodology is that you can take many separate applications that have been built with Fusebox and combine them together by creating a master fusebox that redirects users to the application of their choice. You can see an example of that in Figure 10-5.

Learning Different Fuse Types

There are four main types of fuses that are used in Fusebox:

- **Display**   Display fuses contain code and text formatting. They will most commonly be used for standard header, footer, and navigation elements. Display fuse files usually have the prefix dsp.

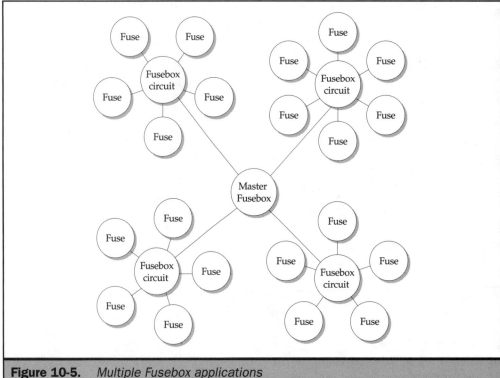

Figure 10-5. *Multiple Fusebox applications*

- **Action**   Action fuses are used to perform specific functions that make your application work. Fuse action files start with the prefix act.

- **Query**   Query files contain queries. Query files have the prefix qry.

- **Application**   Application files are used to set up your environment, using things such as the cfapplication tag. They use the prefix app.

Documenting with Fusedocs

In the previous examples, I used my own flavor of a documentation header, but one part of the Fusebox methodology provides its own brand of documentation, called *Fusedocs*. Fusedocs should be written prior to coding. They will help you define your application's logic.

There are three main sections to a Fusedoc:

- **Properties**   The properties section changes based on the functionality of the file. Common properties are the name of the file, its creator, and the date that it was created. Often, the history of the fuse will be located here.

- **Responsibilities**   The responsibilities section is intended to describe what the particular template does. This is written from the point of view of the fuse. The responsibilities section for the formurl2attributes tag might be: I will convert form and URL variables to the attributes scope. An application architect writes the responsibilities section, and a programmer writes the code that makes this work.

- **Attributes**   The attributes section is used to define the variables that are to be passed in or out of the fuse. There are various properties to an attribute, such as its name, its scope, comments, whether it is optional or not, a default value, and whether or not the value is editable.

The Fusedocs 2.0 specification creates these sections in tag format, similar to HTML or CFML. You will want to remember to comment them out so neither ColdFusion nor your browser tries to translate the information. This is an example Fusedoc:

```
<!---
<fusedoc fuse="dsp_home" language="ColdFusion MX"
         specification="2.0">

 <responsibilities>
  I display the text for the site's home page.
 </responsibilities>

 <properties>
  <history author="Jeffry Houser" company="DotComIt"
           email="jeff@instantcoldfusion.com" role="Architect"
           type="Create" date="03/21/2001">
 </properties>
 <io>
  <in>
  </in>
  <out>
  </out>
 </io>
</fusedoc>
--->
```

We enclose the whole Fusedoc in ColdFusion comment tags. It starts with an open fusedoc tag, where we specify the name of the fuse, the language it was created for, and the version of fusedoc that we are defining. Responsibilities are defined with the responsibilities tag. Properties are defined between an open and close properties tag, with a history tag defining the basics.

The attributes are defined with the io tag, and within that with the in and out tags. Since our dsp_home fuse does not contain any inputs or outputs other than the exit

CODING IN COLDFUSION

point, we leave this spot blank. Attributes are usually defined by the type of attribute (Boolean, String, Query, and so on) followed by the various properties of each type. The document type definition (DTD) for the Fusedocs is available at www.halhelm.com.

Analysis of Fusebox

As with any methodology, Fusebox has good and bad points. Separating chunks of an application into smaller pieces and keeping each individual template set on one task is a plus. It makes the application as a whole much easier to write, debug, and maintain. I like the fact that it includes a specification for documentation, as documentation is very important to the maintenance of an application.

Perhaps the biggest plus of the Fusebox methodology is that it is widely accepted in the ColdFusion community, and is gaining acceptance as a methodology for developing in other languages. In mid-2002, a Fusebox committee is being created to control the future direction of Fusebox. This is a move similar to the one that gave definition and control of HTML to a standards body, and bodes well for future development. Fusebox 3 brings greater integration with individual Fusebox sites, or circuits.

I don't like the use of the custom tag, formurl2attributes, that is common in Fusebox. Copying variables from one scope to another seems to be a waste of valuable resources. A developer should understand variable scopes (Chapter 8) and know where a variable comes from and how to use it without having to move a value between scopes.

Another fallback of the methodology is the fact that every link goes back to the same file. This makes it hard to perform log analysis of the site. Also, you have to do extra processing for every page request to figure out what action to perform. While a master routine was great in traditional programming, in web development, I find it beneficial to approach each page request as a separate program. Using the master fusebox template places on top of the site a layer of complexity that may not be needed. As a site grows larger, your master fusebox template contains more choices and is more likely to slow down the site. I once worked on a site where the master fusebox template contained over 200 lines, with over 50 choices. This was a point where the methodology was taken too far, thus defeating the original purpose of Fusebox, which is to simplify and improve development.

 Make sure you check out www.fusebox.org for all the latest Fusebox information.

Developing with SmartObjects

SmartObjects (SO) takes an object-oriented approach to ColdFusion. This section shows you how to put the SmartObjects methodology to work for you.

Understanding Objects

To start, I will define some common concepts of object-oriented programming. Object-oriented programming (OOP) is done with a different mindset than traditional development.

- **Method**   A method is akin to a function or procedure. In a true object-oriented language, all code resides in methods.

- **Property**   A property is like a variable. It is a name and value pair associated with a class.

- **Class**   A class is a collection of methods and properties.

- **Object**   An object is an instance of a class. To compare this to a standard ColdFusion concept, an array is similar to a class, but it is just a concept until you create an array variable, which is akin to an object.

- **Inheritance**   Inheritance refers to when one class receives all the methods and properties of its parent. In the way that you have received your mother's eyes and father's nose, a class receives all the properties of its parent class, and all the properties of that class' parents, and so on until it is out of classes. Inheritance also allows for overwriting methods and properties with new ones specific to the subclass.

We will move on to see how object-oriented methodologies can be put into practice with ColdFusion.

Applying Objects to ColdFusion

The concept behind SmartObjects is to take a normal directory full of ColdFusion files and convert it into a class. Every CFML template in the directory becomes a method. The class definition is defined using a file called public.cfm. Two custom tags are used to interface with the class: cf_objects instantiates the class, and cf_call calls methods associated with classes. This discussion starts with the public.cfm file.

The public.cfm file uses a third custom tag, cf_class, to define the class. These are the parameters of the custom tag:

- **class**   This contains the name of the class that is being created. You will want to specify the path from the web server root, with periods separating each directory name: for example, Osborne.CompleteReference.Chapter10.SmartObjects.

- **inherit**   This will contain the parent class of the new class.

- **methods**   The methods attribute contains a list of methods that are available to this class, separated by a comma.

The call to the custom tag is all that is contained in the public.cfm file. Here is an example public.cfm file:

```
<CF_Class
 class=" Osborne.CompleteReference.Chapter10.TestClass"
 methods="Display,Edit,Delete">
```

This public.cfm file defines the TestClass class with three methods: Display, Edit, and Delete. If there are any problems, the tag could throw either of two error messages:

■ **SmartObjects.CF_Class.MissingAttribute.Class**   Means that the class attribute was not defined when calling the custom tag.

■ **SmartObjects.CF_Class.MissingClass**   Specifies that the existing class was not able to inherit from another class, because that class was not defined.

 You can download all the SmartObjects custom tag files, as well as examples and other supporting documentation, from smart-objects.com.

After creating the class, you can use the cf_object tag to instantiate it. There are two parameters to this custom tag:

■ **class**   The name of the class that you are creating an object from

■ **object**   The name of your new object

There are three error codes that this object could return:

■ **SmartObjects.CF_Object.MissingAttribute.Class**   States that the class attribute was missing from the custom tag call

■ **SmartObjects.CF_Object.MissingAttribute.Object**   States that the object attribute was missing from the custom tag call

■ **SmartObjects.CF_Object.MissingClass**   States that the class you are trying to instantiate does not exist

To create an instance of the object that was previously created, you would use this code:

```
<cf_object Class="TestClass" Object="MyTestObject">
```

We now have a valid instance of our object and we can call methods against it.

To call methods against an object, we use the cf_call custom tag. There are three main attributes to calling a method:

■ **object**   Contains the variable name of the object you are calling

■ **method**   Contains the name of the method that you want to call

■ **application**   Contains a yes or no value that tells you whether or not you will need cflocation to redirect the user to a new page

The error values to check for in the cf_call custom tag are as follows:

■ **SmartObjects.CF_Call.MissingAttribute.Object**   States that the object attribute was missing from the custom tag call

- **SmartObjects.CF_Call.MissingAttribute.Method** States that the method attribute was missing from the custom tag call

- **SmartObjects.CF_Call.MissingClass** States that the object that was called was of an invalid class

- **SmartObjects.CF_Call.MissingMethod** States that an invalid method was specified in the call

- **SmartObjects.CF_Call.BadObject.DoesNotExist** Specifies that the Object variable specified in the custom tag call does not exist

- **SmartObjects.CF_Call.BadObject.NotStructure** Specifies that the object specified in the custom tag is not a structure variable, and is therefore not valid

- **SmartObjects.CF_Call.BadObject.NoClassRecord** States that the object does not have a class record, and is therefore an invalid object

We can call our display method like this:

```
<cf_call object=" MyTestObject " method=" Display">
```

Although, we did not illustrate the template that makes up the display method here, the template could contain any valid ColdFusion code and perform any action that can be performed in a nonmethod ColdFusion template.

Analyzing SmartObjects

If you want to apply OOP techniques to ColdFusion, then SmartObjects is the way to go. The custom tags provide you with an interface for developing and using classes without showing you the details behind implementation, if you don't need to know them. The built-in error checking in the custom tags is good, and something that a lot of applications are weak on.

However, there are some not-so-perfect things about SO, too. Object-oriented design could be overkill for many ColdFusion projects. If object-oriented design was the way to go for you, you may find the SO implementation limiting. There is no support for object properties, and no way to send parameters to methods.

There is no standardization in this methodology other than objects. Projects built with SmartObjects could vary widely in many areas, from documentation to file structure. The custom tags are not very well documented as far as how to use them. You have to pour over examples to get an inkling of what is going on.

Some Other Methodologies

After looking at two major development methodologies in the ColdFusion space, I want to point out a few more that exist, but are not yet prominent on the radar screen:

- **cfObjects** cfObjects is another look at OOP with ColdFusion. Check it out at www.cfobjects.com.

- **Switch Box** Switch Box is a way to define specific paths (called message vectors) through an application. Point your browser to http://switch-box.org for more information.

- **Black Box** Black Box is a method for development that highlights separation of functionality, or business logic, from display and formatting code.

You can always create your own methodology, or modify one of these existing ones to suit your needs. The most important part of developing is to use a methodology. The second most important thing is to document your methodology. These two actions will save you from wasting a lot of time in the long run.

Summary

In this chapter, you learned about the following:

- The importance of using a development methodology

- Some standard elements that can be used for creating your own methodology

- Fusebox, one of the most popular methodologies

- SmartObjects and the custom tags that make it work

The next chapter will go on to examine Dreamweaver MX and how it can be used within ColdFusion.

Chapter 11

Writing
ColdFusion Code

The next generation of web page editors starts with Macromedia's Dreamweaver MX. Dreamweaver MX combines the features of Dreamweaver and Dreamweaver UltraDev into a single product. Hard-core coders in the audience may remember past versions of Dreamweaver as a GUI tool that changed your code. That is no longer the case. Dreamweaver MX has become a great tool for coders and GUI designers alike.

Configuring Dreamweaver MX

There are many new features in Dreamweaver that will enhance your development experiences with it. This section talks about the various layouts of the interface and how to customize it to suit your needs. We will end this discussion by introducing snippets.

Getting Around in Dreamweaver

The interface for Dreamweaver MX has been enhanced and changed. If you are a user of previous versions of Dreamweaver, then these changes may take you by surprise. Fear not, because you can always revert back to your old way of working while still taking advantage of some of the new Dreamweaver MX features.

Changing the Dreamweaver Workspace

The first thing that we want to examine is how to choose your workspace. Dreamweaver MX provides you with three different types of workspaces, or views, from which to choose.

Figure 11-1 shows the view designed specifically for the coding crowd that is used to using HomeSite or ColdFusion Studio. This view is my preferred view. I'm a ColdFusion Studio user by trade and like to be able to get in to play around with the code.

For all you users upgrading from previous versions of Dreamweaver or UltraDev, you may want to set up your interface to look similar to Dreamweaver 4, as shown in Figure 11-2. If you want to help to ease your transition from previous versions, then this is the layout for you. The Dreamweaver 4 interface is not limited to a single window.

For those of you that love change, Dreamweaver MX provides a whole new interface, as shown in Figure 11-3. This is known as the Dreamweaver MX workspace. This workspace allows you access to all of Dreamweaver's new features while providing an interface that is familiar to most Windows users. The various panels are dockable and provide easy access to ColdFusion's features.

You may be wondering how you can change from one workspace to another. Here are the instructions:

1. Launch Dreamweaver and choose Edit | Preferences to open the Preferences dialog box.

2. Select General. Click the Change Workspace button to open the Workspace Setup window:

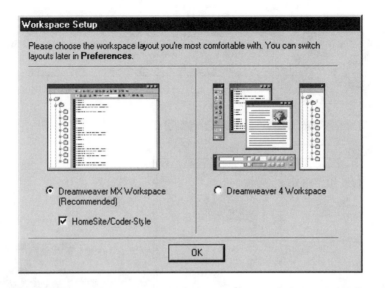

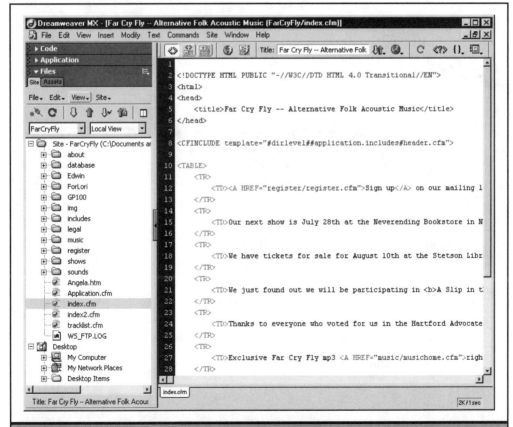

Figure 11-1. *Dreamweaver MX, HomeSite Coder view*

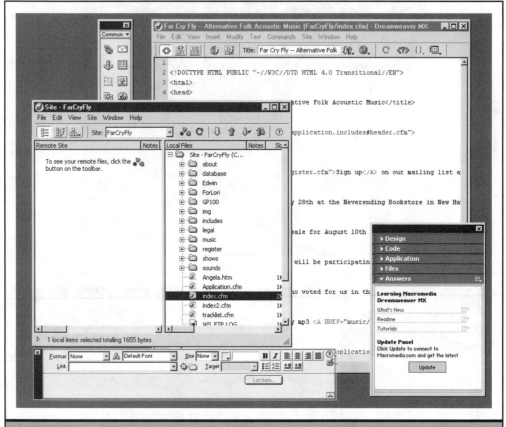

Figure 11-2. *Dreamweaver MX, Dreamweaver 4 view*

3. Select the type of workspace you want, either Dreamweaver 4 or Dreamweaver MX. If you choose the Dreamweaver MX workspace, you have the option to select the HomeSite/Coder-Style layout by checking the box.

4. Click OK to close the Workspace Setup window.

5. Click OK to close the Preferences dialog box.

6. Exit Dreamweaver MX.

7. Relaunch Dreamweaver MX. You will see your new workspace selection.

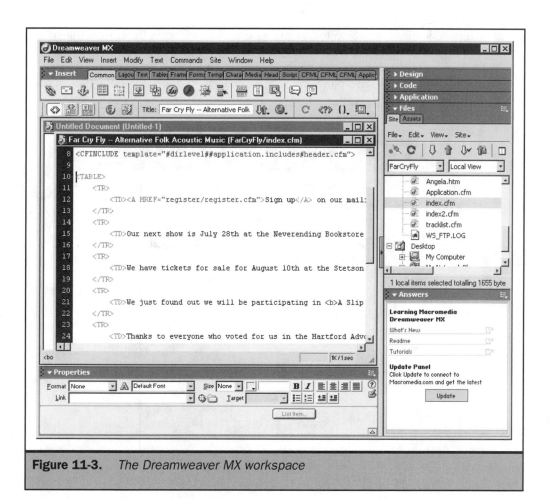

Figure 11-3.   *The Dreamweaver MX workspace*

Using Panels

The Dreamweaver interface contains a number of panels that provide various functions during your development efforts. Each of these panels can be placed into the interface, or float on top of it. This is a list of the different panels:

- **Insert**   Contains commonly used tags, grouped into separate tabs. This panel can contain HTML tags, ColdFusion tags, or tags from other technologies, such as ASP or .NET.

- **Properties**   Shows a lot of properties specific to the location of the cursor in the open document.

- **Files** Contains two tabs, Site and Assets. The Site tab shows the current machine, and any remote sites that you have set up for use. The Assets tab contains properties of the current site, such as images, links, and Shockwave or Flash movies. I like to use this panel because I can easily work with all the files in my web site.

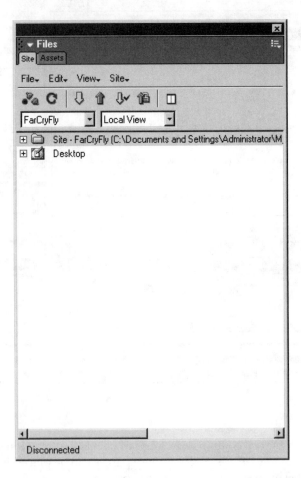

- **Answers** Contains all the information that you need to get help in Dreamweaver.
- **Application** Contains information about databases, data bindings, server behaviors, and components. This is handy if you can connect to a web site via ColdFusion's Remote Development Services (RDS). You can view databases, check out ColdFusion Components and Web services, and create recordsets. I like to use this panel because it gives me easy access to databases.

■ **Code**   Allows you access to inspect tags in the current document, view and edit predefined code segments (called snippets), or search for help on ColdFusion, HTML, JavaScript, or other resources. I like to keep this panel open because of the snippets.

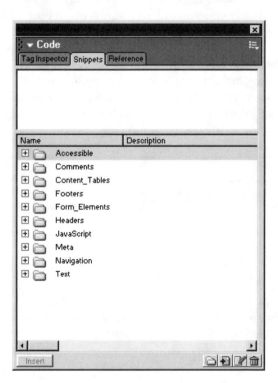

- **Design** Has three tabs: HTML Styles, CSS Styles, and Behaviors. HTML and CSS Styles are the snippets of design. They allow you to create code that will customize a display, including font, size, color, and style. Behaviors are for JavaScript code.

- **Results** Contains debugging information from various debugging tools, such as link checker and tag validation, and other sources such as search results, site reports, and FTP logs.

- **Advanced Layout** Assists you in developing with frames and layers.

- **History** Shows the most recent actions that you have taken in your development.

- **SiteSpring** Used for integration with Macromedia SiteSpring, the Macromedia workflow tool.

- **Timelines** Used to help integrate with Shockwave or Flash movies.

You can turn on or off any of these panels from the Window menu. Most of them reside nicely in the gray docking area, either to the left for people in the HomeSite view, or to the right for people using the Dreamweaver MX view.

Understanding Tag Libraries

There are many tag libraries available to you from within Dreamweaver MX. A tag library is a collection of related tags, such as HTML tags or ColdFusion tags. In Dreamweaver MX, not only can you access a bunch of prebuilt libraries, you can create your own.

Creating a New Tag Library

Before you can start using tag libraries, you need to understand what they are in relation to everything else. When you enter a tag, Dreamweaver will search through the tag libraries to find the tag's pop-up attributes. The following screenshot shows the pop-up menu you get after typing in the cfapplication tag:

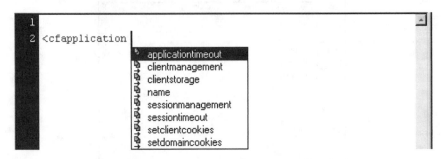

All the attributes are listed in the pop-up menu, and you can choose the attribute you want to add without having to have it memorized.

Suppose you wanted to create a new tag library to contain all of your custom tags. This is how you would do it:

1. Launch Dreamweaver. Select Edit | Tag Libraries to open the Tag Library Editor, shown in Figure 11-4.

2. Click the plus sign to see a list of menu choices. Select the New Tag Library option.

3. Enter the name of your new tag library, CustomTags.

4. Click OK, and your new library will appear in the list.

5. Now you have to tell Dreamweaver when it should check the library for pop-ups. Scroll through the "used in" list and select ColdFusion Components and ColdFusion Template. You have finished creating your tag library.

Creating a New Tag

Creating the tag library is only the first step. It is potentially useless if you don't fill it with some tags. This is how:

1. Launch Dreamweaver if you haven't already and select Edit | Tag Libraries.

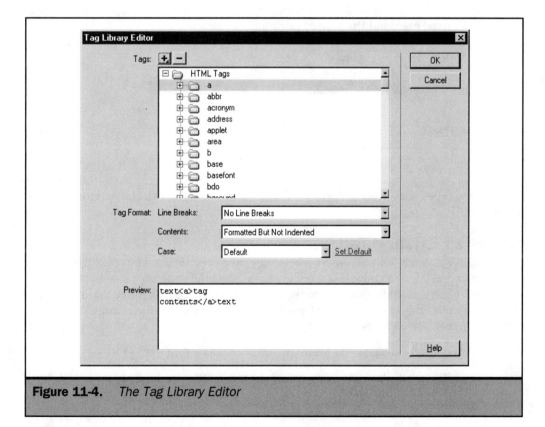

Figure 11-4.   *The Tag Library Editor*

2. Click the plus sign and select New Tags from the menu to open the New Tags dialog box.

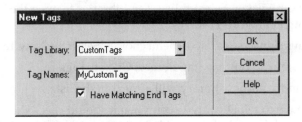

3. Select the library you are adding the tag to and enter the name of the custom tag.

4. Click OK. The tag is created.

5. Select the tag from the list of your new tag library. Click the plus sign and select New Attributes to open the New Attributes window.

6. Type the attribute name and click the OK button.

7. Select the attribute from the list. You can further edit its capabilities, such as whether the attribute will be inserted into the document in lowercase, uppercase, or a mixed case, and the type of attribute.

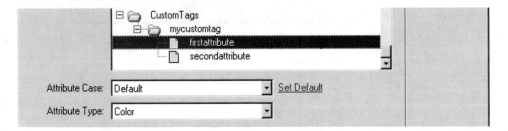

Enumerated types allow you to specify a list of values that you can choose from. Text is the default.

Editing an Existing Tag

Suppose we wanted to edit the pop-up behavior for a specific tag. Let's take a look at the cfapplication tag. We know that there are three potential values for the clientstorage attribute: Registry, Cookie, or the name of a datasource. If we look at the tag in the tag library, we notice that it is set to a text attribute. Suppose we want to change this to offer us some choices. This is how:

1. Launch Dreamweaver if it is not already and select Edit | Tag Libraries.

2. Expand the CFML Tags library, and find the cfapplication tag. Expand the list of cfapplication attributes.

3. Change the Attribute Type drop-down list box from Text to Enumerated. The Values box will open.

Attribute Case:	Default	▼	Set Default
Attribute Type:	Enumerated	▼	
Values:			

4. Enter the names, separated by a comma, in the Values box: Registry, Cookie, EnterYourOwnDataSource.

5. Click OK to save. Now when you type in the clientstorage attribute of the cfapplication tag, you will receive the three options instead of nothing.

```
<cfapplication clientstorage=""
</body>
</html>
```

```
cookie
enteryourowndatasource
registry
```

Creating Snippets

A snippet is a block of code that you want to write once and be able to use again, by inserting it into the document. Snippets are great for things such as JavaScript that you use on a routine basis, or to define default values for a ColdFusion tag that you use commonly. This section shows you how to create snippets and insert them into the document.

Creating a Snippet

One of the most common tags used in a ColdFusion application is the cfapplication tag, as discussed in Chapter 8. There are going to be many common attributes that you use for a cfapplication tag throughout all of your applications. However, it doesn't make sense to create a custom tag or include for it, as discussed in Chapter 16. It makes an ideal snippet.

This is how you can create a snippet in Dreamweaver:

1. Launch Dreamweaver, and expand the Code panel. If the Code panel is not already open, you can select snippets from the Window menu to display it.

2. Create a new folder, if necessary, by clicking the New Snippet Folder button.

3. Click the New Snippet button to open the Snippet dialog box.

4. Enter the name of the snippet: **Default cfapplication Tag**.

5. Enter a description: **This is a generic cfapplication that I can use in my applications**.

6. Select a snippet type: whether you want to wrap your code around a selection or insert a block. Wrapping your code is for tags with start and end tags. Inserting a block is for a selection without start and end tags.

7. Enter your default cfapplication tag in the Insert Code box. The Snippet dialog box will look something like this:

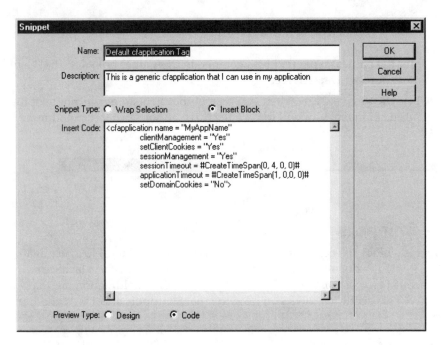

8. Click OK to save your new snippet. It is now ready for use.

Inserting a Snippet

After you have created a snippet, you need to know how to insert it into a page. Dreamweaver MX allows you to do that, as follows:

1. Launch Dreamweaver and create a new page by selecting File | New.

2. Select Dynamic Page from the Category list, and ColdFusion from the Dynamic Page list.

3. Click the Create button to create your new page.

4. Select your snippet from the Snippet list. Click the Insert button.

5. The snippet will be placed into the page.

Working with Sites

This section examines sites in depth. First, you will learn how to create a site. Then, we will talk about the assets of a site. Dreamweaver MX sites are a way to organize and maintain files associated with your web site. Finally, we will demonstrate how to upload a site.

Defining a Site

This is how you can create a site:

1. Launch Dreamweaver and expand the Files panel. If the Files panel is not shown, you can display it by selecting Window | Sites.

2. If you do not have any sites created, you can click the Define A Site link. Otherwise, choose New Site from the Site menu to open the Site Definition dialog box, shown in Figure 11-5.

3. Enter the site name, the local root folder, and the default images folder for the site (or click the folder icon to select these folders graphically).

4. Enter the HTTP address of the site. This will allow Dreamweaver to check links that refer to your own site.

5. In the categories listed at left, click Testing Server. Select ColdFusion in the Server Model drop-down list box. Select the type of access you have to the site— Local/Network, FTP, or WebDAV—and fill in the appropriate information.

6. Click Remote Info in the Category list. This shows you how to access files remotely. You can select FTP, Local, RDS, Visual SourceSafe, or WebDAV. If applicable, you can click the Settings button to change settings for that particular access method.

7. Click Design Notes in the Category list. Design Notes is a feature that will allow you to share extra information about the site files with other developers.

8. You can select Site Map Layout to control the layout of a site map and File View Column to control the file columns of a site.

9. Click OK to create the site. You now have a new site all ready for development from within Dreamweaver MX.

Accessing Site Assets

The Assets tab of the Files panel has two options: Site and Favorites. Selecting Site shows all assets for the current site. Selecting Favorites shows assets that you use across multiple sites. The following options run down the side of the Assets panel:

- **Images**   Contains all images associated with the site.
- **Colors**   Contains colors in the site, including those used in style sheets. This includes text color, background colors, and link colors.

- **URLs**   Lists all the URLs that are used in the site.
- **Flash**   Lists all the Flash movies that are used in the site.
- **Shockwave**   Lists all the Shockwave movies that are used in the site.
- **Movies**   Lists MPEGs, AVI files, and other movie files that don't fit into the Flash or Shockwave categories.
- **Scripts**   Lists all the JavaScript or VBScript files in the site. This tab does not list scripts that show up in pages; it lists only scripts that are used in their own file.
- **Templates**   Lists all the templates that are associated with the current site. Templates are ways to create custom page layouts.
- **Library Items**   Lists all library items associated with the current site. Library items are elements, such as images or text, that are used in multiple pages, and updated frequently. Updating the library item will update corresponding pages that use the item.

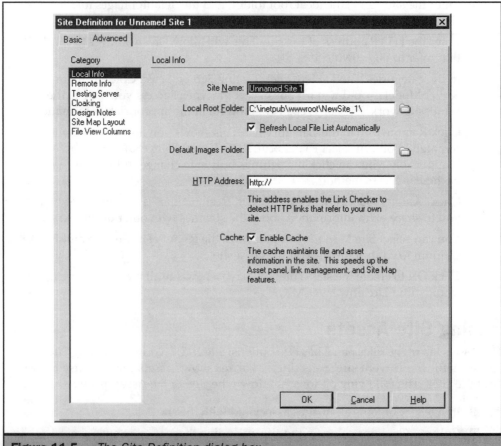

Figure 11-5.   *The Site Definition dialog box*

Uploading a Site

If developing a web site is 90 percent of the work, the other 10 percent is updating your live copy with the development version. You will have problems if you have content created on the live server while new development is taking place on the development server. Dreamweaver provides you with tools to help avoid this.

The first step in uploading your files is to make sure you have a remote server set up:

1. Launch Dreamweaver if it is not already open. Go to the Files panel and select the Site tab. You can choose Window | Site if the Files panel is not already open.

2. From the Site tab, choose Edit Sites to open the Edit Sites window.

3. Choose the name of your site and click Edit.

Tip *You can perform many other actions from this menu, such as duplicating, deleting, editing, and creating sites.*

4. On the Advanced tab of the Site Definition dialog box, click Remote Info in the Category list. Select how you have access to your site. RDS and FTP are the most common, but Dreamweaver also supports SourceSafe, WebDAV, or a local network connection.

5. If you are using SourceSafe, WebDAV, or RDS, click the Settings button and input the appropriate settings. In most cases, this is a username, password, and directory.

6. Click OK to exit the Site Definition dialog box. Then click Done to close the Edit Sites dialog box.

You are now ready to upload files to your web server:

1. Launch Dreamweaver, if it is not already open. Go to the Files panel and select the Site tab. You can choose Window | Site if the Files panel is not already up.

2. Highlight your site, right-click, and select Synchronize to open the Synchronize Files dialog box.

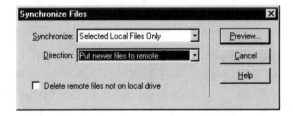

3. You have two options in the Synchronize drop-down list box. You can upload either the entire site or specific files.

4. In the Direction drop-down list box, you have three options. The first is to put new files onto the remote host. The second is to get new files from the remote host. The third works in both ways: it will bring new files down and send new files up.

5. If you want to delete remote files that have been removed from your hard drive, you can click the checkbox. Be careful about doing this if new pages are being created live that you do not have on your local disk.

6. Click the Preview button. You will see a list of all files that need to be uploaded.

7. Click OK. You have uploaded your site.

Working with Databases

If you are dealing with dynamic development, Dreamweaver has some important features for you. You can connect to ColdFusion servers via RDS, by creating a site that is accessed that way. Via RDS you can check out the datasources that are set up in ColdFusion, and create recordsets that can be brought into a template.

Understanding the Application Panel

The Application panel allows you to perform various data-oriented actions. It has four tabs:

- **Databases**   Allows you to access databases via ColdFusion's RDS.
- **Data Bindings**   Allows you to set up things like ColdFusion variables or recordsets.
- **Server Behavior**   Allows you to set up and choose specific server behaviors such as JavaScript functions and parsing through recordsets.
- **Components**   Allows you to look at ColdFusion Components or Web services that are available on your application server.

Accessing a Database in Dreamweaver

Once you have created a datasource and have set up Dreamweaver to access the ColdFusion server, you can access the database from within Dreamweaver. This is how:

1. Launch Dreamweaver if you have not already. Expand the Application panel. If it is not open, you can open it by selecting Window | Databases.

2. If you see a screen like the following, you are not set up to access the ColdFusion server.

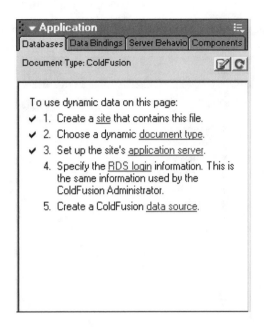

Follow the steps onscreen. For Step 1, create a Dreamweaver site as you learned how to do earlier in this chapter. For Steps 2 and 3, you can click the links to specify the dynamic document type and set up the application server for the site. For Step 4, click the RDS Login text and type your username, if applicable, and password.

3. Another dialog box might pop up, if you didn't already save this information in the site definition.

Configure RDS Server

Host name:	
Port:	80
Full Host Directory:	C:\
Username:	
Password:	☑ Save

OK   Cancel

4. Enter the hostname, username, password, and other relevant information.

You should now be able to see the datasources in the database list:

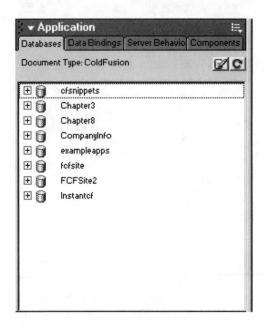

Once you have a datasource listed, you can look at tables and views, and view data. You can also create recordsets for use in your Dreamweaver templates.

Creating a Recordset Without SQL

After you have access to the databases, as described in the preceding section, you can create recordsets for use within your documents. This is how:

1. Launch Dreamweaver if it is not already. Go to the Data Bindings tab of the Application panel. You can select Window | Data Bindings to go straight there.

2. Click the plus sign on the menu and select the Recordset (Query) option. This window will pop up:

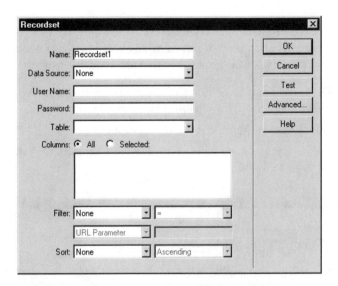

3. Choose a name and datasource for the recordset. Enter the username and password, if applicable.

4. Click the Advanced button to create a complex query.

5. You can select the tables that you want in your query from the database items list. You can add the items to the select, where, or ordering portion of the SQL statement.

6. Click Test when you are finished writing your query. You will see the results.

7. You can specify any URL parameters that are needed to execute the query.

8. Click OK. Congratulations! You've created your query in the current page.

Accessing ColdFusion Components and Web Services

ColdFusion Components (CFCs) are an important new feature introduced in ColdFusion MX. They are discussed in more detail in Chapter 16. Web services will be the wave of the future, and they are discussed in Chapter 31. You can access both of these features from the Components tab in the Application panel.

Creating a ColdFusion Component

ColdFusion Components are a way to modularize and reuse your code. You can access the ColdFusion Components and Web services that are available from the Components tab:

1. Launch Dreamweaver. Select the Components tab from the Application panel. You can go straight there by selecting Window | Components.

2. From the drop-down menu, choose CF Components.

3. Click the plus sign to create a new ColdFusion Component. You will see the Create Component window.

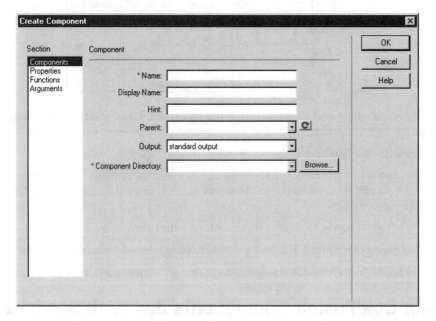

4. Enter the name of the component, the display name, the hint, the parent (if applicable), the output, and the directory that the component will reside in.

5. Click Properties in the Section list. This enables you to enter all the properties that your new component uses. Click the plus sign to add a property, and the minus sign to remove it. You can define its name, display name, the hint, the access level, the type of property, and the default value.

6. Click Functions in the Section list.

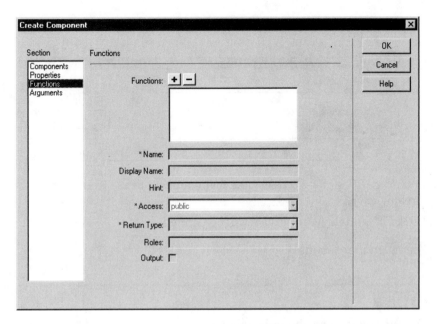

You can define all the functions that are associated with the ColdFusion Component. The plus sign will add a function; the minus sign will remove it. You can define the name of the function, the display name, the hint, the type of access the function has, the type of value it returns, and its roles.

7. Click Arguments in the Section list. This enables you to specify arguments for functions that were defined in Step 6. You can specify the name of the argument, its display name, its type, the default value, and whether or not it is required.

8. Click OK to create your ColdFusion Component.

 You can learn more about ColdFusion Components in Chapter 16.

Accessing Web Services

Creating a Web service, for access from Dreamweaver, is even easier than creating a ColdFusion Component. This is how:

1. Launch Dreamweaver. Select the Components tab from the Application panel. You can go straight there by selecting Window | Components.

2. From the drop-down menu, choose Web Services.

CODING IN COLDFUSION

3. Click the plus sign to create a new Web service. You'll see this window:

4. Enter the URL of the Web services that you want to use from within Dreamweaver.

5. Click OK, and the Web service will be verified.

You can learn more about Web services in Chapter 31.

Summary

In this chapter, you learned about the following:

- The Dreamweaver MX interface
- How to use Dreamweaver MX to create ColdFusion templates
- How to use sites in Dreamweaver MX
- How to access databases through Dreamweaver MX

The next chapter will teach you all about forms and URL variables.

The Complete Reference

ColdFusion MX

Chapter 12

Sharing Variables Between Templates

A web server creates no correlation between page requests. It can't tell who you are, where you came from, or what you've already done in the site. Many methods have been developed to follow a user's path through a web site. ColdFusion uses CFID and CFTOKEN values, as discussed in Chapter 8, to keep track of user information via session and client variables. This chapter discusses other ways to pass data between templates and how they can be applied to ColdFusion.

Passing Parameters via the URL

The most common way to pass parameters from one page to another is to append them to the URL. This section starts by describing the format of a URL. Then, it moves on to show you how to put variables in your URL. It finishes by describing how to access those variables in ColdFusion.

Using the URL Query String

First, we want to look at the format of a URL. This is a standard URL:

http://www.instantcoldfusion.com/index.cfm

The URL starts with the name of the protocol, http://. It is followed by a domain name, www.instantcoldfusion.com. The location of the page that you want to load comes next, including the directory and the filename. The example does not have a directory, but the filename is index.cfm. This is a standard URL.

There is an optional part of the URL, called the query string, that is not in the preceding example. It comes after the filename. The query string contains a list of name-value pairs, separated by the ampersand (&) character. This is a URL that contains a query string:

http://www.instantcoldfusion.com/index.cfm?MyVar=Val&MyVar2=Val2

First, note that a question mark separates the filename from the query string. After that comes our variable list. The URL contains two values, MyVar and MyVar2, with the values of Val and Val2, respectively. In the URL string, you don't need to use quotes around your variables.

Accessing Parameters from ColdFusion

Now that you know how variables get into the URL, you need to know how you can access those variables in ColdFusion. There is a specific scope, the URL scope, that you can use to access variables that have been passed via the URL. We discussed variable scopes in Chapter 8.

Let's take a look at this URL:

http://www.instantcoldfusion.com/Test.cfm?MyVar=Val&MyVar2=Val2

This is test.cfm, the page that will process the variables:

```
<!--- www.instantcoldfusion.com

Description: Page to output URL variables

Entering: N/A
Exiting: N/A

Dependencies: N/A
Expecting: MyVar
   MyVar1

Modification History
Date        Modifier                Modification
**********************************************************
03/27/2002 Jeff Houser, DotComIt   Created
--->

<cfoutput>
 MyVar: #url.MyVar#<br>
 MyVar2: #url.MyVar2#<br>
</cfoutput>
```

When running the page, test.cfm, ColdFusion will output something like this:

```
MyVar: Val
MyVar2: Val2
```

It sees the cfoutput tag and starts looking for the number signs, which tell it to process a variable. When it finds the two variables, it sees that the variables are in the URL scope and returns their value.

URL variables are very common when you want to pass small amounts of information via the URL, such as a unique identifier, when creating a drill-down interface. If you choose not to use cookies for ColdFusion's session management capabilities, then you must pass the CFID and CFTOKEN as URL variables to every page request. If you have lots of variables that you need to pass, you probably want to use a form.

Using Forms

A *form* is a collection of HTML elements that are used to collect information from the user. This section examines form elements and talks about ColdFusion-specific form elements. Then, it shows you how to create a sample form.

Introducing Form Elements

This section introduces the form tag and talks about the various form element tags that exist in HTML. The conversation continues by discussing ColdFusion's cfform tag and the ColdFusion-enhanced version of the standard form elements.

Using the Form Tag

The form tag is one with both a start and end tag. These are the attributes of the form tag:

- **action**   Contains the location that the form submits onto when the Submit button is clicked.

- **enctype**   Specifies the type of data that is being passed by the form. The default value is application/x-www-form-urlencoded. If you are submitting a file, make sure that you set it to multipart/form-data, or you will not be able to access the file on the form's processing page.

- **method**   Defines the type of operation the form will perform. The available options are either post, to send data, or get, to retrieve data. The default is get.

Setting up your form tag is only half the battle. You have to define any number of individual elements for the form between the open and close form tags for the form to do anything. You can see a table of all form elements in Table 12-1. We will examine many of them in more depth later in this chapter

Accepting Text Input

There are various forms of text input that you might want to accept from a user. In a user registration form, you might want to have the user input their name, address, or password. In a customer support form, you may want them to enter their e-mail address, comments, and a description of their concern.

Element	Tag	Attributes	Comment
Small text box	Input	**name:** The variable name that will contain the value on the form processing page **type:** Text **value:** The default value of the text **size:** The size of the text box **maxlength:** The largest possible input that is selected	Accepts short text input from the user

Table 12-1.   *HTML Form Attributes*

Element	Tag	Attributes	Comment
Password	Input	**name:** The variable name that will contain the value on the form processing page **type:** Passwordv **value:** The default value of the text **size:** The size of the text box **maxlength:** The largest possible input that is selected	Just like a text box except that the input will be masked with asterisks
Checkbox	Input	**name:** The variable name that will contain the value on the form processing page **type:** Checkbox **value:** The default value of the text **checked:** Tells whether or not the checkbox is checked; checked does not need a value	Use checkboxes when you want the user to be able to select any number of choices
Radio button	Input	**name:** The variable name that will contain the value on the form processing page **type:** Radio **value**: The default value of the text **checked:** Tells whether or not the radio button is selected; checked does not need a value	Use radio buttons when you want the user to be able to select only a single choice
Button	Input	**name:** The variable name that will contain the value on the form processing page **type:** Button **value:** The default value of the text	Use to place a button on a form
Submit button	Input	**name:** The variable name that will contain the value on the form processing page **type:** Submit **value:** The default value of the text	The Submit button is used to send all the form elements onto the processing page
Reset button	Input	**name:** The variable name that will contain the value on the form processing page **type:** Reset **value:** The default value of the text	The Reset button is used to set all form elements to their default values

Table 12-1.   *HTML Form Attributes* (continued)

CODING IN COLDFUSION

Element	Tag	Attributes	Comment
File	Input	**name:** The variable name that will contain the value on the form processing page **type:** File **value:** The default value of the text	The file type is used to upload a file to the server
Hidden	Input	**name:** The variable name that will contain the value on the form processing page **type:** Hidden **value:** The default value of the text	Hidden form elements are not displayed on the page
Image	Input	**name:** The variable name that will contain the value on the form processing page **type:** Image **value:** The default value of the text	Use to place an image on a form
Select box	Select	**name:** The variable name that will contain the value on the form processing page **multiple:** Tells the select box whether or not to allow multiple attributes; it doesn't have a value **size:** Specifies the initial width of the select box	Used in conjunction with the Option tag
Option		**value:** The default value of the text **selected:** Sets this option as the first value in the select box; it does not have a value	Used in conjunction with the Select tag
Large text box	TextArea	**name:** The variable name that will contain the value on the form processing page **rows:** Specifies the height of the text box **cols:** Specifies the length of the text area	Use large text boxes to collect a user's comments, or other lengthy entries

Table 12-1. *HTML Form Attributes* (continued)

There are three different ways through which you can accept text input: a password box, a text box, and a text area. Text boxes and password boxes are set up using the input tag. The main difference is that a password box will mask the user's input. The following page includes a text box and password box:

```
<!--- www.instantcoldfusion.com

Description: A page to demonstrate form elements

Entering: N/A
Exiting: FormElementsp.cfm

Dependencies: N/A
Expecting: N/A

Modification History
Date      Modifier               Modification
*********************************************************
03/27/2002 Jeff Houser, DotComIt    Created
--->

<form action="FormElementsp.cfm" method="post">
 Text Input: <input type="Text" name="TextInput"><br>
 Password Input: <input type="Password" name="Password"><br>
</form>
```

This is a simple page that includes a form post to a processing page. There is a Text Input box, and a Password Input box.

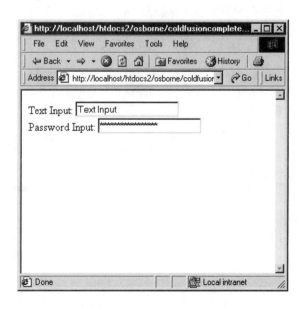

CODING IN COLDFUSION

You will notice that the Text Input box presents its output in plain text and the Password Input box shows its value covered with asterisks.

The textarea tag is used to provide a larger input area to the user, allowing the user to write multiline data. This code creates the page:

```
<!--- www.instantcoldfusion.com

Description: Page to demonstrate the TextArea tag

Entering: FormElementsi.cfm
Exiting: N/A

Dependencies: N/A
Expecting: N/A

Modification History
Date        Modifier               Modification
****************************************************
03/27/2002 Jeff Houser, DotComIt   Created
--->

<form action="FormElementsp.cfm" method="post">
 Text Area <br>
 <textarea rows="10" cols="40"></textarea>
</form>
```

The result of this code is a screen similar to this:

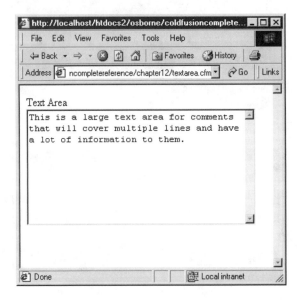

Making Choices with Checkboxes, Radio Buttons, and Select Boxes

There will be times when you want to accept user input, but instead of giving the user free will, you want to have the user select between two or more choices. You can do this by using checkboxes, radio buttons, or a select box. Radio buttons are best when you want to show the user all the choices and have them pick only one.

Checkboxes are great when you want to show the user all the choices, and enable them to select more than one. Select boxes can be set up to accept either a single selection or multiple selections. They are good if you want to preserve real estate on your form. Here is a page with all three elements:

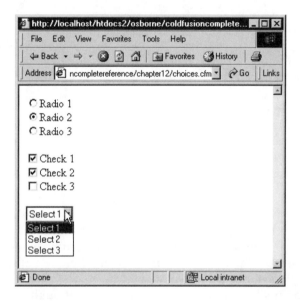

This is the code that creates the page:

```
<!--- www.instantcoldfusion.com

Description: Page to demonstrate checkboxes, radio buttons,
             and list boxes

Entering: N/A
Exiting: N/A

Dependencies: N/A
Expecting: N/A
```

```
Modification History
Date        Modifier                Modification
************************************************************
03/27/2002 Jeff Houser, DotComIt    Created
--->

<form action="FormElementsp.cfm" method="post">
 <input name="RadioButton" type="radio"
                           value="Radio1" checked>Radio 1<br>
 <input name="RadioButton" type="radio" value="Radio2">Radio 2<br>
 <input name="RadioButton" type="radio" value="Radio3">Radio 3<br>
 <br>
 <input name="CheckB" type="Checkbox"
                       value="Check1" checked>Radio 1<br>
 <input name="CheckB" type="Checkbox" value="Check2">Check 2<br>
 <input name="CheckB" type="Checkbox" value="Check3">Check 3<br>
 <br>
 <select name="SelectBox">
  <option value="Select1">Select 1
  <option value="Select2">Select 2
  <option value="Select3">Select 3
 </select>
</form>
```

For radio buttons to work, every element of the radio button set must have the same name. That is how your browser associates the radio buttons together and prevents the user from selecting more than one. You can create multiple sets of radio buttons on a single page by giving the sets different names.

Checkboxes do not have to have the same name, although it is often handy for processing on the back end. A checkbox name will contain a comma-delimited list of all checked entries on the form's processing page. If no checkboxes were checked, then the variable will not exist.

The last element on the page is a select box. The select box allows the user to select one element from a drop-down list. The option text and value are specified with the option tag. The name is specified in the select tag. When the form is submitted, the form-processing page will be able to access a variable with the name in the select tag and the value of the selected option.

Using Built-in ColdFusion Form Elements

ColdFusion provides enhanced versions of many of the standard form elements, as you can see in Table 12-2. Instead of placing these elements inside a form tag, they must be

CF Tag	Attributes	Comment
cfapplet	**appletsource:** The name of the registered applet **name:** The name of the applet **notsupported:** The message to display if the applet is not supported **param_*n*:** Applet parameters	Allows you to use an applet that was registered in the ColdFusion Administrator
cfinput	**type:** Either text, radio, checkbox, or password **name:** The name of the attribute **value:** The default value of the attribute **required:** A yes or no value stating whether this will be required **range:** The minimum and maximum value separated by a comma; applies only to numerical data **validate:** Will validate data input based on date, eurodate, time, float, integer, telephone, zipcode, creditcard, social_security_number, or regular_expression **onvalidate:** The name of a custom JavaScript function you want to call when validating data **pattern:** The pattern to validate against if validate is equal to regular_expression **message:** The message if validation fails **onerror:** A custom JavaScript function to call if validation fails **checked:** If checkbox or radio **passthrough:** For HTML attributes not supported by cfoutput	A ColdFusion replacement for the HTML input
cfselect	**name:** The name of the attribute **required:** A yes or no value stating whether this will be required **message:** The message if validation fails **onerror:** A custom JavaScript function to call if validation fails **size:** The size of the box **multiple:** A Yes/No attribute that specifies whether multiple selections are allowed **query:** The query you want to populate data from **selected:** The default value for the box **value:** The query column value for the items **display:** The query column display text **passthrough:** For HTML attributes not supported by cfoutput	ColdFusion replacement for the HTML select tag; this automatically fills with query data

Table 12-2. *ColdFusion Form Elements*

CODING IN COLDFUSION

CF Tag	Attributes	Comment
cfslider	**name:** The name of the slider input **value:** The default value required; whether or not this attribute is required **range:** The minimum and maximum numbers that can be accepted, separated by a comma **label:** The label to display with the control **refreshlabel:** Yes or No, whether to refresh the label when the slider is moved **scale:** The scale of the slider; if the range is 1 to 100 and the scale is 10, then the display will display 0, 10, 20, 30, and so on up to 100 **onvalidate:** The name of a custom JavaScript function you want to call when validating data **message:** The message if validation fails **onerror:** A custom JavaScript function to call if validation fails **tickmarkmajor:** Yes or No, renders all major tickmarks on scale **tickmarkminor:** Yes or No, renders all minor tickmarks on scale **tickmarkimages:** A list of URLs that contain images for the labels **tickmarklabels:** A list of text that contains text for the labels **lookandfeel:** Accepts motif, windows, or metal **vertical:** If yes, renders slider vertically **notsupported:** The message to display if the applet is not supported	For creating a slider that will allow you to choose a number
cftextinput	**name:** The name of the text input **value:** The default value required; whether or not this attribute is required **range:** The minimum and maximum numbers that can be accepted, separated by a comma **validate:** Will validate data input based on date, eurodate, time, float, integer, telephone, zipcode, creditcard, social_security_number, or regular_expression **onvalidate:** The name of a custom JavaScript function you want to call when validating data **message:** The message if validation fails **onerror:** A custom JavaScript function to call if validation fails **size:** The size of the box **maxlength:** The maximum length of the box **notsupported:** The message to display if the applet is not supported	For creating a text box

Table 12-2. *ColdFusion Form Elements* (continued)

CF Tag	Attributes	Comment
cftree	**name:** The name of the text input **required:** A yes or no value stating whether this will be required **delimiter:** The list separator in the variable path **completepath:** Yes or No, passes the root level of the path **appendkey:** Yes or No, passes cftreeitemkey value along with value of selected tree item **highlighthref:** Yes or No, highlights links associated with a URL **onvalidate:** The name of a custom JavaScript function you want to call when validating data **message:** The message if validation fails **onerror:** A custom JavaScript function to call if validation fails **lookandfeel:** Accepts motif, windows, or metal **border:** Yes or No, to display border **hscroll:** Yes or No, display horizontal scroll bar **vscroll:** Yes or No, display vertical scroll bar **notsupported:** The message to display if the applet is not supported	Displays a tree hierarchy of information
cftreeitem	**value:** The value of the current item **display:** The label of the current item **parent:** The parent of the current item **img:** To specify a custom image, put the location and filename of the image; to use included images, select CD, computer, document, element, folder, floppy, fixed, or remote **imgopen:** The open tree item icon **href:** The URL to associate with the tree item **target:** The target to launch the URL in **query:** The query name that generates data for this item **queryasroot:** Yes or No, to define the query as a root level **expand:** Yes or No, expands the tree to show children	Populates a cftree

Table 12-2.   *ColdFusion Form Elements* (continued)

CODING IN COLDFUSION

CF Tag	Attributes	Comment
cfgrid	**name:** The name of the text input **query:** The query associated with the grid row **insert:** Yes or No, user can insert a row **delete:** Yes or No, user can delete a row **href:** If the grid is from a query, then this is a query column; otherwise it is a URL **hrefkey:** Name of key query column **target:** If href is a URL, the target **appendkey:** Yes or No; if yes, passes selected tree item in the query string of the URL **rowheaders:** Yes or No, displays numeric row headers **colheaders:** Yes or No, displays column headers **selectmode:** This value should be Edit, single, row, column, or browse **picturebar:** Yes or No, displays images for insert, delete, and sort **insertbutton:** Text of the Insert button **deletebutton:** Text of the Delete button **sortascendingbutton:** Text of the Sort button **sortdescendingbutton:** Text of the Sort button **notsupported:** The message to display if the applet is not supported	Used to present data in a table format
cfgridcolumn	**name:** The column name **header:** The text for the column header **width:** The width of the column, in pixels **href:** If the grid is from a query, then this is a query column; otherwise it is a URL **hrefkey:** Name of key query column **target:** If href is a URL, the target **select:** Yes or No, allows user to select the column **display:** Yes or no, if no hides the column **type:** The type of column; can be an image, numeric, Boolean, or string_nocase **values:** A comma-separated list to make this field a drop-down list **valuesdisplay:** Maps elements of drop-down list to string display **valuesdelimiter:** Delimiters used in values and valuedisplay fields	Used to specify a column in the grid
cfgridrow	**data:** A comma-separated list of column values	Used to specify a row in the grid

Table 12-2. *ColdFusion Form Elements* (continued)

placed inside ColdFusion's special cfform tag. These are the attributes for ColdFusion's cfform tag:

- **name** Contains the name of the form and is identical to the attribute of the CFML form tag.

- **action**   Is identical to the HTML action attribute. It can be either post or get.

- **preservedata**   Accepts either of two values, yes or no. If you are submitting a form onto itself, this attribute will tell the ColdFusion form tags whether or not to retain their values. This works on cfinput, cfslider, cftextinput, cftree, and cfselect. If set to no, then the values are reset.

- **onsubmit**   Allows you to call a JavaScript function when the form is submitted. It accepts the name of the JavaScript function. This is the same as the onsubmit attribute in the HTML form tag.

- **target**   Specifies the name of the window where the information is sent.

- **enctype**   Specifies the encryption type that will be placed onto the form before the information is submitted. This is identical to the form enctype attribute.

- **passthrough**   Allows you to specify additional attributes that aren't inherently specified otherwise.

- **codebase**   Contains the location of the downloadable JRE plug-in.

- **archive**   Contains the location for downloading Java classes for ColdFusion functions.

ColdFusion offers specialized versions of text boxes and the select boxes. It also offers Java applet form elements, including cfgrid, which is like a spreadsheet table; cfapplet, which will display custom applets registered in the ColdFusion Administrator; cftree, to display items in a tree-like structure; and cfslider, to provide a sliding control to select values.

Creating a Form

There are two pages that make any form work: an input page and a processing page. This section steps you through the process of creating each page, while building an interface to make a new item in the database we generated in Chapter 9.

Creating the Input Page

First, we will examine the database tables. We have four tables: Brand, Product, ProductCategory, and ProductPrice. You can see the table structure in Figure 12-1.

We are going to create a page that allows us to create a new product. There are five fields in the Product table:

- **ProductID**   The primary key for this table. This is generated automatically.
- **ProductName**   The name of the product.
- **ProductPriceID**   The foreign key relating to the ProductPrice table.
- **BrandID**   The foreign key relating to the Brand table.
- **ProductCategoryID**   The foreign key relating to the ProductCategory table.

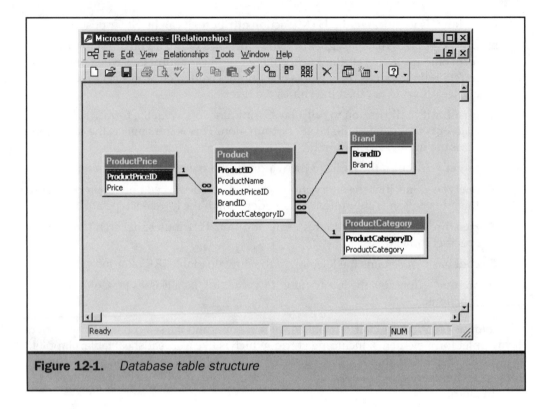

Figure 12-1. *Database table structure*

Since the ProductID is generated automatically, we only need to accept user input for the four remaining items. We could implement them all as text boxes, but it would be hard for an end user to input proper data into the ID fields. A much better way is to have the user view the text that the ID refers to. They choose the text value, but we get the ID value. This can be implemented using queries and select tags. This is how we can create our finished form:

1. Create a blank document, in your CFML editor of choice. Enter your documentation header. Save the file as **Producti.cfm**.

2. Create three queries, one to get the product prices, one to get the brands, and one to get the categories:

```
<!--- query to get the Brands --->
<cfquery name="GetBrands" datasource="Chapter12">
 SELECT Brand.*
 FROM Brand
 ORDER BY Brand.Brand
</cfquery>
```

```
<!--- query to get the Prices --->
<cfquery name="GetPrices" datasource="Chapter12">
 SELECT ProductPrice.*
 FROM ProductPrice
 ORDER BY ProductPrice.Price
</cfquery>


<!--- query to get the Categories--->
<cfquery name="GetCategory" datasource="Chapter12">
 SELECT ProductCategory.*
 FROM ProductCategory
 ORDER BY ProductCategory.ProductCategory
</cfquery>
```

3. Add the open form tag to start creating your form:

```
<form action="Productp.cfm" method="post">
```

4. Add the product name to your form:

```
Product Name: <input type="Text" name="ProductName"><br>
```

5. Create the select boxes for Brand, Price, and Category. To do this, start by creating the select tag named BrandID. Within the open and close select tags, use cfoutput to loop over the GetBrands query. Create option tags, with the value being the BrandID and the display text being Brand. The code should look like this:

```
Brand:
<select name="BrandID">
  <cfoutput query="GetBrands">
   <option value="#GetBrands.BrandID#">#GetBrands.Brand#
  </cfoutput>
</select>
```

| Tip | *As you are developing, remember to scope your variables. In this case, they are scoped to match the query.* |

6. Repeat Step 5 for the GetPrices and GetCategory query:

```
Price:
 <select name="ProductPriceID">
  <cfoutput query="GetPrices">
   <option value="#GetPrices.ProductPriceID#">#GetPrices.Price#
  </cfoutput>
 </select>
 <br>
```

```
Category:
<select name="ProductCategoryID">
 <cfoutput query="GetCategory">
  <option value="#GetCategory.ProductCategoryID#">
    #GetCategory.ProductCategory#
 </cfoutput>
</select>
<br><br>
```

7. Add the Submit button and end form tag:

```
<input type="Submit">
</form>
```

8. Add your close form tag, and you have a fully functional form. Load it in the browser.

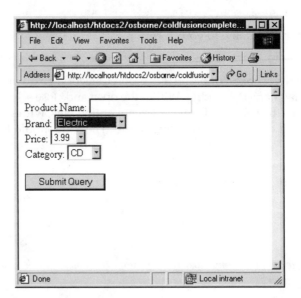

Creating the Processing Page

Creating the input form is half of the battle. The next step is to create the page that processes the form, productp.cfm. ColdFusion creates a form scope that contains all the variables that were submitted in the form. Here is how you can create your processing page:

1. Create a blank document in your favorite CFML editor. Enter your documentation header. You will be expecting four form variables to be defined when you execute this page. Save the file as **Productp.cfm**.

2. Create your insert query. You learned how to do this in Chapter 9. Here is the query:

```
<cfquery datasource="Chapter12">
 INSERT INTO Product (ProductName, ProductPriceID,
                      BrandID, ProductCategoryID)
 VALUES ('#Form.ProductName#',#form.ProductPriceID#,
         #form.BrandID# ,#form.ProductCategoryID#)
</cfquery>
```

3. Add a message confirming the insert, and save the file.

4. Load the input page. Enter some data, click the Submit button, and check the database for the new record.

Creating and Updating Data with Forms and ColdFusion

This section shows you how to use forms in conjunction with cfinsert and cfupdate. These tags take a form's submission and uses it to create new data, or update existing data, respectively. The discussion can start with the cfinsert tag.

Creating a New Database Record with cfinsert

The cfinsert tag takes a form's submission data and inserts it into the specified table of a database. These are the attributes of the cfinsert tag:

- **datasource** The name of the datasource that you want to insert into. This is required.

- **tablename** The name of the table that you want to create a new record in. This is required.

- **tableowner** This contains the table owner, for data sources that support table ownership, such as SQL Server or Oracle.

- **tablequalifier** This contains the table qualifier, if relevant to the database you are using.

- **username** The username, if needed, to access the datasource.

- **password** The password, if needed, to access the datasource.

- **formfields** An optional list of form fields that will be inserted into the table. If this attribute is left out, then all fields are inserted.

To create the input page, we can use the one from the previous example. The processing page replaces the query with the cfinsert tag. This is the tag that we use:

```
<cfinsert datasource="Chapter12"
          formfields="ProductName, ProductPriceID, BrandID,
```

```
                              ProductCategoryID"
             tablename="Product">
```

In the cfinsert tag, we specify the datasource, the list of form fields, and the name of the table that we are inserting into.

Tip *Although it isn't required, I find that I always have the best results when I specify values for the formfield attribute.*

Updating a Database Record with cfupdate

The last thing to examine in this chapter is the cfupdate tag. The cfupdate tag is very similar to the cfinsert tag, except its purpose is to update an existing record instead of creating a new one. This section demonstrates how it works.

Creating the Input Page

The first step is to create our update page, to update an existing record. This would be a good place to use URL variables. First, we can make a page that displays a list of all records, and then we will link to the form update page.

This is how we can create the page that displays all records:

1. Create a blank page in your favorite CFML editor. Add your header documentation. Save it as **Products.cfm**.

2. Create a query to get all the ProductName and ProductID fields in the database:

```
<cfquery datasource="Chapter12" name="GetProducts">
 SELECT Product.ProductID, Product.ProductName
 FROM Product
 ORDER BY Product.ProductName
</cfquery>
```

3. Use cfoutput to loop over the query. For each element, create a link to the next page in our process, Productu.cfm. Pass the ProductID as a URL variable:

```
<cfoutput query="GetProducts">
 <a href="Productu.cfm?ProductID=#GetProducts.ProductID#">
  #GetProducts.ProductName#
 </a><br>
</cfoutput>
```

Believe it or not, creating the page to display all the products was that easy. These three steps are the start of the drill-down interface.

The next step is to flush the Productu.cfm page. This page will be very similar to the producti.cfm page, with one important difference: It will be filled with data, instead of being blank.

Here is how we can create it:

1. Create a blank page in your favorite CFML editor. Add your header documentation. This page will be expecting the ProductID to be defined when executed. Save it as **Productsu.cfm**.

2. Create a query to retrieve all the product information:

```
<cfquery name="GetProduct" datasource="Chapter12">
 SELECT Product.*
 FROM Product
 WHERE Product.ProductID = #url.ProductID#
</cfquery>
```

   This query does not have to be complicated; it is just a straightforward SQL select. We follow this by three queries to get the Brand, Price, and Category data. These queries have not changed from our new page creation form.

3. We want to add a new attribute to the form. We need to be able to pass the ProductID from one template to the next. We can do this using a hidden form field:

```
<input type="hidden" name="ProductID"
       value="<cfoutput>#GetProduct.ProductID#</cfoutput>">
```

   The hidden form field will pass the ProductID as a form element without displaying it on the screen to the user.

4. The next step is to start to populate the form with the relevant data. We can add the value attribute to the ProductName text box:

```
Product Name:
<input type="Text" name="ProductName"
       value="<cfoutput>#GetProduct.ProductName#</cfoutput>"><br>
```

   We use the cfoutput tag to output the first ProductName returned from our GetProducts query. Since we were querying on the primary key, we can be assured that only one record was returned.

5. Next, we want to make sure that the select boxes select the current correct value for the brand, price, and category. We can do this using an if statement. If statements are discussed in more detail in Chapter 13. For now, you just need to understand that it is a way to make a decision in your code. If the current BrandID is equal to the BrandID of the product we are examining, then display the selected text to select the default value. This is the updated Brand select box code:

```
<select name="BrandID">
 <cfoutput query="GetBrands">
  <option value="#GetBrands.BrandID#"
          <cfif GetBrands.BrandID is GetProduct.BrandID>
```

```
          selected
        </cfif>>
  #GetBrands.Brand#
 </cfoutput>
</select>
```

Inside the option tag, we perform the conditional to decide if the GetBrands.BrandID is equal to the GetProduct.BrandID. We can perform similar actions for the ProductPriceID and ProductCategoryID:

```
<select name="ProductPriceID">
 <cfoutput query="GetPrices">
  <option value="#GetPrices.ProductPriceID#"
         <cfif GetPrices.ProductPriceID is
               GetProduct.ProductPriceID>
          selected
         </cfif>>
  #GetPrices.Price#
 </cfoutput>
</select>
<br>

<select name="ProductCategoryID">
 <cfoutput query="GetCategory">
  <option value="#GetCategory.ProductCategoryID#"
         <cfif GetCategory.ProductCategoryID is
               GetProduct.ProductCategoryID>
          selected
         </cfif>>
  #GetCategory.ProductCategory#
 </cfoutput>
</select>
```

6. You can save your document. Load it and it will look something like this:

Creating the Processing Page

The last step in creating our update pages is to create the processing page using the cfupdate tag. The cfupdate tag takes all form data that is passed into it and updates a database record. The primary key takes a form's submission data and inserts it into the specified table of a database.

The cfupdate tag has the exact same attributes as the cfinsert tag. The primary key field must be specified in the form, however, or ColdFusion will throw an error. This is how we will use it on the form processing page:

```
<cfupdate datasource="Chapter12"
          formfields="ProductID, ProductName, ProductPriceID,
                      BrandID, ProductCategoryID"
          tablename="Product">
```

Summary

In this chapter, you learned about the following:

- How to pass parameters via the URL
- HTML and CFML form tags
- How to create a form
- How to used cfupdate and cfinsert to maintain database records

The next chapter will examine conditional logic and demonstrate how to control your code.

The Complete Reference

ColdFusion MX

Chapter 13

Controlling Your ColdFusion Code

Much of the code that we have created before this chapter has been linear. The template executes from start to finish, top to bottom, without question. In the real world, many applications do not work that way. You will want to execute a section of code more than once, or perhaps not execute some code at all. This chapter will demonstrate the ways to make decisions in your code.

Making Decisions with Conditional Logic

The first type of code control logic that we are going to examine is called conditional logic. Conditional logic allows you to make decisions in your code. This section will examine conditional logic and tell you how to use it from within ColdFusion.

Understanding Conditional Logic

Conditional logic is a way to make decisions. You make decisions every day, whether it is choosing the numbers on a lottery ticket, deciding to call in sick to work and go to a beach, or having chocolate cake for lunch instead of salad. Conditional logic is a way to put these decisions into a cause and effect format. The cause is the condition, your choice. The effect is the action that takes place because your condition became true. In conditional logic, you can also perform a different action if that condition did not become true.

These are some examples of where conditional logic might come into play:

- If you win the lottery, you will quit your job; otherwise, you will keep working.
- If the car breaks down, you will be late for the appointment; otherwise, you will be on time.
- If you sleep late, you will miss the sunrise; otherwise, you will see it.

The places where conditionals come into play are endless. These are some web-based examples:

- If the form information verifies correctly, then process the form; otherwise, ask the user for corrected input.
- If the database query returns records, display them; otherwise, do nothing.
- If the user is logged in, show them the information; otherwise, send them to the login screen.

The basis for all ColdFusion conditional logic is Boolean logic. We talked about Boolean logic in Chapter 8, when covering ColdFusion expressions. Boolean operators and decision operators can be used in conditional statements. Table 13-1 contains ColdFusion's Boolean and decision operators.

Operator	Expression Type	Use	Order of Operations
IS EQ EQUAL	Decision	Performs a case-insensitive comparison and returns true if the values are identical.	Eighth
IS NOT NEQ NOT EQUAL	Decision	Performs a case-insensitive comparison and returns false if the values are identical.	Eighth
CONTAINS	Decision	If the value on the left is contained in the value on the right, returns true.	Eighth
DOES NOT CONTAIN	Decision	If the value on the left is contained in the value on the right, returns false.	Eighth
GREATER THAN GT	Decision	If the value on the left is greater than the one on the right, returns true.	Eighth
LESS THAN LT	Decision	If the value on the left is greater than the one on the right, returns false.	Eighth
GREATER THAN OR EQUAL TO GTE GE	Decision	If the value on the left is greater than the value on the right, returns true.	Eighth
LESS THAN OR EQUAL TO LTE LE	Decision	If the value on the left is greater than the value on the right, returns false.	Eighth
NOT	Boolean	If the condition is true, then it becomes false. If the condition is false, then it becomes true.	Ninth
AND	Boolean	If both conditions are true, the result is true; otherwise, the result is false.	Tenth

Table 13-1.   *Boolean and Decision Operators*

Operator	Expression Type	Use	Order of Operations
OR	Boolean	If both conditions are false, the result is false; otherwise, the result is true.	Eleventh
XOR	Boolean	If both conditions are true or both conditions are false, the result is false. If one condition is true and one condition is false, the result is true.	Twelfth
EQV	Boolean	If both conditions are true, or both values are false, the result is true. If one condition is true and the other is false, the result is false.	Thirteenth
IMP	Boolean	If the first condition is true and the second is false, the result is false. Otherwise, the result is true.	Fourteenth

Table 13-1. *Boolean and Decision Operators* (continued)

Choosing the Tags of Conditional Logic

There are two different tags that are used to implement conditional logic in ColdFusion: the cfif tag and the cfswitch tag. The cfif tag is good when you have a limited number of options. The cfswitch tag excels when you are checking a single variable for many potential values.

Making Decisions with cfif, cfelse, and cfelseif

The most common conditional statement is the cfif statement. If the specified condition is true, then ColdFusion will perform certain actions. This is the format for a cfif statement:

```
<cfif expression>
  Perform Actions
</cfif>
```

The cfif tag needs an open and close tag, with the actions residing in between. The only attribute to the cfif tag is an expression. While the most common expressions to use here are Boolean or decision expressions, as previously discussed, you can use any ColdFusion expression. If the expression is 0, false, or no, then the condition is considered false. Anything else will return a true value.

There are many times when you want to perform a default action, if the original action returns false. ColdFusion provides that functionality in the form of the cfelse tag. You can only use one cfelse within the cfif block:

```
<cfif expression>
 Perform Actions
<cfelse>
 Perform Other Actions
</cfif>
```

The cfelse tag does not have any attributes or expressions.

The cfelseif tag is designed to allow you to make more decisions within a cfif block. If expression1 is true, then action1 is performed, or else if expression2 is true, then action2 is performed, or else action3 is performed. It is set up like this:

```
<cfif expression>
 Perform Actions
<cfelseif expression>
 Perform Other Actions
<cfelse>
 Perform Default Actions
</cfif>
```

You can have as many cfelseif tags as you need, so long as they become before the cfelse tag.

We can examine a real-world example of the cfif tag. Suppose we were trying to verify a form. Two fields are required: an E-mail field, named Email, and a password field, named PWord. Before we try to process the form processing page, most likely a database insert, we want to make sure that both of these fields are defined, and present the user with an error if they are not. We can use the IsDefined function to check for the variable's existence:

```
<cfif (NOT IsDefined("form.Email")) OR
      (NOT IsDefined("form.PWord"))>
  Warning! There was a problem.
<cfelse>
```

```
 Perform form processing
</cfif>
```

We want to check to see if the variable exists or not. We do this by using the IsDefined function, which returns a Boolean value, and then reversing its condition with the NOT operator. We can expand on this more to provide a detailed error message:

```
<cfif (NOT IsDefined("form.Email")) OR
      (NOT IsDefined("form.PWord"))>

  Warning, these variables: <br>
 <cfif NOT IsDefined("form.Email")>
  form.Email
 </cfif>
 <cfif NOT IsDefined("form.PWord")>
  form.Email
 </cfif>
 <br>were not defined

<cfelse>
 Perform form processing
</cfif>
```

Here we are using a nested if statement, which means that one if statement is located inside another. You can nest if statements as much as needed. However, too much nesting can make the code hard to read or follow.

It is good to note here that ColdFusion will use short-circuit evaluation in Boolean conditions. In an AND statement, if the first value is equal to false, the result will be false, and there is no need to process the second value. In an OR value, if the first value is true, the whole expression will result to true, and there is no need to process the second value. ColdFusion knows this and processes the conditions as such.

Choosing from Many Options with cfswitch, cfcase, and cfdefaultcase

If you want to perform different actions based on a value of a specific variable, it can become inefficient to use the cfif statement. Examine this example:

```
<cfif variables.Car IS "Dodge">
 Perform Dodge Actions
<cfelseif variables.Car IS "Honda">
```

```
  Perform Honda Actions
<cfelseif variables.Car IS "Toyota">
  Perform Toyota Actions
<cfelseif variables.Car IS "BMW">
  Perform BMW Actions
<cfelse>
  Perform Unknown Actions
</cfif>
```

While the preceding code is easy enough to read, it has to go through many choices, therefore performing many comparison operations before finding BMW, or an undefined action. Case statements are designed to help speed the process. ColdFusion provides us with two tags, cfswitch and cfcase, to perform case statements.

There are two primary portions to a case statement: the switch and the case. The switch is the value that you are checking against. The case is the group of actions that are performed if the switch value is equal to the case value.

The cfswitch tag only has one attribute: expression. It will accept any valid expression as a value. The cfcase tag has two attributes: value and delimiter. The value attribute contains a list of potential values for the expression result defined in the cfswitch tag. The delimiter attribute is the character used to separate multiple values in the value attribute.

This is how we put it all together:

```
<!--- start the cfswitch tag --->
<cfswitch expression="#variables.Car#">

  <!--- Check the Dodge value --->
  <cfcase value="Dodge">
   Perform Dodge Actions
  </cfcase>

  <!--- Check the Honda value --->
  <cfcase value="Honda">
   Perform Honda Actions
  </cfcase>

  <!--- Check the Toyota value --->
  <cfcase value="Toyota">
   Perform Toyota Actions
  </cfcase>
```

```
<!--- Check the BMW value --->
<cfcase value="BMW">
 Perform BMW Actions
</cfcase>
</cfswitch>
```

After a close examination of this code, you might notice two things. First, the Car variable is not defined, so ColdFusion will cause an error when trying to run this code. Second, we have lost our default case.

 The value in a cfcase statement can contain a list, and the code will execute if any single item in the list is equal to the result of the cfswitch expression.

To handle the first issue, we can easily create the car variable with cfset or cfparam. In many real-world cases, we will be accessing the Car variable in the form or URL scopes, not as a local variable. To handle the second issue, ColdFusion provides us with cfdefaultcase. This is a tag with no parameters that must be used inside the cfswitch. Normally, you would want to place the cfdefaultcase tag block after all other cfcase statements. Once the cfdefaultcase is executed, all other cases after it will be ignored. This is our updated code with the cfdefault case in place:

```
<!--- start the cfswitch tag --->
<cfswitch expression="#variables.Car#">

 <!--- Check the Dodge value --->
 <cfcase value="Dodge">
  Perform Dodge Actions
 </cfcase>

 <!--- Check the Honda value --->
 <cfcase value="Honda">
  Perform Honda Actions
 </cfcase>

 <!--- Check the Toyota value --->
 <cfcase value="Toyota">
  Perform Toyota actions
 </cfcase>

 <!--- Check the BMW value --->
 <cfcase value="BMW">
```

```
   Perform BMW Actions
</cfcase>

<cfdefaultcase>
  Perform unknown actions
</cfdefaultcase>
</cfswitch>
```

The cfdefaultcase will be processed after all other cases.

Repeating Sections of Your Code

This section explains looping concepts and then describes the different types of loops that are available in ColdFusion. First, we examine looping concepts and demonstrate some examples of where loops are useful in programming. Then, we demonstrate how to use loops in ColdFusion.

Understanding Loops

A loop is a way to repeat a specific section of code a certain number of times. A loop is similar to a racetrack. You start at one point, and travel a path until you get back to the point at which you started. The number of times the path is traveled before the loop, or race, is over is decided by the type of loop (or race) you are running. There are two main types of loops: index loops and conditional loops.

An index loop is a loop that will execute a specific number of times. There are some standard elements of an index loop:

- **index**   The index is a variable that keeps track of the current loop iteration. You must remember to increment this variable for each loop iteration, or the loop will never stop.
- **start**   The start value contains the number where the loop will start.
- **end**   The end value of the loop. When the index gets here, the loop stops.
- **step**   The step attribute contains the amount that the index will increment after each pass through the loop.

Index loops are great for performing mathematical operations and processing an array.

Note *You may have heard of index loops being referred to as for loops.*

Conditional loops are loops that will loop until a specific condition is met. There are two general types of conditional loops: while loops and repeat loops. The only difference is where the condition is checked. While loops check for the condition before the loop is executed, and repeat loops check for the condition after the loop is executed. A repeat loop will always execute a condition at least once. Conditional loops excel at advanced string processing.

ColdFusion does not support repeat loops in CFML, but you can achieve this functionality in cfscript, as we discuss in Chapter 15.

ColdFusion also has built-in loop types that will let you loop over a query or list. Since many of the variable scopes are stored internally as structures, this is especially handy when, for instance, you want to display all elements in the session scope.

Using Different Types of ColdFusion Loops

ColdFusion provides a tag designed strictly for looping purposes: cfloop. There are three main types of loops available in ColdFusion: index loops, collection loops, and conditional loops. The attributes to the cfloop tag change depending upon the type of loop that you are looping over. We will examine them all.

Index Loops

There are four attributes that the cfloop tag will use to perform an index loop. They are parallels of the four elements of an index loop:

- **index** The index is the name of the variable that will contain the current iteration of the loop.
- **from** The from variable is the initial value of the index.
- **to** The to variable is the final value of the index.
- **step** The step value contains the increment of the index for each loop iteration. The default step is 1.

Let's look at some examples.

You can use an index loop to loop a specific number of times. This will loop five times:

```
<cfloop index="TempIndex" from="1" to="5">
 <cfoutput>
  #TempIndex#,
 </cfoutput>
</cfloop>
```

The output from this will be 1, 2, 3, 4, 5. We can also use an index loop to count down backward:

```
<cfloop index="TempIndex" from="5" to="1" step="-1">
 <cfoutput>
  #TempIndex#,
 </cfoutput>
</cfloop>
```

By assigning the step to a negative number, the output will be 5, 4, 3, 2, 1.

You might want to use an index loop to loop over an array:

```
<cfloop index="ArrayIndex" from="1" to="#arraylen(testarray)#">
 <cfoutput>
  #TestArray[ArrayIndex]#<br>
 </cfoutput>
</cfloop>
```

The output of this will depend on how many elements are in the array and what the elements are.

Conditional Loops

Conditional loops are used to repeat a certain section of code until a specific condition has been met. In CFML, there is a single attribute, condition, that specifies when the loop will end. The value of this attribute is any ColdFusion expression.

Conditional loops are most commonly used for string processing. Here is an example that will loop over a string and return a list of all the ASCII values of the characters in it:

```
<!--- set up some default variables --->
<cfset TempString = "This is a Test String">
<cfset AsciiList = "">

<!--- start the loop --->
<cfloop condition="Len(TempString) GT 0">
 <!--- Add to the Ascii List --->
 <cfset AsciiList = ListAppend(AsciiList,Asc(TempString))>

 <!--- Remove the first character from the string,
       or blank it out if there is only one character left --->
 <cfif (Len(TempString) GT 1)>
  <cfset TempString =  right(TempString, Len(TempString)-1)>
 <cfelse>
  <cfset TempString = "">
 </cfif>
</cfloop>
```

The code starts by setting some variables: the string we want to process and the result list. We loop until the TempString variable is empty. We use the Asc function to pick the ASCII value of the first character in the TempString variable. The value is appended to the AsciiList result variable. The conditional before the end of the loop removes the first character from the TempString, so the next time through the loop, the next character will be processed.

Collection Loops

A collection is a COM object or a structure. There are two attributes that allow cfloop to cycle over one of these:

- **collection**   The collection attribute is the name of the COM object or structure that you want to loop over.

- **item**   The item is a variable name that will contain the current item you are looping through. For a structure, it contains the current key; for a COM object, it contains the properties.

Since many of the variable scopes are stored internally as structures, you can loop over them using this type of loop. The following loop displays all the session variables, and I use it commonly for debugging:

```
<cfloop collection=#session# item="TempKey">
 <cfoutput>
  #TempKey# #session[TempKey]#
 </cfoutput><br>
</cfloop>
```

The preceding code will output the name of the session variable and its value.

Looping over a Query

There are two ways to loop over a query: with cfloop and with cfoutput. Chapter 9 briefly explained how to use cfoutput to loop over a query. This section examines that technique in more detail and describes how we can perform similar things with cfloop.

The attributes to loop over a query with cfoutput are the following:

- **query**   The query attribute is the name of the query you want to loop over.
- **startrows**   The startrows attribute contains the first row of the query you want to display.
- **maxrows**   The maxrows attribute contains the maximum number of rows you want to display from the query.
- **group**   The group attribute is the name of a column that you are grouping against. Grouping in SQL will be discussed in Chapter 21.
- **groupcasesensitive**   The groupcasesensitive attribute accepts a yes or no value, distinguishing whether or not to group in a case-sensitive manner.

The following are the attributes for looping over a query with cfloop:

- **query**   The name of the query that you want to loop over
- **startrow**   The row that you want to start looping at
- **endrow**   The row that you want to end looping at

Looping with cfoutput is great if you need to use the group attribute, or need to output the value. Looping with cfloop is good for processing the data or when you need to loop over a query inside a cfoutput block. You don't normally use cfloop strictly to output data, because then you will need an additional cfoutput tag, which makes the templates less efficient, because there are two more tags to process (the begin and end cfoutputs).

Start with the query from the previous chapter:

```
<cfquery datasource="Chapter12" name="GetProducts">
 SELECT Product.ProductID, Product.ProductName
 FROM Product
 ORDER BY Product.ProductName
</cfquery>
```

We already know how to output this data using cfoutput:

```
<cfoutput query="GetProducts">
 #GetProducts.ProductID#, #GetProducts.ProductName#<br>
</cfoutput>
```

We can also loop over the data with cfloop:

```
<cfloop query="GetProducts">
 <cfoutput>
  #GetProducts.ProductID#, #GetProducts.ProductName#<br>
 </cfoutput>
</cfloop>
```

Both blocks of code perform the same action.

Looping over Lists

The final type of looping that we want to examine is how to loop over a list. There are three parameters that allow us to do this:

- **index**   The variable that contains the current list element.
- **list**   The list that you are looping over.
- **delimiters**   The delimiters for the list that you are looping over. The default is a comma.

CODING IN COLDFUSION

The ability to loop over a list is good for list processing. It would be ideal, for example, to process each element of a check box on a form processing page.

Here is an example:

```
<cfloop index="ListElement" list="1,2,5,4,6,7,9,8,10">
 <cfoutput>
  #ListElement#<br>
 </cfoutput>
</cfloop>
```

The output from this would be each list element on a single line:

```
1
2
5
4
6
7
9
8
10
```

Controlling Code with Other Tags

There are some other code control tags that exist in ColdFusion. They are usually used to interrupt the flow of normal execution. This section discusses the cfbreak, cfabort, and cfexit tags.

Using cfbreak

The cfbreak and cfexit tags are the two simplest tags to interrupt the flow of a template. The cfbreak tag is used specifically for loops. If you use it within a loop, it will cease processing the loop and continue execution of the code that resides after the end of the loop.

The cfabort tag is used mainly as a debugging tag, alongside cfoutput or cfdump. It accepts one attribute, called showerror. ColdFusion will return everything that was processed before the cfabort tag was run and the value of the showerror attribute. To debug with it, you can use cfoutput to output the variables that you want to see, and then use the cfabort tag to stop page processing. You can also use the cfdump tag to output specific variables.

Debugging ColdFusion pages is discussed in more detail in Chapter 18.

Using cfexit

The cfexit tag is the most complicated tag for interrupting the logic flow of an application. It can have different behavior depending on the value of its attribute or where the tag is called. The cfexit tag has one attribute, method. There are three different values for the method attribute: ExitTag, ExitTemplate, and Loop. Table 13-2 shows the various behaviors of the tag.

Value	Called From	Action
ExitTag	Inside a template	Aborts processing of the template; same as cfabort without the error message
	Inside a begin custom tag	Continues processing after the end tag
	Inside an end custom tag	Continues processing after the end tag
ExitTemplate	Inside a template	Aborts processing of the template; same as cfabort without the error message
	Inside a begin custom tag	Continues processing after the first child in the body
	Inside an end custom tag	Continues processing after the end tag
Loop	Inside a template	Throws an error
	Inside a begin custom tag	Throws an error
	Inside an end custom tag	Breaks out of the current tag and continues processing after the tag is called

Table 13-2. *Behavior of the cfexit Tag*

Summary

In this chapter, you learned about the following:

- Conditional logic
- Looping in ColdFusion
- Alternate forms of controlling page flow logic

The next chapter will discuss migrating applications from past versions of ColdFusion to ColdFusion MX.

Chapter 14

Migrating Your Applications to ColdFusion MX

M any of you reading this book likely have had experience with previous versions of ColdFusion. If you are wondering what problems you might run into as you move your applications from ColdFusion 5 to ColdFusion MX, then this is the chapter for you.

Changes in ColdFusion MX

ColdFusion MX is the biggest release of ColdFusion since its inception many years ago. Along with the array of new features, ColdFusion MX has gone through some natural growing pains. Some features are no longer needed and thus removed, while others are changed or modified. This section talks about the changes to the CFML language.

Discontinuing Deprecated Tags and Functions

Coding in CFML is, perhaps, where ColdFusion developers spend the bulk of their time. Knowing what tags are no longer in use can save you debugging time. Knowing what tags are deprecated in favor of a new tag is also helpful. This section illustrates the changes.

Deprecated tags still work in this version of the software, but will probably cease to work in future versions. Obsolete tags are removed from this version of the software altogether. Table 14-1 lists and describes the deprecated and obsolete tags. Table 14-2 shows all the deprecated or obsolete functions.

Tag	Status	Description
cfauthenticate	Obsolete	ColdFusion MX uses a different security model than previous versions of ColdFusion. This is discussed in Chapter 17.
cfimpersonate	Obsolete	ColdFusion MX uses a different security model than previous versions of ColdFusion. This is discussed in Chapter 17.
cfgraph	Deprecated	Use the cfchart, cfchartdata, and cfchartseries tags instead. We discuss these tags in Chapter 20.
cfgraphdata	Deprecated	Use the cfchart, cfchartdata, and cfchartseries tags instead. We discuss these tags in Chapter 20.

Table 14-1. *Deprecated and Obsolete ColdFusion Tags*

Tag	Status	Description
cfregistry	Deprecated in Unix	The registry concept does not apply to Unix machines as it does to a Windows machine. Instead of using cfregistry, store information in a client variable, a text file, a database, or an LDAP file.
cfservlet	Deprecated	This can only call servlets created in JRUN 3.1 or earlier.
cfservletparam	Deprecated	This can only call servlets created in JRUN 3.1 or earlier.

Table 14-1.   *Deprecated and Obsolete ColdFusion Tags* (continued)

CODING IN COLDFUSION

If you are using any of these tags or functions in your existing ColdFusion applications, then you need to rewrite that code to use an alternate method of achieving your goal.

In addition to the removal of some tags and functions, there are some attributes in tags that have been deprecated. Table 14-3 lists and describes attributes that have been deprecated in tags.

Function	Status	Description
AuthenticatedContext( )	Obsolete	ColdFusion MX uses a new security model, as discussed in Chapter 17.
AuthenticatedUser( )	Obsolete	ColdFusion MX uses a new security model, as discussed in Chapter 17.
IsAuthenticated( )	Obsolete	ColdFusion MX uses a new security model, as discussed in Chapter 17.
IsAuthorized( )	Obsolete	ColdFusion MX uses a new security model, as discussed in Chapter 17.
IsProtected( )	Obsolete	ColdFusion MX uses a new security model, as discussed in Chapter 17.

Table 14-2.   *Deprecated and Obsolete ColdFusion Functions*

Tag	Attribute	Value	Description
cfapplication	clientstorage	registry	Obsolete on Unix versions of ColdFusion
cfdirectory	sort	temporary	No longer supported on Windows units
cferror	type	monitor	Obsolete
cfform	enablecab	N/A	Deprecated, do not use
cfinsert	dbtype	dynamic	Obsolete, do not use
cfinsert	dbserver	N/A	Obsolete
cfinsert	dbname	N/A	Obsolete
cfinsert	connectstring	N/A	Obsolete
cfinsert	provider	N/A	Obsolete
cfinsert	providerdsn	N/A	Obsolete
cfgridupdate	dbtype	dynamic	Obsolete, do not use
cfquery	dbtype	dynamic	Obsolete, do not use
cfquery	dbserver	N/A	Obsolete
cfquery	dbname	N/A	Obsolete
cfquery	connectstring	N/A	Obsolete
cfquery	provider	N/A	Obsolete
cfquery	providerdsn	N/A	Obsolete
cfupdate	dbtype	dynamic	Obsolete, do not use
cfupdate	dbserver	N/A	Obsolete
cfupdate	dbname	N/A	Obsolete
cfupdate	connectstring	N/A	Obsolete
cfupdate	provider	N/A	Obsolete
cfupdate	providerdsn	N/A	Obsolete
cfstoredproc	dbtype	dynamic	Obsolete, do not use

Table 14-3. *ColdFusion Tags with Obsolete Attributes*

Tag	Attribute	Value	Description
cflog	thread	N/A	Deprecated; if set to No, ColdFusion will throw an error
cflog	date	N/A	Deprecated; if set to No, ColdFusion will throw an error
cflog	time	N/A	Deprecated; if set to No, ColdFusion will throw an error
cfprocparam	maxrows	N/A	Obsolete; use cfprocresult instead
cfsetting	catchexceptionsbypattern	N/A	Attribute is obsolete

Table 14-3.   *ColdFusion Tags with Obsolete Attributes* (continued)

Changes in Tags and Functions

There are many functions and tags that were modified in ColdFusion MX. Some have deprecated attributes, as discussed in the previous section. Others have modified or expanded functionality. Table 14-4 lists and describes the tags with changes.

Tag	Attribute	Value	Description
cfapplet	N/A		Can now be used outside of the cfform tag.
cfcache	N/A	N/A	The Cfcache.map file contains the template name and timestamp of the source.
cfcache	timespan	N/A	This new attribute defines the number of days between the page being cached and the cache being flushed.

Table 14-4.   *Modified ColdFusion Tags*

Tag	Attribute	Value	Description
cfcache	action	Cache	Caches on both the server and client. In past versions it would only cache on the server.
cfcache	action	Optimal	Same as cache.
cfcache	action	ServerCache	The page caches on the server; this is the behavior that used to be exhibited by giving the value cache.
cfcache	action	Flush	Expires the cache on the server and the client.
cfcache	port	N/A	Now defaults to the value used to access the page. In CF5, it defaulted to 80.
cfcache	protocol	N/A	Now defaults to the value used to access the page. In CF5, it defaulted to HTTP.
cfcatch	N/A	N/A	No longer catches function validation errors.
cfcatch	N/A	Cfcatch.message	Returns a different SQLstate for Type IV database drivers. Gets current values every time an error is thrown. To retain old values, create a new message or variable.
cfcol	header	Empty	If used with cftable colheader, then true will be displayed in the column header.
cftable	colheader	any	If used with cftable colheader, then true will be displayed in the column header.
cfcollection	action	N/A	This attribute is optional, with the default value being list.
cfcollection	name	N/A	Provides a name for the queried results. Required when action is –list.
cfdirectory	N/A	N/A	No longer returns rows for "." and ".." in Windows machines.

Table 14-4. *Modified ColdFusion Tags* (continued)

Tag	Attribute	Value	Description
cfdirectory	action	list	On Unix, only reports readonly and hidden attributes.
cfform	preservedata	Yes	Checked values of checkboxes or radio buttons are ignored.
cfhttp	N/A	N/A	Response headers will now be returned without changing to uppercase or sorting the headers. ColdFusion 5 returned headers alphabetically in all uppercase.
cfhttp	N/A	N/A	Status code: 200 is followed by Ok instead of SUCCESS.
cfhttp	timeout	N/A	Requires JDK 1.4, otherwise ignored.
cfindex	key	N/A	Query Attribute, type="File", and type="Path" can now be used with actions that require key attribute.
cfquery	N/A	N/A	Disallows use of unescaped reserved words in a query of a query.
cfquery	timeout	N/A	Measures timeout value in seconds instead of milliseconds.
cfldap	sort	N/A	Now triggers a server-side sort, not a client-side sort. Use query of a query to perform client-side sorting.
cfldap	action	query	When used with dn in the list of attributes, returns each distinguished name with a comma, followed by a space. CF5 did not return values in a consistent format.
cfldap	referral	N/A	Returns the name of the server before the results.
cfloop	N/A	N/A	Structure keys are returned in the order they were created. StructSort and StructKeySort can be used to sort a structure.

Table 14-4.   *Modified ColdFusion Tags* (continued)

Tag	Attribute	Value	Description
cfmail	N/A	N/A	Undelivered mail is structured differently.
cfparam	N/A	N/A	Complex variables will no longer be assigned to the client scope, which only supports simple values.
cfprocparam	dbvarname	N/A	Is ignored for all drivers.
cfregistry	N/A	N/A	On Windows machines, a lot of information, such as the mail root or verify collection information, is no longer stored in the Registry.
cfreport	N/A	N/A	No longer manages a data connection to crystal reports. It just passes the datasource, username, and password information to the Crystal Reports server and lets it handle it.
cfswitch	N/A	N/A	All code inside a cfswitch must reside within a cfcase or cfdefaultcase.

Table 14-4.   *Modified ColdFusion Tags* (continued)

In ColdFusion MX, in addition to the changes to some of the tags, some functionality changes have occurred within ColdFusion functions. Table 14-5 describes the changes.

Function	Description
ArrayAvg	ColdFusion MX returns 0 when used on an empty array; ColdFusion 5 returns infinity (1.#INF).
ArrayMin	ColdFusion MX returns 0 when used on an empty array; ColdFusion 5 returns infinity (1.#INF).
ArrayMax	ColdFusion MX returns 0 when used on an empty array; ColdFusion 5 returns infinity (1.#INF).

Table 14-5.   *ColdFusion Function Modifications*

Function	Description
ArraySum	ColdFusion MX returns 0 when used on an empty array; ColdFusion 5 returns infinity (1.#INF).
DateDiff	ColdFusion 5 incorrectly calculates a negative difference; for example, the difference between 9:23:30 and 9:22:30 would be –59 seconds. ColdFusion MX corrects this.
DateFormat	ColdFusion MX cannot parse dates in the format of month day, year hour am.
DeleteClientVariables	ColdFusion MX returns false if a variable does not exist. ColdFusion 5 would ignore the function call.
GetBaseTagList	ColdFusion MX returns prefixed custom tags with the format prefix:tag.
GetLocale	If the locale has not been specifically set, ColdFusion MX returns the default locale of the client OS. ColdFusion 5 returned English(US) as the default locale.
GetTempDirectory	ColdFusion MX returns the temporary directory for the Java Application Server instead of the Windows default directory.
IsArray	ColdFusion MX returns true for a query column.
IsDateFormat	If no mask is specified, ColdFusion returns the date in the format of the current locale.
IsTimeFormat	ColdFusion MX supports these masks: h:m:s hh:mm:ss hh:mm:ss:t hh:mm:ss:tt
IsWDDX	ColdFusion MX returns no for complex variables. ColdFusion 5 would return an error.
Len	ColdFusion MX continues processing after an ASCII 0 (NUL) character. ColdFusion 5 would stop.
ListSetAt	ColdFusion MX no longer changes the first delimiter in the list to the first delimiter specified in the function.
ListSort	In a descending textnocase sort, ColdFusion MX returns the elements in a different order than ColdFusion 5. Both are correct because, in a no case sort, apple is equal to APPLE.

Table 14-5.   *ColdFusion Function Modifications* (continued)

CODING IN COLDFUSION

Function	Description
LsCurrencyFormat	When given a negative number, ColdFusion MX will not return a negative number. Using the local argument ColdFusion MX returns the currency in the locale's standard format. Using the International argument ColdFusion MX returns the currency with its international currency code.
LsDateFormat	ColdFusion MX has no limitations on the range of dates that can be used.
LsEuroCurrencyFormat	ColdFusion MX only returns euro currency format if the locale is set to a euro company; otherwise, it returns the locale's currency format.
LsIsCurrency	If euro currency is passed into the function, ColdFusion MX returns yes if the locale is a euro member; otherwise, it returns no.
LsIsDate	ColdFusion MX supports full date and full datetime as parameters, which include the name of the day.
LsParseDateTime	ColdFusion MX no longer supports dates in this format: hh:mm:ss day month year ColdFusion MX will not parse time zone values, such as EST. If the time zone is not set to the time zone of the current locale, the date is modified so that it does.
ParseDateTime	ColdFusion MX processes the offset in the arguments.
REReplace	ColdFusion MX excludes questionable punctuation, such as +, &, and =, in the [[:punch]] class of a regular expression. Adds the following characters to regular expressions as replacement strings to control case conversion: \u, \U, \l, \L, and \E. In ColdFusion 5, these characters must be manually escaped using two slashes.
REReplaceNoCase	ColdFusion MX adds the following characters to regular expressions as replacement strings to control case conversion: \u, \U, \l, \L, and \E. In ColdFusion 5, these characters must be manually escaped using two slashes.
StructKeyList	ColdFusion MX returns structure keys in the order they were created.

Table 14-5. *ColdFusion Function Modifications* (continued)

Using the Code Compatibility Analyzer

ColdFusion MX provides a way to automatically search through your ColdFusion 5 applications, looking for areas that may experience problems with ColdFusion MX. This is called the Code Compatibility Analyzer.

Understanding How the Code Compatibility Analyzer Works

The Code Compatibility Analyzer performs four main functions:

- Highlights your use of obsolete features in ColdFusion MX
- Finds deprecated CFML features in ColdFusion MX
- Points out ColdFusion features that behave differently
- Analyzes your code for CFML syntax errors

Running the ColdFusion Code Compatibility Analyzer cycles through each individual file in a directory, and optionally all of its subdirectories, and highlights the errors in each one. When running the Analyzer, you should follow these best practices. First, make sure you only run it on one application at a time. It is a resource-consuming process, and you don't want to negatively affect other applications on the server. If you can run it on a server that is not hosting live applications, that is even better. Second, make sure you turn off syntax validation if you are only testing for incompatibilities with ColdFusion 5 applications. Syntax validation makes the Analyzer do a lot more work.

Using the Code Compatibility Analyzer

The Code Compatibility Analyzer can be reached from the ColdFusion Administrator. This is how you open it and use it:

1. Launch the ColdFusion Administrator. Select the Code Analyzer Link under Debugging & Logging. The interface for the analyzer will come up:

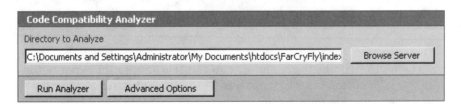

CODING IN COLDFUSION

2. Either type in a filename or directory name or use the Browse Server button to select it. This directory is the location of the file on the disk, and is not relative to the web server's root directory.

3. Click the Advanced Options button to open this window:

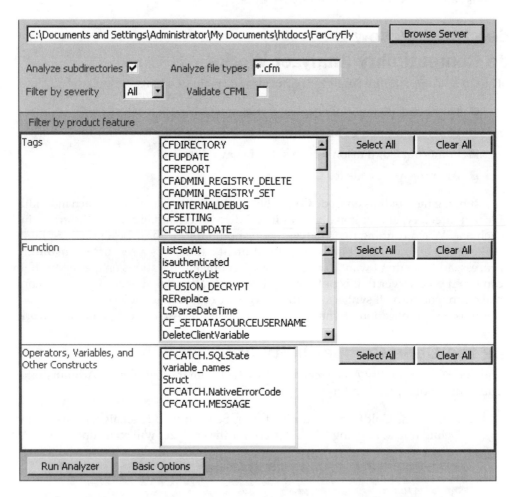

The advanced options allow you to choose which tags, functions, or special variables to examine the code for. You can also specify the types of files to analyze. The default is to just analyze CFM files. You can also filter the results by Errors, Information, or All.

Selecting the Analyze Subdirectories checkbox allows you to analyze subdirectories. If you don't specify a specific filename in the directory to analyze, selecting the Analyze Subdirectories checkbox will process all files in subdirectories of the directory you select, and all files in those subdirectories, and so on.

You can go back to the basic options by clicking the Basic Options button.

4. Click the Run Analyzer button and you will get the results:

	Error	Info	Total
Others	1	0	1
Total	1	0	1

Results Summary

C:\Documents and Settings\Administrator\My Documents
Thursday, April 04, 2002 at 12:33 PM

Actions	Feature	Severity	Document
🔁🔄	Parse Error (1)	Error	C:\Documents and Settings\Administrator\My Documents\htdocs\FarCryFly\index2.

The display gives you a summary of the number of problems that were found in your code.

5. Click each individual page to see an in-depth description of each individual error:

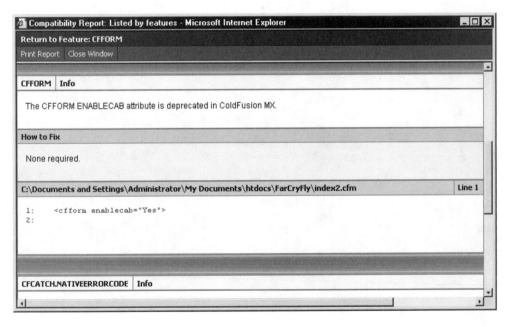

6. Click Print Report to print a report, or Close Window to close the window. You can go back to Step 1 to run the Analyzer on different pages, directories, or applications.

Summary

In this chapter, you learned about the following:

- Elements of CFML that have become either obsolete or deprecated
- How to use the CFML Code Compatibility Analyzer to test your code for changed functionality

The next chapter will discuss ColdFusion's scripting language, CFScript.

The Complete Reference

ColdFusion
MX

Part IV

Demonstrating Advanced Application Development Concepts

The
Complete
Reference

ColdFusion
MX

Chapter 15

Scripting Inside ColdFusion

CFML is a tag-based language that is the heart and soul of ColdFusion. It is similar to HTML, and many people who knew HTML made the jump to ColdFusion easily. In an attempt to sway the JavaScript, Java, and C++ crowd, CFScript was introduced in ColdFusion 4. This chapter teaches you all about it.

Introducing CFScript

This section explains what CFScript is and how you can use it in your ColdFusion development adventures. It starts with an explanation of CFScript, and then demonstrates how to use it to write ColdFusion code.

Scripting in ColdFusion

CFScript was created in an effort to help bridge the gap between JavaScript and CFML. The CFScript syntax is based on JavaScript, which was based on Java, which was based on C. If you know C, Java, or JavaScript, you may be better off learning CFScript as an introduction to ColdFusion, as opposed to CFML.

 Although CFScript is based upon JavaScript, it is still a server-side language. You cannot use it to manipulate a web page after it has been passed to the web browser.

Unfortunate as it may seem, CFScript is historically not a very well documented area of ColdFusion. That is okay, because many have traveled the trenches to figure it out for us. CFScript is similar, but not identical to, JavaScript. Knowing JavaScript will help, but you will be entirely confused if you don't understand the differences between JavaScript and CFScript:

- CFScript uses ColdFusion expressions, which are neither a subset nor superset of JavaScript.
- CFScript is not case sensitive. This can be a blessing for those of you who are used to the case sensitiveness of JavaScript.
- All statements must end in a semicolon. In JavaScript, this isn't always the case. CFScript is stricter on the case.
- Assignment in CFScript is a statement. JavaScript treats assignment as an expression, allowing you to create and change variables in the middle of an assignment. CFScript will not allow this.
- Objects that are part of the Document Object Model (DOM) are implicitly available in JavaScript, but don't exist in CFScript. In CFScript, they don't apply.
- Curly brackets, { }, are used to group together statements. This is true for both JavaScript and CFScript.
- CFML tags are not available in CFScript, although the full range of CFML functions are available.

To access CFML tags inside CFScript, you can use cffunction (see Chapter 16) to create a custom function that calls the tag. The custom function could then be called inside CFScript.

■ CFScript can access variables that were created in the template before the CFScript block. CFML after a CFScript block can access the variables created after the block. CFScript does contain a local variable scope for use in custom functions. These variables cannot be accessed outside the custom function.

Writing CFScript Code

This section shows you how CFScript can work for you. It demonstrates how to add code documentation into a CFScript block and how to apply variable assignment techniques with CFScript. It starts by discussing the CFScript tag in general.

Formatting CFScript Code

CFScript blocks are created with a tag that is aptly named cfscript. The cfscript tag needs both a start and end tag. The CFScript code falls between the open and close tag:

```
<cfscript>
 CFScript statements
</cfscript>
```

As discussed in the previous section, a semicolon is used to separate CFScript statements. Extraneous white space or line breaks are ignored. There is no limit to the number of statements that can reside in a CFScript block.

In the course of your development, you may want to block certain sections of CFScript code altogether. CFScript supports that functionality with the use of curly brackets, { }. Here is an example:

```
<cfscript>
 {
  statement1;
 }
 {
  statement2;
  statement3;
  statement4;
 }
</cfscript>
```

This code is split up into two separate blocks of code. The first segment only contains a single line. It is perfectly acceptable to create a code block with one line. The second block contains three lines. There is no limit to the number of lines that can appear in a code block. You will most commonly use the code blocks when creating conditional or looping statements.

Documenting CFScript Code

CFScript, thankfully, allows you to document your code. Documenting your code makes it easier to maintain in the future, as discussed in Chapter 10. CFScript allows for two kinds of comments: single-line comments and multiline comments. Both are similar to their JavaScript counterparts, although they're different than the HTML or CFML equivalents.

To create a single-line comment in CFScript, you just put two slashes before your comment. You can't use comments in the middle of a CFScript statement, but you can use them on the same line as one. This is an example:

```
<cfscript>
  // CFScript comment here
</cfscript>
```

Multilined comments are also supported. They start out with a forward slash and an asterisk. They end with the same characters in reverse order, an asterisk and then a forward slash:

```
<cfscript>
  /*  This is a the first line of a multiline comment
      This is the second line of a multiline comment
      This is the last line of a multiline comment */
</cfscript>
```

Documentation of your code is very important, and helps make the code more readable and maintainable.

Creating and Outputting Variables in CFScript

This section shows you CFScript in action by demonstrating how to create and output variables in CFScript. Variables are created with assignment. Unlike CFML, there are no equivalents to the cfparam and cfset tags. To create an assignment statement in CFScript, you would format it like this:

```
<cfscript>
  VariableName = Expression;
</cfscript>
```

The VariableName can be any valid variable name in ColdFusion. It is followed by an equal sign and then a ColdFusion expression.

As a general rule, if you are setting variables in a block of at least three, using CFScript is quicker than using multiple cfset or cfparam tags.

After creating your variables, you can manipulate them in many different ways. We will show you how to output the variable using the WriteOutput function. The single parameter of the WriteOutput function is an expression. This code segment will create and output a variable:

```
<cfscript>
 MyVariable = "Test Variable";
 WriteOutput(MyVariable);
</cfscript>
```

In this code, you may notice that we are not using the pound signs around the ColdFusion expression. They are implied in CFScript, so you do not need to specify them.

Caution *CFScript is not commonly used for output operations because it does not mix easily with HTML, as CFML does.*

Applying Conditional Logic in CFScript

Conditional logic is how you make decisions in your code. Chapter 13 discussed conditional logic and how to apply it within CFML. This section teaches you how to use conditional logic in CFScript.

Using If Statements

The most common form of conditional logic is the if statement. CFScript supports all aspects of the if statement, including the initial if, the else, and the else if. We start by looking at a simple if statement:

```
<cfscript>
 if (Expression){
  CFScript Statements;
 }
</cfscript>
```

The if statement starts with the if keyword. It is followed by a ColdFusion expression, surrounded by parentheses. Then we have a code block, marked with curly brackets.

The code that we execute in case the conditional occurs resides in the ColdFusion block. A semicolon must separate each line of code in the block.

CFScript also supports an else statement, with the keyword else:

```
<cfscript>
 if (Expression){
  CFScript Statements;
 } else {
  CFScript Statements;
 }
</cfscript>
```

The structure of the if-else statement is almost identical to a simple if statement. After the if code block, we have the keyword else, followed by a second code block. The second code block contains the else condition.

Note *If your block of code only contains a single statement, you do not have to group it with the curly brackets.*

CFScript does not have a special keyword, such as the cfelseif tag, that allows you to create an else if statement. It is easy to create one by combining the else keyword with the if keyword, as shown here:

```
<cfscript>
 if (Expression){
  CFScript Statements;
 } else if (Expression){
  CFScript Statements;
 } else {
  CFScript Statements;
 }
</cfscript>
```

The statement that follows the else condition is another if statement. You can daisy-chain as many if statements like this as you need.

This is an example of conditional logic in CFScript:

```
<cfscript>
 MyVariable = "Target";
 if (NOT IsDefined("MyVariable")){
  WriteOutput("Warning, MyVariable was not defined.");
```

```
 } else if (MyVariable NEQ "Target"){
  WriteOutput("You missed the Target.");
 } else {
  WriteOutput("You hit the Target.");
 }
</cfscript>
```

First, a variable, MyVariable, is created. Then, the if statement is entered into, which first checks if the variable is defined and then outputs an error. Of course, we know the variable is defined, because we set it up in the previous line, but a real-world situation may not be as simple. The else if statement checks if the MyVariable value is not equal to Target. If it isn't, we output the "You missed the Target." text; otherwise, we output "You hit the Target."

CFScript if statements will short circuit. This means that in a case where multiple conditions exist, it will only evaluate conditions until it can find the result. For example, if you have the condition X or Y, and X is true, it doesn't matter what Y is, because the result will always be true.

Using Switch Statements

The second implementation of conditional logic is in the form of a switch and case statement. We discussed how to implement case statements with CFML in Chapter 13. Case statements are faster than if statements if you are going to be daisy-chaining a lot of else if statements in the path.

There are two main parts to a switch statement: the switch and the case. CFScript appropriately uses the keywords, switch and case, to define each one. This is the basic format of a switch statement:

```
<cfscript>
 switch (Expression){
  case "Value1" : {
   statement1;
   break;
  }
 }
</cfscript>
```

The first statement within our CFScript block is the switch keyword. It is followed by an expression, in much the same way as the if statement is followed by an expression. The expression is enclosed in parentheses. After the expression is an open curly bracket. All the case statements must reside between the open and close curly brackets.

The case keyword comes next. You can have as many case statements as you need inside the switch. After the keyword case is the value that you are checking for. If the value is not equal to the result of the expression, the code will move on to the next case. After the value is a colon, followed by the open curly brackets that signify a group of code. You can list code for multiple cases either by separating them with a comma after the case keyword or by stacking multiple case statements on top of one other before executing the code, like this:

```
<cfscript>
 switch (Expression){
  case "Value1" :
  case "Value2" :
  case "Value3" : {
   statement1;
   break;
  }
 }
</cfscript>
```

The preceding code performs the statement if the Expression is equal to Value1, Value2, or Value3.

The group of code is a list of statements. The last line in the statement is the break keyword, which is the way to tell ColdFusion that you have found your result and it should continue processing the template at the end of the switch block. If you do not use this, there is a possibility that more code segments will be executed, especially the CFScript equivalent of cfdefaultcase.

To create a default condition if no other conditions meet the value specified in the switch, CFScript provides the default statement. The default keyword is the equivalent of the CFML cfdefaultcase. This is how it would be set up:

```
<cfscript>
 switch (Expression){
  case "Value1" : {
   statement1;
   break;
  }

  default : {
   statementdefault;
  }
 }
</cfscript>
```

After our case statements comes the default block. It starts with the default keyword and is followed by a colon. The default block is similar to case blocks; however, due to its nature, you do not have to specify a value. Curly brackets enclose the group of statements that you perform in the default case.

We can rewrite our previous cfif example to use a case statement:

```
<cfscript>
 MyVariable = "Target";

 if (IsDefined("MyVariable")){
  switch (MyVariable) {

   case "Target" : {
    WriteOutput("You hit the Target.");
    break;
   }

   default : {
    WriteOutput("You missed the Target.");
   }
  }
 }
</cfscript>
```

Case statements are ideal if you want to check the value of something, but they are not good for other types of conditions. To provide the same functionality as before, you need to enclose the switch in an if statement. First you must make sure that MyVariable is defined before entering the code. Then the switch is performed on the MyVariable value. There are two possible cases. The first case executes if the value is equal to "Target." The second case, which is the default, executes if the value is not equal to Target. In a real-world situation, you would only want to use a case if you were planning on having more options, but this demonstrates the concepts behind it.

Looping in CFScript

The next thing that we want to examine is how to loop in CFScript. We discussed different types of loops in Chapter 13. This section demonstrates the different types of loops that are available in CFScript.

Using For Loops

There are two main types of for loops in CFScript. One is a standard index loop, as discussed in Chapter 13. The second type provides an easy way to loop over a structure in CFScript. This section examines both types.

Index Loops

The index loop is used to perform a specific action a certain number of times. The four elements of the index loop are the starting point, the ending point, the step, and the index. The starting and ending points are self-explanatory. The index is the variable used to keep track of the current iteration. The step is the amount that the index will increment after an iteration.

This is the format for an index loop:

```
<cfscript>
 For (Initialize Expression ; Condition ; Increment Expression){
  statements;
 }
</cfscript>
```

The syntax here is close to a for loop in JavaScript. It starts with the keyword for. Following that is a ColdFusion expression. Use this expression to initialize your index variable. Then comes a semicolon. After the semicolon is a condition. The loop code will continue to execute until the condition becomes false. The next statement is the expression that will automatically change the value of the index variable.

Here is a simple example that will loop from 1 to 5 and output each iteration along the way:

```
<cfscript>
 For (Index=1; Index LTE 5 ; Index = Index + 1){
  WriteOutput(Index);
 }

</cfscript>
```

The index is initialized to 1. The loop will run until the index is less than or equal to 5. The index is incremented by 1 for each iteration of the loop. The output, as expected, is 12345.

The break keyword can be used to exit out of a loop, just as it can be used in the switch-case statement.

Looping over a Structure

For loops, in a slightly different format, can be used to loop over a structure. We discussed structures in Chapter 8. A structure is an associative array that has name-value pairs. This is the format for a for-in loop:

```
<cfscript>
for (Index in Structure) {
  Statements;
}
</cfscript>
```

This loop will loop for each key in the structure. The index will take on the value of the current key, process the loop code, and then increment. The loop starts with the for keyword. Then we have the name of our index variable, followed by the in keyword. After the in keyword we have the name of our structure. The statement is enclosed in parentheses. The loop block is enclosed in open and close curly brackets.

Here is an example of a for-in loop:

```
<cfscript>
MyStructure=StructNew();
MyStructure.Key1="Value1";
MyStructure.Key2="Value2";
MyStructure.Key3="Value3";

for (MyKey in MyStructure){
  WriteOutput(MyKey & " " & MyStructure[MyKey] & "<br>");
}

</cfscript>
```

The start of this code creates the structure, with three keys and three values. Then we come upon the loop. It starts with the for keyword. We loop over all the keys in the MyStructure variable. The single processing line we use is to output the name of the key and its value.

  You cannot use for-in loops to loop over lists or arrays. Use a normal for loop, looping until the index is equal to the length of the array or list.

Conditional Loops

There are two types of conditional loops in CFScript: while loops and do-while loops. This section explains what they both are and how they work.

While Loops

A while loop is a conditional loop in ColdFusion. It is supported in both CFScript and CFML. A while loop checks a certain condition, runs the loop code, checks the condition again, runs the loop code, and so on until the condition evaluates to false. This is the format for a while loop:

```
<cfscript>
 While (Expression){
  Statements;
 }
</cfscript>
```

It starts with the keyword, while. It is followed by an expression in parentheses. The loop will continue to execute until this condition is false. After the end parenthesis, we have an open curly bracket, and the list of statements. The loop ends with a close curly bracket.

Caution *Make sure that you always execute a statement that will affect your expression, or else the loop will never end, thus locking the server.*

We can use the while loop in a similar manner to the way that we use the for loop. This is a while loop that will loop from 1–5:

```
<cfscript>
 Index = 1;
 while (Index LTE 5){
  WriteOutput(Index);
  Index = Index+1;
 }
</cfscript>
```

First, we set the Index variable using a CFScript assignment. Variable initialization like this is not needed in a for loop. Next comes the keyword while, followed by the condition. We are looping while the index is less than or equal to 5. There are two lines in the loop block. The first is to output the index value. The second will increment the index value.

In the for loops, the index value was automatically incremented. This is not the case with a while loop.

Do-While Loops

Do-while loops are another form of conditional loop. They do not have a parallel in CFML. The main difference between a while loop and a do-while loop is that a do-while loop checks the condition after the loop code is executed. This is contrary to what a standard while loop does. A do-while loop will always execute at least once.

This is the format for a do-while loop:

```
<cfscript>
 do {
  statements;
 } While (expression);
</cfscript>
```

The loop starts with the do keyword. Following that is an open curly bracket and the statements that make up the loop. The close curly bracket comes next, followed by the while keyword. After the while keyword is the expression that is used for loop control. The statement is closed with a semicolon.

We can replicate the functionality of the same example we used in the while loop and for loop:

```
<cfscript>
 Index = 1;
 Do{
  WriteOutput(Index);
  Index = Index+1;
 } while (Index LTE 5);
</cfscript>
```

The do-while loop is structured in much the same way as the while loop is. We initialize the Index variable before entering the loop. The loop starts with the do keyword. The loop body outputs the Index variable and increments the index counter. The condition resides at the end of the loop, stating that we will loop until the index is less than or equal to 5. A semicolon follows the condition, ending the loop. The output here will be the same as the output in the past two loops: 12345.

Note   *Any loop can include the continue or break keywords. When the continue keyword is executed, the loop stops its current iteration and starts the next one. Break will stop the loop completely and continue execution after the end of the loop.*

Summary

In this chapter, you have learned about the following:

- CFScript generally
- Variable assignment in CFScript
- Controlling CFScript code with conditional and looping logic

In future chapters, we will discuss more features of CFScript. Chapter 18 will discuss error handling, and Chapter 16, the next chapter, will discuss user-defined functions and other code modularization options.

The Complete Reference

ColdFusion MX

Chapter 16

Modularizing Your Code

An important programming concept is code modularization. This chapter explains the concept of code modularization and why you would want to do it. It goes on to examine the ways that ColdFusion can support code modularization.

Understanding Code Modularization

Before you can learn how to apply code modularization techniques to ColdFusion, you need to understand what code modularization is. This section explains code modularization and discusses some of the benefits of code modularization.

Using Code Modularization Techniques

The best way to explain code modularization is with an example. Think about the last program that you ran. It might have been a spreadsheet or word processing document. It could have been an HTML editor, such as Dreamweaver or HomeSite. Each of these programs probably has a way to save a file. We examine the algorithm for this next.

To save a file, first the program checks whether the file already has a name. If it does, then the program saves under the current filename. If it does not, then the program performs some actions to get the filename, usually by popping up a dialog box that requests the user to enter a filename. This is the general algorithm, in pseudocode:

```
If Command is Save
 If FileName is not known
  Get the filename
 endif
 Save The File
endif
```

Further examination of the program will probably also reveal a Save As option. This option is very similar to the Save File algorithm, except that the program definitely asks for the filename:

```
If Command is Save
 Get the filename
 Save The File
endif
```

There are two actions that reside in each algorithm: getting a filename and saving the file. You wouldn't want to have to write the same chunk of code two different times in two different, but similar, algorithms. This is where code modularization comes into play. It is the act of writing a single chunk of code to perform a single action, and then using that code in multiple places.

In the web development world, you will probably want to modularize things such as headers, footers, and navigation elements. That way, changes made to one file are automatically filtered through to every page in the site. The second site I ever built—before dynamic web sites were the norm—had over 100 pages. I spent many an hour manually modifying links and img tags as the site changed. I longed for some form of code modularization.

Benefiting from Code Modularization

These are the main benefits of modularizing your code:

- **Code reuse** When you write a code module, you can use it in many places, without having to rewrite it multiple times. This is the primary reason for modularizing code.

- **Speedier development** If you write your code in a modular fashion, you will develop a library of modules, many of which can be plugged into any single application and used. This means that you have less up-front coding time and can develop applications quicker. Take a look at all the custom tags in the Macromedia Developer's Exchange, or the user-defined functions at cflib.org, to see some code you can download and use in your own application.

- **Parallel development** After you separate your code into modules, two different developers can develop two different modules at the same time.

- **Less debugging** As you develop a module, you code and debug it to make sure it works separately from the rest of the application. Once you have done this to satisfaction, you don't have to worry anymore about debugging it.

- **Easier to make changes** If you find something in your code module that is incorrect, or needs fixing, you can change it in one place, instead of in 100 different site templates.

The remainder of this chapter examines the tools that allow you to implement code modularization in ColdFusion.

Implementing Code Modularization with Includes

Includes are a simple form of code modularization that is available in ColdFusion. This section explains what they are and how you can use them.

Making Includes Work for You

An *include* is a way to include the contents of one file inside another. The code is processed just as if the code residing in the include file were placed in the original file. Take this file as an example:

```
<html>
<head>
 <title>Sample Page</title>
</head>

<body>
 This is a Sample Template
</body>
</html>
```

This is a simple HTML document, separated into two parts, the header and the body. Suppose you wanted to take the header and separate it from this file. That would give you two separate files, the main file and the header file. This is the header file:

```
<head>
 <title>Sample Page</title>
</head>
```

This is the main file:

```
<html>
<!--header include here -->
<body>
 This is a Sample Template
</body>
</html>
```

The two separate files allow us to separate the two different sections of our template without changing the functionality of the template. Figure 16-1 demonstrates how an include will work.

It is good to note here how includes deal with variables in ColdFusion templates. Includes are treated as if the included code is not in a separate file at all. All variable scopes that are available to the template are available to the include. The include can access variables created before the include was included. Variables created in the include are available to the calling template, after it calls the include. Other forms of code modularization are not as lenient with variable usage.

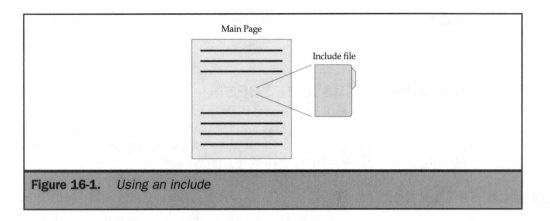

Figure 16-1. *Using an include*

Using the cfinclude Tag

ColdFusion provides a tag, cfinclude, that allows you to use includes in your applications. The most common uses for the cfinclude tag are to store standard page elements such as a navigation bar, store custom functions, or break up overly complicated pages into smaller segments.

The cfinclude tag has a single attribute, called template. It contains the name and location of the file that you want to insert into the current ColdFusion page. The value for the template file must either be relative to the current file or refer to a mapped directory in the ColdFusion Administrator.

The template attribute for a cfinclude tag is relative to the calling page. If an included page contains a second cfinclude, the template attribute needs a value that is relative to the included page, not the original calling page.

This is how we would use the cfinclude tag in the earlier example:

```
<html>
<!--header include here -->
<cfinclude template="header.cfm">
<body>
 This is a Sample Template
</body>
</html>
```

The resulting HTML that is streamed to the browser will be identical to the original page that we started with. When processing the main page, first the html tag is sent to the browser. Then, ColdFusion kicks in and sees the cfinclude file. It gets the header.cfm template and adds that text to the output. It finishes processing the remainder of the template normally.

Creating CFML Custom Tags

The second form of code modularization in ColdFusion is a custom function. There are two types of custom tags: CFML custom tags and CFX custom tags. CFX custom tags (discussed in Chapter 26) are extensions to ColdFusion's functionality that are written in C++ or Java. This section concentrates on CFML custom tags.

Explaining Custom Tags

This section starts by giving a broad overview of what custom tags are. It then examines how to pass variables to and from custom tags, and discusses variables in the special custom tag scope, thistag.

Understanding Custom Tags

There are some limitations to the include method of code modularization. Includes are not completely separate from the template that calls them. This makes them great for simplifying and organizing your code, but it is not ideal for creating black box modules, where you punch in some values and a result value pops back out. There is no way to explicitly pass values in or out of an include. Because they are not processed as an entity separate from the template, includes tend to rely on the code in the main template, and often the main template may rely on actions that take place in the include. Custom tags are designed to bypass these problems.

From a cosmetic point of view, there is little difference between a custom tag file and an include file. They are both CFML templates and can contain a mix of HTML and CFML tags. The real difference is how the two are used from within the main, or calling, template. With an include, the code is just picked up from its resting place, processed, and the result is dropped into the main template's output right where it is located. Custom tags are called with either a special syntax or the cfmodule tag, and are treated differently than includes, with their own variable scopes, place in the computer's stack, and variable memory.

Passing Parameters with Custom Tags

There are three scopes that relate to a custom tag:

- **attributes**   Contains all the variables that are passed into the custom tag
- **caller**   Contains all the values that are passed out of the custom tag back to the calling template
- **thistag**   Contains special variables that relate to the custom tag's execution

The attributes that are passed into the tag are placed into the attributes scope. If you have required (or optional) attributes, you can check for their existence using conditional logic, or by using the cfparam tag if you want to set it to a default value. You can easily decide not to process the information inside a custom tag if variables are not defined. You can even throw your own errors, as discussed in Chapter 18. The caller scope is used to create variables in the template that called the custom tag. This can be done with the cfset tag. This is how you pass values out of the custom tag.

The thistag scope has some special variables associated with it that you can use to control the execution of the custom tag:

- **ExecutionMode**   Specifies which method the tag is in. The valid values are start, end, or inactive. Start and end values are self-explanatory. The inactive mode is used for nested tags. This variable is set to inactive when tags within the open and close custom tag are executing.

- **HasEndTag**   Specifies whether the calling page uses both a start and end tag when it calls the custom tag.

- **GeneratedContent**   Contains all content that was generated by the custom tag. The variable is empty when processing the start tag.

- **AssocAttribs**   Contains all the attributes of all nested tags if the cfassociate tag is used. (A *nested tag* is a tag that is called inside of another tag.) ColdFusion has some built-in tags, such as cfhttp and cfhttpparam, that are designed to be nested.

As with all variables, you can access the variables in the thistag scope in this format:

```
thistag.VariableName
```

where the variable name is equal to one of the four values in the preceding list.

In this discussion of variable scopes, it is worth mentioning that the variable scopes that are associated with an HTTP request can be accessed within a custom tag without specifically passing the values as parameters. These scopes are url, form, cgi, request, cookies, server, application, session, and client. It is generally considered good practice to pass these values as attributes, instead of relying on the scopes.

Calling Custom Tags

Creating your custom tag is only half the battle, albeit the hard half. The next step is to call upon the custom tag. ColdFusion supports two different syntaxes for calling on the custom tag. One syntax uses the cfmodule tag. The second is a custom syntax. This section explains both.

You can call a custom tag by using the following syntax:

```
<cf_mytagname attribute1="value1" attribute2="value2">
```

The tag name starts with two letters, cf, followed by an underscore. After that comes the name of the tag. The name of the tag is identical to the name of a file. If you created a file called MyCustomTag.cfm, you could call it as a custom tag using cf_mycustomtag. After the name of the tag comes an attribute list. The attributes are name-value pairs, just like attributes in standard HTML or CFML functions.

When you call upon a tag using the custom tag syntax, ColdFusion first looks in the current directory for the tag. Next, it looks in the custom tags directory, CustomTags, of the ColdFusion installation. Then, it looks in all the subdirectories of the custom tag directory. Finally, it looks in any additional custom tag directories that were specified in the ColdFusion Administrator.

The second way to call a custom tag is with the cfmodule tag. The cfmodule tag has these attributes:

- **template** Specifies the location of the custom tag. The location is relative to the page that is calling the tag. It will also search all the ColdFusion mapped locations if the file is not found. This is a required attribute if the name attribute is not used.

- **name** Specifies the name of the custom tag. A custom tag is named based on the filename and location of the file, relative to the custom tag directory. You specify the name as Directory.Subdirectory.TagName. In the previous example, ColdFusion would look for TagName.cfm in the directory\subdirectory directory of the CustomTags directory.

- **attributes** Specifies name-value pairs that contain the attributes for the custom tag.

- **attributecollection** Contains a structure variable with attributes to pass into the custom tag. The custom tag will automatically add all the values in this variable to the attributes scope of the custom tag.

The biggest advantage that the cfmodule syntax has over the cf_tagname syntax is that with cfmodule, ColdFusion does not have to search for the file, because you specify where it is. This could give you noticeable performance improvements if the custom tag is buried deep beneath a subdirectory of the custom tag's directory.

 Avoid creating attributes to custom tags that have the same name as any of the cfmodule parameters. This will cause errors when you try to call the custom tag.

This is an example of the cfmodule format:

```
<cfmodule template="mytagname"
          attribute1="value1" attribute2="value2">
```

The cfmodule tag specifies the template attribute, and the two custom attributes.

Coding a Simple Custom Tag

This section teaches you how to create a simple custom tag. Suppose you want to perform a simple mathematical function $X^2 + X + Y$ and return the results. We can implement this using a custom tag. First, we create a custom tag:

```
<!--- www.instantcoldfusion.com

Description: A Custom Tag to perform the mathematical
            function: X^2 + X + Y

Entering: N/A
Exiting: N/A

Dependencies: N/A
Expecting: X : a number
           Y : a number

Modification History
Date       Modifier                Modification
************************************************************
04/07/2002 Jeff Houser, DotComIt   Created
--->

<!--- check if variables are defined --->
<cfif IsDefined("attributes.X") and IsDefined("attributes.Y")>

 <!--- Perform Math Problem --->
 <cfset caller.result =
        attributes.X^2 + attributes.X + attributes.Y>

<cfelse>
 <!--- Variables weren't defined so send back an error --->
 <cfset caller.result="The variables were not defined.">
</cfif>
```

The documentation header specifies the math problem that this custom tag will solve and the two variables that are supposed to be passed into it. The body of the code first checks whether the two variables are defined. If they are, the math operation is performed; otherwise, an error is returned. The result, whatever it is, is sent back by creating a variable in the caller scope.

DEMONSTRATING ADVANCED APPLICATION DEVELOPMENT CONCEPTS

This is the calling template:

```
<!--- www.instantcoldfusion.com

Description: A page to call the Custom Tag

Entering: N/A
Exiting: N/A

Dependencies: CustomTag.cfm
Expecting: N/A

Modification History
Date       Modifier                Modification
***********************************************************
03/07/2002 Jeff Houser, DotComIt   Created
--->

<!--- set the X and Y variables --->
<cfset X = 11>
<cfset y = 2>

<!--- call the custom tag --->
<cfmodule template="CustomTag.cfm" X=#x# Y=#y#>

<!--- output the results --->
<cfoutput>#x#^2 + #X# + #Y# = #result#</cfoutput>
```

The first thing to note in this template is that the documentation header specifies that the CustomTag.cfm file is dependent upon this template's execution. Once inside the template, there are three main sections of note. The first section sets up the X and Y variables. The second section calls the custom tag using the cfmodule tag. The final section outputs the values.

Creating User-Defined Functions

The next form of ColdFusion code modularization is user-defined functions (UDF). ColdFusion offers many built-in functions to perform a variety of tasks, from date arithmetic, to array and structure processing, to query manipulation. With the release of ColdFusion 5, the ability to create your own functions, using CFScript, came into existence. ColdFusion MX raises the bar by adding the cffunction tag, which allows you to create functions from within ColdFusion. This section examines both ways.

Understanding UDF Basics

This section discusses some universal conventions for user-defined functions. It provides some guidelines that should be used when creating a UDF. Then, it describes how variables are passed in and out of the function. Finally, it provides some additional tips that relate to custom functions.

Naming Your User-Defined Function

Here are some general guidelines for creating functions:

- The function must have a unique name, different from all other variables and existing functions.

- The function name cannot start with the letters cf.

- Existing functions, whether custom or built-in, cannot be overridden. An overridden function is a part of the object-oriented programming discipline. When a function is overridden, you create a new function by the same name that offers different functionality. ColdFusion won't allow this.

- You cannot define a function inside another function. ColdFusion will throw an error if this occurs.

- Functions can call themselves, if necessary. This is called *recursion*.

- Functions created with the cffunction tag do not have to return a value. Functions created with CFScript do.

- In CFScript, the return is defaulted to the last variable set, if not specified.

- Create your functions inside a CFM page. Use the cfinclude tag to include the functions in the page that you are creating. This combines the best of both worlds for reuse and file organization.

Scoping Arguments in a Function

When you use a function and pass arguments into it, the arguments are placed in a scope of their own, the arguments scope. The arguments scope exists only during the execution of the function. The arguments scope is a special case in ColdFusion development, because it can be treated as an array or as a structure. You can access variables in the arguments scope in two ways:

```
Arguments[number]
Arguments["Argumentname"]
```

To find the number of arguments in the scope, you can use the ArrayLen or StructCount function.

When calling your custom functions, you should take note of what happens when the values are passed into the function. Simple values are passed by value, as are arrays.

This means that a copy of the value is created and passed into the function. Any changes made to the value are not reflected in the code that calls the function, because they are made to the copy. The copy ceases to exist after the function is called.

All complex values, except arrays, are passed into the function by reference. This means that a reference, or pointer, to the variable is created in memory. When the value is changed in the function, the value is also changed in the calling template. Values that are passed this way include structures, queries, and external objects such as COM objects.

ColdFusion functions also support local variables that will exist only in the function. These local variables are created in a special scope called this. Creating variables in the this scope is different if you create the function in CFScript or CFML. Local variables in a CFScript function are specified using the var keyword. Local variables in a CFML function are created, just like any other variable, in a scope called this.

Learning Additional UDF Quirks

ColdFusion treats UDFs internally as ColdFusion variables. You can wait for a moment while the implications of this sink in. You can set the UDF to a variable, put it in a specific scope, or even use it as the argument to another function. UDFs are initially placed into the variables scope, but you can move them into any scope.

This code moves the MyFunction function into the application scope:

```
<cfset application.MyFunction = variables.MyFunction>
```

Putting the function into the application scope stores the function in persistent memory, making it available to every page in an application.

Considering that functions are treated as ColdFusion variables, there is a special function, IsCustomFunction, that you can use to check whether a variable is a custom function. It accepts one argument, the name of the variable that you are testing. You can test whether a variable is a custom function by using this code:

```
<cfif IsCustomFunction(MyVariable)>
  It is a Custom Function
<cfelse>
  It isn't a Custom Function
</cfif>
```

Make sure you do not enclose the name of the variable in quotes.

Scripting a UDF in CFScript

This section shows how you can use CFScript to create a user-defined function. First we examine the function definition, and then we look at an example. If you want to brush up on your CFScript skills, check out Chapter 15.

Defining a Function in CFScript

Functions are defined in CFScript similarly to the way they are defined in JavaScript:

```
<cfscript>
 function FunctionName ( Parameterlist ){
  // Local variable declarations
  var MyLocalVariable = "Test Value";

  // statements
  Statements;

  // return expression
  return (expression);
 }
</cfscript>
```

A function declaration starts out with the keyword function and is followed by the name of the function. After that comes a comma-delimited list of the required parameters. The code of the function is a block, surrounded by curly brackets.

Tip *The variables that are specified in the argument list are required when using the function. Additional arguments will reside in the arguments scope, and can therefore be optional.*

The code block starts with local variable declarations. Each local variable declaration uses the var keyword in front of it. This specifies the difference between a variable local to the function and a variable that will be available in the template. These variables exist inside the function, but are not available anywhere else in the ColdFusion template that uses the function. Following that comes the code, which performs the function's actions. Anything that can be done in CFScript can be done in a UDF.

Tip *Always define your local variables with the var keyword. These var statements must be at the top of your UDF, before other code.*

To return a value with a CFScript custom function, the return keyword is used, followed by an expression. The result of the expression will be the value that is returned. Both simple and complex values can be returned.

Tip *Includes must be created in the same page that calls them, and must be defined before they are called.*

An Example

Knowing these specific details of a function, we can create a function that performs similar actions to the custom tag we developed in the previous section:

```
<cfscript>
 /* a Custom Function to perform the mathematical
    function: X^2 + X + Y
    Expecting:
      X  : a number
      Y  : a number */

 function MyCustomFunction(x, y){
  // Perform Math Problem
  return (arguments.X^2 + arguments.X + arguments.Y);
 }
</cfscript>
```

The mathematical code is very similar to the custom tag. We do not have to check for the variable's existence because they are listed as required parameters. ColdFusion will throw an error if the variables are not defined.

The custom function can be called just as if it were a predefined ColdFusion function:

```
<cfoutput>#MyCustomFunction(1,2)#</cfoutput>
```

Put all this code in a template and the results will be output, 4.

Using the cffunction Tag

In addition to CFScript, custom functions can be created in CFML using the cffunction tag. This tag is a new addition to CFML, and it greatly expands the usability of custom functions, because now all ColdFusion tags can be used inside them. Custom functions can now do things that they were unable to do in ColdFusion 5, such as perform queries with the cfquery tag. This section shows you how.

Creating CFML Functions

Three different tags can be used to create a custom function. Cffunction is used to define the function, cfargument defines the arguments that are passed into the function, and cfreturn defines the value that is returned from the function.

These are the attributes to the cffunction tag:

- **name** Contains the name of the custom function.
- **returntype** Specifies the type of data returned by the function (optional attribute). Valid values are query, string, numeric, Boolean, date, struct, array, binary, XML, customfunction, and object.

■ **output** Defines how ColdFusion deals with output in the function body. If this
is not specified, the output is treated as normal CFML. If you specify yes, then
ColdFusion treats all text inside the function as if it were inside a cfoutput. If the
attribute contains no, the function is processed as if all output were prevented.

The cfargument tag has these attributes:

■ **name** Contains the name of the argument.

■ **type** Contains the data type of the argument. The valid values for this attribute
are query, string, numeric, Any, Boolean, date, struct, array, binary, variablename,
uuid, guid, numeric, query, string, and a component name.

■ **required** Specifies whether or not the current value is required (Boolean
attribute).

■ **default** Specifies the default value for the attribute if it is not passed into the
argument.

The format for the cfreturn tag is an expression. It does not have any specific attributes,
but can be used like this:

```
<cfreturn expression>
```

With the use of the tags behind us, we can continue on to create a custom function.

Putting Together a CFML Custom Function

With the knowledge of the tags that create custom functions in CFML, we can now create
a custom function. This code re-creates the functionality that we created as both a custom
tag and a CFScript custom function:

```
<!--- Define the custom function to perform the math function --->
<cffunction name="MyCustomFunction" returntype="numeric">
 <!--- define the arguments --->
 <cfargument name="X" required="yes" type="numeric" default="1">
 <cfargument name="Y" required="yes" type="numeric" default="1">

 <!--- Perform Math Problem --->
 <cfreturn arguments.X^2 + arguments.X + arguments.Y>

</cffunction>
```

This CFML function is a cross between the custom tag and the CFScript function. The
name of the custom function is defined in the cffunction tag. The returntype is specified
as numeric, because the function will return a numeric value.

The two arguments, x and y, are defined with the cfargument tag. They are both marked as required with default values set if they are not defined. Giving them default values nulls out the required attribute, because if the value is missing, it will still be defined.

When listing arguments in a custom function, make sure you list the optional arguments last.

The expression that computes the value resides in the cfreturn value. The function is called just like any other function:

```
<cfoutput>#MyCustomFunction(2,1)#</cfoutput>
```

The final version of code modularization we are going to examine is ColdFusion Components.

You can define local variables in a CFML custom function by using the var keyword with cfset, like this: `<cfset var MyLocalVariable="MyValue">`*. These variables should be defined at the top of the UDF.*

ColdFusion Components

ColdFusion Components (CFCs) is a brand-new feature brought out in ColdFusion MX. Like custom tags and user-defined functions, ColdFusion Components offer a way to create specific code modules. Unlike custom tags and user-defined functions, ColdFusion Components are ideal vehicles for communicating with third-party products, such as Flash movies and Web services. They also provide features akin to object-oriented languages, such as inheritance and methods.

Creating a ColdFusion Component

The first step in our examination of ColdFusion Components is to learn how to create one. This section covers the tags that are used within components.

Using the cfcomponent Tag

There are two different ways to create components. The first is to define the component with the cfcomponent tag. The second is to create a ColdFusion template and give it the extension cfc. This section examines both ways.

The cfcomponent tag is used to define a ColdFusion Component. These are its attributes:

- **extends** Contains the name of the parent component from which methods and properties are inherited. It is optional if you are not building a component off another.

- **output** Specifies whether or not output from within methods is suppressed (optional attribute; accepts a Boolean value). If set to yes, all output from within methods is suppressed. If set to no, then output is permitted.

The cfcomponent tag does not provide any functionality; it is just a wrapper that goes around the component's code.

The code that makes up the CFC is a series of methods, defined with the cffunction tag. In addition to the name, returntype, and output attributes, the cffunction tag has additional attributes geared toward components:

- **access** Defines the context from which the method can be evoked: private means the method is available only from within the component; package means that it is available to the component that declares the method or other components in the package; public means it is available to any page executing locally; and remote makes it available remotely via a URL, Flash, or a Web service.

- **roles** Contains a list of security roles that can invoke this method. If this attribute is omitted, anyone can use this function. For more information, see Chapter 17 about securing your ColdFusion applications.

- **exceptions** Contains a comma-delimited list of exceptions. These are used so that the client can use error handling when calling the method.

You would write your code within the cffunction tag just as if you were writing a custom function. Next we will create a sample CFC to see how it all comes together.

Creating a Sample CFC

For a sample CFC, I am going to move away from our arithmetic example in the previous sections toward something that is more representative of what you'll encounter in the real world. In your development travels, you have probably heard of a data structure called a stack. A *stack* is a complex data type, similar to an array or structure, with some special limitations placed on it.

Items always must be placed on the top of the stack. This is called *pushing* an item onto the stack. Items also must be removed from the top of the stack. This is called *popping*. A good example of this is a computer's memory stack. Stacks operate on the first in, last out (FILO) theory. CFCs are the perfect way to create a stack in ColdFusion.

This is how you can create your component:

1. Create an empty page and save it with a cfc extension. Add a documentation header:

```
<!--- www.instantcoldfusion.com

Description: a CFC to create a Stack

Entering: N/A
Exiting: N/A
```

```
Dependencies: N/A
Expecting: N/A

Modification History
Date        Modifier              Modification
***********************************************************
04/07/2002 Jeff Houser, DotComIt   Created
--->
```

2. Add the cfcomponent tag to the CFC file:

```
<cfcomponent output="false">

</cfcomponent>
```

This is actually an optional step, because the fact that you are creating a component is implied if you are writing code within a CFC file.

3. We need three functions for our stack component: one to create the stack, one to push items onto the stack, and one to pop items off the stack. Here is the method to create the stack:

```
<!--- a function to create a new stack --->
<!--- A stack is a Structure containing an array --->
<!--- This is so the stack methods can act as Array or --->
<!--- Structure functions and the stack can be modified --->
<!--- without being returned --->
<cffunction name="StackNew" access="public">
 <cfset this.StackStruct = StructNew()>
 <cfset this.StackStruct.StackArray= ArrayNew(1)>
 <cfreturn this.StackStruct>
</cffunction>
```

The first thing you will notice is that we are implementing the stack as an array inside a structure. This is done because arrays are passed by value into functions, whereas stacks are passed by reference. Implementing the stack as a structure means that we are not obligated to return the stack if we make changes to it.

Code inside a component, but outside of a method, is called when the component is instantiated. It can be used to set up the component. This is akin to a constructor method of OOP.

The function is titled StackNew, and its access is public. The function creates two local variables, a new structure and an element to that structure, called StackArray. The structure is returned by the function.

4. The next function that we want to create is the function to push an element onto the stack. The code is shown here:

```
<!--- a function to add an element onto the stack --->
<!--- using the ArrayPrepend Function to add on top of stack--->
<cffunction name="StackPush" access="public">
```

```
<cfargument name="Stack" required="Yes">
<cfargument name="StackElement" required="Yes">
<cfreturn ArrayPrepend(arguments.Stack.StackArray,
                       arguments.StackElement)>
</cffunction>
```

The StackPush method accepts two arguments, the stack and the element that we are pushing onto it. Both are required. To perform our push action, the ArrayPrepend function is used. The return value is a Boolean value indicating whether or not the push was successful.

| **Note** | *To access a predefined variable in a component, you can use the this scope.* |

5. Remove an item from the top of the stack. This is the code:

```
<!--- a function to remove an element from the stack --->
<!--- This function returns the removed element --->
<cffunction name="StackPop" access="public">
 <cfargument name="Stack" required="Yes">
 <cfset this.item = Stack.StackArray[1]>
 <cfset deleted = ArrayDeleteAt(arguments.Stack.StackArray, 1)>
 <cfreturn this.item>
</cffunction>
```

This code accepts a single argument, the stack. This code is more complicated than the code in the push function. First we need to get the top variable on the array, which we store in a local variable. The next step is to remove the top variable from the array. We return the value that we took off the stack. Congratulations! You have just finished creating your first ColdFusion Component.

This code can be expanded upon to make sure that your users don't try to pop from an empty stack, for example. Other items you may want to add are variable checks. Are the users really passing a stack variable into the methods? You will want to make sure.

Invoking a ColdFusion Component

Creating your component is only half the battle. You need to know how to use it. There are numerous ways to invoke a component. This section explains them and demonstrates how to use them.

Using Your Component

ColdFusion Components can be invoked in any number of ways, as shown in Table 16-1. First, we examine the cfinvoke method. These are the attributes to the cfinvoke tag:

- **component** Contains the name of the component. To find a component in a different directory, you can use the dot notation that was used with custom tags to find the component: Directory.subdirectory.componentname.

- **method** Contains the name of the method you are invoking.
- **returnvariable** Contains the results from the function that are returned.
- **argumentcollection** Contains a structure that holds all the arguments passed into the function.
- **argumentname** Used to specify the arguments that you want to pass into the method. If you want to list arguments separately when you are calling them, you can list them just as if you were passing values into a custom tag.

There is a third method that can be used to pass variables into a method using the cfinvoke tag: use the cfinvokeargument tag. It has two attributes:

- **name** Contains the name of the attribute.
- **value** Contains the value of the attribute.

Here is an example of the cfinvoke tag:

```
<cfinvoke component="MyComponent" method="MyMethod"
        returnvariable="Result" argument1="Value1"
        argument2="value2">
```

Invocation	Description
CFML	Use the cfinvoke or the cfobject tag. This will be discussed in more depth in this chapter.
CFScript	Use the CreateObject function. This will be discussed in more depth in this chapter.
URL control	You can invoke a component via a URL, such as syntax like this: Webserver/cfcname.cfc?method=methodname&argument1=value1&argument2=value2
Form control	Enter the file path to the component in the action attribute and the method name as a form variable. To pass parameters, the name of the form elements must equal the name of the method arguments.
Flash gateway	From within client-side ActionScript, as discussed in Chapter 28.
Web services	With the CFML cfinvoke tag, as discussed in Chapter 31.

Table 16-1. *Ways to Invoke ColdFusion Components*

The example invokes the MyMethod method of the MyComponent component, and returns the results in the variable Result. Two arguments are passed into the component by listing the arguments. We could call the same method, with the same values, by using the cfinvokeargument tag:

```
<cfinvoke component="MyComponent" method="MyMethod"
          returnvariable="Result" >
<cfinvokeargument name="Argument1" value="Value1">
<cfinvokeargument name="Argument2" value="Value2">
```

The method could also be invoked using the argumentcollection attribute:

```
<cfset MyArguments = StructNew()>
<cfset MyArguments.Argument1 = "Value1">
<cfset MyArguments.Argument2 = "Value2">
<cfinvoke component="MyComponent" method="MyMethod"
          returnvariable="Result"
          argumentcollection="MyArguments">
```

The next thing we will examine is the cfobject tag. The cfobject tag will create an instance of the component. It has two attributes:

- **name** Contains the name you are applying to this instance of the component.
- **component** Contains the name of the component.

Although an instance of the component is now created, you still need to use the cfinvoke tag to call specific methods. Here is an example:

```
<cfobject name="MyInstance" component="MyComponent">
<cfinvoke component=" MyInstance" method="MyMethod"
          returnvariable="Result" argument1="Value1"
          argument2="value2">
```

This invocation method is different than previous ones, because the instance of the object is used instead of the component name.

Methods can also be invoked using CFScript, via the CreateObject function. This method is most similar to using the cfobject tag. Here are the parameters:

- **Type** Must be set to component.
- **Name** Contains the name and location of the component.

You can create a component instance using the CreateObject tag like this:

```
<cfscript>
 MyInstance = CreateObject("component", "MyComponent");
</cfscript>
```

After you create a component, you can call methods in CFScript using this syntax:

```
<cfscript>
 MyInstance.MyMethod("Value1","Value2");
</cfscript>
```

Next, we can create a test page to demonstrate the invocation of the stack component.

Invoking the Stack Component

The stack component that we created needs to be tested. The best way to do that is to invoke the component, and then test the results that get returned to make sure that they are expected. First, we can test the stack creation:

```
<!--- create the stack --->
<cfinvoke component="Stack" method="StackNew"
          returnVariable="MyStack">

<!--- Check the return value --->
<cfif IsArray(MyStack.StackArray)>
 The stack is an array<br>
<cfelse>
 The stack isn't an array. <br>
</cfif>
```

This code uses the cfinvoke method to invoke the StackNew method. This method does not need any arguments passed into it. The way that we check whether the stack was correctly created is by checking the MyStack.StackArray variable. This tells us whether the stack was properly initialized.

The next piece of functionality to test is adding elements onto the stack:

```
<!--- invoke the StackPush method --->
<cfinvoke component="Stack" method="StackPush"
          returnVariable="Pushed" Stack="#MyStack#"
          StackElement="Test Value">
```

```
<!--- Test the Pushed Value and the length of the array --->
<cfoutput>
 Pushed: #Pushed# #ArrayLen(MyStack.StackArray)#
</cfoutput><br>

<cfloop index="TempIndex" from="1"
        to="#ArrayLen(MyStack.StackArray)#">
 <cfoutput>
  #MyStack.StackArray[TempIndex]#<br>
 </cfoutput>
</cfloop>
```

First the StackPush method is invoked using the cfinvoke tag. We do two things to test
the value. First we check the value of the Pushed variable, which is returned from the
function, and the updated length of the StackArray variable. The second thing that we
do is to loop over the StackArray using the cfloop tag. Outputting each value of the array
will show us for sure whether or not the push actually worked.

Caution   *In the real world, you wouldn't want to access elements of the stack directly. You would
only want to manipulate through the provided methods.*

The last step is to check the pop method:

```
<cfinvoke component="Stack" method="StackPop"
          returnVariable="Popped" Stack="#MyStack#">

<!--- Display the return value of the pop function --->
<cfoutput>
 Popped: #Popped# #ArrayLen(MyStack.StackArray)#
</cfoutput><br>

<!--- Display all elements in the Stack --->
<cfloop index="TempIndex" from="1"
        to="#ArrayLen(MyStack.StackArray)#">
 <cfoutput>
  #MyStack.StackArray[TempIndex]#<br>
 </cfoutput>
</cfloop>
```

The method is called using the cfinvoke tag. To test the results, we output the returned
value, Popped, and the new size of the StackArray. Then the code loops over the
StackArray to view its modified values.

Using the cfproperty Tag

The cfproperty tag can be used to provide metadata to a ColdFusion Component, when viewing the CFC file in a browser. It can also be used to create custom types, which can be used within components of a package.

The following are the attributes of the cfproperty tag:

- **name**   Contains the name of the new variable type.
- **type**   Contains the ColdFusion variable type. Valid values are any, array, binary, Boolean, date, guid, numeric, query, string, struct, uuid, variablename, or a component name.

Suppose you create a ColdFusion Component, called Address.cfc:

```
<cfcomponent>
 <cfproperty name="Address1" type="String">
 <cfproperty name="Address2" type="String">
 <cfproperty name="City" type="String">
 <cfproperty name="State" type="String">
 <cfproperty name="Zip" type="String">
</cfcomponent>
```

The preceding component contains five cfproperty tags that can be used to make up an address.

Create a second CFC in the same directory. Name this one UseAddress.cfc. This one will have a function, OutputAddress. The function will accept a single parameter, with a type of address:

```
<cfcomponent>
 <cffunction name="ReturnAddress" returntype="Address"
             access="remote" output="yes">
  <cfargument name="InputAddress" type="Address" required="Yes">
  <cfreturn #InputAddress#>
 </cffunction>
</cfcomponent>
```

The component contains a single function, with one parameter, InputAddress. The InputAddress parameter is of type address. When you call this function, ColdFusion will look for Address.cfc and know that the page needs to contain all the property values.

You can call this component like this:

```
<cfset MyAddress = createObject("component","Address")>
```

```
<cfset MyAddress.Address1 = "Address1">
<cfset MyAddress.Address2 = "Address2">
<cfset MyAddress.City = "City">
<cfset MyAddress.State = "State">
<cfset MyAddress.Zip = "Zip">

<cfinvoke component="UseAddress" method="ReturnAddress"
        InputAddress="#MyAddress#" returnVariable="ReturnAddress">
```

First we create an instance of the Address object. The second step is to define the values that make up an address. They are defined as if a structure was created, using the objectname before the name of the property. Following that the component can be invoked, passing the address type into the InputAddress parameter.

  This example is discussed with regard to Web services in Chapter 31.

Learning Other Component Uses

There are some other elements of ColdFusion Components that are worth making note of. They are shown in Table 16-2.

Feature	Comments
Error handling	Try and Catch functions allow for method security. This is discussed in Chapter 18.
Component method security	Method access can be restricted using the role and access attributes. This is discussed in Chapter 17.
Component packages	Components stored in the same directory make up a component package. This helps to group related, but separate, functionality together.
Component inheritance	Allows you to import methods and properties from another component.
Component introspection	This is also known as component metadata. It provides a self-documenting definition of how to use the component without revealing its implementation.

Table 16-2. *Additional Component Features*

The one area that we want to examine further is component metadata. You can discover all the properties, methods, and inheritance of a component by accessing the CFC file from the web browser. The CFC file metadata is displayed as shown in Figure 16-2.

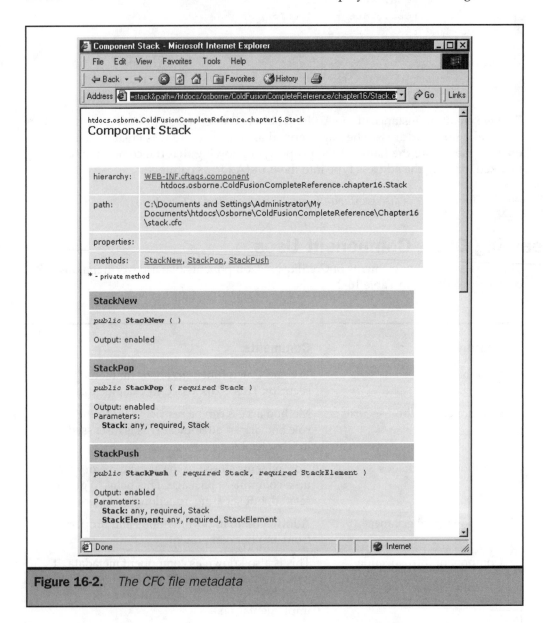

Figure 16-2.   *The CFC file metadata*

ColdFusion also provides these functions to provide this data in different formats:

- **CfcToMCDL**   To return the data in Master Control Document List (MCDL) format. MCDL is a data specification.
- **CfcToHTML**   To display the data in HTML format.
- **CfcToWDDX**   To return the data in WDDX format. WDDX is a form of XML that is discussed in Chapter 27.
- **CfcToWSDL**   To provide the data to a Web service.

Deciding When to Use Which Code Modularization Method

You may be wondering how you can choose between the different modularization types. There is no definitive answer, and many types can be used to solve the same problem. Table 16-3 provides a guide that you can use.

Purpose	cfinclude	Custom Tag	UDF	Component
Provide static display for multiple pages	Preferred			
Deploy headers or footers	Preferred			
Include one page in another	Preferred			
Divide pages into smaller units	Preferred			
Use variables in calling page	Alternate	Preferred	Preferred	Preferred
Implement recursion		Preferred	Preferred	Preferred
Distribute code		Preferred	Preferred	Preferred
Use subtags		Preferred		
Provide data manipulation		Alternate	Preferred	

Table 16-3.   *Preferred Methods for Using Code Modularization*

Purpose	cfinclude	Custom Tag	UDF	Component
Exchange data between modularization code		Alternate	Preferred	Preferred
Integrate with Flash		Alternate	Alternate	Preferred
Use built-in security			Alternate	Preferred
Encapsulate properties and methods				Preferred
Create Web services				Preferred
Implement object-oriented methodologies				Preferred

Table 16-3. *Preferred Methods for Using Code Modularization* (continued)

Summary

In this chapter, you learned about the following:

- Code modularization in ColdFusion
- How to use includes and custom tags
- How to create custom functions in CFScript and CFML
- ColdFusion Components

The next chapter will discuss how to secure your ColdFusion applications.

The Complete Reference

ColdFusion MX

Chapter 17

Securing Your ColdFusion Applications

hapter 4 discussed some best practices for securing your server. This chapter will discuss how to secure your ColdFusion applications. A whole new security model comes with ColdFusion MX. This chapter talks about what this security model is and how you can add security features in your applications.

Introducing ColdFusion MX's New Security Framework

There are two parts to adding security features into your application. Authentication is the first part. This is where you check to see if the user is allowed access to your application. The second part is user authorization. This is where you check to see if the current user is allowed to access the secured resource.

Authenticating Users

The first step in any authentication scheme is to decide what type of security your application needs. This section raises some questions to help you decide that, and then helps you create a database structure that reflects those needs. Finally, this section describes how to create a login page.

Designing Your Application's Security Model

The first thing you need to do before implementing a security system is to design it. The following are questions you should ask yourself when deciding how to design your security system:

- What functions of your application should have restricted access?
- Do different people in the organization have different access needs?
- Is there some crossover between the needs of different departments?
- Do some people have similar access needs, while others do not?

I will demonstrate how to step through this process with an example. Suppose you enter a contract to build a dynamic web site for a company that takes pictures of houses for real estate agents and publishes them to a web site. The salespeople need to be able to create new clients in the system. The photographers need to be able to create new houses in the system as they photograph the houses. The photographers may try to limit their duties to taking pictures and pass the data entry duties onto data entry people. The clients want to be able to get into their house descriptions and modify text. The boss wants to be able to perform every function in the system, including creating and modifying users and their access.

How do you turn this information into a useable security model for the web site? I like to do it one step at a time:

1. Define the roles (sometimes called groups) that have access to your web site. In this case, you have the boss, the salespeople, the photographers, the clients, and the data entry people.

2. Define the types of data that you want to control access to. This project has two areas: clients and houses.

3. Try to draw a chart, showing who has access to what data. You can see the chart I created in Figure 17-1.

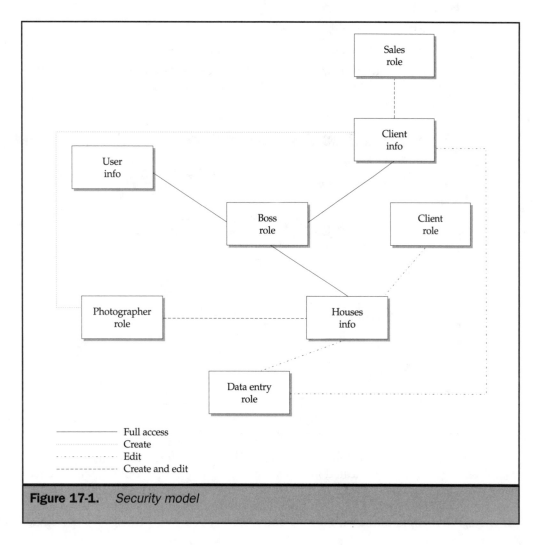

Figure 17-1. *Security model*

The security diagram often helps me to visualize the project. We can distinguish these facts from it:

- Salespeople can create and edit clients
- Clients can edit houses
- Data entry people can edit houses
- Data entry people can edit client info
- Photographers can create and edit houses
- Photographers can create clients
- The boss can create, edit, and delete houses
- The boss can create, edit, and delete clients
- The boss can create, edit, and delete users of the system

4. From this, you can create the table structure. The user information includes the groups, or roles, and user information. An intersection table connects the two. You need a Houses table and a Clients table. This is the table structure:

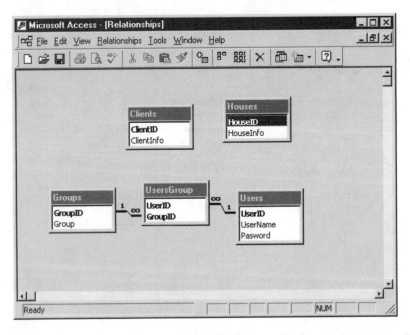

Although this system does provide a solid base from which to build, this application could easily get more complicated in a real-world situation. You wouldn't want a client to be able to modify any house or client data of another client. You would restrict them to their own data. Depending on the company, similar issues could exist for the photographers, salespeople, and even the data entry people. You could change the system to accommodate this by creating an intersection table that associates the Users table with the Clients table and one that associates the Users table with the Houses table.

Logging in with cflogin and cfloginuser

The next step is to create the ability to log in a user. In this manner, ColdFusion MX provides strong enhancements over previous versions of ColdFusion, in which login systems had to be built completely from scratch. There are two tags, cflogin and cfloginuser, that handle the login procedures.

The cflogin tag has no attributes. It is the equivalent of this conditional statement:

```
<cfif user is not logged in>
 Process login code
<cfelse>
 do nothing
</cfif>
```

For the cflogin tag to work, it needs both a start and end tag. The cfloginunser tag must reside inside the cflogin block. If the user has already logged in via the cflogin tag, then the cflogin block will be ignored.

These are the attributes to the cfloginuser tag:

- **name** The username of the user who is logging in.

- **roles** A list of roles that are assigned to a user. Roles are akin to groups, and are used to provide, or deny, access to specific features.

- **password** The password of the user that is logging in.

The cfloginuser tag does not actually verify the user against an LDAP directory or custom datasource, so do not execute this tag until you have successfully logged the user in through other means. This tag creates the ColdFusion framework internal to ColdFusion that keeps different users separate from each other.

This is how we create the templates that will make our login scheme a reality:

1. Make sure that you have an Application.cfm file with a cfapplication tag set up in the root directory. This should suffice:

   ```
   <CFAPPLICATION name="Chapter17" Sessionmanagement="Yes"
                  sessiontimeout="#createtimespan(1, 0, 0, 0)#">
   ```

2. Create the following login form. The input page accepts the username and password. The processing page will verify that information against the database.

   ```
   <!--- www.instantcoldfusion.com

   Description: A page to accept login information
               (username and password)
   ```

```
Entering: N/A
Exiting: loginp.cfm

Dependencies: N/A
Expecting: N/A

Modification History
Date      Modifier                 Modification
**********************************************************
04/09/2002 Jeff Houser, DotComIt   Created
--->

<form action="loginp.cfm" method="post">
 Name: <input type="Text" name="UserName"><br>
 Password: <input type="password" name="Pasword"><br>
 <input type="Submit">
</form>
```

The form is very simple and contains just the two fields that we need, Name and Password. (The password field is named, pasword, with one s. This is done to avoid problems with the reserved word, password.)

3. Create the form processing page:

```
<!--- www.instantcoldfusion.com

Description: A page to process Login information

Entering: Logini.cfm
Exiting: N/A

Dependencies: N/A
Expecting: form.username
   form.pasword

Modification History
Date      Modifier                 Modification
**********************************************************
04/09/2002 Jeff Houser, DotComIt   Created
--->


<!--- verify the user against the database --->
<cfquery datasource="Chapter17" name="VerifyUser">
 SELECT * FROM Users
 WHERE Users.UserName = '#form.UserName#' AND
```

```
       Users.pasword = '#form.Pasword#'
</cfquery>

<cfif VerifyUser.RecordCount is 1>
 Executing Database Query
 <!--- If the user information verified, get the --->
 <!--- user's groups --->
 <cfquery datasource="Chapter17" name="GetGroups">
  SELECT Groups.GroupID
  FROM UsersGroup, Groups
  WHERE UsersGroup.UserID = #VerifyUser.UserID# AND
    UsersGroup.GroupID = Groups.GroupID
 </cfquery>

 <cflogin>
  <cfloginuser name="#VerifyUser.Username#"
               password="#VerifyUser.Pasword#"
               roles="#ValueList(GetGroups.GroupID)#">
 </cflogin>

 Congratulations, you have logged in.  <br>

<cfelse>
 We were unable to log you in, please try again.<br>

</cfif>
```

The first action of the login-processing page is to check to see if the user entered a valid username and password combination. We perform that check by querying the database. If a result is returned, then the user was properly verified and we perform a second query to get all the groups that the user belongs to. After that, we use the cflogin and cfloginuser tags to log the user in. To specify the user's roles, I used the ValueList function to return the query column as a list.

| Note | *In the method that is used here, we are using the ID fields for the roles, not textual names. Whichever you use is just a matter of personal preference.* |

4. Check the Application.cfm file to see if the user is logged in. If the user is not logged in, redirect them to the login page using the cflocation tag. You cannot perform this check on the same page as the login page.

Consider this scenario. You try to access a page. The Application.cfm executes, and sees that you are not logged in. The cflocation tag redirects to the login page in the same directory. The Application.cfm executes. It sees that you are not logged in. The cflocation tag redirects to the login page, and it all starts again.

I like to keep the login scripts in the root directory and the remainder of the application underneath it. This is the Application.cfm for our subdirectory:

```
<cfapplication name="Chapter17" Sessionmanagement="Yes"
               sessiontimeout="#createtimespan(1,  0, 0,  0)#">

<!---if the user didn't log in, make sure they do --->
<cflogin>
 <cflocation url="../logini.cfm">
</cflogin>
```

The key thing to notice in this template is that it contains the same cfapplication tag as the one in the parent directory. You want to make sure that the name of the application is the same because this is one of the elements that ColdFusion uses to keep track of sessions.

The last step is to provide a way to log out your users. ColdFusion provides this in the form of cflogout. This tag accepts no attributes. It just automatically resets the user variables. A user will also be logged out if their session variables time out.

Authorizing Users

After you set up your login and logout functionality, you are in a position to access your application located in the subdirectory. You need to know how to access your groups, or roles, once you have logged in. ColdFusion provides the IsUserInRole function to determine this. The function contains a single attribute, a list of the roles that you are checking against.

When creating your code, you can use this function to decide whether the user has access to a specific resource. If the user has access, you can allow them to execute the code. If the user does not have access, you can redirect the user elsewhere, or show them nothing at all. Look at the following example of a navigation bar:

```
<a href="Index.cfm">Home<a/>

<!--- create a house, boss, and photographers --->
<cfif IsUserInRole("1,3")>
 <a href="CreateHouse.cfm"> Create House</a>
</cfif>

<!--- create a client, boss, and sales agents --->
<cfif IsUserInRole("3,4")>
<a href="CreateClient.cfm"> Create Client</a>
</cfif>
```

```
<!--- edit a house, boss, and data entry --->
<cfif IsUserInRole("2,3")>
 Authorized for 3<br>
</cfif>
```

Depending on the roles and how you use them, you can turn on, or off, any aspect of the display.

   ColdFusion MX also provides a function, GetAuthUser, that will return the username of the user who is currently logged in.

Integrating with LDAP

Lightweight Directory Access Protocol (LDAP) was created as a standard way to store authentication information across multiple platforms. ColdFusion integrates with LDAP directories via the cfldap tag. This section explains what LDAP is and demonstrates how to access an LDAP directory from within ColdFusion.

Understanding LDAP

An LDAP directory is a collection of information, akin to a telephone book, that is arranged and accessed via a hierarchy. The standard was created in the mid-1990s when the need existed to access ISO x.500 directories from personal computers with limited processing power. Many products will act as LDAP servers, such as iPlanet, Lotus Domino, and Microsoft Active Directory Services.

LDAP structures are hierarchical, meaning that there is a root node, and everything resides underneath it. Items that exist on the same level are considered equal. If we were to try to design a structure for our company that takes pictures of houses, it might look like Figure 17-2.

At the root node is the company. There are two nodes underneath it, users and groups. The groups reside under the group node, and the users reside under the users node. Individual groups are on the same level as individual users. The group entry would contain a list of users in the groups. The individual user entries would contain information such as username and password. This structure is, conceptually, very similar to the database we created in the first section of this chapter.

There are four main concepts that are universal to all LDAP directories:

- **Entry**   Each node of an LDAP directory is an entry. Entries consist of a collection of attributes and must follow the rules defined in the schema.

- **Attribute**   An attribute is a single entity of an entry. Each single attribute has a type and a value. The type determines how the value is treated and what information it can contain. Attributes could contain a user's name, location, e-mail address, and organization.

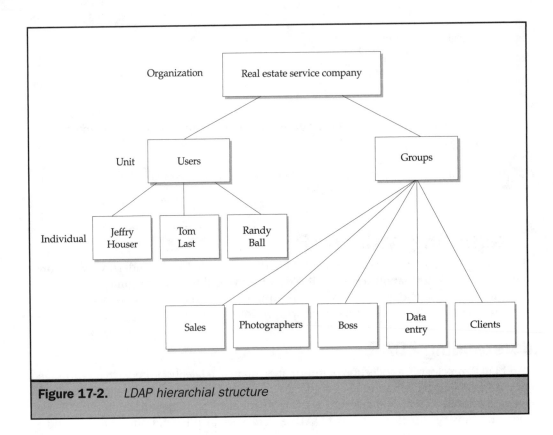

Figure 17-2. *LDAP hierarchial structure*

Tip *A list of standard attributes is located at http://developer.netscape.com/docs/manuals/ directory/schema2/41/attindex.htm. You should also check the documentation of your LDAP server, if available.*

- **Distinguished name** A distinguished name is something that uniquely identifies an entry. It is made up of the relative distinguished name (RDN) for the current entry and all that entry's parents. The RDN is the key that identifies all children among their parent entity.

- **Schema** A schema is a set of rules that defines the information that can be stored in a directory. Its two primary elements are the object class and the attribute type. Both object classes and attribute types contain a name and a unique identifier. The object class also contains a list of required and optional attribute types that the object can contain and, if applicable, the class that the object inherits from. Attribute types include an indicator as to whether the type is single- or multivalued and the rules that are used to verify the data.

Although this section didn't contain an exhaustive in-depth tutorial of LDAP, it is enough information for you to access an LDAP directory via ColdFusion.

Authenticating Users Against an LDAP Server

This section teaches you about the cfldap tag, which is what you use to access and modify cfldap server information via ColdFusion. This section ends by demonstrating the cfldap tag's usage.

Learning about the cfldap Tag

The cfldap tag is used to access an LDAP directory from within ColdFusion. The cfldap tag allows you to create, delete, read, and edit the following information stored within an LDAP directory:

- **server**   The hostname or IP address of the LDAP server.
- **port**   The port number that the LDAP server resides on. The default is 389.
- **username**   The username of the user accessing the server. The default is anonymous. Required if secure = cfssl_basic.
- **password**   The password of the user that is accessing the server. Required if secure = cfssl_basic.
- **action**   Defines the action that the tag will perform: query, to retrieve information; add, to add a new entry; modify, to change an existing entry; modifydn, to modify a distinguished name; or delete, to delete an entry.
- **name**   The name of the variable that the information you retrieve from the LDAP will be returned to. Required if action is query.
- **timeout**   The maximum length of the timeout. The default is 60 seconds.
- **maxrows**   Contains the maximum number of entries that the LDAP query will return.
- **start**   Contains the name of the distinguished name of the node that you are going to start your search on. Required if action is query.
- **scope**   Specifies the scope of the search: to the current level (onelevel), the current entry (base), or the current entry and all levels below it (subtree).
- **attributes**   If the action is a query, this is a comma-delimited list of attributes to return. To get all attributes, specify, *. If the action is add or modify, this is a comma-delimited list of attributes. If the action is modifydn, ColdFusion doesn't check these values before passing them onto the LDAP server.
- **filter**   Defines the search criteria. The default is objectclass =*.
- **sort**   A comma-delimited list of columns that the results will sort on.
- **sortcontrol**   The type of sort: asc, for ascending; nocase, for case insensitive; or desc, for a descending sort.
- **dn**   The distinguished name. Required if action is add, modify, modifydn, or delete.
- **startrow**   The first row of the LDAP query that will be returned in the ColdFusion query. The default is 1.

- **modifytype** Defines how to process multivalued attributes. Options are add, delete, and replace.

- **rebind** If the rebind attribute is set to yes, then ColdFusion attempts to execute the query using the original credentials. If set to no, referred connections are anonymous.

- **referral** The number of hops allowed by a referral.

- **secure** An optional attribute that defines the type of security to use when accessing the LDAP server. Valid values are CFSSL_Basic or certificate_db.

- **separator** Specifies the delimiter that separates multivalued attributes in the returned query. The default is a comma.

- **delimiter** Specifies the separator for name-value pairs.

Many of the attributes are not required for our query purposes, because we just need to retrieve data, without updating or changing data.

Verifying the User Data

We can verify against the LDAP in a similar manner to our custom database verification. We can even use the same login input page. This is the updated login processing page:

```
<!--- www.instantcoldfusion.com

Description: A page to process Login information

Entering: Logini.cfm
Exiting: N/A

Dependencies: N/A
Expecting: form.username
   form.pasword

Modification History
Date        Modifier                 Modification
*********************************************************
04/09/2002 Jeff Houser, DotComIt    Created
--->


<!--- verify the user against the database
       we need to log in as the directory manager to verify
       the user --->
<cfldap action="query" name="VerifyUser"
```

```
            attributes="UID,dn,username,password"
            start="u=Users"
            scope="subtree"
            server="localhost"
            filter= "(&(username=#form.Username#)
                   (Password=#form.Pasword#)"
            username="cn=directory manager"
            password="Password">

<cfif CerifyUser.RecordCount is 1>
 <!--- If the user information verified, get the --->
 <!--- user's groups --->
 <cfldap action="query" name="GetGroups"
          attributes="GroupID"
          start="u=Groups"
          scope="subtree"
          server="localhost"
          filter= "(&(username=#form.Username#)"
          username=" #VerifyUser.dn#"
          password="form.Pasword">

 <cflogin>
  <cfloginuser name="# VerifyUser.dn#"
               password="#form.Pasword#"
               roles="#ValueList(GetGroups.GroupID)#">
 </cflogin>

 Congratulations, you have logged in.   <br>

<cfelse>
 We were unable to log you in, please try again.<br>

</cfif>
```

DEMONSTRATING
ADVANCED APPLICATION
DEVELOPMENT CONCEPTS

The first cfldap tag verifies that the user has entered their information properly. The *u* in the start attribute stands for unit. We are looking for a node in the users unit where the username is equal to form.username and the password is equal to form.password. To perform this query against the LDAP server, we must be logged in as the directory manager, to make sure we have access to the whole directory. The cn stands for common name.

The second cfldap tag returns all the groups that the user is associated with. We look in the groups unit, specified with the start parameter, and on all the sublevels. We filter by using the username. This time the user who logs in to the LDAP directory is the user who is trying to log in. That is acceptable now that we verified the user exists. The remainder of the template uses the cflogin and cloginuser accordingly.

Protecting Other Resources

This final section discusses some other ways to protect ColdFusion features and data. ColdFusion Components, discussed in Chapter 16, have security features built in. This section also shows you how to protect non-HTML content such as sound files, images, or PDFs.

Securing Your ColdFusion Components

ColdFusion Components (CFCs) are a way to bring object-oriented concepts into ColdFusion MX. If you are not familiar with ColdFusion Components, you can read all about them in Chapter 16. A CFC is a way to group a bunch of functionality, called methods, together. The methods are defined via the use of the cffunction tag. There are two attributes on the cffunction tag that pertain to security measures:

- **access** Specifies the type of function that you are creating. Valid values are: private, which means that the function can only be called by functions from within the existing CFC; public, which means anyone can use this CFC method; remote, which is designed for remote access via Web services, through a URL, or by Flash; and package, which means that the function can only be called by functions in the CFC package. Remember that a package is a collection of all CFCs in a single directory.

- **roles** Relate back to the roles that were specified when the user logged in with the cfloginuser tag. If the user is not in the role specified in this attribute, he or she cannot access the function.

Suppose that while creating the real estate service company's web site, we decided to use a CFC to handle the creation, editing, and display of a house. We would want to restrict the creation function to the Photographers and the Boss. The EditHouse function would be restricted to Photographers, Data Entry People, Clients, and the Boss. Deleting a house would be restricted to the Boss. This would be the skeleton of the CFC:

```
<cfcomponent>
 <cffunction name="DisplayHouse" access="Public" output=""Yes">
   <!--- house display code --->
 </cffunction>

 <cffunction name="EditHouse" access="Public" output=""Yes"
```

```
                    roles="Photographers, DataEntry, Client, Boss">
  <!--- house edit code --->
</cffunction>


<cffunction name="CreateHouse" access="Public" output="""Yes"
            roles="Photographers, Boss">
  <!--- house creation code --->
</cffunction>


<cffunction name="DeleteHouse" access="Public" output="""Yes"
            roles="Boss">
  <!--- house creation code --->
</cffunction>


</cfcomponent>
```

The specific code of each function is not filled in, but this would be a skeleton of the structure, with the specific access levels restricting the use of each function to the proper roles.

Delivering Files with cfcontent

Suppose that the same real estate service company was offering high-resolution scans of images. They want to prevent unauthorized people from going directly to the images and viewing them. People can go directly to the images if they reside in a web-accessible directory. Since the image files are not ColdFusion templates, the Application.cfm will not run and users will be able to download the images directly.

ColdFusion provides a tag, cfcontent, to handle this type of issue. You can store your files in a non-web-accessible directory and then deliver them to qualified users with cfcontent. These are the attributes to the tag:

- **type**   A required attribute that specifies the file mime type of the file that is going to be returned.
- **deletefile**   A Boolean attribute that specifies whether or not the file gets deleted after delivery to the client.
- **file**   An optional attribute that specifies the name of the file that you want to deliver to the client.
- **reset**   An optional Boolean attribute that specifies whether or not to preserve the output that precedes the call to cfcontent. If the file attribute exists, this attribute has no effect.
- **encoding**   An optional attribute that specifies the encoding type of the generated output. This value could be any valid character encoding. The default is ISO-8859-1.

To put cfcontent to use, you first need to log in the user. Put the files that you want to deliver in a directory that is not accessible from the Web. You could actually put the files in any directory, but if they are web-accessible, it defeats the purpose of using this method to secure files.

Deliver the files, like this:

```
<cfcontent file="C:\MyDirectory\MyImage.jpg"
           type="image/jpeg">
```

The only way to view this file from the Web is to load the ColdFusion page that contains the cfcontent command.

> **Note**   *The cfcontent tag's use is not limited to delivering photos. Any type of file could be delivered with this tag, such as QuickTime movies, MP3 sound files, or Adobe PDF files.*

Summary

In this chapter, you learned the following:

- How to secure your applications with the cflogin and cfloginuser tags
- How to integrate ColdFusion with LDAP directories
- Security features of ColdFusion Components
- How to protect files with cfcontent

The next chapter will teach you tips for debugging and troubleshooting your ColdFusion applications.

The Complete
Reference

Chapter 18

Debugging and Optimizing Your Applications

319

This chapter teaches you how to debug and optimize your ColdFusion templates. It starts by showing how you can find syntax errors in your templates as you write them. It then teaches you about error-handling concepts in ColdFusion. Finally, it discusses ways you can optimize the code in your site.

Finding Errors in Your Application

This section discusses the debugging options that are available in ColdFusion MX. It examines each element of the debugging output and describes the different types of debugging panels. It finishes by showing you some common syntax errors that ColdFusion might return and how you can use these errors to eliminate syntax problems in your code.

Gathering Debugging Information

The first universal step to finding errors in your applications is to turn on debugging information. This section explains all the different debugging data that is available to you and the different display methods.

Understanding Debugging Output

The debugging output provides you with a lot of different information based on the execution of your page. Debugging can be enabled from the ColdFusion Administrator, as discussed in Chapter 6. This chapter shows you some output and demonstrates how it all works together.

ColdFusion's debugging output provides information under the following headings:

- **Debugging Information** Displays general information at the bottom of the page, including the template, the time stamp, the locale, the ColdFusion version, the browser (user agent), the remote IP address, and the name of the host.

Debugging Information
ColdFusion Server Enterprise 6,0,0,43030

Template	/htdocs/InstantColdFusion/index.cfm
Time Stamp	11-Apr-02 11:57 AM
Locale	English (US)
User Agent	Mozilla/4.0 (compatible; MSIE 5.5; Windows NT 5.0)
Remote IP	127.0.0.1
Host Name	127.0.0.1

■ **Execution Time** Provides a detailed description of the execution time of the template. All includes and custom tags are listed here, as well as the Application.cfm and OnRequestEnd.cfm files, if applicable.

Execution Time

Total: 3000 ms

```
1156 ms (16) C:\Documents and Settings\Administrator\My Documents\htdocs\InstantColdFusion\index.cfm
829 ms (218) C:\Documents and Settings\Administrator\My Documents\htdocs\InstantColdFusion\application.cfm
218 ms (0)    C:\Documents and Settings\Administrator\My Documents\htdocs\InstantColdFusion\inc\app_login.cfm
16 ms (0)     C:\Documents and Settings\Administrator\My Documents\htdocs\InstantColdFusion\inc\header.cfm
0 ms (0)      C:\Documents and Settings\Administrator\My Documents\htdocs\InstantColdFusion\inc\app_errors.cfm
0 ms (0)      C:\Documents and Settings\Administrator\My Documents\htdocs\InstantColdFusion\inc\app_scope.cfm
0 ms (0)      C:\Documents and Settings\Administrator\My Documents\htdocs\InstantColdFusion\inc\app_variables.cfm
0 ms (0)      C:\Documents and Settings\Administrator\My Documents\htdocs\InstantColdFusion\inc\footer.cfm
781 ms        STARTUP, PARSING, COMPILING, LOADING, & SHUTDOWN
```

■ **SQL Queries** Specifies the time it took to execute the query, the name of the datasource, the number of records that were returned, the file location of the file that ran the query, and the query text. This information is useful if you are trying to isolate query bottlenecks.

SQL Queries

```
getUser (Datasource=instantCF, Time=140ms, Records=0) in C:\Documents and Settings\Administrator

              select *
              from users
              where users.lcv = '40188271146'
```

■ **Scope Variables - Application Variables** Displays variables in particular scopes. You can choose which variables and scopes you want displayed in the ColdFusion Administrator. You can start with the application variables.

Scope Variables

Application Variables:

```
datasource=instantCF
errordir=error/
applicationname=InstantColdFusion
includedir=inc/
```

■ **CGI Variables**   Special variables that contain information about the page request, including directory paths and server names.

```
CGI Variables:

SCRIPT_NAME=/htdocs/InstantColdFusion/index.cfm
HTTPS_KEYSIZE=
CERT_KEYSIZE=
AUTH_USER=
SERVER_NAME=localhost
REQUEST_METHOD=GET
AUTH_PASSWORD=
AUTH_TYPE=
HTTPS_SECRETKEYSIZE=
CERT_SERVER_SUBJECT=
CERT_SERIALNUMBER=
PATH_INFO=/htdocs/InstantColdFusion/index.cfm
HTTP_COOKIE=CFID=401; CFTOKEN=88271146
SERVER_PORT=80
REMOTE_USER=
QUERY_STRING=
CERT_SERVER_ISSUER=
CERT_SECRETKEYSIZE=
HTTP_REFERER=
```

Unless I am specifically dealing with CGI variables in an application, I like to turn these off in the ColdFusion Administrator.

■ **Cookie Variables**   The cookies that the server has set on the browser. ColdFusion uses cookies as part of its application framework, as described in Chapter 8. I like to keep these on. They are shown in Figure 18-1.

■ **Request Variables**   Variables that exist only during the page request (see Figure 18-1). Variable scopes are described in Chapter 8.

■ **Server Variables**   Special variables that contain server information, such as the version of ColdFusion and the operating system of the server (see Figure 18-1). I usually turn these off.

■ **Session Variables**   User-specific variables (see Figure 18-1). I like to keep a watch on these.

■ **Debug Rendering Time**   The time it took to create the debugging output.

Debug Rendering Time: 515 ms

The time it takes to create the debugging output is included in this value, so with the debugging turned off, this value will probably be slightly less.

Note   *Complex variables such as arrays or structures will not display each individual element.*

Cookie Variables:

CFID=401
CFTOKEN=88271146

Request Parameters:

tempsession=Struct (22)

Server Variables:

os=Struct (5)
coldfusion=Struct (7)

Session Variables:

salutation=
lcv=40188271146
cfid=401
email=
company=
firstname=
urltoken=CFID=401&CFTOKEN=88271146
fax=
address1=
lastname=
userid=
address2=
title=
isloggedin=false
stateid=
zip=
sessionid=INSTANTCOLDFUSION_401_88271146

Figure 18-1.   *Cookie, request, server, and session variable debug output*

Using the Different Debugging Styles

There are two different debugging styles that you can choose from the ColdFusion Administrator. One is the classic style, and the other, new to ColdFusion MX, is called dockable. The classic style is the one that I prefer. It displays all documentation information after the template's execution, at the bottom of the page. The dockable style works differently.

 Tip *You can switch between debugging styles in the ColdFusion Administrator.*

Change your debug settings to display the dockable format, and load a page. At the bottom of the page, you will see this:

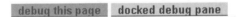

If the window did not pop up automatically, click the Debug This Page link. The debugging window should pop up:

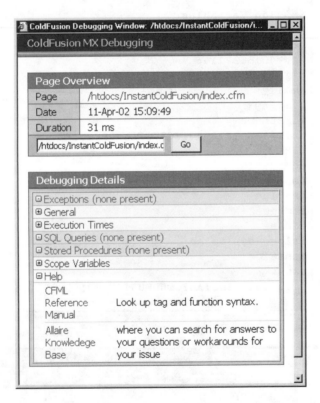

This window has all the same information that the class has, but in a more compressed space so that you can expand the information you want to see and collapse the information that you do not. When the window comes up, all information will be collapsed.

If you do not like switching between different windows, you can click the Docked Debug Pane link. This will split your current window and show the debugging output in a frame, next to the window that you are surfing in (see Figure 18-2). The docked format is new in ColdFusion MX and seeks to improve the debugging and optimization of your code.

You can customize the debugging output if it suits your needs. The debugging templates are located in CFusionMX\wwwroot\WEB-INF\debug.

Isolating Syntax and Logic Errors

This section discusses some common syntax errors you may come across when developing your ColdFusion application, and shows you how to interpret the ColdFusion errors. The section finishes by examining some common tags that are used for isolating programming errors in ColdFusion templates.

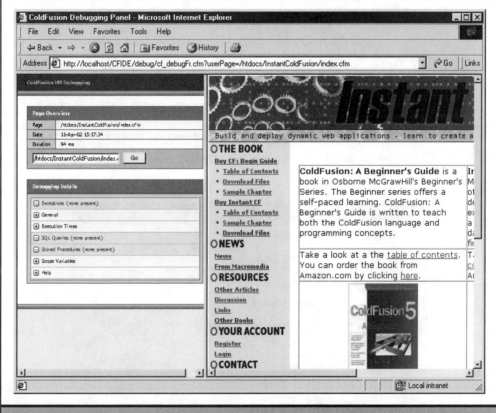

Figure 18-2. *The docked Debugging panel*

Viewing Common Errors

To start, I want to define some of the common errors that you may come across when developing your ColdFusion applications. Many of these errors are due to typos and are easily debugged.

■ **Database error** ColdFusion passes SQL queries into the database without any verification of the query. Because of this, database errors can be hard to debug from ColdFusion. Here is an example of one:

ColdFusion passes the query text to the ODBC driver, and if there is an error, ColdFusion raises an exception. To debug your queries, it is best to use an alternate tool, such as SQL Server's Query Analyzer or the Queries view in Microsoft Access, so that you can see the output of the query. Such a tool also may give you more information as to the problem than is provided via ODBC. If you are creating dynamic queries based on ColdFusion variables, the next step is to find out what values are in the variables that make up your query.

■ **Invalid tag or tag attribute** Invalid tag errors are almost always due to typos. This is an example:

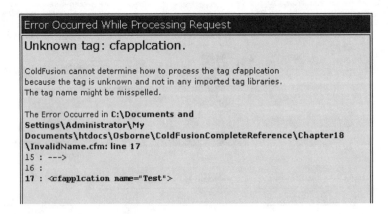

These errors usually give you more information than database errors. You are given the error type (unknown tag) along with the line that the error occurred on and the file that the error occurred in. The code sample provides the few lines of code that precede the one that caused an error. To correct these, just go to the line number and change the tag. If you have an invalid parameter, ColdFusion MX will helpfully provide you with a list of all valid parameters.

■ **Undefined variable** Variable definition problems, other than typos, are usually due to you trying to access an undefined variable. The errors are similar in format to the invalid tag errors. You are given a line number and a description of the problem.

This type of error will happen most commonly when some of your smarter users try to modify URL outputs, or in HTML forms where you use checkboxes. If the checkboxes are not checked, no variable exists on the form processing page. The best way to avoid these errors is to use the IsDefined function to check for a variable's existence before accessing it, or to use the cfparam tag to define a default value to variables that are not defined.

■ **Mismatched tags** If you have an open tag but not a close tag, ColdFusion throws an error. This is most common with mismatched cfif statements.

Understanding Common Tags for Debugging Templates

Discovering syntax errors in your application is relatively easy. Finding problems with your business logic is not always so easy. Just because ColdFusion processes the code properly does not mean that the code will operate correctly.

Look at this real-world example. Suppose you are creating a record in a database and need the unique ID of this new record so you can perform additional processing on this page, such as creating additional relationships based on the new record. An example of this is creating a user in a database and then immediately adding that new user into a group. We discussed users and groups in Chapter 17.

You write the following code:

```
<!--- Create the user --->
<cfquery name="CreateUser" datasource="Chapter18">
 INSERT INTO  Users (UserName, Pasword)
 VALUES ('Jeff', 'Houser')
</cfquery>

<!--- Get the new user's ID --->
<cfquery name=" GetNewUserID" datasource="Chapter18">
 SELECT TOP 1 UserID
 FROM Users
 ORDER BY Users.UserID DESC
</cfquery>
```

The first query creates the user. The second query gets the largest UserID from the database, assuming that it is related to the existing user.

The password field is named pasword with one s. This is done to avoid problems with the reserved word, password.

The previous code will probably work every time you test it on your development server. However, what happens when you start to have load on the server? Consider the following scenario.

Two people are creating a new account at once:

1. User1 creates an account and clicks the Submit button.
2. User2 creates an account and clicks the Submit button.
3. User1's CreateUser query runs, creating his account.
4. User2's CreateUser query runs, creating his account.
5. User1's GetNewUserID query executes, returning User2's ID.
6. User2's GetNewUserID query executes, returning User2's ID.

Did you notice the error? The system would now be setting up User2 with all of User1's information, in addition to all of User2's information. If User1 was being set up as a server administrator and User2 was being set up as a data entry person, you just gave your data entry user all the access of a server administrator. This is usually not ideal.

In short, your code is correct from a CFML perspective, but wrong from a business logic perspective. How do we fix it? In this case, the simplest fix is to wrap both statements in a cftransaction block. A SQL transaction is a series of queries performed as a group. The cftransaction tag is a way to define transactions from within ColdFusion. It will prevent User2 from being created before User1 is finished.

How do you discover business logic errors? There is no single method for finding errors in an application, but I like to start by isolating the block of code that has the error and go from there. You can use a group of ColdFusion tags together that will help you isolate problems: cfabort, cfoutput, cfdump, and cflog.

The first two tags that we want to examine are used to output the value of variables: cfoutput and cfdump. We previously discussed the cfoutput tag. In this case, it needs no attributes. We can just list the variables that we want to output, surrounded by pound signs. The cfdump tag is like cfoutput, used for this purpose, with built-in formatting and support for complex variables. It has one attribute, var, that accepts the name of the variable that you want to output.

Make sure that you enclose the variable name in pound signs, or cfdump will mistake it for a string and output the variable name, not the variable value.

After outputting variables, you usually want to stop the processing of the page with cfabort. The cfabort tag uses a single attribute, showerror, which contains the message that is displayed before the template processing stops. This is an optional attribute. Outputting the variables and then stopping the template from processing will help you figure out if the error is located before, or after, the place where you stopped the template.

The cflog tag is designed to save information about your application without interrupting the existing logic flow. You can use it to add custom information to a log file, or even create your own, application-specific logs. These are the attributes:

- **text**   Contains the text that you want to add to the log.

- **log**   Specifies either Application or Scheduler if you want to write to the Application or Scheduler log files. This is ignored if the file attribute is specified.

- **file**   Specifies the name of the file that you want to add your log information to. When specifying this attribute, do not include the file extension. If you want to add something to the myapplication.log file, for example, use myapplication.

- **type**   Specifies the type of data that you want to log: information, warning, error, or fatal information.

- **thread**   Specifies whether or not to put the threadID in the log file (Boolean attribute).

- **date**   Specifies whether the date is placed in the log (Boolean attribute). Answering no to this will throw an error, because it is deprecated.

- **time**   Specifies whether the time is placed in the resulting log file (Boolean attribute). Answering no to this will throw an error, because the attribute is deprecated.

- **application**   Specifies the name of the application that the error occurred in. The name of the application is specified in the cfapplication file.

The cflog tag is great for collecting information about the use of your application.

Using cftrace

ColdFusion MX provides a new tag, cftrace, which is a combination of cflog, cfabort, and cfdump. The cftrace tag will output variable values, save debugging data to the cftrace.log file, and abort page processing. Its output can also be integrated with Dreamweaver MX.

These are the attributes of the cftrace tag:

- **abort**   Specifies whether or not to abort the processing page when the tag is called (Boolean attribute).

- **category**   Contains a string that is used to specify trace groups.

- **inline** Specifies whether or not output is sent to the page as the tag executes (Boolean attribute).

- **text** Contains the text that you want placed in the text portion of the log.

- **type** Accepts four values—information, warning, error, and fatal information—and places this information in the type portion of the log.

- **var** Specifies the name of a simple or complex variable (optional attribute). This variable will be displayed on the browser.

The use of the cftrace tag is very subjective, considering that the text and category attributes can contain values for anything you want. Using these attributes not only is very beneficial, but is almost a necessity when you plan to analyze the log information.

Suppose that you are creating an application, and you want to follow what happens every time a particular form is submitted. You might add a cftrace tag like this:

```
<cftrace var="form" text="Form Variables'"
        category="My Form" inline="no">
```

This tag will not interrupt the flow of the page, but will add information to the cftrace log. A trace entry is made in the debugging output.

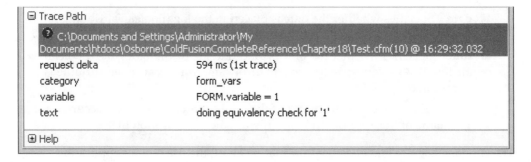

If you set the inline attribute to yes, the trace output is also showed as part of the application template.

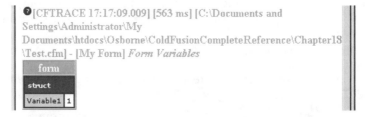

This allows for instant gratification of your debugging output needs.

Creating Error Handlers

After you finish writing your application, too many times you stop once you can prove functionality. This usually is due to budget or time constraints, or other considerations. However, just because an application is functional does not mean that it is perfect. This section teaches you the types of errors that can happen during run time, and how you can handle them.

Examining Errors that Occur in Web Development

First, we discuss some common definitions that you need to know when learning how to handle errors. Then, we discuss some of the common types of errors that can, and will, occur in web development.

Understanding Error Definitions

The following are some common terms that are used in error handling that you need to know to understand the rest of this section:

- **Exception**   Another name for an error.
- **Throw**   Used to define when an error occurs.
- **Catch**   The resolution of an error; sometimes called "trapping the error."

The reasoning for the throw and catch analogy is this: Programs execute in a straight line, from top to bottom, and when an error happens, it interrupts the normal flow of the program. The code automatically stops processing the normal path and jumps right to the error handling code. The execution is thrown from one place to another, just like a baseball is thrown. The error handling code catches the error, just as someone would catch the baseball. When you catch the error, you are able to put the program back on track.

Explaining the Different Types of Errors

These are the types of errors that you may experience when creating your web applications:

- **Syntax errors**   Occur because of errors in your ColdFusion code (as discussed earlier in this chapter). These are usually due to typos and can be easily fixed. There should be none of these errors in your application by the time it goes live.

- **Business logic errors**   Occur because your code performs the wrong functionality. These errors are harder to track down than syntax errors. Hopefully, by the time you go live, you are sure that none of these problems exist.

- **Missing page errors**   Occur because a page is missing, whether it is a missing ColdFusion template, a custom tag, or a dead link. Oftentimes, these errors are due to invalid relative links. Sometimes they occur when other sites link to yours, or you link to other sites.

- **User input errors**   Occur when the user inputs invalid information. Whenever you ask the user for information, you should verify that the information they give you is what you want. If you are asking for a number and given text, your application needs to notice and tell the user they made a mistake in their input.

- **Security errors**   Occur when a user tries to access something that they should not have access to. The most common way to address these problems is to redirect the user to a login page.

- **Database errors**   Occur because of a failed database operation. Perhaps the database server went down, or unverified user input made your query invalid.

Ideally, you don't want any of these errors to happen on your site, but often they are unavoidable. Something will go wrong. You need to know how to spot potential problems and handle them so that the user does not get an ugly-looking error.

Creating a Generic Error Handler

This section shows you how you can set up a generic error handler. A generic error handler is a handler that you set up to handle your errors if all else fails. They are usually just used to display a pretty page to your end user and log as much information as you can about them.

Setting Up ColdFusion to Catch Errors

Chapter 3 describes how to set up the site-wide handlers from the ColdFusion Administrator. The site-wide error handler will work for every application located on the ColdFusion server. On the Settings page of the ColdFusion Administrator, you can define the error templates to handle missing templates and all other errors.

Missing Template Handler

Specify the relative path to a template to execute when the ColdFusion application server cannot find a requested template.

Site-wide Error Handler

Specify the relative path to a template to execute when the ColdFusion Application Server encounters errors while processing a request.

ColdFusion also provides a way to create application-specific error handlers via the cferror tag. Normally, you want to keep the cferror tag in the Application.cfm file. These are its attributes:

- **type**   Specifies the type of error to watch for (required attribute). Valid values are request, validation, and exception.

■ **template** Contains the name of the page that will be executed if a specific type of error occurs.

■ **mailto** Does not e-mail the error to anyone, but rather makes an e-mail address available on the error processing page.

■ **exception** Contains the type of errors that this handler will catch, a list of which is provided in Table 18-1.

There are three classifications of errors that can be specified in the type attribute. These classifications define the features you have accessible in the error template and the special variables.

■ **Request** Request error types have access to the special variables, which are explained next, but do not have access to CFML tags. Request errors should only be used as a backup in sites with user requirements.

■ **Exception** Exception error types have access to all the applicable variables and the full range of the CFML language.

■ **Validation** Validation errors are just like exception errors, except they have access to special validation variables. This type of exception will only be called if you specify that a value must be required using a hidden field called *fieldname*_required.

Exception	Description
Application	Catches application-specific errors
Database	Catches database style errors
Template	Catches exceptions with ColdFusion pages
Security	Catches security errors
Object	Catches errors with objects created by the cfobject tag
MissingInclude	Catches missing files
Expression	Catches all expression errors
Lock	Catches all custom exceptions
CustomType	Catches a custom type that was defined with the cfthrow tag
Any	Catches any exception

Table 18-1. *ColdFusion Exceptions*

The monitor exception type is deprecated in ColdFusion MX. Make sure that you do not use it.

Many special variables exist for use with the error-handling templates. These variables, listed next, contain different information about the error, which you can use to debug it. These variables are contained in a structure, called error, that is created automatically upon the creation of an error.

- **Error.Diagnostics**   Contains the detailed error message from the ColdFusion server. It is available in exception and request errors.

- **Error.MailTo**   Contains the value that was specified in the mailto attribute of the cferror tag. It is available in exception and request errors.

- **Error.DateTime**   Contains the date and time that the exception occurred. It is available in exception and request errors.

- **Error.Browser**   Contains the name of the browser that the user was browsing with when the error occurred.

- **Error.GeneratedContent**   Contains the content that was generated by the failed request. It is available in exception errors.

- **Error.RemoteAddress**   Contains the IP address of the client that caused the error. It is available in exception and request errors.

- **Error.HTTPReferer**   Contains the page that the client was on before the error occurred. It is available in exception and request errors.

- **Error.Template**   Contains the name of the template that caused the error. It is available in exception and request errors.

- **Error.QueryString**   Contains the query string that was in the URL that caused the error. The variable is available in exception and request error types.

- **Error.ValidationHeader**   Contains the header text for the validation message. It is available for validation errors only.

- **Error.InvalidFields**   Provides a list of form fields that did not pass the validation tests. This is available in validation errors.

- **Error.ValidationFooter**   Contains the footer text for the validation message. It is available in validation errors only.

You can use these variables to collection information in a log, display an error message to the user, or even send e-mail to yourself regarding the error.

Creating the Handler Page

This section shows you how create a standard error page. To do so, follow these steps:

1. Create an empty template. Add your documentation header:

```
<!--- www.instantcoldfusion.com

Description: Page to handle exception type errors

Entering: N/A
Exiting: N/A

Dependencies: N/A
Expecting: N/A

Modification History
Date        Modifier              Modification
**********************************************************
04/13/2002 Jeff Houser, DotComIt    Created
--->
```

2. Create a log entry in this application's log:

```
<cflog file="MyApplication" type="Error"
        text="There was an exception error: #error.Diagnostics#
              in #Error.Template# ">
```

The code uses the cflog tag to create an entry in this application's log file.

3. Send an e-mail to yourself, or to the web master, stating the error's information. This can be done using the cfmail tag, which is discussed in more detail in Chapter 22.

```
<cfmail to="#error.MailTo#" from=error@instantcoldfusion.com
        subject="There was an Exception Error">

DateTime: #Error.DateTime#<br>
Diagnostic: #Error.Diagnostics#<br>

Generated Content: #Error.GeneratedContent#<br>
HTTP Referrer: #Error.HTTPReferer#<br>

Template: #Error.Template#<br>
Browser: #Error.Browser#<br>

Remote Address: #Error.RemoteAddress#<br>
QueryString: #Error.QueryString#<br>

</cfmail>
```

The cfmail tag is used with three parameters: to, the user who the e-mail is sent to; from, the e-mail address that the e-mail is sent from; and subject, the subject of the e-mail. The body of the message e-mail contains all the informational error variables.

4. Display a message to the user who experienced the error. Showing them a blank page doesn't achieve anything more than showing them an ugly error message.

```
Sorry, you have encountered an error.  We will work to fix it
ASAP!<br>
```

5. With your error page created, make sure that you add the cferror tag to your application.cfm page:

```
<cferror type="exception" template="ErrorTemplate.cfm"
        exception="any" mailto="jeff@instantcoldfusion.com">
```

Without the cferror tag, no one will ever see your error template, in the rare case that errors do occur.

Creating a Specific Error Handler

ColdFusion allows you to handle errors in CFScript and CFML. This section shows you how to catch predefined errors in a specific code section in your application, and how you can create your own error handler, if necessary.

Catching Errors in CFScript and CFML

There are two tags that ColdFusion uses to handle errors in CFML: cftry and cfcatch. Both have an open and close tag. The cftry tag accepts no attributes. It marks a block of ColdFusion code, saying, "Try to execute this block of code and let me know if there is an error." If an error occurs, the cftry tag starts looking for cfcatch blocks.

The cfcatch blocks must reside inside a cftry block. There is no limit to the number of cfcatch blocks that you can have, but you must have at least one. The cfcatch tag accepts a single attribute, type. The type attribute contains the name of the exception that you want to catch. You can refer to Table 18-1 for the list of exceptions.

Suppose you had some database code that inserted values into a database. Your application is very secure and you have created different user accounts at the database level. The user logged in and you have stored the username and password in two session variables. This is your insert code:

```
<cfquery datasource="Chapter18" name="InsertQuery"
        username="#session.Username#"
        password="#session.Password#">
 INSERT INTO MyTable (MyData1, MyData2, MyData3)
 VALUES ('Data 1', 'My Data 2', 'Three')
</cfquery>
```

What happens when the user does not have access to create tables in this database? A database error will be returned to ColdFusion. This could be caught with the cferror tag, but that will interrupt the normal processing flow. The best way to fix this is with cftry and cfcatch:

```
<cftry>
 <!--- Perform database insert --->
 <cfquery datasource="Chapter18" name="InsertQuery"
          username="#session.Username#"
          password="#session.Password#">
  INSERT INTO MyTable (MyData1, MyData2, MyData3)
  VALUES ('Data 1', 'My Data 2', 'Three')
 </cfquery>

 <!--- if there was an error, catch it --->
 <cfcatch type="database">
   Warning, you do not have access to these pages.
 </cfcatch>
</cftry>
```

The query is now encompassed in a cftry block. If an error occurs, ColdFusion will look for the cfcatch statement. The code in the relevant cfcatch error will be executed and code will continue normally after the cftry error.

There are many special variables that are accessible from within the cfcatch tag. These are similar to the error variables that exist in the error templates called by cferror. They contain specific information regarding the type of tag. The special error variable is called cfcatch, and these are the variables associated with it:

- **cfcatch.Type**   Contains the type of the exception that was just caught.
- **cfcatch.Message**   Contains a diagnostic error message.
- **cfcatch.Detail**   Contains the error message generated by the ColdFusion interpreter.
- **cfcatch.TagContext**   Contains the names and positions of each tag and full pathnames of all files. This is called the tag stack and is useful when dealing with custom tags.
- **cfcatch.NativeErrorCode**   Contains the database error code, if applicable. This is only available in database errors.
- **cfcatch.SQLState**   Contains the SQLState as returned by the database, if it was a database error. The default for this value is negative 1.
- **cfcatch.ErrNumber**   Contains the ColdFusion internal error number. It is only applicable to expression errors.
- **cfcatch.MissingFileName**   Contains the name of the missing file, if the exception was a MissingInclude exception.

■ **cfcatch.LockName** Contains the name of the lock, or anonymous if you were not using a named lock; available for failed lock operations. Named locks are most common when accessing application, session, and server variables.

■ **cfcatch.LockOperation** Contains the name of the operation that failed: timeout, unknown, or create Mutex. A Mutex is an object that allows for multiple threads to access it simultaneously. Create Mutex errors are due to ColdFusion being unable to get access to the object.

■ **cfcatch.ErrorCode** Contains the error code specified in the cfthrow tag (discussed later in this chapter); defined only for a custom error type.

■ **cfcatch.ExtendedInfo** Contains the error message specified in the cfthrow tag; also defined exclusively in custom tags.

You can use these variables within the cfcatch block to display error information to the user, log the error with the cflog tag, or to perform any additional processing that you may need. Here is an example:

```
<cftry>
 <!--- Perform database insert --->
 <cfquery datasource="Chapter18" name="InsertQuery"
         username="#session.username#"
         password="#session.password#">
  INSERT INTO MyTable (MyData1, MyData2, MyData3)
  VALUES ('Data 1', 'My Data 2', 'Three')
 </cfquery>

 <!--- if there was an error, catch it --->
 <cfcatch type="database">
   Warning, you do not have access to these pages.<br>
  <cfoutput>
   <!--- Display the SQL Errors --->
   Database Error Code: #cfcatch.NativeErrorCode#<br>
   SQL State: #cfcatch.SQLState#<br>
  </cfoutput>
 </cfcatch>
</cftry>
```

The preceding code displays the error messages to the user.

If you cannot handle the error in a cfcatch block and want to throw it again, you can do so with the cfrethrow tag. The tag accepts no attributes.

CFScript also provides two commands that allow you to catch errors: try and catch. They operate in a very similar manner to the CFML tags:

```
try {
 Code that may cause an exception
}
catch(ExceptionType ExceptionVariable){
 Code to handle exception
}
```

The main difference here is that the catch code is not put inside the try block; it is placed after the try block. The two variables that follow the catch keyword are the ExceptionType, which refers to the type of error that you are trying to catch (as shown earlier in Table 18-1), and the ExceptionVariable, which is the name of the variable that will contain the related error information. This is equivalent to the cfcatch.Type variable.

Creating Your Own Errors

That last item to examine in this section is how you can create your own custom exceptions. The most common use for creating a custom exception is within a custom tags, but you can use the functionality anywhere. These are the attributes of the cfthrow tag:

- **type** Defines the type of the error that you are throwing. The default value is application.
- **message** Describes the error. It is accessed in the cfcatch block by cfcatch.message.
- **detail** Specifies a detailed description of the events that caused the error. ColdFusion automatically appends the location of the error at the end of your text. You can access this using the cfcatch.Detail variable.
- **errorcode** Contains whatever you place in it. It is accessed in the cfcatch block by cfcatch.ErrorCode.
- **extendedinfo** Also contains information that you want to supply. It is accessed from the cfcatch.ExtendedInfo variable.

Perhaps you created a custom tag to display two simple values:

```
<!--- Output the values --->
<cfoutput>
 #attributes.LastName#, #attributes.FirstName#
</cfoutput>
```

Before you execute this code, you want to make sure the variables are defined:

```
<!--- verify that the variables are defined --->
<cfif not IsDefined("attributes.LastName") and
      not IsDefined("attributes.FirstName')>
```

```
<cfthrow type="Undefined Variables"
          Detail="The required variables for this custom tag
                    are LastName and FirstName">
</cfif>

<!--- Output the values --->
<cfoutput>
 #attributes.LastName#, #attributes.FirstName#
</cfoutput>
```

While you are at it, you may as well check to make sure that the variables have simple types. This can be done using the IsSimpleValue function:

```
<!--- verify that the variables are defined --->
<cfif not IsDefined("attributes.LastName") and
      not IsDefined("attributes.FirstName")>
 <cfthrow type="UndefinedVariables"
          Detail="The required variables for this custom tag
                    are LastName and FirstName">
</cfif>

<!--- check to make sure that the variables are of simple types --->
<cfif not IsSimpleValue (attributes.LastName) and
      not IsSimpleValue ( attributes.FirstName)>
 <cfthrow type="ComplexValues"
          Detail="The required variables for this custom tag
                    are LastName and FirstName">
</cfif>

<!--- Output the values --->
<cfoutput>
 #attributes.LastName#, #attributes.FirstName#
</cfoutput>
```

The cfthrow tag must be contained within a cftry block. You can call your custom tag like this:

```
<cftry>
 <!--- call custom tag --->
 <cf_MyTag LastName="" FirstName="">

 <!--- catch the errors --->
 <cfcatch type=" UndefinedVariables">
```

```
  <cfoutput>#cfcatch.Detail#</cfoutput>
</cfcatch>

<cfcatch type=" ComplexValues">
 <cfoutput>#cfcatch.Detail#</cfoutput>
</cfcatch>

</cftry>
```

Creating your own errors is an important thing to do in custom tags.

Optimizing Code

This section discusses some different ways to optimize your ColdFusion applications. Some of the best optimization methods involve good database design (Chapter 9) and the use of advanced database functionality (Chapter 21). If you can offload the work from your ColdFusion Application Server, the efficiency of the end result will be improved. This section concentrates on things you can do inside ColdFusion to help improve performance.

Targeting Areas for Optimization

The first step in any optimization is to find out what areas of your application are not performing at peak. Load testing, as discussed in Chapter 5, is a good start. This section explains how you can use ColdFusion to generate specific errors of functionality in your ColdFusion application.

Evaluating Performance with GetTickCount

A lot of performance data is available in the debugging output of your ColdFusion page. You can create your own performance data for portions of a template using the GetTickCount function, which accepts no attributes and returns a value from the time clock of the computer. In and of itself, the value is not too useful. The usefulness lies when you subtract the results of two separate GetTickCount functions, thus getting the number of milliseconds that the application took to run.

Perhaps you wanted to compare cfloop to cfoutput when looping over a query. GetTickCount is what you would use. Consider this code:

```
<!--- Perform the Query --->
<cfquery datasource="Chapter18" name="MyQuery">
 SELECT Field1
 FROM MyTable
```

```
</cfquery>

<!--- get the TickCount before the loop --->
<cfset LoopTick1 = GetTickCount()>

<!--- Loop over the query and output the value --->
<cfloop query="MyQuery">
 <cfoutput>
  #MyQuery.Field1#
 </cfoutput>
</cfloop>
<br>

<!--- get the TickCount after the loop --->
<cfset LoopTick2 = GetTickCount()>

<!--- compute the Loop execution time --->
<cfset LoopTime = LoopTick2 - LoopTick1>

<!--- get the TickCount before the cfoutput --->
<cfset OutputTick1 = GetTickCount()>

<!--- Loop over the query and output the value --->
<cfoutput query="MyQuery">
 #MyQuery.Field1#
</cfoutput>
<br>

<!--- get the TickCount after the cfoutput --->
<cfset OutputTick2 = GetTickCount()>

<!--- compute the cfoutput execution time --->
<cfset OutputTime = OutputTick2 - OutputTick1>

<!--- Output the Results --->

<cfoutput>
 cfloop Time: #LoopTime#<br>
 cfoutput Time: #OutputTime#<br>
</cfoutput>
```

The first thing that we do is query the database. Then, the code uses the GetTickCount function and stores it in LoopTime1. It loops over the query and outputs all the values in it. Next, it gets the LoopTime2 value. Finally, it computes the amount of time that it took to run the loop, by subtracting the second number from the first.

The second block of code, dealing with cfoutput, performs similar actions. It uses the GetTickCount function to fill the OutputTick1 variable. Then, it uses cfoutput to loop over the query and output its values. Finally, it takes the final tick and computes the OutputTime variable. The last few lines of code output the values:

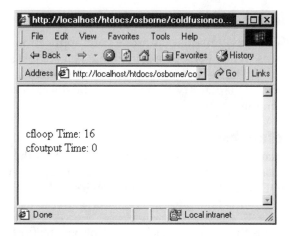

Deciding What to Optimize

When you are optimizing your application, you will probably have limited time. It is best to point your efforts to specific areas for optimization. This is what I like to do:

- **Database design**   A good database design is a good contributor to a healthy application. I like to start by evaluating the database design against the functionality that we are creating on the web site.

- **Business logic**   The items I like to look for next are major flaws within the logic of the application. For example, are you using ColdFusion to read from a file and import into a database, when other methods, such as Microsoft Data Transfer Services in SQL Server, would be more efficient? Are you making judicious use of application and session variables? Are variables being properly locked?

- **Home page**   Next I like to take a good look at the home page. It will most likely be the page that is hit most often in your web site. Do you have a lot of dynamic content on it? Does the content have to be dynamic? Would it be more efficient to generate a static home page once a day instead of once every time someone goes to it?

DEMONSTRATING
ADVANCED APPLICATION
DEVELOPMENT CONCEPTS

- **Database queries** Next I like to examine database queries. Is ColdFusion performing calculations that would be better off given to the database? Would stored procedures or views improve the efficiency of your application?

- **Code tweaks** After all else is said and done, and you still have time left, the final thing to look at is code specifics. Do you have a lot of loops inside each other? Will CFScript improve efficiency over a specific code segment?

The next section of this chapter discusses caching issues.

Caching in ColdFusion

One of the easiest things you can do to improve your application's performance is to cache queries and pages. When you cache something, you are just storing it in memory for quicker access. We will talk about caching ColdFusion pages and caching queries. You may want to review Chapter 3, where we examine the caching attributes of the ColdFusion Administrator.

Caching with cfcache

The easiest way to cache a page is with the cfcache tag. It saves the page's contents in memory. This tag must be placed at the top of a ColdFusion page. You will want to do this in cases where you are not creating content changes each time the page executes. These are the attributes of the tag:

- **action** Contains these actions: cache, to cache a page; flush, to refresh a cached page; clientcache, to cache a page on the browser; and optimal, to cache on both the client and server. The default value is cache.

- **username** If authentication is needed, contains the username needed.

- **password** If authentication is needed, contains the password needed.

- **protocol** Defines the method used for page caching, http://, the default, or https://.

- **directory** Contains the absolute directory path of the page. The default is the current page that is processing.

- **cachedirectory** Contains the absolute path of the directory to cache pages to.

- **expireurl** Takes a URL with wildcards to define what should be flushed. For example, if you want to flush MyPage.cfm?MyVar=1 and MyPage.cfm?MyVar=2, you might set this attribute to MyPage.cfm*.

- **port** Contains the port number of the web server. It defaults to 80.

The cfcache tag is the easiest way to improve the efficiency of your page.

If you have a page that mixes static content with dynamic content, the cfsavecontent tag will help you store the static content to a variable. This in essence allows you to cache the portions of your page that will not change much. The cfsavecontent tag accepts one parameter, variable, which is the name of the variable that you want to store your content to. The cfsavecontent tag needs both a begin and end tag, with the content that you want to save in between. Look at this example:

```
<cfif IsDefined("application.MyNavigationBar")>
 <cfsavecontent variable="application.MyNavigationBar">
  Insert Navigation Bar Code
 </cfsavecontent>
</cfif>
```

You will notice that the MyNavigationBar is put into the application scope. This is done so that the variable will exist once for every user. Before creating the variable, we check for its existence. To use it, we just output as we would any other variable.

Caching Queries with cfquery

The biggest performance drain on your application will most likely come from database queries. Often, the database is located in a separate server, so ColdFusion has to access it via ODBC across a network. The easiest performance boost that you can give is by caching queries. It changes the execution time of a query from x milliseconds to 0 milliseconds in no time.

You can cache queries very easily using the cachedwithin attribute, which specifies the amount of time that the query will remain in the cache. The cachedwithin attribute accepts a timespan value created with the CreateTimeSpan function, which accepts four number attributes: days, hours, minutes, and seconds. This is how you use it:

```
<cfquery datasource="MyDataSource" name="MyQuery"
         cachedwithin="#CreateTimeSpan(1,0,0,0)#">
 Query Statements Here
</cfquery>
```

This will cache the query for one day. Whenever the query is run, ColdFusion will check to see if the query exists in memory. If it doesn't exist, ColdFusion runs the query and stores it in memory. If it does exist, then ColdFusion checks to see how old the current query is. If the query is older than the time frame specified with the CreateTimeSpan function, the query is run again; otherwise, the cached query is used.

> **Tip** *The CreateTimeSpan function returns a number. If you are trying to tweak every last bit of performance out of your system, then you can execute the CreateTimeSpan function, find its results, and hard code those results instead. One day is equal to a value of 1, 12 hours is equal to a value of .5, and so on.*

Presenting the Appearance of Speed

The nature of ColdFusion is that a page is processed from start to finish and then streamed back to the user. If you have pages that contain a lot of processing or take a long time to load, this is not desirable. You can use the cfflush tag to send portions of the page to the user.

The cfflush tag has a single attribute, interval. It is used to specify the number of bytes that need to be accumulated before the information is streamed back to the browser. This does not make the application any more responsive; it just makes it appear faster to the end user, because they have to wait less time for feedback.

The very first time that the cfflush tag is used, all HTML headers are sent to the page. Subsequent returns do not contain the headers. When choosing the amount of data that you want to flush, it is a good idea not to make the number too small. Some browsers will ignore numbers if they are too small. On the other hand, if you set the number too large, it defeats the purpose of flushing the data. I like to set the number somewhere between 200–400K.

ColdFusion tags that require HTML headers to operate properly cannot be used after the first cfflush tag. These tags are cfcontent, cfcookie, cfform, cfheader, cfhtmlhead, and cflocation.

Summary

In this chapter, you learned about the following:

- The different methods of debugging in ColdFusion
- How to handle errors with cftry and catch
- How to optimize your applications with caching
- ColdFusion's debugging output, in detail

The next chapter will examine how you can maintain file and directories from within ColdFusion.

The Complete Reference

ColdFusion MX

Chapter 19

Maintaining File and Directory Structures

Sometimes you need to work with the files and directories on a server. Perhaps you need to read information from a file and use it within ColdFusion, or maybe you need to create a file from within ColdFusion. Perhaps you have users who are uploading files in an application, and you want to save the files to your server and create a directory for each specific user. All of these things can be done with ColdFusion's file and directory management tags.

Using the cffile Tag

The cffile tag enables you to perform many file handling tasks, such as creating files, reading and writing from files, renaming files, and uploading files. This section shows you how to use the cffile tag to accomplish these tasks.

Uploading a File

This section demonstrates how you can use the cffile tag to upload a file onto the server. It will show an example where you can accept a file from a user and upload it.

Learning How to Upload

Perhaps the most common use I have had for the cffile tag is to have a user submit files via an HTML form, such as a resume or image file, and to upload those files. The cffile tag has one important attribute, action, which specifies the action that will take place. These are the valid attributes to upload a file:

- **action** To upload a file, set the action attribute to upload. This is a required attribute.

- **filefield** Contains the name of the form field that contained the file. This is a required attribute.

- **destination** Contains the absolute path of the directory you are uploading your file to. This is a required attribute. In ColdFusion MX, a trailing slash is not needed. This was required in ColdFusion 5.

- **nameconflict** Defines what to do if there is a name conflict. Its values are: error, to throw an error and not save the file; skip, to not save the file; overwrite, to replace the file; and makeunique, to create a custom, unique filename for the current file. The default value is error.

- **accept** Contains a list of comma-delimited mime types that are accepted by cffile. If you leave this blank, all file types will be accepted.

- **mode** Specifies on Unix-based operating systems, such as Solaris, HP-UX, or Linux, the octal values of the chmod command, in the order of owner, group, and other. You can look up chmod in your Unix documentation. Windows units will ignore this attribute.

■ **attributes**   Specifies the attributes that will be set to the file when it is uploaded. Valid values are archive, readonly, hidden, and normal. This is intended to set permissions on Windows units, and you can specify a comma-delimited list of the relevant attributes. If you leave this attribute out, then the current file attributes are maintained.

After the file is uploaded, ColdFusion creates some special status variables that you can use to access information about the file and the upload. You can access them with the cffile prefix. This is the list:

■ **cffile.AttemptedServerFile**   Contains the initial name of the file that ColdFusion used when trying to save the uploaded file.

■ **cffile.ClientDirectory**   Contains the location of the uploaded file on the client's system.

■ **cffile.ClientFile**   Contains the full name of the file that the client uploaded, including the extension.

■ **cffile.ClientFileExt**   Contains the extension of the file that the client uploaded.

■ **cffile.ClientFileName**   Contains the name of the file that the client uploaded, without an extension.

■ **cffile.ContentSubtype**   Contains the MIME content subtype of the saved file.

■ **cffile.ContentType**   Contains the MIME content type of the saved file.

■ **cffile.DateLastAccessed**   Contains the date and time that the uploaded file was last accessed.

■ **cffile.FileExisted**   Contains a Boolean value stating whether the uploaded file already existed.

■ **cffile.FileSize**   Contains the size of the uploaded file, in bytes.

■ **cffile.FileWasAppended**   Contains a Boolean value stating whether or not ColdFusion appended the uploaded file to another file.

■ **cffile.FileWasOverwritten**   Contains a Boolean value stating whether or not ColdFusion overwrote a file during the upload.

■ **cffile.FileWasRenamed**   Contains a Boolean value stating whether or not the uploaded file was renamed.

■ **cffile.FileWasSaved**   Contains a Boolean value stating whether or not the file was saved.

■ **cffile.OldFileSize**   If a file was overwritten, this variable contains the size, in bytes, of the overwritten file.

■ **cffile.ServerDirectory**   Contains the name of the directory that the file was saved to.

■ **cffile.ServerFile**   The name of the file, as it was saved on the server, including the extension.

DEMONSTRATING
ADVANCED APPLICATION
DEVELOPMENT CONCEPTS

■ **cffile.ServerFileExt** Contains the name of the file extension, as the file was saved on the server.

■ **cffile.ServerFileName** Contains the name of the file, as it was saved on the server, without the extension.

■ **cffile.TimeCreated** Contains the date and time that the file was uploaded.

■ **cffile.TimeLastModified** Contains the date and time of the last update to the uploaded file.

Next we can look at an example of how to upload a file.

  If you are migrating from ColdFusion 5, you should no longer access the file upload information variables using the file prefix. It still works, but is deprecated. Use the cffile prefix instead.

Creating a File Upload Example

To create an example of the file upload procedure, we need two pages, the form input page and the form processing page. The form input page is very simple:

```
<!--- www.instantcoldfusion.com

Description: Input page to upload a file

Entering: N/A
Exiting: FileUploadp.cfm

Dependencies: N/A
Expecting: N/A

Modification History
Date        Modifier                Modification
**********************************************************
03/17/2002 Jeff Houser, DotComIt    Created
--->


<!--- Start the form --->
<form action="FileUploadp.cfm" enctype="multipart/form-data"
      method="post">

 <!--- The file input box --->
 The File: <input type="File" name="MyFile"><br>
 <input type="Submit" name="submit">

</form>
```

The documentation header starts the page. The only code on the page is an HTML form. The form tag specifies the enctype as multipart/form-data because that is needed to send files via a form. The single input box is of type form, with the name MyFile.

The processing page processes the form on the back end:

```
<!--- www.instantcoldfusion.com

Description: Processing Page to upload a file

Entering: FileUploadi.cfm
Exiting: N/A

Dependencies: N/A
Expecting: form.MyFile

Modification History
Date        Modifier              Modification
*********************************************************
04/17/2002 Jeff Houser, DotComIt   Created
--->

<!--- upload the file --->
<cffile action = "upload" fileField = "MyFile"
  destination = "C:\MyLocation" nameConflict = "Error">

<!--- output a confirmation message --->
<cfoutput>
 Your File, #cffile.serverFile#, was uploaded.
</cfoutput>
```

This template uploads the file. The documentation header states that it is expecting the form.MyFile variable to be defined when this page is executed. The cffile tag is used with the action attribute equal to upload. In case of a name conflict, an error is thrown. You can catch these errors using techniques described in Chapter 18. The last part of the template provides a confirmation message to the user. I chose to output the name of the file, but you could output anything that you desire.

Reading from and Writing to Files

The cffile tag also allows you to read from and write to a file. There are two types of reading: reading text and reading binary.

Reading from a File

You may want to read from a text file and insert the data into a database, or read a binary file so that you can turn it into a binary object for other uses. ColdFusion supports both of these options.

If you want to read from a text file, these are the attributes:

- **action**   Must be set to read.
- **file**   Must contain the absolute pathname of the file.
- **variable**   Contains the name of the variable that will contain the file's contents.
- **encoding**   Contains the encoding type of the file that you are reading. The default is ISO-8859-1, although any valid encoding type will suffice.
- **charset**   Contains the name of the Java character set that is used for file contents. A character set is a group of related characters, usually including the alphabet letters, numbers, and other specialized characters such as commas and quotation marks.

The file will read the complete file text into a single variable. You can then manipulate that variable as needed.

Caution   *The cffile tag is not built for reading from large text files, such as server logs. This can cause undue stress, and a crash, on the server.*

To read a binary file, you set up the cffile tag with these attributes:

- **action**   Must be set to readbinary
- **file**   Specifies the absolute pathname of the file
- **variable**   Accepts the name of the variable that you are adding the file's contents to

Reading binary files is often used in conjunction with the ToBase64 function, which converts the binary data to Base64. It accepts two parameters: the name of the variable containing the binary data file, and the encoding type. It is useful to do this when transferring files to another site, via web protocols, such as HTTP or SMTP. Using the web protocols from within ColdFusion is discussed in Chapter 22.

Writing to a File

There are two different actions that you can write to a file using the cffile tag: write and append. Write will write information to the beginning of the file. Append will append the information to the end of the file.

These are the attributes for writing or appending to a file:

- **action**   Must be set to write to write to a file. It must be set to append to add information to a file.

- **file**   Contains the full pathname of the file that you are writing to.

- **output**   Accepts the content that you are creating.

- **mode**   Specifies on Unix-based operating systems, such as Solaris, HP-UX, or Linux, the octal values of the chmod command, in the order of owner, group, and other. You can look up chmod in your Unix documentation. Windows units will ignore this attribute.

- **addnewline**   Contains a Boolean attribute that specifies whether or not the new line character is written to the text file. The new line character is written to the file after the text you specify in output.

- **encoding**   Accepts the character encoding of a given attribute. The encoding attribute does not apply if the action is set to append.

- **attributes**   Specifies the attributes that will be set to the file when it is uploaded. Valid values are archive, readonly, hidden, and normal. This is intended to set permissions on Windows units, and you can specify a comma-delimited list of the relevant attributes. If you leave this attribute out, then the current file attributes are maintained.

- **charset**   Contains the name of the Java character set that is used for file contents.

If the file already exists, all text inside the file will be overwritten when you write to a file. Appending text to a file will add the text to the end. This method is used to store a user's output. You will most commonly want to use these methods to create static HTML files from dynamic content, such as in a scheduled task to create a static version of the home page.

Performing Standard File Operations

The cffile tag also lets you perform standard file actions, such as moving, renaming, copying, and deleting files. This section demonstrates how.

To move a file, you set up the cffile tag with these attributes:

- **action**   Must be set to move.

- **source**   Specifies the absolute directory location of the file on the web server.

- **destination**   Specifies the new absolute directory location of the file on the web server.

- **mode**   Specifies on Unix-based operating systems, such as Solaris, HP-UX, or Linux, the octal values of the chmod command, in the order of owner, group, and other. You can look up chmod in your Unix documentation. Windows units will ignore this attribute.

- **attributes**   Specifies the attributes that will be set to the file when it is uploaded. Valid values are archive, readonly, hidden, normal, and system. This is intended to set permissions on Windows units, and you can specify a comma-delimited list of the relevant attributes. If you leave this attribute out, then the current file attributes are maintained.

- **charset**   Contains the name of the Java character set that is used for file contents.

To rename or copy a file, the cffile tag has the same attributes:

- **action**   Contains either rename, for renaming a file, or copy, to copy a file.

 Tip   *If you are copying a file, but do not want to overwrite an existing one, you can use the FileExists function to check for the variable's existence before using the cffile tag.*

- **source**   Contains the source location of the file.

- **destination**   Contains the full pathname of the renamed file.

- **mode**   Specifies on Unix-based operating systems, such as Solaris, HP-UX, or Linux, the octal values of the chmod command, in the order of owner, group, and other. You can look up chmod in your Unix documentation. Windows units will ignore this attribute.

- **attributes**   Specifies the attributes that will be set to the file when it is uploaded. Valid values are archive, readonly, hidden, normal, and system. This is intended to set permissions on Windows units, and you can specify a comma-delimited list of the relevant attributes. If you leave this attribute out, then the current file attributes are maintained.

The last operation that you can perform with the cffile tag is to delete a file. It accepts these attributes:

- **action**   Must be set to delete.
- **file**   Contains the absolute path of the file that you are deleting.

The cffile tag is a powerful tag with many options that allow it to integrate with the underlying operating system.

Performing Directory Maintenance

Just as you can maintain files by using the cffile tag, you can maintain directories by using the cfdirectory tag. The cfdirectory tag enables you to get a listing of all files in a directory, create directories, rename directories, and delete directories. This section shows you how to do all of these things.

Getting a File List from a Directory

To get a list of all files in a directory, you use the cfdirectory tag with these attributes:

- **action** Must be equal to list.
- **directory** Specifies the name of the directory you want to get a list of files in.
- **name** Specifies the name of the variable that will contain the directory list.
- **filter** Specifies a filter to apply on the directory list. For example, if you want to show all CFM templates, your filter would be *.cfm.
- **sort** Accepts values that you want to sort on. You have to specify the name of the field that you are sorting on: Name, Size, Type, DateLastModified, or Attributes. You can specify asc after the field name for an ascending sort, or specify desc for a descending sort. Multiple sorts can be separated by commas.

After you use the cfdirectory tag, ColdFusion creates a query object with these columns.

- **Name** Specifies the name of the directory entry. Neither '.' nor '..' is returned in the query. This is a change in functionality from ColdFusion 5.
- **Size** Specifies the size of the entry.
- **Type** Specifies the type of entry. Valid values are file for a file, or dir for a directory.
- **DateLastModified** Specifies the date that the entry was last modified.
- **Attributes** Contains the file attributes of the file, if the current entry is a file.
- **Mode** Contains the permissions of the file in a Unix or Linux directory. This attribute does not exist in Windows.

We can get the directory listing using this code:

```
<cfdirectory action="list" name="DirList" sort="name asc"
            directory="C:\MyDir\">
```

This creates a query object named DirList. The following code will loop over the query and output the relevant directory information:

```
<cfoutput query="DirList">
 #DirList.Name#, #DirList.Size#, #DirList.Type#,
 #DirList.DateLastModified#, #DirList.Attributes# <br>
</cfoutput>
```

The most common use of this functionality is to retrieve a list of directories in an application where you are storing user-specific files in a user-specific directory.

Performing Directory Maintenance

The cfdirectory tag also enables you to create new directories, rename directories, and delete directories, if your application has the need for that. Following the preceding example, suppose you are creating directories for each user in an application. When someone registers, you need to create a new directory for them. These are the attributes needed to create a new directory:

- **action**   Must be set to create.
- **directory**   Specifies the absolute path of the directory that you are creating.
- **mode**   Used to set up permissions on the directory in a Linux/Unix machine. It accepts the octal commands from chmod.

You can easily create a directory like this:

```
<cfdirectory action="create"
             directory="C:\Users\MyNewDirectory">
```

What if someone wants to change his or her username? You will want to rename their directory to reflect this. You will use these attributes:

- **action**   Must be set to rename
- **directory**   Accepts the absolute file path of the directory you are renaming
- **newdirectory**   Accepts the absolute file path of the directory's new name

The tag in action looks something like this:

```
<cfdirectory action="rename"
             directory="C:\Users\MyNewDirectory"
             NewDirectory="C:\Users\AnotherNewDirectory">
```

Suppose the user wants to delete their account altogether because they do not like the new changes to your company's privacy policy. This can be done with these two attributes:

- **action**   Should be set to delete to remove the directory
- **directory**   Must contain the full path of the directory that you want to delete

As you remove the user from your system, use these attributes:

```
<cfdirectory action="delete"
             directory=" C:\Users\AnotherNewDirectory">
```

If you try to delete a file or directory that you do not have permissions to delete, ColdFusion will throw an error. You can catch that error using error-handling features, as described in Chapter 18.

Executing Other File Handling Functions

ColdFusion also provides you with additional functions for handling code. They are shown in Table 19-1.

Function	Parameters	Description
DirectoryExists	**Path:** An absolute path to the directory	Returns true if the directory exists, false otherwise.
FileExists	**Path:** The absolute path to the file	Returns true if the file exists, false otherwise.
GetCurrentTemplatePath	N/A	Returns the absolute path of the page currently executing. If executed inside an include tag, the location of the include will be returned.
GetBaseTemplatePath	N/A	Returns an absolute path of the base page currently executing. If called from an include, will return the location of the calling page.
GetDirectoryFromPath	**Path:** The absolute path to the file	Returns the absolute path without a filename.
GetFileFromPath	**Path:** The absolute path to the file	Returns the filename without the directory structure.
GetTempDirectory	N/A	Returns the absolute path to the directory that ColdFusion uses for temporary files.

Table 19-1. *File Handling Functions*

DEMONSTRATING
ADVANCED APPLICATION
DEVELOPMENT CONCEPTS

Function	Parameters	Description
GetTempFile	**Dir:** The name of the directory **Prefix:** The prefix of the temporary file	Creates a temporary file in a directory whose name starts with the first three characters of the prefix.
ExpandPath	**Path:** A relative or absolute path to a directory or file	Returns the absolute path from any given relative path.

Table 19-1. *File Handling Functions* (continued)

Summary

In this chapter, you learned about the following:

- ColdFusion's file handling capabilities
- How to upload files with the cffile tag
- How to manage directories with the cfdirectory tag
- The functions that relate to file and directory management

The next chapter will teach you how you can create graphs from within ColdFusion.

Chapter 20

Creating Graphs with ColdFusion

This chapter shows you how to create graphs from within ColdFusion using the cfchart tag. Graphs are a great way to provide a visual representation of your data, especially from queries, if you want to run reports. This chapter demonstrates how you can create graphs and how you can use them in your own development.

Graphing Within ColdFusion

ColdFusion MX can make 11 different types of graphs, using a combination of three different tags: cfchart, cfchartseries, and cfchartdata. This section examines each of the tags and explains how they can be used together to create graphs.

Setting Up Your Graphs

The cfchart tag defines a container for the cfchartdata and cfchartseries tags. It is used to set up the general graph parameters. These are its attributes:

- **format**   Accepts Flash, JPG, or PNG. The default is Flash.
- **chartheight**   Specifies the height of the graph in pixels. The default value is 240.
- **chartwidth**   Specifies the width of the graph in pixels. The default value is 320.
- **scalefrom**   Specifies the Y-axis minimum value. The default value is determined by the data.
- **scaleto**   Specifies the Y-axis maximum value. The default value is determined by the data.
- **showxgridlines**   A Boolean attribute that specifies whether or not to display grid lines along the X axis. This attribute defaults to no.
- **showygridlines**   A Boolean attribute that specifies whether or not to display grid lines along the Y axis. This attribute defaults to yes.
- **gridlines**   Specifies the number of gridlines to include on the value axis. The default is 3, which stands for the top, bottom, and zero. If set to 0, no gridlines will be displayed.
- **seriesplacement**   If a chart has more than one series of data, then this attribute will specify this dataset's relative position in the series. Values are default, cluster, stacked, or percent.
- **foregroundcolor**: Defines the color of the text, labels, and gridlines of the graph. The default is black. Hex values and named colors are both supported.
- **databackgroundcolor**   Specifies the color of the area around chart data. The default is white. Values are accepted in hex or as named colors.

- **borderbackgroundcolor** Specifies the color of the text between the background and border, labels, or the legend. The accepted values should either be in hex or as named colors. The default is white.

Tip *For hex values, where you want to use the pound sign, you have to escape the pound sign by placing two pound signs instead of one: ##FFFFFF.*

- **showborder** A Boolean attribute telling whether or not the border should be shown. The default value is no.

- **font** Specifies the text name of the font that you want to use to display graph text. The valid values are arial, times, courier, and arialunicodeMS. The default is arial.

- **fontsize** Specifies the size of the font. The default is 11.

- **fontbold** A Boolean value that specifies whether or not the font is bolded. This attribute defaults to no.

- **fontitalic** A Boolean attribute that specifies whether or not the font should be displayed in italics. The default is no.

- **labelformat** Defines the format for the Y-axis labels. Valid values are number, currency, percent, and date.

- **yaxistitle** Specifies text for the Y-axis title.

- **xaxistitle** Specifies the text for the title to be displayed on the X axis.

- **sortxaxis** A Boolean value that specifies whether or not to sort the column labels along the axis. The default is to not sort them.

- **show3d** A Boolean value that specifies whether or not the chart should be given a three-dimensional appearance. The default value is no.

- **xoffset** Specifies the number of units that the chart will be horizontally angled, if show3d is set to yes. The default is .1.

- **yoffset** Specifies the number of units that the chart will be vertically angled, if show3d is set to yes. This value should be between negative 1 and 1. Negative 1 means the angle will be 90 degrees to the left and 1 means 90 degrees to the right. The default is .1.

- **rotated** A Boolean attribute that specifies whether or not the bar will be rotated at 90 degrees. To create a horizontal bar chart, set this option to yes. The default value is no.

- **showlegend** A Boolean value that specifies whether or not to show the legend of the graph. The default is yes.

- **tipstyle** Determines the action that will open a window to display specifics of a specific chart element. The default is mouseover. Other options are mousedown and off. Off will not open up a second window to display specific data.

- **tipbgcolor** Specifies the color of the tip. This applies to Flash-format graphs only. The default is white.

- **showmarkers** Specifies whether or not the data points are displayed. The default is yes. This applies only to line, curve, or scatter graph types, as specified in the type attribute of cfchartseries.

- **markersize** Specifies the pixel size of the data point markers. This will be set automatically if left out.

- **pieslicestyle** Accepts two values: solid and sliced. Solid displays a pie unsliced. Sliced, the default value, separates each piece of the pie.

- **url** Specifies the URL to open if the user clicks a data series. Variables can be specified within the URL string, and you can specify them dynamically based on what part of the graph the user clicks. $Value$ will insert the value of the selected row, $itemlabel$ will pass the label of the clicked item, and $serieslabel$ will pass the label of the selected series. You may set this value to

  ```
  MyPage.cfm?IL=$ItemLabel$&SL=$SeriesLabel$&Val=$value$
  ```

- **name** Specifies a variable name of the graph. Using this tag suppresses display, but stores the data as an encoded binary graph.

The cfchart tag uses both a start and end tag. The cfchartseries and cfchartdata tags must be created inside the cfchart block. These tags will be examined next.

 In ColdFusion 5, the cfgraph and cfgraphdata tags were used to create charts. These tags are deprecated in ColdFusion MX.

Defining Your Data

The two remaining tags for creating graphs are cfchartdata, which is used to define data points on the graph, and cfchartseries, which is used to define the style of the graph and to specify and configure query data, if applicable. These are the attributes for cfchartseries:

- **type** Defines the type of graph you are creating. Valid values are bar, line, pyramid, area, cone, curve, cylinder, step, scatter, and pie. Bar and cylinder are identical if the show3d attribute of cfchart is set to no. Cone and pyramid are also identical in 2D mode.

- **query** Specifies the name of the query that you are populating the chart with.

- **itemcolumn** Contains the name of the query column that will contain the label for the graph data. This is a required attribute if the query attribute is specified.

- **valuecolumn** Contains the name of a query column that will be used to specify the data values that will be graphed. This is a required attribute if the query attribute is specified.

- **serieslabel** Contains a text value that specifies the label of this data series. This is an optional attribute.

- **seriescolor** Specifies the color of the main element that will be used in this data series. For a bar chart, this is the color of the bar; for a pie chart, this is the color of the first piece of pie. Other graph types have similar elements. This value can be set using a hex value or a named color.

- **paintstyle** Specifies the style of the data series. Valid values are plain, solid, raise, shade, or light. The default value is plain.

- **markerstyle** Specifies the shape of the marker that specifies the data point. This attribute is valid only for line, curve, and scatter plots where the show3d attribute of cfchart is set to no. The default value is rectangle. Other values are triangle, diamond, circle, letter, mcross, snow, and rcross.

- **colorlist** An optional attribute that specifies the slices for each piece of pie if the chart is a pie chart.

To color a pie graph, ColdFusion first looks to the seriescolor attribute. If it is omitted, then ColdFusion will automatically color the slices. If seriescolor is specified, the first pie slice gets the specified color. Then, ColdFusion looks to the colorlist attribute to get the remainder of the colors after the first piece of pie.

 ColdFusion MX will only create graphs on numerical data. Dates, times, or currency must be converted to integers or real numbers.

The cfchartdata tag has two attributes:

- **item** Contains the data point name
- **value** Contains the data point value

You can use the cfchartdata tag to specify individual points on your chart. It can be used alone, or with a query specified in cfchartseries. The cfchartdata tag must always be located inside an cfchartseries block.

Creating a Graph with cfchart

This section shows you different ways that you can populate your graph data from within ColdFusion. It demonstrates queries, manual specification of data points, and combining different types of graphs. It finishes by showing you how to save your chart as a variable.

Specifying Your Data Points Manually

ColdFusion MX allows you to specify manual data points on a graph using the cfchartdata tag. Suppose you had created a survey for your web site. You have a user table that contains your users, an answer table that contains the answers, and a table that intersects the two. You want to create a chart that shows all the answers and how many people chose a particular answer. This section shows you how to do this.

1. Get the data out of the database. We can create a query to get the information:

```
<cfquery name="GraphQuery" datasource="Chapter20">
 SELECT Answers.Answer
 FROM Answers, UserAnswers
 WHERE Answers.AnswerID = UserAnswers.AnswerID
</cfquery>
```

This query gets the Answers.Answer text. It joins the Answers and UserAnswers queries. This makes sure that the answer is returned once for each time that it was chosen.

2. Get a list of all the answers and the total number of times that each one was chosen. The text needs to be used to refer to the total number of times it was chosen. There is a name and a value. That sounds like a variable. Since there are a group of them, we can use a structure:

```
<!--- code to calculate totals --->
<!--- Create the structure --->
<cfset DataStruct=StructNew()>

<!--- Loop over the Query --->
<cfloop query="GraphQuery">

 <cfif StructKeyExists(DataStruct, GraphQuery.Answer)>
  <!--- If the key exists in the structure, increment it --->
  <cfset DataStruct[GraphQuery.Answer] =
                            DataStruct[GraphQuery.Answer]+1>
 <cfelse>
  <!--- If the key does not exist, create it with the default
        value of 1 --->
  <cfset Temp = StructInsert(DataStruct, GraphQuery.Answer, 1)>
 </cfif>
</cfloop>
```

First the code creates a new, empty structure. Then it loops over the query. If there is already a structure key that corresponds to the current Answer text, increment its value. If there isn't, create the key and give it an initial value of 1.

3. Set up the chart. This code will do that:

```
<cfchart sortXAxis="Yes">
 <cfchartseries type="Line">
```

The code shows the cfchart and cfchartseries tags. It specifies that the X axis will be sorted. This controls the order in which the labels and graph data are displayed. The cfchartseries tag specifies that the chart will be a line graph.

4. Create the cfchartdata tags. This can be done by looping over the structure with a cfloop:

```
<cfloop collection=#DataStruct# item="TempKey">
  <cfchartdata item="#TempKey#"
              value="#DataStruct[TempKey]#">
</cfloop>
```

The item attribute is the name of the key, which is the answer. The value is the value of the structure, or the total number of times that the answer was given.

5. Close the cfchartdata and cfchart tags:

```
  </cfchartseries>
</cfchart>
```

Load the page and you can look at the graph.

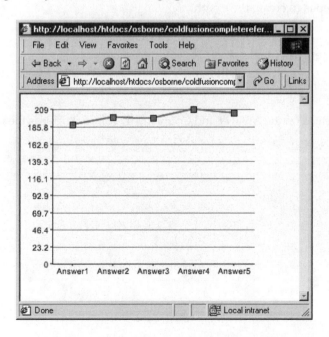

Graphing a Query

Is there a better way to create the graph from the last section? As a matter of fact, there is. You can create a query that will automatically be returned with the values.

The first step is to write a query to get the data and perform the computations:

```
<cfquery name="GraphQuery2" datasource="Chapter20">
 SELECT Answer, COUNT(UserID) AS CountAnsID
 FROM Answers, UserAnswers
 WHERE Answers.AnswerID = UserAnswers.AnswerID
 GROUP BY Answer
</cfquery>
```

A lot of things are happening with this query. First, in the select clause, an aggregate function is used. The count function returns the number of specified items. It returns the number of UserIDs. After the count function is an alias, which gives a name to the value. Without that, there is no way to access the results of the aggregate function. Next in the query comes the from and where clauses. They join the Answers and UserAnswers tables. The last line of the query is a group clause, using the keywords GROUP BY, and the name of the field. The group clause returns each value for the column, Answer, only once. It automatically removes duplicates.

Tip *Query grouping and aggregate functions are discussed in more detail in Chapter 21.*

The next step is to create the graph:

```
<cfchart>
 <cfchartseries type="Line" query="GraphQuery2"
                itemcolumn="Answer" valuecolumn="CountAnsID">
</cfchart>
```

The graph is created on the Answer and CountAnsID columns. This is the resulting graph:

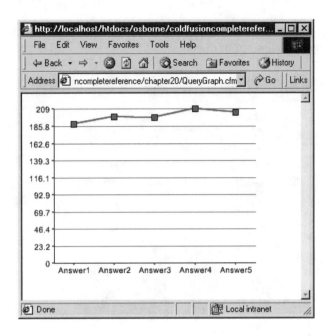

Combining Data Series

When creating graphs within ColdFusion MX, you can also combine two different data sets, defined with the cfchartseries tag, into a single graph. The two data sets can use this to plot two different lines over each other, or two different forms of data. Using the survey example, perhaps you want to chart the results of two different surveys at the same time.

Each item on the X axis can have only one value in each series. ColdFusion will graph the value for the last specified point.

The cfchart has an attribute, seriesplacement, that specifies the way that different cfchartseries tags will interoperate with each other. The values are cluster, stacked, or percent. The percent attribute will tally up the total for each item for each X value and display the series as an element of the chart:

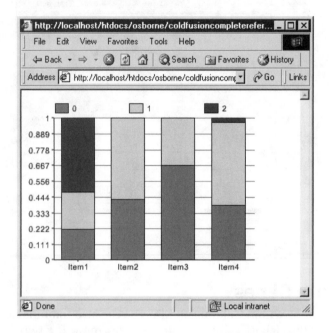

If you stack items, the elements of the second series will be placed on top of elements of the first series. The third series will be placed on top of the second series, and so on.

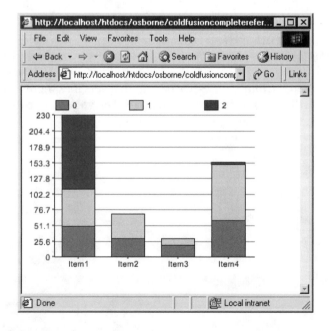

The last form of combining data is to cluster it. That means that the two different types of data are placed next to each other on the graph.

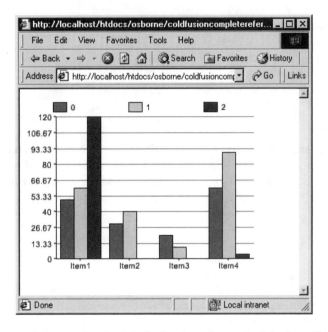

The different series can also be labeled using the serieslabel attribute of the cfchartseries tag. You can also choose colors with the seriescolor attribute. These actions will make your graph easier to read in the long run, because you can associate colors and text with the items on the graph.

The survey example can be expanded upon to allow for more than one survey question. We do this by adding a new table for questions and placing the QuestionID in the Answers table. This will allow us to keep track of which answers go to which question.

We can implement the graph for two questions, by first performing two queries:

```
<!--- Get the Data for the first question --->
<cfquery name="GetQuestion1" datasource="Chapter20">
 SELECT Questions.Question, Answers.Answer,
        COUNT(UserAnswers.UserID) AS MaxAnsID
 FROM Answers, UserAnswers, Questions
 WHERE Answers.AnswerID = UserAnswers.AnswerID AND
       Answers.QuestionID = Questions.QuestionID AND
       Questions.QuestionID = 1
 GROUP BY Questions.Question, Answers.Answer
</cfquery>

<!--- Get the Data for the second question --->
```

```
<cfquery name="GetQuestion2" datasource="Chapter20">
 SELECT Questions.Question, Answers.Answer,
        COUNT(UserAnswers.UserID) AS MaxAnsID
 FROM Answers, UserAnswers, Questions
 WHERE Answers.AnswerID = UserAnswers.AnswerID AND
       Answers.QuestionID = Questions.QuestionID AND
       Questions.QuestionID = 2
 GROUP BY Questions.Question, Answers.Answer
</cfquery>
```

These queries are very similar to the one that was examined when creating a chart with a single series of data. The join adds the Questions table, based on the QuestionID. The question text is also added to the select clause and the group clause.

The second step is to create the graph with both data plots. This is the code:

```
<cfchart seriesPlacement="default">

<!--- create a graph of the first query --->
 <cfchartseries type="Line" query="GetQuestion1"
                itemcolumn="Answer" valuecolumn="MaxAnsID"
                serieslabel="#GetQuestion1.Question#">

<!--- create a graph of the second query --->
 <cfchartseries type="Line" query="GetQuestion2"
                itemcolumn="Answer" valuecolumn="MaxAnsID"
                serieslabel="#GetQuestion2.Question#">
</cfchart>
```

The code contains two cfchartseries tags, one for each query. The serieslabel for each one refers to the Question column that comes from the query. This is the resulting graph:

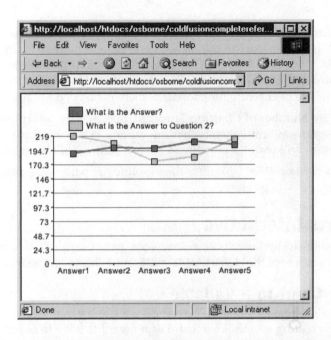

Making Use of Additional cfchart Features

There is some other existent chart functionality that is worth mentioning. This section gives you a refresher on the chart settings in the ColdFusion Administrator. It also shows you how you create a drill-down chart structure by making portions of the chart links and how to save a chart as a variable.

Administering ColdFusion Charts

Log in to the ColdFusion Administrator and click the Charting link under Server Settings in the navigation bar. From there, you can change multiple settings that pertain to creating graphs from within ColdFusion. These are the settings that you can modify:

- **Cache Type** You can set the cache to either memory or disk. Memory caches are quicker, but are limited in space.

- **Maximum Number of Images in the Cache** Specifies the maximum number of chart images to store in the cache at one time. When too many images are in the cache, then ColdFusion will delete the oldest one to make room for the new one. The default value is 50, and the largest this value can be is 250. Unless you are using lots of charting functionality, there is no need to raise this number.

- **Maximum Number of Charting Threads** Specifies the total number of threads that can perform simultaneous charting actions. When the maximum is reached, ColdFusion will wait for one thread to stop before it allows the next one to start.

- **Disk Cache Location** Specifies the absolute file path of the place where disk cache images will be stored.

Making Charts Interactive

This section demonstrates how you can save your chart into a variable and how you can use the url attribute of the cfchart tag to make your charts clickable to another page.

Saving the Chart to a Variable

The cfchart tag allows you to create a chart and save it to a variable. This is useful if you are consistently creating specific charts and don't want to have to redo the processing for each chart, or want to perform other actions on the chart such as e-mailing it or saving it to a file so the user can access it in the future.

You can save the chart to a file using the name attribute of the cfchart tag in combination with the cffile tag. Here is an example:

```
<!--- Create the chart --->
<cfchart seriesPlacement="default" name="MyChart" format="jpg">
 <cfchartseries type="Line" query="GetQuestion1"
                itemcolumn="Answer" valuecolumn="MaxAnsID"
                serieslabel="#GetQuestion1.Question#">
 <cfchartseries type="Line" query="GetQuestion2"
                itemcolumn="Answer" valuecolumn="MaxAnsID"
                serieslabel="#GetQuestion2.Question#">
</cfchart>
```

This creates the chart with two separate series of data, from the queries that were created in the previous section. The name attribute tells ColdFusion to store the chart in the MyChart variable instead of displaying it. The chart will not be displayed to the user. We can save this chart to a file, like this:

```
<cffile action="WRITE" file="C:\MyDirectory\MyChart.jpg"
        output="#MyChart#" charset="ISO-8859-1">
```

This will save the chart to the file by using the cffile's write action.

If you save your chart to a JPG or PNG file, mouseover tips and URLs will not be saved with the file. If you want to preserve these settings, make sure you generate a Flash file.

Creating a Drill-Down Chart Structure

You can create drill-down charts using ColdFusion's chart-handling facilities. You do this by using the url attribute of the cfchart tag. Suppose we want users to be able to click a coordinate of our chart and retrieve a list of all users who chose the answer that corresponds to the coordinate in question. This is the code that creates the chart:

```
<!--- Create chart with the URL attribute --->
<cfchart url="UrlChart2.cfm?value=$Value$
          &ItemLabel=$ItemLabel$&SeriesLabel=$SeriesLabel$">
 <cfchartseries type="Line" query="GetQuestion1"
            itemcolumn="Answer" valuecolumn="MaxAnsID"
            serieslabel="#GetQuestion1.Question#">
 <cfchartseries type="Line" query="GetQuestion2"
            itemcolumn="Answer" valuecolumn="MaxAnsID"
            serieslabel="#GetQuestion2.Question#">
</cfchart>
```

This section of code creates the chart with the url attribute. Inside the url attribute, a relative URL is created, pointing to the URLChart2.cfm page. Special attributes are passed via the URL: ItemLabel, SeriesLabel, and Value. These values are different for each point on the graph. In the url attribute, the special variables are delimited by a dollar sign before and after the special value.

When someone is viewing the chart and clicks the point, they are transported to the URLChart2.cfm page:

```
<!--- www.instantcoldfusion.com

Description: Page to display the extra drill down chart data

Entering: N/A
Exiting: N/A

Dependencies: N/A
Expecting: url.Itemlabel
           url.serieslabel
           url.value

Modification History
Date       Modifier              Modification
*********************************************************
```

DEMONSTRATING ADVANCED APPLICATION DEVELOPMENT CONCEPTS

```
04/18/2002 Jeff Houser, DotComIt    Created
--->

<!--- Get all users who chose that answer --->
<cfquery datasource="Chapter20" name="GetAnswers">
 SELECT Users.*
 FROM Users, UserAnswers, Answers
 WHERE Users.UserID = UserAnswers.UserID AND
       UserAnswers.AnswerID = Answers.AnswerID AND
       Answers.Answer = '#url.ItemLabel#'
</cfquery>

<!--- output the graph information that was clicked on --->
<br>
<cfoutput>
 <b>#url.Value#</b> users chose <b>#url.ItemLabel#</b> in
 <b>#url.SeriesLabel#</b> survey.<br><br>
</cfoutput>

<!--- Show the list of all users who voted this way --->
These are the users who voted this way:<br>

<cfoutput query="GetAnswers">
 #GetAnswers.User#<br>
</cfoutput>
```

The template starts with the documentation header. This page displays all the users who have chosen the accepted answer for the question. The first real code that it performs is a query. The query joins the Users, UserAnswers, and Answers table to get the list of all users who have answered the question with this particular answer.

The next action that is performed in the template is to display some text describing this page. It states the number of users who have chosen the answer for the particular question. The last portion of the template uses cfoutput to loop over the query and display the usernames of all the users who have voted in this manner:

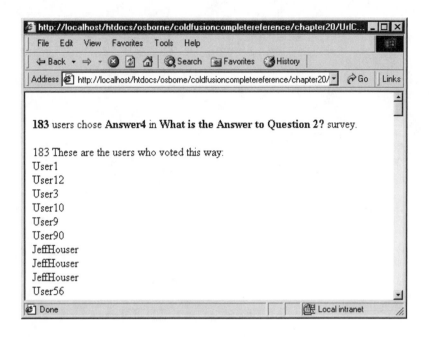

Summary

In this chapter, you learned about the following:

- ColdFusion's charting and graphing functions
- How to graph query data
- How to specify data points manually
- How to mix different graphs together to make a single graph

The next chapter will teach you some advanced SQL functionality, including some stored procedures and how to query a query.

The Complete Reference

ColdFusion MX

Chapter 21

Learning Advanced Database Concepts

This chapter teaches you some advanced database concepts. It describes how to offload some work onto the database. It covers using aggregate functions in your SQL queries, and how to perform SQL grouping. It also shows you how to use stored procedures in Oracle and SQL Server, as well as ColdFusion's Query of Queries functionality. If you need a refresher on basic database concepts, you can turn to Chapter 9.

Understanding Advanced SQL

This section teaches you some advanced SQL concepts. It demonstrates SQL grouping and shows you how you can use it in your own applications. It also teaches you many of the common aggregate functions that are available in SQL.

Grouping Your SQL Statements

This section teaches you about SQL grouping and how you can set up your queries to use grouping. It also explains how to use the grouped query data from within ColdFusion.

Understanding SQL Grouping

The best way to understand what SQL grouping can be used for is by an example. Suppose there is a table named Categories, like this:

CategoryID	Category
1	Red
2	Blue
3	Orange
4	Yellow

Separate from the Categories table, the application has a table called Products:

ProductID	ProductName
1	Apple
2	Banana
3	Cucumber
4	Licorice
5	Popsicle
6	Sour Ball
7	Bubble Gum

These two tables must relate to each other, so there is an intersection table that links to the two:

CategoryID	ProductID
1 (Red)	1 (Apple)
1 (Red)	4 (Licorice)
1 (Red)	5 (Popsicle)
1 (Red)	6 (Sour Ball)
2 (Blue)	5 (Popsicle)
2 (Blue)	6 (Sour Ball)
3 (Orange)	5 (Popsicle)
3 (Orange)	6 (Sour Ball)
4 (Yellow)	2 (Banana)
4 (Yellow)	5 (Popsicle)
4 (Yellow)	6 (Sour Ball)

Since the intersection table only contains IDs, I added the text that each ID refers to in parentheses after the number.

Nothing shown so far is new. You can do a simple select on the data to retrieve the data:

```
SELECT Categories.Category , Products.Product
FROM Categories, Products, CategoryProducts
WHERE Categories.CategoryID = CategoryProducts.CategoryID AND
      CategoryProducts.ProductID = Products.ProductID
```

The query will return data, like this:

Category	Product
Red	Apple
Red	Licorice
Red	Popsicle
Red	Sour Ball
Blue	Popsicle

Category	Product
Blue	Sour Ball
Orange	Popsicle
Orange	Sour Ball
Yellow	Banana
Yellow	Popsicle
Yellow	Sour Ball

This table is similar to the intersection table, except it contains the text data instead of IDs. You will also notice that the category field has a lot of duplicates.

What happens when you want to create a listing or report like the following?

```
Red:
 Apple
 Licorice
 Popsicle
 Sour Ball
Blue:
 Popsicle
 Sour Ball
Orange:
 Popsicle
 Sour Ball
Yellow:
 Banana
 Popsicle
 Sour Ball
```

You need to display the category, then all the products inside that category. One way to do this is to execute a query to get all the categories. As you loop over the category, you can execute another query to get the products based on the CategoryID. Don't ever do this. In this sample case, you will run five queries to get all the data. In a real-world situation, the number will probably be significantly higher. You can do this by executing a single query that uses SQL grouping.

Implementing SQL Grouping

There are two things you need to do to use SQL grouping. The first is to learn the SQL grouping clause. The second is to learn how to use grouping from your ColdFusion code. Many CFML tags contain attributes that allow you to group data.

In a SQL statement, the grouping clause comes after the conditional portion of the SQL statement and before the ordering portion of the SQL statement. Here is an example:

```
SELECT Categories.Category , Products.Product
FROM Categories, Products, CategoryProducts
WHERE Categories.CategoryID = CategoryProducts.CategoryID AND
      CategoryProducts.ProductID = Products.ProductID
GROUP BY Categories.Category, Products.Product
```

The grouping clause starts with the two keywords GROUP BY. Following the keywords comes a list of fields that the query is going to be grouped on. Every column in the select statement that is not in an aggregate function should be listed here. This will successfully group your data.

The cfoutput and cfmail tags have the grouping attributes that allow for grouping within ColdFusion. These are the two attributes:

- **group** Specifies the name of the column that the output will be grouping on.

- **groupcasesensitive** Accepts a Boolean value that specifies whether or not the grouping will be case sensitive. Case-sensitive groupings consider "Yellow" and "yellow" to be two different elements. Case-insensitive groupings consider them to be the same.

You use these attributes with cfoutput by nesting cfoutput blocks. The outer cfoutput block will have the group and query attributes. The inner cfoutput block will have no attributes. Here is an example, running off of the query text that we previously specified:

```
<!--- Outer loop --->
<cfoutput query="MyQuery"  group="Category">
 #MyQuery.Category#<br>

 <!--- Inner Loop --->
 <cfoutput>
    #MyQuery.Product#<br>
 </cfoutput>

</cfoutput>
```

The outer loop specifies the query, MyQuery, and the column that we are grouping on, Category. It outputs the category values. The inner loop contains no attributes and outputs the name of the Product. The results of this query are similar to the output shown earlier in this chapter, with the products listed under each individual category.

DEMONSTRATING
ADVANCED APPLICATION
DEVELOPMENT CONCEPTS

The cfmail tag can also be used to group information. (You can find more information about cfmail in Chapter 22.) The outer loop is specified in the cfmail tag. The inner loop uses cfoutput. Using the MyQuery query, this is the code:

```
<!--- Outer cfmail loop --->
<cfmail to="jeff@farcryfly.com" from="jeff@farcryfly.com"
        query="MyQuery" group="Category" subject="Test">

 #MyQuery.Category#<br>

 <!--- Inner Mail Loop --->
 <cfoutput>
    #MyQuery.Product#<br>
 </cfoutput>

</cfmail>
```

The cfmail tag accepts the query and group attributes. The inner loop uses the cfoutput tag. The results of this method are that a single e-mail message is sent for each category, and the body of the e-mail message contains the products associated with that category.

 You can group more than two levels.

Using Aggregate Functions and Other Keywords

This section teaches you about some pertinent keywords that you can use when writing your SQL queries. It also discusses some aggregate functions that you can use to manipulate the data before sending the result set back to yourself.

Selecting Rows with DISTINCT and TOP

This section examines some of the keywords and functions that are a part of SQL that can help you alter the data that is returned by a particular query. This section first looks at some keywords, and then looks at the aggregate functions. There are two keywords that commonly are used in query statements: DISTINCT and TOP.

Perhaps you want to get a list of all categories that are associated with a particular product. The DISTINCT keyword would help you do so. It is used to return unique rows from the query set. Duplicate rows are removed. The DISTINCT keyword comes after the SELECT keyword, but before the list of fields that you want to select. Here is an example:

```
SELECT DISTINCT Categories.Category
FROM Categories, CategoryProducts
WHERE Categories.CategoryID = CategoryProducts.CategoryID
```

The DISTINCT keyword follows the SELECT keyword, but comes before the Category field. This query will get all categories that also exist in the CategoryProducts table, but will return each one of them just once.

The TOP keyword is used to limit the number of items that are returned from a query. It is used in conjunction with a number. You can return 1 row, 100 rows, or any number of rows that you choose. This is similar, in concept, to the maxrows attribute of the cfquery tag. The difference is that using the TOP keyword will limit the number of records returned from the query, thus limiting your bandwidth usage. Using maxrows returns all records from the query's result set, but only places a subset of them in the ColdFusion query object.

This is an example of using the TOP keyword to return only a single category:

```
SELECT TOP 1 Categories.Category
FROM Categories
```

The preceding code will return the top category. This is often useful if you want to retrieve sample data for development purposes.

Manipulating Data with Aggregate Functions

This section shows you how to use SQL aggregate functions to manipulate data before sending the data to ColdFusion. Aggregate functions are functions that operate on a query column and return the results as a single value. Some common aggregate functions are listed in Table 21-1.

Aggregate Function	Description
MIN	Returns the smallest value in the column
MAX	Returns the largest value in the column
COUNT	Returns the total number of values in the column
SUM	Adds all the values in the column and returns the result
AVG	Adds all the values in the column, divides the result by the number of columns, and returns the result

Table 21-1. *SQL Aggregate Functions*

To use an aggregate function, you just specify the name of the function in the select clause of the SQL statement. The column that you are operating on is placed between parentheses next to the function. Here is an example:

```
SELECT Count(Categories.Category) AS CategoryCount
FROM Categories
```

The preceding query will return a single row that contains the number of categories in the Categories table. You will notice that after the function, the keyword AS appears, followed by a custom variable name that you can specify. This is called an alias. Since the result of the function has no name, we have to assign it one so that it can be accessed in our ColdFusion code, later.

Let's say you want to know how many products are in the category Red. You could use this query:

```
SELECT Count(Categories.CategoryID) AS CategoryCount
FROM CategoryProducts
WHERE CategoryProducts.CategoryID = 1
```

This will return the results that you need.

The other functions are used to perform mathematical functions. To demonstrate these functions, we will add a price column to the product table. If you want to know what is the highest-priced product in your database, you can use the MAX function. If you want to know what is the lowest-priced product, you can use the MIN function. The average price is given to you by the AVG function. The total can be achieved using the SUM function. All these functions can be used in the same query:

```
SELECT MIN(Price) AS MinPrice, MAX(Price) AS MaxPrice,
       SUM(Price) AS TotalPrice, AVG(Price) AS AvgPrice
FROM Products
```

This will return the proper values based on the data in the database.

Using SQL Server's Stored Procedures

Each database employs its own language for stored procedures, and the capabilities and limitations are quite different across the different databases available for ColdFusion developers. This section examines stored procedures in SQL Server.

Creating Stored Procedures in SQL Server

Stored procedures in SQL Server are written in Transact-SQL, or T-SQL, Microsoft's implementation of the Structured Query Language. You will recognize much of T-SQL since it is close to the ANSI standard for SQL. There are extensions to T-SQL that provide the syntax and conventions for writing SQL Server's stored procedures. If you do not commonly write stored procedures, you may need a reference handy to help guide you through the particulars.

 The subject of stored procedures for each of these databases is worthy of a large book by itself, and the discussion that follows only touches on key syntax and concepts.

Creating a Stored Procedure

In SQL Server's Enterprise Manager, stored procedures exist in a node under the database. There are several ways to create a stored procedure, but we are going to first look at creating a simple procedure directly in the database schema so that you can familiarize yourself with the basic syntax. Most developers prefer to write their procedures in SQL Server's Query Analyzer, with its handy tools, or in an editor such as ColdFusion Studio that provides a bit more authoring flexibility than the property box. But, for the sake of simplicity, we are going to create a procedure directly through Enterprise Manager.

To begin, open Enterprise Manager, connect to your database, and expand the Databases node. Right-click Stored Procedures and select New Stored Procedure.

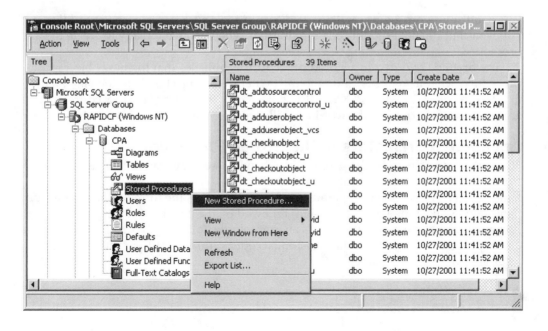

DEMONSTRATING
ADVANCED APPLICATION
DEVELOPMENT CONCEPTS

The Stored Procedure Properties dialog box that opens is where we'll place our T-SQL that defines the stored procedure.

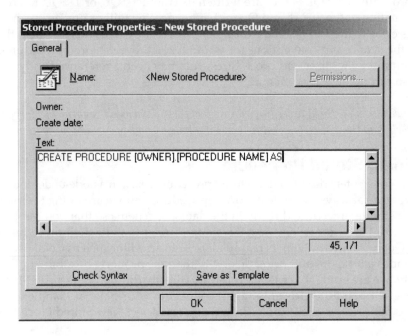

When authoring procedures with text editors or tools such as ColdFusion Studio, you would paste the resultant code into this box when you were ready to create the procedure.

The first line required in a stored procedure establishes that the new object is a procedure, what its name is, and who the owner of the object is. The first statement in a procedure is CREATE PROCEDURE, followed by the name of the procedure. If there are no variables to declare, the word AS will complete the opening statement.

Accepting Parameters in the Stored Procedure

Stored procedures may accept parameters when invoked, and can return parameters from the code. Input and output parameters must be declared between the procedure name and the AS statement. A parameter declaration takes the form of the parameter's name (always beginning with an @ sign) followed by the data type of the parameter. A comma separates each parameter. As an example, the following block of T-SQL creates a new procedure called procStartSession, accepting three input parameters and returning two output parameters:

```
CREATE PROCEDURE DBO.procStartSession
  @username varchar(12),
```

```
@password varchar(12),
@entryPage varchar(64),
@userID int OUTPUT,
@sessionID char(12) OUTPUT
AS
```

The keyword OUTPUT follows the last two parameters, indicating that they will be returned as outbound parameters by the procedure. SQL Server implicitly assumes the first three parameters are input parameters, since there is no keyword following the data type.

Controlling the Program Flow

Once the parameters have been declared, the program flow may begin. Stored procedures are most often a hybrid between program-flow and SQL statements. The complete set of available T-SQL statements and functions is available from SQL Server documentation (and the list is large). Most operations that developers are familiar with can be performed in T-SQL, including conditional operations, through the form of an IF...ELSE statement and looping logic in the form of BEGIN...END or WHILE statements.

What language could possibly be without everyone's favorite IF...ELSE statement? T-SQL is no exception, and allows conditional checks inside of procedures. The syntax begins with IF followed by a Boolean test. If the Boolean test returns true, then the statement immediately following is executed. If it returns false, and there is an ELSE statement, then the statement following the ELSE is executed. Since we often need to execute multiple statements after a condition is met, we can wrap a collection of statements between the words BEGIN and END. Here is an example:

```
IF @entryPage = 'special.cfm'
 SET @sestimeout = 400
ELSE
BEGIN
 SET @sestimeout = 800
 IF @entryPage = 'buynow.cfm'
 BEGIN
  INSERT INTO BigBuyers (UserID,BuyingDate)
  VALUES (@UserID,GETDATE())
  UPDATE tdUser SET LastBuy = GETDATE()
  WHERE UserID = @UserID
 END
END
```

In the preceding example, we have a compound conditional with an ELSE clause. In the second IF statement, we have two operations we need to perform: an insert and an update. To do this, we wrap the routine in a BEGIN...END statement. Also note that we have used a T-SQL function called GETDATE() to generate today's date for the SQL. We could have provided today's date as an input parameter, but it is always preferable to have SQL Server exploit its own functions when possible. Mathematical operators follow familiar conventions, and a complete list is available in SQL Server's help file.

Loops are performed with a WHILE statement. The loop syntax begins with the word WHILE followed by an expression. As long as the expression is true, the loop will continue. Ensure that the condition being inspected in the expression is being modified in the loop, or else an infinite loop will occur. The BEGIN...END statement will hold together multiple statements for the loop. A BREAK statement also can be added to the loop to break out of the loop when a condition is met. For an example of the WHILE statement, we can produce four records with a foreign key that we are working with using the following:

```
SET @varcount = 0
WHILE (SELECT count(*) FROM txQuestions
        WHERE userID = @userID) < 4
BEGIN
 SET @varcount = @varcount + 1
 INSERT INTO txQuestions (userID,quested,groupID)
 VALUES (@userID,@count,@groupID)
 IF (SELECT count(*) FROM txQuestions
     WHERE groupID = @groupID) > 24
  BREAK
 ELSE
  CONTINUE
END
```

If the user has less than four questions in the table, the loop will execute. If the user's group has 25 questions currently in the table, the loop will discontinue, and the code will continue processing after the END of the WHILE loop. For the @varcount variable to function properly, it has to be declared earlier in the procedure.

Exploiting Additional SQL Server Features

SQL Server also provides some important system functions, the two most popular of which are @@IDENTITY and @@ROWCOUNT. The system function @@IDENTITY pulls back the identity value of the row that was just inserted, and @@ROWCOUNT retrieves the count of rows affected by the subsequent operation. From ColdFusion, such operations would require multiple round trips to the database. Using stored procedures, however, we can perform this in a single request. To see how this works, we can look at creating a new session for our user with the following code:

```
CREATE PROCEDURE DBO.procStartSession
 @userName varchar(12),
```

```
@password varchar(12),
@entryPage varchar(64),
@userID int OUTPUT,
@sessionID char(12) OUTPUT
AS

--Grab the current userID for this person
SELECT @userID = userID FROM tdUser
WHERE username = @username and password = @password
 IF @@ROWCOUNT = 0
 BEGIN
  --New user, create a user in the table
  INSERT INTO tdUser (username,password,creationDate)
  VALUES (@username,@password,GETDATE())
  SELECT @userID = @@IDENTITY
 END
--Create a session and grab the sessionID
INSERT INTO tdSession (userID,sesDate)
VALUES (@userID, GETDATE())
SELECT @sessionID = @@IDENTITY
```

This T-SQL first attempts to assign a userID to the variable @userID based on the parameters provided. If no record was selected, determined by the check of @@ROWCOUNT, then the code will insert a new record. After inserting the record, the code will check for the new ID and set it to the userID parameter. Finally, with the @userID, the procedure will make a session entry and again will select the last identity and assign it to the @sessionID parameter.

One of the real strengths of stored procedures is the ability to interact with other objects in the database, including other stored procedures. For example, common calculations performed in an organization may be abstracted to a user-defined function or a procedure in SQL Server (note, user-defined functions are only available in SQL Server 2000). Then, when you need to make the calculation in any procedure, you can call the function or procedure for this operation.

To call a procedure in T-SQL, begin with the keyword EXEC followed by the procedure name. Next, you must provide the mandatory parameters required by the procedure in a comma-separated list. These parameters may be specified either by assignment or by position. In the following example, we declare some local variables and set them to test values, to demonstrate calling a procedure with variables as parameters:

```
DECLARE @varusername varchar(12)
DECLARE @varpassword varchar(12)
DECLARE @varentryPage varchar(64)
```

```
DECLARE @varsessionID char(12)
DECLARE @varuserID int
SET @varusername = 'test'
SET @varpassword = 'test'
SET @varentryPage = 'thispage.cfm'
EXEC dbo.procStartSession @username = @varusername,
@password = @varpassword, @entryPage = @varentryPage,
@userID = @varuserID OUT, @sessionID = @varsessionID OUT
```

The execution command could also have set the parameters to static values with a statement such as this:

```
EXEC dbo.procStartSession @username = 'test',
        @password = 'test', @entryPage = 'thispage.cfm',
        @userID = @varuserID OUT, @sessionID = @varsessionID OUT
```

In both instances, the variables @varsessionID and @varuserID will be available for the remainder of the procedure that called dbo.test2.

User-defined functions may be used as a value in an insert, update, or select statement, and can be set to local variables as well. To call a user-defined function in T-SQL, simply write the function out and populate its parameters. Local variables may be used in parameters, or they can be hard-coded with values:

```
SELECT f_calculate_cost(@itemID, 5, @quantity) AS total_cost,
                itemDesc, itemSKU
                FROM tdItem WHERE itemID = @itemID
```

In the first column of the record, the function will produce the result of the calculation based on the parameters provided. The parameters include two variables and a hard-coded constant of 5. Calculations that are common in your application should be rendered as functions for easier development and centralization.

SQL Server also has a collection of system procedures that accomplish a large variety of tasks. Many of them assist the database administrator in the routine maintenance of the database. Others, like xp_send_mail, may offer valuable assistance to a ColdFusion application by offloading tasks from the application server to the database server. The cfmail tag is a taxing event for the application server, and under heavy load this feature can quickly become the breaking point. Offloading this functionality to SQL Server, which in turn can execute the task asynchronously, removes a performance vulnerability from the application. For xp_send_mail to work, however, the server must be configured properly.

Using SQL Server's Authoring Tools

As mentioned at the beginning of the discussion on SQL Server's procedures, there are several tools with which to author a stored procedure. SQL Server has a Create Procedure Wizard, but it is woefully inadequate for all but the simplest of procedures. Text editors can be employed to create the code that in turn is pasted into a text area of a new stored procedure dialog box. Most editors offer meaningful color-coding when the code is saved as a SQL file. One of the better places to author and work with stored procedures is SQL Query Analyzer.

SQL Query Analyzer is available from Enterprise Manager under the Tools menu. You can create your procedure using the Query pane. One of the advantages is that the Object Browser on the left side provides a visual representation of the parameters and dependencies of objects in SQL Server. Since you will want to interact with existing objects, this information can really speed up the process of creation.

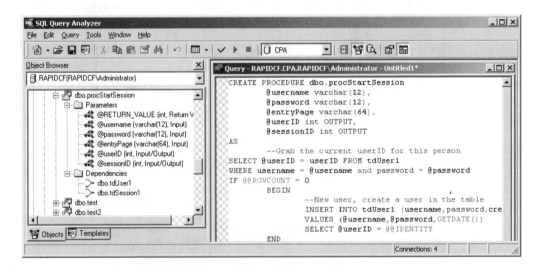

Some of the tools that come with SQL Query Analyzer are invaluable when tuning your stored procedure. Perhaps the most important is the Estimated Execution Plan. On the toolbar at top, clicking the Estimated Execution Plan button will populate the results pane with details on the execution plan for your procedure.

This tool will help identify particularly slow operations, and will assign an estimated cost for each move in your procedure. With this information, you can focus in on performance culprits fairly easily.

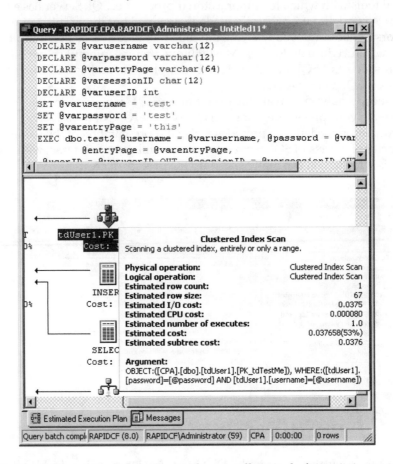

SQL Query Analyzer provides other tools, as well, to include statistics, tracing, and debugging options.

Using Oracle's Stored Procedures

This section teaches you about stored procedures in Oracle. It begins by introducing PL/SQL, Oracle's stored procedure language, and finishes by showing you some tools that can be used to create stored procedures.

Creating a Stored Procedure

Oracle's SQL is quite different from SQL Server or ANSI SQL. The most prominent difference arises in joins. Instead of using INNER JOIN or OUTER JOIN in the FROM clause of a query, Oracle SQL specifies the joined fields in the WHERE clause. After the initial shock of this convention, most developers discover that this syntax is actually considerably easier and more flexible. In a short time, very complicated joins can be written by hand without the aid of tools, unlike SQL Server, with its complex nested join syntax.

Oracle stored procedures are written in PL/SQL, or Procedural Language/SQL. The PL/SQL language is a more focused language than SQL Server's T-SQL, but is quite similar in practice. Some of the differences at first appear bizarre, but with short practice, developers learn that PL/SQL is actually a very powerful and accommodating language.

Stored procedures occupy their own branch in the object tree of Oracle's DBA Studio. To find procedures, open DBA Studio and expand the database that you intend to work in. Procedures are located under Schema. If you have multiple schemas in your database, the various schemas will appear under the Procedure branch.

To create a procedure, you must have sufficient privileges. In many situations, you may not have this permission, and will have to send your code to a DBA. If you do have Create Procedure permission, right-click the Procedure branch and select Create. A Create Procedure box will appear (see Figure 21-1). Enter the name of the procedure in the Name text box. Be sure to select the correct schema in the drop-down list, or else the procedure may not be available to your user context.

The opening syntax for a procedure is the statement CREATE OR REPLACE PROCEDURE followed by the schema and the procedure name and punctuated with the keyword AS. The OR REPLACE is not necessary on the first creation, but often is included because any corrections will require its addition. In practice, this would look like the following:

```
CREATE OR REPLACE PROCEDURE cpa.procAddItem
AS
```

Learning the PL/SQL Language

This section shows you all you need to know to write stored procedures in PL/SQL. It demonstrates important PL/SQL concepts.

Using Parameters in PL/SQL

In PL/SQL, the parameters rest between the procedure name and the AS keyword, and are wrapped by parentheses. Each parameter is listed, followed by an IN, OUT, or IN OUT mode and the data type. Commas separate each parameter defined. Instead of

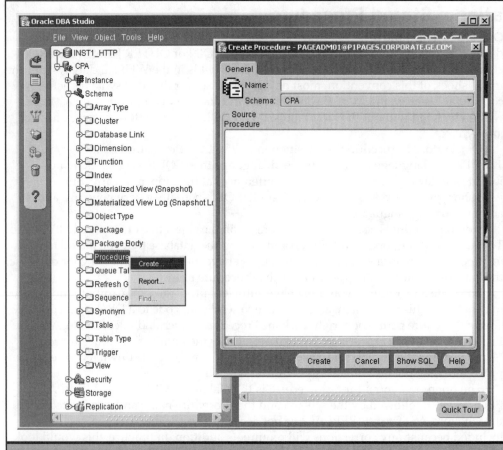

Figure 21-1. *Creating a stored procedure in Oracle's DBA Studio*

specifying the actual data type, the optional %TYPE may be used. This solicits the type information directly from the table the parameter is from. In practice, the parameter declaration looks like the following example:

```
CREATE OR REPLACE PROCEDURE cpa.procAddItem
  (vModel IN NUMBER,
   vModelYear IN NUMBER,
   vMileage IN NUMBER,
   vPrice IN NUMBER,
   vDealerID IN NUMBER,
```

```
   vSynopsis IN varchar2(512),
    itemID OUT NUMBER)
 AS
BEGIN
 /* ... Bunch of Procedure stuff here ... */
END;
```

Parameters in PL/SQL do not have any characters, such as an @ sign, signifying their role. To prevent ambiguity, most developers prefix the variables with a v, var, or a v and an underscore, although this is not required. Immediately following the AS keyword, the keyword BEGIN demarks the point where the procedure starts. The END keyword followed by a semicolon identifies the end of the procedure. Here we introduce a common theme that differentiates PL/SQL from T-SQL: the omnipresent semicolon. Each operation in PL/SQL ends with a semicolon. Forgetting the semicolon often results in a cryptic error message about one of the objects in the vicinity of where the phrase should have ended.

Controlling the Program Flow

With the explanation of the declaration out of the way, we can now delve into the specifics of PL/SQL. Program flow in PL/SQL is a familiar dance between SQL statements and flow-control statements. PL/SQL supports conditional statements and loop logic.

The conditional check syntax in Oracle is fairly simple, but distinct from T-SQL. It begins with the keyword IF followed by a Boolean expression and the keyword THEN. The operation is closed with an END IF and a semicolon. An ELSE may be used between the THEN and END IF keywords.

```
IF vPrice > 40000 THEN
  INSERT INTO premiumInv (itemID,dealerID)
  VALUES (vItemID, vDealerID);
ELSE
  INSERT INTO saleInv (itemID, dealerID)
  VALUES (vItemID, vDealerID);
  vInflatedPrice := vPrice + (vPrice * 0.20);
END IF;
```

In the second conditional in the preceding example, a variable is set to inflate the price by 20 percent (a common sales tactic that inflates the asking price to lend the impression that the item is a bargain). When setting a variable in PL/SQL, a colon precedes the equal sign. For equality inspections, where we are testing the left side against the right side, a normal equal sign is used. In a cruel twist from Oracle, the else if operation is carried out with the keyword ELSIF. The previous word is not a typo; the second *E* is intentionally omitted from the word.

Oracle uses the keywords FOR, IN, LOOP, and END LOOP to execute a programmatic for loop. To begin the loop, the FOR keyword is followed by the counter variable. The IN keyword sets up the range for the iterations. The range is expressed as two integers separated by two periods in between. These integers may be variables declared earlier in the code. The keyword LOOP transitions the code into the executed logical block. At the end of the block of code that the loop will iterate through, the keyword END LOOP with a semicolon punctuates the operation. Here is an example:

```
DECLARE
vTop INTEGER :=24;
BEGIN
 FOR i IN 5..vTop LOOP
  vTotal := i + vTotal;
  IF vTotal < 20 THEN
    FOR j IN REVERSE 1..3 LOOP
    INSERT INTO oblivion (fooCount,barCount)
    VALUES (i,j);
   END LOOP;
  END IF;
  IF vTotal > 100 THEN
   EXIT;
  END IF;
 END LOOP;
END;
```

In the preceding convoluted compound loop, we can view a handful of features in Oracle for loops. First, the outside loop is able to use a variable, vTop, to set the top value of the loop. After a simple assignment that adds the current loop value to vTotal, a second loop will execute if vTotal is less than 20. The second loop, however, will start at 3 and loop down to 1 in reverse order due to the keyword REVERSE following the IN keyword. Both counter variables are available in the inside loop for the INSERT INTO statement. Following the inside loop, if vTotal has exceed 100, the loop will terminate due to the EXIT keyword.

PL/SQL also offers a WHILE loop. Like its sibling in T-SQL, the WHILE loop executes as long as a Boolean condition remains true:

```
WHILE length(vSynopsis) < 512 LOOP
 vSynopsis := vSynopsis ||' '|| f_random_word();
END LOOP;
```

In the example, the loop will build the synopsis up until it is 512 characters long. Since the last run may make it longer than 512 characters, the variable would require trimming if it truly needed to be less than 512 characters long. Note, the syntax for concatenating in Oracle is two pipes (| |). The single quotes with a space will concatenate a space between vSynopsis and the string returned by the user-defined function f_random_word( ).

Setting Variables from Database Information

To set a variable with a value from the database, we use a SELECT query with an INTO keyword. This type of query is often called a singleton SELECT, since it is pulling only one row. The value from the SELECT will be available for the remainder of the procedure.

```
SELECT dealerDesc INTO vDealerDesc
FROM tdDealer
WHERE dealerID = vDealerID
```

This query will throw an error if more than one record is returned. Consequently, if your conditional is not a unique constrained primary key or some other field that has a unique constraint, you will want to apply some exception handling to the query.

When a new record is inserted, we often require the identity just assigned that new record. With SQL Server, system functions provide us that ability. In Oracle, we can request the identity after the insertion with the keyword RETURNING:

```
INSERT INTO tdDealer
  (dealerDesc, dealerState, dealerBrand)
VALUES (vDealerDesc, vDealerState, vDealerBrand)
RETURNING dealerID INTO vDealerID;
```

The new ID will be available through the variable vDealerID.

Understanding Transactions

PL/SQL facilitates easy transactional control when performing multiple-step operations. If a step of your process fails, you can roll back to points identified in your code. This prevents corrupted data when an error occurs, or when a process is short-circuited. The keyword SAVEPOINT identifies the start of the transactional block. Assigning a value to the savepoint allows you to set multiple points to roll back to. If your transaction completes without any issues, the keyword COMMIT will commit the transaction. If an exception occurs, ROLLBACK will roll the transaction back to the specified savepoint.

```
SAVEPOINT S1;
  DELETE FROM premiumInv WHERE itemID = vItemID;
  DELETE FROM saleInv WHERE itemID = vItemID;
  IF SQL%NOTFOUND THEN
   ROLLBACK TO S1;
```

```
END IF;
DELETE FROM dealerSales WHERE itemID = vItemID;
IF SQL%FOUND THEN
  COMMIT;
ELSE
  ROLLBACK TO S1;
END IF;

SAVEPOINT S2;
 DELETE FROM tdItemDetail WHERE itemID = vItemID;
 DELETE FROM tdItem WHERE itemID = vItemID;
 IF SQL%FOUND THEN
   COMMIT;
 ELSE
   ROLLBACK TO S2;
 END IF;
```

The preceding code is a good example of the strength of stored procedures. To remove an item that is a foreign key in multiple tables, we must delete all the records where the item is a foreign key first, and then we can delete the record where the item is the primary key. To do so in this scenario would have required five round trips to the database from ColdFusion. Executing the scenario in a stored procedure is significantly faster, is more reliable, and can be run from a console such as SQL*Plus.

The preceding example uses two savepoints. Using SQL%NOTFOUND and SQL%FOUND, we can determine if the query successfully deleted a row or more. If the second or third delete statement fails to delete a record, the transaction rolls back to the savepoint with the name S1. If the fifth delete fails to delete a record, then the transaction only rolls back to the savepoint named S2. In very large "cleanup" procedures, careful selection of savepoints and rollbacks will ensure the integrity of the data.

Building Oracle Stored Procedures with Authoring Tools

There are numerous ways to build an Oracle stored procedure. Most DBAs and many developers simply write the stored procedure in a text editor and then run the SQL file in SQL*Plus. SQL*Plus is an interface to the database that works similarly to a Unix console. SQL*Plus can provide information about errors and feedback on the execution plan.

Third-party vendors also provide rich tools for developing Oracle database objects such as stored procedures. One of the more popular is TOAD by Quest Software. TOAD offers a complete interface with myriad tools to help in development.

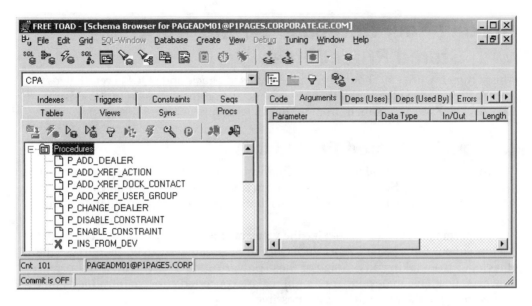

TOAD's environment is fairly easy to use and provides several advanced tools as well.

Finding More Information

Stored procedures are capable of far more than has been covered in this chapter. In most databases, stored procedures can interact to some extent with third-party objects to send targeted e-mail messages, build dynamic files, and perform a wide range of operations. ColdFusion developers also can overcome JDBC limitations by working with data through stored procedures. Most databases have rich libraries of books covering details of their stored procedures.

While stored procedures are valuable, they can be time-consuming to develop. Some ColdFusion templates will benefit more than others from a change to stored procedures. At the top of the list are those templates with multiple-step database operations. If you must insert or delete from a normalized schema, stored procedures are particularly valuable, removing the necessity for numerous round trips to the database. Checkout pages in shopping carts likewise benefit, since there are usually a few tables requiring updates or inserts. In high-traffic pages, stored procedures can return meta information quickly while providing scalability. Also, stored procedures are especially valuable for often-repeated calculations, or complicated business logic.

You can find more information about PL/SQL or T-SQL by checking the documentation of the relevant database server.

DEMONSTRATING
ADVANCED APPLICATION
DEVELOPMENT CONCEPTS

Making Your Database Do the Work with Stored Procedures

This section teaches you about stored procedures in Oracle and SQL Server. It gives you an overview and explains why they are beneficial, and then goes on to demonstrate how to create and access them from within ColdFusion.

Understanding Stored Procedures

Stored procedures are vital to a quality ColdFusion application. Their significance cannot be underestimated. Stored procedures often can transform marginal ColdFusion applications into scalable, fast applications that are able to perform under demanding conditions.

While most developers recognize the value of stored procedures, few use them to their potential. Often, a bad experience early in a developer's career discourages the developer from taking advantage of these powerful tools. Given their importance, however, ColdFusion developers should make a concerted effort to introduce stored procedures into their code whenever possible.

Stored procedures provide speed, scalability, and modularity, the three most sought-after qualities in web applications. Specific advantages include the following:

- **Less traffic through the network**   Often, a stored procedure can accomplish that which would take two or three queries to achieve. Each round trip to the database is a costly event.

- **Stored procedures are precompiled**   Most database servers precompile stored procedures and pass parameters in as bind variables, thereby eliminating unnecessary steps at run time.

- **Cleaner transactional control**   Transactional control of complicated, multistep SQL operations is better handled on the database server than from the application server.

- **Smaller footprint on the JDBC layer**   The JDBC code for a stored procedure typically is smaller than that for a comparable query.

- **Code reuse**   Once developed, you can use the stored procedure in other templates or even in other applications. The other applications do not have to be ColdFusion applications, either. This is important when strategizing for integration with JSP servers.

- **Decentralize development effort**   Stored procedures offer an excellent opportunity to "black box" tasks, wherein a team member can develop the business logic as another develops the presentation layer, without stepping on each other's toes.

So, if stored procedures are so great, why don't we see them more often? The primary reason lies in their complexity. Writing a query in ColdFusion is a straightforward exercise. Building a stored procedure and calling it from ColdFusion does require a greater initial investment in development time. Stored procedures are tougher to write than queries and are not as easy to debug. Also, many developers may not have permissions to create procedures on the database. These developers have to work through a database administrator and the associated delays that entails.

Integrating ColdFusion with Stored Procedures

ColdFusion interacts with stored procedures with three specific tags: cfstoredproc, cfprocparam, and cfprocresult. In concert, these tags call the procedure, pass it parameters, and expose the result set to the template.

Using the cfstoredproc Tag

The core tag for interacting with stored procedures is cfstoredproc. This tag specifies the procedure to be called and sets some basic attributes for the event. The cfstoredproc tag wraps around the other tags employed with stored procedures, and must end with a closing cfstoredproc tag. The tag has the following seven attributes available, the first two of which are required (the remaining five are optional):

- **procedure**   Used to specify the name of the stored procedure that you are calling. Most developers include either a *p* or the word proc in the name to differentiate it from other database objects.

Avoid using system conventions in the name, such as sp_ or xp_, in SQL Server, since these indicate system procedures.

- **datasource**   Used to specify the name of the datasource that contains the procedure.
- **returncode**   Allows you to access the status code returned by the stored procedure (accepts a Boolean value). The status code is stored in the cfstoredproc.StatusCode variable. Each database returns a proprietary set of status codes providing feedback about the execution of your procedure. These can be helpful when developing, to confirm the status of your request. The default value for this attribute is no.
- **debug**   Determines whether or not debug information is available for each statement (accepts a Boolean value). If you set it to yes, then debug information is available for each statement. If you set it to no, the default value, then debug information is not available.
- **blockfactor**   Specifies the number of rows retrieved from the server at a time (accepts a whole number value between 1 and 100, with 1 being the default value).

If your procedure typically returns three to five rows, and seldom returns more, you should set your blockfactor to 5. Doing so would retrieve all five records in a single fetch. In this example, if three records are returned, JDBC will dynamically resize the blockfactor to the smaller size. Attention to blockfactor is most important when scalability and performance are imperative for your application.

- **username**   Used to specify a username, if needed, to access the datasource. It is used in conjunction with the password attribute.

- **password**   Used specify a password to access the datasource, if needed. It is used in conjunction with the username attribute.

Thus, at a minimum, the syntax for calling a stored procedure from ColdFusion is as follows:

```
<cfstoredproc procedure="ProcHelloWorld" datasource="myDB">
</cfstoredproc>
```

This tag would send a request to invoke the stored procedure ProcHelloWorld on the server myDB.

Using the username and password attributes may expose a security hole in your application, if code is displayed when errors occur. The more appropriate, and common, solution is to set up a new datasource that uses the username and password. More information about securing your ColdFusion applications can be found in Chapter 17.

Using the cfprocparam Tag

Most often, stored procedures require parameters in order to function properly. These parameters, or input variables, are provided to the procedure via the cfprocparam tag, which is nested inside the cfstoredproc tag. A cfprocparam tag is a stand-alone tag, and does not have a closing tag.

The cfprocparam tag handles both parameters to be sent to the stored procedures and those returned by the procedure. Each parameter passed to a stored procedure requires its own cfprocparam tag. Similarly, output parameters are likewise specified with their own cfprocparam tag. The tag has eight attributes with which to massage the input data and specify particulars of returned values:

- **type**   Used to differentiate between input and output variables (optional attribute). For input parameters, the value for this attribute is in. For bind variables that return values from the procedure, the value is out or inout. The latter parameters would have an OUT keyword in their declaration clause of the procedure, as we will see when we explore the actual procedures themselves.

- **cfsqltype**   Specifies the data type for the parameter. When ColdFusion sends or receives a variable from a procedure, it must associate the proper data type with that variable. Possible values for this attribute use a composite name with a CF_SQL_ prefix to the data type's common name. The valid values for this attribute are CF_SQL_BIGINT, CF_SQL_BIT (correlates with BIT types for SQL Server), CF_SQL_BLOB, CF_SQL_CLOB, CF_SQL_CHAR, CF_SQL_DATE (correlates with SMALLDATETIME for SQL Server, DATE for Oracle), CF_SQL_DECIMAL, CF_SQL_DOUBLE, CF_SQL_FLOAT, CF_SQL_IDSTAMP, CF_SQL_INTEGER, CF_SQL_LONGVARCHAR, CF_SQL_MONEY, CF_SQL_MONEY4, CF_SQL_NUMERIC, CF_SQL_REAL, CF_SQL_REFCURSOR, CF_SQL_SMALLINT, CF_SQL_TIME, CF_SQL_TIMESTAMP, CF_SQL_TINYINT, CF_SQL_VARCHAR (VARCHAR for SQL Server or VARCHAR2 for Oracle).

- **dbvarname**   Identifies the specific parameter of the stored procedure. This parameter is required if your procedure was developed with named notation— that is, if the name of the parameter rather than the order in which it appears is what identifies it in the request. Even when using named notation, it is a good practice to observe the ordinality of the parameters. Given that some database administrators may have enabled case sensitivity, it is also prudent to observe case when entering this value.

- **variable**   Specifies the variable name that your ColdFusion template will use to access the returned value. This parameter is required when the parameter type is OUT or INOUT. As with all ColdFusion variables, the value cannot begin with a number, and should not have punctuation in it.

- **value**   Specifies the parameter's value. This attribute is required for IN and INOUT parameters, unless the null="yes" parameter is used. Of course, the data passed in this parameter should conform to the data type specified in the cfsqltype attribute of the tag.

- **maxlength**   Sets a limit to the size of the parameter. This attribute is useful when passing values to a fixed-length variable, such as a parameter with the data type of VARCHAR2(50) or CHAR(50). This will prevent sending user-provided data that exceeds the size allotted in the database. The scale attribute similarly conforms input data for numbers, by dictating the number of decimal places for the parameter.

- **scale**   Specifies the number of decimal places in a parameter (optional attribute). The default value is 0.

- **null**   Specifies that the value of the parameter will be passed to the stored procedure as NULL. It accepts a Boolean value and defaults to no. Specifying "yes" in this parameter negates the value attribute. This is an optional attribute.

As an example of calling a stored procedure from ColdFusion, we could call a SQL Server stored procedure called ProcAddUser providing it with basic user information with the following syntax:

```
<cfstoredproc procedure="ProcAddUser" datasource="Chapter31">
  <cfprocparam type="in" cfsqltype="CF_SQL_DATE"
               dbvarname="BirthDate" value="#form.BirthDate#">
  <cfprocparam type="in" cfsqltype="CF_SQL_VARCHAR"
               dbvarname="LastName" value="#form.LastName#">
  <cfprocparam type="in" cfsqltype="CF_SQL_VARCHAR"
               dbvarname="fName" value="#form.fName#">
  <cfprocparam type="in" cfsqltype="CF_SQL_VARCHAR"
               dbvarname="Email" value="#form.Email#">
  <cfprocparam type="in" cfsqltype="CF_SQL_CHAR"
               dbvarname="State" value="#form.State#" maxlength="2">
  <cfprocparam type="in" cfsqltype="CF_SQL_BIT"
               dbvarname="SsSubscriber" value="#form.SsSubscriber#">
  <cfprocparam type="in" cfsqltype="CF_SQL_INTEGER"
               dbvarname="Income" value="#form.Income#">
  <cfprocparam type="in" cfsqltype="CF_SQL_SMALLINT"
               dbvarname="Dept" value="#form.Dept#">

  <!--- Now, grab the new ID and user's session info --->
  <cfprocparam type="out" cfsqltype="CF_SQL_INTEGER"
               dbvarname="NewID" variable="UserID">
  <cfprocparam type="out" cfsqltype="CF_SQL_INTEGER"
               dbvarname="NewSession" variable="SessionID">
</cfstoredproc>
```

The preceding code inputs basic information about a new user by setting parameters with form values. The user's birth date is entered with a data type of date; the user's name and e-mail are entered with a varchar data type; and the user's income is entered with an integer data type. The state is entered as a char(2) with a maxlength set to conform the input to the length of the data type. The isSubscriber flag is entered as a bit, and the foreign key of Dept (usually from a drop-down list) is entered with a smallint data type. Of course, all of these data types are determined in the declaration clause of the stored procedure. ColdFusion simply must conform to those decisions. The procedure in this example also returns two values to ColdFusion: userID and sessionID, both of which are integers.

This example also demonstrates one of the strengths of a stored procedure. We created a new session in the database for the user and selected the user's identity. To add a user to a relational database, often we must insert into multiple tables. This requires several trips to the database from ColdFusion, a costly price of inserting into properly normalized databases. With a procedure, we can send all of the parameters in a single request, and let the procedure insert into the various tables. Not only does this considerably reduce the round-trip activity between the application layer and the database, the stored procedure can take advantage of inherent features of the database to further speed the process.

Using the cfprocresult Tag

What if we need to pull back more than just a couple of ID numbers or simple strings? How can we draw back a row or a record set from the procedure? To do this, we must include the last tag in ColdFusion's stored procedure family, the cfprocresult tag.

When we execute a query using cfquery, we are provided a single result set that we may expose in our code using a variety of tools, foremost of which is the cfoutput tag. Executing a stored procedure provides us similar ability when we use the cfprocresult tag. This tag, always imbedded in a cfstoredproc tag pair, provides us the ability to identify and name result sets returned by a procedure.

The cfprocresult tag has three valid attributes:

- **name** Used to specify the name with which you may access the result set (required attribute).

- **resultset** Allows you to segregate result sets when multiple result sets are returned from a procedure. The value must be a number, and references which result set should inherit the name attribute assigned in the same tag. Only result sets that will later be used in the template require a cfprocresult tag.

- **maxrows** Functions like its sibling in the cfquery tag, and limits the number of rows returned in the result set (optional attribute). Typically, however, the preferred method of limiting results is in the actual stored procedure, where queries and results can be manipulated to produce the desired results.

Putting Stored Procedures to Work

For an example of the complete set of tags, we can use the following hypothetical scenario. You have a set of templates that adds inventory to your used-Porsche dealership web site. After adding a vehicle, the current list of inventory must appear, as well as a list of dealers and basic information pertaining to the dealer that normally would require a separate query. You have authored a stored procedure that accepts the information on the newly listed vehicle, populates the appropriate tables, selects the newly revised inventory, and queries for the specifics on the dealer as well. The ColdFusion template on the page that receives the form submission could work as follows:

```
<!--- www.instantcoldfusion.com

Description: Page to Demonstrate a Stored Procedure

Entering: N/A
```

```
Exiting: N/A

Dependencies: N/A
Expecting: N/A

Modification History
Date        Modifier                Modification
************************************************************
05/22/2002 Chris Graves, RapidCF    Created
--->

<!--- Call the stored procedure
<cfstoredproc procedure="ProcAddCar" datasource="MyDSN">
 <cfprocparam type="in" cfsqltype="CF_SQL_SMALLINT"
              dbvarname="Dealer_ID" value="#form.Dealer_ID#">
 <cfprocparam type="in" cfsqltype="CF_SQL_SMALLINT"
              dbvarname="Model_Year" value="#form.Model_Year#">
 <cfprocparam type="in" cfsqltype="CF_SQL_SMALLINT"
              dbvarname="Model" value="#form.Model#">
 <cfprocparam type="in" cfsqltype="CF_SQL_INTEGER"
              dbvarname="Mileage" value="#form.Mileage#">
 <cfprocparam type="in" cfsqltype="CF_SQL_INTEGER"
              dbvarname="Price" value="#form.Price#">
 <cfprocparam type="in" cfsqltype="CF_SQL_INTEGER"
              dbvarname="Sales_Rep" value="#form.Sales_Rep#">
 <cfprocparam type="in" cfsqltype="CF_SQL_VARCHAR"
              bvarname="Synopsis" value="#form.Synopsis#"
              maxlength="512">

 <!--- Out parameters will populate variables in the page --->
 <cfprocparam type="out" cfsqltype="CF_SQL_CHAR"
              dbvarname="Dealer_IMG" variable="Dealer_IMG">
 <cfprocparam type="out" cfsqltype="CF_SQL_VARCHAR"
              dbvarname="Dealer_Name" variable="Dealer_Name">
 <cfprocparam type="out" cfsqltype="CF_SQL_DATE"
              dbvarname="Dealer_Last_Sale" variable="Dealer_Last_Sale">

 <!--- Result sets will build the current inventory and dealer list --->
 <cfprocresult name="Inventory" resultset="1">
 <cfprocresult name="Dealer_List" resultset="2">
</cfstoredproc>

<!--- now display some Dealer information --->
<cfoutput>
 <img src="# Dealer_List.Dealer_IMG#"><br>
 #Dealer_List.Dealer_Name#'s current inventory.<br>
 Last sale made on # Dealer_List.Dealer_Last_Sale#<br>
</cfoutput>
```

```
<table>
 <cfoutput query="Inventory">
  <tr>
   <td>
    <b>#Inventory.Model#</b> #Inventory.Model_Year#
    #Inventory.Mileage# #Inventory.Price#
   </td>
  </tr>
 </cfoutput>
</table>

<table>
 <cfoutput query="Dealer_List">
  <tr>
   <td>
    #Dealer_List.Dealer_Name# #Dealer_List.Dealer_Last_Sale#
   </td>
  </tr>
 </cfoutput>
</table>
```

Now we have all the tools necessary to call a stored procedure, pass it parameters, accept values, and pull result sets. The key ingredient missing in the preceding equation, however, is the stored procedure itself.

Querying a Query

With ColdFusion 5, Macromedia added the feature to run a SQL query against a record set that already existed in memory. This feature is referred to as a Query of Queries. This section shows you how to implement the Query of Queries in ColdFusion and tells you places where you can use it.

Learning to Query Your Query

This section shows you what you need to know to use the Query of Queries functionality in ColdFusion. It goes over the basics and shows you how to implement it. Then, it discusses some of the SQL features that are supported by the Query of Queries.

Understanding Query of Queries

The ability to query a query is a way to manipulate a ColdFusion query object. Before you can manipulate that query object, you must create it. There are many ways to create a query object in ColdFusion; most commonly, the cfquery tag is used. Other tags, such as cfdirectory or cfhttp, also will do the job. You can also create a query in CFScript using the QueryNew function. You can look at your ColdFusion documentation for a complete list of tags that will return queries.

After you have the query in memory, the next step is to manipulate it. You can do that by using the cfquery tag. There are only two attributes that are needed to perform a query against a query:

- **name**   Used to specify the name of the variable that will contain the resultant query object.

- **dbtype**   Should be set to query when performing a Query of Queries.

Many of the other attributes, such as datasource, username, password, blockfactor, and timeout, do not apply to a Query of Queries. You aren't accessing a datasource, you're accessing something in memory. You don't need a username or password to access an in-memory object. The blockfactor attribute relates to how data is returned from the database to ColdFusion. The data has already been returned to ColdFusion.

Note   *For a full explanation of the cfquery tag, including all of its attributes, check out Chapter 9.*

Suppose that we want to create a drill-down interface of categories and products—the same database we were using earlier in this chapter to describe aggregate functions. We can start with this query:

```
<!--- execute the cached query --->
<cfquery datasource="Chapter21" name="GetInfo" cachedwithin="1">
 SELECT Categories.CategoryID, Categories.Category ,
        Products.Product
 FROM Categories, Products, CategoryProducts
 WHERE Categories.CategoryID = CategoryProducts.CategoryID AND
       CategoryProducts.ProductID = Products.ProductID
</cfquery>
```

This code will execute the query to get all the category and product information. It is cached, so it will execute once and the resulting record set will stay in memory. The drill-down interface will have two pages, one for categories and one for products. This query will be on each page.

The first page in the drill-down list will list all the categories and offer a link to the second page. First, we need to get all the Category and CategoryID columns from the query. This is where the ability to query a query comes into play:

```
<!--- Perform the Query of Queries to get distinct categories --->
<cfquery dbtype="Query" name="DrillDown">
 SELECT DISTINCT CategoryID, Category
 FROM GetInfo
```

```
   ORDER BY Category
</cfquery>
```

The Query of Queries specifies the dbtype as query and specifies the name as DrillDown. The datasource is left out. This query selects the distinct Category and CategoryID, from the query GetInfo. The Query orders the data. The next step is to output the query information:

```
<!--- output the Categories --->
<cfoutput query="DrillDown">
 <A HREF="DrillDown2.cfm?CategoryID=#DrillDown.CategoryID#">
  #DrillDown.Category#
 </A><br>
</cfoutput>
```

The code loops over the Query of Queries just as if it were a database query. The code displays a link to the DrillDown2.cfm page, passing the CategoryID as a parameter, and displays the category text as the link.

The DrillDown2.cfm page needs to use the CategoryID to get a list of products. This is the Query of Queries:

```
<!--- execute the cached query to get the Products--->
<cfquery dbtype="Query" name="DrillDown">
 SELECT Product
 FROM GetInfo
 WHERE GetInfo.CategoryID = #url.CategoryID#
 ORDER BY Category
</cfquery>
```

This query selects from the same GetInfo query. It gets a list of all products, based on the CategoryID, which is passed in the URL.

The final step is to output the product info:

```
<!--- Output the Products --->
<cfoutput query="DrillDown">
 #DrillDown.Product#<br>
</cfoutput>
```

The cfoutput tag loops over the query DrillDown. It displays the Product for each loop iteration.

Understanding Supported SQL

The Query of Queries feature set does not meet all the ANSI standards, but supports many of them. This is a list of things that you can do with Query of Queries:

- **Dot notation**   If a table has dots in its name, you can still access the table by using Query of Queries.

- **Joins**   A join is a way to get data from two different tables. A Query of Queries does not support outer joins, nor does it support the inner join syntax that uses the keywords INNER JOIN.

- **Union**   The Union operator combines the results of two or more SELECT statements into a single table. ColdFusion accept this if the two tables have the same number of columns and both data types are numeric, character, dates, or identical. By default, the union operator will remove all duplicates from the result set. You can avoid this by using the keyword ALL. You can use parentheses to change the order of evaluations when performing a union on more than one SELECT statement.

Caution	*Query of Queries does not support ODBC-formatted dates.*

- **Aliasing**   Query of Queries supports column aliases. This is when you use the AS operator to refer to a column or table under a different name. SELECT ProductID AS PID from Products is an example.

- **Comparison operators**: Query of Queries supports many different comparison operators. You can use the keyword IS, and it checks if an expression is true, false, or NULL. Mathematical comparison operators are >, >=, <>, !=, <, or <= and can be used to compare two expressions.

- **BETWEEN operator**   This operator is used to check that an expression is between two other expressions. It is set up like this:

  `expression BETWEEN expression AND expression`

- **IN operator**   This operator is used to check if an expression is in the specified list.

- **LIKE operator**   This operator is used to perform wildcard searches. The wildcards are the underscore (_), to represent a single character; percent sign (%), to represent zero or more characters; square brackets ([ ]), to specify a character range; and square brackets with a caret ([^])to represent characters not in the specified range. By default, searches are case sensitive. You can use the functions Upper or Lower to make the search case insensitive. Wildcards can be escaped with a forward slash (\ ).

- **Aggregate functions**   The AVG, COUNT, MAX, MIN, and SUM aggregate functions are supported by the Query of Queries.

- **Group By and Having** Query of Queries supports the use of Group By and Having clauses. Grouping was discussed earlier in this chapter. The Having clause is used to place restrictions on which records are returned to the record set after the query has been grouped. It is similar to a WHERE clause.

- **Ordering** You can order your queries using the ORDER BY clause. You can order ascending (ASC) or descending (DESC) on any column that exists in the query you are querying against.

- **NULL values** If you try to access columns that contain NULL values in a Query of Queries, it will not work. The workaround is to make sure that the result is not NULL before accessing it. This is an example condition: MyColumn IS NOT NULL AND MyColumn = 'A'.

- **Escape reserved words** You can escape reserved words by surrounding the reserved word with brackets. It is considered bad practice to use reserved words in your tables or columns, or as ColdFusion variables.

Using Query of Queries

There are many benefits that you can achieve by using a Query of Queries:

- If you need to access similar data multiple times, accessing and manipulating a query in memory is much quicker than accessing the database each time. You should be careful about persistent storage of large result sets in server memory, though.

- If you want to combine data from two different databases, this is the best way to do it. You can easily join two different queries using the Query of Queries functionality. This is by far the most useful application of this feature.

- You can create a drill-down interface without having to access the database at each step of the drill down. You can create a query that contains all the data you need and then pass the query to each template of your drill-down interface by saving it as a persistent variable. You can use the Query of Queries feature to get the data you need at each step of the drill down.

- If you want to manipulate cached query data, this is a good way to create variations of your pages without having to access the database again. A good example of this is creating Forward and Next buttons to parse through your data. Run your query once and cache it. You can select the specific items you want to display using the Query of Queries.

There can be a lot of benefits to using the Query of Queries functionality. However, you must take care to not use it for something that could be offloaded to the database in the first place, by using stored procedures, aggregate functions, or other database functionality.

DEMONSTRATING ADVANCED APPLICATION DEVELOPMENT CONCEPTS

Summary

In this chapter, you learned about the following:

- Aggregate functions
- Stored procedures in Oracle and SQL Server
- How to use ColdFusion's Query of Queries functionality

The next chapter will teach you how to integrate with Internet protocols, including HTTP and POP mail accounts.

The Complete Reference

ColdFusion MX

Part V

Integrating ColdFusion with Other Technologies

The
Complete
Reference

ColdFusion
MX

Chapter 22

Mixing ColdFusion
with Internet Standards

his chapter demonstrates how ColdFusion can be mixed with Internet protocols.
It teaches you how to send and receive e-mail, retrieve remote files using HTTP,
and transfer files using FTP. All of this can be done within ColdFusion.

Sending and Receiving E-Mail

This section shows you how you can send and check your e-mail from within ColdFusion.
You could use these features to create a web-based e-mail program, similar to Hotmail
or Yahoo!. ColdFusion provides two tags, cfmail and cfpop, that allow you to interact
with e-mail.

Sending E-Mail from Within ColdFusion

To send SMTP e-mail from within ColdFusion, you must use the cfmail tag. You may
want to do this to e-mail to your user the tracking information after you have shipped
their order or to send the user a verification e-mail after they have registered on your
site. These are the attributes of the cfmail tag:

- **to**   Specifies who the e-mail is sent to (required attribute).

- **from**   Specifies who the e-mail is sent from (required attribute).

- **cc**   Takes a comma-delimited list of people who you want to send the e-mail to,
  via carbon copy (optional attribute).

- **bcc**   Takes a comma-delimited list of people who you want to send the e-mail
  to, via blind carbon copy (optional attribute).

- **subject**   Specifies the subject that will be given to the e-mail (required attribute).

- **type**   Brings extended functionality into standard e-mail (optional attribute).
  Currently, the only valid value is HTML, which should be used if you are sending
  an HTML e-mail. If you leave this attribute out, the e-mail is sent as plain text.

- **query**   Accepts the name of a query that you want to loop over. If you want
  to send an e-mail for each record in the query, use this tag (optional attribute).

- **maxrows**   Specifies the maximum number of messages to send. The default
  value is the size of the query.

- **startrow**   Specifies the first row in a query that the cfmail tag will start processing.
  The default value is 1 (optional attribute).

- **group**   If you are sending e-mail based on a query, you can use SQL grouping
  with the group attribute. Grouping was discussed in Chapter 21. You may want
  to use this feature to, for example, send to all users an e-mail containing a list of
  all orders that they had placed at your site (optional attribute).

- **groupcasesensitive**   Specifies whether or not the grouping is case sensitive (Boolean attribute). It is used in conjunction with the query and group attributes (optional attribute).

- **mimeattach**   Specifies the path to a file that you want to attach to the e-mail. If you want to attach more than one file, you can do so with the cfmailparam tag (optional attribute).

- **server**   Specifies the name of the mail server. ColdFusion does not include a built-in e-mail server; it will only integrate with an existing e-mail server. This is required if there is no value specified in the ColdFusion Administrator.

Caution	*ColdFusion is not an e-mail server. To send e-mail, you must specify the server in either the cfmail tag or the ColdFusion Administrator, as discussed in Chapter 6.*

- **port**   Specifies the port that the mail server listens to on the server that you are using to send the mail. This is usually 25.

- **mailerid**   Specifies the name of the mailer program, as is defined in the X-mailer SMTP header. The default is ColdFusion Application Server. You can change this value to make the mail server think that the mail server was set by an alternate program.

- **timeout**   Specifies the number of seconds to wait for the mail server (optional attribute).

- **spoolenable**   Specifies whether messages are saved until the sending operation is complete or are queued but not stored (Boolean attribute). If set to yes, the default, messages are saved until the sending operation is complete. If set to no, messages are queued but not stored. This attribute is new in ColdFusion MX.

If you want to send an e-mail with more than one attachment or with a custom e-mail header, you need to use the cfmailparam tag. The cfmailparam tag must reside within a cfmail tag block. The tag has these attributes:

- **file**   Contains the location of the file that you are attaching to your e-mail (optional attribute).

- **name**   Specifies the name of the header. You cannot use the name and file attribute in the same cfmailparam tag (optional attribute).

- **value**   Contains the value of the header (optional attribute).

You can have as many cfmailparam tags as you need. If you are attaching files, you must have one cfmailparam attribute per file.

Receiving E-Mail Within ColdFusion

It is also possible to retrieve e-mail from a POP3 mail server. The cfpop tag will retrieve e-mail messages from a remote server and delete them if necessary. These are the attributes for the tag:

- **server**   Contains the name of the pop server that you are using to retrieve mail. It can be a domain name or an IP address (required attribute).

- **port**   Specifies the POP port of the mail server. The default value is 110.

- **username**   Contains the name of the user that is logging in to the mail server. The default value is anonymous.

- **password**   Contains the password used to access the mail server. This is used in conjunction with the username attribute (optional attribute).

- **action**   Specifies the action that the tag will perform. Valid options are getheaderonly, getall, and delete. The getall value returns e-mail headers, text, and attachments. The getheaderonly option returns only e-mail headers. Since it returns less data than getall, it is quicker. Setting this value to delete will delete e-mail on the server.

- **name**   Specifies the name of the query object that will contain the e-mail information sent back from the server if the action attribute is getheaderonly or getall.

- **messagenumber**   Specifies the list of messages to affect when performing the action specified in action. The default is to affect all messages, unless you are deleting messages, in which case you must specify the message number of the e-mails that you want to delete, using either this attribute or the uid attribute.

- **uid**   Specifies a list of unique identifiers for e-mail messages. If you are deleting messages, then you must specify this or the messagenumber attribute. If you are using the action getheaderonly or getall, then leaving this attribute out will return all messages.

- **attachmentpath**   Specifies the directory location in which attachments will be stored if the action is getall.

- **timeout**   Specifies the length of time that ColdFusion will wait for a response from the mail server. The default value is 60 seconds.

- **maxrows**   Specifies the number of messages returned. It starts with the number specified in the startrow attribute. This attribute is ignored if the messagenumber attribute is specified.

- **startrow**   Specifies the first row to return in the recordset. If the messagenumber attribute is specified, this attribute is ignored. The default value is 1.

- **generateuniquefilenames**   Specifies whether or not attachments should be saved with a unique filename if naming conflicts exist (Boolean attribute). The default value is no.

After calling the cfpop tag, a query object is created. These are the fields that are available in the query:

- **Date**   Contains the date of the message. It is available when returning header information with action=getheaderonly and action=getall.

- **From**   Contains the e-mail address of the user who sent the message. It is available when returning header information with action=getheaderonly and action=getall.

- **MessageNumber**   Contains the unique ID of the e-mail message. It is available when returning header information with action=getheaderonly and action=getall.

- **ReplyTo**   Contains the default return address of the sent e-mail. It is available when returning header information with action=getheaderonly and action=getall.

- **Subject**   Contains the subject of the e-mail message. It is available when returning header information with action=getheaderonly and action=getall.

- **CC**   Contains a list of all e-mail addresses that were carbon copied to the original user. It is available when returning header information with action=getheaderonly and action=getall.

- **To**   Contains the e-mail address that the e-mail was sent to. It is available when returning header information with action=getheaderonly and action=getall.

- **Body**   Contains the body text of the e-mail. It is only available when returning header information with action=getall.

- **Header**   Contains header text of the e-mail. It is only available when returning header information with action=getall.

- **Attachments**   Contains a list of names of all attachments to the current e-mail. It is only available when returning header information with action=getall.

- **AttachmentFiles**   Contains the actual file data of the attachments of the current e-mail. It is only available when returning header information with action=getall.

The next section shows you how you can put these tags into action.

Creating a Simple Web-Based E-Mail Program

This section shows you the cfpop and cfmail tags in action. It steps you through the creation of a simple web-based e-mail program that will allow you to send and receive e-mails.

Getting E-Mails from the Server

To view e-mails that reside on our server, we need two pages. The first displays a list of all e-mails. The second displays the message detail for an e-mail message. These are the steps we can take to create these two pages:

1. Open your favorite CFML editor and create a blank page. Add a documentation header:

```
<!--- www.instantcoldfusion.com

Description: A page to retrieve e-mail from a Web Box

Entering: N/A
Exiting: N/A

Dependencies: N/A
Expecting: N/A

Modification History
Date       Modifier             Modification
*********************************************************
04/22/2002 Jeff Houser, DotComIt   Created
--->
```

This sets up the documentation for the page. There is no surprise there.

2. Get our e-mail headers using the cfpop tag:

```
<cfpop action="getheaderonly"
        username="test@instantcoldfusion.com" password="test"
        server="mail.instantcoldfusion.com" name="GetHeaders">
```

The action is set to getheaderonly. The server is set to the name of the mail server. The username and password allow you to log in. The name, GetHeaders, tells ColdFusion to create a query with the results.

3. Output the header information:

```
<cfoutput query="GetHeaders">
  #GetHeaders.Date#, #GetHeaders.From#, #GetHeaders.Subject#
  <a href="ShowMessage.cfm
                   ?MessageNumber=#GetHeaders.MessageNumber#">
  Display
```

```
</a><br>
</cfoutput>
```

The display section loops over the query. It outputs the Date, From, and Subject fields. It also creates a link to a second page, ShowMessage.cfm. This is the page we create next, which will show all the detail from a particular message. The MessageNumber is passed as a URL variable. The link is closed and so is the output. This is what our screen may look like:

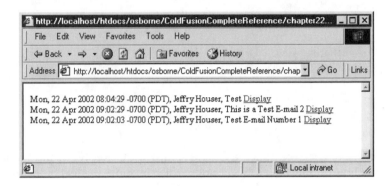

4. Create a new page in your favorite CFML editor. Drop in your documentation header:

```
<!--- www.instantcoldfusion.com

Description: Page to display an e-mail message

Entering: N/A
Exiting: N/A

Dependencies: N/A
Expecting: url.MessageNumber

Modification History
Date       Modifier            Modification
********************************************************
04/22/2002 Jeff Houser, DotComIt    Created
--->
```

This page will be the page to display the message. A message number must be passed into it.

5. The first step in our page is to get the full body of the message:

```
<cfpop action="getall" server="mail.instantcoldfusion.com"
    username="test@instantcoldfusion.com" password="test"
    name="GetMessage" messagenumber="#url.MessageNumber#">
```

We get the message using the cfpop tag with the action set to getall. The server, username, and password are identical to the previous page where we retrieved headers. We name the resulting query, GetMessage, and specify the message number using the MessageNumber attribute.

6. Display the message. We use the cfoutput tag to loop over the query and display the pertinent information:

```
<cfoutput query="GetMessage">
 Date: #GetMessage.Date# <br>
 From: #GetMessage.From#<br>
 To: #GetMessage.To#<br>
 CC: #GetMessage.CC#<br>
 ReplyTo: #GetMessage.ReplyTo#<br>
 Subject: #GetMessage.Subject# <br>
 Body:<br>
 #HTMLCodeFormat(GetMessage.Body)#<br>
</cfoutput>
```

This block of code outputs the Date, From, To, CC, ReplyTo, and Subject fields. The last line outputs the Body variable, which includes the text of the message. The Body field is surrounded by the HTMLCodeFormat function. This will preserve the layout of the Body field, as opposed to displaying it as a single string. This is a message page:

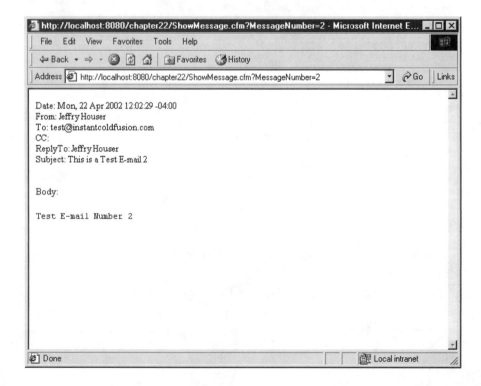

Creating E-Mail via the Browser

The next step in the web-based e-mail process is to create messages and send them using the cfmail tag. This process also needs two pages, the page for the user to input their information and the page to process their input. Here is how we create the pages to send e-mail:

1. Open your CFML editor and create a blank page. Add in a documentation header:

```
<!--- www.instantcoldfusion.com

Description: Page to create an e-mail message

Entering: N/A
Exiting: Mailp.cfm

Dependencies: N/A
Expecting:

Modification History
Date       Modifier                Modification
**********************************************************
04/22/2002 Jeff Houser, DotComIt   Created
--->
```

This page creates the form that allows us to compose a mail message.

2. Create your form. The form needs five elements, corresponding to the parts of the e-mail message:

```
<form action="mailp.cfm" method="post"
      enctype="multipart/form-data">
 To: <input type="Text" name="To"><br>
 CC: <input type="Text" name="CC"><br>
 Subject: <input type="Text" name="Subject"><br>
 Body: <br>
 <textarea name="Body" rows="15" cols="30"></textarea><br>
 <input type="Submit" name="Submit" value="Send">
</form>
```

Standard text input boxes are used for the To, CC, and Subject fields. The Body field will probably be multiline and thus an input text box won't be sufficient.

It uses a textarea tag to create a larger space for the message to be composed. The page looks like this:

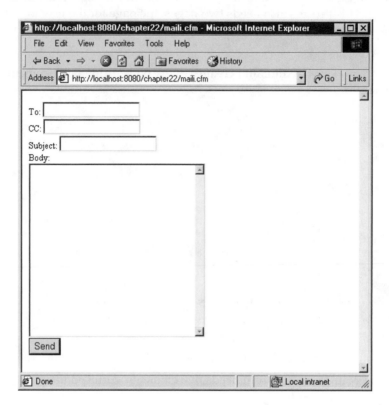

Save the page, and you can move on to creating the next one.

3. Create a blank page in your CFML editor. Add a documentation header:

```
<!--- www.instantcoldfusion.com

Description: Page to send an e-mail based on form information.

Entering: Maili.cfm
Exiting: N/A

Dependencies: N/A
Expecting: form.To
           form.CC
           form.Subject
           form.Body
```

```
Modification History
Date        Modifier                  Modification
**********************************************************
04/22/2002 Jeff Houser, DotComIt      Created
--->
```

The To, CC, Subject, and Body fields must be defined for this page to work properly. This page is entered from the Maili.cfm page.

4. Send the e-mail, using the cfmail tag:

```
<cfmail to="#Form.To#" from="test@instantcoldfusion.com"
        cc="#Form.CC#" subject="#Form.Subject#">

 #form.Body#
</cfmail>
```

The form fields specify who the mail is sent to, whether anyone is carbon copied, and the subject. The name of the person sending the e-mail is hard-coded. In a real-world application, where the code is used by many users, you would probably want to set this up as a session or client variable. The form Body field is located in the middle of the e-mail.

5. Provide the user with some feedback. They will want to know that the message was successfully sent. Here is the code:

```
<cfoutput>
 Your mail was sent successfully to #form.To#
</cfoutput>
```

The cfoutput tag surrounds some confirmation text. The To field is displayed to the user.

Interacting with Other Protocols

This section demonstrates how ColdFusion can work with other Internet protocols, such as HTTP and FTP. The cfhttp and cfftp tags can use these protocols to access information on other Internet servers.

Performing HTTP Operations with cfhttp

This section teaches you about the cfhttp tag. It demonstrates how to use the cfhttp tag and explains the cfhttpparam tag and how you can use it when accessing remote servers. It finishes by demonstrating the variables that are accessible after executing a cfhttp tag.

Learning the cfhttp Tag Attributes

The Hypertext Transfer Protocol (HTTP) is the protocol that defines how data is transferred back and forth between the web server and web browser. ColdFusion can mimic the actions of a web browser by using the cfhttp tag. You can use it to request data from another server or to remotely post data to another server.

These are the attributes to the cfhttp tag:

- **url** Contains the absolute URL of the HTTP resource you are accessing. This will most likely contain the name of the protocol, http or https; the hostname or IP address of the server; and the directory structure of the file you want. This is a required attribute.

- **port** Contains the port that the web server is requesting (the default is port 80).

- **method** Contains either get or post. These are the two actions that can occur from the cfhttp tag, just like the action tag from a form.

- **username** Specifies the username if the server you are accessing requires a username and password for authentication.

- **password** Specifies the password of the user who needs to be authenticated by the web server.

- **name** Contains the name of the query object that is created as a result of the cfhttp operation.

- **columns** Contains the name of the query columns in the resulting query if you are using cfhttp with the get operation and want to turn the results into a query. The column attribute specifies the name of the columns of the query.

- **firstrowasheaders** Determines how ColdFusion processes the first row of the recordset returned by cfquery (Boolean attribute). If the attribute is set to yes, then the first row is turned into columns, and the columns attribute, if specified, is ignored. If set to no and the columns attribute is not specified, columns are created in the form of column_1, column_2, and so on. If set to no and the columns attribute is specified, this attribute is ignored. This attribute is new in ColdFusion MX.

- **path** Specifies the file path if you want to store the results of the cfhttp operation in a file. If the path is not specified, a variable is created (cfhttp.FileContent) with the results.

- **file** Contains the name of the file that is created to store the results of the cfhttp action. You should specify a filename without path information.

- **delimiter** Specifies the delimiter that separates different columns of data and is required to create a query from the operation. The default value is a comma, but you can specify any other value you wish.

- **textqualifier** Specifies the start and finish of the column in the file you are getting. The default value is two double quotes. The column delimiter is required to create a query.

- **resolveurl** Specifies whether or not relative URLs in the returned page are fully resolved into absolute URLs (optional attribute that accepts a Boolean value). Items that are fully resolved include image source tags, anchor references, form actions, applet code bases, script sources, embedded sources, embedded plug-in space, body backgrounds, frame sources, background sources, object data, object classids, object codebases, and an object usemap.

- **proxyserver**   Contains the hostname or IP of the proxyserver, if applicable (optional attribute).

- **proxyport**   Contains the port number that the proxy server is located on (optional attribute).

- **useragent**   Specifies the value of the HTTP_User_Agent request header that you give to the request (optional attribute).

- **throwonerror**   Specifies whether or not to throw an error (Boolean attribute). If there is an error requesting the file and this value is yes, ColdFusion throws an error. The error can be caught using standard error-catching methods, as discussed in Chapter 18. If the value is set to no, no error is thrown (optional attribute).

- **redirect**   Specifies whether or not ColdFusion will allow itself to be redirected by the server it is calling (Boolean attribute). If it is set to yes, ColdFusion will allow itself to be redirected by the server it is calling. Only four redirects will be allowed before an error is thrown. If this attribute is set to no, and the throwonerror attribute is set to yes, the redirection will fail and throw an error. If set to yes, the request is redirected. ColdFusion will throw an error after four redirections. JavaScript and meta header redirects are ignored.

Caution   *Much of the documentation on the redirect attribute is incorrect. The cfhttp variable is never created if an error occurs, so you cannot access the StatusCode or ResponseHeader variables.*

- **timeout**   Specifies a value, in seconds, of how long ColdFusion will wait for a response from the server. You can specify timeout values in a URL using a special RequestTimeout variable or in the ColdFusion Administrator. If either of these values is less than the value specified in the timeout attribute, the lesser of the two timeouts will be chosen. If no timeout is specified, then ColdFusion will wait indefinitely for the request to complete, which could lock up the server.

One of the most common uses of the cfhttp command is to retrieve data from a remote server, such as a WDDX or XML feed. This method will be discussed more in Chapter 27, but here is a quick example:

```
<cfhttp url="http://www.macromedia.com/desdev/
              resources/macromedia_resources.xml"
        method="get">
</cfhttp>
```

This code grabs an XML feed from the Macromedia web site. This feed in particular contains a list of all the recent articles to Macromedia's developer's center.

Learning How to Use the cfhttpparam Tag

You probably noticed that the cfhttp tag accepts both a start and end tag. What do you put in between the start and end tag? You place cfhttpparam tags between them. If you are posting data to a server, you can use a group of these tags to define the state of the application, including form variables, CGI variables, cookie variables, a file, and URL variables. These are the attributes to the cfhttpparam tag:

- **name**   Contains the name of the variable data that is passed (required attribute).
- **type**   Contains the type of data that is being passed (required attribute). Valid values are URL, FormField, Cookie, CGI, and File.
- **value**   Contains the value of URL, FormField, CGI, or Cookie (optional attribute).
- **file**   If you are passing a file type to the processing page, use the file attribute to specify the absolute directory location of the file (optional attribute).

You can use the cfhttpparam tag to set up the state of the application you are executing on a remote server. Suppose you are calling a page, called Loginp.cfm. When this page is called, it is expecting two variables to be defined, a username and a password. You could call this page like this:

```
<cfhttp url="http://myserver.com/Loginp.cfm "
        method="post">
 <cfhttpparam name="username" value="Me" type="form">
 <cfhttpparam name="password" value="Pass" type="form">
</cfhttp>
```

With those two form variables defined in the request, the remote server does not know whether the page was submitted via a Submit button on a login form or via your ColdFusion server using cfhttp. This method can be used to perform remote searches on eBay or Google, register at Yahoo!, or submit a story to SlashDot.org.

Accessing cfhttp's Return Content

After running your cfhttp tag, you can access special variables that contain the results of the cfhttp operation. The variables are accessed using the format cfhttp.*VariableName*. These are the variables:

- **cfhttp.FileContent**   Contains the results of the operation. This could be binary data, depending on the mimetype.
- **cfhttp.MimeType**   Defines the mime type of the return value.
- **cfhttp.Header**   Contains the HTTP header of the request as single string.

- **cfhttp.ResponseHeader[HTTP_Header_Key]**   Returned as a structure. It contains each element of the header in the response as a separate value.
- **cfhttp.StatusCode**   Contains any errors that exist, if cfhttp was trying to turn the file into a query.

After calling the XML feed, you can output the variables using a ColdFusion template, as we did in previous examples. Here is some sample code:

```
<cfoutput>
 Header as Structure: <br>
 <cfdump var="#cfhttp.responseheader#">
 <br>

 Header as String: #cfhttp.Header#<br><br>
 MIMEType of return data: #cfhttp.mimetype# <br><Br>

 FileContent:<br> #HTMLEditFormat(cfhttp.filecontent)# <br><Br>
</cfoutput>
```

Additional processing can be done on the variables as needed.

Transferring Files with cfftp

You can access File Transfer Protocol (FTP) servers from within ColdFusion. FTP is a protocol designed for moving files from one server to another. This section shows you how to use it.

Connecting to an FTP Server

Before you can perform any actions over an FTP site, you need to connect to the site. The tag that allows you to connect to FTP sites is the cfftp tag. These are the attributes for the cfftp tag:

- **action**   Should be set to open to connect to an FTP server (required attribute).
- **username**   Specifies the username that you can use to log in to the FTP site (required attribute).
- **password**   Specifies the password that you use to log in to the FTP site (required attribute).
- **server**   Contains the domain name or IP address of the server that you are connecting to (required attribute).
- **timeout**   Specifies how long ColdFusion will wait for a response from the FTP server. The default value is 30 seconds.
- **port**   Specifies the port that the FTP server resides on. The default value is 21.

- **connection**   Used to give a name to the connection. You use this name to cache the connection and access it later.

- **proxyserver**   Contains the name of the proxy server that you are connecting through.

- **retrycount**   Specifies the number of times that ColdFusion will try to connect before failing. The default value is 1.

- **stoponerror**   Tells ColdFusion whether to throw an error when an error occurs. If set to yes, an appropriate error is thrown. If set to no, these values are created: cfftp.Succeeded, cfftp.ErrorCode, and cfftp.ErrorText.

- **passive**   Specifies whether or not cfftp will connect to the FTP server in passive mode (optional Boolean attribute). The default value is no.

The first thing you will want to do is connect to an FTP server and cache the connection. Connecting to the server is a resource-intensive operation, so caching the connection will give you performance improvements.

 To keep the connection open across multiple page requests, you should store the connection in an application or session variable.

This is how you can open and cache a connection:

```
<cfftp connection="MyFTPConnection" action="open"
       username="Jeff" password="MyPassword"
       server="ftp.myserver.com" stoponerror="Yes">
```

You have now created the MyFTPConnection variable in the variables scope. The variable contains an open FTP session.

 For local server operations, do not use the cfftp tag. Stick to cffile, cfdirectory, or cfcontent.

Performing FTP Directory Operations

Now that you have connected to the FTP site, what actions can you perform on it? These are the attributes that allow you to perform directory operations:

- **action**   The action attribute is required and is used to define the action you want to perform. Its possible values are the following: changedir, to change the directory; createdir, to create a directory; listdir, to get a list of all files and directories in the directory; removedir, to delete the directory; getcurrentdir, to get the current directory; existsdir, to check whether a directory exists; existsFile, to check whether a file exists; exists, to check whether a remote object exists; remove, to delete a directory; getcurrenturl, to return the URL for the FTP server; and rename, to rename a file or directory.

- **name**   Specifies the name of the variable that will contain the directory listing. A query object is created with the directory listing information. This attribute is required if action is equal to listdir.

- **connection**   Contains the name of the connection, if you are using a cached connection.

- **directory**   Contains the name of the directory that you are going to perform your action on. It is required if the action is changedir, createdir, listdir, or existsdir.

- **item**   Contains the object of the exists or remove actions. Valid values are file or directory.

- **existing**   Defines the current name of the directory if action is equal to rename.

- **new**   Defines the new name for the directory if the action is set to rename.

The results of your operation are stored in a variable called cfftp.ReturnValue. If the action is getcurrentdir, its value is the current directory. If the action is getcurrenturl, the action is to return the current URL. If the action is existsdir, existsfile, or exists, the value returned is yes or no.

You can perform these actions to a noncached FTP connection if you specify the server, username, and password attributes.

If you list the directory, these are the columns that are in the query that ColdFusion creates:

- **Name**   Contains the filename of the current element.

- **Path**   Contains the complete path, relative to the FTP root directory, of the current element.

- **URL**   Contains the complete URL for the current file or directory.

- **Length**   Contains the size of the file.

- **LastModified**   Contains the date and time that the file or directory was last modified.

- **Attributes**   Contains the value either normal or directory.

Caution   *Platform-specific values, such as hidden or system, are no longer returned in the attributes variable.*

- **IsDirectory**   Contains a Boolean value indicating whether or not the object is a file or directory.

- **Mode**   Contains the octal string permissions (applies only to Unix or Linux machines).

INTEGRATING COLDFUSION
WITH OTHER
TECHNOLOGIES

After you connect to an FTP server, using the code in the previous section, you can get and display a directory list using this code:

```
<!--- Get the current directory --->
<cfftp connection="MyFTPConnection" action="GetCurrentDir"
     stoponerror="Yes">

<!--- display the current directory --->
<cfoutput>
 The current directory is #cfftp.ReturnValue#<br>
</cfoutput>

<!--- get the current directory list --->
<cfftp connection="MyFTPConnection" action="dirlist"
     directory="#cfftp.ReturnValue#" name="DirList"
     stoponerror="Yes">

<!--- Display the directory listing --->
<cfoutput query="DirList">
 #DirList.Name#, #DirList.Length# #DirList.Attributes#
 #DirList.IsDirectory#<br>
</cfoutput>
```

This code will show the directory listing of your FTP server. First it gets the current directory. Then it outputs that value. Next, it uses that value to get the directory listing. Finally, it outputs the results of that directory.

Performing File Operations with cfftp

File operations can be performed over FTP. You can upload, download, delete, or perform a number of other actions using the cfftp tag. These are the attributes:

- **action** The action attribute is required and is used to define the action you want to perform. Its possible values are as follows: getfile, to get a file; putfile, to put a file on the FTP server; existsfile, to check whether a file exists; exists, to check whether a file exists; remove, to delete a file; and rename, to rename a file.

- **connection** Contains the name of the connection, if you are using a cached connection.

- **transfermode** Contains the method that is used to transfer files. The options are binary, ASCII, or auto. The default value is auto.

- **asciiextensionlist** Contains a list of file extensions that will force ASCII transfer mode. The default value is txt;htm;html;cfm;cfml;shtm;shtml;css;asp;asa. This only applies if transfermode is set to auto.

- **failifexist**   Specifies what to do if a local file exists with the same name as a file on the server (Boolean value). If it is set to yes, which is the default, a file upload or download will fail if a local file exists with the same name as one on the server. If set to no, the file is overwritten.

- **localfile**   Contains the name and location of the file on the local file system (required attribute if the action is getfile or putfile).

- **remotefile**   Contains the name of the file on the remote system (required attribute if action is getfile, putfile, or existsfile).

- **item**   Contains the object of the exists or remove actions. Valid values are file or directory.

- **existing**   Defines the current name of the directory if action is equal to rename.

- **new**   Defines the new name for the directory or file if the action is set to rename.

You can upload a file using this command:

```
<cfftp connection="MyFTPConnection" action="putfile"
       localfile="C:\MyFile.cfm" remotefile="MyFile.cfm">
```

This will upload MyFile.cfm to the current directory specified in MyFTPConnection. You can then download that file using this code:

```
<cfftp connection="MyFTPConnection" action="getfile"
       localfile="C:\MyFile.cfm" remotefile="MyFile.cfm">
```

Closing an FTP Connection

After you have finished with your work on the FTP site, you need to close the connection. You do this also with the cfftp tag. These are the attributes:

- **action**   Defines the action of the tag. It should be set to close to close the connection. This is a required attribute.

- **connection**   Used to give a name to the connection. You use this name to cache the connection and access it later.

- **stoponerror**   Tells ColdFusion whether to throw an error when an error occurs. If set to yes, an appropriate error is thrown. If set to no, these values are created: cfftp.Succeeded, cfftp.ErrorCode, and cfftp.ErrorText.

Close the connection with this command:

```
<cfftp connection="MyFTPConnection" action="close"
       stoponerror="Yes">
```

Summary

In this chapter, you learned the following:

■ How to create e-mail using cfmail

■ How to check an e-mail account using cfpop

■ How to retrieve remote data using cfhttp and cfftp

The tags in this chapter, most specifically cfhttp and cfmail, have sparked quite a controversy in past versions of ColdFusion. For some servers, they seem to work great, but other servers have problems at the slightest sign of these tags. There have been many alternate tags created to perform the actions better than ColdFusion. If you experience problems or want expanded functionality, search the Macromedia Developer's Exchange for options. The next chapter will teach you how to integrate ColdFusion with J2EE servers.

Chapter 23

Using ColdFusion with Java and J2EE Application Servers

Since ColdFusion MX is now built to run on top of a J2EE server, integrating ColdFusion with JSP pages, tags, and other Java objects is much easier. This chapter shows you how to integrate these technologies.

Understanding Java Technologies

Variations of Java technologies come in many different flavors. These are some common Java technologies that you may come across when developing web applications:

- **JavaScript** JavaScript is a client-side technology that is built into browsers. To use JavaScript from within ColdFusion, you just place it inside your ColdFusion templates, and ColdFusion streams it to the browser just like standard HTML. In-depth examination of JavaScript is beyond the scope of this book, but JavaScript does have similarities to CFScript, discussed in Chapter 15. Many people would not consider JavaScript a Java technology since it has little in common with other Java technologies, other than its syntax and name.

- **Java applets** Java applets are programs written in Java that are designed to run in a browser. Most browsers support Java. You can include Java applets in ColdFusion templates by using either the HTML applet tag or ColdFusion's cfapplet tag. The cfapplet tag references applets registered in the ColdFusion Administrator. We discussed the tag in Chapter 12, and discussed registering applets in Chapter 6.

- **Java Server Pages** ColdFusion supports Java Server Pages (JSP) in two different ways. The first is to include JSP pages in a ColdFusion template using the GetPageContext function. If you do this, then both types of pages can share the persistent scopes. The second way is to import JSP tag libraries using the cfimport tag.

  ColdFusion templates are not JSP templates, though, and you will not be able to use include, taglib, or page directives in ColdFusion templates. Use cfimport and cfinclude to access JSP tag libraries instead. JSP expression, declaration, and scriptlet elements are also unavailable. You will have to use ColdFusion elements and expressions. The CFML interpreter ignores JSP comments, so make sure you stick to CFML comments. Standard JSP tags are also unavailable if the tags are not available as JAR files. ColdFusion tags and the PageContext object must be used instead.

- **Java servlets** Java servlets are Java programs written to execute on the server. They are similar to JSP pages, except that they are not exposed. You can access these servlets by using ColdFusion's GetPageContext function.

Caution *In past versions of ColdFusion, the cfservlet tag was used to call Java servlets. This tag is deprecated in ColdFusion MX.*

- **Java objects**   Java objects include the standard classes that make up the J2EE interface, custom classes, and Enterprise Java Beans. You can access these methods by using ColdFusion's cfobject tag.

Integrating ColdFusion with JSP

This section shows you how to integrate ColdFusion MX with JSP. It discusses the PageContext class and how to access it from within ColdFusion. It also discusses how to share persistent scopes between JSP and ColdFusion, as well as how to import JSP libraries with the cfimport tag.

Understanding the PageContext Class

ColdFusion is built to run on top of a J2EE server, and therefore each ColdFusion template is one level of abstraction above Java Server Pages (JSP). This section starts by explaining the PageContext class of a Java Server.

Explaining the PageContext Class

The PageContext class in Java Server Pages is akin to the Document Object Model of a web page. It is a way to access specific elements of a page. A class is a group of associated methods and properties. Methods are akin to functions, and properties are akin to variables.

The PageContext class is designed as a way to provide implementation-dependent features of a JSP run-time engine. Its benefits for provides any number of useful facilities when you are writing a JSP page:

- **JspWriter**   JspWriter provides a way to create output from within your JSP page. You probably won't need this functionality from within your ColdFusion pages, because you can use ColdFusion's output mechanisms.

- **Session management**   The PageContext object provides a way to access and manage session usage. Since ColdFusion MX is built on top of a J2EE engine, it is very easy to share the request, session, and application scopes between a JSP page and a ColdFusion page. JSP does not have a parallel for other ColdFusion scopes, such as client or form.

- **Page directives**   The PageContext object provides a mechanism for exposing page directive attributes. A directive is a set of instructions to the JSP server that can set properties but do not produce output.

- **Request Forwarding**   The PageContext object provides a mechanism that allows you to forward the current request to other active requests, or include the current request in another active request. This ability will probably be the most useful to ColdFusion developers, and will warrant the most discussion.

- **Error handling**   The PageContext object provides JSP error-handling features. In a ColdFusion template, you will probably want to use ColdFusion's error handling, and not JSP error handling.

Getting the PageContext Object from Within ColdFusion

ColdFusion MX provides equivalent features to many of the standard JSP tags. Two JSP tags that may be useful in ColdFusion development are the jsp:forward and jsp:include tags. ColdFusion has tags that perform similar, but different, functions.

The jsp:include tag will include static and dynamic resources into the current page. Processing will automatically resume in the calling page once the included page is processed. It is similar to the cfinclude tag, except that the only available scopes are request, session, and application. A cfinclude tag will have access to all variable scopes. A jsp:forward tag will stop processing of the current page and call another page, executing it as if it were the same page. This function redirects the client to the new page. This is quite different from cfinclude, which operates on the server side.

You cannot directly use the jsp:include and jsp:forward tags within ColdFusion. The PageContext class, however, contains an include method and a forward method that allow you to get the same functionality. The first step is to create a page context variable using the GetPageContext function. This is an example:

```
<cfset PageContext = GetPageContext()>
```

The function accepts no parameters. It just returns the PageContext object of the JSP for use from within ColdFusion.

The jsp:include function accepts one parameter, the page that you want to include. After you have created the PageContext variable, you can call the include function inside CFScript, like this:

```
<cfscript>
 PageContext.include("MyPage.jsp");
</cfscript>
```

The forward method accepts the same single attribute:

```
<cfscript>
 PageContext.forward("MyPage.jsp");
</cfscript>
```

 Caution *When calling a JSP page using either forward or include, your URL must be case sensitive, or the code will not work.*

You can pass variables to the forward and include functions as URL variables, appended to the JSP page. Here is an example:

```
<cfscript>
 PageContext.include("MyPage.jsp?MyVar=MyVar");
```

```
PageContext.forward("MyPage.jsp?MyVar=MyVar");
</cfscript>
```

 Note *Although these two functions are probably the most common that you will need, you can use any method in the PageContext class. Go to http://java.sun.com/j2ee/sdk_1.2.1/ techdocs/api/javax/servlet/jsp/PageContext.html for more information on PageContext.*

Integrating JSP with ColdFusion

This section shows you some other ways that JSP can integrate with ColdFusion. It shows you how to import custom JSP tags for use from within ColdFusion and how both JSP and ColdFusion can use variable scopes to share data.

Importing JSP Custom Tags into ColdFusion

This is how you can import a JSP custom tag into ColdFusion:

1. The JSP custom tag will consist of two files: *taglibname*.jar and *taglibname*.tld. These files should be provided to you from the person who developed the custom tag. You need to place these two files in a directory that is accessible by ColdFusion. Commonly, these files are placed in the web-inf folder of your web server's root directory.

2. From within your ColdFusion page, use the cfimport tag to import the custom tag library. The cfimport tag is akin to the JSP taglib directive. These are the attributes for the cfimport tag:

   ■ **taglib** Set the taglib attribute with the URL of the tag library, a JAR file, or the tag library descriptor (TLD) file. This attribute is mutually exclusive with the webservice attribute.

   ■ **prefix** The prefix attribute specifies the name of the variable that will contain the tag library. You will be able to reference the functions from this tag library. The default value is blank.

   ■ **webservice** If you are accessing the custom tag library as a web service, specify its location here. This attribute is mutually exclusive with the taglib attribute.

Note *The cfimport tag does not work within the Application.cfm file or in a cfinclude page. It must reside on the page that calls the library functions.*

The following example calls upon the random function, which is part of the Apache Jakarta project. The Jakarta project provides open source tag libraries for all to use.

```
<cfimport taglib="/htdocs/lib/random.jar" prefix="MyRand">
```

The previous code will successfully load the random.jar library. The random library will be used to create a random password in the following steps.

You can find more information about the Jakarta project at http://jakarta.apache.org/taglibs/index.html.

3. After you load the library, you can call methods from the library by using the JSP action syntax. Here is an example:

```
<MyRand:string id="RandPass" length="9"
               charset="A-Za-z0-9_=+" />
```

The JSP syntax starts with the name of the JSP library instance, MyRand. A colon comes next, followed by the name of an element type, string. It is followed by a list of attributes that are associated with the element type. The first is id, set to RandPass. The id attribute defines a variable that will be created by the tag. The remaining attributes specify specific attributes for the method in question. The string method will create a random stream of letters that is nine characters long, within the character set specified by the charset attribute.

This JSP action uses a special close tag syntax, where the backward slash is placed at the end of the tag before the > bracket. This is part of the XML and XHTML specifications.

4. After defining the method call, you need to make it accessible by putting the result in a ColdFusion variable:

```
<cfset myPassword = RandPass.random>
```

The JSP variable, randPass, is called and the password is created in the ColdFusion variable. This finishes the example.

Sharing Variable Scopes Between ColdFusion and JSP

If your application includes both ColdFusion and JSP pages, data in the session, application, and request scopes can be shared between the two pages. The request scope is shared only if you use the forward or include methods. The session and application scopes will hold true for href links and cfhttp calls, as well as the forward and include methods.

To share session variables, J2EE session management must be enabled in the ColdFusion Administrator. We demonstrated how to do this in Chapter 3.

This is a simple example of sharing variable scopes between ColdFusion and JSP:

1. Create some variables in the shared scopes:

```
<!--- set up the cfapplication so application and session
      variables will be available --->
<cfapplication name="MyApp" sessionmanagement="yes">

<!--- Set up the variable in the application scope --->
<cflock scope="application" type="exclusive" timeout="30">
 <cfset application.TestAppVar="My Test App Var">
</cflock>

<!--- Set up the variable in the session scope --->
<cflock scope="session" type="exclusive" timeout="30">
 <cfset session.TestSesVar="My Test Session Var">
</cflock>

<!--- Set up the variable in the request scope --->
<cfset request.TestReqVar = "My Test Request Variable">
```

This code sets up the scope of the application with the cfapplication tag and then creates three test variables, one in each of the scopes that can be shared.

2. Call the Java Server Page:

```
<cfscript>
 GetPageContext().include("VariableSharing.jsp");
</cfscript>
```

Using ColdFusion's GetPageContext function and JSP's include method, we are able to launch the VariableSharing.jsp page.

3. Create your JSP page, VariableSharing.jsp, using code similar to this:

```
<%@page import="java.util.*" %>

request.TestReqVar: <%= request.getAttribute("TestReqVar")%>

session. TestSesVar:
    <%=((Map)session.getAttribute("MyApp")).get("TestSesVar")%>

application.TestAppVar:
<%=((Map)(application.getAttribute("MyApp"))).get("TestAppVar")%>
```

The first thing that the JSP page does is import the java.util library. This is a standard library of JSP functions. Then it outputs the variables from the three shared scopes. To get the request variable within a JSP page, an expression is used. The expression is denoted by <%=. The request scope uses the name of the scope, request, and the getAttribute method. The expression is closed with the characters %>. The value of the method is the name of the variable that you want to return.

> **Note**   *URL variables can be accessed the same way that request variables are accessed.*

A different method is used to return a session or application variable. First, the getAttribute method is used to get all the variables from the MyApp application. Then, the get method is used to get the specific variable name. The map keyword casts the variable to a Java Map object.

ColdFusion can also access variables that were created in a JSP page, as long as they were created in the same scopes. This is how:

1. Create your variables from within the JSP page:

```
<%@page import="java.util.*" %>

<% request.setAttribute("TestReqVar",
                        "My Test Request Variable");%>
<% ((Map)session.getAttribute("MyApp"))
        .put("TestSesVar", "My Test Session Var");%>
<% application.setAttribute("MyApp.TestAppVar",
                           "My Test App Var");%>
```

The first line of the code imports the java.util class. The next three lines create a variable in each of the scopes. The variables are created in a similar manner to the way that they were retrieved in the previous section. The request and application variables are created with the setAttribute method instead of the getAttribute method. The session variable is created using the put method, instead of the get method.

2. Include the ColdFusion page inside the JSP page:

```
<jsp:include page="JSPVariableSharing.cfm" />
```

To do this, the jsp:include action is used. It accepts a single attribute, page, which is the name of the ColdFusion page that needs to be included.

3. Output the variables using the cfoutput tag and some ColdFusion expressions:

```
<!--- set up the application --->
<cfapplication name="MyApp" sessionmanagement="yes">

<cfoutput>

  <!--- Output the Request Variable --->
  request.TestReqVar: #request.TestReqVar#<br>

  <!--- Output the session Variable --->
  <cflock scope="session" type="readonly">
    session.TestSesVar: #session.TestSesVar#<br>
```

```
    </cflock>

    <!--- Output the application Variable --->
    <cflock scope="application" type="readonly">
     application.TestAppVar: #application.TestAppVar#<br>
    </cflock>
   </cfoutput>
```

This code first sets up the application framework with the cfapplication tag. Then, it outputs the variables in standard ColdFusion fashion, starting with the request, then the session, and finally the application.

Addressing Other ColdFusion and Java Issues

This section sums up some final issues regarding ColdFusion and Java. It discusses how data types are converted when data is moved between a ColdFusion page and a Java technology. It also demonstrates how Java objects can be invoked using the cfobject tag.

Converting Data Types Between ColdFusion and Java

ColdFusion is a very loosely typed language. It is easy to change a variable from one type to another. Java, on the other hand, is strongly typed. Java needs variable declarations, and you have to stick to your declaration, or explicitly change it. ColdFusion will try to convert to Java types before calling a Java method. Table 23-1 shows how ColdFusion handles changing variable types. This table shows the default conversions. You can change the conversion using the JavaCast function.

If you have a class that has multiple implementations of the same method that differ only in parameter types, ColdFusion may be confused as to which method to call. You can fix these ambiguous data types by using the JavaCast function, which accepts two parameters:

- **Type**   Contains the name of the Java type that you are casting the variable into. Valid values are Boolean, int, long, double, and string.

- **Variable**   Contains the name of the ColdFusion variable that is being cast (required parameter).

This function is useful if you need to invoke Java objects, as described next.

Invoking Java Objects from Within ColdFusion

If you need to create an instance of a Java object, you can use the cfobject tag. Java objects are different from JSP pages. They are compiled classes, which reside on the server. When ColdFusion calls a class, a Java Virtual Machine (JVM) embedded in ColdFusion executes it.

ColdFusion Type	Java Type
String or list	String
Integer	Short, int, or long. Short or int may result in a loss of precision.
Real number	Float or double may result in the loss of some precision.
Boolean	Boolean
Array	java.util.vector If the array has a consistent data type, it can be converted to a Java array of data types: byte[ ], char[ ], boolean[ ], int[ ], long[ ], float[ ], double[ ], String[ ], or Object[ ]
Date-time	java.util.date
Structure	java.util.Map
Query object	java.util.Map
XML document object	N/A
ColdFusion component	N/A

Table 23-1. *Converting ColdFusion Data Types to Java Data Types*

These are the attributes that you can use in a cfobject tag:

- **type** Must be set to Java to instantiate an object.
- **action** Should be set to create to create the object.
- **class** Accepts the name of the class object that you want to create (required attribute).
- **name** Contains the name of the ColdFusion variable that will contain the object (required attribute).

This is how you can use the cfobject tag to instantiate a Java object:

1. Load the class with the cfobject tag:

```
<cfobject type="Java" class="MyClass" name="MyObject">
```

Tip *You can also create an object using the CreateObject function.*

2. The cfobject tag loads the class, but it does not initialize it. Only static methods and fields are accessible before the class is initialized. To initialize it, you need to load its constructor method:

```
<cfset Instance=MyObject.init()>
```

The init statement is a ColdFusion identifier that automatically calls the class constructor. A constructor method is one that initializes any variables or other code that need to be initialized inside the class. The class is now ready for your use.

The most common thing that you will want to do with your class is to deal with properties or methods. You can retrieve properties if they are exposed for your usage. To set a property, use

```
<cfset MyObject.PropertyName = "Value">
```

To get the property, use

```
<cfset PropertyValue = MyObject.PropertyName>
```

You can call methods by using a similar format:

```
<cfset ReturnValue = MyObject.MyMethod(Attribute1, Attribute2)>
```

Methods, just like ColdFusion functions, may have zero or more attributes depending on the method's purpose.

Summary

In this chapter, you learned about the following:

- Java technologies and how they relate to ColdFusion
- Java Server Pages and the PageContext class
- How to share information between ColdFusion templates and JSP templates
- Some other issues dealing with ColdFusion and Java

The next chapter will teach you how to create search engines with Verity.

INTEGRATING COLDFUSION
WITH OTHER
TECHNOLOGIES

Chapter 24

Creating Search Engines with Verity

C oldFusion MX comes with a Verity server built in. The Verity server is a full-text search engine that will help you create advanced searches for your web site. The server will run in two different modes: VDK, which is maintained through ColdFusion, and K2, which is maintained separately from ColdFusion. This chapter shows how you create and use both kinds of collections.

Creating Verity Collections

This section explains what a Verity collection is. It also explains how you can create Verity collections and populate them with the numerous data types.

Understanding Verity Collections

Before you can create and populate Verity collections, you need to understand what a Verity collection is. Simply stated, a Verity collection is a collection of data. It is a specialized database that contains descriptions of the indexed information. This database is optimized for extremely fast searching. A Verity collection can easily be compared to the index created by a relational database management system (RDBMS). A collection is a map that contains pointers to the information, just like an index points to information in a database table.

When you put information into a Verity collection, it is called *indexing* that information. There are three different types of information that can be put into a Verity collection:

- **Text files**   Verity can index text files, including HTML documents.

- **Binary files**   Verity can index many binary files, including documents created using Microsoft Word, Adobe PDF, Lotus Word Pro, Microsoft Excel, and Lotus Freelance. You can check your ColdFusion documentation for a full list of supported documentation types.

- **ColdFusion queries**   Using Verity, you can index ColdFusion query objects. This includes not only database queries created using the cfquery tag, but also the result sets from cfldap, cfpop, and other tags that return query objects.

Indexing all of these types of data in a single collection is a way to create a single search engine that will allow for searching across all the content on your site. Verity collections are optimized for search and therefore operate more efficiently than other available searching methods.

Creating VDK Verity Collections

There are two different ways in which you can create a collection from within ColdFusion. One is to use the ColdFusion Administrator. The other is to create the collection using CFML in a ColdFusion template.

Using the ColdFusion Administrator to Create a Collection

This is how you can create a collection via the ColdFusion Administrator:

1. Launch your ColdFusion Administrator and click the Verity Collections link under Data & Services. You will see the Verity Collections page:

Add New Verity Collections

Name	
Path	C:\CFusionMX\verity\collections Browse Server
Language	English

Create Collection

Connected Local Verity Collections

Actions	Alias Name	Mapped	Online	External	Language	Path

There are currently no available collections.
Please use the form above to create or map to a collection.

Connected K2 Verity Collections

Alias Name	Online	External	Path

There are currently no available K2 collections.

2. Enter the name of the collection in the Name box. Select the language of the collection in the Language drop-down list. Finally, enter the path where you want the connection to be located. I usually do not change this setting.

3. Click the Create Collection button, and your collection is created.

Connected Local Verity Collections

Actions	Alias Name	Mapped	Online	External	Language	Path
⊙⊙⊙⊙⊗	Chapter24	NO	YES	NO	english	C:\CFusionMX\verity\collections\

The collection is displayed in the Connected Local Verity Collections box.

Using CFML to Create a Collection

Collections can also be created in CFML using the cfcollection tag. To create a collection with this tag, you give it these attributes:

- **action**   Must be set to create a collection.
- **collection**   Accepts the name of the collection (required attribute). New in ColdFusion MX, spaces are allowed in the collection name.
- **path**   Specifies the absolute path to the place where the collection will be stored. The collection can be stored anywhere, but a common location is C:\CFusionMX\verity\collections.
- **language**   Specifies the language that the collection will be created in (optional attribute). The default value is English.

To create a collection, you can just run a ColdFusion template with this line:

```
<cfcollection action="create" collection="Chapter24"
              path="C:\CFusionMX\Verity\Collections">
```

This tag creates a collection called Chapter24 in the Collections subdirectory of ColdFusion's Verity directory. The cfcollection tag is great in situations where you do not want to expose the ColdFusion Administrator to your users, but still want them to be able to create and access Verity collections.

Tip *Always wrap a cflock tag around the cfcollection tag. This prevents two cfcollection tags from executing simultaneously and causing errors for both users.*

Populating Verity Collections

When you create a Verity collection, you have not yet put any data in it. The collection is an empty collection, devoid of any data. An empty collection is potentially useless. This section shows you how to add files, queries, and other data to your collection.

Indexing Text and Binary Files

Just as in collection creation, you can index collections either using the ColdFusion Administrator or in a ColdFusion template. This section shows you how to perform each method.

Indexing from the ColdFusion Administrator

These are the steps that you can follow to index a collection from the ColdFusion Administrator:

1. Launch the ColdFusion Administrator. Click the Verity Collections link under Data & Services. This opens the Verity Collections page, which includes a list of all collections. Click the Index button next to the link that you want to index.

2. Clicking the Index button opens this dialog box:

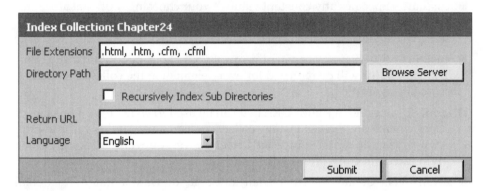

3. Enter the extensions for the files that you want to index.

If you list .cfm or .cfml in the File Extensions list box, the ColdFusion code will be indexed, not the resulting HTML of the processed code. Normally, you will not want to do this.

Select the language of the collection and the directory path. If you want to index all subdirectories below the current directory, select the Recursively Index Sub Directories checkbox.

4. Enter a return URL. This will make it easy for you to create return links to your pages. The return URL will probably be something like http://www.myserver.com/MyIndexedDirectory/.

5. Click the Submit button to index the collection. You will be returned to the collection page.

Filling Your Collection Using CFML

If you do not have access to the ColdFusion Administrator, you are still able to index collections through the use of CFML's cfindex tag. These are the attributes that you need to use to index documents:

- **collection** Contains the name of the collection that you want to index (required attribute).
- **action** Must be set to update to add data to your collection.
- **type** Must be set to file if you want to index a specific file, or to path if you want to index a group of files in the specified path. Set it to path if you want to index only files that pass an extension filter.

INTEGRATING COLDFUSION WITH OTHER TECHNOLOGIES

- **title** Should be set to a title for the collection, which will allow you to search the collection by title, or display a title separate from the key.

- **key** Specifies the absolute path of the files that you are indexing if the type is set to file or path.

- **custom1** Specifies any constant value of your choosing (optional attribute). The same value will be returned for every element in the collection when searching against it.

- **custom2** Specifies any constant value of your choosing (optional attribute). The same value will be returned for every element in the collection when searching against it.

- **urlpath** Specifies a return URL that can be used to create return links to pages when searching against the collection. You must set this value to http:// www.myserver.com/MyIndexedDirectory/ if you were indexing the MyIndexedDirectory directory of your web server.

- **extensions** Contains a list of extensions that you want to index. The default extensions are .htm, .html, .dbm, .dbml, .cfm, and .cfml.

Caution *I recommend not ever using the default value for the extensions attribute. You probably will not want to index CFML code, but rather the results of that CFML code.*

- **recurse** Specifies whether or not to index the directories recursively (Boolean attribute).

- **language** Specifies the language of the collection. The default value is English.

To index files using this method, you could execute a template that contains this code:

```
<cfindex collection="Chapter24" action="update" type="path"
        key="C:\InetPub\wwwroot\MySite" Recurse="Yes"
        urlpath="http://localhost/MySite/">
```

Indexing Queries and Other Dynamic Data

Sometimes you will want to index dynamic data, such as queries from a database. There is no way to do this from the ColdFusion Administrator, but thankfully, it can be done using the cfindex tag. These are the attributes that you give the cfindex tag to index via a query:

- **collection** Contains the name of the collection that you want to index (required attribute).

- **action** Must be set to update to add data to your collection.

- **type** Must be set to custom to index a query.

- **title**   Contains the name of the columns from the query that are going to be indexed.

- **key**   Contains a column name from the query. This field must be unique for each element in the query. A primary key often is used.

- **body**   Accepts a comma-delimited list of query columns, which will be stored in the collection.

- **custom1**   Specifies any constant value of your choosing (optional attribute). The same value will be returned for every element in the collection when searching against it.

- **custom2**   Specifies any constant value of your choosing (optional attribute). The same value will be returned for every element in the collection when searching against it.

Tip	*When indexing a query result set, a common use for either of the custom attributes might be to give it a value of MyPage.cfm?MyIndex=. When creating the query search, you can return links to the page that displays the information by using the urlpath, custom value, and key.*

- **urlpath**   Specifies a return URL that can be used to create return links to pages when searching against the collection. You must set this value to http://www.myserver.com/MyIndexedDirectory/ if you are indexing the MyIndexedDirectory directory of your web server.

- **query**   Contains the name of the query that generates the link.

- **language**   Specifies the language of the collection. The default value is English.

You might want to index query data, because it allows you to give your users the ability to access data without accessing the database. Searching against a Verity collection is more efficient than querying a database.

To index a query, you must first run the query, then run the cfindex tag against the query. Here is some code that uses the survey database we used in Chapter 20. It indexes all the survey questions.

```
<!--- Query the database --->
<cfquery datasource="Chapter24" name="IndexQuery">
 SELECT Questions.*
 FROM Questions
</cfquery>

<!--- index the query --->
<cfindex collection="Chapter24" action="update" type="custom"
         title="QuestionID" key="QuestionID" body="Question"
```

```
Custom1="DisplayQuestion?QuestionID="
URLPath="../MySite" Query="IndexQuery">
```

First, the code executes the query to get all the questions. Then, the cfindex tag adds the query information into the Chapter24 collection. The type of indexing we are doing is custom. The title and key fields are set to QuestionID. The body is question. If we were indexing a table with more fields, more fields would most likely be listed here. The urlpath uses a URL that is relative to where you plan to search from. It specifies one directory level up and down from the MySite directory. The name of the query, IndexQuery, is listed last.

Performing Other Actions Against Verity Collections

There are other actions that you may want to perform on a Verity collection. This section shows you how to perform them, and then gives you details on the information that you can retrieve from a collection.

Maintaining Verity Collections

In addition to creating and populating collections, there are other actions that may need to be performed. These actions can be performed either in the ColdFusion Administrator or by using the cfindex or cfcollection tag. Here is what you can do:

■ **Repair**   If a collection becomes corrupt, you can repair it. This action can be done using the cfcollection tag or the ColdFusion Administrator. From the ColdFusion Administrator, you can click this icon:

To repair the collection using the cfcollection tag, you only need to specify the name of the collection in the collection attribute, and set the action attribute to repair.

Caution   *The repair option must complete before other actions on the collection begin.*

■ **Optimize**   Every so often, you may want to optimize your collection. This will make sure that things are running at their peak efficiency. To optimize from the ColdFusion Administrator, click this button:

To optimize using the cfcollection tag, specify the name of the collection in the collection attribute and set the action attribute to optimize.

■ **Purge** When you purge a collection, you delete all of the information inside it, but leave the collection intact. This is the purge icon from the ColdFusion Administrator:

The cfindex tag can purge a collection if you set the action attribute to purge, specify the name of the collection in the collection attribute, and set the action attribute to optimize.

■ **Delete** All good things must come to an end, and that may some day include killing your Verity collection. To do so from the ColdFusion Administrator, use this icon:

If you want to use the cfindex tag, just set the action attribute to delete and the collection attribute to the name of the collection you are about to delete. If you want to use the cfcollection tag, just set the action to delete and the collection attribute to the name of the collection.

■ **Refresh** Refreshing a tag can only be done using the cfindex tag. When you refresh a collection, first it is purged, and then it is updated. Set the action attribute to refresh, and set the collection attribute to the name of the collection in question.

Getting Information on a Verity Collection

If you want to get information out of a Verity collection for use within a ColdFusion template, you can execute the cfcollection tag with these attributes:

■ **action** Must be set to list.

■ **name** Specifies the name of the return variable for this collection.

After the cfcollection tag is run, a query variable, named from the name attribute, is created with these values:

- **External** Set to Yes if the collection is external, No if the collection is not external, and not found if the collection is registered but not located at the mapped path. This information is not available if the collection is located in a K2 Server collection. We discuss the K2 Server in the following section.

Note *Mapped collections are empty collections that point to data in another collection. The mapped collection can be used as an alias for the one it points to.*

- **Language** Contains the language that the collection is set to. This information is not available if the collection is a K2 Server collection.

- **Mapped** Specifies whether or not the collection is a mapped collection (Boolean attribute). This information is not available if the collection is a K2 Server collection.

- **Name** Contains the name of the collection if it is a ColdFusion registered collection. If the collection is registered at a K2 Server, then the name value contains its alias.

- **Online** Specifies whether or not the collection is online (Boolean attribute). If the External variable is not found, then this value is always no. This value is only available for K2 Server collections.

- **Path** Contains the absolute path to the collection location. If the collection is mapped or registered by the K2 Server, the collection name is located in the Path variable.

- **Registered** Contains CF for ColdFusion collections, or K2 for K2 Server registered collections.

Using the Verity K2 Server

ColdFusion MX includes a restricted version of the Verity K2 Server. The K2 Server is a scalable search engine that supports simultaneous indexing and distributed repositories. It can handle hundreds of simultaneous users. ColdFusion uses Verity in VDK mode by default. This section shows you how to set up and use the Verity K2 Server.

Configuring the Verity K2 Server

This section teaches you some of the things that you need to do to set up ColdFusion to use your Verity K2 Server. It also tells you about the three different kinds of collections and how they are represented in the Verity INI files.

Setting Up ColdFusion to Use the K2 Server

There are three steps that you must take to set up ColdFusion to use the K2 Server:

1. **Edit the k2server.ini file**   The k2server.ini file is located at installationdirectory\ lib on Windows units and opt/coldfusion/verity/platform/bin/ on Unix units. The platform refers to the operating system that the software was installed on. You will not need to edit many of the settings located in the INI file. The portNo and Coll-n entries deserve examination, though.

    Open the file in a text editor. The portNo entry specifies the port number of the Verity server. The default value is 9901. The Coll-n is a block of entries that are used to specify information about the collection. The collpath contains the absolute collection path, and the collalias contains an alias to the collection. Every alias must be unique. This is an example:

    ```
    [Coll-0]
    collPath=c:\cfusionmx\verity\collections\MyCollection\file
    collAlias=Chapter24
    onLine=2
    ```

    The number after the Coll- must be incremented by one for each subsequent collection that you add to the file. The collAlias value must be unique for every collection on the server. There are other parameters that you can specify with relation to the file, but discussion of them is beyond the scope of this book.

if you make changes to the INI file, you must stop and start the K2 Server before they will take effect.

2. **Start the K2 Server**   You can start the K2 Server from the command line. The executable is located in the cfusionmx\lib\ directory on Windows units. On Unix machines, it is located in opt/coldfusion/verity/platform/bin/. The platform refers to the OS that the software was installed on. Execute the K2Server.exe file to start the server. You need to specify the location of the INI file using the inifile parameter at the command line.

To install the K2 Server as a service on Windows units, set –ntserver 1 as the command-line parameter. You can also set it up as a service manually by using this line to the K2Server.ini file: vdkHome=c:/cfusionmx/lib/common.

3. **Set hostname and port** The last step is to register, for lack of a better word, the Verity K2 Server with ColdFusion. This is done from the ColdFusion Administrator. Click the Verity K2 Server link under Data & Services to open the Verity K2 Server page:

Add Verity K2 Server

K2 Server Host Name	localhost
K2 Server Port	9901

Connect

Connected Verity Collections

Actions	Name	Port	Online	Broker	Doc Count	Doc Count Limit
⊠	localhost	9901	YES	NO	0	250000

Connected K2 Verity Collections

Alias Name	Online	External	Path
Chapter24	YES	YES	{localhost:9901} c:\cfusionmx\verity\collections\Chapter24\file\

Enter the name of the server, probably localhost, and the port. Click the Connect button, and ColdFusion will connect to the server. The K2 Server connections will be listed on both the Verity K2 Server page and the Verity Collections page.

You may have to stop the K2 Server, perhaps to load an updated INI file or shut down the machine. On a Windows machine, you can shut down the service either from the Services icon in the Control Panel, or by executing the following from the command line:

```
k2server –ntservice 0
```

If you are running the K2 Server in a command window, you can shut it down by using control-c. On Unix machines, a script is included to stop the K2 Server. It is located in the /opt/coldfusion/verity/platform/bin directory and is named stopk2server.

Understanding the Different Type of Collections

There are three different ways to create a Verity collection. The first is to create it in ColdFusion, as discussed earlier in this chapter. You can also create collections using Verity-specific tools such as a Verity spider or a utility called MKVDK. Both options will be discussed later in this chapter. This section shows you how each of these collections is represented in the k2server.ini file.

A collection populated by a ColdFusion query is a custom collection. The collPath attribute should point to the custom directory of the collection:

```
[Coll-0]
collPath=c:\cfusionmx\verity\collections\MyCollection\custom
collAlias=Chapter24K2
onLine=2
```

If the collection is created from ColdFusion as a file collection, the collPath value points to the file directory of the collection name. This is an example entry:

```
[Coll-0]
collPath=c:\cfusionmx\verity\collections\MyCollection\file
collAlias=Chapter24K2
onLine=2
```

Collections that are created using Verity tools such as the Verity spider or the MKVDK utility do not make a distinction between file collections and query collections. As such, the collpath points only to the collection directory, like this:

```
[Coll-0]
collPath=c:\cfusionmx\verity\collections\MyCollection\
collAlias=Chapter24K2
onLine=2
```

Managing Collections

Verity includes a tool, called a spider, that can be used to index web sites that are located on the same machine that the ColdFusion server resides on. The spider supports Internet standards, including HREF links and frames.

Populating with the Verity Spider

The Verity spider is located in the CFusionMX\lib_nti40\bin directory, with a filename of vspider.exe. Here is a list of the command-line options:

- **Collection**   Contains the name of the collection that you want to create or update.

- **Start**   Specifies the starting point for the indexing job. You set this to the name of a file or URL where you want to start your indexing.

- **Refresh**   Used for updating a collection. The spider will update documents that have changed, add new documents, and remove documents that are no longer in the repository.

- **Cmdfile**   Accepts the name of an ASCII file that contains preferences.

- **Help**   Displays all the valid options available with the vspider executable.

- **Jobpath**   Specifies the location of the Verity spider databases and job-related files and directories. These files include logs, admin files, bulk insert files, and temporary files.

- **Style**   Specifies the path to the style files of the collection. If not specified, the default path is used, which is located at collectionname\common\styles. A style is used to specify the content of a collection. For example, ColdFusion collections are set up with a style to contain the Key, Custom1, Custom2, and URL attributes.

- **Auth**   Specifies an authorization file to access secure paths.

- **Cgiok**   Allows indexing of URLs that contain a query string, denoted by the ? symbol. You will want to set this when indexing ColdFusion documents.

- **Host**   Lets you list multiple web hosts that the spider will index. Separate each host with a space.

- **Loglevel**   Specifies the type of messages that will be logged. Valid values are summary, skip, verbose, debug, and trace.

- **Nooptimize**   Prevents the spider from optimizing a collection. This will increase the performance of the spider.

- **Purge**   Purges a collection.

- **Repair**   Repairs a collection.

Note   *The preceding list of options is not exhaustive. Check your ColdFusion documentation for a complete list.*

This is an example of how you might use the spider:

```
vspider -collection c:\cfusionmx\verity\collections\MyCollection\
        -start http://localhost/ -cgiok -host localhost
```

The name of the collection is specified, as MyCollection, by giving its location on disk. It starts indexing at the localhost and will index all URL variables.

Caution *You cannot use the Verity spider that is included in ColdFusion to index remote servers. This is a limitation that can be overcome by purchasing the full K2 Server from Verity.*

Using the mkdvk Utility

Verity includes a utility, called mkdvk, that can assist in managing collections. It is located in the same directory as the vspider.exe file: CFusionMX\lib\platform\bin. You use the mkdvk file to create a new collection. It first sets up the style files for the collection, and then reads the files and passes the information to the Verity engine. Next, the gateway opens the document files and parses them. The Verity partition is created, including an index and an attribute table. Finally, the assist data is generated.

Here is a list of options that work with the mkdvk utility:

- **collection**   Accepts the name of the collection that you are working on.
- **create**   Creates a collection.
- **delete**   Deletes the collection.
- **insert**   Adds documents to an existing collection. This is the default value for the utility.
- **update**   Adds documents to the collection, first replacing everything in the collection.
- **extract**   Removes field values from the documents, using field extraction rules.
- **repair**   Fixes a damaged collection.
- **purge**   Deletes all documents from the collection without deleting the actual collection.
- **path**   Specifies the documents you want to index.
- **filespec**   Used to define the type of documents that you want to index. This is a comma-delimited list of extensions.
- **bulk**   Informs the utility that it is looking for many documents.
- **style**   Specifies the directory that contains the style files used in creating the collection.
- **description**   Specifies a description for the collection. You can enter any text that you wish.
- **words**   Tells Verity to build a word list for every partition of the collection.
- **about**   Displays information about the collection, such as its description and the date it was last modified.
- **datapath**   Specifies the absolute path of the collection's documents.
- **mode**   Sets the indexing mode. The values are case sensitive and include generic, fastsearch, newsfeedldx, newsfeedopt, bulkload, and readonly. The default value is generic.

- **help**   Displays all valid options for the program.

- **optimize**   Optimizes the collection, based on the specs you specify. Here is a list of some common options: maxclean, to perform an exhaustive housecleaning of the documents; maxmerge, to merge partitions to create partitions that are as large as possible; squeeze, to recover lost space taken up by deleted documents; and publish, to prepare a collection for best search performance.

- **nooptimize**   Specifies that documents will not be optimized as they are being indexed.

- **noindex**   Specifies that documents will not be added or deleted to the collection.

- **locale**   Specifies the language of the collection. The default value is English.

You can check your ColdFusion documentation for a full list of mkdvk options.

There are many other command-line utilities available for you to use to maintain your Verity collections. You can find out about them by consulting your ColdFusion documentation.

Using Verity Functions

Table 24-1 provides a list of all of ColdFusion's functions that may assist you when dealing with the Verity K2 Server.

Function	Parameters	Description
IsK2ServerOnline	N/A	Checks whether the Verity K2 Server is online. It returns a Boolean value.
IsK2ServerABroker	N/A	Determines if the K2 Server is a broker. A broker surpasses the limitations imposed on the K2 Server included in ColdFusion MX.
IsK2ServerDocCountExceeded	N/A	Determines whether the limit for the number of documents that can reside on the K2 Server has been exceeded.
GetK2ServerDocCount	N/A	Returns the number of documents in the collections on the K2 Server.
GetK2ServerDocCountLimit	N/A	Returns the total number of documents that can reside in the K2 Server.

Table 24-1.   *Verity K2 Server Functions*

Creating Verity Search Templates

This section demonstrates how you can create a search template to search against your Verity collections. It starts by creating the search templates and finishes by discussing some advanced search features of Verity.

Creating Search Queries

There are two types of searches you can run against a Verity collection: simple and explicit. A simple expression consists of one or more words, and the STEM and MANY modifiers are used by default. In explicit searches, the operators must be specified. This section examines some of the common search operators.

The following are the types of operators that can be used in a search:

- **Concept**   Identify a concept in a document by combining search elements.
- **Relational**   Search fields in a collection. They are similar to searches that you would use when performing a database query, and compare the specified value to the field values such as Custom1, Custom2, and Key.
- **Evidence**   Specify basic and intelligent word searches.
- **Proximity**   Specify the relative locations of words to each other.
- **Score**   Are not used to help the search, but rather to manage the score that is returned for a particular document that meets the given criteria.

The types of operators that can be used in a Verity expression are listed and described in Table 24-2.

Operator	Type	Description
AND	Concept	Selects documents that contain all of the search elements.
OR	Concept	Selects documents that contain at least one of the search elements.
ACCRUE	Concept	Selects documents that include at least one of the search elements.
ALL	Concept	Selects documents that contain all of the search items.
ANY	Concept	Selects documents that contain at least one of the search items.

Table 24-2.   *Verity Operators*

Operator	Type	Description
=	Relational	Selects documents that have fields that are equal to the specified value. Used for numeric and date comparisons.
!=	Relational	Selects documents that have fields that are not equal to the specified value. Used for numeric and date comparisons.
>	Relational	Selects documents where the specified value is greater than the value in the search fields. Used for numeric and date comparisons.
>=	Relational	Selects documents where the specified value is greater than or equal to the search fields. Used for numeric and date comparisons.
<	Relational	Selects documents where the fields are less than the specified value. Used for numeric and date comparisons.
<=	Relational	Selects documents where the specified value is less than or equal to the value of a field. Used for numeric and date comparisons.
CONTAINS	Relational	Selects documents by matching the word or phrase that you specify to the fields.
MATCHES	Relational	Selects documents by choosing exact matches between the search item and values stored in a specific document field.
STARTS	Relational	Selects documents by matching the search element with characters at the start of a word.
ENDS	Relational	Selects documents by matching the search element with characters at the end of a word.
SUBSTRING	Relational	Selects documents by matching the search element with any portion of the document.
STEM	Evidence	Searches on word variations. For example, searching on "Running" would also search on "run."
WILDCARD	Evidence	Matches wildcard characters in search strings.
WORD	Evidence	Performs a basic word search, selecting documents that include one or more instances of the specific word you enter.

Table 24-2. *Verity Operators* (continued)

Operator	Type	Description
THESAURUS	Evidence	Expands the search to include words that you did not enter, but that have a similar meaning to the words you did enter.
SOUNDEX	Evidence	Expands the search to include words that sound like the ones you entered.
TYPO/*N*	Evidence	Expands the search to include words you entered, plus words that are similar. Approximate pattern matching is used to identify similar words.
NEAR	Proximity	Selects all documents that contain the search elements. The closer the terms are together, the higher their score.
NEAR/*N*	Proximity	Selects documents that contain two or more of the search words within *N* words of each other. *N* must be between 1 and 1024.
PARAGRAPH	Proximity	Selects documents that include all of your specified words in the same paragraph.
PHRASE	Proximity	Selects documents that include a specified grouping of two or more words.
SENTENCE	Proximity	Selects documents that include all the specified words.
IN	Proximity	Selects documents contained within the specified values.
YESNO	Score	Forces all scores of 0 to become 1.
PRODUCT	Score	Multiplies the scores for each search element in your query and outputs the results.
SUM	Score	Adds the scores for all documents returned so that they equal 1.
COMPLIMENT	Score	Calculates the scores of documents by subtracting the score of a document from 1.
CASE	Modifiers	Performs a case-sensitive search.
MANY	Modifiers	Counts the density of words, stemmed variations, or phrases in a document and produces a relevance ranking. Use with WORD, WILDCARD, STEM, PHRASE, SENTENCE, or PARAGRAPH.
NOT	Modifiers	Excludes documents that contain the words in question. This can be used with AND and OR.

Table 24-2.   *Verity Operators* (continued)

Operator	Type	Description
ORDER	Modifiers	Specifies that search elements must occur in the same order that they are specified in the query. Place the order operator before PARAGRAPH, SENTENCE, or NEAR/*N*.

Table 24-2. *Verity Operators* (continued)

Searching from Within ColdFusion

This section shows you how to create templates to perform a simple search. The template group needs two separate files, the input page and the processing page. This section steps you through the creation of both of them.

Creating the Search Input Page

This is how you can create a search page for searching with Verity:

1. Create an empty page in your favorite CFML editor. Add your documentation header:

```
<!--- www.instantcoldfusion.com

Description: Verity Search Input Page

Entering: N/A
Exiting: Searchp.cfm

Dependencies: N/A
Expecting: N/A

Modification History
Date      Modifier                Modification
*********************************************************
04/26/2002 Jeff Houser, DotComIt   Created
--->
```

The documentation header states that the second page in our process is the Searchp.cfm page and includes a short description of this template.

2. To accept input, an HTML form is used. Start the form:

```
<form action="Searchp.cfm" method="post">
```

The form posts its data on the Searchp.cfm page.

3. Collect the search text box from the user and add a Submit button to the form:

```
Enter Your Search <input type="Text" name="Criteria">
<input type="submit" name="Submit">
```

4. Close the form:

```
</form>
```

Save your template and load it in your browser:

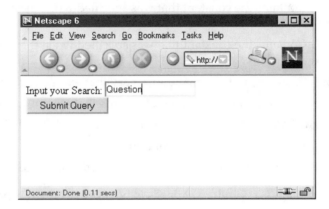

The Results Page

To search on the results page, we must use the cfsearch tag. The cfsearch tag searches the Verity collection and creates a ColdFusion query. These are its attributes:

- **name**   Contains the name of the resulting query variable.
- **collection**   Contains the name of the collection that you are searching against (required attribute). You can also specify the absolute path to the collection instead of the collection name. This attribute will accept multiple collections, if you separate them with a comma.
- **type**   Specifies the type of search you are performing, either simple or explicit. The default is simple.
- **criteria**   Specifies the search expression (required attribute). The type of search that is being conducted will determine the value of this attribute.
- **maxrows**   Specifies the maximum number of rows to return. The default is to return all rows.
- **startrow**   Specifies the first row to return from the resulting query. The default is 1.
- **language**   Specifies the default value for the language attribute is English.

After you execute the search, these are the values that are contained in the resulting query:

- **URL**   Contains the value that was specified when the information was indexed.
- **Key**   Contains the unique identifier of the item in the collection.
- **Title**   Contains the title of the collection.
- **Score**   Contains the resulting score of the document in question.
- **Custom1**   Contains the constant that was specified when the collection was indexed.
- **Custom2**   Contains the constant that was specified when the collection was indexed.
- **Summary**   Contains the automatic summary that was generated by cfindex.
- **RecordCount**   Contains the number of records that were returned.
- **CurrentRow**   Contains the row number of the record that is being processed.
- **ColumnList**   Contains a list of all columns in the query.
- **RecordsSearched**   Contains the number of records that were searched.

After the search page is submitted, it needs to be processed by this page:

```
<!--- www.instantcoldfusion.com

Description: The Search Processing Page

Entering: Searchi.cfm
Exiting: N/A

Dependencies: N/A
Expecting: form.Criteria

Modification History
Date        Modifier                Modification
*********************************************************
04/26/002 Jeff Houser, DotComIt    Created
--->

<!--- Search the collection --->
<cfsearch collection="Chapter24b" criteria=#form.criteria#
          name="MySearch">
```

```
<!--- Output the total number of results --->
<cfoutput>
 #MySearch.RecordCount# Records were returned<br><br>
</cfoutput>

<!--- output other search related data --->
<cfoutput query="MySearch">
 Key: #MySearch.key#<br>
 Title: #MySearch.Title#<br>
 Score: #MySearch.Score#<br>
 ColumnList: #MySearch.ColumnList# <br>
 Summary: #MySearch.Summary#<br>
 View:
  <a href="#MySearch.URL##MySearch.Custom1##MySearch.Key#">
   My Search
  </a>
</cfoutput>
```

The page starts with the documentation header, demonstrating the purpose of the page and the expected variable, form.criteria. The first thing that happens in the page is that the collection is searched with the cfsearch tag. Then the total number of returned records is displayed to the user. Then the data from the search is displayed to the user. In most site searches, we would want to create a link using the URL return value, so the last line of the template creates the URL that points to a page that displays the custom value.

Note *This code could be easily expanded to allow for more complex searches.*

Summary

In this chapter, you learned about the following:

- Verity collections
- How ColdFusion creates, populates, and maintains Verity collections
- The Verity K2 Server
- How to created a search engine for your site

Then next chapter will teach you how to integrate ColdFusion with WHTML to create wireless applications.

Chapter 25

Writing ColdFusion for Wireless Applications

This chapter shows you how you can use ColdFusion to write wireless applications. Wireless devices such as mobile phones and personal digital assistants have been including web-surfing capabilities for quite some time. Standard web pages aren't designed for such a small screen, and computer web browsers are generally too big and bloated to run on these devices. The answer resides in a new protocol and a new set of streamlined browsers. This chapter examines that protocol, the Wireless Application Protocol (WAP), and how you can integrate it with ColdFusion.

Learning the Language of Wireless

This section gives an overview of wireless applications. It discusses the WAP protocol and demonstrates building a web page with Wireless Markup Language (WML).

Understanding Wireless Applications

From a user's perspective, there is little difference between web surfing from a computer or from a wireless device. There are hyperlinks that can be clicked and buttons to be pressed. Behind the scenes, though, there are more obvious differences. The data is not transferred over wires, such as on the Internet; it is transferred via wireless radio signals at speeds that do not come close to the speeds at which a standard computer can connect to the Internet.

WAP is an effort to define a standard for using wireless devices over the Internet. Wireless devices are characterized by small screens and limited processing power. Conceptually, wireless Internet and traditional Internet are similar. A web browser in a wireless device requests information from a web server. The web server returns the data, and the web browser displays it.

HTTP, the protocol for transporting web pages, is not designed or optimized for the low bandwidth usage of wireless applications. Something called a WAP gateway is placed between the wireless device and the web server. The WAP gateway gets the data via HTTP, and then breaks it up into smaller chunks before sending it to the wireless device. Thankfully, the people who create wireless devices use their own gateways, so web hosting providers do not have to deal with creating their own.

The first WAP specification (WAP 1.0) was released in 1998. Through some minor updates, the WAP 2.0 specification was released in January 2002. Here are some of the highlights of it:

- Includes support for Internet protocols such as TCP/IP and HTTP. Wireless applications can now more easily coexist with existing technologies.

- Includes higher-speed transfer technologies such as General Packet Radio Service (GPRS) and 3rd Generation Cellular (3G).

- Provides an application development environment that will enable interaction with wireless devices.

- Addresses characteristics of these devices, such as limited battery life, smaller screens, and limited memory.

- Minimizes the processing power needed to run wireless applications.

- Incorporates flexibility in UI design, allowing different manufacturers to differentiate themselves from each other.

There are three major components of the WAP 2.0 specification:

- **Protocol stack support** The WAP stack is a list of pages that the user has visited. The WAP 2.0 protocol includes support for IP, which opens up a range of full Internet services, including the Wireless Session Protocol (WSP), which is the wireless equivalent of HTTP; Wireless Transaction Protocol (WTP), which is designed for thin clients with very little, or no, processing power; Wireless Transport Layer Security (WTLS), which is akin to HTTPS and is used to provide privacy and ensure data integrity; and Wireless Datagram Protocol (WDP), which is similar to TCP.

- **WAP Application Environment** The WAP Application Environment is often referred to as a WAP browser. It is closely aligned with the web model, where users request data and the servers send data. However, it also allows for the servers to actively push data to the user in real time. It embraces developing Internet standards, including eXtended Hypertext Markup Language Mobile Profile (XHTMLMP) and WML.

- **Additional services** Additional services include WAP Push, which is used to send data to devices via a Push Proxy and is used for real-time applications; User Agent Profile, which allows clients to describe their preferences to an application server; data synchronization, which allows for support of the SyncML language for synchronizing different data sources; and Pictograms, which allow for the use of tiny images in a consistent fashion.

 For more information and the latest WAP specification, check out www.wapforum.org.

Creating Wireless Web Pages

The main language that is used in wireless development is Wireless Markup Language (WML). It is similar to HTML in format. This section concentrates on WML, since that is the most common markup language used in wireless development.

A Sample WML Document

When browsing via a wireless application, users are often paying for the time that they spend online, sometimes per minute. Thus, it is, or at least should be, a primary goal of wireless applications to allow users to navigate the web applications quickly to get to the information that they need.

INTEGRATING COLDFUSION WITH OTHER TECHNOLOGIES

HTML is made up of pages or documents, but WML uses the metaphor of cards and decks. A card contains content and control logic. The control logic specifies how the user can move between cards. A deck is made up of one or more cards. An application can be made up of multiple decks. Decks are usually transmitted to the wireless device in one group, thereby diminishing the delay when moving between cards. A deck is located in a single file.

The general format of a WML file starts with a header:

```
<?xml version="1.0"?>
<!DOCTYPE wml PUBLIC "-//WAPFORUM//DTD WML 1.1//EN"
                     "http://www.wapforum.org/DTD/wml_1.1.xml">
```

The header consists of an XML document declaration and the doctype information. The doctype declaration points to the data table definition for WML 1.1.

Note   *Save WML documents with a .wml extension.*

From the previous chapters, you know that documentation is all-important in any type of development. You can add comments in your WML file the same way that you would add them in an HTML file. Enclose the comments in between <!-- and -->, just like this:

```
<!-- Your comment here -->
```

The next step in our document is to create the deck. This is done with open and close wml tags:

```
<?xml version="1.0"?>
<!DOCTYPE wml PUBLIC "-//WAPFORUM//DTD WML 1.1//EN"
                     "http://www.wapforum.org/DTD/wml_1.1.xml">

<!-- Create the deck -->
<wml>
</wml>
```

The next step is to add a number of cards to the deck:

```
<?xml version="1.0"?>
<!DOCTYPE wml PUBLIC "-//WAPFORUM//DTD WML 1.1//EN"
                     "http://www.wapforum.org/DTD/wml_1.1.xml">

<!-- Create the deck -->
<wml>
```

```
<!-- Create the card -->
<card id="MyName">
</card>
</wml>
```

Cards reside between the open and close card tags. There are three attributes that can be used for most WML elements:

- **xml:lang**   Used to define the human language of the data (optional attribute).
- **class**   Used to group together several different elements under the same name. This is useful only if external programs are going to access your data. Wireless browsers usually ignore this attribute.
- **id**   Used to provide a unique name to an element within a deck.

Next, add some content to the card:

```
<?xml version="1.0"?>
<!DOCTYPE wml PUBLIC "-//WAPFORUM//DTD WML 1.1//EN"
                     "http://www.wapforum.org/DTD/wml_1.1.xml">


<!-- Create the deck -->
<wml>

 <!-- Create the card -->
 <card id="MyName">
  <p>Welcome to The Site</p>
 </card>
</wml>
```

When you are developing in HTML, you create links between pages. In WML, you create links either between decks or between cards. This is an example that places a link in MyName card to the MyName2 card:

```
<?xml version="1.0"?>
<!DOCTYPE wml PUBLIC "-//WAPFORUM//DTD WML 1.1//EN"
                     "http://www.wapforum.org/DTD/wml_1.1.xml">


<!-- Create the deck -->
<wml>
```

```
<!-- Create the card -->
<card id="MyName">
 <p>Welcome to The Site</p>
 <p><a href="#MyName2">Go to MyName2</a></p>
</card>

<!-- Create a second card -->
<card id="MyName2">
 <p>Welcome to the second site</p>
</card>
</wml>
```

The link is similar to an HTML href using a bookmark. It points the wireless browser to a card name within the same deck, preceded by a #. You can link to other decks by specifying deckname#card. You can also link to other sites just as if there were no difference from normal HTML.

WML is a format of XML, so its definition is defined in a DTD file. The file can be found at www.wapforum.org/DTD/wml20-flat.dtd.

Using Anchor Elements

In addition to the <a> tag that is used to link between cards and decks, there is an anchor tag. The anchor tag allows you more control over the actions that happen when the user selects a link. You can use the anchor tag in conjunction with a go tag to perform similar actions to the ones that the <a> tag performs. This is how it works:

```
<!-- Create the card -->
 <card id="MyName">
  <p>Welcome to The Site</p>
  <p>
   <anchor>
    Go to MyName2
    <go href="#MyName2"/>
   </anchor>
  </p>
 </card>

<!-- Create a second card -->
<card id="MyName2">
 <p>Welcome to the second site</p>
</card>
```

Note that the go tag uses shorthand for closing a tag. Instead of specific open and close tags, the go tag is closed in one swoop, ending the tag with />.

You can also use a prev tag. This is the equivalent of the Back button in a web browser. This is how you would use the prev tag in the MyName2 card:

```
<!-- Create a second card -->
 <card id="MyName2">
  <p>Welcome to the second site</p>
  <p><anchor>Back<prev/></anchor></p>
 </card>
```

When surfing via a wireless device, this gives the user the option to go back to previously viewed pages.

Collecting User Data

WML allows you to collect information from the user. This is similar to the way that HTML forms allow you to collect information. The first step in this process is to understand how variables are used in WML. Although the concept of a variable is familiar to users of ColdFusion (if it isn't to you, read Chapter 8), it is new in a markup language. HTML does not have variables.

In WML, a variable is a way that you can share information between cards. Variables are created with the setvar tag. It has two attributes, name and value. This is similar to the ColdFusion cfparam tag. Here is an example:

```
<setvar name="MyVar1" value="Scrumpy"/>
```

The variables can be triggered by user interaction. Take a look at these two cards:

```
<!-- Create the card -->
 <card id="MyName">
  <p>Welcome to The Site</p>
  <p>
   <anchor>
    Go to MyName2
    <go href="#MyName2">
     <!-- Create the variable -->
     <setvar name="MyVar1" value="Scrumpy"/>
    </go>
   </anchor>
  </p>
 </card>
```

When the link to go to the second card is selected, the variable is created. You can access the values of a variable by prepending the variable name with a dollar sign:

```
<!-- Create a second card -->
<card id="MyName2">
 <p>$MyVar</p>
</card>
```

The wireless browser will recognize the variable and output its value.

The biggest use of variables is to fill them with values based on user input. The WML input tag allows you to take input from the user. The most important attribute to the input tag is the name attribute. It is used to specify the variable name of the user's input. Here is a simple example:

```
<card>
 <p>
  Enter Your Info <input name="MyVar1"/>
  Thank You
 </p>

</card>
```

When the code is processed, the wireless browser will ouput the label text "Enter Your Info" and then pause for user input. After the user answers the question, the card will continue processing by saying "Thank You."

Other than the name attribute, here are some of the more commonly used attributes of the input tag:

- **value** Specifies a default value for the tag.
- **type** Can be set to text, password, checkbox, radio, submit, reset, or hidden.
- **size** Specifies the length of the user input.
- **maxlength** Specifies the maximum number of characters a user can enter.
- **checked** If using a radio button or checkbox, specifies that the default state of the box be checked.

 As with HTML, you can also use select boxes in WML. Examination of these is beyond the scope of this book, though.

Using Emulators to Test Your Wireless Applications

You will most likely be developing your wireless application on a computer, not on a wireless device. How do you test your code without having a wireless device handy?

It is not in the best interests of the wireless companies to force you to buy one of their devices to deliver content to them. The answer resides in a program called an emulator.

An emulator is a program that mimics the functionality of a wireless program. Emulators run on a normal computer, and you can get emulators for just about any type of wireless device. There is no common browser between wireless devices, so you may find that each wireless device translates your WML code differently. Most companies that create wireless devices with WAP capability offer emulators. Here are a few of them:

- **Openwave SDK**   The Openwave SDK is one of the most common SDKs used for development. You can find out more at www.openwave.com. This product used to be called phone.com.

- **Nokia**   Nokia offers a wide range of wireless devices, and as such offers its own software development kit for testing your wireless applications. You can get emulators for just about every phone Nokia offers. Check them out at www.nokia.com.

- **Gelon**   Gelon is a web-based emulator. You type in your web site address and the emulator pops up the site in a window that is similar to a wireless phone. Check it out at www.gelon.net.

- **SmartPhone**   SmartPhone is an emulator that emulates many of the most popular phone formats. You can find more information about it at www.yospace.com.

This list of emulators is just a sampling of the full range of them. If you are developing your application for a specific market, try to find an emulator from the company that makes the wireless device.

 Browsers that are built for wireless applications are created to be lean. They are not as forgiving of poor code as many of the computer-based web browsers.

Integrating WAP and CFML

This section describes some of the issues that you need to address when developing wireless applications with ColdFusion. It talks about setting up your ColdFusion pages to be viewed by a wireless browser, managing sessions, and sending data from the client to the ColdFusion server.

Defining Your Page Type

ColdFusion and HTML pages, by default, have a MIME type of text/html. Wireless browsers cannot view pages of this type. They need a MIME type of text/vnd.wap.wml to properly display the web pages. The cfcontent tag allows you to specify the MIME type of the current file. The cfcontent tag, introduced in Chapter 17, is used to deliver files to a web browser that would not otherwise have been accessible. Here we can use it to specify the type of content that we are returning in the ColdFusion template.

To specify the MIME type of a file, the cfcontent tag only needs the type attribute. You use the attribute to specify the name of the MIME type. This is how we would use it for our wireless application:

```
<cfcontent type="text/vnd.wap.wml">
```

It is a best practice to put this cfcontent tag in the Application.cfm page of your wireless application's directory. That way, all pages will automatically be sent to the browser with the proper MIME type setting.

Session Management

The next issue surrounding ColdFusion wireless development is how to handle session management. As we discussed in Chapter 8, ColdFusion keeps track of sessions by using two cookies: CFID and CFTOKEN. However, not all wireless browsers support the use of cookies. This can cause a problem if your application requires them.

Thankfully, there is another way to handle state management in ColdFusion. You need to pass the two cookies via the URL query string whenever you link from one deck to another. Since moving between cards in a deck does not load a new page from the server, the URL attributes do not need to be passed.

Look at this deck, Session1.cfm, as an example:

```
<!--- www.instantcoldfusion.com

Description: Wireless Application Page to test passing session
             variables

Entering: N/A
Exiting: N/A

Dependencies: N/A
Expecting: N/A

Modification History
Date        Modifier                Modification
*********************************************************
04/29/2002 Jeff Houser, DotComIt    Created
--->

<!--- set a ColdFusion variable --->
<cflock scope="session" type="exclusive" timeout="30">
```

```
<cfset session.MyTestVar ="This is a Test Session Variable">
</cflock>


<?xml version="1.0"?>
<!DOCTYPE wml PUBLIC "-//WAPFORUM//DTD WML 1.1//EN"
                    "http://www.wapforum.org/DTD/wml_1.1.xml">


<!--- Create the deck --->
<wml>

 <!-- Create the card -->
 <card id="Session1Card1">
  <p>Welcome to Session1Card1</p>
  <!--- output the session variable --->
  <cflock scope="session" type="readonly" timeout="30">
   <p><cfoutput>#session.MyTestVar#</cfoutput></p>
  </cflock>
  <!--- Link to another card --->
  <p><a href="#Session1Card2">Go to MyName2</a></p>
 </card>

 <!-- Create a second card -->
 <card id="Session1Card2">
  <p>Welcome to Session1Card2</p>
  <!--- output the session variable --->
  <cflock scope="session" type="readonly" timeout="30">
   <p><cfoutput>#session.MyTestVar#</cfoutput></p>
  </cflock>
  <p>
  <!--- Link to another deck --->
   <a href="Session2.cfm#Session2Card1?cfid=
           <cfoutput>#cfid#&amp;cftoken=#cftoken#</cfoutput>">
     Go to Session2
   </a>
  </p>
 </card>
</wml>
```

As with all others, this page starts with a documentation header. It then creates a session variable. The cfapplication tag and the cfcontent tag were set up in the Application.cfm. Then comes the wml document header information. Next comes the deck with two cards. The first deck outputs the session value and has a link to the second card. The second deck outputs the session value and has a link to the second deck. The cfid and cftoken values are passed via the URL. You will notice that the ampersand, which is used to set up the query string of the URL, is escaped using &. This is because the emulator won't work otherwise. Loading this page in the Openwave emulator will show the following:

Image courtesy of Openwave Systems Inc.

Selecting the link will go to the following screen:

Image courtesy of Openwave Systems Inc.

Next, we look at Session2.cfm, the second deck:

```
<!--- www.instantcoldfusion.com

Description: Wireless Application Page to test passing session
              variables
```

```
Entering: N/A
Exiting: N/A

Dependencies: N/A
Expecting: N/A

Modification History
Date        Modifier              Modification
*********************************************************
04/29/2002 Jeff Houser, DotComIt    Created
--->

<?xml version="1.0"?>
<!DOCTYPE wml PUBLIC "-//WAPFORUM//DTD WML 1.1//EN"
                    "http://www.wapforum.org/DTD/wml_1.1.xml">

<!-- Create the deck -->
<wml>

 <!-- Create the card -->
 <card id="Session2Card1">
  <p>Welcome to Session2Card1</p>
  <!--- Output the session variable --->
  <cflock scope="session" type="readonly" timeout="30">
   <p><cfoutput>#session.MyTestVar#</cfoutput></p>
  </cflock>
  <p><a href="#Session2Card2">Go to MyName2</a></p>
 </card>

 <!-- Create a second card -->
 <card id="Session2Card2">
  <p>Welcome to Session2Card2</p>
  <!--- Output the session variable --->
  <cflock scope="session" type="readonly" timeout="30">
   <p><cfoutput>#session.MyTestVar#</cfoutput></p>
  </cflock>
 </card>
</wml>
```

The Session2.cfm page is very similar to the Session1.cfm page. There are two cards. The first one displays the session variable and provides a link to the second card:

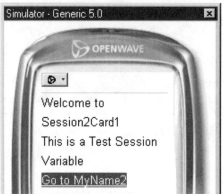

Image courtesy of Openwave Systems Inc.

The second card displays the session variable:

Image courtesy of Openwave Systems Inc.

Sending Data to the Server

It is very common in web development to want to accept values from a user and manipulate them on the server. This is done through HTML forms and the use of the form variables. You already learned how to accept user input from a wireless application. How do you send that data back to ColdFusion?

If we really wanted to, we could send the data back to the server using URL variables. This is not considered ideal, though. The WML specification includes a better way, which is through a tag called postfield. There are two attributes to the postfield tag that are worthy of note:

- **name**   Contains the variable name that is going to be sent back to the server.
- **value**   Contains the value of the name that will be sent back to the server.

Here is a simple example of using the postfield tag:

```
<!--- www.instantcoldfusion.com

Description: WML page to post data

Entering: N/A
Exiting: N/A

Dependencies: N/A
Expecting: N/A

Modification History
Date        Modifier               Modification
*********************************************************
04/28/2002 Jeff Houser, DotComIt    Created
--->

<?xml version="1.0"?>
<!DOCTYPE wml PUBLIC "-//WAPFORUM//DTD WML 1.1//EN"
                     "http://www.wapforum.org/DTD/wml_1.1.xml">

<!--- Create the deck --->
<wml>

 <!--- Create the card --->
 <card id="Form1Card1">
  <p>
   <anchor>
    Test Post
    <go href="Formp.cfm" method="post">
     <postfield name="TestVariable" value="MyValue"/>
    </go>
   </anchor>
  </p>
 </card>

</wml>
```

The deck contains one card. It has a single link, created using the go tag, that passes TestVariable onto Formp.cfm page. This is the Formp.cfm page:

```
<!--- www.instantcoldfusion.com

Description: Page to process form input

Entering: N/A
```

```
Exiting: N/A

Dependencies: N/A
Expecting: form.TestVariable

Modification History
Date        Modifier                Modification
**********************************************************
04/29/2002 Jeff Houser, DotComIt    Created
--->

<?xml version="1.0"?>
<!DOCTYPE wml PUBLIC "-//WAPFORUM//DTD WML 1.1//EN"
                    "http://www.wapforum.org/DTD/wml_1.1.xml">

<!--- Create the deck --->
<wml>

 <!-- Create the card -->
 <card id="Form2Card1">
  <p>
   <cfoutput>#form.TestVariable#</cfoutput>
  </p>
 </card>

</wml>
```

This page simply outputs the value of the test variable. When information is posted from a wireless application to a server, a form scope is created just as if an HTML form were submitted.

Tip   *The postfield tags must always be contained in a go tag. The go tag must be contained within an anchor element.*

This is an example that accepts some user input:

```
<!--- www.instantcoldfusion.com

Description: Page to accept user input

Entering: N/A
Exiting: UserInputp.cfm

Dependencies: N/A
Expecting: N/A
```

```
Modification History
Date        Modifier              Modification
********************************************************
04/29/2002 Jeff Houser, DotComIt   Created
--->

<?xml version="1.0"?>
<!DOCTYPE wml PUBLIC "-//WAPFORUM//DTD WML 1.1//EN"
                     "http://www.wapforum.org/DTD/wml_1.1.xml">

<!--- Create the deck --->
<wml>

 <card id="GetInput">
  <p>
   <!--- Get User Info --->
   Enter Your Info <input name="MyVar1"/>
   <!--- Post User Input --->
   <anchor>
    Post
    <go href="UserInputp.cfm" method="post">
     <postfield name="MyVar1" value="$(MyVar1)"/>
    </go>
   </anchor>

  </p>
 </card>
</wml>
```

This page starts with the documentation header. It is a deck that contains a single card. The card gets one field of user input and then posts that field to the UserInputp.cfm page. The value attribute of our postfield tag contains a variable, MyVar1. This is how we access the values that the user entered. Here is the page:

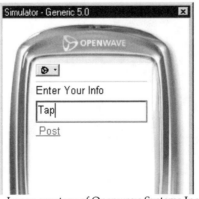

Image courtesy of Openwave Systems Inc.

This is the page that processes our user input:

```
<!--- www.instantcoldfusion.com

Description: Page to process User Input

Entering: UserInputi.cfm
Exiting: N/A

Dependencies: N/A
Expecting: form.MyVar1

Modification History
Date        Modifier                Modification
************************************************************
04/29/2002 Jeff Houser, DotComIt    Created
--->

<?xml version="1.0"?>
<!DOCTYPE wml PUBLIC "-//WAPFORUM//DTD WML 1.1//EN"
                     "http://www.wapforum.org/DTD/wml_1.1.xml">

<!--- Create the deck --->
<wml>

 <!-- Create the card -->
 <card id="Form2Card1">
  <p>
   <!--- output the value --->
   <cfoutput>#form.MyVar1#</cfoutput>
  </p>
 </card>

</wml>
```

This page, once again, is a deck with a single card. The card outputs the value of the form variable, but does little else. Here is the page:

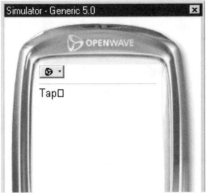

Image courtesy of Openwave Systems Inc.

When creating your applications you will probably want to perform more advanced ColdFusion processing on the form variables. The rest of the book talks about a lot of things you can do to variables.

 Not all wireless browsers support post operations. Test your application thoroughly if you want to use this approach.

Summary

It is not possible to explore every aspect of WML in one chapter. You should check out the resources mentioned throughout this chapter. In this chapter, you learned about the following:

- The Wireless Application Protocol (WAP)
- WML and some of its basic tags
- How to integrate CFML and WML

The next chapter will take you in a different direction by showing you how you can expand custom tags using the CFX API.

The Complete Reference

Chapter 26

Extending ColdFusion with CFX Custom Tags

This chapter teaches you how you can extend the functionality that ColdFusion offers by writing custom programs in either C++ or Java. This opens a broad range of functionality to ColdFusion developers. CFX tags have many uses, such as to get information about image files, maintain users on the underlying operating system, and even compress files.

Creating CFX Tags in Java

This section teaches you all you need to know about creating CFX tags in Java. It presents the interface that you can use to share data between ColdFusion and the custom tag. It also shows you how to create a sample custom tag from within Java. However, this section does not teach you the Java language, or how to set up or install Java development tools. (For more information on Java, try *Java 2: The Complete Reference, Fifth Edition* by Herb Schildt. McGraw-Hill/Osborne, 2002.)

Understanding the Java CFX Classes

Four interfaces are available from within Java that allow you to integrate with ColdFusion: CustomTag, Request, Response, and Query. This section discusses each one of the objects and how you can use them from within your Java classes. Table 26-1 lists and describes all the functions, their parameters, and the interface that implements them.

The CustomTag interface is used for implementing custom tags. It has a single method, processRequest, which has two parameters, a request object and a response object. The function does not return anything.

The Request interface allows you to interact with the request that called the CFX tag. It allows you to manage attributes with the attributeExists, getAttribute, getAttributeList, and getIntAttribute methods. It can also get queries using the getQuery method and check for the debug attribute using the getDebug method. The debug attribute specifies whether debug information should be shown to the user or suppressed.

The Response interface allows you to send information back to the calling page. You can create a query using the addQuery method or create a variable using the setVariable method. Output can be generated using the write or writeDebug functions.

The Query interface allows you to manipulate query data, whether it be a query object that was passed into the custom tag or a query object that you want to pass out of the custom tag. You can add rows by using the addRow function; retrieve column information by using getColumns and getColumnIndex; retrieve specific indexes by using the getData function; set the value of a column by using setData; retrieve the name of the query by using the getName function; and retrieve the length of the query by using getRowCount.

To create a custom tag in Java, you have to make sure that the Java CFX classes, previously described, are available to your Java compiler. There is a file named cfx.jar that is located in the lib directory of your ColdFusion installation. You must either set the classpath variable to include this directory or move the cfx.jar file into a directory

Function	Parameters	Returns	Interface	Description
processRequest	**request:** Request object **response:** Response object	Void	CustomTag	Called to process the call to the custom tag.
attributeExists	**string:** Attribute name	Boolean	Request	Checks to see if an attribute was passed into the tag.
debug	N/A	Boolean	Request	Checks if the tag contained the debug attribute.
getAttribute	**string:** Attribute name	String	Request	Returns the value of a specific attribute.
getAttributeList	N/A	String	Request	Returns a list of all attributes.
getIntAttribute	**string:** Attribute name	int	Request	Returns an attribute's value as an integer. Returns –1 or throws an exception if the attribute name is not valid.
getIntAttribute	**string:** Attribute name **int:** Default integer	int	Request	Returns an attribute's value as an integer, or the default value if not applicable.
getQuery	N/A	Query	Request	Retrieves a query. If no query was passed, returns null.
getSetting	**string:** Name of setting	String	Request	Retrieves a global custom tag setting.
addQuery	**string:** Name of query **string[ ]:** Array of query column names	Query	Response	Creates a query in the calling template.
setVariable	**string:** Name of variable **string:** Value of variable	void	Response	Creates or sets a variable in the calling template.
write	**string:** String to output	void	Response	Outputs text back to the user.
writeDebug	**string:** Value to output	void	Response	Outputs a message back to the user.
AddRow	N/A	int	Query	Adds an empty row to a query.
getColumnIndex	**string:** Name of column	int	Query	Returns the index of the specified column.
getColumns	N/A	String[ ]	Query	Returns an array of columns.
getData	**int:** Row **int:** Column	String	Query	Returns data at the specified row and column intersection.
getName	N/A	String	Query	Returns the name of the query.

Table 26-1.   *ColdFusion Java Interfaces*

Function	Parameters	Returns	Interface	Description
getRowCount	N/A	int	Query	Returns the number of rows in a query.
setData	**int:** Row **int:** Column **string:** Value	Void	Query	Sets a field in a query at the specified row and column intersection point.

Table 26-1. *ColdFusion Java Interfaces* (continued)

that is accessible from your classpath. The classpath is a variable that tells your Java compiler where to find the Java classes.

Creating a Custom Tag

A CFX custom tag is stored in a Java .class file. The .class file is a compiled version of the source code contained in a .java file. This section will show you how to create the code, but compiling it into a .class file is compiler-specific and beyond the scope of this book. We will create a custom tag that can be used to read a single line from a file. ColdFusion does not provide inherent functionality to do this. The cffile tag will only read a file in all at once and is not intended for large files. By separating the file per each line, we should be able to handle much larger files than would be practical with the cffile tag.

This is how we create our CFX tag:

1. Import the relevant class libraries:

```
import com.allaire.cfx.* ;
import java.io.* ;
```

The two libraries that are imported are the custom tag library, com.allaire.cfx, and the java io library, java.io.

2. Set up the class:

```
public class GetLine implements CustomTag
{
}
```

The class is named GetLine and implements the class CustomTag from the com.allaire.cfx library.

3. Our class only needs a single method, so we set that up next:

```
public void processRequest( Request request, Response response )
 throws Exception
{
}
```

The processRequest method is called automatically when the final CFX custom tag is called. All our processing code will reside in this method. It passes two objects as parameters, Request and Response, each referring to request and response objects, respectively. The method resides within brackets that open and close the class declaration.

4. Inside the method, the first thing that we want to do is make sure that our necessary variables are passed into the tag. To process this tag, we need to know the name of the file and the location that we are reading from. This tag returns two values. First, it returns the next line from the file. Second, it returns the location of the file pointer.

```java
// check if file variable is defined
if ( !request.attributeExists( "File" ) ){
    throw new Exception("Missing attribute (File)" ) ;
}


if ( !request.attributeExists( "ReturnLine" ) ){
    throw new Exception("Missing attribute (ReturnLine)" ) ;
}

if ( !request.attributeExists( "ReturnLocation" ) ){
    throw new Exception("Missing attribute (ReturnLocation)" ) ;
}


long CurrentLine = 0;

// Check for Line to get.  If blank, default to 0
if (  request.attributeExists( "CurrentLocation" ) )
{
  // get CurrentLineAttribute
  CurrentLine = request.getIntAttribute( "CurrentLocation" ) ;
}
```

This code checks for the values in the request variable using the attributeExists method. If the CurrentLocation variable is undefined, the code creates it and assigns it a default value, 0. This will read from the start of the file. This is an optional attribute to the custom tag.

5. Set up the file for use within the Java class. This is the code:

```java
// initialize the file
RandomAccessFile MyFile =
        new RandomAccessFile(request.getAttribute("File"), "r");
```

We set up the object named MyFile. The constructor for RandomAccessFile takes two values, the name of the file and a mode attribute. The getAttribute value is used to specify the location of the file. The mode value is hard-coded as an r, which means that we are opening the file for reading. To open the file for reading and writing, we must specify rw as the mode attribute. The RandomAccesFile class allows us to access anywhere in the file, unlike some other classes that offer a more iterative approach.

6. Find the current place in the file where we want to start reading the line. We passed in, or set a default value, to the CurrentLine variable:

```
// skip to the current place in the file
MyFile.seek(CurrentLine);
```

The seek method will move to the location in the file that we specified.

7. Now that we are at the current location in the file, we can use the readLine method to get the line:

```
// Read the Line
String Line = MyFile.readLine();
response.setVariable(request.getAttribute("ReturnLine"),Line);
```

After reading the line into a string variable, we use the setVariable method of the response object to create the result variable in the calling template. The name of the new variable is the value of the ReturnLine attribute that was passed into the custom tag.

8. Get the updated location in the file. After reading information from the file, the pointer is automatically incremented. The getFilePointer method will return its current location:

```
// get the current file pointer
long Pter = MyFile.getFilePointer();
response.setVariable(request.getAttribute("ReturnLocation"),
                     Long.toString(Pter));
```

The ReturnLocation variable is created in the calling template similarly to the way that the ReturnLine variable was created. The long data type must be converted to a string before sending it back to the calling template. That is done with the Long.toString method.

9. Close the file:

```
MyFile.close();
```

This finishes the method. Compile it into a class file, and you are all set.

Calling the Custom Tag

Once you have created and compiled your CFX tag, you need to register it from the ColdFusion Administrator. This was discussed in Chapter 6. Register the GetLine file with these parameters:

- **Tag Name** Should be cfx_getline.
- **Class Name** Should be GetLine. Remember that Java is case sensitive, so this has to match the case of the name of the class file.
- **Comments** Can be anything you want them to be.

This may be a good time to check the Java settings by clicking the Java and JVM link under Server Settings.

The next step is to create the page:

```
<!--- Get the first line from the custom tag --->
<CFX_GetLine currentlocation="0" file="C:\ testFile.cfm"
    returnline="MyReturnLine" returnlocation="MyReturnLoc">

<!--- Output the First Line of the page --->
<cfoutput>
 Return Line: #MyReturnLine#<br>
 Return Loc: #MyReturnLoc#<br>
</cfoutput>
<br>

<!--- Output the values from the custom tag --->
<CFX_GetLine currentlocation="#MyReturnLoc#"
             file="C:\ testFile.cfm" returnline="MyReturnLine"
             returnlocation="MyReturnLoc">

<!--- Output the second line of the page --->
<cfoutput>
   Return Line: #MyReturnLine#<br>
   Return Loc: #MyReturnLoc#<br>
</cfoutput>
```

This page will read and output the first two lines from the file. The second time it calls the custom tag, the end location that was passed back from the first call is used to continue reading from the specified location. Some limitations of this tag are discussed at the end of the chapter. For now, let's look at how we can implement something similar in C++.

Creating CFX Tags in C++

This section shows you how you can re-create our Java ReadLine custom tag in the C++ language. It starts by explaining the C++ classes that can be used to create a custom tag in C++. It then goes through the process of creating a tag to read a single line from a file. Finally, it shows you how you can use the tag after registering it.

Understanding the C++ CFX Classes

The C++ classes and methods that allow you to access ColdFusion variables are described in Table 26-2. There are four different classes: CCFXException, CCFXQuery, CCFXRequest, and CCFXStringSet.

The CCFXRequest class is used to interact with the ColdFusion request. It is a combination of the Request and Response Java classes. It allows you to work with variables by using AttributeExists, GetAttribute, GetAttributeList, and SetVariable; deal with queries and strings by using GetQuery, AddQuery, and CreateStringSet; offer output back to the user by using write and WriteDebug; throw exceptions by using ThrowException and ReThrowException; and get information about the tag by using GetCustomData and SetCustomData.

Method	Parameters	Returns	Class	Description
AttributeExists	**LPCSTR:** Name of attribute	Boolean	CCFXRequest	Checks if attribute exists.
GetAttribute	**LPCSTR:** Name of attribute	LPCSTR	CCFXRequest	Returns the attribute's value.
GetAttributeList	N/A	CCFXStringSet	CCFXRequest	Returns StringSet object of all attributes.
GetQuery	N/A	CCFXQuery	CCFXRequest	Returns query object that was passed to the tag.
Write	**LPCSTR:** String to output	N/A	CCFXRequest	Outputs text to the user.
SetVariable	**LPCSTR:** Name of variable **LPCSTR:** Value of variable	N/A	CCFXRequest	Creates variable in calling page.
AddQuery	**LPCSTR:** Name of query **CCFXStringSet:** List of query columns	CCFXQuery	CCFXRequest	Creates a query in the calling page.
Debug	N/A	Boolean	CCFXRequest	Returns true if the tag has the debug attribute, false otherwise
WriteDebug	**LPCSTR:** Text	N/A	CCFXRequest	Outputs Debug text
CreateStringSet	N/A	CCFXStringSet	CCFXRequest	Creates a CCFXStringSet object

Table 26-2.   *C++ ColdFusion Classes and Methods*

Method	Parameters	Returns	Class	Description
ThrowException	**LPCSTR:** Short error **LPCSTR:** Diagnostic information	N/A	CCFXRequest	Throws an error.
ReThrowException	**CCFXException:** Exception	N/A	CCFXRequest	Rethrows an exception that couldn't be handled.
SetCustomData	**LPVOID:** Pointer to custom data	N/A	CCFXRequest	Sets custom tag data. Used to pass data to procedures within tag implementation.
GetCustomData	N/A	LPVOID	CCFXRequest	Returns pointer to custom tag in stack.
AddString	**LPCSTR:** String to add	int	CCFXStringSet	Adds a string to the set.
GetCount	N/A	int	CCFXStringSet	Returns number of items in set.
GetString	**int:** Index of string	LPCSTR	CCFXStringSet	Returns string at specified reference.
GetIndexForString	**LPCSTR:** String to check for	int	CCFXStringSet	Returns index of specified string.
AddRow	N/A	int	CCFXQuery	Adds a row to a query.
GetColumns	N/A	CCFXStringSet	CCFXQuery	Returns a string set of all columns.
GetData	**int:** Row **int:** Column	LPCSTR	CCFXQuery	Returns the data at the specified index.
GetName	N/A	LPCSTR	CCFXQuery	Returns the name of the query.
GetRowCount	N/A	LPCSTR	CCFXQuery	Returns number of rows in query.
SetData	**int:** Row **int:** Column **LPCSTR:** Data	N/A	CCFXQuery	Sets a value at the specified index.
GetError	N/A	LPCSTR	CCFXException	Returns basic user information.
GetDiagnostics	N/A	LPCSTR	CCFXException	Returns detailed diagnostics about error.

Table 26-2.   *C++ ColdFusion Classes and Methods* (continued)

The CCFXStringSet class is used to deal with string collections. It is the equivalent of an array of strings in ColdFusion. To create a string, you can use AddString. To get the string, you can use GetString or GetIndexForString. The GetCount function tells you how many strings are in the collection.

You can create, access, and modify queries using the CCFXQuery class. To get information from a query, use GetColumns, GetData, GetName, or GetRowCount. To set data, you can use the AddRow or SetData method.

The final class is the CCFXException class. It allows you to do deal with exceptions that are thrown by the tag. It has two methods: GetError, to get the general error information, and GetDiagnostics, to get the full diagnostic information.

Creating the C++ Custom Tag

With an understanding of the classes behind you, you can create your custom tag in C++. C++ must compile into a DLL to be used as a custom tag. Because of this, any programming language that can be used to create a DLL can be used to create a CFX custom tag. The custom classes that are provided by Macromedia must be converted to that alternate programming language. Macromedia provides the classes in a file called cfx.h. It is located in the cfx\include directory of your ColdFusion installation.

When you install ColdFusion for the first time on your machine, you have an option to install a CFXAPI Tag Development Kit. This option automatically installs a CFX Custom Tag Wizard for use from Microsoft Visual C++ Studio. Using this wizard is, by far, the easiest way to create a custom tag.

This is how to finish your custom tag after using the wizard:

1. The relevant file where we write the tag functionality is Request.cpp. The first step in the code is to include the necessary files:

```
#include "stdafx.h"  // Standard MFC libraries
#include "cfx.h"     // CFX Custom Tag API
#include <fstream.h> // File Streams
```

There are three files included here: stdafx.h, which encompasses commonly used directives; cfx.h, which contains the ColdFusion classes; and fstream.h, which will allow us to access the files.

2. Set up the method that will automatically be called when we call the custom tag:

```
void ProcessTagRequest( CCFXRequest* pRequest ){
}
```

3. Within the method, include some error-handling features:

```
Try{
 // Code here
}

// Catch Cold Fusion exceptions & re-raise them
catch( CCFXException* e )
```

```
{
 pRequest->ReThrowException( e ) ;
}

// Catch ALL other exceptions and throw them as
// Cold Fusion exceptions (DO NOT REMOVE! --
// this prevents the server from crashing in
// case of an unexpected exception)
catch( ... )
{
 pRequest->ThrowException(
   "Error occurred in tag CFX_READLINE",
   "Unexpected error occurred while processing tag." ) ;
}
```

This code is filled in automatically by the CFX Custom Tag Wizard, and is not something that I wrote specifically for this tag. It performs error checking, just in case there are errors in any of the code that was written. The real meat of the tag lies in the try block.

4. Initialize the variables. As with the tag we wrote in Java, three variables are expected to be passed into this tag:

```
// check if file variable is defined
if ( pRequest->AttributeExists( "File" )==FALSE ){
 pRequest->ThrowException("CFX_ReadLine",
                           "Missing attribute (File)");
}

// check if the ReturnLine variable exists
if ( pRequest->AttributeExists( "ReturnLine" )==FALSE ){
 pRequest->ThrowException("CFX_ReadLine",
                           "Missing attribute (ReturnLine)");
}

// check if the ReturnLocation variable exists
if ( pRequest->AttributeExists( "ReturnLocation" )==FALSE ){
 pRequest->ThrowException("CFX_ReadLine",
                           "Missing attribute (ReturnLocation)");
}

long CurrentLine = 0;
// Check for Line to Get.  If Blank, default is 0
if ( pRequest->AttributeExists("CurrentLocation")==TRUE ){
 // get CurrentLineAttribute
 CurrentLine = atol(pRequest->GetAttribute("CurrentLocation"));
}
```

As with the Java tag, there are four attributes passed in here. We check to make sure that the File, ReturnLine, and ReturnLocation are set. If the CurrentLine is not set, we give it a default value of 0. That will put us at the beginning of the file.

5. Initialize the file:

```
// initialize the file
ifstream MyFile;
MyFile.open(pRequest->GetAttribute("File"));
```

To get the file, we use the ifstream class. The open method sets up the file so we can read from it. We pass the File attribute into it.

6. After the file is set up, we need to find the place where our new line starts:

```
// skip to the current place in the file
MyFile.seekg (CurrentLine);
```

The seekg method of the ifstream object moves to the specified position in the file.

7. After getting to the position in the file, we can read the line. This is the code:

```
// Read the Line
char Line[256];
MyFile.getline(Line, 256);
```

To read a line from the file, using the ifstream object, we can use the getline method. The getline method accepts three parameters. The first is an array of characters. C++ does not have a built-in string object. The second is the limit to the number of characters that are going to be read. You can set this value to anything that you need. The third value is the end of line character. If you leave it out, a default end of line character is used. This code uses the default.

8. Return the values to the user:

```
// return the line
LPCSTR ReturnLineName = pRequest->GetAttribute("ReturnLine");
pRequest->SetVariable(ReturnLineName,Line);

// get the current file pointer
char Loc[1];
ltoa(MyFile.tellg(), Loc, 10);

// return the location
LPCSTR ReturnLocationName =
                    pRequest->GetAttribute("ReturnLocation");
pRequest->SetVariable(ReturnLocationName,Loc);
```

The first step is to send back the ReturnLine value. First, we get the specified name of the variable, using the LPCSTR type. Then, we return the value using the SetVariable method of the pRequest object. The second step is to get the return pointer of the file. We use the tellg method of the ifstream object. The ltoa function is used to convert the long into a character. The three parameters of this function are the value you want to covert, the variable you are putting the result in, and the base that the conversion will take place in. We want our results in base 10.

9. Close the file:

```
// close the file
MyFile.close();
```

The file is closed using the close method. You can now compile the code into a DLL file.

Calling the Custom Tag

To use the custom tag from within a ColdFusion template, you need to register it from the ColdFusion Administrator. This was discussed in more detail in Chapter 6. You can select the CFX Tags link under Extensions in the ColdFusion Administrator. Click the Register C++ CFX button. You will need to enter this information:

- **Tag Name**   Specifies the tag that you want to use to create the DLL.

- **Server Library**   Needs to contain the absolute directory path to the server's DLL.

- **Procedure**   Specifies the name of the procedure in the DLL to call. Most likely this will be ProcessTagRequest.

- **Keep Library Loaded**   Tells ColdFusion whether or not to load the library in memory and keep it there. If you are going to be using this custom tag a lot, then checking this box will improve performance.

- **Description**   Can be anything you want to set it to.

The code that we use to call this tag is similar to the code that we used to call the Java tag. I named the C tag CFX_CGetLine instead of CFX_GetLine. Here is the code:

```
<!--- Get the first line from the custom tag --->
<CFX_CGetLine currentlocation="0" file="C:\ testFile.cfm"
    returnline="MyReturnLine" returnlocation="MyReturnLoc">

<!--- Output the First Line of the page --->
<cfoutput>
 Return Line: #MyReturnLine#<br>
 Return Loc: #MyReturnLoc#<br>
</cfoutput>
<br>
```

```
<!--- Output the values from the custom tag --->
<CFX_CGetLine currentlocation="#MyReturnLoc#"
              file="C:\ testFile.cfm" returnline="MyReturnLine"
              returnlocation="MyReturnLoc">

<!--- Output the second line of the page --->
<cfoutput>
  Return Line: #MyReturnLine#<br>
  Return Loc: #MyReturnLoc#<br>
</cfoutput>
```

Once again, this example code will run the tag twice, returning the first two lines from the file. The second time the tag is run, we pass it the returned location from the first time the tag was run.

Enhancing the Custom Tag

The custom tag that was developed in this chapter is probably not ready for a production environment. Although it is good enough to demonstrate the creation of a custom tag, the tag created does not have the error-checking requirements that would be necessary to make it a viable solution in a production environment. Some issues that you may need to address are the following:

- What happens when someone tries to retrieve data past the end of the file?
- What happens if an invalid filename is passed into the tag?
- What happens if the file is perfectly valid, but cannot be accessed for some reason, such as it is locked by another process?
- What happens if the ReturnLine or ReturnLocation variables are passed into the tag with invalid variable names as values?
- What happens if the CurrentLocation variable is not an integer?

These are just some of the issues that may need to be addressed further before I would recommend rolling this tag out in a production environment.

 You can check out www.intrafoundation.com to find a similar tag that includes many of the error-handling functionalities just described.

Summary

In this chapter, you learned about the following:

- Java custom tag classes
- How to create CFX custom tags with C++
- How to create a custom tag in Java and C++

The next chapter will teach you how to use XML and WDDX within your ColdFusion applications.

The
Complete
Reference

ColdFusion
MX

Chapter 27

Sharing Data with WDDX or XML

The future of data sharing resides in XML. XML is a way to define a standard data format so that applications, whether they are web-based or not, can use the same data. One of the most common uses of XML is to share data between separate applications. XML is platform independent and can be used on any operating system, including Windows, Linux, or Unix, and from within any programming language, whether it be ColdFusion, .NET, or C++. In addition to covering XML in depth, this chapter introduces WDDX, which is an implementation of XML that was originally developed by Allaire, the company that created ColdFusion.

Creating and Using XML Documents

This section describes what XML is. It demonstrates the XML functions and methods from within ColdFusion and steps you through the creation of an example application that might use XML.

Describing XML

This section offers a brief overview of XML and shows you how you can apply XML concepts in your own development. It explains document type definitions (DTDs) and how you can use existing DTDs to create your own XML documents.

Understanding XML

XML stands for Extensible Markup Language. In the buzzword flurry, it is hard to pin down exactly what XML is. XML is a language used to define your data. It is a language used to define other markup languages. It is a set of rules that can be used to create a markup language of your own design. It has a tag-based syntax, similar to HTML. XML is designed to be expanded upon to meet individual needs, whereas HTML is a strict standard. The easiest way to describe it is with an example.

Suppose that you are a company that builds copiers. Your products are sold through a series of independent dealers, but customers still come to you for support. You need to be able to create corporate data sheets on each of your products. Many of your dealers want to be able to create customized data sheets that highlight their dealer information, as opposed to the information from your corporation. Additionally, you want to be able to provide the dealers with information to use on their web site, without being committed to the look and feel of the corporation's web site.

The answer to your data sharing needs lies in XML. You can create an XML feed of the product specifications and use that XML feed to create the data sheets on your own site. You then can tell your dealers where to get the feed, thereby giving them access to the same information that you have, and enabling them to use it to create custom brochures and post the data on their web sites.

The power of XML resides in the sharing of data. There are two different aspects of XML that you need to note. The first is the aspect that defines the language, which most commonly is a document type definition (DTD). A DTD defines the structure of the data. The second aspect is the XML document, which is created based on the rules set forth in the DTD. There are many DTDs in existence that were created for one purpose or another, so you may not have to create one from scratch to suit your needs.

Using Macromedia's Document Type Definitions

Your DTD document is made up of any number of four different DTD tags: an element declaration, an attribute-list declaration, an entity declaration, and a notation declaration. Entity declarations are just a way to include other DTDs in the current one. This is useful for simplifying a DTD. Notation declarations are used to give a name to a DTDs or to certain parts of a DTD. Full exploration of notation and entity declarations is beyond the scope of this chapter, but attribute-list and element declarations will be examined in more depth.

> **Tip**   *I strongly suggest examining some existing DTDs before trying to create your own.*

Macromedia offers an XML resource feed for developers. You can use it to display resources and articles from the Macromedia developer center on your own home page. This section explains the DTD elements by using this resource feed as an example.

You can view the Macromedia resource feed DTD at www.macromedia.com/desdev/resources/macromedia_resources.dtd. Here is what we see when we look at it:

```
<!ELEMENT macromedia_resources (resource*)>
```

The DTD starts with an element. Elements of a DTD are specified using the < angle bracket and an exclamation point. This is different than HTML, which only uses < to specify tags. The name of the element is macromedia_resources. After that comes the type of the element. Valid types are Empty, Any, Mixed, or children. Empty and Any are specified by the keywords Empty and Any, respectively. Children data are designed for tags that have subtags. You would specify the name of the child element. Mixed types contain character data, interspersed with child elements. In this case, we have a subtag named resource. The asterisk means that zero or more of this element can occur.

Next, you will notice an attribute-list DTD tag. Attribute-list DTD tags specify the attributes for a particular element. This is the attribute-list:

```
<!ATTLIST
        macromedia_resources
        xmlns:macromedia_resources
        CDATA
        #REQUIRED>
```

It starts with the keyword ATTLIST. It is followed by the attribute name, which in this case is xmlns:macromedia_resources. After the name comes a list of associated attributes.

The attributes could be text values, names of other elements, or one of the keywords #Required, #Implied, or #Fixed. If it is #Fixed, then a default value must be specified. This attribute list will be used to specify the URL location of the DTD. It is character data and required.

This is not an exhaustive explanation of XML DTDs. Check out www.w3.org/TR/1998/ REC-xml-19980210.html or www.w3.org/TR/REC-xml for more information.

Next comes the resource element:

```
<!ELEMENT resource (
                title,
                author,
                url,
                product+
                )>
```

The resource element is made up of four other elements: title, author, url, and product. The comma specifies the and operator. So, resource is made up of a title element, an author element, and a url element. The plus sign after product specifies that there must be one or more product elements.

An attribute to the resource element is defined next:

```
<!ATTLIST resource
            type(
                Article |
                Column |
                TechNote |
                Tip |
                Tutorial |
                White_Paper |
                Sample_Application |
                Component |
                Extension
                )
            #REQUIRED>
```

The attribute to the resource element is type. The vertical var (|) is used to specify the or element. This means that the type attribute can have a value of Article, Column, TechNote, Tip, Tutorial, White_Paper, Sample_Application, Component, or Extension.

Next come the title, author, and url elements:

```
<!ELEMENT title  (#PCDATA)>
<!ELEMENT author  (#PCDATA)>
<!ELEMENT url  (#PCDATA)>
```

These three elements are simple elements, containing text (PCDATA) values.

Next comes the product element. You will remember that the product element differs from the other elements in the fact that there can be one or more product elements. This is its element declaration:

```
<!ELEMENT product  (category*)>
```

The element declaration specifies that the product is made up of zero or more category elements. There is also a name attribute that can be used with the product element:

```
<!ATTLIST
        product
        name (
                Dreamweaver |
                Fireworks |
                Dreamweaver_UltraDev |
                HomeSite |
                ColdFusion |
                Macromedia_Flash_Player |
                Macromedia_Generator |
                Macromedia_Spectra |
                Macromedia_Flash |
                FreeHand |
                Director |
                Sitespring |
                Authorware |
                Shockwave_Player |
                JRun |
                Fontographer |
                SoundEdit_16)
        #REQUIRED>
```

The name attribute of the product element is required. Its valid values are Dreamweaver, Fireworks, Dreamweaver_UltraDev, HomeSite, ColdFusion, and so on.

INTEGRATING COLDFUSION
WITH OTHER
TECHNOLOGIES

Finally, the category definition is in the DTD:

```
<!ELEMENT category   (#PCDATA)>
<!ATTLIST
        category
        name
        CDATA
        #REQUIRED>
```

The category contains character data. Its only attribute is a name attribute. In practice, the category element is not being used at the time of this writing.

Examining an XML Document

With an understanding of the Macromedia DTD, you are ready to examine the XML document that it is created from. The document starts with an XML declaration:

```
<?xml version="1.0" ?>
```

This is used to specify which version of XML is used to create the document.

Next comes the macromedia_resources tag:

```
<macromedia_resources xmlns:macromedia_resources=
                    "http://www.macromedia.com/desdev/
                    resources/macromedia_resources.dtd">
```

The tag specifies the location of the resource feed.

Next comes the list of resources. Here is an example of one:

```
<resource type="Article">
 <title>The Story Behind Macromedia Studio MX</title>
 <author>Kevin Lynch</author>
 <url>http://www.macromedia.com/desdev/mx/studio/articles/smx.html</url>
 <product name="ColdFusion" />
 <product name="Dreamweaver" />
 <product name="Fireworks" />
 <product name="FreeHand" />
 <product name="Macromedia_Flash" />
 </resource>
```

The resource starts with the resource tag. It specifies the type as an attribute. This resource is an article. Then comes the title, author, and URL information. Following that is a list of product tags, with the attribute specifying each individual product that this article is associated with.

Accessing XML from Within ColdFusion

This section examines the functions and tags that allow you to access and use XML from within ColdFusion. It goes on to show you an example of the Macromedia XML resource feed and teach you how to integrate it into your web site.

Using ColdFusion's XML Tags and Functions

To deal with XML documents within ColdFusion, you need to create a new XML document object. Table 27-1 lists and describes all the XML functions and tags available in ColdFusion.

Name	Tag/ Function	Parameters	Description
cfxml	Tag	**variable:** Name of the XML document object **casesensitive:** Whether or not the XML object will be considered case sensitive (default is no)	Creates an XML document object by defining it between open and close cfxml tags.
IsXMLDoc	Function	**value:** Name of XML document object	Checks whether given value is an XML document object.
IsXMLElement	Function	**value:** Name of XML document object element	Checks whether the given value is an element of the XML document.
IsXMLRoot	Function	**value:** Name of XML document object element	Checks whether the given value is the root element of an XML document.
XMLChildPos	Function	**element:** Name of XML element **childname:** Child element to search under **n:** Index of child element you want to search through	Returns the position of a child element within an XML document object.
XMLNew	Function	**casesensitive:** Boolean value indicating whether or not the new object will be case sensitive	Returns an empty XML document.

Table 27-1. *ColdFusion XML Tags and Functions*

Name	Tag/ Function	Parameters	Description
XMLFormat	Function	**String:** The string you want to format in XML	Returns the value you specified with XML characters escaped.
XMLParse	Function	**XmlString:** XML document object **casesensitive:** Boolean value indicating whether or not the new object will be case sensitive	Converts a string variable into an XML document object.
XMLSearch	Function	**xmldoc:** The XML document object **xpathstring:** XPath expression	Uses an XPath expression to search the XML document. XPath is beyond the scope of this book. Go to /www.w3.org/ TR/xpath for more information.
XMLTransform	Function	**xml:** An XML document or string **xslstring:** The XSLT transformation to apply	Applies XSLT (Extensible Stylesheet Language Transformation) to a specified XML document or string. XSLT is beyond the scope of this book.

Table 27-1. *ColdFusion XML Tags and Functions* (continued)

Creating an XML Document Object

You can create an empty XML document using the XMLNew function. You can also create a new element by using the cfxml tag. This section demonstrates how to use the cfxml tag. As discussed in the previous section, the cfxml tag has two attributes, the variable name and casesensitive attribute. For the time being, the Macromedia resource feed will be abandoned in favor of something simpler, but it will be revisited later in this chapter.

Suppose we are creating an XML document that defines a record collection. Here is an example document:

```
<cfxml variable="MyXMLDoc" caseSensitive="No">
 <cdcollection>
  <album type="cd">
   <band>Far Cry Fly</band>
   <name>Audience Participation</name>
   <song track="2">Simple Melody</song>
   <song track="7">Falling</song>
  </album>

  <album type="tape">
   <band>Spin Doctors</band>
   <name>Pocket Full of Kryptonite</name>
   <song track="7">Two Princes</song>
   <song track="1">Jimmy Olsen Blues</song>
  </album>
 </cdcollection>
</cfxml>
```

The root of the XML document is the cdcollection tag. The cdcollection is made up of a bunch of different albums. Each album constitutes a child of the cdcollection. Albums contain children of their own, including band, name, and songs.

An XML document starts with a top-level element and can have any number of subelements nested inside it. Figure 27-1 shows a representation of the cdcollection document. The top level is a document object. Inside the document object is the root element, cdcollection. Inside the cdcollection, each album is listed. Inside the album are the specific elements of that album, including the band, name, and songs. Attributes and values of the album are located at the same level.

XML data is stored internally as a mix of ColdFusion structures and arrays. Table 27-2 shows a list of elements of an XML document and how they are stored. In a simple description, attributes are stored as a structure. Nodes and children are stored as arrays. Everything else is stored as a string.

At first glance, it may seem tricky to put the XML document and the table together. To learn how to access the values in the XML document object, it is best to compare them side by side:

XML Structure	How to Access
<cdcollection>	No data to access
<album type="cd">	MyXMLDoc.cdcollection.album[1].XmlAttributes.Type
<band>Far Cry Fly</band>	MyXMLDoc.cdcollection.album[1].band.XMLNodes[1].XMLValue
<name>Audience Participation</name>	MyXMLDoc.cdcollection.album[1].name.XMLNodes[1].XMLValue

XML Structure	How to Access
<song track="2">Simple Melody</song>	MyXMLDoc.cdcollection.album[1].song[1].XMLNodes[1].XMLValue MyXMLDoc.cdcollection.album[1].song[1].XmlAttributes.Track
<song track="7">Falling</song>	MyXMLDoc.cdcollection.album[1].song[2].XMLNodes[1].XMLValue MyXMLDoc.cdcollection.album[1].song[2].XmlAttributes.Track
</album>	No data to access
</cdcollection>	No data to access

It is worthy to note that when you are accessing the songs or albums, if you leave out the array element, it defaults to 1. You can use this technique on any of the arrays in an XML document.

You probably noticed in the previous table that the variable names used to access specific entities within the XML structure are rather long. There is a solution. You can take specific elements and set variables to them:

```
<cfset MyAlbum = MyXMLDoc.cdcollection.album>
```

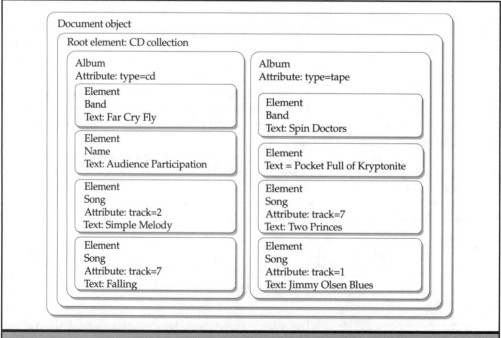

Figure 27-1.   *A graphical representation of an XML document*

Entry Name	Type	Relates To	Description
XMLRoot	No data	Document object structure	Top-level root element.
XMLComment	String	Document object structure	A string that contains all comments in the document prolog (beginning) or epilogue (end).
XMLDoctype	XMLNode	Document object structure	Specifies the doctype attribute of the document. It only exists if a doctype is specified.
XMLName	String	Element	The name of the element.
XMLNSPrefix	String	Element	The prefix of the namespace.
XMLNSURL	String	Element	The URL of the namespace.
XMLText	String	Element	Contains all data in the element, excluding children data.
XMLComment	String	Element	Contains all comments in the current element, but not in children elements.
XMLAttributes	Structure	Element	A structure of all attributes and their values to the current element.
XMLChildren	Array	Element	An array of all of this element's children elements. This is an array of structures.
XMLParent	XMLNode	Element	The parent of the current node.
XMLNodes	Array	Element	An array of all nodes in this element.
XMLName	String	Node	The node name.
XMLType	String	Node	The node type. Valid values are CDATA, COMMENT, ELEMENT, ENTITYREF, PI, TEXT, ENTITY, NOTATION, DOCUMENT, FRAGMENT, or DOCTYPE.
XMLValue	String	Node	The value of the current node.

Table 27-2.   *XML Elements and Their ColdFusion Types*

You now have a single variable that contains the album information. You can output the values by looping over them:

```
<cfloop index="Index" from="1" to="#ArrayLen(MyAlbum)#">
 <cfoutput>
  Album Type: #MyAlbum[Index].XmlAttributes.Type#<br>
  Band: #MyAlbum[Index].band.XMLNodes[1].XMLValue#<br>
  Name: #MyAlbum[Index].name.XMLNodes[1].XMLValue#<br>
  Song Name: #MyAlbum[Index].song[1].XMLNodes[1].XMLValue#<br>
  Track Number: #MyAlbum[Index].song[1].XmlAttributes.Track#<br>
  Song Name: #MyAlbum[Index].song[2].XMLNodes[1].XMLValue#<br>
  Track Number: #MyAlbum[Index].song[2].XmlAttributes.Track#<br>
 </cfoutput>
</cfloop>
```

With more real-world data, you would probably want to apply a similar method to the songs with the original loop:

```
<cfloop index="AlbumIndex" from="1" to="#ArrayLen(MyAlbum)#">
 <cfoutput>
  Album Type: #MyAlbum[AlbumIndex].XmlAttributes.Type#<br>
  Band: #MyAlbum[AlbumIndex].band.XMLNodes[1].XMLValue#<br>
  Name: #MyAlbum[AlbumIndex].name.XMLNodes[1].XMLValue#<br>
  <!--- get the songs array into a variable --->
  <cfset AlbumSongs= MyAlbum[AlbumIndex].song>
  <!--- Loop over it --->
  <cfloop index="SongIndex" from="1" to="#ArrayLen(AlbumSongs)#">
   Song Name: #AlbumSongs[SongIndex].XMLNodes[1].XMLValue#<br>
   Track Number: #AlbumSongs[SongIndex].XmlAttributes.Track#<br>
  </cfloop>
 </cfoutput><br>
</cfloop>
```

Instead of manually outputting the song list, which can have more than one entry, the song array is set to the AlbumSongs variable. By looping over the AlbumSongs variable, we can write code that will work no matter how many songs are listed.

Retrieving the Macromedia Resource Feed DTD

This section puts the previous examples to use by writing a function that will retrieve and output the Macromedia XML resource feed and turn it into a ColdFusion query. First, we can examine a shortened version of the XML document:

```
<?xml version="1.0" ?>
<macromedia_resources xmlns:macromedia_resources=
                      "http://www.macromedia.com/desdev/
                       resources/macromedia_resources.dtd">
 <resource type="Article">
  <title>The Story Behind Macromedia Studio MX</title>
  <author>Kevin Lynch</author>
  <url>http://www.macromedia.com/desdev/mx/studio/articles/smx.html</url>
  <product name="ColdFusion" />
  <product name="Dreamweaver" />
  <product name="Fireworks" />
  <product name="FreeHand" />
  <product name="Macromedia_Flash" />
  </resource>
 <resource type="Tutorial">
  <title>New Macromedia Studio MX Application Development Center</title>
  <author>Macromedia</author>
  <url>http://www.macromedia.com/desdev/mx/studio/</url>
  <product name="ColdFusion" />
  <product name="Dreamweaver" />
  <product name="Fireworks" />
  <product name="FreeHand" />
  <product name="Macromedia_Flash" />
  </resource>
</macromedia_resources>
```

As you know from examining the DTD earlier in this chapter, the document root is macromedia_resources. It contains a list of resources. The resources are made up of a title, author, url, and a list of product tags that specify the product that this resource relates to.

This is how we can create a function to get the resource feed and turn it into a ColdFusion query. In our process, we use two functions: one to get the resource feed and a second to turn it into a ColdFusion query.

1. Create the function definition:

   ```
   <cffunction name="GetMacromediaXMLResourceFeed">
   </cffunction>
   ```

2. Get the resource feed by using the cfhttp tag:

   ```
   <CFHTTP url="http://www.macromedia.com/desdev/
               resources/macromedia_resources.xml"
               method="GET">
   </CFHTTP>
   ```

3. After getting the feed, we need to translate it into a ColdFusion XML document object. We can return the document object in the same line of code:

   ```
   <cfreturn #XMLParse(cfhttp.FileContent)#>
   ```

This code takes the FileContent returned by the cfhttp tag and passes the string through the XMLParse function, which creates the XML document from the string.

4. With a function to get the resource feed, we now write a function to parse the XML document object and turn it into a ColdFusion query. To do these actions, CFScript is the best choice:

```
<cfscript>

 function TranslateResourceFeed(S){
 }
</cfscript>
```

The previous code sets up the function definition. One variable is passed into the function, S, which is expected to contain an XML document object, created from the Macromedia resource feed.

5. Define some default variables:

```
// Create the Query
var ResultQuery = QueryNew("Type, Title, Author,
                            URL, ProductName");


// Get a pointer to the Resource Array
var MacromediaResources = S.macromedia_resources.resource;


// This will be a pointer to the Product Names used in
// the loop
var ProductNames = "";


// Loop Counter Variables
var ResourceIndex= 1;
var ProductIndex = 1;


// Var RowNumber for use of keeping track of current record
var RowNumber = 0;
```

First, the result query is created. The QueryNew function is used, as we discussed in Chapter 21. The query will have a column for Type, Title, Author, URL, and ProductName. Next, the resource array is set to the variable MacromediaResources. An array to the Products array is initialized to zero. The pointer won't be used or set until later in this chapter. Two loop control variables, ResourceIndex and ProductIndex, are initialized next. Finally, a RowNumber variable is used to keep track of the current record in the result query.

6. To create our query, two loops are needed. One loop will loop over the resource array, MacromediaResources. The second loop will be located inside the first loop and will loop over the product array, ProductNames. This code loops over the MacromediaResources array:

```
for (ResourceIndex =1;
     ResourceIndex LTE ArrayLen(MacromediaResources );
     ResourceIndex=ResourceIndex+1) {

 ProductNames =  MacromediaResources[ResourceIndex].product;
}
```

This loop initializes the ProductNames array using the ResourceIndex variable. Inside this loop another loop must be located:

```
for (ProductIndex =1;
     ProductIndex LTE ArrayLen(ProductNames );
     ProductIndex=ProductIndex+1) {

 // add a new row to the query
 RowNumber = QueryAddRow(ResultQuery);

 // populate Query
 QuerySetCell(ResultQuery, "Type",
             MacromediaResources[ResourceIndex].
                          XMLAttributes.Type, RowNumber);
 QuerySetCell(ResultQuery, "Title",
             MacromediaResources[ResourceIndex].
                     title.XMLNodes[1].XMLValue, RowNumber);
 QuerySetCell(ResultQuery, "Author",
             MacromediaResources[ResourceIndex].
                     author.XMLNodes[1].XMLValue, RowNumber);
 QuerySetCell(ResultQuery, "URL",
             MacromediaResources[ResourceIndex].
                     url.XMLNodes[1].XMLValue, RowNumber);

 QuerySetCell(ResultQuery, "ProductName",
        ProductNames[ProductIndex].XMLAttributes.Name, RowNumber);
}
```

The inner loop loops over the ProductNames array. It creates a new row in the ResultQuery variable. Then the QuerySetCell function is used to add the specific values to the query. The loop ends and the next iteration of the outer loop (MacromediaResources) starts.

7. The final step of our function is to return the ResultQuery:

```
Return ResultQuery;
```

The statement uses the Return keyword to send the ResultQuery variable back to the function's caller.

8. You can try these two functions with code like this:

```
<cfoutput>
 <cfset MyName = #TranslateResourceFeed(
                         GetMacromediaXMLResourceFeed())#>
 <cfdump var="#MyName#">
</cfoutput>
```

The cfdump output will be similar to the following:

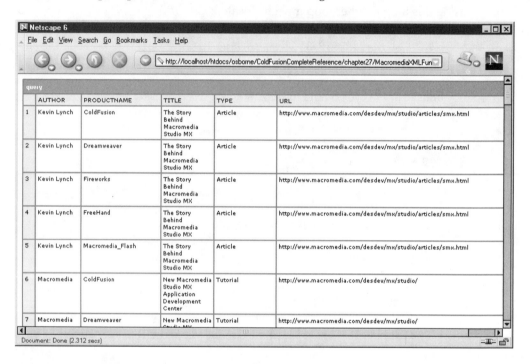

Using WDDX in ColdFusion

This section introduces you to Web Distributed Data Exchange (WDDX). It is the name for an XML DTD that makes it easy to share ColdFusion variables with other applications. WDDX was introduced as part of ColdFusion before XML was fully understood. As ColdFusion includes more native XML features and XML becomes an industry standard, the benefits of WDDX decrease, but if you want to share data between ColdFusion applications, there is no better or easier tool than WDDX.

Using the cfwddx Tag

The process of transforming data from its native language to WDDX is known as *serializing* the data. The process of transforming data from WDDX back to its native language is known as *deserializing* the data. ColdFusion provides a tag, cfwddx, that allows you to perform serialization and deserialization of ColdFusion data.

These are the attributes to the cfwddx tag:

- **action** The action attribute is required. It should be set to one of the following: cfml2wddx, to change from CFML to WDDX format; wddx2cfml, to change from WDDX to CFML; cfml2js, to change from CFML to JavaScript; or wddx2js, to change from WDDX to JavaScript format.

- **input** Accepts the value that that tag will process (required attribute). If you give it a variable name, make sure that you surround it with pound signs, so the value is returned and not the variable name.

- **output** Specifies the name of the variable that will contain the results of the action. If this attribute is omitted, the result is output into the HTML stream.

- **toplevelvariable** If you are converting from WDDX or CFML to JavaScript, this specifies the name of the JavaScript variable that will contain the WDDX object.

- **usetimezoneinfo** Specifies whether to use time zone information when serializing from CFML to WDDX (Boolean attribute). The default is yes.

- **validate** Specifies whether to validate WDDX input before changing WDDX to CFML or JavaScript (Boolean attribute). If set to yes, it validates WDDX input before changing WDDX to CFML or JavaScript. The default value is no.

It is very easy to use the WDDX tag to transform variables from one format to another. To transform a CFML structure to a WDDX object, use this code:

```
<cfwddx action="cfml2wddx" input="#MyColdFusionVariable#"
        output="MyWDDXVariable">
```

To transform the data back, you can get it using the cfhttp tag and deserialize it with cfwddx:

```
<cfhttp url="http://localhost/MyWDDX.cfm" resolveurl="no">
<cfwddx action="wddx2cfml" input="#cfhttp.FileContent#"
        output=" MyColdFusionVariable">
```

The DTD for WDDX can be found at www.openwddx.org/downloads/dtd/ wddx_dtd_10.txt. You can check out the www.openwddx.org site for more WDDX information.

Finding Uses for WDDX in Your Development

There are numerous uses for the WDDX technology:

- You can share query, structure, or other ColdFusion information between two ColdFusion applications. Since WDDX is built into ColdFusion, sharing the information between the two sites is very easy. On the presenting site, use the cfwddx tag with the action set to cfml2wddx. On the receiving site, use the cfwddx tag with the action set to wddx2cfml.

- You can use WDDX to serialize complex variables into strings and then store them as client variables. This provides flexibility in situations where client variables are a better choice than session variables.

- If you want to easily make your ColdFusion variables available to JavaScript objects, use ColdFusion's cfwddx tag with the action set to cfml2js.

- Transforming WDDX objects directly to JavaScript can also be done using the cfwddx tag with the wddx2js action.

- There is WDDX support built into many languages, so you can use the cfwddx tag to share your data with anyone using other technologies, such as Active Server Pages (ASP) or PHP Hypertext Processor (PHP).

- Use WDDX to store a denormalized data structure in a database. In some cases, a denormalized data structure can improve performance because you have to perform fewer joins to get the data you need. Denormalized data does make it harder to keep the data up-to-date, though. When using this method, I prefer to keep my data normalized in the database for data modifications and routinely run a scheduled task that will update a separate denormalized table for the complex joins.

Summary

In this chapter, you learned about the following:

- Extensible Markup Language
- How to create a function to transform Macromedia's XML resource feed into a ColdFusion query
- WDDX and it uses within ColdFusion

The next chapter will show you how to use ColdFusion with Flash.

The
Complete
Reference

ColdFusion
MX

Chapter 28

Integrating
ColdFusion MX
and Flash MX

With the release of its MX suite of products, Macromedia has taken great strides to make each MX product closely integrate with other MX products. ColdFusion and Flash MX are no exception. This chapter teaches you about developing Flash applications and how Flash can work together with ColdFusion.

Understanding Macromedia Flash

This section teaches you about Macromedia Flash and how it can be used in web development. It introduces ActionScript, which is the language of Flash.

Explaining Macromedia Flash

Macromedia has stated unequivocally that it sees full-blown application development in the near future for Flash. Traditionally, Flash has been used exclusively for client-side development. Flash has become the industry-standard platform for developing rich animations, games, and cutting-edge media presentations on the Web. Because Flash programs are executed in the run-time environment of a browser plug-in, developers are for the most part shielded from the cross-browser compatibility issues commonly associated with DHTML and other client-side scripting languages.

In recent years, companies have begun examining Flash as a presentation layer solution for serious web-enabled business applications. Flash MX may change this forever, as companies can now consider Flash for more than just the presentation layer of their business applications. Entire web-enabled and stand-alone applications can be developed in Flash MX. ColdFusion developers need to master two key new features in Flash MX to be able to work with other Flash developers on a common project, design Flash-enabled sites, and implement ColdFusion/Flash MX code-based applications.

The first major new feature is the ability to call remote Web services from Flash movies. Before Flash MX, a developer who needed to make his or her Flash movie leverage server-side processing or business logic had to write ActionScript (the Flash scripting language) that would request a dynamic page URL (which in turn spat back name-value pairs). While Flash MX is still primarily a client-side technology, MX enables users to request Web services across a network. This functionality, coupled with the ability to create ColdFusion Components (see Chapter 16) that expose themselves as Web services (Chapter 31), allows for the easy exchange of data between ColdFusion and Flash applications.

The second Flash MX core new feature that helps developers to leverage the power of ColdFusion from their Flash applications is server-side ActionScript. ActionScript, the European Computer Manufacturer's Association (ECMA)-based language used to write code in the Flash environment, can now also be used to write ActionScript files that reside on the server and have the ability to invoke certain ColdFusion MX Application Server functionality without having to make an HTTP request for a CFML template. These server-side ActionScript files can easily be invoked from Flash applications.

This chapter cannot teach you everything you need to know about Flash to start creating Flash applications. What it will teach you is how ColdFusion MX and Flash MX "talk" to each other, and how ColdFusion applications can be written in such a way as to allow Flash developers to leverage the might of your ColdFusion applications. We will examine not only the specifics of how to write Flash-compatible ColdFusion code, but also the ActionScript syntax necessary to leverage ColdFusion from within Flash MX applications. I recommend familiarizing yourself with the Flash IDE, picking up a good book on Flash MX ActionScript, and practicing these techniques. (*Macromedia Flash MX: The Complete Reference* by Brian Underdahl, McGraw-Hill/Osborne, 2002, is a good choice.) Understanding how to build business applications with Flash MX will likely prove to be a very valuable weapon in your web development arsenal.

Explaining ActionScript

ActionScript is an ECMA-compliant scripting language used to script objects and write business logic in the Flash environment. In Flash MX, ActionScript is now, for all intents and purposes, an object-oriented language. It also happens to be a loosely typed language, meaning variables are dynamically cast from data type to data type as needed in the code. Everything in Flash fits into an object model—a movie-based object model (commonly referred to as MOM). Does all of this sound familiar? If you've done any work with JavaScript, it should. JavaScript is also an ECMA-compliant scripting language that is capable (for all intents and purposes) of object-oriented application development. In fact, you'll find that, for the most part, JavaScript and ActionScript code look almost identical in syntax. JavaScript is also loosely typed, and uses an object model as well (its object model is document based—commonly referred to as DOM).

As mentioned before, Flash allows for business logic to be written in ColdFusion and isolated from the Flash-based presentation layer of an application. Traditionally, Flash (and DHTML/HTML) user interfaces used standard HTTP GET and POST operations to communicate back and forth across the Internet with a ColdFusion application server in order to be dynamically driven. Flash MX communicates with ColdFusion MX via AMF (Action Message Format), which has support for data typing and complex data binding as well as incremental recordset retrieval and other advanced communication layer features. The major advantage to using AMF is the conversion of ActionScript native data types to ColdFusion native data types, and vice versa. We'll look at how to pass values back and forth between ColdFusion and Flash in the next sections, but you can review the data types and their equivalents in Table 28-1.

ColdFusion Data Type	ActionScript Data Type
Boolean	Boolean
string	string
number	number
date	date object
structure	ActionScript object
array of structures	array
XML (an XML String)	ActionScript XML object
NULL	NULL

Table 28-1.   *ColdFusion and Flash Data Types*

Writing Flash-Compatible ColdFusion Templates

There are two different ways to pass data back and forth between Flash and ColdFusion. The first way is to access ColdFusion templates directly from Flash. The second way is to access a ColdFusion Component as a Web service. This section examines both ways.

Passing Values Between Flash and ColdFusion

To pass values to and accept values from Flash from within a ColdFusion template, you use the flash scope. There are three variables ColdFusion developers need to know and understand: flash.Params, flash.Result, and flash.PageSize.

When a flash file requests and passes parameters to a ColdFusion template, those variables exist as keys in a structure known as flash.Params. You reference these values in one of two ways: with array syntax or with structure dot notation. When named parameters are passed from Flash, you reference the value(s) as flash.*ParameterName*. If an array of parameter values is passed from Flash, the values are referenced with array syntax like so: flash.Params[ArrayIndex].

For example, if you have a ColdFusion template that accepts a single parameter—a number representing the unique ID of an employee in an employee records table—the query would look something like this:

```
<cfquery name="GetEmployeeDetails" datasource="Chapter28">
  SELECT * FROM Employee
  WHERE EmployeeID = #flash.EmpID#
</cfquery>
```

If an array was passed from Flash, the code will look like this:

```
<cfquery name="GetEmployeeDetails" datasource="Chapter28">
 SELECT * FROM employee
 WHERE employeeID = #flash.Params[1]#
</cfquery>
```

Suppose you want to send the results of this query back to Flash. To send the result set back to Flash, your code needs to use the flash.result variable. Our code would now look like this:

```
<cfquery name="GetEmployeeDetails" datasource="Chapter28">
 SELECT * FROM Employee
 WHERE EmployeeID = #flash.EmpID#
</cfquery>
<cfset flash.Result = GetEmployeeDetails>
```

Now suppose that rather than selecting detail information for one employee, our page accepts a department ID and selects all employee information for all employees that work for this department. To limit the number of records sent back to a Flash movie at a time, you use the flash.PageSize variable. If we want our ColdFusion page to return five records at a time to the Flash movie, the code would look like this:

```
<cfquery name="GetDeptEmployeeDetails" datasource="Chapter28">
 SELECT * FROM employee
 WHERE employeeCategoryID = #flash.categoryid#
</cfquery>

<cfset flash.PageSize = 5>
<cfset flash.Result = GetEmployeeDetails>
```

In this example, we've specified that only five records at a time will be returned for use by the Flash movie. This keeps the Flash movie small and allows it to load faster. Behind the scenes, recordset loading control shifts from ColdFusion to Flash, and ColdFusion will ignore the flash.PageSize variable after the initial record set is requested. After this initialization, the Flash RecordSet object controls the incremental delivery with its SetDeliveryMethod function.

It is important to note that while the techniques previously discussed will allow a ColdFusion template to accept arguments from and pass values back to Flash, they also prevent the ColdFusion template from behaving the way templates traditionally behave. If a client (Internet user) were to request the template directly from a web browser (or the file were included using cfinclude), errors would be thrown since the flash scope now does not exist. Conditional logic should be employed in order to allow the template to also be cfincluded or browsed directly, like so:

```
<!--- www.instantcoldfusion.com

Description: Page to demonstrate a page that will work when
             called for Flash and accessed directory via the web.

Entering: N/A
Exiting: N/A

Dependencies: N/A
Expecting: flash.EmpID or form.EmpID

Modification History
Date        Modifier                 Modification
*************************************************************
06/03/2002 Simon Horwith, Figleaf   Created
--->

<!--- Copy the EmpID from the form or Flash scope for use in
      the query, otherwise display message and abort.   --->
<cfif IsDefined("flash.EmpID")>
 <cfset variables.EmpID = flash.EmpID>
<cfelseif IsDefined("form.EmpID")>
 <cfset variables.EmpID = form.EmpID>
<cfelse>
 You Must Supply an Employee ID from a form or from a Flash Movie!
 <cfabort>
</cfif>

<!--- Query Database --->
<cfquery name="GetEmployeeDetails" datasource="Chapter28">
 SELECT * FROM Employee
 WHERE EmployeeID = #variables.EmpID#
</cfquery>

<!--- Return Result to Flash --->
<cfset flash.Result = GetEmployeeDetails>

<!--- If called from Flash, Everything from here down will be
      ignored. --->
<cfoutput query="GetEmployeeDetails">
```

```
#GetEmployeeDetails.FirstName#
#GetEmployeeDetails.LastName#<br>
</cfoutput>
```

When calling local server ColdFusion templates from Flash, the web root directory that contains the ColdFusion template is represented as the service name in Flash, and the name of the file (CFM template) is represented as a function of that service. If, in the last example, the ColdFusion template were saved as GetDepTemps.cfm and saved in the C:\InetPub\WWWRoot\DeptInfo directory, it would be seen (and called) from Flash as the GetDeptEmps function of the DepInfo service. We'll examine the ActionScript specifics of calling ColdFusion templates later in this chapter.

Designing Flash MX-Compatible ColdFusion Components

ColdFusion MX, with its underlying Java architecture, allows developers to build CFML applications in a more object-oriented manner. A benefit of this approach to development is a complete separation of business processes from the presentation layer. ColdFusion Components implement this business logic as objects with callable methods and properties. By exposing a ColdFusion Component to the rest of the world as a Web service (allowing remote access to its methods and properties via SOAP), component functionality can be called from other local ColdFusion templates, Flash MX applications, or any other SOAP-enabled environment.

Tip	*For more information on ColdFusion Components, check out Chapter 16.*

By defining core business logic as callable components with methods and properties that return standard data types, code need not be modified or rewritten in order to work with different environments. If components are written to accept standard data typed arguments (if any), perform the requested operation, and return the results as a standard data typed variable, there needn't be any regard for what type of application made the request. This is a more ideal way to construct applications than writing Flash-specific CFML code in your ColdFusion templates. Once components have been written, the only thing that needs to be done to the ColdFusion code so that it can be called from Flash movies is to allow remote invocation for any function you want to remotely call. This is accomplished by specifying "access="remote" in the cffunction tag.

Another feature of components is that you can browse them and their descriptions from the Flash MX authoring environment Service Browser. The Service Browser is part of the Flash Remoting Components, which can be downloaded from http:// download.macromedia.com/pub/flash/flashremoting/FlashRemotingCmpntsInstall.exe. Once the Flash Remoting Components are installed, opening the Service Browser will reveal your default gateway (if it's not there, add it). You can then add any services you want, using the directory path from the web root to the component, separated by dots, with the component filename (without extension) at the end. For example, after creating hellotest.cfc in the comptest directory off of my root, my Service Browser shows the following:

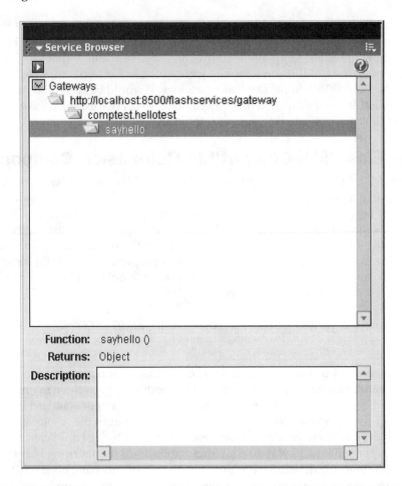

Components can be written comments in the description attribute of the cffunction tag. These comments will show up as documentation in the Flash Service Browser. A self-documenting component named "hellotest" that has a "sayhello" function that uses component metadata to document itself would look like this:

```
<cfcomponent>
 <cffunction name="SayHello"
             description="Returns a hello world message"
             access="remote">
  <cfset MSG = "Hello World">
```

```
<cfreturn MSG>
</cffunction>
</cfcomponent>
```

The code would appear like so in the Service Browser:

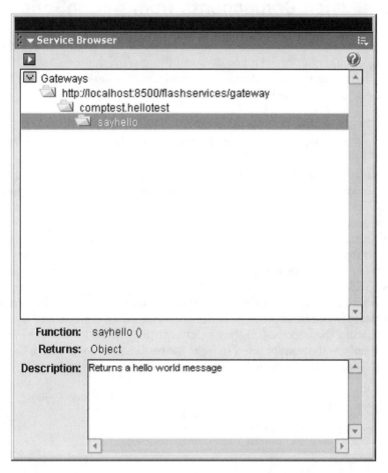

So far, we've examined the new ColdFusion MX coding techniques that expose CFML code to Flash movies. As a best practice, I'd use ColdFusion Components to interact with Flash. Using the flash scope in "regular" templates, calling ColdFusion file URLs via HTTP, and using other workarounds to execute CFM templates from Flash aren't as efficient, robust, or easy to implement as ColdFusion Components. In addition to calling ColdFusion templates from Flash, the MX family has introduced a new method of leveraging the ColdFusion server from Flash—server-side ActionScript. We'll first examine the ActionScript syntax used to call components, and then we'll take a look at what server-side ActionScript can do for us.

Learning ActionScript

This section introduces you to some aspects of ActionScript. There is no way to cover everything about ActionScript in a single chapter, so you should check your documentation from both ColdFusion MX and Flash MX for more information.

Calling ColdFusion Components from ActionScript

This section takes a general look at the syntax required to call Web services from ActionScript. ColdFusion Components are ridiculously easy to call from Flash movies; it's knowing enough ActionScript to do something with the result sent back from ColdFusion that poses the real dilemma for most ColdFusion developers. Flash movies communicate with a ColdFusion server via the Flash Gateway.

Note *As mentioned earlier, you need to install the Flash Remoting Components from http:// download.macromedia.com/pub/flash/flashremoting/FlashRemotingCmpntsInstall.exe.*

Once you have installed the Service Browser, open it and add your local gateway (or some other gateway) if it's not already listed. The URL should look something like http://localhost:8500/flashservices/gateway. Once the gateway is there, you click Add Service and then specify the web root path (separated by dots) and filename (without extension) to the ColdFusion Component you want to make browsable. Its functions and their descriptions will then be viewable in the Service Browser. It is not necessary to use the Service Browser, but it is a nice way to see what services are available, as well as the functions available to each service.

When coding Flash applications, it's considered a best practice to have a separate layer to hold all of your business logic code. This separates the visual and user interactive related code from the process(es) they might require. In your "actions" layer, code ActionScript objects that can be used to hold the results sent back from a ColdFusion Component. The syntax would look like this:

```
//Create an object to catch the CFC results to load into
// my select list
GetCategories = function(){
}

//The struct from the ColdFusion Component will be passed to
// this method as an ActionScript Object.
GetCategories.ProtoType.onResult = function(CFCResult){

//determine how many result sets have been returned from
// the server side component
CategoriesCount = CFCresult.GetLength();
```

```
//for each result received...
for (Var i=0; i<_CategoriesCount; I++){
 //create an object to the store the values of that row
 var Row = CFCResult.GetItemAt(I);
 //populate the categories combobox component with the given
 // category value
 Categories.AddItem(Row.Category, Row.Category);
 }
}

//If any errors occur, this method will be called.
GetCategories.ProtoType.OnStatus = function(Error){
// no list was built, so allow the user to type
Categories.SetEditable(1);
```

You will notice in the previous code that comments are preceded with two slashes, //, just like in JavaScript or CFScript.

You also need to include the netServices ActionScript file somewhere in the movie, to leverage the Flash Gateway Connection functionality. This simple line of code (most likely in the actions layer) will accomplish that:

```
#include "NetServices.as"
```

Another good practice is to create an object in the actions layer that will hold a connection to the CFC Web service. The code should look something like this:

```
//create an object to hold my gateway connection
MyGatewayConnection = NetServices.CreateGatewayConnection();
//create an object to hold the service call
GetEmployeesServerTalk = GatewayConnection.GetService
                 ("MyComponents.Categories",new GetCategories());
```

This code tells Flash to pass the results it receives from any MyComponents.Categories function to the GetCategories( ) Flash Object. The only thing left to do is put the code that actually calls the Web service in the movie, which looks like this:

```
GetEmployeesServerTalk.GetCategories();
```

Creating one ActionScript object to hold the connection and another ActionScript object to accept all of the return data in this manner allows for easy reuse of the connection and reexecution of its result(s)—which is ideal, especially when making multiple round trips to the server from your Flash MX movies.

Leveraging ColdFusion with Server-Side ActionScript

A new functionality included in the release of ColdFusion and Flash MX is server-side ActionScript. This section shows you how to use server-side ActionScript to access HTTP and database operations from within Flash movies.

Introducing Server-Side ActionScript

The server-side ActionScript file is called from a client-side Flash movie via the Flash Gateway, just like any other Web service. To use server-side ActionScript, you create a file with an .asr extension and store it in any directory or subdirectory off of the web root (or off of any web server mapped drive). There are two new ActionScript functions available for leveraging a ColdFusion server: CF.Query and CF.HTTP.

Calling a server-side ActionScript file is relatively the same as calling any other remote Web service. Include the NetServices.as file, specify the default gateway URL, and create a connection to it. To set the default gateway to use, you can use the SetDefaultGateWayUrl( ) function like so:

```
NetServices.SetDefaultGateWayUrl
  ("http://localhost:8500/flashservices/gateway")
```

You then set a variable equal to the connection as before:

```
myGatewayConnection = NetServices.createGatewayConnection();
```

The next thing your movie must do is create an instance of the server-side ActionScript, like so:

```
CategoryService = MyGatewayConnection.GetService
                        ("CategoryScripts", this)
```

In the previous code segment, the name of the ASR file is categoryscripts.asr. To then call a function defined in categoryscripts.asr, you use the following syntax:

```
CategoryService.FunctionName(FunctionParameter1,
                        FunctionParameter2, etc.)
```

As with other functions, the order of arguments passed is the same as the order expected by the function. You then use the results as you would the results of any other service call in your ActionScript, when getting back a query record set. When calling a function that uses CF.HTTP, you will be returned various HTTP return values as properties (Header, StatusCode, Text, Mimetype, Charset, Filecontent, and ResponseHeader).

Querying a Datasource from Server-Side ActionScript

There are two different ways to query a datasource with the CF.Query function: named argument and positional argument. A named argument specifies the name of the argument. A positional argument associates the argument value with the name of the argument, based on the position of the argument in the argument list. The syntax for named argument querying looks like the following:

```
CF.Query({
  datasource:"datasource name",
  sql:"SQL Statement",
  username:"Username",
  password:"Password",
  maxrows: max_number_of_rows,
  timeout:milliseconds_to_wait_before_timingout
})
```

The following is the syntax for positional argument querying:

```
CF.query(datasource, sql, username, password, maxrows)
```

When a record set comes back to Flash, it exists as a recordset class object. Table 28-2 illustrates the methods that are available for use in a record set.

Method	Description
AddItem	Appends a row to the end of a record set
AddItemAt	Inserts a row into a specific position in a record set
AddView	Requests notification of any changes in the state of a record set
Filter	Creates a new record set containing rows from the original record set
GetColumnNames	Returns all of the recordset column names
GetItemAt	Retrieves a specific row from a record set
GetItemID	Gets the unique ID for a specific row in a record set

Table 28-2.   *Methods to Use on a Record Set*

INTEGRATING COLDFUSION
WITH OTHER
TECHNOLOGIES

Method	Description
GetLength	Returns the total number of rows in a record set
GetNumberAvailable	Returns the number of records in a record set that have been downloaded from the server
IsFullyPopulated	Returns a Boolean value that is used to determine whether or not a record set can be manipulated
IsLocal	Returns whether or not a record set is server-associated or local
RemoveAll	Removes all rows in a record set
RemoveItemAt	Removes a specific row in a record set
ReplaceItemAt	Replaces all of the contents of a specific row in a record set
SetDeliveryMode	Changes the delivery mode of a server-associated record set
SetField	Overwrites the value of one field in a specific row
Sort	Sorts all records in a record set by a specific comparison function
SortItemsBy	Sorts all the rows in a record set by a specific column

Table 28-2. *Methods to Use on a Record Set* (continued)

A simple example of server-side ActionScript to return all categories from a Category table would look like this:

```
Function GetCats(){
 MyCats = CF.Query({datasource: "myDSN",
                    sql: "SELECT * FROM category"})

 if (MyCats)
  return MyCats;
 else
  return null;
}
```

Using HTTP from Server-Side ActionScript

The CF.HTTP() method allows server-side ActionScript to request a URL with GET or POST. The ability to get web addresses with GET is of particular use, but you can also post via the URL if need be. The simple syntax looks like the following:

```
Function SimpleGetURL(URL){
 TheContents = CF.HTTP(URL);
 return TheContents.Get("FileContent");
}
```

Like CF.Query, CF.HTTP has both a named argument and a positional argument syntax. The named argument syntax looks like this:

```
CF.HTTP ({
 Method: "GET or POST",
 url:"a URL",
 username:"username",
 password:"password",
 resolveurl:"yes or no",
 params:an_array_variable,
 path:"a path",
 file: "a filename"
})
```

These arguments do the same thing as their cfhttp counterparts. The syntax for a positional call would look like this:

```
CF.HTTP(method, url, params, username, password)
```

When passing parameters to CF.HTTP, you pass an array of objects. The following are the object keys that are allowed:

Parameter	Parameter Descriptions
name	Variable name for the data being passed
type	Type of transaction (URL, FormField, Cookie, CGI, or File)
value	Value of the variable being passed

After requesting a URL via CF.HTTP, the following data is returned back to Flash:

Return Value	Return Value Description
text	A Boolean indicating whether or not the requested URL contains text data
charset	The character set specified in the content-type HTTP response header
header	The raw HTTP response header
filecontent	The returned file contents
mMimetype	The MIME type ("text/html", "image/gif", etc.)
responseheader	The response header; if there is more than one instance of a header key, this will be an array
statuscode	HTTP error code (400: Bad Request, 405: Method Not Allowed, 404: Not Found, etc.)

Summary

In this chapter, you learned about the following:

- Flash MX and ActionScript in general
- How to share data between a Flash movie and a ColdFusion template
- Server-side ActionScript
- How to call a ColdFusion Web service from within a Flash movie

The next chapter will teach you about adding web-based content editors to your web site.

The
Complete
Reference

ColdFusion
MX

Chapter 29

Adding Web-Based
Content Editors
to Your Site

541

Occasionally, you will want to offer your clients the capability to modify and edit content online. The easier you make it for your clients to edit the content, the better off you are. While you could give them access to the pages and some books on HTML and CFML, doing so will most surely mean a support headache for you later on. A more elaborate option is to give your users the ability to edit content online using a graphical interface. This chapter discusses three of the most commonly used products designed strictly for this purpose: ActivEdit, eWebEditPro, and soEditor.

Delivering Content with ActivEdit from CFDev.com

One of the most popular content editors is ActivEdit from CFDev.com. It is a component built using ActiveX and DHTML. You can access ActivEdit as a ColdFusion custom tag, allowing you to easily integrate it into ColdFusion applications built on ColdFusion 4 and above. This section shows you how to use it.

Setting Up ActivEdit

You can download the ActivEdit archive of the file from www.cfdev.com. Unzip the archive using your favorite unzip program and run the setup program. The custom tag, activedit, will automatically be placed in the custom tag directory of your ColdFusion installation. An example application and documentation will be placed in the activedit directory of your web server's root directory.

 There is a free developer version of the activedit tag.

The heart of ActivEdit resides in a CFML custom tag, ActiveEdit.cfm. The custom tag can be called using the cf_activedit syntax. Open and close tags are both needed, similar to the textarea HTML form element. These are the attributes to the custom tag:

- **inc** Specifies the include directory for the ActivEdit files (required attribute). If you are inserting an image, or uploading a file, the directory specified here is the one that will contain the files to handle these actions.

- **name** Specifies the name of the form field (required attribute).

- **image** Specifies whether the image button will be visible on the default toolbar (Boolean attribute). The image button allows you to add an image to your text.

- **imagepath** Contains the absolute path of the image folder on the server (required attribute if the image attribute is set to yes).

- **imageurl** Contains a URL that points to the image folder (required attribute if the image attribute is set to yes). If the baseurl attribute is specified, this attribute can be relative to the baseurl value.

- **baseurl** Specifies the URL that will be prepended to all relative URLs in the document. You will most likely want to set this to the root of your domain.

- **upload** Specifies the upload of images to the directory specified in imagepath (Boolean attribute).

- **height** Specifies the height of the form control.

- **width** Specifies the width of the form control.

- **toolbar** Used to allow customization of the toolbars. Explanation of this is beyond the scope of this book. You can check the ActivEdit documentation for more information.

- **allowtable** Toggles the visibility of table controls (Boolean attribute).

- **cutcopypaste** Toggles the visibility of the controls for cutting, copying, and pasting text (Boolean attribute).

- **redoundo** Used to allow the display of Undo and Redo buttons (Boolean attribute).

- **find** Toggles the visibility of the Find button (Boolean attribute).

- **buttoncolor** Specifies the color of the buttons in ActivEdit (accepts an HTML color value). The default value is the Windows button color.

- **border** Specifies the type of border around the ActivEdit control in cascading style sheet (CSS) notation. The default value is 1px outset.

- **alloweditsource** Toggles the ability to edit the source generated by the tag.

- **breakonenter** Specifies whether the control will insert an HTML line break, <br>, when using the ENTER key. The <p> tag is used instead.

- **defaultfont** Specifies the name of the font for the ActivEdit control. CSS notation should be used to specify this value. The default is 10pt Verdana.

This custom tag can be put into use fairly easily.

ActivEdit has two features that can be used to expand the technology's functionality. Both of these features are beyond the scope of this book, but you can find out more by reading your ActivEdit documentation. The first feature is the ActivEdit application programming interface (AEAPI). It is a way that you can set up JavaScript code to respond to specific events. You can use this type of functionality to do things such as change the background color.

The second piece of expanded functionality is a spell-checking custom tag, CFX_JspellCheck. On the form-processing page, you can send it the data that was entered into the activedit tag, and it will spell check it and return a list of incorrect words, as either a JavaScript array or a WDDX structure. The return value can be used to point out misspelled words and offer suggestions for changes. You can find out more about WDDX in Chapter 27, and check your ActivEdit documentation for more information on the spell checker.

Using ActivEdit in Your Application

This section shows you how to put the activedit tag to use. Suppose you want to create a section of your Intranet site that contains employee pages. Each employee will be able to access their page and display any information they wish. In most cases, you will not be able to count on the employees knowing HTML or ColdFusion. This is where ActivEdit comes into play.

Creating Your Database

The data that the user is creating needs to be stored in the database. This can be accomplished with a single employee table. Here are the fields you might need in the table and what each contains:

- **EmployeeID**   A unique identifier for each employee
- **Username**   The employee's username
- **Pasword**   The employee's password
- **FirstName**   The employee's first name
- **LastName**   The employee's last name
- **PageContent**   The content for the employee's page

Other fields you may want to include would depend upon other things that you would want to do with the employee's information, but these fields are fine for our purposes.

Using the activedit Tag

The next step is to create form pages that offer the imaginary employees a way to edit their information. As with all form pages, this one contains an input page and a processing page. This code is written assuming that the user has already logged in and we have created a session variable with their UserID. You can check Chapter 17 for information about login and logout scripts.

Here is the input page:

```
<!--- www.instantcoldfusion.com

Description: Page to Accept Employee information

Entering: N/A
Exiting: AEEmployeep.cfm

Dependencies: N/A
```

```
Expecting: N/A

Modification History
Date        Modifier              Modification
***********************************************************
05/06/2002 Jeff Houser, DotComIt    Created
--->

<!--- get the current data --->
<cflock type="readonly" scope="session" timeout="10">
 <cfquery datasource="Chapter29" name="GetCurrentPageContext">
  SELECT PageContent
  FROM Employees
  WHERE Employees.EmployeeID = #session.EmployeeID#
 </cfquery>
</cflock>


<!--- Create the form --->
<form action="AEEmployeep.cfm" method="post">

 <!--- Drop in ActivEdit --->
 <cf_activedit inc="inc/" name="PageContent" upload="1" image="yes"
               imagepath="C:\webroot\Chapter29"
               imageurl="images/" width="580">
  <cfoutput>
   #GetCurrentPageContext.PageContent#
  </cfoutput>
 </cf_activedit>

 <input type="submit" value="Submit">
</form>
```

This page starts with the documentation header. The first processing that the page does is to get the current value of the PageContent column for the current user. It does this by performing a query. The query is wrapped in a cflock block, because a session variable is accessed in the query.

The next step is to create the form. The form posts data onto the AEEmployeep.cfm page. Since a session variable is once again being accessed, the cflock tag is needed.

The next step uses the activedit tag to create the specialized form element:

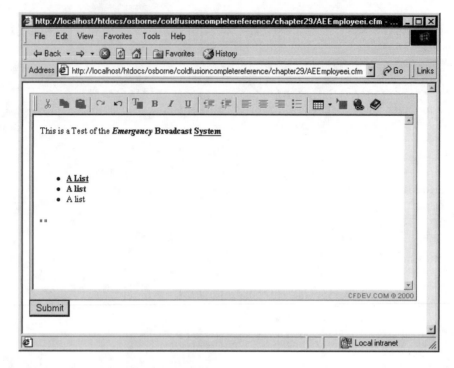

The default value of the editing window is filled in between the activedit open and close tags. It is set as the default value of editing window, similar to the way a textarea tag might be used. The page finishes with a Submit button and the end form tag.

The form processing page is a little simpler:

```
<!--- www.instantcoldfusion.com

Description: Page to Process the Employee Information

Entering: AEEmployeei.cfm
Exiting: N/A

Dependencies: N/A
Expecting: form.EmployeeID
   form.PageContent

Modification History
Date       Modifier                Modification
*********************************************************
05/06/2002 Jeff Houser, DotComIt    Created
--->
```

```
<!--- Insert the Query --->
<cflock type="readonly" scope="session" timeout="10">
 <cfquery datasource="Chapter29" name="UpdateQuery">
  UPDATE Employees
  SET PageContent = '#form.PageContent#'
  WHERE Employees.EmployeeID = #session.EmployeeID#
 </cfquery>
</cflock>

<!--- Output the Values that were stored --->
<cfoutput>
 #form.PageContent#
</cfoutput>
```

The page starts with the documentation header, as always. It specifies that the PageContent and EmployeeID variables need to be defined when executing this page, and that this page is executed after the AEEmployeei.cfm page. This page performs two actions. First, it inserts the data in the database. Second, it outputs the data. With the data in the database, it can now be used anywhere in this site or other sites that have access to the database.

Editing Data with eWebEditPro from Ektron

This section shows you how eWebEditPro can be configured into your web site. eWebEditPro is a product from Ektron corporation. Earlier versions of it were included in Macromedia's Spectra, so it works nicely with any ColdFusion-based application. It is a highly customizable program. This section shows you how to use it.

Understanding eWebEditPro Custom Tag

There are two parts to eWebEditPro, the client portion and the server portion. You can download the server portion at www.ektron.com and install it on your ColdFusion server. The first time that a client hits the page that uses the Ektron editor, the program is downloaded and installed on the client machine. This is a one-time installation, so the client does not have to worry about installing it every time they access the server.

As with ActiveEdit, eWebEditPro is implemented as a CFML custom tag. You will probably find the file in the ewebeditpro2 directory of your web server's root. The file is named ewebeditpro2.cfm. I like to copy it to the custom tag directory of my ColdFusion installation. These are the attributes for the ewebeditpro2 custom tag:

- **path**   Specifies the name of the web directory where ewebeditpro was installed. The default value is set to /ewebeditpro2.

- **maxcontentsize**   Specifies the largest number of characters that can be saved in the content window.

- **name**   Specifies the name of the editor window. This name should be a valid JavaScript identifier. The name attribute also specifies the name of the resulting form variable.

- **editorname**   Used as an alternate to name. If you have to launch the custom tag using cfmodule instead of the cf_ewebeditpro2 syntax, the editorname attribute also specifies the name of the resulting form variable.

- **width**   Specifies the width of the editor window, in pixels or as a percentage.

- **height**   Specifies the width of the editor window, in pixels or as a percentage.

- **value**   Specifies the default text that will appear in the editor window.

- **license**   Specifies the license key of the editor.

- **locale**   Specifies the URL of the localization directory. This applies if you are using eWebEditPro in a language other than English.

- **config**   Specifies the location of an XML configuration file. Configuring the editor window via XML is beyond the scope of this book.

- **stylesheet**   Specifies the CSS file that is used to format the window content.

- **bodystyle**   Specifies CSS information without placing it in a file.

- **hideaboutbutton**   Tells the editor whether or not to display the About button on the toolbar (Boolean attribute). The default value is false.

- **ondblclickelement**   Specifies the action that is executed when a link is clicked. This is a JavaScript function.

- **onexeccommand**   Specifies the event that is triggered if a toolbar button is clicked or a drop-down or context menu is selected. Specify the name of a JavaScript function in this attribute.

- **onfocus**   Specifies the event that occurs when the editor becomes the active element of the page.

- **onblur**   Specifies the actions to occur when the editor loses focus as the active page element.

Here is an example page that uses the editor window:

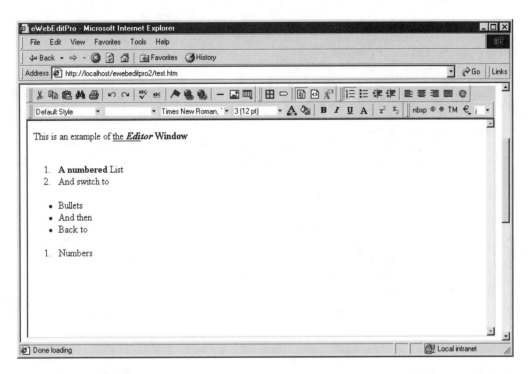

eWebEditPro is a configurable product. The toolbars can be dragged around the window, or even turned off. The user can switch back and forth between an HTML code view and the WYSIWYG (what you see is what you get) view. Links, tables, and images can easily be added or removed using the toolbar buttons. The content can even be saved. Additional setup options are available to the server administrator through a specialized configuration utility. You can manually create an XML configuration document, if necessary.

   When someone saves web content from the eWebEditPro editor, JavaScript reads the text into a hidden form field.

Adding eWebEditPro to Your Site

This example uses eWebEditPro in the same manner that ActivEdit was used. This is the input page:

```
<!--- www.instantcoldfusion.com

Description: Page to change Employee information using
            Ektron eWebEditPro
```

```
Entering: N/A
Exiting: EktronEmployeep.cfm

Dependencies: N/A
Expecting: N/A

Modification History
Date        Modifier                Modification
*********************************************************
05/06/2002 Jeff Houser, DotComIt    Created
--->

<!--- get the current data --->
<cflock type="readonly" scope="session" timeout="10">
 <cfquery datasource="Chapter29" name="GetCurrentPageContext">
  SELECT PageContent
  FROM Employees
  WHERE Employees.EmployeeID = #session.EmployeeID#
 </cfquery>
</cflock>

<!--- create the form --->
<form action=" EktronEmployeep.cfm" method="post">

 <!--- Drop in eWebEditPro custom tag --->
 <cfoutput>
  <cf_ewebeditpro2 name="PageContent" Width="100%" Height="75%"
                   value="#GetCurrentPageContext.PageContent#">
 </cfoutput>
 <input type="submit" value="Submit">

</form>
```

This page starts with the documentation header. It uses a query to retrieve the data for the user. The form tag submits the file onto EktronEmployeep.cfm. The form field contains the ewebeditpro2 custom tag call. The name is specified as PageContent. The width and height are specified. The default value is given as the value returned from the query. The page finishes with a Submit button and a close form tag. The processing page is no different than the processing page we examined earlier in this chapter.

Using soEditor from SiteObjects

This section examines a final web-based content manager, soEditor, available from SiteObjects (www.siteobjects.com). It works in the same manner as the previous examples. A custom tag is provided. soEditor can tell if your browser supports its advanced features. If your browser doesn't support the advanced features, soEditor offers a standard textarea element.

Setting Up the soEditor Tag

soEditor can be downloaded from www.siteobjects.com. It is based off a CFML custom tag, just as ActivEdit and eWebEditPro are. The soEditor custom tag is named soeditor_pro. These are its attributes:

- **form**   Contains the name of the form that the soEditor is included in. It is required, and its value is case sensitive.

- **field**   Contains the name of the form field that you want to create (required attribute).

- **scriptpath**   Specifies the name of the directory that contains the soEditor files (required attribute). Normally, you set this to /soeditor/. It is imperative that the leading and trailing slashes are included in this value. soEditor will use this to find specific images and other files it needs.

- **width**   Specifies the width of the text box, in pixels or as a percentage.

- **height**   Specifies the height of the text box, in pixels or as a percentage.

- **cols**   Contains the number of columns that will be available in the box. This is included for cross-browser compatibility and is similar to width.

- **rows**   Contains the number of rows that will be available in the box. This is included for cross-browser compatibility and is similar to height.

- **pageedit**   Specifies whether or not the text being edited contains the HTML header information, such as the html, head, and body tags.

- **wordcount**   Specifies whether or not the word count will be displayed (Boolean attribute). The default value is false.

- **validateonsave**   Checks whether or not any text is contained in the field when the form is submitted.

- **validationmessage**   Contains the message to display if the validation fails.

- **html**   Specifies the default content that will be loaded into the editor. This is analogous to the value attribute of the input tag.

- **allowupload**   Specifies whether or not image uploading is allowed on the server.
- **allowfoldercreation**   Specifies whether or not the image folder will be created on the server if it does not exist.
- **spellcheck**   Specifies whether or not the spellcheck button is displayed on the toolbar. You can check the soEditor documentation for more information about the spell checker.

There are over 90 attributes for this custom tag, many of which are used to define the layout of the soEditor toolbar. The previous list only contains the required and commonly used attributes. You should check out your soObject documentation for more information.

Editing the Page

We can easily re-create our previous example using this tag. This is the updated page:

```
<!--- www.instantcoldfusion.com

Description: Page to change Employee information using Site
             Objects soEditor

Entering: N/A
Exiting: AEEmployeep.cfm

Dependencies: N/A
Expecting: N/A

Modification History
Date        Modifier                Modification
********************************************************
05/06/2002 Jeff Houser, DotComIt    Created
--->

<!--- get the current data --->
<cflock type="readonly" scope="session" timeout="10">
 <cfquery datasource="Chapter29" name="GetCurrentPageContext">
  SELECT PageContent
  FROM Employees
  WHERE Employees.EmployeeID = #session.EmployeeID#
 </cfquery>
</cflock>
```

```
<form name="SOForm" action="SOEmployeep.cfm" method="post">

<!--- Drop in ActivEdit --->
<cfoutput>
 <cf_soeditor_pro form="SOForm" field="PageContent"
                  scriptpath="/siteobjects/soeditor/pro/"
                  html="#GetCurrentPageContext.PageContent#">
</cfoutput>

<input type="submit" value="Submit">
</form>
```

The code starts with the documentation header. You will notice that a name was added
to the form tag. Then it uses the soeditor_pro tag to create the form element:

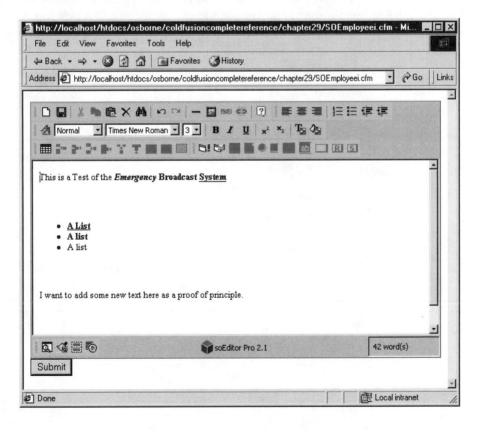

The custom tag uses the three required attributes: form, field, and scriptpath. It also specifies the html attribute to fill in the value with a default value. The page finishes with a Submit button and the close form tag. The processing page is the same in this case as it was with ActivEdit and eWebEditPro.

Summary

In this chapter, you learned about the following:

- Web-based content editors
- How to develop an application that uses content editors, including CFDev.com's ActivEdit, Ektron's eWebEditPro, and SiteObjects' soEditor.

Although this chapter examined only one example for the use of online content editors, there are many more uses that you will discover as you develop more. Each editor has its own strengths and weaknesses, and you should choose the one that best meets your needs. The next chapter will teach you all about interfacing ColdFusion with COM objects.

The
Complete
Reference

ColdFusion
MX

Chapter 30

Calling COM and
CORBA Objects
from ColdFusion

This chapter teaches you how you can call COM and CORBA objects from within ColdFusion. It starts with a general explanation of what COM and CORBA are, and then teaches you how you can use a COM object to fill in a PDF form via the Web.

Introducing COM and CORBA

This section introduces the COM and CORBA technologies, then shows you how you can access the technologies from ColdFusion using the cfobject tag.

Understanding COM

COM stands for Component Object Model. CORBA stands for Common Object Request Broker Architecture. COM is one of the most widely used component models in the world. It is a Microsoft invention and remains primarily Windows-based. CORBA is brought to us by the Object Management Group (OMG). Both technologies provide a way for different programs to share data and functionality with each other.

You do not need to know how COM and CORBA work to use the objects from within ColdFusion. You need to know the properties and methods of the object. You also need to know what data is expected by the methods and what data you should expect back to you. If you want to know more details about how COM and CORBA work, however, read on.

COM is an architecture that allows applications to be built from a collection of binary components, usually DLL or EXE files. The way COM works is to provide a way for one component to create an instance, or object, of another. The object that is created encapsulates all properties and methods of the component that it called. Properties are like variables and contain data. Methods are akin to functions and perform a series of predefined actions. Once the object is created, COM drops out of the picture. The two components can talk to each other directly. This is beneficial to component creators because they no longer have to develop custom interfaces for every program that wants to use the component. It is beneficial to the developers who use the component because they are able to access any component object that adheres to the COM standards.

Note *Microsoft offers a version of COM called Distributed Component Object Model (DCOM), which is designed for network usage.*

CORBA is, conceptually, very similar to COM, in that it provides a way for programs to interact with each other. Unlike COM, CORBA is developed to be a cross-platform standard. CORBA is designed for distributed computing and client/server operations. It allows for the remote invocation of objects. The application knows how to access the object, but does not know its location or the details of its implementation. For every CORBA object, an Interface Definition Language (IDL) interface must be created. It is this interface that allows the program to access the properties and methods of a CORBA object. You request an object through its object request broker (ORB). The ORB handles all references to the underlying code.

 For more information about CORBA, go to www.omg.com. Find more information about COM by pointing your browser to www.microsoft.com/com/default.asp.

Creating COM and CORBA Objects

With a brief overview of COM and CORBA behind us, this section demonstrates how you can access these types of objects from within ColdFusion. You can create and manipulate objects using CFML tags and CFScript blocks.

Creating Objects Within ColdFusion

There are two different ways that you can create COM or CORBA objects from within ColdFusion. One is to use the cfobject tag. The second is to use the CreateObject function. This section demonstrates both ways.

To create an object with the cfobject tag, you would give the tag these attributes:

- **type**   Should be set to com to call a COM object (required attribute).

- **action**   Should be set to either create or connect (required attribute). You will usually use create for a DLL, and use connect for an EXE program.

- **class**   Contains the ProgID of the component object to invoke (required attribute). The ProgID should be provided by the make of the COM object. If not, you can find it by using a Microsoft utility called oleview.

 If you do not have documentation on the COM object, you can find out its ProgID by using OLEView, a Microsoft utility available at www.microsoft.com/com/ resources/oleview.asp.

- **name**   Contains the name of the variable that will point to the object (required attribute).

- **context**   Defines the context in which you are instantiating the COM object (optional attribute). Its values are inproc, local, and remote. The inproc value stands for in-process and is used when calling an object that is running off the processing space as ColdFusion. The local value is for an out-of-process object, which is when the object is on the same server but not sharing any server processing space with ColdFusion. The remote value is used for an out-of-process object that is running remotely on a network.

- **server**   Specifies the URL or IP of the server where the object is located. This attribute is required if the context is remote.

The cfobject tag can also be used to call CORBA objects. It uses a similar, but different, set of attributes:

- **type**   Specifies the type of object to call. Should be set to corba to call a CORBA object (required attribute).

- **context**   Specifies the context of the CORBA call. Its values are ior and nameservice. The context attribute is an optional attribute. If set to ior, ColdFusion uses Interoperable Object Reference (IOR) to access the object. If set to nameservice, then ColdFusion uses naming services to access this option.

- **class**   Contains the absolute path to the file that contains the IOR Reference if the context attribute is set to ior. This is a required attribute. If the context attribute is set to nameservice, this attribute should contain the forward-slash-delimited naming convention of the object.

- **name**   Contains the name of the variable that will point to the object (required attribute).

- **locale**   Specifies the Java configuration that contains the properties file.

You can create a COM object like this:

```
<cfobject type="com" action="create"
          class="MyClass" name="MyClassObject">
```

This creates an object from the MyClass COM object and assigns it to the variable MyClassObject.

To create a CORBA object, it must first be registered from the ColdFusion Administrator. Details on how to do this were discussed in Chapter 6. You might call the object like this:

```
<cfobject type="corba" context="ior"
          class="C:\MyClass.ior" name="MyClassObject">
```

This code will create the MyClass CORBA object in ColdFusion, with the name MyClassObject.

You can also create COM and CORBA objects using the CreateObject function. This is very similar to the way that objects are created with the cfobject tag. To create a COM object, the CreateObject function accepts these four arguments:

- **type**   Should be set to com to call a COM object.

- **class**   Contains the ProgID of the component object to invoke (required attribute).

- **context**   Defines the context in which you are instantiating the COM object (optional attribute). Its values are inproc, local, or remote.
- **server**   Specifies the URL or IP of the server that contains the object. This attribute is required if the context is remote.

To create a CORBA object with the CreateObject function, these attributes would be as follows:

- **type**   Specifies the type of object to call. It should be set to corba to call a CORBA object (required attribute).
- **context**   Specifies the context used to call the CORBA object. Its values are ior and nameservice. If set to ior, ColdFusion uses Interoperable Object Reference (IOR) to access the object. If set to nameservice, then ColdFusion uses naming services to access this option. The context attribute is an optional attribute.
- **class**   Specifies the absolute path to the file that contains the IOR reference if the context attribute is set to ior. Specifies the forward-slash-delimited naming convention of the object if the context is set to nameserivce. This is a required attribute.
- **locale**   Specifies the location of the Java configuration that contains the properties file.

Missing from both of these lists is the name argument. The function returns the object, so there is no need to give it a specific name.

Here are some examples that mimic the previous cfobject examples. This code creates a COM object:

```
<cfset MyClassObject = CreateObject("com", "MyClass", "Local")>
```

This code creates a CORBA object:

```
<cfset MyClassObject = CreateObject("corba", "ior",
                                    "MyClass.ior")>
```

You can also use the function to create objects from within CFScript:

```
<cfscript>
  MyCOMObject = CreateObject("com", "MyClass", "Local");
  MyCorbaObject = CreateObject("corba", "ior", "MyClass.ior");
</cfscript>
```

INTEGRATING COLDFUSION
WITH OTHER
TECHNOLOGIES

Using Objects from Within CFScript

After creating the objects in memory, you need to know how to call the methods and access the properties that are associated with the object in question. This is very easy to do, although many of the specifics will depend on the object and the methods or properties that you can access through it.

You can call a method using the following syntax:

```
ObjectVariable.MethodName(AttributeList)
```

After the name of the object variable comes a period followed by the name of the method. The parentheses surround the list of attributes. A comma separates attributes. You can use this approach to calling methods within a cfset tag or inside CFScript.

You access properties in much the same way as you call methods:

```
ObjectVariable.PropertyName
```

It is a ColdFusion expression, similar to how you would access the value of a ColdFusion structure key. The name of the object variable comes first, followed by the name of the property.

 For a lot of good information about using ColdFusion with COM, check out www.cfcomet.com.

Filling Out PDF Forms in ColdFusion

This section demonstrates COM objects by showing you how you can fill out PDF forms from within ColdFusion. First, it demonstrates the basics on how to create a PDF form. Then, it examines a program called ActivePDF Toolkit, which enables you to populate HTML forms.

Creating a PDF Form

The first step in our process is to create a PDF form, and add PDF fields to it. You need Adobe's Acrobat to do this. Open Microsoft Word (or any word processor of your choice) and type these lines:

```
This is a Test PDF Document

Name:
```

```
Address:
Address2:
City:
State:
Zip:
```

Now create your PDF file from this document. You can do this using Acrobat Distiller or PDFWriter, both of which are part of Acrobat. This is what your PDF will look like:

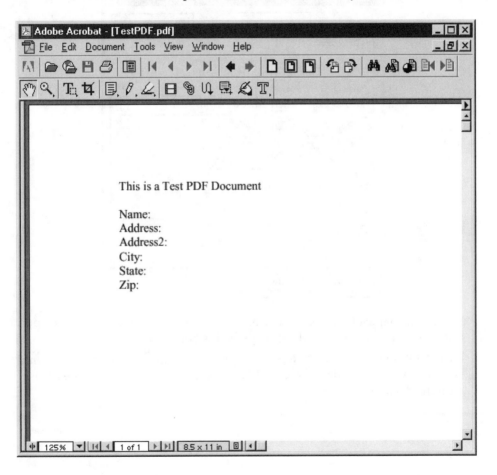

Now open the PDF you created and do the following:

1. Click the Form button, which will show all existing fields (at the moment, there shouldn't be any) and allow you to create new fields.

2. Create six fields, one next to each text identifier. In the PDF, fields are created by clicking the screen and dragging the mouse pointer. When you release the mouse button, this window pops up:

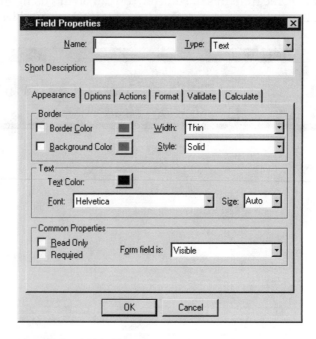

3. Enter the name of the field. There are numerous other options you can apply to the field that are beyond the scope of this book.

4. Click OK to save the field. Repeat the process for all fields in the document: Name, Address1, Address2, City, State, and Zip. You will see all the fields on the document:

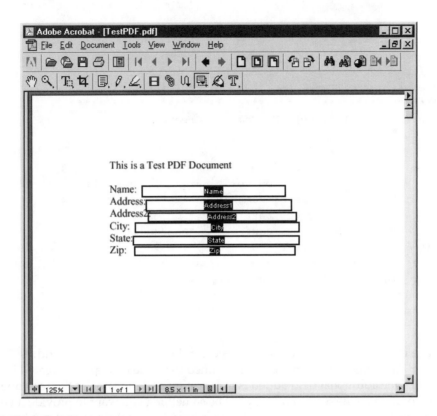

5. Save the document.

Populating the Form via ColdFusion

After creating the PDF form field, the next step is to create the web pages that will process and fill the form. Input can be accepted from the user using an HTML form. The form-processing page is where we will use COM to populate the form fields and create a new form.

Creating the Input Page

The first step is to create the input form page. Here is the code:

```
<!--- www.instantcoldfusion.com

Description: Page to submit data onto ActivePDF pdf

Entering: N/A
Exiting: AcitvePDFp.cfm

Dependencies: N/A
```

INTEGRATING COLDFUSION WITH OTHER TECHNOLOGIES

```
Expecting: N/A

Modification History
Date        Modifier                Modification
*******************************************************
05/08/2002 Jeff Houser, DotComIt    Created
--->

<form action="ActivePDFp.cfm" method="post">
 New PDF Name: <input type="text" name="PDFName"><br>
 Name: <input type="text" name="Name"><br>
 Address 1: <input type="text" name="Address1"><br>
 Address 2: <input type="text" name="Address2"><br>
 City: <input type="text" name="City"><br>
 State: <input type="text" name="State"><br>
 Zip: <input type="text" name="Zip"><br>
 <input type="Submit" name="submit">
</form>
```

This page is a simple form input page. It asks for the Name, Address1, Address2, City, State, and Zip fields. These are identically named to the fields that you created in your PDF form. One additional field added is the location and filename of the resulting PDF. This is a location on the server and may not be something you want to provide if people are going to be accessing your application remotely. Here it is displayed in a browser:

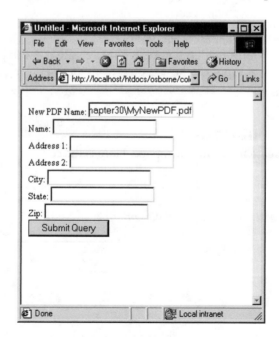

Using COM to Process the Data

After creating the input page, the next step is to process the data using COM. To do this, you need to download and install the ActivePDF Toolkit from www.activepdf.com. This is a very well-documented COM object, and using it is easy.

This section examines the processing page. Here is how we structure the page:

1. Add the documentation header to the page:

```
<!--- www.instantcoldfusion.com

Description: Page to process data into ActivePDF pdf and fill
            out form fields

 Path:
  open output destination file
  open input PDF form
  set form field values
  copy input form into destination file
  close output destination

Entering: N/A
Exiting: N/A

Dependencies: N/A
Expecting: form.Name
    form.Address1
    form.Address2
    form.City
    form.State
    form.Zip
    form.PDFName

Modification History
Date        Modifier                Modification
*********************************************************
05/08/2002 Jeff Houser, DotComIt    Created
--->
```

The seven form fields are listed as being required for this page to process correctly. This documentation also states the algorithm that the page will have to perform to populate the PDF form. First, it will create the destination file. Next, it will open the input file. Then, it will give values to the form fields, copy the input file to the destination file, and close the output file. Each process will be examined with more explanation as it comes up.

2. Before we can start using the ActivePDF Toolkit, we need to create an instance of it. The object could be created using either the cfobject tag or the CreateObject function. This example uses the cfobject tag:

```
<cfobject type="com" action="create"
          class=APToolkit.Object name="MyPDF">
```

You can download and install the ActivePDF Toolkit from www.activepdf.com. It needs to be installed before you can call upon the COM object. ActivePDF is a company that offers a lot of PDF creation programs. The object that is created here is an instance of APToolkit.Object. It is put into the ColdFusion variable MyPDF.

> **Tip**   *When using the cfobject tag to instantiate a class, it is considered a best practice to use proper error handling with cftry and cfcatch.*

3. The remainder of our processing can be performed in a CFScript block. This is the start of the CFScript block:

```
<cfscript>
 // Create New PDF
 MyPDF.OpenOutputFile(form.PDFName);
```

One method is called here. The OpenOutputFile method uses the name and location of the PDF that we specified to create a blank PDF.

4. The next line of CFScript code is shown here:

```
MyPDF.OpenInputFile("C:\MyDoc\TestPDF.pdf");
```

The OpenInputFile points to the PDF form.

5. With the PDF loaded in memory, the fields in the form can start to be populated:

```
MyPDF.SetFormFieldData("Name", form.Name,1);
MyPDF.SetFormFieldData("Address1", form.Address1,1);
MyPDF.SetFormFieldData("Address2", form.Address2,1);
MyPDF.SetFormFieldData("City", form.City,1);
MyPDF.SetFormFieldData("State", form.State,1);
MyPDF.SetFormFieldData("Zip", form.Zip,1);
```

This block of code uses the SetFormFieldData method to populate the form fields with data. The first parameter of the method is the name of the PDF form field. The second parameter is the value that you want to put into the PDF form field. This code places the submitted value from the PDF forms. The last value contains a list of attributes that will be placed into the field. The value is set to 1, which means that none of the attributes change.

6. Use the CopyForm method:

```
MyPDF.CopyForm(1,0);
```

The CopyForm method takes the filled-out PDF form and imprints the data and layout onto the blank PDF. It has two attributes. The first attribute is a number and specifies the first page that will be copied to the resulting form. The second attribute specifies the last page that will be copied into the resulting PDF. If the second value is set to zero, then all of the pages in the PDF will be copied.

7. Close the two files that were opened:

```
MyPDF.CloseOutputFile();
MyPDF.CloseInputFile();
```

The CloseOutputFile method closes the new PDF that was created. The CloseInputFile method closes the PDF form that we created the new PDF from. This is done so that they do not remain open in memory.

8. Close the CFScript block and display a confirmation to the user:

```
</cfscript>

Thanks, your PDF is created!
```

This is the resulting PDF:

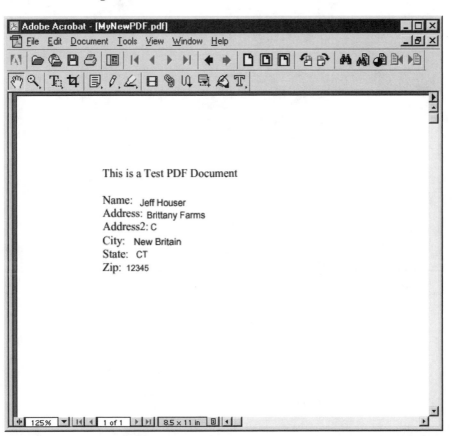

The applications of this code could be far reaching, especially if you start saving the data in a database. You could very easily fill out a form, print it, sign it, and send it in. In the future, a new copy of the form could easily be created without any data entry errors. This could benefit many companies.

Summary

In this chapter, you learned about the following:

- COM and CORBA technologies in general
- How to access COM and CORBA objects from within ColdFusion
- How to fill out PDF forms using a COM object

The next chapter will teach you all about creating and accessing Web services from within ColdFusion.

The Complete Reference

ColdFusion MX

Chapter 31

Using Web Services in ColdFusion

This chapter teaches you how you can access Web services from within ColdFusion. It gives you a broad overview of what Web services are and the technologies that surround them. The chapter finishes by showing you how to create and use Web services via ColdFusion.

Understanding Web Services

This section explains to you what Web services are and how they can be beneficial. It also gives an overview of the technologies that make up Web services.

Explaining Web Services

The term Web service has been the buzzword of choice in early 2002, although it is unclear exactly what a Web service is. In its simplest form, a Web service is a way to run one program from another. Often this is done over the Internet or some other network. The network is usually the Internet, although that is not the only way to use a Web service.

Two of the key elements of a Web service are that it is called across a network and is self-defining. Web services have a built-in mechanism for defining how the service works. The person who offers the Web service must provide a definition of the API using WSDL (Web Services Description Language). WSDL is an XML-formatted document that includes the operations the Web service can perform, including the relevant parameter's return values for each operation.

When someone makes a Web service available, they are said to be *publishing* that Web service. To publish a Web service, you must create the WSDL file that defines the methods and parameters of the service and make that service available. The program that calls upon the service is said to be *consuming* the Web service. To consume a Web service, the calling program must first parse the WSDL file to determine its interface, and then request the service.

Web services can be used for many purposes. Perhaps you manage a bank and want to be able to accept credit cards online for your vendors. Although there are methods of doing this that existed long before Web services, a Web service is the perfect medium for providing this functionality. Maybe you want to provide other information to e-commerce sites, such as a shipping rates program that calculates the shipping rate based on the weight of items you are selling. Perhaps you are a company that sells your product through a group of dealers. You could create a Web service so that a particular dealer could check current stock levels in your warehouse.

Mixing Technologies to Make a Web Service

Three main standards are involved with Web services: WSDL, SOAP, and UDDI. UDDI (Universal Description, Discovery, and Integration) is a way to find Web services. ColdFusion does not have any built-in support for UDDI, but you can find out more information about it at www.uddi.org. This section examines WSDL and SOAP in more detail.

Explaining SOAP

SOAP (Simple Access Open Protocol) is the largest standard for providing Web services. It is designed to be simple, flexible, and easily distributable. The following are some of the features SOAP offers:

- SOAP provides a mechanism for defining the unit of communication. All information is stored in an envelope. Envelopes are made up of multiple messages. A message is a single piece of information divided into an XML body and any number of headers.

- SOAP provides a way to handle errors that occur in the source. The mechanism for doing this is called a *fault*.

- SOAP is designed to be extensible via the use of SOAP headers. This provides a way to add more features without changing the specification.

- A way to bind SOAP messages to HTTP is built into the protocol. HTTP is the most common method of data transfer on the Internet.

For more information on SOAP, check out the World Wide Web Consortium's site at www.w3.org/TR/SOAP/.

Defining Your Web Services with WSDL

WSDL (Web Services Description Language) is an XML-based language that is used to define the functionality of the Web service. If you haven't already, you can find more information about XML and DTDs in Chapter 27.

These are the main elements of the WSDL DTD:

- **definitions** Contains namespace definitions that are used to avoid naming conflicts between multiple Web services. It is the root element of the file.

- **types** Defines the types that are used by the Web service messages. It is a subtag of definitions.

- **message** Defines the name and data type of the input and output parameters of the Web service. It is a subtag of definitions.

- **porttype** Defines the operations performed by the Web service. It is a subtag of definitions.

- **binding** Defines the protocol that the Web service can be accessed by. It is a subtag of definitions.

- **operation** Defines operations that can be invoked remotely. It is usually a subtag of binding.

- **input**   Defines the values that are sent to the operation. It is a subtag of operation.

- **output**   Defines the values that are sent back from the operation. It is a subtag of operation.

- **fault**   Defines the error messages that might get returned from the operation. It is a subtag of operation.

- **service**   Defines a group of related operations. It is a subtag of definitions.

- **port**   Defines a full operation, including its inputs and outputs. It is a subtag of service.

When you create a Web service in ColdFusion, you create a CFC. ColdFusion is able to create the WSDL document automatically. For those of you who have a thirst for knowledge, check out www.w3.org/TR/wsdl for more information about WSDL.

Creating a Web Service from Within ColdFusion

This section teaches you how to create a ColdFusion Component and shows you how you can publish it to the world to be used as a Web service.

Creating a Web Service

You can create a Web service from within ColdFusion, by creating a ColdFusion Component (CFC). Suppose you were creating a Web service for an online music store. Given the name of a song, the service will return the name of the band that sings it. This section shows you how to create this type of Web service.

Designing the Database

The first step in our process is to design the database. Two tables are needed to accomplish the task. First, we need an Artists table, to contain the names of all the artists who have recorded songs. These are the fields in the table:

- **ArtistID**   Contains a unique identifier for the artist.
- **ArtistName**   Contains the name of the artist.

The second table that we need is a Songs table. Knowing the artist, we need to know the songs recorded by that artist:

- **SongID**   Contains the unique identifier for the song.
- **SongName**   Contains the name of the song.
- **ArtistID**   Contains the unique identifier of the artist who performed the song. This column will be a foreign key.

The table structure looks like this:

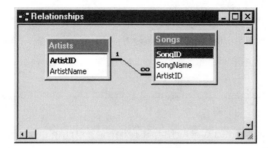

Creating the CFC

The second step is to create the ColdFusion Component that will become the Web service. Only one function is needed in our component, GetArtist. It will accept the name of the song and return the name of the artist who wrote the song.

 If you haven't already, take a look at Chapter 16 for a more in-depth look at ColdFusion Components.

This is how we can create the component:

1. Create an empty file in your favorite CFML editor. Save the file with a .cfc extension. Add your documentation header:

```
<!--- www.instantcoldfusion.com

Description: A CFC that will be called as a Web service
    It will allow users to send in a song.  This will send back
    the artist name.

Entering: N/A
Exiting: N/A

Dependencies: N/A
Expecting: N/A

Modification History
Date       Modifier                Modification
*********************************************************
05/10/2002 Jeff Houser, DotComIt   Created
--->
```

The header documents this CFC. It is a ColdFusion Component and will be used to create a Web service. The single method will allow users to send in a song, and the function will return the name of the artist that performed the song.

2. Define the component, using the cfcomponent tag:

```
<cfcomponent output="false">
</cfcomponent>
```

3. Create our function definition inside the component:

```
<cffunction name="GetArtist" returntype="string"
           access="remote" output="no">
  <cfargument name="SongName" type="string" required="Yes">
</cffunction>
```

The function is named GetArtist. It returns a string and the access is remote. This function does not produce any output. The function contains a single argument, as defined by the cfargument tag. The name is SongName, which accepts a string value and is required.

4. Inside the function declaration, the function code needs to exist. The bulk of the code resides within a query:

```
<cfquery datasource="Chapter31" name="FindArtist">
 SELECT Artists.ArtistName
 FROM Artists, Songs
 WHERE Songs.SongName = '#arguments.SongName#' AND
       Songs.ArtistID = Artists.ArtistID
</cfquery>
```

This query performs a join on the Artists and Songs tables, where the ArtistID is equal. It further limits the return set by selecting all the songs where the SongName is equal to the input value of the function.

5. Return the value:

```
<cfif FindArtist.RecordCount is 0>
 <cfreturn "Not in Database">
<cfelse>
 <cfreturn FindArtist.ArtistName>
</cfif>
```

There are two options in the return code. We want to return either the artist or a message stating that the artist is not located in the database. We can use the RecordCount variable of the query to see if the query returned any results. If it did, we return the artist. If it did not, we return the message stating the artist is not located in the database.

At this point, you have created a ColdFusion Component. You may not realize that you have also created a Web service. When the function definition was created, the access attribute of the cffunction tag was set to remote. This allows the component to be called as a Web service. There is relatively little difference between creating a Web service and creating a component.

Examining the WSDL Definitions for the File

After creating the Web service, you can load it in a browser to see the metadata associated with the Web service:

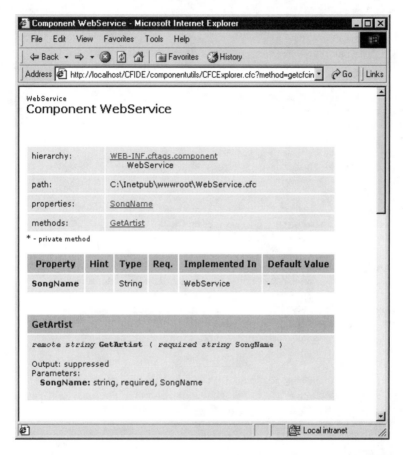

You can also view the WSDL of the Web service by opening the CFC in the browser and adding wsdl to the query string. This is the WSDL code for WebService.cfc?wsdl:

```
<?xml version="1.0" encoding="UTF-8" ?>
<wsdl:definitions targetNamespace=http://DefaultNamespace
        xmlns:wsdl="http://schemas.xmlsoap.org/wsdl/"
        xmlns:xsd="http://www.w3.org/2001/XMLSchema"
        xmlns:wsdlsoap="http://schemas.xmlsoap.org/wsdl/soap/"
        xmlns:intf="http://DefaultNamespace"
        xmlns:impl="http://DefaultNamespace-impl"
        xmlns:SOAP-ENC="http://schemas.xmlsoap.org/soap/encoding/"
```

```
          xmlns="http://schemas.xmlsoap.org/wsdl/">

<wsdl:message name="getSongNameResponse">
 <wsdl:part name="return" type="SOAP-ENC:string" />
</wsdl:message>

<wsdl:message name="GetArtistResponse">
 <wsdl:part name="return" type="SOAP-ENC:string" />
</wsdl:message>

<wsdl:message name="GetArtistRequest">
 <wsdl:part name="SongName" type="SOAP-ENC:string" />
</wsdl:message>

<wsdl:message name="setSongNameRequest">
 <wsdl:part name="SongName" type="SOAP-ENC:string" />
</wsdl:message>

<wsdl:message name="CFCInvocationException" />
<wsdl:message name="setSongNameResponse" />
<wsdl:message name="getSongNameRequest" />

<wsdl:portType name="WebService">
 <wsdl:operation name="GetArtist" parameterOrder="SongName">
  <wsdl:input message="intf:GetArtistRequest" />
  <wsdl:output message="intf:GetArtistResponse" />
  <wsdl:fault name="CFCInvocationException"
              message="intf:CFCInvocationException" />
 </wsdl:operation>

 <wsdl:operation name="getSongName">
  <wsdl:input message="intf:getSongNameRequest" />
  <wsdl:output message="intf:getSongNameResponse" />
  <wsdl:fault name="CFCInvocationException"
              message="intf:CFCInvocationException" />
 </wsdl:operation>

 <wsdl:operation name="setSongName" parameterOrder="SongName">
  <wsdl:input message="intf:setSongNameRequest" />
  <wsdl:output message="intf:setSongNameResponse" />
 </wsdl:operation>
</wsdl:portType>

<wsdl:binding name="WebService.cfcSoapBinding"
              type="intf:WebService">
 <wsdlsoap:binding style="rpc"
           transport="http://schemas.xmlsoap.org/soap/http" />
 <wsdl:operation name="GetArtist">
  <wsdlsoap:operation soapAction="" />
```

```
  <wsdl:input>
    <wsdlsoap:body use="encoded"
        encodingStyle="http://schemas.xmlsoap.org/soap/encoding/"
        namespace="http://DefaultNamespace" />
  </wsdl:input>
  <wsdl:output>
    <wsdlsoap:body use="encoded"
        encodingStyle="http://schemas.xmlsoap.org/soap/encoding/"
        namespace="http://DefaultNamespace" />
  </wsdl:output>
</wsdl:operation>

<wsdl:operation name="getSongName">
  <wsdlsoap:operation soapAction="" />
  <wsdl:input>
    <wsdlsoap:body use="encoded"
        encodingStyle="http://schemas.xmlsoap.org/soap/encoding/"
        namespace="http://DefaultNamespace" />
  </wsdl:input>
  <wsdl:output>
    <wsdlsoap:body use="encoded"
        encodingStyle="http://schemas.xmlsoap.org/soap/encoding/"
        namespace="http://DefaultNamespace" />
  </wsdl:output>
</wsdl:operation>

<wsdl:operation name="setSongName">
  <wsdlsoap:operation soapAction="" />
  <wsdl:input>
    <wsdlsoap:body use="encoded"
        encodingStyle="http://schemas.xmlsoap.org/soap/encoding/"
        namespace="http://DefaultNamespace" />
  </wsdl:input>
  <wsdl:output>
    <wsdlsoap:body use="encoded"
        encodingStyle="http://schemas.xmlsoap.org/soap/encoding/"
        namespace="http://DefaultNamespace" />
  </wsdl:output>
</wsdl:operation>
</wsdl:binding>

<wsdl:service name="WebServiceService">
  <wsdl:port name="WebService.cfc"
            binding="intf:WebService.cfcSoapBinding">
    <wsdlsoap:address location="http://localhost/WebService.cfc" />
  </wsdl:port>
</wsdl:service>
</wsdl:definitions>
```

The WSDL file starts with the definitions tag, which defines the various XML schemas that this WSDL file follows. Following that comes a string of numerous messages that define the parameters and return values of this Web service. Next comes the portType tag, which defines this as a Web service. Inside the portType tag are various operations that are performed by the Web service. Next the operations that are performed are defined. After the portType tag comes the binding tag, which defines the protocols that will be used to run the Web service. It also defines all the operations and their input and output values. The last tag is the service tag, which defines the location of the service.

The data types that are returned from the CFC methods will automatically translate into WSDL data types, as shown in Table 31-1. ColdFusion automatically generates the WSDL file, so you don't have to worry about creating it yourself. It is good to understand the format of the WSDL file, though, so that you can easily understand and use Web services that you did not create.

Using Properties with CFCs and Web Services

There is a tag that relates to Web services called cfproperty. It can be used to create your own variable types for Web services. First, you need to know the attributes to the cfproperty tag:

- **name**   Contains the name of the new variable type.

- **type**   Contains the ColdFusion variable type. Valid values are any, array, binary, Boolean, date, guid, numeric, query, string, struct, uuid, variablename, or a component name.

Let's say, for example, that you wanted to create an Address variable type for use in your ColdFusion Components. You can do so with this code:

```
<cfcomponent>
 <cfproperty name="Address1" type="String">
 <cfproperty name="Address2" type="String">
 <cfproperty name="City" type="String">
 <cfproperty name="State" type="String">
 <cfproperty name="Zip" type="String">
</cfcomponent>
```

Save this code in a file called Address.cfc. Now when you define arguments in other CFCs, you can use the Address type:

```
<cfcomponent>
 <cffunction name="OutputAddress" returntype="Address"
             access="remote" output="yes">
  <cfargument name="InputAddress" type="Address" required="Yes">
  <cfreturn InputAddress>
 </cffunction>
</cfcomponent>
```

CFML Data Type	WSDL Data Type
Numeric	SOAP-ENC: double
Boolean	SOAP-ENC: boolean
String	SOAP-ENC: string
Array	SOAP-ENC: array
Binary	Xsd:base64Binary
Data	xsd:dateTime
guid	SOAP-ENC: string
uuid	SOAP-ENC: string
Void	N/A
Struct	Map
Query	QueryBean
Any	complexType
Component definition	complexType

Table 31-1. *ColdFusion to WSDL Data Types*

This method accepts an input of type Address and returns it. In a real-world situation, you would want to perform other processing on the data. The upcoming section, "Consuming a Web Service from Within ColdFusion," will discuss how to pass these custom types into a Web service.

Publishing a Web Service

Creating a Web service is only half the battle—thankfully the harder half. The next step is to publish your Web service. You can do this easily within ColdFusion:

1. Create your ColdFusion Component file. Make sure that the methods that you want to be available via Web services have their access attribute set to remote.

2. Place the CFC file, or files, in a web-accessible directory.

3. Tell people where to find the CFC file, and how to display the metadata and WSDL file.

Now your Web service is available to be consumed by anyone who wants to use it.

Consuming a Web Service from Within ColdFusion

This section teaches you how you can access a Web service from within ColdFusion. It shows you how to call methods from a Web service and how to process the data that gets sent back to you.

Invoking a Web Service

This section teaches you how to consume a Web service, whether it was built in ColdFusion, .NET, or some other language. Web services can be consumed using both CFML and CFScript.

Instantiating the Web Service with CFML

If you need to consume a Web service using CFML, you can use the cfinvoke tag. These are the relevant attributes:

- **webservice** Specifies the WSDL file of the Web service. If you are referencing a ColdFusion Component, you want to set this to http://servername/mycfc.cfc?wsdl. If you are referencing another type of Web service, the provider has to tell you where to point this.

- **returnvariable** Contains the variable name that will hold the results of the executed method.

- **username** Specifies the username if authentication is needed to get to the Web service.

- **password** Specifies the password if authentication is needed to get to the Web service.

- **method** Specifies the name of the Web service method you want to invoke (required attribute).

- *argumentlist* Specifies the names and values of the arguments that are being passed into the method specified in the method attribute. Attributes are listed by name-value pairs in the form of *myargument="MyValue"*.

- **argumentcollection** Specifies the name of a structure that contains all the parameters to be passed into the method specified in the method attribute.

We can call the Web service named WebService.cfc, created earlier in this chapter, like this:

```
<cfinvoke component="WebService" method="GetArtist"
          returnVariable="Artist" songname="Go Away">
```

We can also call it using the argumentcollection attribute:

```
<cfset ArgumentStruct = StructNew()>
<cfset ArgumentStruct.SongName = "Two Princes">
<cfinvoke component="WebService" method="GetArtist"
          returnVariable="Artist"
          argumentcollection="#ArgumentStruct#">
```

There is an additional tag, cfinvokeargument, that can be used to pass arguments to a Web service. These are its arguments:

- **name**   Contains the name of the attribute that you are passing into the Web service.

- **value**   Contains the value of the attribute that you are passing into the Web service.

This is an example of how to use the cfinvokeargument tag:

```
<cfinvoke component="WebService" method="GetArtist"
          returnVariable="Artist">
 <cfinvokeargument name="SongName" value="In Bloom">
</cfinvoke>
```

Instantiating the Web Service with CFScript

You can also access Web services with CFScript, using the CreateObject function. The function accepts two parameters:

- **type**   Must be set to webservice.
- **urltowsdl**   Specifies the web location of the WSDL file.

Using CFScript, you can create an object that will point to the WSDL file without actually calling a method. This is contrary to how the cfinvoke tag works. Here is an example of calling a Web service in CFScript:

```
<cfscript>
 ObjectArtist = CreateObject("webservice",
                             "http://localhost/WebService.cfc?wsdl");
</cfscript>
```

After creating the object, you still need to be able to call upon the functionality of it. You can do this just as if you had created an object and were calling the method. The name of the function that you are calling comes after the name of the object:

```
<cfscript>
 Artist = ObjectArtist.GetArtist("Runaway Train");
</cfscript>
```

The parameter list is located in parentheses after the name of the method.

 You can create an alias for a WSDL in the ColdFusion Administrator. This was described in Chapter 6. Once you create the alias, you can reference that alias instead of the URL location of the WSDL file.

Passing Custom Data Types into a Web Service

If you are accessing a Web service with a custom data type, you need to know how to call upon that custom data type. Earlier in the chapter, we created a custom data type called Address. It had five different unique string values: Address1, Address2, City, State, and Zip.

You want to call a Web service that uses this Address data type. You can pass it a parameter of type Address by creating a structure that contains all five elements of the Address data type. Here is the code:

```
<cfset TempAddress = StructNew()>
<cfset TempAddress.Address1 = "Address1">
<cfset TempAddress.Address2 = "Address2">
<cfset TempAddress.City = "City">
<cfset TempAddress.State = "State">
<cfset TempAddress.Zip = "Zip">
```

Once the structure is created, it can be passed into the Web service as an argument:

```
<cfinvoke webservice = http://localhost/UseAddress.cfc?wsdl
  method = "ReturnAddress" returnVariable = "MyReturn">

 <cfinvokeargument name="InputAddress" value="#TempAddress#">
</cfinvoke>
```

When a custom data type, such as Address, is returned from a Web service, ColdFusion puts it into a structure for access.

This is a simple function that accepts and returns the same value:

```
<cffunction name="ReturnAddress" returntype="Address"
            access="remote" output="yes">
 <cfargument name="InputAddress" type="Address" required="Yes">
 <cfreturn InputAddress>
</cffunction>
```

We can call the function with this code:

```
<cfset TempAddress = StructNew()>
<cfset TempAddress.Address1 = "Address1">
<cfset TempAddress.Address2 = "Address2">
<cfset TempAddress.City = "City">
<cfset TempAddress.State = "State">
<cfset TempAddress.Zip = "Zip">

<!--- Invoke the Web service that Returns the
      Custom Data Type --->
<cfinvoke webservice = "http://localhost/UseAddress.cfc?wsdl"
  method = "ReturnAddress" returnVariable = "MyReturn">

 <cfinvokeargument name="InputAddress" value="#TempAddress#">
</cfinvoke>

<!--- output the values --->
<cfoutput>
 #MyReturn.Address1#<br>
 #MyReturn.Address2#<br>
 #MyReturn.City#<br>
 #MyReturn.State#<br>
 #MyReturn.Zip#<br>
</cfoutput>
```

The code calls the Web service with the Address variable type, and returns it. The output sees that the same values have been returned.

While the return value is referenced in a similar manner to a structure, it is not a structure.

Summary

In this chapter, you learned about the following:

- Web services and associated technologies, such as SOAP and WSDL
- How to create a Web service in ColdFusion
- How to consume a Web service from within ColdFusion

The next chapter will examine BlueDragon, a CFML application server that competes with Macromedia's ColdFusion.

The
Complete
Reference

ColdFusion
MX

Chapter 32

Discovering BlueDragon

BlueDragon is a third-party CFML interpreter brought to us by the combined forces of New Atlanta and n-ary. It is designed as an alternate to Macromedia's ColdFusion Server. Like ColdFusion MX, BlueDragon is based on J2EE server technology. Unlike ColdFusion MX, BlueDragon has been around for three years as a J2EE CFML interpreter. This chapter is written based on the public beta of BlueDragon 3.0.

Installing BlueDragon

This section steps you through the installation process of BlueDragon. It talks about the software and hardware that you need to get BlueDragon to work.

Preparing to Install

BlueDragon comes in two different flavors. One version is a stand-alone product; the second is a plug-in for existing J2EE servers. This chapter concentrates on the stand-alone version of the software.

The first thing you will need to do is to choose your operating system. BlueDragon will work on the Windows server-based operating systems (XP, 2000, NT 4.0), SPARC Solaris 2.6+, and Red Hat Linux 6.2+. Your choice of web server will depend, in part, on the operating system that you are installing on.

After choosing the operating system, make sure you have a machine with acceptable hardware requirements. BlueDragon's requirements are equal to those of the Sun Java Runtime Engine. These are modest hardware requirements that any recent machine will surpass. On the Windows side of things, you need a Pentium 166 and 32MB of RAM.

On any operating system, you can use a built-in web server, although it is not recommended for production sites. If you are installing on a Windows unit, you can choose from Microsoft IIS, Netscape Enterprise Server, iPlanet Web Server, or Apache Web Server. SPARC Solaris systems accept the same list, minus Microsoft IIS, which is based off of Windows. Linux systems will only support the Apache Web Server.

 BlueDragon does not support Windows consumer operating systems such as Windows 98, 95, or Me.

Here are some things that you should do in preparation for installing BlueDragon:

- **Download the installer**   You can do this from www.newatlanta.com. If you are downloading for Windows, the file is BlueDragon_Server_30.exe. The Solaris file is BlueDragon_Server_30-solaris.sh, and the Linux file is BlueDragon_Server_30-linux.sh.

- **Configure your ports**   The built-in web server is set to listen to port 8080. If you have another product configured to listen to that port, you should change it to listen to another.

- **Uninstall conflicting programs**   You do not want to run BlueDragon on a machine that also has any versions of ColdFusion or any servlet JSP engines such as JRun or TomCat. You should uninstall these programs before trying to install BlueDragon.

- **Disable Java servlet support**   If you are planning on running BlueDragon on top of Netscape Enterprise or iPlanet, you must first disable the built-in Java servlet support. You can check documentation on your web server or on BlueDragon for more information on how to do this.

You are now ready to start the installation process.

Installing the BlueDragon Software

This section shows you how to install the BlueDragon software. It also tells you what files are installed and where they are located on your server.

Stepping Through the Installation Process

This is how you can install BlueDragon:

1. Launch the installer. If you are on a Windows-based unit, just double-click the installer. If you are on a Unix- or Linux-based machine, you can use the following command:

   ```
   sh ./BlueDragon_Server_30-solaris.sh
   ```

   If you are on a Linux machine, you can use this command:

   ```
   sh ./BlueDragon_Server_30-linux.sh console
   ```

   The installer screen will pop up.

2. Click Next and review the readme file.

3. Click Next and review the license agreement. If you agree to the license agreement, select the appropriate radio button and click Next. Otherwise, click Cancel.

4. Enter the installation directory on the next screen.

5. On the Built-in Web Server Port Number screen, select a port for the built-in web server.

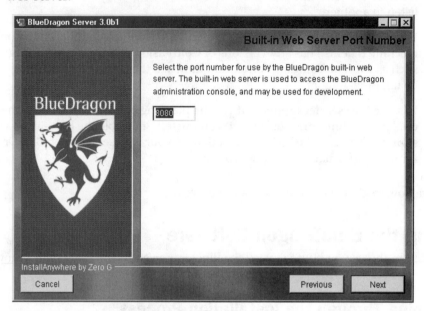

It is important that you assign a unique port here. You do not want two programs trying to listen to the same port.

6. On the External Web Server Adapter screen, select the web server adapter that you wish to install, if any.

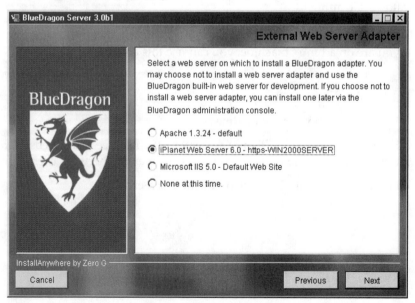

Web sever adapters are plug-ins that allow BlueDragon to work with an external web server. The BlueDragon installer will automatically detect the web servers you have installed on your system.

7. If you are installing the web server adapter for Netscape or iPlanet, you have to choose the port number that BlueDragon will use to communicate with the web server.

It is important that this port number does not conflict with any other software. The default port number, 8888, is used for server administration for Netscape Enterprise Server and iPlanet Server. If you are running either of these web servers, make sure that you change the default value.

Note   *The default port number will probably change in later releases.*

8. Select a password for the BlueDragon Administration Console. You have to enter the password a second time to confirm it.

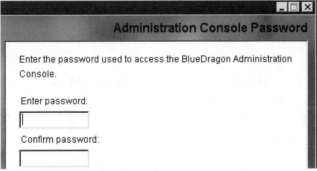

9. Verify your installation options on the Pre-Installation Summary screen. Click the Install button. The system will install BlueDragon. Click Done to finish your installation.

10. If you installed a web server adapter, you have to restart that web server before BlueDragon will work.

You can verify your installation in Windows by looking for the BlueDragon service in the Services control panel. In Unix or Linux, BlueDragon is installed as a daemon and the installer starts it. An index.cfm page is installed into the root directory of the web site. If the page loads properly, the configuration was properly installed.

Looking at the Installation Directories

Table 32-1 shows the subdirectories that will be installed in your BlueDragon installation directory. If you need to know where to find something, this will tell you where to look. The default installation directory for Windows is C:\Program Files\New Atlanta\BlueDragon. The default installation directory for Unix is /usr/local/New_Atlanta/BlueDragon.

Directory	Description
bin	Contains binary files that relate to the BlueDragon server.
classes	Used to store classes that reference either Java CFX custom tags or classes that are instantiated with cfobject.
config	Contains configuration files used by the BlueDragon server.
customtags	Contains CFML custom tags. This operates the same way as Macromedia's CFML custom tag directory.
docs	Contains the documentation for BlueDragon.
install	Contains files that are used by the BlueDragon installer.
jre	Contains the built-in BlueDragon Java run-time environment.
lib	Contains Java files that make the BlueDragon server work.
logs	Contains all log files.
mail	Contains files used by BlueDragon to send e-mail. A log file, mail.log, is in this directory.
servlets	The directory in which Java servlet files should be placed.
uninstall	Contains files for the BlueDragon uninstaller.
wwwroot	The root directory for the built-in web server.

Table 32-1.   *BlueDragon Installation Directory*

Administering a BlueDragon Server

This section teaches you all the information that you need to know to administer your BlueDragon server. It shows you how to use the BlueDragon administrator and how you can set up databases for access from within CFML code.

Using the Administrator

Point your browser to http://localhost:8080/bluedragon/admin.cfm. This takes you to the BlueDragon administrator login screen. Enter the same password that you entered during the installation process and then click Log in. The main BlueDragon administrator page opens, as shown in Figure 32-1.

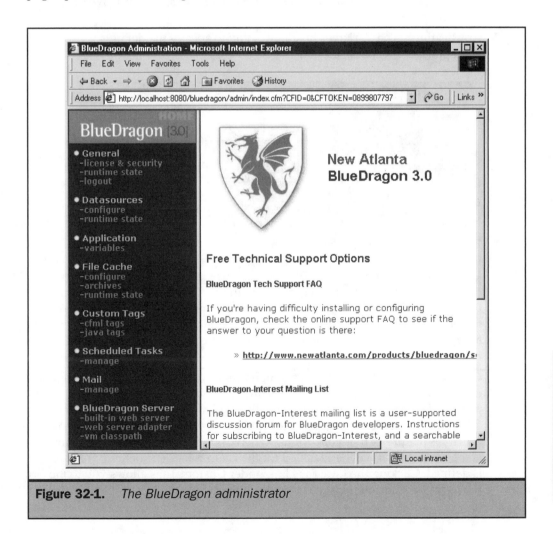

Figure 32-1.   *The BlueDragon administrator*

INTEGRATING COLDFUSION
WITH OTHER
TECHNOLOGIES

Here is a list of sections in the BlueDragon administrator and the actions that you can perform:

- **General** In the General section, you can click the License & Security link to specify a list of IP addresses that are allowed to access the administrative section or change the password for logging in to the administrator. You can click Logout, or access the Runtime State page, which allows you to view information about the current process, including files in the cache, datasources in action, and the Java Virtual Machine.

- **Datasources** In the Datasources section, you can click the Configure link to set up datasources for use from within your BlueDragon application. You can also click the Runtime State link to get information about currently active database connections.

- **Application** The Variables link allows you to specify the defaults for session and application variable timeout.

You can also use this link to specify whether you want to store client information in the Registry or as cookie values.

- **File Cache** You load the File Cache Management page by clicking the Configure link under the File Cache option. This page allows you to specify a trusted cache and the maximum number of files that can be stored in the cache. A trusted cache will not check the file in memory with the file on disk before serving it to the end user. This will improve performance on production servers, where the files are not changing on a routine basis. Other options under the File Cache menu are Archives (not yet implemented) and Runtime State, which allows you to get information about the current cache.

- **Custom Tags** The Custom Tags options allow you to handle CFML and Java custom tags. Clicking the CFML Tags link takes you to the CFML Custom Tag page. It allows you to create a mapping that will map to a custom tag. This works differently from Macromedia's ColdFusion server. The mapping name that you specify is the prefix that you will use when calling the custom tag. The directory is the location that will be searched for the custom tag. The default prefix, CF_, is defined. Clicking the Java Tags link under Custom Tags allows you to modify the list of CFX custom tags that were built in Java.

■ **Scheduled Tasks** Selecting the Manage link allows you to maintain your list of scheduled tasks. You can create a new task or edit an existing task.

■ **Mail** Selecting the Manage link allows you to specify the mail server that you want to use when calling the mail tags in your code.

■ **BlueDragon Server** This heading offers three options. Click Built-In Web Server to modify the port number of the built-in web server. You can see the web server adapters that are installed by selecting the Web Server Adapter link. The VM Classpath link will show you information about the Java virtual machine.

Accessing Databases with BlueDragon

One of the most important parts of ColdFusion development is the ability to access a database. This section shows you how to set up a datasource so that you can access it from within ColdFusion. BlueDragon comes with JTurbo, a product from New Atlanta that includes JDBC database drivers for Microsoft SQL Server, Oracle, and MySQL. It also comes with an ODBC bridge that allows you to connect to any ODBC-based datasource. You can use any third-party JDBC drivers to connect directly to any other database of your choice by adding the location of the driver into your classpath.

This is how you can set up a datasource:

1. Launch the BlueDragon Administration Console. Click the Configure link under Datasources.

2. Click the Add Data Source button. Enter the name of your datasource, the name of the database, and a description. Select the type of driver that you will use for this datasource.

3. Step 2 in the datasource setup process is used to specify the location of the database if you are accessing a client/server database.

INTEGRATING COLDFUSION WITH OTHER TECHNOLOGIES

If you are creating a datasource using the Other or the ODBC bridge option, then you will bypass Step 2. Enter the information about the database server and click Next.

4. The third step for adding the datasource contains lots of miscellaneous information. Fill in the relevant database information. The Driver Class box should be filled in automatically, as should the Database URI box if you are accessing a database server. You can enter the default username and password, as well as select various checkboxes for SQL permission that can be executed against this datasource. Click the Next button.

5. The final step in creating the datasource lets you verify the information you have submitted and gives you the option to change any of it. Click Cancel if you do not want to create the datasource.

Understanding CFML Differences

Since BlueDragon is an alternate implementation of Macromedia's CFML language, there are some minor differences in the language, based on what is supported and implemented. BlueDragon is currently compatible with most of the ColdFusion 5 language, but not all. A CFMX-compatible release is due out in the third quarter of 2002. This section explores some of the differences in the language.

Here is a list of differences:

■ **Variable scopes** In ColdFusion MX, specifying the variable scope as a prefix to the variable is optional, although not recommended. In BlueDragon, specifying the scope is not optional unless you are referencing a variable in the variables scope.

■ **URL and form variables** In BlueDragon, there is no difference between URL and form variable scopes. They are aliases of each other. In Macromedia's ColdFusion Server, URL variables are used to reference variables in the query string, and form variables are used to reference variables that were submitted via an HTTP post.

■ **Caller scope** The caller scope is used in custom tags to access values on the calling page. Both Macromedia ColdFusion and BlueDragon allow the caller scope to access local variables on the page. ColdFusion will allow you to access other scopes on the page using a syntax similar to caller.form.MyVariable. This is invalid in BlueDragon.

■ **Unsupported tags** BlueDragon does not have support for a lot of the built-in features that are used to communicate with add-on software such as Verity or SiteMinder. These CFML tags are not supported in BlueDragon: cfapplet, cfassociate, cfauthenticate, cfcollection, cfgrid, cfgridcolumn, cfgridrow, cfgridupdate, cfimpersonate, cfindex, cfprocessingdirective, cfreport, cfsearch, cfsetting, cftransaction, and cfwddx.

- **cfgraph changes** BlueDragon will only develop graphs in JPG format. ColdFusion 5 can create graphs in JPG, GIF, and Flash formats. The fileformat attribute is ignored because of this.

- **Database tags** On cfinsert, cfquery, cfstoredproc, and cfupdate, BlueDragon does not support the connectstring, dbname, dbserver, provider, or providerDSN attributes. The dbtype attribute is not supported on anything but cfquery. ColdFusion MX also removed support for many of these attributes, due to the limitations of JDBC drivers.

- **COM support** BlueDragon does not support COM or CORBA objects. The cfobject tag or CreateObject function will only support java as the type.

- **cfparam** The cfparam tag cannot be used to make cookies in BlueDragon. This works in ColdFusion. The cfcookie tag should be used instead.

- **cfregistry** BlueDragon will simulate the Registry on non-Windows systems. It is therefore possible to use the cfregistry tag on all operating systems. Macromedia ColdFusion limits the cfregistry use to Windows units.

- **cfset** In BlueDragon, it is not possible to create or modify cookie or CGI values with cfset. The cfcookie tag can be used for cookies. If you use a dot in a variable name, BlueDragon will create a structure with a single key. This is how ColdFusion MX works, but not how ColdFusion 5 works.

- **cftree and cftreeitem** In cftree, the completepath, delimiter, and onvalidate attributes are not supported. For cftreeitem, img and imgopen are not supported.

- **IsDefined** When you perform a query in ColdFusion, the query variable is not created if the query returns no values. You can use the IsDefined function to check for the existence of a query variable. In BlueDragon, the query is always created. To check whether values were returned by the query, check whether QueryName.RecordCount is greater than 0. ParameterExists, a deprecated replacement for IsDefined, is not implemented in BlueDragon.

- **ParagraphFormat** When using the ParagraphFormat function, ColdFusion will convert new line characters into spaces. BlueDragon will covert them into HTML line breaks, <br>.

- **Custom tags** BlueDragon does not support C++ custom tags, although it does support custom tags written in Java. ColdFusion 5 and MX support both types of custom tags.

- **Client variables** Client variables can be stored as cookies or in the Registry. They cannot be stored in a datasource.

Testing many of the samples from earlier in this book resulted in no problems when running against BlueDragon. ColdFusion MX–specific features are not supported, such as CFCs and cfloginuser, but you can use includes, database tags, and all of the ColdFusion 5 tags and functions.

Tip   *You can check your BlueDragon documentation for more updates about CFML compatibility.*

Summary

In this chapter, you learned about the following:

- The BlueDragon CFML interpreter
- The differences between BlueDragon and Macromedia's ColdFusion Server
- How to test some applications in BlueDragon

I hope you found this book informative and useful. You can look at the appendixes for places to find further information.

The
Complete
Reference

Part VI

Appendixes

The Complete Reference

ColdFusion MX

Appendix A

ColdFusion Tag and Function List

599

This appendix gives you a list of all of ColdFusion's tags and functions along with their parameters and attributes, a short description, and default values where applicable.

Short References

This section provides a reference list of specific tags and functions, sorted by category.

Application Framework

cfapplication	cfassociate	DeleteClientVariable	cferror
cfexecute	GetClientVariablesList	GetFunctionList	GetProfileSections
GetProfileString	GetServiceSettings	cfimport	cflock
cfmodule	cfprocessingdirective	cfregistry	cfscript
SetEncoding	cfsetting	URLSessionFormat	

Array Functions

ArrayAppend	ArrayAvg	ArrayClear	ArrayDeleteAt
ArrayInsertAt	ArrayIsEmpty	ArrayLen	ArrayMax
ArrayMin	ArrayNew	ArrayPrepend	ArrayResize
ArraySet	ArraySort	ArraySum	ArraySwap
ArrayToList	IsArray	ListToArray	StructKeyArray

Bit Functions

BitAnd	BitMaskClear	BitMaskRead	BitMaskSet
BitNot	BitOr	BitSHLN	BitSHRN
BitXor			

Code Modularization

cfargument	cfassociate	cfcomponent	cffunction
GetBaseTagData	GetBaseTagList	GetMetaData	cfinclude

cfinvoke	cfinvokeargument	IsCustomFunction	cfmodule
cfobject	cfproperty		

Data Conversion

ArrayToList	FormatBaseN	Hash	InputBaseN
ListToArray	StructKeyArray	StructKeyList	ToBase64
ToBinary	ToString	XMLFormat	XMLParse
XMLTransform			

Data Output and Formatting

cfchart	cfchartdata	cfchartseries	CJustify
cfcol	cfcontent	DateFormat	DecimalFormat
DollarFormat	cfflush	FormatBaseN	cfheader
HTMLCodeFormat	HTMLEditFormat	LJustify	cflog
LSCurrencyFormat	LSEuroCurrencyFormat	LSNumberFormat	LSParseCurrency
LSParseDateTime	LSParseEuroCurrency	LSParseNumber	LSTimeFormat
NumberFormat	cfoutput	ParagraphFormat	cfprocessingdirective
PreserveSingleQuotes	RJustify	cfsilent	StripCR
cftable	TimeFormat	WriteOutput	YesNoFormat

Database and Query Manipulation and Display

cfcol	cfinsert	IsQuery	cfloop
cfobjectcache	cfoutput	PreserveSingleQuotes	cfprocparam
cfprocresult	cfquery	QueryAddColumn	QueryAddRow
QueryNew	cfqueryparam	QuerySetCell	QuotedValueList
cfstoredproc	cftable	cftransaction	cfupdate
ValueList			

Date and Time

CreateDate	CreateDateTime	CreateODBCDate	CreateODBCDateTime
CreateODBCTime	CreateTime	CreateTimeSpan	DateAdd
DateCompare	DateConvert	DateDiff	DateFormat
DatePart	Day	DayOfWeek	DayOfWeekAsString
DayOfYear	DaysInMonth	DaysInYear	FirstDayOfMonth
GetHTTPTimeString	GetLocale	GetTimeZoneInfo	Hour
IsDate	IsLeapYear	IsNumericDate	LSDateFormat
LSIsDate	LSParseDateTime	LSTimeFormat	Minute
Month	MonthAsString	Now	ParseDateTime
Quarter	Second	TimeFormat	Week
Year			

Debugging and Error Handling

cfabort	cfbreak	cfcatch	cfdump
cferror	GetBaseTemplatePath	GetCurrentTemplatePath	GetException
GetMetricData	GetTemplatePath	GetTickCount	IsDebugMode
cflog	cfreport	cfrethrow	cfthrow
cftrace	cftry		

Dynamic Evaluation

DE	Evaluate	IIf	SetVariable

Extensibility

cfchart	cfchartdata	cfchartseries	cfcollection
cfcomponent	CreateObject	cfexecute	cfftp
cffunction	cfindex	cfinvoke	cfinvokeargument

cfmodule	cfobject	cfproperty	cfreport
cfreturn	cfsearch	cfscript	cfwddx
cfxml	XmlChildPos	XmlElemNew	XmlFormat
XmlNew	XmlParse	XmlSearch	XmlTransform

File and Directory Management

cfdirectory	DirectoryExists	ExpandPath	cffile
FileExists	cfftp	GetBaseTemplatePath	GetCurrentTemplatePath
GetDirectoryFromPath	GetFileFromPath	GetProfileSections	GetProfileString
GetTempDirectory	GetTempFile	GetTemplatePath	cfprocessingdirective

Flow Control and Decisions

cfabort	cfbreak	cfcase	cfdefaultcase
DirectoryExists	cfelse	cfelseif	cfexit
FileExists	cfif	Iif	cfinclude
IsArray	IsAuthenticated	IsBinary	IsBoolean
IsCustomFunction	IsDate	IsDebugMode	IsDefined
IsK2ServerABroker	IsK2ServerDocCountExceeded	IsK2ServerOnline	IsLeapYear
IsNumeric	IsNumericDate	IsObject	IsQuery
IsSimpleValue	IsStruct	IsUserInRole	IsWDDX
IsXMLDoc	IsXMLElement	IsXMLRoot	cflocation
cfloop	LSIsCurrency	LSIsDate	LSIsNumeric
cfrethrow	StructIsEmpty	StructKeyExists	cfswitch
cfthrow	cftry	YesNoFormat	

Form Elements

cfapplet	cfform	cfgrid	cfgridcolumn
cfgridrow	cfgridupate	cfhtmlhead	cfinput
cfldap	cfmail	cfmailparam	cfpop
cfselect	cfslider	cftextinput	cftree
cftreeitem			

International Functions

DateConvert	GetLocale	GetTimeZoneInfo	LSCurrencyFormat
LSDateFormat	LSEuroCurrencyFormat	LSIsCurrency	LSIsDate
LSIsNumeric	LSNumberFormat	LSParseCurrency	LSParseDateTime
LSParseEuroCurrency	LSParseNumber	LSTimeFormat	SetEncoding
SetLocale			

Internet Protocol

cfcookie	cfftp	GetHttpRequestData	GetHttpTimeString
HTMLCodeFormat	HTMLEditFormat	cfhttp	cfhttpparam
cfldap	cfmail	cfmailparam	cfpop
SetEncoding	URLDecode	URLEncodedFormat	URLSessionFormat

Java Integration

GetException	GetPageContext	cfimport	IsObject
JavaCast	cfobject		

List Functions

ArrayToList	GetBaseTagList	GetClientVariableList	GetToken
Len	ListAppend	ListChangeDelims	ListContains
ListContainsNoCase	ListDeleteAt	ListFind	ListFindNoCase
ListFirst	ListGetAt	ListInsertAt	ListLast
ListLen	ListPrepend	ListQualify	ListRest
ListSetAt	ListSort	ListToArray	ListValueCount
ListValueCountNoCase	QuotedValueList	ReplaceList	StructKeyList
ValueList			

Mathematical Process

Abs	ACos	ArrayAvg	ArraySum
ASin	ATn	Ceiling	Cos

DecrementValue	Exp	Fix	FormatBaseN
IncrementValue	InputBaseN	Int	Log
Log10	Max	Min	Pi
Rand	Randomize	RandRange	Round
Sgn	Sin	Sqr	Tan
Val			

Page Processing

cfcache	cfcontent	cfflush
GetBaseTemplatePath	GetCurrentTemplatePath	GetDirectoryFromPath
cfheader	cfhtmlhead	cfinclude
cflocation	cfprocessingdirective	cfsavecontent
cfsetting	cfsilent	

Regular Expressions

| REFind | REFindNoCase | REReplace | REReplaceNoCase |

Security

| Decrypt | Encrypt | GetAuthUser | Hash |
| IsUserInRole | cflogin | cfloginuser | cflogout |

String Processing

Asc	Chr	CJustify	Compare
CompareNoCase	CreateUUID	DayOfWeekAsString	Decrypt
Encrypt	Find	FindNoCase	FindOneOf
FormatBaseN	GetToken	Hash	Insert
JavaCast	JSStringFormat	LCase	Left
Len	LJustify	LSIsCurrency	LSIsDate

LSIsNumeric	LSParseCurrency	LSParseDateTime	LSParseEuroCurrency
LSParseNumber	Ltrim	Mid	MonthAsString
NumberFormat	ParagraphFormat	ParseDateTime	PreserveSingleQuotes
REFind	REFindNoCase	RemoveChars	RepeatString
Replace	ReplaceList	ReplaceNoCase	REReplace
REReplaceNoCase	Reverse	Right	RJustify
Rtrim	SpanExcluding	SpanIncluding	StripCR
ToBase64	ToBinary	ToString	Trim
UCase	URLDecode	URLEncodedFormat	Val
XMLFormat			

Structure Functions

Duplicate	GetFunctionList	GetHTTPRequestData	GetMetricData
GetTimeZoneInfo	IsStruct	StructAppend	StructClear
StructCopy	StructCount	StructDelete	StructFind
StructFindKey	StructFindValue	StructGet	StructInsert
StructIsEmpty	StructKeyArray	StructKeyExists	StructKeyList
StructNew	StructSort	StructUpdate	

Variable Manipulation

cfcookie	DE	Decrypt	DeleteClientVariable
cfdump	Encrypt	Evaluate	Hash
cfoutput	cfparam	cfregistry	cfsavecontent
cfschedule	cfset	SetEncoding	SetLocale
SetProfileString	SetVariable		

Verity Integration

cfcollection	GetK2ServerDocCount	GetK2ServerDocCountLimit
cfindex	IsK2ServerABroker	IsK2ServerDocCountExceeded
IsK2ServerOnline	cfsearch	

XML and WDDX

GetMetaData	IsWDDX	IsXmlDoc	IsXmlElement
IsXmlRoot	cfwddx	cfxml	XmlChildPos
XmlElemNew	XmlFormat	XmlNew	XmlParse
XmlSearch	XmlTransform		

ColdFusion Tags and Functions

cfabort   A tag used to stop the processing of a ColdFusion page.

Attribute	Req/Opt	Default	Description
showerror	Optional	N/A	Contains the error to display when the tag executes.

Abs   A function to return the absolute value of a number without its sign.

Parameter	Req/Opt	Default	Description
number	Required	N/A	Specifies the number.

ACos   A function used to perform an arccosine.

Parameter	Req/Opt	Default	Description
number	Required	N/A	Specifies the cosine of the angle, between 1.0 and –1.0.

cfapplet   A tag used to reference a Java applet that was registered in the ColdFusion Administrator.

Attribute	Req/Opt	Default	Description
appletsource	Required	N/A	Name of the registered applet.
name	Required	N/A	The form variable name of the applet.
height	Optional	N/A	The height of the applet, in pixels.

Attribute	Req/Opt	Default	Description
width	Optional	N/A	The width of the applet, in pixels.
vspace	Optional	N/A	The space above and below the applet, in pixels.
hspace	Optional	N/A	The space to the left and right of the applet, in pixels.
align	Optional	N/A	The alignment of the applet. Valid values are left, right, bottom, top, texttop, middle, absmiddle, baseline, or absbottom.
notsupported	Optional	Browser must support Java to view ColdFusion Java Applets!	The text to display if the browser does not support Java.
param_*n*	Optional	N/A	The name-value pairs of the required parameters for this applet.

cfapplication   A tag used to set up ColdFusion's application framework.

Attribute	Req/Opt	Default	Description
name	Required for session and application variables; optional for client variables	N/A	The name of your application.
clientmanagement	Optional	No	Yes to enable client variables; no to go without them.
clientstorage	Optional	registry	Specifies how client variables are stored. Valid values are registry, cookie, or the name of a datasource.
setclientcookies	Optional	Yes	Yes enables client cookies. No turns them off.

Attribute	Req/Opt	Default	Description
sessionmanagement	Optional	No	Yes enables session variables. No turns them off.
sessiontimeout	Optional	Specified in ColdFusion Admin.	Specifies the lifespan of session variables. You can set this using the CreateTimeSpan function.
applicationtimeout	Optional	Specified in ColdFusion Admin.	Specifies the lifespan of application variables. You can set this using the CreateTimeSpan function.
setdomaincookies	Optional	No	Yes to set CFID and CFTOKEN as domain cookies, for clustered servers. No to set them as normal cookies.

cfargument A tag used to define a parameter in a custom function.

Attribute	Req/Opt	Default	Description
name	Required	N/A	Specifies the name of the argument.
type	Optional	any	Specifies the type of the argument: any, array, binary, Boolean, date, guid, numeric, query, string, struct, uuid, variablename, or component name.
required	Optional	no	A Boolean value that specifies whether this is a required parameter for the function.
default	Optional	N/A	The default value of the argument.

ArrayAppend A function used to add a value to the end of an array. Returns true on success.

Parameter	Req/Opt	Default	Description
array	Required	N/A	Specifies the name of the array.
value	Required	N/A	Specifies the value to append.

ArrayAvg   A function used to return the average of all values in an array.

Parameter	Req/Opt	Default	Description
array	Required	N/A	Specifies the name of the array.

ArrayClear   A function used to delete all values in an array. Returns true on success.

Parameter	Req/Opt	Default	Description
array	Required	N/A	Specifies the name of the array.

ArrayDeleteAt   A function used to delete a single array value. Returns true on success.

Parameter	Req/Opt	Default	Description
array	Required	N/A	Specifies the name of the array.
position	Required	N/A	Specifies the position of the value to delete.

ArrayInsertAt   A function used to insert a value into an array. Returns true on success.

Parameter	Req/Opt	Default	Description
array	Required	N/A	Specifies the name of the array.
position	Required	N/A	Specifies the position in which to insert the value.
value	Required	N/A	Specifies the value to insert.

ArrayIsEmpty   A function used to check if an array is empty. Returns true if array is empty.

Parameter	Req/Opt	Default	Description
array	Required	N/A	Specifies the name of the array.

ArrayLen   A function used to return the length of an array.

Parameter	Req/Opt	Default	Description
array	Required	N/A	Specifies the name of the array.

ArrayMax   A function used to return the largest value in an array.

Parameter	Req/Opt	Default	Description
array	Required	N/A	Specifies the name of the array.

ArrayMin   A function used to return the smallest value in an array.

Parameter	Req/Opt	Default	Description
array	Required	N/A	Specifies the name of the array.

ArrayNew   A function used to create a new array. Returns the new array.

Parameter	Req/Opt	Default	Description
dimension	Required	N/A	Specifies dimension of the array: 1, 2, or 3.

ArrayPrepend   A function used to add an item to the beginning of an array. Returns true on success.

Parameter	Req/Opt	Default	Description
array	Required	N/A	Specifies the name of the array.
value	Required	N/A	Specifies the value to prepend.

ArrayResize   A function used to change the size of an array. Returns true on success.

Parameter	Req/Opt	Default	Description
array	Required	N/A	Specifies the name of the array.
minimumsize	Required	N/A	Specifies the smallest allowed size of the array.

ArraySet   A function used to set the elements of a one-dimensional array to a specified value. Returns true on success.

Parameter	Req/Opt	Default	Description
array	Required	N/A	Specifies the name of the array.
start_pos	Required	N/A	Specifies the index of the first value to set.
end_pos	Required	N/A	Specifies the index of the last value to set.
value	Required	N/A	Specifies the value to set the elements to.

ArraySort   A function used to sort an array. Returns true on success.

Parameter	Req/Opt	Default	Description
array	Required	N/A	Specifies the name of the array.
sorttype	Required	N/A	Specifies the sort type: numeric, text, or textnocase.
sortorder	Optional	N/A	Specifies the sort order, either ASC or DESC.

ArraySum   A function used to add all elements in an array and return the value.

Parameter	Req/Opt	Default	Description
array	Required	N/A	Specifies the name of the array.

ArraySwap   A function used to swap two elements of an array. Returns true on success.

Parameter	Req/Opt	Default	Description
array	Required	N/A	Specifies the name of the array.
position1	Required	N/A	Specifies the position of the first element to swap.
position2	Required	N/A	Specifies the position of the second element to swap.

ArrayToList   A function used to convert the array to a list and return the list.

Parameter	Req/Opt	Default	Description
array	Required	N/A	Specifies the name of the array.
delimiter	Optional	, (comma)	Specifies the list separator.

Asc   A function used to return the ASCII value of the first character of a string.

Parameter	Req/Opt	Default	Description
string	Required	N/A	Specifies the string to process.

ASin   A function used to return the arcsine of a number.

Parameter	Req/Opt	Default	Description
number	Required	N/A	Specifies the sine of the angle. Must be between 1.0 and –1.0.

cfassociate   A tag used to allow subtag data to be saved with the base tag.

Attribute	Req/Opt	Default	Description
basetag	Required	N/A	The name of the base tag.
datacollection	Optional	AssocAttribs	The structure in which the data will be stored.

Atn   A function used to return the arctangent of a number.

Parameter	Req/Opt	Default	Description
number	Required	N/A	Specifies the tangent of the angle.

BitAnd   A function used to return a bitwise logical AND operation.

Parameter	Req/Opt	Default	Description
number1	Required	N/A	A 32-bit signed integer.
number2	Required	N/A	A 32-bit signed integer.

BitMaskClear   A function used to return a bitwise mask clear operation.

Parameter	Req/Opt	Default	Description
number	Required	N/A	A 32-bit signed integer.
start	Required	N/A	Specifies the start bit for the mask, between 0 and 31.
length	Required	N/A	Specifies the length of the mask to be cleared, between 0 and 31.

BitMaskRead   A function used to perform a bitwise mask read operation and return the integer result.

Parameter	Req/Opt	Default	Description
number	Required	N/A	A 32-bit signed integer.
start	Required	N/A	Specifies the start bit for the mask, between 0 and 31.
length	Required	N/A	Specifies the length of the mask to be cleared, between 0 and 31.

BitMaskSet   A function used to perform a bitwise mask set operation and return the result.

Parameter	Req/Opt	Default	Description
number	Required	N/A	A 32-bit signed integer.
mask	Required	N/A	A 32-bit signed integer to use as the mask.
start	Required	N/A	Specifies the start bit for the mask, between 0 and 31.

Parameter	Req/Opt	Default	Description
length	Required	N/A	Specifies the length of the mask to be cleared, between 0 and 31.

BitNot   A function used to return a bitwise logical NOT operation.

Parameter	Req/Opt	Default	Description
number	Required	N/A	A 32-bit signed integer.

BitOr   A function used to return the results of a bitwise logical OR operation.

Parameter	Req/Opt	Default	Description
number1	Required	N/A	A 32-bit signed integer.
number2	Required	N/A	A 32-bit signed integer.

BitSHLN   A function used to return the results of a bitwise shift left, no rotation operation.

Parameter	Req/Opt	Default	Description
number	Required	N/A	A 32-bit signed integer.
count	Required	N/A	Specifies the number of bits to shift the number, in the range of 0–31.

BitSHRN   A function used to return the results of a bitwise shift right, no rotation operation.

Parameter	Req/Opt	Default	Description
number	Required	N/A	A 32-bit signed integer.
count	Required	N/A	Specifies the number of bits to shift the number, in the range of 0–31.

BitXor   A function used to return the results of a bitwise logical XOR operation.

Parameter	Req/Opt	Default	Description
number1	Required	N/A	A 32-bit signed integer.
number2	Required	N/A	A 32-bit signed integer.

cfbreak   A tag used to break out of a loop.
No attributes

cfcache   A tag used to store a copy of the processed ColdFusion page in the server's memory.

Attribute	Req/Opt	Default	Description
action	Optional	cache	Valid values are cache, to cache the page on both the server side and client side; flush, to flush the cached page; clientcache, to cache on the client side only; servercache, to cache on the server side only; or optimal, which is the same as cache.
directory	Optional	*cf_root*/cache	Contains the path to the cache directory.
timespan	Optional	Keep page cached until manually flushed	Interval until the page is flushed. You can populate this with the CreateTimeSpan function.
expireURL	Optional	Flush all pages	Used with action=flush and contains the URL to be flushed.
username	Optional	N/A	The username to access this page, if required.
password	Optional	N/A	The password to access this page, if required.
port	Optional	The port of the current page	The port number of the web server from which the page was requested.
protocol	Optional	The protocol of the current page	Either http:// or https://.

cfcase   A tag used to define a case. Used with the cfswitch tag.

Attribute	Req/Opt	Default	Description
value	Required	N/A	The value, or list of values, that is being compared to the expression result specified in the cfswitch.
delimiters	Optional	, (comma)	The character that separates different values.

cfcatch   A tag used to catch an error. Used within a cftry block.

Attribute	Req/Opt	Default	Description
type	Optional	Any	The type of expression to catch. Valid values are application, database, template, security, object, missinginclude, expression, lock, custom_type, searchengine, or any.

Ceiling   A function used to return the closest integer that is greater than the given number.

Parameter	Req/Opt	Default	Description
number	Required	N/A	Specifies a real number.

cfchart   A tag used to generate and display charts.

Attribute	Req/Opt	Default	Description
format	Optional	Flash	Specifies the format of the chart: jpg, png, or flash.
chartheight	Optional	240	Specifies the chart height, in pixels.
chartwidth	Optional	320	Specifies the chart width, in pixels.
scalefrom	Optional	Determined by data	Specifies the minimum Y-axis value.
scaleto	Optional	Determined by data	Specifies the maximum Y-axis value.

Attribute	Req/Opt	Default	Description
showxgridlines	Optional	No	A Boolean value that specifies whether or not the X gridlines should be displayed.
showygridlines	Optional	Yes	A Boolean value that specifies whether or not the Y gridlines should be displayed.
gridlines	Optional	3	The number of gridlines to display. The default is 3, top, bottom, and zero. Set it to 0 to display no lines.
seriesplacement	Optional	Default	If a chart has more than one series, this specifies the relative positions of the series: default, cluster, stacked, or percent.
foregroundcolor	Optional	Black	Specifies the color of the text, gridlines, and labels.
databackgroundcolor	Optional	White	Specifies the color area around the chart.
borderbackgroundcolor	Optional	White	Specifies the color between the data background and the border.
showborder	Optional	No	A Boolean value that specifies whether or not to show the border.
font	Optional	Arial	Specifies the name of the font. Valid values are arial, times, courier, or arialunicodeMS.
fontsize	Optional	11	Specifies the size of the font.
fontbold	Optional	No	A Boolean value that specifies whether or not the font will be bold.
fontitalic	Optional	No	A Boolean value that specifies whether or not the font will be italic.
labelfont	Optional	Number	The format for the Y-axis labels. Valid values are number, currency, percentage, or date.
xaxistitle	Optional	N/A	Specifies the title of the X axis.
yaxistitle	Optional	N/A	Specifies the title of the Y axis.
sortxaxis	Optional	No	A Boolean value that specifies whether or not to sort the X-axis data.

Attribute	Req/Opt	Default	Description
show3d	Optional	No	A Boolean value that specifies whether or not the graph will be shown in 3-D format.
xoffset	Optional	.1	If show3D is set to yes, specifies the number of units the display will be angled horizontally.
yoffset	Optional	.1	If show3D is set to yes, specifies the number of units the display will be angled vertically.
rotated	Optional	No	If set to yes, rotates a chart 90 degrees clockwise. This is used to make horizontal bar charts.
showlegend	Optional	Yes	A Boolean value to specify whether or not the legend is shown. Yes shows it; no hides it.
tipstyle	Optional	mouseover	Specifies the action that will open the window to display information about the current element. Valid values are mousedown, mouseover, or off.
tipbgcolor	Optional	white	The name of the color. Applies only to Flash graphs.
showmarkers	Optional	Yes	A Boolean value that specifies whether or not to show the data point markers.
markersize	Optional	Automatic	Specifies the size of the data point markers, in pixels.
pieslicestyle	Optional	Sliced	The style of the pie, if chartseries is set to pie. Valid values are solid or sliced.
url	Optional	N/A	URL to open if a user clicks a data series.
name	Optional	N/A	Contains the page variable name. Used primarily with Flash users.

cfchartdata   A tag used to specify the data within a chart. Used with the cfchart tag.

Attribute	Req/Opt	Default	Description
item	Required	N/A	The name of the item.
value	Required	N/A	The value of the item.

cfchartseries   A tag used to specify the style in which to display a chart. Used with cfchart.

Attribute	Req/Opt	Default	Description
type	Required	N/A	Specifies the style of the chart: bar, line, pyramid, area, cone, curve, cylinder, step, scatter, or pie.
query	Optional	N/A	Name of the ColdFusion query from which to get the data.
itemcolumn	Required if query is specified	N/A	Name of column that contains the item label data.
valuecolumn	Required if query is specified	N/A	Name of the column that contains the item value data.
serieslabel	Optional	N/A	A label for this specific series.
seriescolor	Optional	N/A	A color for this specific series.
paintstyle	Optional	plain	Sets the display style of the series. Valid values are plain, raise, shade, or light.
markerstyle	Optional	rectangle	Specifies the icon that marks the data point. Valid values are rectangle, triangle, diamond, circle, letter, mcross, snow, or rcross.
colorlist	Optional	N/A	If chartseries is set to pie, this can be set to a list of pie slice colors.

Chr   A function used to return the ASCII character of the given value.

Parameter	Req/Opt	Default	Description
number	Required	N/A	Specifies a value between 1 and 255.

CJustify   A function used to center a string in the specified length, and return the new string.

Parameter	Req/Opt	Default	Description
string	Required	N/A	Specifies a string or variable to be centered.
length	Required	N/A	Specifies the length of the string.

cfcol   A tag used to define the table column header, width, alignment, and text of columns in a table created with the cftable tag.

Attribute	Req/Opt	Default	Description
header	Required	N/A	Specifies the column header text.
width	Optional	20	Specifies the column width.
align	Optional	Left	Specifies the column alignment, either left, right, or center.
text	Required	N/A	Specifies the text to display in the column.

cfcollection   A tag used to create, register, and administer Verity collections.

Attribute	Req/Opt	Default	Description
action	Optional	List	Specifies the action to perform. Valid values are create, repair, delete, map, optimize, or list.
collection	Required	N/A	Specifies the name of the collection.
path	Optional	N/A	Specifies the absolute path to the Verity collection.
language	Optional	English	Specifies the language of the collection.
name	Required if action is list	N/A	Specifies the name of the query returned if the action is list.

Compare   A function used to perform a case-sensitive comparison of two strings. If string1 is less than string2, returns 1; if string1 is greater than string2, returns –1. Returns 0 if equal.

Parameter	Req/Opt	Default	Description
string1	Required	N/A	Specifies the first string.
string2	Required	N/A	Specifies the second string.

CompareNoCase A function used to perform a case-insensitive comparison of two strings. If string1 is less than string2, returns 1; if string1 is greater than string2, returns –1. Returns 0 if equal.

Parameter	Req/Opt	Default	Description
string1	Required	N/A	Specifies the first string.
string2	Required	N/A	Specifies the second string.

cfcomponent A tag used to define a ColdFusion Component.

Attribute	Req/Opt	Default	Description
extends	Optional	N/A	Contains the name of the parent component.
output	Optional	N/A	A Boolean value used to specify whether or not the output is permitted in the component.

cfcontent A tag used to send a file from the server to the client.

Attribute	Req/Opt	Default	Description
type	Optional	N/A	Specifies the MIME type, optionally including the character encoding.
deletefile	Optional	No	Specifies whether or not to delete the file after the download operation.
file	Optional	N/A	The name of the file to get. Is mutually exclusive to the reset attribute.
reset	Optional	Yes	A Boolean value that specifies whether to preserve or discard previous output. Ignored if the file attribute is used.

cfcookie A tag used to set a cookie on the client's browser.

Attribute	Req/Opt	Default	Description
name	Required	N/A	Specifies the name of the cookie.
value	Optional	N/A	Specifies the value of the cookie.
expires	Optional	now	Specifies the expiration date of the cookie. Accepts a date, a number (for days), now, or never.

Attribute	Req/Opt	Default	Description
secure	Optional	N/A	If set to yes, transmits the cookie securely; otherwise, it transmits the cookie normally.
path	Optional	N/A	Specifies the URL, within a domain, that the cookie applies to.
domain	Required if path attribute specified	N/A	Specifies the domain for which the cookie is valid.

Cos   A function used to return the value of a cosine function.

Parameter	Req/Opt	Default	Description
number	Required	N/A	Specifies the angle, in radians, to calculate the cosine.

CreateDate   A function used to return a date/time object, without the time.

Parameter	Req/Opt	Default	Description
year	Required	N/A	Specifies the year of the new date.
month	Required	N/A	Specifies the month of the new date.
day	Required	N/A	Specifies the day of the new date.

CreateDateTime   A function used to return a date/time object.

Parameter	Req/Opt	Default	Description
year	Required	N/A	Specifies the year of the new date.
month	Required	N/A	Specifies the month of the new date.
day	Required	N/A	Specifies the day of the new date.
hour	Required	N/A	Specifies the hour of the new date object.
minute	Required	N/A	Specifies the minute of the new date object.
second	Required	N/A	Specifies the second of the new date object.

CreateObject A function used to return an object, either a COM, CFC, CORBA, Java, or Web service object.

Parameter	Req/Opt	Default	Description
type	Required	N/A	Specifies the type of object: COM, CORBA, Java, component, or webservice.
COM or Java class/ Component/ CORBA context/ urltowsdl	Required	N/A	For COM: Specifies the PROGID of object. For Component: Specifies the name of a component. For CORBA: Specifies IOR or NameService. For Java: Specifies Java ClassName. For Web Service: Specifies the location of the WSDL file.
COM context/ CORBA Class	Required	N/A	For COM: Specifies inProc, Local, or Remote. For Component: Doesn't apply. For CORBA: If context is IOR, specifies absolute path of COM object. If context is NameService, specifies name of slash-delimited naming context of service. For Java: Does not apply. For Web Service: Does not apply.
COM servername CORBA Locale	Required	N/A	For COM: Specifies the servername of the object. For Component: Doesn't apply. For CORBA: Specifies Java config file that holds properties. For Java: Does not apply. For Web Service: Does not apply.

CreateODBCDate A function that returns an ODBC date object.

Parameter	Req/Opt	Default	Description
date	Required	N/A	Specifies the date or date/time object.

CreateODBCDateTime A function that returns an ODBC date/time object.

Parameter	Req/Opt	Default	Description
date	Required	N/A	Specifies the date/time object.

CreateODBCTime A function that returns an ODBC time object.

Parameter	Req/Opt	Default	Description
date	Required	N/A	Specifies the date or date/time object.

CreateTime   A function that returns a time variable.

Parameter	Req/Opt	Default	Description
hour	Required	N/A	Specifies a number in the range of 0–23.
minute	Required	N/A	Specifies a number in the range of 0–59.
second	Required	N/A	Specifies a number in the range of 0–59.

CreateTimeSpan   A function that returns a date/time object that defines a time period.

Parameter	Req/Opt	Default	Description
days	Required	N/A	Specifies the number of days of the timespan.
hours	Required	N/A	Specifies the number of hours in the timespan.
minutes	Required	N/A	Specifies the number of minutes in the timespan.
seconds	Required	N/A	Specifies the number of seconds in the timespan.

CreateUUID   A function that returns a unique identifier. It returns a 35-character representation of a 128-bit integer.
No parameters

DateAdd   A function that adds one date to another and returns the results.

Parameter	Req/Opt	Default	Description
datepart	Required	N/A	Specifies the part of the date that you want to add: yyyy (year), q (quarter), m (month), y (day of year), d (day), w (weekday), ww (week), h (hour), m (minute), or s (second).
number	Required	N/A	Specifies the number of units to add to the date.
date	Required	N/A	Specifies the date to be added to.

DateCompare   A function that performs a comparison of two dates. If the first date is earlier than the second date, –1 is returned. If the first date is later than the second date, 1 is returned. If they are equal, 0 is returned.

Parameter	Req/Opt	Default	Description
date1	Required	N/A	Specifies the first date/time object.
date2	Required	N/A	Specifies the second date/time object.
datepart	Optional	N/A	Specifies the precision of the comparison: s (seconds), n (minutes), h (hours), d (days), m (month), or yyyy (year).

DateConvert   A function used to convert a date between local time and Universal Time Coordinate and return the result.

Parameter	Req/Opt	Default	Description
Type	Required	N/A	Specifies the type of conversion: local2UTC or UTC2local.
date	Required	N/A	Specifies the first date/time object.

DateDiff   A function used to return the number of units by which date1 is less than date2.

Parameter	Req/Opt	Default	Description
datepart	Required	N/A	Specifies the part of the date that you want to add: yyyy (year), q (quarter), m (month), y (day of year), d (day), w (weekday), ww (week), h (hour), m (minute), or s (second).
date1	Required	N/A	Specifies the first date.
date2	Required	N/A	Specifies the second date.

DateFormat   A function used to return a formatted date.

Parameter	Req/Opt	Default	Description
date	Required	N/A	Specifies the date to be added to.

Parameter	Req/Opt	Default	Description
mask	Optional	N/A	Specifies the characters that show how to display the date. Valid values are short, medium, long, full, d (day of month as digits with no leading zero), dd (day of month as digits with leading zero), ddd (day of week as three letters), dddd (day of week as full name), m (month as digits, with no leading zero), mm (month as digits, with leading zero), mmm (month as three letters), mmmm (month as full name), y (year as two digits, with no leading zero), yy (year as two digits, with leading zero), yyyy (year as four digits), or gg (period/era string).

DatePart   A function used to return part of a date.

Parameter	Req/Opt	Default	Description
datepart	Required	N/A	Specifies the portion to be returned: yyyy (year), q (quarter), m (month), y (day of year), d (day), w (weekday), ww (week), h (hour), m (minute), or s (second).
date	Required	N/A	Specifies the date/time object.

Day   A function used to return the day in a month.

Parameter	Req/Opt	Default	Description
date	Required	N/A	Specifies the date/time object.

DayOfWeek   A function used to return the day of the week as a number.

Parameter	Req/Opt	Default	Description
date	Required	N/A	Specifies the date/time object.

DayOfWeekAsString A function used to return the day of the week as a string.

Parameter	Req/Opt	Default	Description
date	Required	N/A	Specifies the date/time object.

DayOfYear A function used to return the day of a year.

Parameter	Req/Opt	Default	Description
date	Required	N/A	Specifies the date/time object.

DaysInMonth A function used to return the number of days in a month.

Parameter	Req/Opt	Default	Description
date	Required	N/A	Specifies the date/time object.

DaysInYear A function used to determine the number of days in a year.

Parameter	Req/Opt	Default	Description
date	Required	N/A	Specifies the date/time object.

DE A function used to postpone the evaluation of a string as an expression. Used most commonly with the iif function. Returns the parameter surrounded by double quotation marks.

Parameter	Req/Opt	Default	Description
string	Required	N/A	The string to evaluate after the delay.

DecimalFormat A function used to return a number to a decimal-formatted string.

Parameter	Req/Opt	Default	Description
number	Required	N/A	Specifies the number to format.

DecrementValue   A function used to decrement the specified value by one and return the result.

Parameter	Req/Opt	Default	Description
number	Required	N/A	Specifies the number to decrement.

Decrypt   A function used to return a decrypted string that was encrypted using the Encrypt function.

Parameter	Req/Opt	Default	Description
encrypted_string	Required	N/A	Specifies the encrypted string.
seed	Required	N/A	Specifies the key that was used to encrypt the seed.

cfdefaultcase   A tag used with cfswitch to define the default case statement. No attributes

DeleteClientVariable   A function used to delete a client variable. Returns true if successful.

Parameter	Req/Opt	Default	Description
Name	Required	N/A	Specifies the name of the client variable to delete.

cfdirectory   A tag used to perform directory maintenance on the ColdFusion server.

Attribute	Req/Opt	Default	Description
action	Optional	List	Specifies the action to perform. Valid values are list, create, delete, or rename.
directory	Required	N/A	Specifies the absolute pathname of the directory.
name	Required if action is list	N/A	Specifies the name of the return set.
filter	Optional	N/A	Filters the directory listing. Only applies if action is list.
mode	Optional	N/A	Used to set octal permissions on Unix.

Attribute	Req/Opt	Default	Description
sort	Optional	ASC	Specifies the sort order of the result. Only applies if action is list.
newdirectory	Required if action is rename	N/A	Specifies the new directory name.

DirectoryExists   A function that checks whether a directory exists. Returns true if it does, false otherwise.

Parameter	Req/Opt	Default	Description
Path	Required	N/A	Specifies the absolute path of the directory.

DollarFormat   A function that returns a number formatted in U.S. dollar format.

Parameter	Req/Opt	Default	Description
number	Required	N/A	Specifies the number to format.

cfdump   A tag that outputs any variable's value. Used for debugging.

Attribute	Req/Opt	Default	Description
var	Required	N/A	Specifies the variable value to be displayed. Valid variable types are array, CFC, Java object, simple, query, structure, UDF, WDDX, or XML.
expand	Optional	Yes	Specifies whether to expand or collapse the display.
label	Optional	N/A	A String header for the output.

Duplicate   A function that returns a clone, or deep copy, of a variable.

Parameter	Req/Opt	Default	Description
variable_name	Required	N/A	The name of the variable you want to copy.

cfelse A tag that specifies the default condition of an if statement. Used with cfif. No parameters

cfelseif A tag that specifies an elseif condition of an if statement. Used with cfif.

Attribute	Req/Opt	Default	Description
Expression	Required	N/A	An expression that specifies the condition.

Encrypt A function used to return an encrypted version of a string. Used with Decrypt.

Parameter	Req/Opt	Default	Description
string	Required	N/A	Specifies the string to encrypt.
seed	Required	N/A	Specifies the seed to use for encrypting.

cferror A tag used to set up a custom error page for an application.

Attribute	Req/Opt	Default	Description
type	Required	N/A	The type of error. Valid values are application, database, template, security, object, missinginclude, expression, lock, custom_type, or any.
template	Required	N/A	The relative path to the custom error page.
mailto	Optional	N/A	Specifies the e-mail address to be available in the error pages.
exception	Optional	N/A	Specifies the type of exception that the tag generates: either a cftry exception or a custom exception in cfthrow.

Evaluate A function used to evaluate one or more expressions from left to right. Returns the final expression result.

Parameter	Req/Opt	Default	Description
Expression	Required	N/A	Specifies the expression, or expressions, to be evaluated.

cfexecute   A tag used to execute a process on the ColdFusion server.

Attribute	Req/Opt	Default	Description
name	Required	N/A	Specifies the absolute path to the application you want to run.
arguments	Optional	N/A	Specifies command-line arguments to the file.
outputfile	Optional	N/A	Specifies a file in which to direct output generated by the executable.
timeout	Optional	0	The length of time that ColdFusion waits for the output from the program. If set to value, ColdFusion starts the process and does not wait for return output.

cfexit   A tag that aborts processing of the current CFML custom tag.

Attribute	Req/Opt	Default	Description
method	Optional	exittag	Specifies how to exit. Valid values are exittag, exittemplate, or exitloop.

Exp   A function that returns the constant, e, raised to the specified power. The constant e equals the base of the natural logarithm and its value is 2.71828.

Parameter	Req/Opt	Default	Description
number	Required	N/A	Specifies the exponent to apply to e.

ExpandPath   A function used to return the absolute path of a given relative path.

Parameter	Req/Opt	Default	Description
relativepath	Required	N/A	Specifies the relative path of the directory.

cffile   A tag that allows for file maintenance.

Attribute	Req/Opt	Default	Description
action	Required	N/A	Type of operation to perform. Valid values are upload, move, rename, copy, delete, read, readbinary, write, or append.

Attribute	Req/Opt	Default	Description
filefield	Required for upload	N/A	When uploading a file through a form submission, specifies the name of the form field that contains the file.
File	Required for delete, read, write, append, or readbinary	N/A	When deleting, writing, appending, or reading a file, contains the absolute pathname of the file.
Output	Required for write or append	N/A	When writing or appending to a file, contains the contents.
variable	Required for read or readbinary	N/A	When reading from a file, contains the name of the variable that will contain the file's contents.
Source	Required for move, copy, or rename	N/A	When moving, copying, or renaming a file, the absolute path of the file.
destination	Required for upload, move, copy, or rename	N/A	When uploading, moving, copying, or renaming a file, contains the absolute pathname of the file on the server.
nameconflict	Optional	Error	When uploading a file, defines the action to take if a name conflict exists. Options are error, skip, overwrite, and makeunique.
accept	Optional	N/A	When uploading a file, specifies the MIME types that will be accepted.
mode	Optional	N/A	When uploading, renaming, copying, writing, appending, or moving a file, specifies the Octal permissions for Unix-based machines.
attributes	Optional	N/A	When uploading, renaming, copying, writing, appending, or moving a file, specifies the Windows-based permissions: readonly, hidden, and normal.
charset	Optional	UTF-8	When moving, writing, appending, or reading a file, specifies the Java character set name of the file contents.
addnewline	Optional	Yes	When writing or appending to a file, specifies whether a newline character is added to the file.

FileExists   A function that checks if a file exists. If the file exists, returns true; otherwise, returns false.

Parameter	Req/Opt	Default	Description
absolutepath	Required	N/A	Specifies the absolute path of the file.

Find   A function that returns the start position where one string is located inside of another. If it is not found, 0 is returned. The search is case sensitive.

Parameter	Req/Opt	Default	Description
substring	Required	N/A	Specifies the string to search for.
string	Required	N/A	Specifies the string to search in.
start	Optional	N/A	Specifies the character to start the search at.

FindNoCase   A function that returns the start position where one string is located inside of another. If it is not found, 0 is returned. The search is case insensitive.

Parameter	Req/Opt	Default	Description
substring	Required	N/A	Specifies the string to search for.
string	Required	N/A	Specifies the string to search in.
start	Optional	N/A	Specifies the character to start the search at.

FindOneOf   A function used to return the first occurrence of a character in the specified set.

Parameter	Req/Opt	Default	Description
set	Required	N/A	Specifies the characters to search for.
string	Required	N/A	Specifies the string to search in.
start	Optional	N/A	Specifies the character to start the search at.

FirstDayOfMonth   A function used to return the day number of the first day of a month.

Parameter	Req/Opt	Default	Description
date	Required	N/A	Specifies a date/time object.

Fix   A function used to convert a real number to an integer and return the result.

Parameter	Req/Opt	Default	Description
number	Required	N/A	Specifies the number to operate on.

cfflush   A tag used to flush the current page and send all data to the client before processing finishes.

Attribute	Req/Opt	Default	Description
Interval	Optional	N/A	Specifies the number of bytes that need to be reached before flushing the data.

cfform   A tag used to build a CFML custom form. *See also* cfinput, cfselect, cfslider, cftextinput, cftree, cfgrid, and cfapplet.

Attribute	Req/Opt	Default	Description
name	Optional	CFForm_1	Specifies the name of the form.
action	Optional	N/A	Specifies the page to execute when the form is submitted.
scriptsrc	Optional	/cfide/scripts/ cfform.js	Allows the user to control the location of the script file.
preservedata	Optional	No	When a form is submitted back onto itself, this attribute specifies whether to preserve special form field values or reset them.
onsubmit	Optional	N/A	Specifies a JavaScript function to execute after input validation.
passthrough	Optional	N/A	Specifies HTML attributes that are not supported by cfform.
codebase	Optional	/CFIDE/classes/ cf-j2re-win.cab	URL of downloadable JRE plug-in.
archive	Optional	/CFIDE/classes/ CFJava2.jar	URL of downloadable Java class files.

FormatBaseN   A function used to return a number converted to a string in the specified radix.

Parameter	Req/Opt	Default	Description
number	Required	N/A	Specifies the number to operate on.
radix	Required	N/A	Specifies the base of the result.

cfftp   A tag used to access an FTP server via ColdFusion.

Attribute	Req/Opt	Default	Description
action	Required	N/A	Specifies the action to perform: open, close, changedir, createdir, listdir, removedir, getfile, putfile, rename, remove, getcurrentdir, getcurrenturl, existsdir, existsfile, or exists.
username	Required for open	N/A	Contains the username for access to the server.
password	Required for open	N/A	Contains the password for access to the server.
server	Required for open	N/A	Contains the IP address or domain name of the FTP server.
name	Required for listdir	N/A	Name of the result set that will contain the directory listing.
ASCIIExtensionList	Optional	txt;htm;html;cfm;cfml; shtm;shtml;css;asp;asa	Delimited list of file extensions that force ASCII transfer mode.
transfermode	Optional	Auto	Specifies the transfer mode. Valid values are ASCII, Binary, or Auto.
failifexists	Optional	Yes	Specifies whether to fail the operation if a local value exists of the same name.
Directory	Required for changedir, createdir, listdir, or existsdir	N/A	Specifies the directory to perform the operation.
localfile	Required for getfile or putfile	N/A	Specifies the name of the file on the local file system.
remotefile	Required for getfile, putfile, or existsfile	N/A	Specifies the name of the file on the remote system.
item	Required for exists or remove	N/A	Specifies the object of the actions, either file or directory.
existing	Required for rename	N/A	Specifies the current name of the file or directory.
new	Required for rename	N/A	Specifies the new name of the file or directory.
timeout	Optional	30	Specifies the timeout value, in seconds, for all operations.
port	Optional	21	Specifies the port to connect to.

Attribute	Req/Opt	Default	Description
connection	Optional	N/A	Specifies the name of the FTP connection.
proxyserver	Optional	N/A	Specifies the name of the proxy server, if applicable.
retrycount	Optional	1	Specifies the number of retries before an error is reported.
stoponerror	Optional	No	Specifies the action to occur when an error occurs. If set to yes, processing is halted. If set to no, error variables are created and processing continues.
passive	Optional	No	Specifies whether or not to enable passive mode. Yes enables it, no disables it.

cffunction   A tag used to create a user-defined function or a method in a ColdFusion Component.

Attribute	Req/Opt	Default	Description
name	Required	N/A	Specifies the name of the component.
returntype	Required for a Web service	Any	Specifies the type returned by the component. Valid values are any, array, binary, Boolean, date, guid, numeric, query, string, struct, uuid, variablename, void, or another component.
roles	Optional	Empty	Specifies the roles that can access this method of the component.
access	Optional	Public	Specifies the access of the function. Valid values are private, package, public, or remote.
output	Optional	Yes	A Boolean value that specifies whether the function is processed as if it were in a cfoutput or processes as cfsilent.

GetAuthUser   A function used to return the name of the authenticated user.
No parameters

GetBaseTagData   A function used to find a parent tag and return its data.

Parameter	Req/Opt	Default	Description
tagname	Required	N/A	Specifies the ancestor name to return data for.
instancenumber	Optional	1	Specifies the number of ancestor levels.

GetBaseTagList   A function used to return a list of ancestor tag names.
No parameters

GetBaseTemplatePath   A function used to return the absolute path of the base template.
No parameters

GetClientVariablesList   A function used to return a list of non-read-only client variables.
No parameters

GetCurrentTemplatePath: A function used to return the path of the current template.
No parameters

GetDirectoryFromPath   A function used to return the directory, without filename, from the specified path.

Parameter	Req/Opt	Default	Description
path	Required	N/A	Specifies an absolute path.

GetException   A function used to retrieve a Java exception object from a Java exception.

Parameter	Req/Opt	Default	Description
object	Required	N/A	Specifies the name of the Java object.

GetFileFromPath   A function used to return the filename from a given path.

Parameter	Req/Opt	Default	Description
path	Required	N/A	Specifies an absolute path.

GetFunctionList   A function used to return a list of all ColdFusion functions.
No parameters

GetHttpRequestData   A function used to return HTTP request headers and body.
No parameters

GetHttpTimeString   A function used to return the time, in Universal Time Coordinate, from the object.

Parameter	Req/Opt	Default	Description
datetime	Required	N/A	Specifies a ColdFusion or Java date/time object.

GetK2ServerDocCount   A function used to return the number of documents the Verity K2 Server can search.
No parameters

GetK2ServerDocCountLimit   A function that returns the maximum number of documents the Verity K2 Server is permitted to search against.
No parameters

GetLocale   A function used to return a string that contains the current locale.
No parameters

GetMetaData   A function used to return metadata associated with an object deployed on a ColdFusion server. Returns key-value pairs as XML or a component descriptor.

Parameter	Req/Opt	Default	Description
object	Required	N/A	Specifies the object.

GetMetricData   A function used to return metric data about server performance.

Parameter	Req/Opt	Default	Description
mode	Required	N/A	Valid values are perf_monitor, to return a structure of values; simple_load, to indicate overall server load; prev_req_time, to return the time, in milliseconds, it took to process the last request; or avg_req_time, to return the average request time, in milliseconds.

GetPageContext   A function used to return the ColdFusion MX PageContext object.
No parameters

GetProfileSections A function used to return a structure, created from an initialization file. Each structure key will be a section of the initialization file. Values will contain lists of the data.

Parameter	Req/Opt	Default	Description
inifile	Required	N/A	Specifies the absolute path to the INI file.

GetProfileString A function used to return a single value from an initialization file.

Parameter	Req/Opt	Default	Description
inifile	Required	N/A	Specifies the absolute path to the INI file.
section	Required	N/A	Specifies the section to retrieve that value from.
entry	Required	N/A	Specifies the name of the value to get.

GetServiceSettings A function used to return a structure that contains information about the ColdFusion service.
No parameters

GetTempDirectory A function used to return the location of the temporary directory that ColdFusion uses.
No parameters

GetTempFile A function used to create a temporary file in a directory whose name starts with the first three characters of the prefix. It returns the name of the new file.

Parameter	Req/Opt	Default	Description
dir	Required	N/A	Specifies the location to create the file.
prefix	Required	N/A	Specifies the prefix of the temporary file.

GetTickCount A function used to time CFML code segments, by taking the difference between two values.
No parameters

GetTimeZoneInfo A function used to return a structure with local time zone information relative to Universal Time Coordinate.
No parameters

GetToken   A function used to return the token found at the specified position.

Parameter	Req/Opt	Default	Description
string	Required	N/A	Specifies a string to search.
index	Required	N/A	Specifies the position of the token.
delimiters	Required	N/A	Specifies the delimiter, or a list of delimiters.

cfgrid   A tag used to create a grid control. Used with cfform.

Attribute	Req/Opt	Default	Description
name	Required	N/A	The name of the text input.
height	Optional	300	The height of the control.
width	Optional	300	The width of the control.
autowidth	Optional	No	Specifies whether or not all columns display within the grid width.
vspace	Optional	N/A	The number of pixels above or below the applet.
hspace	Optional	N/A	The pixel space on the left and right of the applet.
align	Optional	N/A	The alignment of the box: top, bottom, left, baseline, texttop, absbottom, middle, and absmiddle right.
query	Optional	N/A	The query associated with the grid control.
insert	Optional	No	If set to yes, the user can insert new rows.
delete	Optional	No	If set to yes, the user can delete a row.
sort	Optional	No	If set to yes, sort buttons are displayed on the grid control.
font	Optional	N/A	Specifies the font of the data.
fontsize	Optional	N/A	Specifies the size of the font.
italic	Optional	No	If set to yes, displays data in italics.
bold	Optional	No	If set to yes, displays data in bold.
textcolor	Optional	Black	Specifies the color of text in grid.
href	Optional	N/A	Contains the URL or query column that contains a link from each grid cell.
hrefkey	Optional	N/A	Contains the name of column to be appended to each URL.
target	Optional	N/A	The href target of the URL.
appendkey	Optional	Yes	If set to yes, appends the gfgridkey to the end of each URL.

Attribute	Req/Opt	Default	Description
highlighthref	Optional	Yes	If set to yes, highlights links on the grid.
onvalidate	Optional	N/A	Specifies the name of a JavaScript function you want to call when validating data.
onerror	Optional	N/A	Specifies the JavaScript function to call if validation fails.
griddataalign	Optional	Left	Specifies alignment of data. Valid value are Left, Right, or Center.
Gridlines	Optional	Yes	If set to yes, grid lines are displayed.
rowheight	Optional	N/A	Specifies minimum row height.
rowheaders	Optional	Yes	If set to yes, row headers are displayed.
rowheaderalign	Optional	Left	Specifies alignment of row headers. Valid values are Left, Right, or Center.
rowheaderfont	Optional	N/A	Specifies font for row headers.
rowheaderfontsize	Optional	N/A	Size of header font, in points.
rowheaderitalic	Optional	No	If set to yes, puts headers in italic.
rowheaderbold	Optional	No	If set to yes, makes headers bold.
rowheadertextcolor	Optional	Black	Specifies color of the header text.
colheaders	Optional	Yes	If set to yes, column headers are displayed.
colheaderalign	Optional	Left	Specifies alignment of column headers. Valid values are Left, Right, or Center.
colheaderfont	Optional	N/A	Specifies font of the column header.
colheaderfontsize	Optional	N/A	Specifies size of column header font.
colheaderitalic	Optional	No	If set to yes, displays column headers in italic.
colheaderbold	Optional	No	If set to yes, displays the column header in bold.
colheadertextcolor	Optional	N/A	Specifies color of the header text.
bgcolor	Optional	N/A	Specifies background color of grid.
selectcolor	Optional	N/A	Specifies color for selected grid items.
selectmode	Optional	Browse	Specifies selection mode for grid control. Valid values are Edit, single, row, column, or browse.
maxrows	Optional	N/A	Specifies maximum number of rows in grid.
picturebar	Optional	No	If set to yes, displays images for insert, delete, and sort buttons.
insertbutton	Optional	insert	Specifies text of insert button.
deletebutton	Optional	delete	Specifies text of delete button.
sortascendingbutton	Optional	A -> Z	Specifies text of sort ascending button.
sortdescendingbutton	Optional	Z -> A	Specifies text of sort descending button.

cfgridcolumn   A tag used with cfgrid to specify grid columns.

Attribute	Req/Opt	Default	Description
name	Required	N/A	Specifies the column name.
header	Optional	Yes	Specifies text for the column header.
width	Optional	Column head width	The width of the column in pixels.
font	Optional	Specified in cfgrid	Specifies the font to display the text.
fontsize	Optional	Specified in cfgrid	Specifies the size of the font.
italic	Optional	Specified in cfgrid	If set to yes, displays font italicized.
bold	Optional	Specified in cfgrid	If set to yes, displays the font bolded.
textcolor	Optional	N/A	Specifies the color of text in the column.
bgcolor	Optional	N/A	Specifies background color of the column.
href	Optional	N/A	If the grid is from a query, then this is a query column; otherwise, it is a URL.
hrefkey	Optional	N/A	Specifies the name of a query column.
target	Optional	N/A	Specifies the target of href is a URL.
select	Optional	N/A	If set to yes, the user can select inside the grid control.
display	Optional	Yes	If set to yes, displays column.
type	Optional	N/A	Specifies type of column. Valid values are image, numeric, Boolean, or string_nocase.
headerfont	Optional	Specified in cfgrid	Specifies the font of the column header.
headerfontsize	Optional	Specified in cfgrid	Specifies the font size of the header.
headeritalic	Optional	Specified in cfgrid	If set to yes, column header is displayed in italics.
headerbold	Optional	Specified in cfgrid	If set to yes, column header is displayed in bold.
headertextcolor	Optional	N/A	Specifies the color of the header text.
dataalign	Optional	Specified in cfgrid	Specifies column alignment: left, right, or center.
headeralign	Optional	Specified in cfgrid	Specifies column alignment: left, right, or center.
numberformat	Optional	N/A	Specifies a number format mask.
values	Optional	N/A	Formats a cell as a drop-down box.
valuesdisplay	Optional	N/A	Maps elements of drop-down list to string display.
valuesdelimiter	Optional	, (comma)	Specifies the delimiters used in values and valuedisplay attributes.

cfgridrow　A tag used in conjunction with cfgrid to specify a row of data.

Attribute	Req/Opt	Default	Description
data	Required	N/A	Delimited list of column values.

cfgridupdate　A tag used with cfgrid to update data after it is submitted.

Attribute	Req/Opt	Default	Description
grid	Required	N/A	Specifies the name of the grid.
datasource	Required	N/A	Specifies the name of the datasource to update data in.
tablename	Required	N/A	Specifies the name of the table that data will be updated in.
username	Optional	N/A	Specifies username to access the datasource.
password	Optional	N/A	Specifies the password to access the datasource.
tableowner	Optional	N/A	Specifies the table owner, if applicable.
tablequalifier	Optional	N/A	Specifies the table qualifier, if applicable.
keyonly	Optional	No	If set to yes, the where clause is limited to key values. If set to no, the where clause includes key values and original values that were changed.

Hash　A function used to convert a string to a 32-bit hexadecimal string and return the value.

Parameter	Req/Opt	Default	Description
string	Required	N/A	Specifies the value to hash.

cfheader　A tag used to generate custom HTTP response headers.

Attribute	Req/Opt	Default	Description
name	Required if statuscode is not specified	N/A	Specifies the header name.
value	Optional	N/A	Specifies the header value.

Attribute	Req/Opt	Default	Description
statuscode	Required if name is not specified	N/A	Specifies the status code.
statustext	Optional	N/A	Text that explains the status code.

Hour   A function used to return the hour from the specified date.

Parameter	Req/Opt	Default	Description
date	Required	N/A	Specifies the date/time object.

HTMLCodeFormat   A function used to escape special HTML characters and use the pre tag.

Parameter	Req/Opt	Default	Description
string	Required	N/A	Specifies the value to process.
version	Optional	2.0	Specifies the HTML version: 2.0, 3.2, or –1 (latest version).

HTMLEditFormat   A function used to escape special HTML characters. This does not use the pre tag.

Parameter	Req/Opt	Default	Description
string	Required	N/A	Specifies the value to process.
version	Optional	2.0	Specifies the HTML version: 2.0, 3.2, or –1 (latest version).

cfhtmlhead   A tag used to output text to the header section of an HTML page. Used for JavaScript or meta tags.

Attribute	Req/Opt	Default	Description
text	Required	N/A	The text you want added to the head.

cfhttp A tag used to retrieve data via HTTP, using POST or GET. It can get comma-delimited files and turn them into ColdFusion queries.

Attribute	Req/Opt	Default	Description
url	Required	http	Specifies the absolute hostname of the file you want to retrieve.
port	Optional	80	Specifies the port of the remote server.
method	Optional	get	Specifies the method, either post or get, to retrieve the URL.
username	Optional	N/A	Specifies the username for authentication to the server.
password	Optional	N/A	Specifies the password for authentication to the server.
name	Optional	N/A	Specifies the name of the query that is constructed from the results.
columns	Optional	N/A	Specifies the name of the columns if the results are being returned as a query.
firstrowasheader	Optional	Yes	If set to yes, the first line of the file is used as column headers.
path	Optional	N/A	Specifies path to store a file of the results.
file	Required if method is post and path is specified	N/A	Specifies the name of the file to save the results in.
delimiter	Required to create a query	, (comma)	Specifies the delimiter that can be used to separate columns.
textqualifer	Required to create query	"" (double quotes)	Specifies the start and end of a column.
resolveurl	Optional	No	If set to yes, all internal relative URLs will be turned into absolute URLs.
proxyserver	Optional	N/A	Specifies the proxy server.
proxyport	Optional	80	Specifies the port of the proxy server.
useragent	Optional	N/A	Specifies the agent request header.
throwonerror	Optional	No	If set to yes, throws an exception if there is an error.
redirect	Optional	Yes	If set to yes, will accept a redirect. Otherwise, stops execution.
timeout	Optional	N/A	Specifies the value timeout in seconds.
charset	Optional	The server charset, or if none, UTF-8	Specifies the Java charset name for the file.

cfhttpparam   A tag used to send parameters to a cfhttp call.

Attribute	Req/Opt	Default	Description
name	Required	N/A	Specifies the name of the parameter.
type	Required	N/A	Specifies the type of value: url, formfield, cookie, cgi, or file.
value	Optional if type is file	N/A	Specifies the value of the parameter for url, formfield, cookie, and cgi types.
file	Required if type is file	N/A	Specifies the name of the file.

cfif   A tag used to make decisions in the code.

Attribute	Req/Opt	Default	Description
expression	Required	N/A	Specifies an expression that returns a condition.

IIf   A function used to evaluate a conditional Boolean dynamic expression, and run the specified expression based on the result.

Parameter	Req/Opt	Default	Description
condition	Required	N/A	Specifies an Boolean expression.
expression1	Required	N/A	Specifies the expression to be evaluated if condition is true.
expression2	Required	N/A	Specifies the expression to evaluate if condition is false.

cfimport   A tag used to import JSP custom tag libraries.

Attribute	Req/Opt	Default	Description
taglib	Required	N/A	Specifies the location of the tag library.
prefix	Optional	N/A	Specifies the prefix that the tag library will be accessed by.
webservice	Optional	N/A	Specifies the URL of a WSDL file.

cfinclude   A tag used to embed a ColdFusion or HTML page inside another.

Attribute	Req/Opt	Default	Description
template	Required	N/A	Specifies the relative location of the template.

IncrementValue   A function used to add one to the specified number and return the result.

Parameter	Req/Opt	Default	Description
number	Required	N/A	Specifies the number to increment.

cfindex   A tag used to populate a Verity search.

Attribute	Req/Opt	Default	Description
collection	Required	N/A	Specifies the name of the collection to index data into.
action	Required	N/A	Dictates action to perform: update, delete, purge, or refresh.
type	Optional	If query attribute is specified, custom; otherwise, file	Specifies the type of data to be indexed. Valid values are file, path, or custom.
title	Optional	N/A	Specifies the title for the collection.
key	Required if type is file, path, or custom	Empty String	If type is file or path, set this to the absolute pathname. If type is custom or anything else, set this to a query column.
body	Required if custom	N/A	Set either to a query column or an ASCII text value.
custom1	Optional	N/A	Specifies a custom field for which you can store whatever you want.
custom2	Optional	N/A	Specifies a custom field for which you can store whatever you want.
urlpath	Optional	N/A	If type is file or path, this specifies a URL that is prefixed to the return values.

Attribute	Req/Opt	Default	Description
extensions	Optional	HTM, HTML, CFM, CFML, DBM, DBML	A list of file extensions to index.
query	Required if type is custom	N/A	The name of the query that the collection is generated from.
recursive	Optional	No	If set to yes, the directories will be indexed recursively.
language	Optional	English	Specifies the language of the indexing.

cfinput   A tag used to create radio buttons, checkboxes, or text boxes in a cfform tag.

Attribute	Req/Opt	Default	Description
type	Optional	text	Specifies the type of input box: text, radio, checkbox, or password.
name	Required	N/A	Specifies the name of the form element.
value	Optional	N/A	Specifies the initial value for the element.
required	Optional	no	Specifies whether this is required or not.
range	Optional	N/A	Specifies the minimum value and maximum value, separated by a comma, of the form field.
validate	Optional	N/A	Used to verify the format of the input. Valid values are date, eurodate, time, float, integer, telephone, zipcode, creditcard, social_security_number, or regular_expression.
onvalidate	Optional	N/A	Specifies a JavaScript function to validate user input.
pattern	Required if validate is regular_expression	N/A	Specifies a regular expression to validate input.
message	Optional	N/A	Specifies the message text to display if validation fails.
onerror	Optional	N/A	Specifies the custom JavaScript function to execute if validation fails.
size	Optional	N/A	Specifies the size of the input control.

Attribute	Req/Opt	Default	Description
maxlength	Optional	N/A	Specifies the maximum length accepted in the input control.
checked	Optional	N/A	If set to yes, the checkbox or radio button is checked by default.
passthrough	Optional	N/A	Used to specify HTML parameter code that is not supported by this tag.

InputBaseN   A function used to convert a string, using the radix, into an integer.

Parameter	Req/Opt	Default	Description
string	Required	N/A	Specifies the string to convert.
radix	Required	N/A	Specifies the base of the number, between 2 and 36.

cfinsert   A tag used to insert form data into a database.

Attribute	Req/Opt	Default	Description
datasource	Required	N/A	Specifies the name of the datasource.
tablename	Required	N/A	Specifies the name of the table to insert into.
tableowner	Optional	N/A	Specifies the owner of the table, if applicable.
tablequalifer	Optional	N/A	Specifies the qualifier of the table, if applicable.
username	Optional	N/A	Specifies the username needed to access the datasource.
password	Optional	N/A	Specifies the password needed to access the datasource.
formfields	Optional	All form data	Specifies the list of form fields that are to be inserted into the database.

Insert   A function used to insert a substring into a string at the specified position.

Parameter	Req/Opt	Default	Description
substring	Required	N/A	Specifies the value to insert.
string	Required	N/A	Specifies the value that is being inserted into.
position	Required	N/A	Specifies the position to insert at.

Int   A function used to calculate the closest integer smaller than the specified number.

Parameter	Req/Opt	Default	Description
number	Required	N/A	Specifies a number.

cfinvoke   A tag used to invoke a method from a ColdFusion Component or Web service.

Attribute	Req/Opt	Default	Description
component	Depends on method of invocation	N/A	Component object, or reference to a component object.
method	Depends on method of invocation	N/A	Specifies name of method to call.
returnvariable	Optional	N/A	Specifies the name of result variable.
argumentcollection	Optional	N/A	Specifies the name of a structure that contains method arguments.
username	Optional	N/A	Specifies the username to access the component or Web service.
password	Optional	N/A	Specifies the password to access the component or Web service.
webservice	Required	N/A	Specifies the URL of the WSDL file to invoke a Web service.
input_param	Depends on component	Depends on component	Used to specify input parameters.

cfinvokeargument   A tag used to pass data onto a ColdFusion Component or Web service invoked with cfinvoke.

Attribute	Req/Opt	Default	Description
name	Required	N/A	Specifies the name of the argument.
value	Required	N/A	Specifies the value of the argument.

IsArray   A function used to check if the specified variable is an array. If it is, returns true.

Parameter	Req/Opt	Default	Description
value	Required	N/A	Specifies the variable name.
dimension	Optional	N/A	Specifies the dimension of the array.

IsBinary   A function used to check if the specified variable is in binary. If it is, returns true.

Parameter	Req/Opt	Default	Description
value	Required	N/A	Specifies the variable name.

IsBoolean   A function used to check if the specified variable is Boolean. If it is, returns true.

Parameter	Req/Opt	Default	Description
value	Required	N/A	Specifies the variable name.

IsCustomFunction   A function used to check if the value is a custom function. If it is, returns true.

Parameter	Req/Opt	Default	Description
value	Required	N/A	Specifies the variable name.

IsDate A function used to check if the value is a date. If it is, returns true.

Parameter	Req/Opt	Default	Description
value	Required	N/A	Specifies the variable name.

IsDebugMode A function used to return true if debugging is turned on in the ColdFusion Administrator.
No parameters

IsDefined A function used to return true if the specified variable is defined.

Parameter	Req/Opt	Default	Description
variable	Required	N/A	Specifies the name of the variable.

IsK2ServerABroker A function used to determine if the K2 Server is a broker.
No parameters

IsK2ServerDocCountExceeded A function used to specify if the number of documents that can be searched by the ColdFusion-registered K2 Server has been exceeded.
No parameters

IsK2ServerOnline A function used to check if the K2 Server is online.
No parameters

IsLeapYear A function used to return true if the specified year is a leap year.

Parameter	Req/Opt	Default	Description
year	Required	N/A	Specifies the year.

IsNumeric A function used to return true if the specified value is numeric.

Parameter	Req/Opt	Default	Description
value	Required	N/A	The value that you want to check.

IsNumericDate   A function used to return true if the specified value is a numeric date.

Parameter	Req/Opt	Default	Description
number	Required	N/A	Specifies the value to check.

IsObject   A function used to determine if the specified value is an object.

Parameter	Req/Opt	Default	Description
value	Required	N/A	Specifies the value to check.
type	Optional	N/A	Specifies the data type of the argument: any, array, binary, Boolean, date, guid, numeric, query, string, struct, uuid, variable name, or component name.
component parameter	Optional	N/A	Specifies context-specific arguments for components.

IsQuery   A function used to return true if the specified function is a query.

Parameter	Req/Opt	Default	Description
value	Required	N/A	Specifies the value to check.

IsSimpleValue: A function used to return true if the specified function is a simple value.

Parameter	Req/Opt	Default	Description
value	Required	N/A	Specifies the value to check.

IsStruct: A function used to return true if the specified value is a structure.

Parameter	Req/Opt	Default	Description
value	Required	N/A	Specifies the value to check.

IsUserInRole A function used to return true if the current user is in the specified role.

Parameter	Req/Opt	Default	Description
role	Required	N/A	Specifies the role to check.

IsWDDX A function used to return true if the specified value is a WDDX packet.

Parameter	Req/Opt	Default	Description
value	Required	N/A	Specifies the value to check.

IsXmlDoc A function used to return true if the specified value is an XML document object.

Parameter	Req/Opt	Default	Description
value	Required	N/A	Specifies the value to check.

IsXmlElement A function used to return true if the specified value is an XML element.

Parameter	Req/Opt	Default	Description
value	Required	N/A	Specifies the value to check.

IsXmlRoot A function used to return true if the specified value is an XML document root.

Parameter	Req/Opt	Default	Description
value	Required	N/A	Specifies the value to check.

JavaCast A function used to convert a ColdFusion variable into a Java variable.

Parameter	Req/Opt	Default	Description
type	Required	N/A	Specifies the type to convert to: Boolean, int, long, double, or string.

Parameter	Req/Opt	Default	Description
variable	Required	N/A	Specifies the name of the ColdFusion variable.

JSStringFormat   A function used to escape special JavaScript characters and return the result.

Parameter	Req/Opt	Default	Description
string	Required	N/A	Specifies the value to convert.

LCase   A function used to convert all characters in a string to lowercase and return the result.

Parameter	Req/Opt	Default	Description
string	Required	N/A	Specifies the value to convert.

cfldap   A tag used to access an LDAP directory server.

Attribute	Req/Opt	Default	Description
server	Required	N/A	Specifies LDAP server hostname or IP address.
port	Optional	389	Specifies port of LDAP server.
username	Required if secure=CFSSL_Basic	Anonymous	Specifies UserID for access to the LDAP server.
password	Required if secure=CFSSL_Basic	N/A	Specifies password for access to the LDAP server.
action	Optional	query	Specifies action to perform: query, add, modify, modifydn, or delete.
name	Required for query	N/A	Specifies name of LDAP query.
timeout	Optional	60	Specifies maximum length of time, in seconds, to wait for processing.
maxrows	Optional	N/A	Specifies maximum number of records to return.

Attribute	Req/Opt	Default	Description
start	Required if action is query	N/A	Specifies distinguished name to start the search.
scope	Optional	onelevel	Specifies scope of the search. Valid values are onelevel, base, or subtree.
attributes	Required for query, add, adddn, and modify	N/A	Specifies a list of attributes to return, or update.
filter	Optional	Objectclass=*	Specifies search criteria for action = query.
sort	Optional	N/A	Specifies a list of attributes that the query will be sorted on.
sortcontrol	Optional	ASC	Specifies sort of the resulting query. Valid values are nocase, ASC, or DESC.
dn	Required if action is add, modify, modifydn, or delete	N/A	Specifies distinguished name.
startrow	Optional	1	If creating a query, specifies the first LDAP row to be inserted into the query.
modifytype	Optional	replace	Specifies how to process an attribute in a multivalued list. Valid values are add, delete, or replace.
rebind	Optional	No	If set to yes, attempts to rebind a referral callback.
referral	Optional	N/A	An integer value that specifies the number of hops allowed for a referral.
secure	Optional	N/A	Specifies the security to employ.
separator	optional	, (comma)	Specifies the delimiter to separate attribute values of a multivalued attribute.
delimiter	Optional	N/A	Specifies the separator for name-value pairs if the attributes attribute has more than one item or an attribute uses a semicolon.

Left   A function used to return a new string that contains the specified count characters, starting from the left side of the string.

Parameter	Req/Opt	Default	Description
string	Required	N/A	Specifies the string to process.
count	Required	N/A	Specifies the number of characters to return.

Len   A function used to return the length of a string or binary object.

Parameter	Req/Opt	Default	Description
Value	Required	N/A	Specifies the value to process.

ListAppend   A function used to add a new value to the end of a list and return the new list.

Parameter	Req/Opt	Default	Description
list	Required	N/A	Specifies the list.
value	Required	N/A	Specifies the value to add.
delimiter	Optional	, (comma)	Specifies the list delimiter.

ListChangeDelims   A function used to change the delimiter of a list and return the new list.

Parameter	Req/Opt	Default	Description
list	Required	N/A	Specifies the list.
newdelimiter	Required	N/A	Specifies the new delimiter.
olddelimiter	Optional	, (comma)	Specifies the old list delimiter.

ListContains   A function used to check if a list contains the specified value. The search is case sensitive.

Parameter	Req/Opt	Default	Description
list	Required	N/A	Specifies the list.

Parameter	Req/Opt	Default	Description
value	Required	N/A	Specifies the value to check for.
delimiter	Optional	, (comma)	Specifies the list delimiter.

ListContainsNoCase   A function used to check if a list contains the specified value. The search is case insensitive.

Parameter	Req/Opt	Default	Description
list	Required	N/A	Specifies the list.
value	Required	N/A	Specifies the value to check for.
delimiter	Optional	, (comma)	Specifies the list delimiter.

ListDeleteAt   A function used to remove an element from a list and return the new list.

Parameter	Req/Opt	Default	Description
list	Required	N/A	Specifies the list.
position	Required	N/A	Specifies the position of the element to remove.
delimiter	Optional	, (comma)	Specifies the list delimiter.

ListFind   A function used to return the index of the specified element. The search is case sensitive.

Parameter	Req/Opt	Default	Description
list	Required	N/A	Specifies the list.
value	Required	N/A	Specifies the value to find.
delimiter	Optional	, (comma)	Specifies the list delimiter.

ListFindNoCase   A function used to return the index of the specified value. The search is case insensitive.

Parameter	Req/Opt	Default	Description
list	Required	N/A	Specifies the list.

Parameter	Req/Opt	Default	Description
value	Required	N/A	Specifies the value to find.
delimiter	Optional	, (comma)	Specifies the list delimiter.

ListFirst   A function used to return the first element of a list.

Parameter	Req/Opt	Default	Description
list	Required	N/A	Specifies the list.
delimiter	Optional	, (comma)	Specifies the list delimiter.

ListGetAt   A function used to return the value at the specified position.

Parameter	Req/Opt	Default	Description
list	Required	N/A	Specifies the list.
position	Required	N/A	Specifies the position of the element.
delimiter	Optional	, (comma)	Specifies the list delimiter.

ListInsertAt   A function used to insert an item into a list and return the modified list.

Parameter	Req/Opt	Default	Description
list	Required	N/A	Specifies the list.
position	Required	N/A	Specifies the position of the element.
value	Required	N/A	Specifies the value to insert.
delimiter	Optional	, (comma)	Specifies the list delimiter.

ListLast   A function used to return the last element of a list.

Parameter	Req/Opt	Default	Description
list	Required	N/A	Specifies the list.
delimiter	Optional	, (comma)	Specifies the list delimiter.

ListLen   A function used to return the length of a list.

Parameter	Req/Opt	Default	Description
list	Required	N/A	Specifies the list.
delimiter	Optional	, (comma)	Specifies the list delimiter.

ListPrepend   A function used to add an item to the beginning of a list and return the result.

Parameter	Req/Opt	Default	Description
list	Required	N/A	Specifies the list.
value	Required	N/A	Specifies the value to add.
delimiter	Optional	, (comma)	Specifies the list delimiter.

ListQualify   A function used to insert a string at the beginning and end of each list element.

Parameter	Req/Opt	Default	Description
list	Required	N/A	Specifies the list.
qualifier	Required	N/A	Specifies the qualifier value.
delimiter	Optional	, (comma)	Specifies the list delimiter.
elements	Optional	N/A	Specifies the elements to qualify: all, for all elements, or char, for character elements.

ListRest   A function used to return a list without the first element.

Parameter	Req/Opt	Default	Description
list	Required	N/A	Specifies the list.
delimiter	Optional	, (comma)	Specifies the list delimiter.

ListSetAt A function used to set a value at the specified list position and return the new list.

Parameter	Req/Opt	Default	Description
list	Required	N/A	Specifies the list.
position	Required	N/A	Specifies the position of the list to change.
value	Required	N/A	Specifies the value to change.
delimiter	Optional	, (comma)	Specifies the list delimiter.

ListSort A function used to sort a list and return the modified list.

Parameter	Req/Opt	Default	Description
list	Required	N/A	Specifies the list.
sort_type	Required	N/A	Specifies the type of sort: numeric, text, or textnocase.
sort_order	Optional	N/A	Specifies the sort order: asc or desc.
delimiter	Optional	, (comma)	Specifies the list delimiter.

ListToArray A function used to convert a list into a one-dimensional array.

Parameter	Req/Opt	Default	Description
list	Required	N/A	Specifies the list.
delimiter	Optional	, (comma)	Specifies the list delimiter.

ListValueCount A function used to return the number of instances of the specified value. The search is case sensitive.

Parameter	Req/Opt	Default	Description
list	Required	N/A	Specifies the list.
value	Required	N/A	Specifies the value to look for.
delimiter	Optional	, (comma)	Specifies the list delimiter.

ListValueCountNoCase   A function used to return the number of instances of the specified value. The search is case insensitive.

Parameter	Req/Opt	Default	Description
list	Required	N/A	Specifies the list.
value	Required	N/A	Specifies the value to look for.
delimiter	Optional	, (comma)	Specifies the list delimiter.

LJustify   A function used to left-justify a string in the specified length.

Parameter	Req/Opt	Default	Description
string	Required	N/A	Specifies the string to left-justify.
length	Required	N/A	Specifies the length of the new string.

cflocation   A tag used to redirect the current page to another page.

Attribute	Req/Opt	Default	Description
url	Required	N/A	Specifies the URL to redirect to.
addtoken	Optional	N/A	If client management is enabled, appends CFID and CFToken to the end of the URL.

cflock   A tag used to prevent synchronous access to code or data.

Attribute	Req/Opt	Default	Description
timeout	Required	N/A	Specifies the timeout to wait for access to the data.
scope	Optional	N/A	Specifies the scope of the lock: application, server, or session. This is mutually exclusive with the name attribute.
name	Optional	N/A	Specifies a name for the lock. This is mutually exclusive with the scope.

Attribute	Req/Opt	Default	Description
throwonerror	Optional	Yes	If yes, an exception is generated after the timeout passes; otherwise, execution continues.
type	Optional	Exclusive	Specifies the type of lock: either exclusive or read-only.

cflog A tag used to save information into a log file of your choosing.

Attribute	Req/Opt	Default	Description
text	Required	N/A	Specifies the message to put into the log.
log	Optional	N/A	Specifies which log to place information into, either application or scheduler. This attribute is ignored if file is used.
file	Optional	N/A	Specifies the filename of the log, without extension.
type	Optional	Information	Specifies type of exception: information, warning, error, or fatal information.
application	Optional	Yes	If set to yes, saves the application name in the log entry.

Log A function used to perform the natural log of a number.

Parameter	Req/Opt	Default	Description
number	Required	N/A	Specifies the number to perform the log on.

Log10 A function used to perform the natural log of a number to base 10.

Parameter	Req/Opt	Default	Description
number	Required	N/A	Specifies the number to perform the log on.

cflogin   A tag used to log in a user. Used with cfloginuser.

Attribute	Req/Opt	Default	Description
idletimeout	Optional	1800	Specifies the time interval for the user to be logged off.
applicationtoken	Optional	Application Name	Specifies a unique application identifier.
cookiedomain	Optional	N/A	Specifies the domain in which to set the cookie.

cfloginuser   A tag used to identify an authenticated user to ColdFusion.

Attribute	Req/Opt	Default	Description
name	Required	N/A	Specifies the user's name.
password	Required	N/A	Specifies the user's password.
roles	Required	N/A	Specifies the user's roles.

cflogout   A tag used to log out a user.
No attributes

cfloop   A tag used to loop in ColdFusion, either until a condition is true, a certain number of times, or through a structure or list.

Attribute	Req/Opt	Default	Description
index	Required for index or list loop	N/A	Specifies the value that will contain the current loop iteration in an index or list loop.
from	Required for index loop	N/A	Specifies the start value of an index loop.
to	Required for index loop	N/A	Specifies the end value of an index loop.
step	Optional for index loop	1	Specifies the amount the index will change in an index loop.

Attribute	Req/Opt	Default	Description
condition	Required for conditional loops	N/A	Specifies the expression that will stop the loop when it becomes true.
query	Required for query loop	N/A	Specifies the query to loop over in a query loop.
startrow	Optional for query loop	N/A	Specifies the first row to start looping over in a query loop.
endrow	Optional for query loop	N/A	Specifies the last row to loop over in a query loop.
list	Required for list loop	N/A	Contains the list to loop over.
delimiters	Optional for list loop	, (comma)	Specifies the comma to loop over.
item	Required for collection loop	N/A	Specifies the current index of the object or structure in a collection loop.
collection	Required for collection loop	N/A	Specifies the name of the variable that contains the object or structure to loop over.

LSCurrencyFormat   A function used to format currency in a locale-specific manner.

Parameter	Req/Opt	Default	Description
number	Required	N/A	Specifies the currency value.
type	Optional	N/A	Specifies the type of currency: local, international, or none.

LSDateFormat   A function used to format a date/time object in a locale-specific format.

Parameter	Req/Opt	Default	Description
date	Required	N/A	Specifies the date/time object to format.

Parameter	Req/Opt	Default	Description
mask	Optional	N/A	Specifies the mask used to display dates: short, medium, long, full, d (the day of month with no leading zeros), dd (the day of month with leading zero), ddd (the day of week in a three-letter abbreviation), dddd (the full name of the day of week), m (the month with no leading zero), mm (the month with leading zeros), mmm (a three-letter month abbreviation), mmmm (the month full name), y (a two-digit year with no leading zeros), yy (a two-digit year with leading zero), yyyy (a four-digit year), or gg (period/era string, not processed).

LSEuroCurrencyFormat   A function used to format the number in the local currency format.

Parameter	Req/Opt	Default	Description
currency	Required	N/A	Specifies the currency value.
type	Optional	N/A	Specifies the type of format: local, international, or none.

LSIsCurrency   A function used to return true if the string is formatted in the currency format.

Parameter	Req/Opt	Default	Description
string	Required	N/A	Specifies the value to check.

LSIsDate   A function used to determine whether a string is a date formatted in locale-specific format.

Parameter	Req/Opt	Default	Description
string	Required	N/A	Specifies the value to check.

LSIsNumeric A function used to return true if the specified value is a locale-specific number.

Parameter	Req/Opt	Default	Description
string	Required	N/A	Specifies the value to check.

LSNumberFormat A function used to format a locale-specific number.

Parameter	Req/Opt	Default	Description
number	Required	N/A	Specifies the number to format.
mask	Optional	N/A	Specifies the mask of the number, made up of these characters: "_" or "9" (digit placeholders), "." (decimal), "0" (pad with zeros), "( )" (parentheses for negative numbers), "+" (plus sign), "−" (negative sign), "," (separates every third decimal place with a comma), "L,C" (to left-justify or center numbers in mask width), "$" (to display a dollar sign), and "^" (to separate left and right formatting).

LSParseCurrency A function used to format local-specific currency as a number.

Parameter	Req/Opt	Default	Description
string	Required	N/A	Specifies the string to format.

LSParseDateTime A function used to format a locale-specific date as a string.

Parameter	Req/Opt	Default	Description
datetime	Required	N/A	Specifies the date/time object to format.

LSParseEuroCurrency A function used to format a locale-specific currency string as a string.

Parameter	Req/Opt	Default	Description
currency	Required	N/A	Specifies the currency value to format.

LSParseNumber A function used to format a locale-specific string as a number.

Parameter	Req/Opt	Default	Description
string	Required	N/A	Specifies the string to parse.

LSTimeFormat A function used to format the time part of a locale-specific date/time object.

Parameter	Req/Opt	Default	Description
String	Required	N/A	Specifies the date/time value.
mask	Optional	N/A	Specifies the mask used to display dates: short, medium, long, full, d (the day of month with no leading zeros), dd (the day of month with leading zero), ddd (the day of week in a three-letter abbreviation), dddd (the full name of the day of week), m (the month with no leading zero), mm (the month with leading zeros), mmm (a three-letter month abbreviation), mmmm (the month full name), y (a two-digit year with no leading zeros), yy (a two-digit year with leading zero), yyyy (a four-digit year), or gg (period/era string, not processed).

LTrim A function used to return leading spaces from a string and return the result.

Parameter	Req/Opt	Default	Description
String	Required	N/A	Specifies the string to process.

cfmail A tag used to send e-mail from ColdFusion.

Attribute	Req/Opt	Default	Description
to	Required	N/A	Specifies the e-mail address the e-mail is sent to.
from	Required	N/A	Specifies the e-mail address the e-mail is sent from.

Attribute	Req/Opt	Default	Description
cc	Optional	N/A	Specifies the e-mail addresses to carbon copy the e-mail.
bcc	Optional	N/A	Specifies the e-mail addresses to blind carbon copy the e-mail.
subject	Required	N/A	Specifies the subject of the e-mail.
type	Optional	N/A	Specifies the type of the e-mail. The only valid value is HTML. If left out, the e-mail is sent as text.
maxrows	Optional	N/A	Specifies the maximum number of e-mail messages to send.
mimeattach	Optional	N/A	Specifies the path of the file to attach to the message.
query	Optional	N/A	Specifies the query to send messages for.
group	Optional	CurrentRow	Specifies the name of the query column to group on.
groupcasesensitive	Optional	Yes	A Boolean value. If yes, specifies that grouping is case sensitive.
startrow	Optional	1	Specifies the first row of the query to process.
server	Required if not specified in ColdFusion Admin.	N/A	Specifies the hostname or IP address of the SMTP mail server. The value here will override the one in that administrator.
port	Optional	−1	Specifies the port of the SMTP server. This is usually 25.
mailerid	Optional	ColdFusion Application Server	Specifies the name of the mailerID to be passed in the X-mailer header.
timeout	Optional	−1	Specifies the number of seconds to wait for the SMTP server.
spoolenable	Optional	Yes	If yes, saves a copy of message until message is sent. Otherwise, queues message for sending without saving a copy.

cfmailparam   A tag used inside a cfmail block to attach a file or add a custom header to an e-mail message.

Attribute	Req/Opt	Default	Description
file	Required if name not specified	N/A	Specifies the location of the file you want to attach.
name	Required if file not specified	N/A	Specifies the name of the header.
value	Optional	N/A	Specifies the value of the header.

Max   A function used to return the greater of two numbers.

Parameter	Req/Opt	Default	Description
Number1	Required	N/A	Specifies a number.
Number2	Required	N/A	Specifies a number.

Mid   A function used to extract a substring from a string.

Parameter	Req/Opt	Default	Description
string	Required	N/A	Specifies the string to process.
start	Required	N/A	Specifies the first character to return.
count	Required	N/A	Specifies the number of characters to return.

Min   A function used to return the smaller of two numbers.

Parameter	Req/Opt	Default	Description
Number1	Required	N/A	Specifies a number.
Number2	Required	N/A	Specifies a number.

Minute   A function used to return the minute portion of the specified date.

Parameter	Req/Opt	Default	Description
date	Required	N/A	Specifies a date/time object.

cfmodule   A tag used to invoke a CFML custom tag.

Attribute	Req/Opt	Default	Description
template	Required if name is not used	N/A	Specifies a path to the template that contains the tag, either using a ColdFusion mapping or a relative path.
name	Required if template is not used	N/A	Specifies the name of the custom tag, using the directory.subdirectory.name format.
attributecollection	Optional	N/A	Specifies a structure that contains all attributes to be sent to the custom tag.
attributes	Optional	N/A	Specifies individual attributes to be sent to the custom tag.

Month   A function used to extract the month value from a date/time object.

Parameter	Req/Opt	Default	Description
date	Required	N/A	Specifies a date/time object.

MonthAsString   A function used to return the name of the month based on the given number.

Parameter	Req/Opt	Default	Description
number	Required	N/A	Specifies the number of the month.

Now   A function used to return a date/time object reflecting the current date and time. No attributes

NumberFormat   A function used to return a number formatted according to the mask.

Parameter	Req/Opt	Default	Description
number	Required	N/A	Specifies the number to format.
mask	Optional	N/A	Specifies the mask of the number, made up of these characters: "_" or "9" (digit placeholders), "." (decimal), "0" (pad with zeros), "( )" (parentheses for negative numbers), "+" (plus sign), "–" (negative sign), "," (separates every third decimal place with a comma), "L,C" (to left-justify or center numbers in mask width), "$" (to display a dollar sign), and "^" (to separate left and right formatting).

cfobject   A tag used to create a ColdFusion object that points to a ColdFusion Component, COM object, CORBA object, Web service, or Java object.

Attribute	Req/Opt	Default	Description
type	Optional	N/A	Specifies the object type, either COM, CORBA, or Java.
action	Required for COM or Java	N/A	Specifies the action to perform. For COM: create 3or connect. For Java: create.
class	Required for COM, Java, or CORBA	N/A	Specifies the PROGID of the COM object to invoke, or if a CORBA object, the location of the IOR file or the slash-delimited naming context for nameservice. For Java, specifies the Java class.
name	Required for COM, CORBA, Java, Web service, or component	N/A	Specifies the name of the instantiated component.
context	Optional	For COM, uses a Windows Registry setting	Specifies the context to invoke the COM or CORBA object in. For COM: inproc, local, or remote. For CORBA: ior or nameservice.
server	Required for COM and context is remote	N/A	Specifies the name of the server.

Attribute	Req/Opt	Default	Description
component	Required for component	N/A	Specifies the name of the CFC to be instantiated.
locale	Optional	N/A	In a CORBA object, specifies the arguments to be called to the init_orb function.
webservice	Required for Web service	N/A	Specifies the URL of the WSDL file.

cfobjectcache   A tag used to flush a cached query.

Attribute	Req/Opt	Default	Description
action	Required	N/A	Set this value to clear.

cfoutput   A tag used to display the results of a database query or other ColdFusion operation.

Attribute	Req/Opt	Default	Description
query	Optional	N/A	Specifies the name of the query to loop over.
group	Optional	N/A	Specifies the query to group on.
groupcasesensitive	Optional	Yes	A Boolean value that specifies whether to group case sensitive or case insensitive.
startrow	Optional	1	Specifies the first query record to process.
maxrows	Optional	N/A	Specifies the maximum number of rows to display.

ParagraphFormat   A function used to replace single newline characters with spaces and double newline spaces with paragraph tags.

Parameter	Req/Opt	Default	Description
string	Required	N/A	Specifies the string to format.

cfparam A tag used to test for a parameter's existence and data type and, if not defined, to create the variable with a default value.

Attribute	Req/Opt	Default	Description
name	Required	N/A	Specifies the name of the parameter to test.
type	Optional	N/A	Specifies the type to validate the value against. Valid values are any, array, binary, Boolean, date, numeric, query, string, struct, UUID, or variablename.
default	Optional	N/A	Specifies the value to set the parameter to if it is not defined.

ParseDateTime A function used to format a date/time object according to U.S. conventions.

Parameter	Req/Opt	Default	Description
datetime	Required	N/A	Specifies the date/time object.
conversion	Optional	N/A	Specifies pop, to convert to UTC, or standard, to do no conversion.

Pi A function used to return the mathematical constant, pi, up to 15 digits. No parameters

cfpop A tag used to retrieve e-mail from a POP3 server.

Attribute	Req/Opt	Default	Description
server	Required	N/A	Specifies the IP address or hostname of the mail server.
port	Optional	110	Specifies the port of the mail server.
username	Optional	Anonymous	Specifies the username to access the mail server.
password	Optional	N/A	Specifies the password to access the mail server.
action	Optional	getheaderonly	Specifies the action to perform. Valid values are getheaderonly, getall, or delete.

Attribute	Req/Opt	Default	Description
name	Required for getall or getheaderonly	N/A	Specifies the name of the index query.
messagenumber	Required for delete if UID is not used	N/A	Specifies a comma-delimited list of message numbers to perform actions on.
uid	Required for delete if messagenumber is not used	N/A	Specifies a comma-delimited list of unique IDs to perform actions on.
attachmentpath	Optional	N/A	
timeout	Optional	60	Specifies the timeout to wait for the server.
maxrows	Optional	999999	Specifies the total number of messages to return.
startrow	Optional	1	Specifies the first message to return in the query.
generateuniquefilenames	Optional	No	Accepts a Boolean value; if set to yes, generates unique filenames for all attachments to files.

PreserveSingleQuotes   A function used to prevent ColdFusion from automatically escaping single quotes. This function returns no value.

Parameter	Req/Opt	Default	Description
variable	Required	N/A	Specifies the variable you want to not modify.

cfprocessingdirective   A tag used to suppress extra whitespace and other CFML output.

Attribute	Req/Opt	Default	Description
suppresswhitespace	Optional	N/A	Accepts a Boolean value for whether to suppress whitespace or not.
pageencoding	Optional	N/A	Used to specify the character encoding of the page.

cfprocparam   A tag used to pass parameters onto a stored procedure. Used with cfstoredproc.

Attribute	Req/Opt	Default	Description
type	Required	in	Specifies the type of parameter. Either in, out, or inout.
variable	Required if type is out or inout	N/A	Specifies the ColdFusion variable name.
dbvarname	Required for named notation	N/A	Specifies the name of the stored procedure parameter.
value	Required if type is out or inout	N/A	Specifies the value of the parameter.
cfsqltype	Required	N/A	Specifies the SQL parameter type: CF_SQL_BIGINT, CF_SQL_BIT, CF_SQL_BLOB, CF_SQL_CHAR, CF_SQL_CLOB, CF_SQL_DATE, CF_SQL_DECIMAL, CF_SQL_DOUBLE, CF_SQL_FLOAT, CF_SQL_IDSTAMP, CF_SQL_INTEGER, CF_SQL_LONGVARCHAR, CF_SQL_MONEY, CF_SQL_MONEY4, CF_SQL_NUMERIC, CF_SQL_REAL, CF_SQL_REFCURSOR, CF_SQL_SMALLINT, CF_SQL_TIME, CF_SQL_TIMESTAMP, CF_SQL_TINYINT, or CF_SQL_VARCHAR.
maxlength	Optional	0	Specifies the maximum length of the parameter.
scale	Optional	0	Specifies the number of decimal places in the parameter.
null	Optional	no	Specifies whether the parameter is passed as a NULL value or not.

cfprocresult   A tag used to define the result set from a stored procedure. Used with the cfstoredproc tag.

Attribute	Req/Opt	Default	Description
name	Required	N/A	Specifies the name for the query set.
resultset	Optional	1	Specifies a result set, if the stored procedure returns more than one.
maxrows	Optional	All	Specifies the maximum number of rows returned.

cfproperty   A tag that specifies components as complex types for Web service authoring.

Attribute	Req/Opt	Default	Description
name	Required	N/A	Specifies the name of the property.
type	Optional	N/A	Specifies the type of the component. Valid types are any, array, Boolean, date, guid, numeric, query, string, struct, uuid, variablename, or component name.

Quarter   A function used to return a number of the quarter of the year in which a date falls.

Parameter	Req/Opt	Default	Description
date	Required	N/A	Specifies a date/time object.

cfquery   A tag used to pass a SQL query to a datasource and return the results.

Attribute	Req/Opt	Default	Description
name	Required	N/A	Specifies the name of the resulting query object.
datasource	Required	N/A	Specifies the name of the datasource.
dbtype	Optional	query	Specifies that a query of a query is being performed. Query is the only valid value for this attribute.
username	Optional	N/A	Specifies the username to the datasource.
password	Optional	N/A	Specifies the password to the datasource.
maxrows	Optional	−1 (all)	Specifies the largest number of rows to return in the record set.
blockfactor	Optional	1	Specifies the number of rows to get from the server at once.
timeout	Optional	N/A	Specifies the maximum number of seconds that ColdFusion will wait for the query result set.

Attribute	Req/Opt	Default	Description
cachedafter	Optional	N/A	Specifies a date after which the query will start being cached.
cachedwithin	Optional	N/A	Specifies the time space of the cached query. The CreateTimeSpan function can be used to specify this value.
debug	Optional	N/A	If set to yes and debugging is enabled in the ColdFusion Administrator, then debugging information is displayed. If set to no, the display is suppressed.

QueryAddColumn   A function used to add a new column to a query and return true if successful.

Parameter	Req/Opt	Default	Description
query	Required	N/A	Specifies the query to which to add the column.
column	Required	N/A	Specifies the name of the column to add.
array	Required	N/A	Specifies the array to populate the new column.

QueryAddRow   A function used to add new rows to a query. The value returned is the total number of rows in the query.

Parameter	Req/Opt	Default	Description
query	Required	N/A	Specifies the query to which to add the column.
number	Required	N/A	Specifies the number of rows to add to the query.

QueryNew   A function used to create a new, empty, query object.

Parameter	Req/Opt	Default	Description
columnlist	Required	N/A	Specifies a list of columns to add to the query.

cfqueryparam A tag used to verify the value of a query parameter.

Attribute	Req/Opt	Default	Description
value	Required	N/A	Specifies the value you want to check.
cfsqltype	Optional	CF_SQL_CHAR	Specifies the SQL parameter type: CF_SQL_BIGINT, CF_SQL_BIT, CF_SQL_BLOB, CF_SQL_CHAR, CF_SQL_CLOB, CF_SQL_DATE, CF_SQL_DECIMAL, CF_SQL_DOUBLE, CF_SQL_FLOAT, CF_SQL_IDSTAMP, CF_SQL_INTEGER, CF_SQL_LONGVARCHAR, CF_SQL_MONEY, CF_SQL_MONEY4, CF_SQL_NUMERIC, CF_SQL_REAL, CF_SQL_REFCURSOR, CF_SQL_SMALLINT, CF_SQL_TIME, CF_SQL_TIMESTAMP, CF_SQL_TINYINT, or CF_SQL_VARCHAR.
maxlength	Optional	Length of string value	Specifies the maximum length of the parameter.
scale	Optional	0	Specifies the number of decimal places in the parameter.
null	Optional	No	A Boolean value that specifies whether or not this is a NULL parameter.
list	Optional	No	A Boolean value that, if set to yes, specifies the value is a list.
separator	Optional	, (comma)	Specifies the delimiter of the list attribute.

QuerySetCell A function used to set the value of a query cell. Returns true if successful.

Parameter	Req/Opt	Default	Description
query	Required	N/A	Specifies the name of the query object.
column	Required	N/A	Specifies the column to set.
value	Required	N/A	Specifies the value to insert into the column.
rownumber	Optional	Last row	Specifies the row number in which to set the cell.

QuotedValueList A function used to return a delimited list of values from a query column.

Parameter	Req/Opt	Default	Description
query.column	Required	N/A	Specifies the name of the query and the column.
delimiter	Optional	, (comma)	Specifies the delimiter that separates data.

Rand A function used to return a random number in the range of 0–1. No parameters

Randomize A function used to seed the ColdFusion random number generator. Returns a nonrandom decimal number.

Parameter	Req/Opt	Default	Description
number	Required	N/A	Specifies a number.

RandRange A function used to return a random number in the specified range.

Parameter	Req/Opt	Default	Description
number1	Required	N/A	Specifies the low number.
number2	Required	N/A	Specifies the high number.

REFind A function used to search a string using regular expressions. If returnsubexpression is false, returns the position where the match begins. If true, returns a structure with len and pos arrays. The search is case sensitive.

Parameter	Req/Opt	Default	Description
regularexpression	Required	N/A	Specifies the regular expression.
string	Required	N/A	Specifies the string to search.
start	Optional	1	Specifies the place to start search.
returnsubexpression	Optional	false	Specifies whether to return substrings or not.

REFindNoCase A function used to search a string using regular expressions. If returnsubexpression is false, returns the position where the match begins. If true, returns a structure with len and pos arrays. The search is case insensitive.

Parameter	Req/Opt	Default	Description
regularexpression	Required	N/A	Specifies the regular expression.
string	Required	N/A	Specifies the string to search.
start	Optional	1	Specifies the place to start search.
returnsubexpression	Optional	false	Specifies whether to return substrings or not.

cfregistry   A tag used to read, write, and delete information from the Windows Registry. This tag will not work on a Unix machine.

Attribute	Req/Opt	Default	Description
action	Required	N/A	Specifies the action to perform. Valid values are getall, get, delete, or set.
branch	Required for getall, delete, or set	N/A	Specifies the name of the Registry branch.
entry	Required for get, set, or delete	N/A	Specifies the Registry value to access.
variable	Required for get	N/A	Specifies the variable from which to return the value.
type	Optional	String	Specifies the type of data to retrieve: string, dword, key, or any.
name	Required	N/A	Specifies the name of the record set.
sort	Optional, used with getall	ASC	Specifies the sort information for the return query object. You can sort on the column names: Entry, Type, or Value.
Value	Optional, used with set	N/A	Specifies the value to set the data to. If omitted, either an empty string or a zero will be set.

RemoveChars   A function used to remove characters from a string and return the result.

Parameter	Req/Opt	Default	Description
string	Required	N/A	Specifies the string in which to search.
start	Required	N/A	Specifies the position to start search.
count	Required	N/A	Specifies the number of characters to remove.

RepeatString A function used to create a string that contains repeats of the specified string.

Parameter	Req/Opt	Default	Description
string	Required	N/A	Specifies the string in which to search.
count	Required	N/A	Specifies the number of repeats.

Replace A function used to replace occurrences of specified substring1 in the specified string with substring2. The search is case sensitive.

Parameter	Req/Opt	Default	Description
string	Required	N/A	Specifies the string to search.
substring1	Required	N/A	Specifies the string to find.
substring2	Required	N/A	Specifies the replacement string.
scope	Optional	one	Specifies what to replace: one or all.

ReplaceList A function used to replace occurrences of elements from the first list with corresponding elements from the second list.

Parameter	Req/Opt	Default	Description
string	Required	N/A	Specifies the string to search.
list1	Required	N/A	Specifies a list of strings to find.
list2	Required	N/A	Specifies a list of strings to replace.

ReplaceNoCase A function used to replace occurrences of specified substring1 in the specified string with substring2. The search is case insensitive.

Parameter	Req/Opt	Default	Description
string	Required	N/A	Specifies the string to search.
substring1	Required	N/A	Specifies the string to find.
substring2	Required	N/A	Specifies the replacement string.
scope	Optional	one	Specifies what to replace: one or all.

cfreport   A tag used to generate a report in Crystal Reports, on Windows systems.

Attribute	Req/Opt	Default	Description
datasource	Optional	N/A	Specifies the name of a datasource.
type	Optional	Standard	Specifies the type of report: standard, Netscape, or Microsoft.
timeout	Optional	N/A	Specifies the maximum timeout, in seconds, to wait for the connection to Crystal Reports.
report	Required	N/A	Specifies the path to store the reports.
orderby	Optional	N/A	Specifies the ordering of the report results.
username	Optional	N/A	Specifies the username for access to the datasource.
password	Optional	N/A	Specifies the password for access to the datasource.
formula	Optional	N/A	Specifies the named formula.

REReplace   A function used to search and replace using regular expressions. The search is case sensitive.

Parameter	Req/Opt	Default	Description
string	Required	N/A	Specifies the string to search.
regularexpression	Required	N/A	Specifies the regular expression.
substring	Required	N/A	Specifies the replacement string.
scope	Optional	one	Specifies what to replace: one or all.

REReplaceNoCase   A function used to search and replace using regular expressions. The search is case insensitive.

Parameter	Req/Opt	Default	Description
string	Required	N/A	Specifies the string to search.
regularexpression	Required	N/A	Specifies the regular expression.
substring	Required	N/A	Specifies the replacement string.
scope	Optional	one	Specifies what to replace: one or all.

cfrethrow   A tag used to rethrow an active exception.
No attributes

cfreturn   A tag that returns a value from a function or method created with cffunction.

Attribute	Req/Opt	Default	Description
expr	Required	N/A	The expression to be returned.

Reverse   A function used to return the specified string with all characters reversed.

Parameter	Req/Opt	Default	Description
string	Required	N/A	Specifies the string to process.

Right   A function used to return a new string that contains the specified count characters, starting from the right side of the string.

Parameter	Req/Opt	Default	Description
string	Required	N/A	Specifies the string to process.
count	Required	N/A	Specifies the number of characters to return.

RJustify A function used to right-justify a string in the specified length.

Parameter	Req/Opt	Default	Description
string	Required	N/A	Specifies the string to right-justify.
length	Required	N/A	Specifies the length of the new string.

Round   A function used to round a number to the nearest integer.

Parameter	Req/Opt	Default	Description
number	Required	N/A	Specifies the number to return.

RTrim   A function used to trim trailing spaces off a string.

Parameter	Req/Opt	Default	Description
string	Required	N/A	Specifies the string to process.

cfsavecontent   A tag used to save generated content into a specified variable.

Attribute	Req/Opt	Default	Description
variable	Required	N/A	Specifies the name of the variable to save the content into.

cfschedule   A tag used to create, run, or delete scheduled tasks.

Attribute	Req/Opt	Default	Description
action	Required	N/A	Specifies the action to perform: delete, update, or run.
task	Required	N/A	Specifies the name of the task.
operation	Required if update	N/A	Specifies the task that the scheduler performs. This value is set to httprequest.
file	Required if publish is yes	N/A	Specifies the filename for the published file.
path	Required if publish is yes	N/A	Specifies the path to the published file.
startdate	Required if update	N/A	Specifies the date to start the scheduled task.
starttime	Required if update	N/A	Specifies the time to start the scheduled task.
url	Required if update	N/A	Specifies the URL to execute.
publish	Optional	No	Accepts a Boolean value as to whether or not to save the results to a file.

Attribute	Req/Opt	Default	Description
enddate	Optional	N/A	Specifies the date when the scheduled task will stop.
endtime	Optional	N/A	Specifies the time that the scheduled task will stop.
interval	Required if update	1 hour	Specifies the interval for the scheduled task: once, daily, weekly, monthly, or a number of seconds.
requesttimeout	Optional	N/A	Specifies the timeout for the page to execute.
username	Optional	N/A	Specifies the username for the protected server.
password	Optional	N/A	Specifies the password for the protected server.
proxyserver	Optional	N/A	Specifies the hostname or IP address of the proxy server.
resolveurl	Optional	No	A Boolean value that specifies whether or not to resolve URLs from the retrieved document.
port	Optional	80	Specifies the port of the HTTP server.
proxyport	Optional	80	Specifies the port of the proxy server.

cfscript   A tag used to perform CFScript actions.
No attributes

cfsearch   A tag used to search against a Verity collection.

Attribute	Req/Opt	Default	Description
name	Required	N/A	Specifies the name of the search query.
collection	Required	N/A	Specifies the name of the collection to search or an absolute path to an unregistered collection.
type	Optional	simple	Specifies the type of search, either simple or explicit.
criteria	Optional	N/A	Specifies the search criteria.

Attribute	Req/Opt	Default	Description
maxrows	Optional	All	Specifies the maximum number of rows to return in the result set.
startrow	Optional	1	Specifies the first row to return in the result set.
language	Optional	English	Specifies the language of the search.

Second A function used to return the second value from a date/time object.

Parameter	Req/Opt	Default	Description
date	Required	N/A	Specifies the date/time object.

cfselect A tag used with the cfform tag to create a select box.

Attribute	Req/Opt	Default	Description
name	Required	N/A	Specifies the name of the select box.
size	Optional	N/A	Specifies the number of entries in the drop-down list.
required	Optional	No	Specifies whether the value is required or not.
message	Optional	N/A	Specifies the message to display if the field is required, but not filled in.
onerror	Optional	N/A	Specifies a JavaScript function to call if validation fails.
multiple	Optional	No	Specifies whether to allow for multiple selections or not.
query	Optional	N/A	Specifies the name of the query used to populate the drop-down list.
selected	Optional	N/A	Specifies a list of options to select in the drop-down list.
value	Optional	N/A	Specifies a query column for the value of each element.

Attribute	Req/Opt	Default	Description
display	Optional	Value of value attribute	Specifies a query column for the display text of each element.
passthrough	Optional	N/A	Specifies any other attributes that are not explicitly specified here.

cfset   A tag used to create a ColdFusion variable.

Attribute	Req/Opt	Default	Description
variablename	Required	N/A	Specifies the name and value of the new variable.

SetEncoding   A function used to set the character encoding of Form and URL variables. Returns no value.

Parameter	Req/Opt	Default	Description
scope_name	Required	N/A	Specifies the URL or Form variable.
charset	Required	N/A	Specifies the Java character set for the file.

SetLocale   A function used to set the locale for a ColdFusion application user.

Parameter	Req/Opt	Default	Description
locale	Required	N/A	Specifies the locale to change to.

SetProfileString   A function used to set an entry in an initialization file. Returns an empty string upon success.

Parameter	Req/Opt	Default	Description
inipath	Required	N/A	Specifies the absolute path to the initialization file.
section	Required	N/A	Specifies the section of the initialization file.

Parameter	Req/Opt	Default	Description
entry	Required	N/A	Specifies the name of the entry to set.
value	Required	N/A	Specifies the value from which to set the entry.

cfsetting   A tag used to control the output of a ColdFusion template.

Attribute	Req/Opt	Default	Description
enablecfoutputonly	Required	N/A	If set to yes, blocks output of all text that is not in a cfoutput tag.
showdebugoutput	Optional	Yes	If set to yes, displays debug output; otherwise, suppresses it.
requesttimeout	Optional	N/A	Specifies the time limit after which ColdFusion processes the page as an unresponsive thread.

SetVariable   A function used to set a variable and return the new value.

Parameter	Req/Opt	Default	Description
name	Required	N/A	Specifies the name of the new variable.
value	Required	N/A	Specifies the value of the variable.

Sgn   A function used to return 1 for a positive number, −1 for a negative number, or 0 for 0.

Parameter	Req/Opt	Default	Description
number	Required	N/A	Specifies the number whose sign to return.

cfsilent   A tag used to suppress all output.
No attributes

Sin   A function used to return the arcsine of an angle.

Parameter	Req/Opt	Default	Description
number	Required	N/A	Specifies the angle, in radians.

cfslider   A tag used to place a slider control on a form.

Attribute	Req/Opt	Default	Description
name	Required	N/A	Specifies the name of the control.
label	Optional	N/A	Specifies the label of the control.
refreshlabel	Optional	Yes	A Boolean value that specifies whether to refresh the label when the slider moves.
range	Optional	0,100	Specifies the numeric range of values.
scale	Optional	N/A	Specifies the slider scale of the slider.
value	Optional	Minimum in range	Specifies the default value of the control.
onvalidate	Optional	N/A	Specifies the JavaScript function to call on validation.
message	Optional	N/A	Specifies the message to display if validation fails.
onerror	Optional	N/A	Specifies the JavaScript function to execute if validation fails.
height	Optional	40	Specifies the pixel height of the control.
width	Optional	N/A	Specifies the pixel width of the control.
vspace	Optional	N/A	Specifies the vertical spacing above and below the control, in pixels.
hspace	Optional	N/A	Specifies the horizontal spacing to the left and right of the control, in pixels.
align	Optional	N/A	Specifies alignment of the slider: top, left, bottom, baseline, texttop, absbottom, middle, absmiddle, or right.
tickmarkmajor	Optional	No	If set to yes, displays major tickmarks on the scale.
tickmarkminor	Optional	N/A	If set to yes, displays minor tickmarks on the scale.
tickmarkimages	Optional	N/A	Specifies a list of URLs to images that will be used instead as tickmarks.

Attribute	Req/Opt	Default	Description
tickmarklabels	Optional	No	Specifies the labels for the tickmarks. If set to yes, displays numeric labels. You can use a comma-delimited list of text values to display here. If set to no, nothing is displayed.
lookandfeel	Optional	Windows	Specifies look and feel of control. Valid values are windows, motif, or metal.
vertical	Optional	No	Specifies whether to render the control vertically or not.
bgcolor	Optional	N/A	Specifies the background color of the slider control.
textcolor	Optional	N/A	Specifies the color of the text on the control.
font	Optional	N/A	Specifies the name of the font for the label text.
fontsize	Optional	N/A	Specifies the font size for the label text.
italic	Optional	No	If set to yes, displays the label text in italics.
bold	Optional	No	If set to yes, displays the label text in bold.
notsupported	Optional	N/A	Specifies a message to display if the control is not supported.

SpanExcluding   A function used to retrieve characters, starting from the first character in a string and searching until one is found that matches a character in the specified set. The search is case sensitive.

Parameter	Req/Opt	Default	Description
string	Required	N/A	Specifies the string to search.
set	Required	N/A	Specifies the set of characters to stop at.

SpanIncluding   A function used to retrieve characters, starting from the first character in a string and searching until one is found that matches a character in the specified set. The search is case sensitive.

Parameter	Req/Opt	Default	Description
string	Required	N/A	Specifies the string to search.
set	Required	N/A	Specifies the set of characters to stop at.

Sqr   A function used to return the square root of a number.

Parameter	Req/Opt	Default	Description
Number	Required	N/A	Specifies the number whose square root to get.

cfstoredproc   A tag used to execute a stored procedure in a database. Used with cfstoredprocparam.

Attribute	Req/Opt	Default	Description
procedure	Required	N/A	Specifies the name of the stored procedure in the database.
datasource	Required	N/A	Specifies the name of the datasource.
username	Optional	N/A	Specifies the username for access to the datasource.
password	Optional	N/A	Specifies the password for access to the datasource.
blockfactor	Optional	1	Specifies the number of rows returned to ColdFusion at a time.
debug	Optional	No	A Boolean value that specifies whether or not debug information is listed for each statement.
returncode	Optional	No	Specifies whether or not to return a status code by the procedure.

StripCR   A function used to remove return characters from a string.

Parameter	Req/Opt	Default	Description
string	Required	N/A	Specifies the value to process.

StructAppend   A function used to append one structure to another. Returns true upon success.

Parameter	Req/Opt	Default	Description
structure1	Required	N/A	Specifies the structure to append to.
structure2	Required	N/A	Specifies the structure to append from.
Overwrite	Required	N/A	Specifies whether keys in structure2 will overwrite corresponding keys in structure1.

StructClear   A function used to remove all keys from a structure. Returns true upon success.

Parameter	Req/Opt	Default	Description
structure	Required	N/A	Specifies the structure to process.

StructCopy   A function used to copy a structure. Returns the structure.

Parameter	Req/Opt	Default	Description
structure	Required	N/A	Specifies the structure to process.

StructCount   A function used to return the number of keys in a structure.

Parameter	Req/Opt	Default	Description
structure	Required	N/A	Specifies the structure to process.

StructDelete   A function used to delete a key from a structure. Returns true upon success.

Parameter	Req/Opt	Default	Description
structure	Required	N/A	Specifies the structure to process.
key	Required	N/A	Specifies the key to delete.
indicateexisting	Optional	false	Specifies whether to return yes if key exists.

StructFind   A function used to return the value associated with the specified key.

Parameter	Req/Opt	Default	Description
structure	Required	N/A	Specifies the structure to process.
key	Required	N/A	Specifies the key to return.

StructFindKey   A function used to return an array of structures that contain the specified key. This is a deep search, including nested arrays and structures.

Parameter	Req/Opt	Default	Description
top	Required	N/A	Specifies the ColdFusion object to start search.
value	Required	N/A	Specifies the value to search for.
scope	Required	N/A	Specifies one, to return the first match, or all, to return all matches.

StructFindValue   A function used to return an array of structures that contain the specified value. This is a deep search, including nested arrays and structures.

Parameter	Req/Opt	Default	Description
top	Required	N/A	Specifies the ColdFusion object to start search.
value	Required	N/A	Specifies the value to search for.
scope	Optional	one	Specifies one, to return the first match, or all, to return all matches.

StructGet   A function used to return a structure from the specified path.

Parameter	Req/Opt	Default	Description
Path	Required	N/A	Specifies the pathname or variable that contains the structure.

StructInsert   A function used to insert a value into a structure. Returns true upon success.

Parameter	Req/Opt	Default	Description
structure	Required	N/A	Specifies the structure to insert into.
key	Required	N/A	Specifies the key to create.
value	Required	N/A	Specifies the value to insert into the key.
allowoverwrite	Optional	false	If set to yes, allows overwriting an existing key.

StructIsEmpty   A function used to return true if the specified structure is empty.

Parameter	Req/Opt	Default	Description
structure	Required	N/A	Specifies the structure to process.

StructKeyArray   A function used to return an array of all keys in the structure.

Parameter	Req/Opt	Default	Description
structure	Required	N/A	Specifies the structure to process.

StructKeyExists   A function used to return true if a key exists in the specified structure.

Parameter	Req/Opt	Default	Description
structure	Required	N/A	Specifies the structure to process.
key	Required	N/A	Specifies the key to check for.

StructKeyList   A function used to return a list of all keys in the structure.

Parameter	Req/Opt	Default	Description
structure	Required	N/A	Specifies the structure to process.
delimiter	Optional	, (comma)	Specifies the delimiter for the resulting list.

StructNew   A function used to create and return a new structure. No parameters

StructSort   A function used to sort a structure and return an array of sorted top-level key names.

Parameter	Req/Opt	Default	Description
base	Required	N/A	Specifies the ColdFusion structure.
sorttype	Required	N/A	Specifies the sort type: numeric, text, or textnocase.
sortorder	Required	N/A	Specifies the sort order: ASC or DESC.
pathtosubelement	Required	N/A	Specifies the path to apply to each top-level key.

StructUpdate   A function used to update a value in a structure. Returns true upon completion.

Parameter	Req/Opt	Default	Description
structure	Required	N/A	Specifies the structure to process.
key	Required	N/A	Specifies the key to update.
value	Required	N/A	Specifies the new value.

cfswitch   A tag used with cfcase and cfdefaultcase to perform conditional logic.

Attribute	Req/Opt	Default	Description
expression	Required	N/A	Specifies the expression that each case statement will compare its value against.

cftable   A tag used to build a table in a ColdFusion page. Used with the cfcol tag.

Attribute	Req/Opt	Default	Description
query	Required	N/A	Specifies the name of the query to create a table from.
maxrows	Optional	N/A	Specifies the maximum number of query rows to display in the table.

Attribute	Req/Opt	Default	Description
colspacing	Optional	2	Specifies the colspacing attribute of the table.
headerlines	Optional	2	Specifies the number of lines to use for the table header.
htmltable	Optional	N/A	Specifies to render the table using HTML 3.0. The value of this attribute does not matter.
border	Optional	N/A	Specifies whether or not to put a border around the table. The value of this attribute does not matter.
colheaders	Optional	N/A	Specifies whether or not column headers should be displayed. Used in conjunction with cfcol.
startrow	Optional	1	Specifies the first query row to create the table from.

Tan   A function used to return the tangent of an angle.

Parameter	Req/Opt	Default	Description
Number	Required	N/A	Specifies the angle, in radians.

cftextinput   A tag used to create a text input box.

Attribute	Req/Opt	Default	Description
name	Required	N/A	Specifies the name of the control.
value	Optional	N/A	Specifies the default value of the control.
required	Optional	No	If set to yes, specifies that the field is required.
range	Optional	N/A	Specifies the minimum/maximum value range, separated by a comma. Valid only for numeric data.
validate	Optional	N/A	Specifies the type of validation to occur: date, eurodate, time, float, integer, telephone, zipcode, creditcard, social_security_number, or regular_expression.

Attribute	Req/Opt	Default	Description
onvalidate	Optional	N/A	Specifies JavaScript function to call during field validation.
pattern	Required if validate is regular_expression.	N/A	Specifies JavaScript regular expression pattern to validate input.
message	Optional	N/A	Specifies the message to display if validation fails.
onerror	Optional	N/A	Specifies the JavaScript function to execute if validation fails.
size	Optional	N/A	Specifies the number of characters to be displayed before the horizontal scroll bar shows up.
font	Optional	N/A	Specifies the name of the font for the text.
fontsize	Optional	N/A	Specifies the font size for the text.
italic	Optional	No	If set to yes, displays the text in italics.
bold	Optional	No	If set to yes, displays the text in bold.
height	Optional	40	Specifies the pixel height of the control.
width	Optional	200	Specifies the pixel width of the control.
vspace	Optional	N/A	Specifies the vertical spacing above and below the control, in pixels.
hspace	Optional	N/A	Specifies the horizontal spacing to the left and right of the control, in pixels.
align	Optional	N/A	Specifies alignment of the slider: top, left, bottom, baseline, texttop, absbottom, middle, absmiddle, or right.
bgcolor	Optional	N/A	Specifies the background color of the slider control.
textcolor	Optional	N/A	Specifies the color of the text on the control.
maxlength	Optional	N/A	Specifies the maximum length of the control.
notsupported	Optional	N/A	Specifies a message to display if the control is not supported.

cfthrow   A tag used to create a custom exception. Exceptions can be caught
with cfcatch.

Attribute	Req/Opt	Default	Description
type	Optional	Application	Specifies the type of error, either an application or a custom type
message	Optional	N/A	Specifies a message to describe the exception.
detail	Optional	N/A	Specifies a description of the error.
errorcode	Optional	N/A	Specifies a custom error code.
extendedinfo	Optional	N/A	Specifies a custom error code.
object	Optional	N/A	Specifies the value of the cfobject name attribute. This attribute is mutually exclusive to all other attributes.

TimeFormat   A function used to return formatted time from a date/time object.

Parameter	Req/Opt	Default	Description
time	Required	N/A	Specifies the date/time object to covert.
mask	Optional	N/A	Specifies the mask used to display dates: short, medium, long, full, h (hour, no leading zeros for 12-hour clock), hh (hour, with leading zeros for 12-hour clock), H (hours, no leading zeros for 24-hour clock), HH (hours, no leading zeros for 24-hour clock), m (minutes with leading zeros), mm (minutes without leading zeros), s (seconds with no leading zeros), ss (seconds with leading zeros), t (one-character marker string, A or P), or tt (two-character marker string, AM or PM).

ToBase64   A function used to return Base64 representation of a string or binary object.

Parameter	Req/Opt	Default	Description
object	Required	N/A	Specifies the name of string or object.
encoding	Optional	Encoding on page where function is called	Specifies how characters are represented in the byte array.

ToBinary   A function used to return the binary representation of Base64-encoded data.

Parameter	Req/Opt	Default	Description
base64string	Required	N/A	Specifies the Base64 string to convert.

ToString   A function used to convert a value to a string.

Parameter	Req/Opt	Default	Description
Value	Required	N/A	Specifies the value you want to convert.
encoding	Optional	Encoding on page where function is called	Specifies how characters are represented in the byte array.

cftrace   A tag used to display and log debugging data.

Attribute	Req/Opt	Default	Description
abort	Optional	No	If set to yes, calls the cfabort tag upon execution.
category	Optional	N/A	Specifies a string for identifying trace groups.
inline	Optional	No	If set to yes, displays trace code in addition to the summary.
text	Optional	N/A	Specifies a user-defined string or simple variable.
type	Optional	Information	Specifies the type of entry to make into the log: information, warning, fatal information, or error.
var	Optional	N/A	Specifies the name of the complex variable to display, akin to cfdump.

cftransaction   A tag used to group database queries together into a single transaction.

Attribute	Req/Opt	Default	Description
action	Optional	begin	Specifies action to perform: begin, commit, or rollback.
isolation	Optional	N/A	Specifies the type of ODBC lock: read_uncommitted, read_committed, repeatable_read, or serializable.

cftree   A tag used with the cfform tag to insert a tree control onto a form.

Attribute	Req/Opt	Default	Description
name	Required	N/A	Specifies the name of the control.
required	Optional	No	If set to yes, specifies that the field is required.
delimiter	Optional	\\	Specifies the character used to separate elements in a path.
completepath	Optional	No; tree name return as root	If set to no, passes treename.path as a form variable, otherwise the value is not passed.
appendkey	Optional	Yes	If set to yes, passes key into HREF values.
highlighthref	Optional	Yes	Specifies links that are associated with a tree item.
onvalidate	Optional	N/A	Specifies JavaScript function to validate user input.
message	Optional	N/A	Specifies the message to display if validation fails.
onerror	Optional	N/A	Specifies the JavaScript function to execute if validation fails.
lookandfeel	Optional	windows	Specifies look and feel of control: motif, windows, or metal.
font	Optional	N/A	Specifies the name of the font for the text.
fontsize	Optional	N/A	Specifies the font size for the text.
italic	Optional	No	If set to yes, displays the text in italics.
bold	Optional	No	If set to yes, displays the text in bold.
height	Optional	320	Specifies the pixel height of the control.

Attribute	Req/Opt	Default	Description
width	Optional	200	Specifies the pixel width of the control.
vspace	Optional	N/A	Specifies the vertical spacing above and below the control, in pixels.
hspace	Optional	N/A	Specifies the horizontal spacing to the left and right of the control, in pixels.
align	Optional	N/A	Specifies alignment of the control: top, left, bottom, baseline, texttop, absbottom, middle, absmiddle, or right.
border	Optional	Yes	If set to yes, displays a border around the control.
hscroll	Optional	Yes	If set to yes, permits horizontal scrolling.
vscroll	Optional	Yes	If set to yes, permits vertical scrolling.
notsupported	Optional	N/A	Specifies a message to display if the control is not supported.

cftreeitem   A tag used to populate a tree created with cftree.

Attribute	Req/Opt	Default	Description
value	Required	N/A	Specifies the value to pass when the form is submitted.
display	Optional	value	Specifies the label for the tree item.
parent	Optional	N/A	Specifies the parent for the tree item.
img	Optional	folder	Specifies the imagename, filename, or URL of the image to display for this item. Built-in images are cd, computer, document, element, folder, floppy, fixed, or remote.
imgopen	Optional	N/A	Specifies the icon to display for an open tree item, either a relative path or a ColdFusion image.
href	Optional	N/A	Specifies the URL to associate with the tree item.
target	Optional	N/A	Specifies the target value of the href attribute.

Attribute	Req/Opt	Default	Description
query	Optional	N/A	Specifies the name of the query to generate data.
queryasroot	Optional	N/A	Accepts a Boolean value. If set to yes, defines a query as the root item of the tree.
expand	Optional	Yes	Specifies whether or not this item is expanded by default.

Trim   A function used to remove leading and trailing spaces from the specified value.

Parameter	Req/Opt	Default	Description
string	Required	N/A	Specifies the string to process.

cftry   A tag used in conjunction with cfcatch to catch errors.
No attributes

UCase   A function used to convert the specified string to uppercase.

Parameter	Req/Opt	Default	Description
string	Required	N/A	Specifies the string to process.

cfupdate   A tag used to update a database record based on a form submission.

Attribute	Req/Opt	Default	Description
datasource	Required	N/A	Specifies the name of the datasource.
tablename	Required	N/A	Specifies the name of the table to insert into.
tableowner	Optional	N/A	Specifies the owner of the table, if applicable.
tablequalifer	Optional	N/A	Specifies the qualifier of the table, if applicable.
username	Optional	N/A	Specifies the username needed to access the datasource.

Attribute	Req/Opt	Default	Description
password	Optional	N/A	Specifies the password needed to access the datasource.
formfields	Optional	All form data, except keys	Specifies the list of form fields that are to be inserted into the database. Database key must be present on form.

URLDecode A function used to decode a URL string.

Parameter	Req/Opt	Default	Description
string	Required	N/A	Specifies the URL-encoded string to process.
charset	Optional	N/A	Specifies the character set.

URLEncodedFormat A function used to return a URL-encoded string, with relevant characters escaped as necessary.

Parameter	Req/Opt	Default	Description
string	Required	N/A	Specifies the string to process.
charset	Optional	N/A	Specifies the character set.

URLSessionFormat If the client does not accept cookies, this function returns a URL with all client identification appended to it. Otherwise, it does nothing.

Parameter	Req/Opt	Default	Description
URL	Required	N/A	Specifies the URL.

Val A function used to convert numeric characters in a string to a number and return the number.

Parameter	Req/Opt	Default	Description
string	Required	N/A	Specifies the string to process.

ValueList   A function used to return a list of values for each record in a query result.

Parameter	Req/Opt	Default	Description
query.column	Required	N/A	Specifies the query column to process.
delimiter	Optional	N/A	Specifies the list delimiter.

cfwddx   A tag used to serialize and deserialize ColdFusion data structures in the WDDX format.

Attribute	Req/Opt	Default	Description
action	Required	N/A	Specifies the action to perform: cfml2wddx, wddx2cfml, cfml2js, or wddx2js.
input	Required	N/A	Specifies the value to process.
output	Required if wddx2cfml	N/A	Specifies the name out of the ColdFusion output variable.
toplevelvariable	Required if wddx2js or cfml2js	N/A	Specifies the name of the JavaScript output variable.
usetimezoneinfo	Optional	Yes	If set to yes, uses an hour and minute offset. Otherwise, uses local time zone information.
validate	Optional	No	If set to yes, validates WDDX against an XML parser.

Week   A function used to return the ordinal date of the week.

Parameter	Req/Opt	Default	Description
date	Required	N/A	Specifies a date/time object.

WriteOutput   A function used to write output to the HTML stream.

Parameter	Req/Opt	Default	Description
Value	Required	N/A	Specifies the value to output.

cfxml   A tag used to create XML document objects in ColdFusion.

Attribute	Req/Opt	Default	Description
variable	Required	N/A	Specifies the name of the XML variable.
casesensitive	Optional	N/A	Specifies whether the XML document object is case sensitive or not.

XmlChildPos   A function used to return the position of a child element in an XML object.

Parameter	Req/Opt	Default	Description
element	Required	N/A	Specifies the element to search.
childname	Required	N/A	Specifies the element to search for.
N	Required	N/A	Specifies the index of the child to search.

XmlElemNew   A function used to return a new, XML element.

Parameter	Req/Opt	Default	Description
xmlobject	Required	N/A	Specifies the name of an XML object.
childname	Required	N/A	Specifies the name of the element.

XmlFormat   A function used to escape special XML characters.

Parameter	Req/Opt	Default	Description
string	Required	N/A	Specifies the string to process.

XmlNew   A function used to create a new XML document object.

Parameter	Req/Opt	Default	Description
casesensitive	Optional	No	If yes, makes the XML object case sensitive.

XmlParse A function used to covert a string into an XML document object.

Parameter	Req/Opt	Default	Description
xmlstring	Required	N/A	Specifies the string that contains the XML.
casesensitive	Optional	No	If yes, makes the XML object case sensitive.

XmlSearch A function to use an XPath expression to search an XML document, represented as a string.

Parameter	Req/Opt	Default	Description
xmldoc	Required	N/A	Specifies the XML document object.
xpathstring	Required	N/A	Specifies the XPath expression.

XmlTransform A function used to return the XML document after the XSLT information is applied.

Parameter	Req/Opt	Default	Description
xmlstring xmlobj	Required	N/A	Specifies the XML document object, or a string representation of one.
xlsstring	Required	N/A	Specifies the XSLT information to apply.

Year A function used to return the year of a date/time object.

Parameter	Req/Opt	Default	Description
date	Required	N/A	Specifies the date/time object.

YesNoFormat A function used to return yes for a nonzero value, or no otherwise.

Parameter	Req/Opt	Default	Description
value	Required	N/A	Specifies the value to process.

Appendix B

Discovering Special ColdFusion Variables

709

This appendix shows you some special ColdFusion variables that you can use within your development. It talks about variables associated with the client scope, the server, custom tags, and objects or values that are implicitly returned or created by certain tags.

Scope Variables

This section lists some special variables that are associated with specific variable scopes. You can find more information about variable scopes in Chapter 8.

Client Variables

If client variables are enabled in the cfappliation tag, these variables will automatically be created for each user of your application:

- **client.CFID**   Used with CFToken to keep track of sessions. This value increments for each new user.

- **client.CFToken**   Used with CFID to keep track of sessions. This value is a random value for each new user.

- **client.HitCount**   Contains the number of times that the user visited the site.

- **client.LastVisit**   Contains the date and time of the last visit.

- **client.TimeCreated**   Contains the date and time that the user was created.

- **client.URLToken**   Contains the query string that will be appended to the end of a URL to keep track of the user session. It is in the format

  ```
  CFID=xx&CFToken=xxx
  ```

  It needs to be used only if session management is turned off.

Server Variables

Server variables contain information about ColdFusion and the operating system. They are all read-only variables.

- **server.ColdFusion.ProductName**   Contains the name of the ColdFusion product; this will most likely contain the value ColdFusion Server.

- **server.ColdFusion.ProductVersion**   Contains the version of the ColdFusion server that you are running.

- **server.ColdFusion.ProductLevel**   Contains whether you are running off of ColdFusion Pro or ColdFusion Enterprise.

- **server.ColdFusion.SerialNumber**   Contains the serial number of your ColdFusion installation.

- **server.ColdFusion.SupportedLocales**   Contains a list of locales that are supported by this installation of ColdFusion.
- **server.OS.Name**   Contains the name of the operating system that ColdFusion is operating on top of.
- **server.OS.AdditionalInformation**   Contains additional information about the operating system, if applicable.
- **server.OS.Version**   Contains the version of the server that ColdFusion is operating on.
- **server.OS.BuildNumber**   Contains the build number of the operating system that ColdFusion is operating on top of.

Memory Variables

Memory variable are in the form of application and session variables. They must be enabled in the cfapplication tag.

- **application.ApplicationName**   Contains the name of the application, as specified using the name attribute of the cfapplication tag.
- **session.CFID**   Contains a value used with CFToken to keep track of sessions. This value increments for each new user.
- **session.CFToken**   Contains a value used with CFID to keep track of sessions. This value is a random value for each new user.
- **session.URLToken**   Contains the query string that will be appended to the end of a URL to keep track of the user session. It is in the format

```
CFID=xx&CFToken=xxx
```

It needs to be used only if session management is turned off.

Custom Tag Variables

If you are executing a custom tag, some special custom tag variables are available to you. More information about custom tags can be found in Chapter 16.

- *thistag*.**ExecutionMode**   Contains Start, End, or Inactive. It specifies whether the start tag is being processed or the end tag is being processed. Inactive is used for nested custom tags.
- *thistag*.**HasEndTag**   Specifies whether or not the tag was called with an end tag (Boolean value).
- *thistag*.**GeneratedContent**   Contains all output that is created by the custom tag.
- *thistag*.**AssocAttribs[index]**   Contains all the attributes of nested tags, if cfassociate is used to associate them.

Form Variables

There is only a single form variable that is available implicitly—**form.FieldNames**. This variable contains a list of all the fields names that were on the form before it was submitted. Information about HTML forms can be found in Chapter 12.

CGI Variables

There are various Common Gateway Interface variables that are accessible to a ColdFusion page request. You can access them using the cgi variable scope.

- **Server_Software**   Contains the name and version of the web server.
- **Server_Name**   Contains the server's hostname, DNS alias, or IP address.
- **Gateway_Interface**   Contains the revision number of the CGI specification that the server complies to.
- **Server_Protocol**   Contains the name and revision of the protocol that the request used to request information.
- **Server_Port**   Contains the port number to which the request was sent.
- **Request_Method**   Contains the method with which the request was made. This will probably be GET or POST.
- **Path_Info**   Contains the URL path, without the hostname.
- **Path_Translated**   Contains the directory path of the template on the server.
- **Script_Name**   Contains the virtual path to the script that is executing.
- **Query_String**   Contains the URL's Query String.
- **Remote_Host**   Contains the hostname making the request. If the server does not have this information, it sets Remote_Addr and does not set Remote_Host.
- **Remote_Addr**   Contains the IP address of the remote host.
- **Auth_Type**   Contains the authentication method that validates the user, if supported by the server.
- **Remote_User**   Contains the username that the user has authenticated against. If this variable does not exist, look for Auth_User, which is sometimes used as an alias for Remote_User.
- **Remote_Ident**   Contains the name of the remote user, if RFC 931 identification is supported.
- **Content_Type**   Contains the content type of the data attached to the request.
- **Content_Length**   Contains the length of the Content_Type.

- **HTTP_Referer**   Contains the URL of the document that linked to the current page.
- **HTTP_User_Agent**   Contains the name of the browser that the client is using to make the request.
- **HTTP_IF_Modified_Since**   Contains the last time the page was modified. This is used in browser-side caching.
- **Cert_Subject**   Contains client information, such as the client name and e-mail address, as provided by the server.
- **Cert_Issuer**   Contains information about who issued the client certificate.
- **Client_Cert_Encoded**   Contains the client's certificate, base-64 encoded.

Query Columns Created from ColdFusion Tags

Many ColdFusion tags return query objects. This section shows you the tags that do so and the columns available in those queries. More information about creating SQL queries can be found in Chapter 9 and Chapter 21.

Query Variables

A query object has these special predefined variables:

- *QueryName*.**CurrentRow**   Contains the current row of the query that is being processed. Used mainly in loops.
- *QueryName*.**RecordCount**   Contains the total number of records in the query.
- *QueryName*.**ColumnList**   Contains a list of all the columns that are in the query.

Specialized Query or Stored Procedure Variables

After a query or stored procedure is executed, some special variables are created that are not a part of the query object:

- **cfquery.ExecutionTime**   Contains the length of time it took to execute the query after a query is executed. The prefix for this variable is not the name of the query variable.
- **cfstoredproc.ExecutionTime**   Contains the length of time it took to execute the stored procedure, after a stored procedure is executed. The prefix for this variable is not the name of the query variable.
- **cfstoredproc.StatusCode**   Contains the status code after a Stored Procedure is executed. The prefix for this variable is not the name of the query variable.

cfdirectory Tag

The cfdirectory tag gives you information about the files and directories on the server machine. You can find more information about this tag in Chapter 19. The tag returns a query with these fields:

- *QueryName*.**Name**   Contains the name of the directory.
- *QueryName*.**Size**   Contains the size of the directory.
- *QueryName*.**Type**   Contains File if the current entry is a file, or Dir if the current entry is another directory.
- *QueryName*.**DateLastModified**   Contains the date that the current entry was last modified.
- *QueryName*.**Attributes**   Contains a list of all the file attributes.
- *QueryName*.**Mode**   Contains the octal string on Unix or Linux files.

cfftp Tag

The cfftp tag allows ColdFusion to interact with an FTP server. You can find information about this tag in Chapter 22. The query returned by this tag contains these columns:

- *QueryName*.**Name**   Contains the filename of the current element.
- *QueryName*.**Path**   Contains the file path, without a drive specification.
- *QueryName*.**URL**   Contains a URL to the current entry.
- *QueryName*.**Length**   Contains the file size of the current element.
- *QueryName*.**LastModified**   Contains the date that the element was last modified.
- *QueryName*.**Attributes**   Contains the attributes of the current element.
- *QueryName*.**IsDirectory**   Contains a Boolean value specifying whether or not the current element is a directory.
- *QueryName*.**Mode**   Contains the octal string on Unix and Linux machines.

cfpop Tag

The cfpop tag enables ColdFusion to retrieve information from any POP e-mail server. This tag was discussed in Chapter 22. The query returned by this tag contains these fields:

- *QueryName*.**Date**   Contains the date of the message.
- *QueryName*.**From**   Contains the contact information of the person who sent the e-mail.
- *QueryName*.**Body**   Contains the text of the e-mail message.

- *QueryName*.**Header**   Contains the header information of the e-mail.
- *QueryName*.**MessageNumber**   Contains the message number of the e-mail.
- *QueryName*.**ReplyTo**   Contains the e-mail address in the replyto field.
- *QueryName*.**Subject**   Contains the subject of the e-mail message.
- *QueryName*.**CC**   Contains the carbon copy field of the e-mail message.
- *QueryName*.**To**   Contains the e-mail address of the person that this e-mail was sent to.
- *QueryName*.**Attachments**   Contains the text of the attachments to the current e-mail.
- *QueryName*.**AttachmentFiles**   Contains the filenames of the attachments to the current e-mail.
- *QueryName*.**UID**   Contains a unique identifier for the current message.

cfregistry Tag

The cfregistry tag will return a query with these fields:

- *QueryName*.**Type**   Contains the type of the registry entry, either string, dword, key, or any.
- *QueryName*.**Entry**   Contains the name of the value.
- *QueryName*.**Value**   Contains the value of the entry.

cfsearch Tag

The cfsearch tag is used to search Verity collections, as described in Chapter 24. After the cfsearch tag is executed, a query object is created with query information in it. This is the query information that is contained in the query object:

- *QueryName*.**URL**   Contains the URL of the current document.
- *QueryName*.**Key**   Contains the key of the current document.
- *QueryName*.**Title**   Contains the title of the document.
- *QueryName*.**Score**   Contains the score of the current record.
- *QueryName*.**Custom1**   Contains the custom1 value that was specified when the record was indexed.
- *QueryName*.**Custom2**   Contains the custom2 value that was specified when the record was indexed.
- *QueryName*.**Summary**   Contains the summary for the current record.
- *QueryName*.**RecordsSearched**   Contains the total number of records that were searched.

ColdFusion Error Variables

This section describes variables that are available after an error occurs. These variables contain specific error information and will help you in debugging the error.

cfcatch Tag

You can catch unexpected errors with cftry and cfcatch, as discussed in Chapter 18. When a cfcatch block is executed, these special variables are available:

- **cfcatch.Type**   Contains the exception type. It will have one of these values: application, database, template, security, object, missinginclude, expression, lock, custom_type, or searchengine.
- **cfcatch.Message**   Contains the exception's diagnostic message.
- **cfcatch.Detail**   Contains a detailed message from the ColdFusion interpreter.
- **cfcatch.ErrNumber**   Contains the internal expression error number. Only available for expression errors.
- **cfcatch.NativeErrorCode**   Contains the native database error returned from the ODBC drivers. Only available in database errors.
- **cfcatch.SQLState**   Contains the SQLState associated with the error. Only available for database errors.
- **cfcatch.LockName**   Contains the name of the lock that caused an error. The default value is anonymous if there is no error. Only available in lock errors.
- **cfcatch.LockOperation**   Contains the lock operation that caused an error, either Timeout, Create Mutex, or unknown. Only available for lock errors.
- **cfcatch.MissingFileName**   Contains the name of the missing file. Only available for MissingInclude errors.
- **cfcatch.TagContext**   Contains the location of the tag in the stack.
- **cfcatch.ErrorCode**   Contains a custom error code. Only available for custom errors.
- **cfcatch.ExtendedInfo**   Contains an expanded custom error message. Only available for custom errors.

cferror Tag

When the cferror tag catches an error, the following special error variables are available to you inside the error-processing page. We discussed this in more detail in Chapter 18.

- **error.Diagnostics**   Contains a detailed diagnostic from the ColdFusion server. Available for exception and request errors.

■ **error.MailTo**   Contains the e-mail address that was specified in the cferror tag. Available for exception and request errors.

■ **error.DateTime**   Contains the date and time that the error occurred. Available for exception and request errors.

■ **error.Browser**   Contains the name of the browser that the error occurred in. Available for exception and request errors.

■ **error.GeneratedContent**   Contains the content that was generated by the failed request. Available for exception errors.

■ **error.RemoteAddress**   Contains the IP address of the remote client. Available for exception and request errors.

■ **error.HTTPReferer**   Contains the page that linked the client to the page where the error occurred. Available for exception and request errors.

■ **error.Template**   Contains the name of the page that the error occurred in. Available for exception and request errors.

■ **error.QueryString**   Contains the query string of the client request. Available for exception and request errors.

■ **error.ValidationHeader**   Contains the validation header text. Available for validation errors.

■ **error.InvalidFields**   Contains the list of fields that did not validate. Available for validation errors.

■ **error.ValidationFooter**   Contains the validation message footer text. Available for validation errors.

■ **error.RootCause**   The Java Servlet exception reported by the JVM as the cause of the exception. This is a Java object.

■ **error.Type**   Contains the type of exception for exception errors. It will have one of these values: application, database, template, security, object, missinginclude, expression, lock, custom_type, or searchengine.

■ **error.Message**   Contains the exception's diagnostic message. Available for exception errors.

■ **error.Detail**   Contains a detailed message from the ColdFusion interpreter. Available for exception errors.

■ **error.ErrNumber**   Contains the internal expression error number. Only available for exception expression errors.

■ **error.NativeErrorCode**   Contains the native database error returned from the ODBC drivers. Only available in exception database errors.

■ **error.SQLState**   Contains the SQLState associated with the error. Only available for exception database errors.

- **error.LockName**   Contains the name of the lock that caused an error. The default value is anonymous if there is no error. Only available in exception lock errors.

- **error.LockOperation**   Contains the lock operation that caused an error, either Timeout, Create Mutex, or unknown. Only available for exception lock errors.

- **error.MissingFileName**   Contains the name of the missing file. Only available for exception MissingInclude errors.

- **error.TagContext**   Contains the location of the tag in the stack. Only available for exception errors.

- **error.ErrorCode**   Contains a custom error code. Only available for exception custom errors.

- **error.ExtendedInfo**   Contains an expanded custom error message. Only available for exception custom errors.

Error Types

There are advanced error types that you can specify in the type attribute of the cfcatch tag. The exception names are designed to be self explanatory, so here they are:

- COM.Allaire.ColdFusion.CFEXECUTE.OutputError
- COM.Allaire.ColdFusion.CFEXECUTE.Timeout
- COM.Allaire.ColdFusion.FileException
- COM.Allaire.ColdFusion.HTTPAccepted
- COM.Allaire.ColdFusion.HTTPAuthFailure
- COM.Allaire.ColdFusion.HTTPBadGateway
- COM.Allaire.ColdFusion.HTTPBadRequest
- COM.Allaire.ColdFusion.HTTPCFHTTPRequestEntityTooLarge
- COM.Allaire.ColdFusion.HTTPCGIValueNotPassed
- COM.Allaire.ColdFusion.HTTPConflict
- COM.Allaire.ColdFusion.HTTPContentLengthRequired
- COM.Allaire.ColdFusion.HTTPContinue
- COM.Allaire.ColdFusion.HTTPCookieValueNotPassed
- COM.Allaire.ColdFusion.HTTPCreated
- COM.Allaire.ColdFusion.HTTPFailure
- COM.Allaire.ColdFusion.HTTPFileInvalidPath
- COM.Allaire.ColdFusion.HTTPFileNotFound

- COM.Allaire.ColdFusion.HTTPFileNotPassed
- COM.Allaire.ColdFusion.HTTPFileNotRenderable
- COM.Allaire.ColdFusion.HTTPForbidden
- COM.Allaire.ColdFusion.HTTPGatewayTimeout
- COM.Allaire.ColdFusion.HTTPGone
- COM.Allaire.ColdFusion.HTTPMethodNotAllowed
- COM.Allaire.ColdFusion.HTTPMovedPermanently
- COM.Allaire.ColdFusion.HTTPMovedTemporarily
- COM.Allaire.ColdFusion.HTTPMultipleChoices
- COM.Allaire.ColdFusion.HTTPNoContent
- COM.Allaire.ColdFusion.HTTPNonAuthoritativeInfo
- COM.Allaire.ColdFusion.HTTPNotAcceptable
- COM.Allaire.ColdFusion.HTTPNotFound
- COM.Allaire.ColdFusion.HTTPNotImplemented
- COM.Allaire.ColdFusion.HTTPNotModified
- COM.Allaire.ColdFusion.HTTPPartialContent
- COM.Allaire.ColdFusion.HTTPPaymentRequired
- COM.Allaire.ColdFusion.HTTPPreconditionFailed
- COM.Allaire.ColdFusion.HTTPProxyAuthenticationRequired
- COM.Allaire.ColdFusion.HTTPRequestURITooLarge
- COM.Allaire.ColdFusion.HTTPResetContent
- COM.Allaire.ColdFusion.HTTPSeeOther
- COM.Allaire.ColdFusion.HTTPServerError
- COM.Allaire.ColdFusion.HTTPServiceUnavailable
- COM.Allaire.ColdFusion.HTTPSwitchingProtocols
- COM.Allaire.ColdFusion.HTTPUnsupportedMediaType
- COM.Allaire.ColdFusion.HTTPUrlValueNotPassed
- COM.Allaire.ColdFusion.HTTPUseProxy
- COM.Allaire.ColdFusion.HTTPVersionNotSupported
- COM.Allaire.ColdFusion.POPAuthFailure
- COM.Allaire.ColdFusion.POPConnectionFailure
- COM.Allaire.ColdFusion.POPDeleteError

- COM.Allaire.ColdFusion.Request.Timeout
- COM.Allaire.ColdFusion.SERVLETJRunError
- COM.Allaire.ColdFusion.HTTPConnectionTimeout

Special ColdFusion Variables

There are times when ColdFusion creates special variables, such as when a file is uploaded. This section shows you the variables that are created.

cffile Variables

When you upload a file, the following special variables regarding the operation are created. This was discussed in Chapter 19.

- **cffile.AttemptedServerFile**　Contains the first name that ColdFusion used to save the file.
- **cffile.ClientDirectory**　Contains the client's directory location of the file.
- **cffile.ClientFile**　Contains the client's name of the file.
- **cffile.ClientFileExt**　Contains the extension of the uploaded file.
- **cffile.ClientFileName**　Contains the filename, without extension, of the uploaded file.
- **cffile.ContentSubType**　Contains the content subtype of the saved file.
- **cffile.ContentType**　Contains the content type of the saved file.
- **cffile.DateLastAccessed**　Contains the date and time that the file was last accessed.
- **cffile.FileExisted**　Contains a Boolean value that specifies whether or not a file existed in the uploaded path.
- **cffile.FileSize**　Contains the size of the file that was uploaded.
- **cffile.FileWasAppended**　Contains a Boolean value that specifies whether or not the uploaded file was appended to an existing file.
- **cffile.FileWasOverwritten**　Contains a Boolean value that specifies whether or not a file was overwritten by the uploaded file.
- **cffile.FileWasRenamed**　Contains a Boolean value that specifies whether or not a file was renamed to avoid name conflicts.
- **cffile.FileWasSaved**　Contains a Boolean value that specifies whether or not the file was saved.
- **cffile.OldFileSize**　Contains the size of the file that was overwritten, if applicable.

- **cffile.ServerDirectory**   Contains the server directory of the uploaded file.
- **cffile.ServerFile**   Contains the server filename, including extension.
- **cffile.ServerFileExt**   Contains the server file extension of the file.
- **cffile.ServerFileName**   Contains the server filename of the file.
- **cffile.TimeCreated**   Contains the time that the file was uploaded.
- **cffile.TimeLastModified**   Contains the date and time that the uploaded file was last modified.

cfftp Variables

The cfftp tag can return some values indicating whether or not the operation was successful. This tag was discussed in Chapter 22.

- **cfftp.Succeeded**   Contains a Boolean value that specifies whether or not the operation succeeded.
- **cfftp.ErrorCode**   Contains the ErrorCode sent back from the FTP server, if applicable.
- **cfftp.ErrorText**   Contains the ErrorText sent back from the FTP server, if applicable.

cfhttp Variables

The cfhttp tag can be used to retrieve data from a remote server. The tag was discussed in Chapter 22. These are the variables created after a cfhttp call:

- **cfhttp.FileContent**   Contains the content of the HTTP request.
- **cfhttp.MimeType**   Contains the MIME type of the page returned.
- **cfhttp.Header**   Contains the raw response header.
- **cfhttp.ResponseHeader[http_hd_key]**   Contains the response headers from the HTTP request.
- **cfhttp.StatusCode**   Contains the HTTP error code and associated error string, if the throwonerror attribute of the cfhttp tag is set to no.

The
Complete
Reference

Appendix C

Finding Additional Online and Print Resources

This appendix gives you some great web- and print-based resources that you can access to get more information about ColdFusion, or any of the other technologies that are discussed in this book. It talks about ColdFusion reference sites, places to go for training, and finishes off with some other resources that you may find useful.

ColdFusion Reference Sites

- **www.macromedia.com** The home page of Macromedia, the company that owns and continues development of ColdFusion.
- **www.macromedia.com/desdev/** Macromedia's portal for designers and developers.
- **www.instantcoldfusion.com** The web site for this book.
- **www.optimizingcoldfusion.com** The web site for *Optimizing ColdFusion* by Chris Cortes.
- **www.michaelbuffington.com** The home page of Michael Buffington, author of *ColdFusion: A Developer's Guide*.
- **www.thenetprofits.co.uk/coldfusion/faq/** A source of frequently asked questions on ColdFusion.
- **www.sys-con.com/coldfusion/** *ColdFusion Developer's Journal* home page.
- **www.cfcomet.com** A resource that contains information about using ColdFusion and COM.
- **www.cflib.org** The ColdFusion Common Function library project. A source for user-defined functions.
- **www.cfczone.org** An open source resource for ColdFusion Components.
- **www.defusion.com** Articles on ColdFusion.
- **cfhub.com** Another reference for ColdFusion information.
- **www.teratech.com/coldcuts** ColdFusion code samples.
- **www.fusioncube.net** An informational site on ColdFusion.
- **www.cfnewbie.com** Resources for developers who are new to ColdFusion.
- **www.cfbughunt.org** A site dedicated to identifying bugs in ColdFusion.
- **livedocs.macromedia.com** Online documentation for Macromedia products.

ColdFusion Development Methodologies

- **www.fusebox.org**   This site for Fusebox, the most widely accepted development methodology.
- **www.cfobjects.com**   cfObjects is a framework for developing applications in ColdFusion, with a hint of object-oriented programming.
- **www.black-box.org**   A site for BlackBox, a ColdFusion development methodology.
- **www.smart-objects.com**   A site for SmartObjects, another methodology aligning ColdFusion and object-oriented development.
- **www.iiframework.com**   Another framework for developing ColdFusion applications.
- **www.grokfusebox.com**   A great resource for ColdFusion-related information, particularly on developing with Fusebox.

Mailing Lists and Publications

- **www.houseoffusion.com**   The best source for ColdFusion e-mail discussion lists.
- **www.sys-con.com/coldfusion/list.cfm**   *ColdFusion Developer's Journal* mailing list.
- **www.sys-con.com/coldfusion**   *ColdFusion Developer's Journal* home page.
- **www.tallylist.com**   Numerous mailing list archives.
- **www.fusionauthority.com**   *Fusion Authority*, a weekly ColdFusion e-zine.
- **www.cfadvisor.com**   The web site for *CF Advisor*, a ColdFusion magazine.
- **www.coldfusionmonthly.com**   A monthly ColdFusion magazine.
- **www.cftipsplus.com**   A resource for ColdFusion tips and articles.

Training and Certification

- **www.vue.com**   The home page for the company that administers Macromedia certification tests.
- **cfcertification.com**   Online guides for studying for Macromedia certification.
- **www.centrasoft.com**   Home of CF_Buster, a program designed to help prepare for ColdFusion certification.
- **www.brainbench.com**   An independent third-party certification company.
- **www.brainbuzz.com**   Another independent third-party certification company.
- **www.smartplanet.com**   Online courses in a variety of topics.

Other Technologies

- **www.flashcfm.com** Information for developing with Flash and ColdFusion.
- **www.openwddx.org** The WDDX home page.
- **www.sswug.org** SQL Server Worldwide User's Group.
- **www.mssqlserver.com** A SQL Server resource.
- **www.swynk.com** The biggest resource for Microsoft BackOffice products, such as SQL Server, Exchange, IIS, and Windows 2000.
- **www.sqlmag.com** *SQL Server Magazine* home page.
- **www.apache.org** A free web server.
- **www.activepdf.com** The home page for the ActivePDF toolkit and other server-side PDF generation software.
- **www.webperformanceinc.com** The web site for Web Performance Trainer, described in Chapter 5.
- **www.verity.com** The home site for the Verity search engine tool. A limited version of this tool is included in ColdFusion MX.
- **www.wapforum.org** A resource for wireless application development, including the WAP specifications.
- **www.ucc.ie/xml** The XML FAQ.
- **www.ektron.com** The home of eWebEditPro.
- **www.siteobjects.com** The home of soEditor and other ColdFusion complementary software.
- **www.cfdev.com** The home of ActiveEdit software.
- **intrafoundation.com** A source for many Java and C++ CFX custom tags.

Other References

- **www.cf-community.com** A place for ColdFusion developers to go to get away from it all.
- **www.newatlanta.com** The home of BlueDragon, the original J2EE CFML interpreter.
- **www.cfm-resources.com** A place for free ColdFusion hosting.
- **www.irt.org** Information on a lot of languages, including ColdFusion.
- **forta.com** The home page for ColdFusion's technical evangelist.
- **www.cfconf.org** An informational site on ColdFusion conferences.

- **hshelp.com**   A reference site for VTML, the customizing language of HomeSite and ColdFusion Studio.
- **w3.org**   The official site of the World Wide Web Consortium.
- **www.extremeprogramming.org**   A site dedicated to explaining the Extreme Programming methodology.
- **www.cfugorama.com**   A resource for ColdFusion user groups.

The Complete Reference

ColdFusion MX

Appendix D

Using the Online Files

All of the files that are used in this book are available online at www.instantcoldfusion.com and www.osborne.com. The files come in a single zip archive. You need a program, such as WinZip (www.winzip.com), to unzip the archive. The files are separated into folders, by chapter. Files for Chapter 1 are located in the Chapter1 directory, files for Chapter 2 are located in the Chapter 2 directory, and so on. The zip archive includes ColdFusion templates, database files, and any other applicable files.

Index

F

G

H

I

J

X

Y

INTERNATIONAL CONTACT INFORMATION

AUSTRALIA
McGraw-Hill Book Company Australia Pty. Ltd.
TEL +61-2-9415-9899
FAX +61-2-9415-5687
http://www.mcgraw-hill.com.au
books-it_sydney@mcgraw-hill.com

CANADA
McGraw-Hill Ryerson Ltd.
TEL +905-430-5000
FAX +905-430-5020
http://www.mcgrawhill.ca

GREECE, MIDDLE EAST,
NORTHERN AFRICA
McGraw-Hill Hellas
TEL +30-1-656-0990-3-4
FAX +30-1-654-5525

MEXICO (Also serving Latin America)
McGraw-Hill Interamericana Editores S.A. de C.V.
TEL +525-117-1583
FAX +525-117-1589
http://www.mcgraw-hill.com.mx
fernando_castellanos@mcgraw-hill.com

SINGAPORE (Serving Asia)
McGraw-Hill Book Company
TEL +65-863-1580
FAX +65-862-3354
http://www.mcgraw-hill.com.sg
mghasia@mcgraw-hill.com

SOUTH AFRICA
McGraw-Hill South Africa
TEL +27-11-622-7512
FAX +27-11-622-9045
robyn_swanepoel@mcgraw-hill.com

UNITED KINGDOM & EUROPE
(Excluding Southern Europe)
McGraw-Hill Education Europe
TEL +44-1-628-502500
FAX +44-1-628-770224
http://www.mcgraw-hill.co.uk
computing_neurope@mcgraw-hill.com

ALL OTHER INQUIRIES Contact:
Osborne/McGraw-Hill
TEL +1-510-549-6600
FAX +1-510-883-7600
http://www.osborne.com
omg_international@mcgraw-hill.com

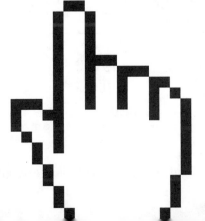

Complete References

Herbert Schildt
0-07-213485-2

Jeffery R. Shapiro
0-07-213381-3

Chris H. Pappas & William
H. Murray, III
0-07-212958-1

Herbert Schildt
0-07-213084-9

Ron Ben-Natan & Ori Sasson
0-07-222394-4

Arthur Griffith
0-07-222405-3

For the answers to everything related to your technology, drill as deeply as you
please into our Complete Reference series. Written by topical authorities, these
comprehensive resources offer a full range of knowledge, including extensive product
information, theory, step-by-step tutorials, sample projects, and helpful appendixes.

OSBORNE
www.osborne.com

For more information on these and other Osborne books, visit our Web site at www.osborne.com